ORGANIZATIONAL BEHAVIOR 1

ESSENTIAL THEORIES OF MOTIVATION AND LEADERSHIP

JOHN B. MINER

M.E.Sharpe
Armonk, New York
London, England

Library of Congress Cataloging-in-Publication Data

Miner, John B.
  Organizational behavior I. Essential theories of motivation and leadership
/ by John B. Miner.
    p. cm.
  Includes bibliographical references and index.
    ISBN 0-7656-1523-1 (cloth : alk. paper) —ISBN 0-7656-1524-X (pbk.: alk. paper)
  1. Employee motivation. 2. Leadership. 3. Organizational behavior. I.
Title: Organizational behavior one. Essential theories of motivation and
leadership. II. Title: Organizational behavior. 1, Essential theories of
motivation and leadership. III. Title: Essential theories of motivation and
leadership. IV. Title.

HF5549.5.M63M5638 2005
302.3'5—dc22   2005003746

Printed in the United States of America

The paper used in this publication meets the minimum requirements of
American National Standard for Information Sciences
Permanence of Paper for Printed Library Materials,
ANSI Z 39.48-1984.

∞

BM (c) 10   9   8   7   6   5   4   3   2   1
BM (p) 10   9   8   7   6   5   4   3

DEDICATION

To the intellectual leaders who coined the ideas and much of the research that made this book possible:

J. Stacy Adams	Gary P. Latham
Bernard M. Bass	Edward E. Lawler
Fred E. Fiedler	Kurt Lewin
George B. Graen	Edwin A. Locke
Stephen G. Green	Robert G. Lord
J. Richard Hackman	Fred Luthans
W. Clay Hamner	David C. McClelland
Frederick Herzberg	Terence R. Mitchell
Robert J. House	Greg R. Oldham
Arthur G. Jago	Lyman W. Porter
Steven Kerr	Victor H. Vroom
Robert Kreitner	Philip W. Yetton

and the many who worked with them.

CONTENTS

List of Tables and Figures   ix
Preface   xi
Acknowledgments   xv

PART I. SCIENTIFIC INTRODUCTION

Chapter 1.   Science and Its Theory   3
Chapter 2.   The Conduct of Research and the Development of Knowledge   18

PART II. THEORIES OF MOTIVATION

Chapter 3.   From Social Psychology and Personality Theory: Kurt Lewin   37
Chapter 4.   Achievement Motivation Theory: David McClelland   46
Chapter 5.   Motivation-Hygiene Theory: Frederick Herzberg   61
Chapter 6.   Job Characteristics Theory: Richard Hackman, Edward Lawler, and Greg Oldham   75
Chapter 7.   Expectancy Theories: Victor Vroom, and Lyman Porter and Edward Lawler   94
Chapter 8.   Operant Behavior and Organizational Behavior Modification: Clay Hamner, and Fred Luthans and Robert Kreitner   114
Chapter 9.   Equity Theory: J. Stacy Adams   134
Chapter 10.   Goal-setting Theory: Edwin Locke and Gary Latham   159
Chapter 11.   Attribution Theory—Managerial Perceptions of the Poor Performing Subordinate: Terence Mitchell and Stephen Green   184

PART III. THEORIES OF LEADERSHIP

Chapter 12.   Normative Decision Process Theory: Victor Vroom, Philip Yetton, and Arthur Jago   207
Chapter 13.   Contingency Theory of Leadership: Fred Fiedler   232
Chapter 14.   Vertical Dyad Linkage and Leader–Member Exchange Theory: George Graen   256
Chapter 15.   Information Processing Theory of Leadership: Robert Lord   280
Chapter 16.   Substitutes for Leadership: Steven Kerr   300
Chapter 17.   Role Motivation Theory: John Miner   319
Chapter 18.   Charismatic Leadership Theory: Robert House   337
Chapter 19.   Transformational Leadership Theory: Bernard Bass   361

Name Index   387
Subject Index   400

LIST OF TABLES AND FIGURES

TABLES

3.1	Methods Used to Create Leadership Climates	40
4.1	Development of the Power Motive and Managerial Performance	51
4.2	Relationships Between Socialized Power and Promotion Among Non-technical Managers	56
5.1	Pre- and Post-Measures of Job Satisfaction for Job Enrichment Projects	68
6.1	Correlation Between Motivating Potential Score and Outcome Variables Moderated by Growth Need Strength and Context Satisfactions	86
7.1	Percentage of Those with Various Instrumental Perceptions Who Are High Performers	102
7.2	Multiple Correlations for Seven Outcomes of Effort–Reward Probabilities Alone and in Combination with Value of Reward (Valence) as Predictors of Job Effort and Performance	104
8.1	Strategies for Shaping and Modeling	121
9.1	Possible Inputs to and Outcomes from an Employment Exchange	136
9.2	The Amount of Inequity Experienced Under Various Input and Outcome Conditions	137
9.3	Errors Detected per Page and Number of Pages Proofed Under Varying Conditions of Equity	142
11.1	Managerial Attributions Regarding Poor Group and Individual Performance Hypothesized from Theory at Link #1 of the Attributional Model	192
11.2	Significant Correlations Between Attributions for Performance and Corrective Actions Recommended	197
12.1	Feasible Sets of Leader Behaviors for Each of Fourteen Group Problem Types	212
12.2	Correlations Between Aspects of the Problem Situation and the Degree of Participativeness of the Reported Leader Behavior	218
12.3	Validity Evidence from Six Studies Representing Normative Tests	220
13.1	Fiedler's Early Classification of Interactive Task Groups	236
13.2	Contingency Theory Variables, Level of Analysis, Measures Used, and Sources of Data	242
14.1	Normative Model for the Development of Dyadic Career Realities	260
14.2	Relationships Between LMX and Outcome Variables	268
14.3	The Development of Dansereau's Dyadic Approach to Leadership	272
15.1	Comparison and Evaluation of Information Processing Models	284
15.2	Potential Means That Can Be Used by Executives to Influence Organizational Performance	288
16.1	Neutralization Effects of Substitutes for Leadership on Two Types of Leader Behavior	303
16.2	Effects of Various Organizational Characteristics on Members' Task-relevant Information and Motivation in Mechanistic and Organic Organizations	305

16.3   Effective Coping Strategies That Might Be Used to Deal with Specific
        Leadership Problems   309
17.1   Schema of Strategic Factors That May Contribute to Ineffective Performance   322
19.1   Mean Corrected Correlations Between MLQ Scales and Effectiveness Criteria
        With (Subordinate Ratings) and Without (Organizational Measures) Common
        Method Bias .   374

FIGURES

1.1   The Components of Theories and How They Function   8
3.1   Kurt Lewin's Force-field Analysis of the Change Process   41
6.1   The Complete Job Characteristics Model   78
6.2   Links Between the Implementing Principles and the Core Job Characteristics   80
7.1   The Original Porter-Lawler Model   99
7.2   Lawler's Portrayal of the Basic Expectancy Theory Model   101
8.1   A Model of the Social Learning Process   123
8.2   The 1980s Expanded Model of Organizational Behavior Modification   123
8.3   Reversal Analysis of the Effects of Organizational Behavior Modification
        Intervention on the Number of Defective Products Produced   126
9.1   Model of the Psychological Processes Involved in Referent Selection   146
9.2   Theoretical Roads to Understanding Organizational Justice   152
10.1 Model of How Feedback Leads to Action   166
10.2 Model of the High Performance Cycle   168
10.3 Model of the Relationships Among Goals, Plans (Task Strategies), and
        Performance   169
10.4 Model of the Motivation Sequence   170
11.1 The Basic Attributional Model   188
11.2 The Attributional Model of Leader Response to Subordinate Poor Performance   190
12.1 Decision Tree for Arriving at Feasible Sets of Leader Behaviors for Different
        Group Problem Types   211
12.2 Decision Tree for Arriving at Feasible Sets of Leader Behaviors for Different
        Group and Individual Problem Types   214
13.1 Effects of Leadership Training on Subsequent Performance as Moderated by
        Situational Favorableness   240
13.2 The Octants of Contingency Theory   243
13.3 Decision Tree for Cognitive Resource Theory   249
14.1 Description of the Role-making Process   261
15.1 Model of Information Processing Directed by Cognitive Schema   282
15.2 Catastrophe Model of Changing Social Perceptions   286
16.1 Causal Model Showing the Roles of Leader Behaviors, Moderators, and Mediators   307
17.1 Steps in the Control Process as Applied to Instances of Ineffective Performance   323
17.2 Outlines of the Four Forms of Role Motivation Theory   .   325
18.1 The Initial Model of Charismatic Leadership   340
18.2 Model of the Charismatic Leadership Process   344
19.1 Outline of the Work Pursued by Bernard Bass Until the Early 1980s   362
19.2 Transactional and Transformational Leadership   364

PREFACE

Essential Theories of Motivation and Leadership is the third in a series of books dealing with microlevel organizational behavior theories, spread unevenly over a twenty-five-year period. The predecessors were *Theories of Organizational Behavior* (1980), and *Organizational Behavior: Foundations, Theories, and Analyses* (2002).

All of these books presuppose some prior work in such fields as organizational behavior, management, and the like. Given an introduction of this kind, readers should find little in this book that overlaps with their prior learning. The reason for this is that basic courses typically take a content- or problem-centered approach. In contrast, this book takes a different tack, focusing on the best theories in the field of micro-organizational behavior and the contributions these theories have made to understanding organizations. Dealing with these theories and the research on them requires not only some basic study in the area, but also an introduction to statistics. With this kind of preparation, readers should have no difficulty comprehending the material presented here, even though some of the theories are by their nature quite demanding.

WHY THEORY?

There are several advantages to being exposed to a book that focuses on theory, as this does. One is that theories become the nodes for ideas around which knowledge is concentrated. This concentration of knowledge surrounding theories makes for a comprehensive, yet more parsimonious, coverage of the subject matter of a field. Good theories tend to attract research, and consequently much of what we really know about motivation and leadership within organizations is encompassed within the theoretical framework. In short, casting a net that catches only theories, and then only those theories that have been shown by research to be the better ones at the present time, provides an ideal perspective on organizational behavior subject matter.

A second point is that concentrating on theories permits a degree of insight into how organizational science really operates that is not possible otherwise. This is so because the interplay between theory development and research is at the very heart of any scientific discipline. To understand this process one has to approach the subject matter of a field through its theories. This becomes particularly important for a field like organizational behavior, where the ties between professional school education and practice are not as close as they are in medicine, for instance. To bring the educational process and actual practice closer together, there needs to be a reciprocal relationship and thus mutual understanding. Much has been written on how academics need to understand the practitioner perspective better, and I applaud such efforts; but if the relationship is to be truly reciprocal, practitioners also need to understand how knowledge is generated in organizational behavior. This book, with its emphasis on theory, provides a unique window to look inside the science of organizational behavior.

WHY THESE THEORIES?

The theories presented in this volume were selected from a larger listing of thirty-eight theories of motivation and leadership originally created to include the most significant theories of the field, if not necessarily the most valid. This larger listing was developed from existing books devoted to surveying the organizational behavior theoretical literature. These thirty-eight were reduced to the nineteen presented here by applying criteria specified in the following manner:

Importance rating. The seventy-one organizational behavior experts who responded to a survey rated the thirty-eight theories on a 7-point scale (with 7 as the high value) with regard to the theory's importance to the field. For the nineteen selected theories, the mean such rating was 4.82, while the mean rating for the theories not included in this book was 3.80. The criterion applied to ensure inclusion in this volume was a rating of 5.00 or above; eight theories met this criterion.

Institutionalization. An institution may be defined as a cognitive, normative, or regulative structure or activity that provides stability and meaning to social behavior. Thus, theories that have the backing of institutionalization are widely known and endorsed. The distribution of importance ratings for each theory was analyzed to determine whether or not the frequencies in the upper half of the distribution departed from normal curve expectations, and if so, whether or not this deviation represented an exaggeration of the frequencies sufficient to produce statistical significance. Those theories that achieved significance were said to be institutionalized; all five of them are included in this book.

Estimated validity. Validity was determined by the author based on an assessment of the research on the theory, both as to its quantity and the support it provided. The "goodness" of the theoretical statements was considered as well, as were evaluations by other reviewers including meta-analyses. These summary ratings were made on a 5-point scale (with 5 as the high point). The mean estimated validity for the nineteen selected theories was 4.05, and for the theories not included here, it was 2.26. Any theory with a rating of 4 or 5 was automatically selected, and there were sixteen of these.

Estimated usefulness. Usefulness in practice was also established by the author depending on the extent to which such applications existed, the extent of the research on these applications, and the support for practical use provided by this research. Endorsements by practitioners provided in the literature were considered, too, but no attempt was made to establish the facts regarding the extent of actual use in practice; the latter were believed to be so subject to faddism as to be unreliable. Again, the estimated usefulness ratings were made on a 5-point scale (with 5 as the high point). For the nineteen theories included in this volume, the mean such evaluation was 3.32, and for the nineteen theories excluded, it was 1.95. The criterion for inclusion was a rating of 4 or 5, and there were eight of these.

In addition to the criteria for a labeling as "essential" provided from these four sources, certain theories that consistently met the next highest rating category were included as well. These consistently "almost good enough" theories are judged to be worthy of inclusion, not on the basis of their performance relative to any single criterion, but because of their total summed scores. They were not institutionalized, but had an importance rating in the 4.00–4.99 range, an estimated validity of 3, and an estimated usefulness of 3. There were two such theories.[1]

A point needs to be made regarding the date of origin of these theories. They extend back to the 1930s and run to the 1980s; yet this is not a history book. Without exception these theories can be found cited in the current literature, and most of them will be found there many times. Several reasons exist for this situation. One consideration is that it takes a number of years for a theory to accumulate enough research to permit an adequate evaluation. Thus, theories of the 1990s and beyond are almost automatically excluded. Furthermore, during the 1960s and 1970s, a large number of individuals came to organizational behavior from other disciplines, thus creating new combinations of knowledge and a particularly fertile ground for theory generation.

Perhaps more important than any other consideration, however, is that organizational behavior theorists tend to keep revising and developing their theories once they get started, and they typically do not stop much before they die. A few of those whose theories are considered in this book have indeed stopped theorizing because they are no longer among us, but most are still at it. This means that many theories of organizational behavior that began decades ago are also very current and continue to dominate the field.

STRUCTURE OF THE BOOK

As noted in the contents, this book is divided into three parts. In Part I are two chapters intended to set the scene for what follows. The objective is to provide the background on scientific method, theory construction and evaluation, measurement considerations, research design, the nature of knowledge in organizational behavior, and other considerations needed to truly understand the theoretical discussions in Parts II and III. Perhaps some readers have a sufficient degree of orientation on such matters so as to be able to skip this introduction and move directly to the theories themselves. Nevertheless, these two chapters contain a considerable amount of material that is new; over 40 percent of the references cite publications dated 2000 or later. I recommend at least a quick skim, and for those who are reasonably new to the field, this should be the needed background to decipher what follows.

Parts II and III take up essential theories of motivation and leadership, respectively. A bit of leadership can be found in Part II and some motivation in Part III, but do not be too concerned about this. The boundaries are somewhat artificial at best. Motivation and leadership have always been closely allied subject matter for organizational behavior, and they appear to be moving closer to each other over time. Frequently, as theories are expanded and developed by their authors, they move from one content area to the other and ultimately come to bridge both fields. There are increasing reasons for incorporating both motivation and leadership in a single book or course of study.

STRUCTURE OF THE CHAPTERS

After the book's introductory material, the remaining chapters follow a generally consistent format. An outline covering the various headings of the chapter provides a roadmap facilitating progress through the discussion and a guide to finding a way out should the reader get lost en route. The introductory material, including what is labeled "Background," is intended to place the theory at hand in its context, both intellectual and historical. What are the sources of the theorist's ideas, and what sort of environment nurtured them? I have tried here to provide for readers something of a biographical understanding of the theorist as a person. Note in this regard that these are all men. There was little by way of diversity of any kind within organizational behavior at the time these theories emerged. It is different now, and I assume that in the future a book such as this will possess a much more diversified cast of characters.

An important feature at the beginning of each chapter is a box (or in a few cases, boxes) that presents the ratings of the theory to be considered and its decade of origin. The ratings are those discussed earlier in this preface—the importance rating, institutionalization if appropriate, estimated validity, and estimated usefulness—each expressed using a set of stars. This information should prove helpful going into the discussion, to guide the reader as to what to expect with each theory.

Following the introductory material for each chapter, the theory is presented in developmental sequence. In a few instances this represents an early comprehensive statement with only a few changes subsequently, but much more frequently the development of the theory extends over years. Some theories are still in transition at this writing. This theoretical statement is followed by an "Evaluation and Impact" section that considers the appropriate research, usually starting with the research conducted by the theory's author(s). In many cases these initial investigations by the theorists set the pattern for subsequent studies by others. In analyzing the research I am rarely able to consider all possible studies, but every effort is made to take up the more significant ones. Meta-analyses and evaluative reviews are relied upon heavily in reaching conclusions.

Applications, if there are any and in almost all instances there are, are considered at appropriate points in the presentation. Usually there is less research, and less by way of evaluations by others, where applications are concerned, but I have presented whatever is available in both instances. In my opinion, in an applied field such as organizational behavior, it is as important to evaluate theories in terms of their relevance for practice as to consider their validity.

In the "Conclusions" section of each chapter, I attempt to explain and document how the estimated validity and estimated usefulness ratings were made for that particular theory. Thus, both positive and negative features are noted and then balanced to arrive at the final rating as reflected in the stars awarded in the box at the beginning of each chapter.

The chapter-end references are numerous, providing both a developmental chronology of theoretical statements and a record of significant research. This is partly to document statements made in the text, but it also provides a list of sources to follow up should the reader wish to learn more about a particular theory. The total number of references runs to over a 1,000, with an average of fifty-six per chapter. More than 30 percent of these have been published in 2000 or more recently, supporting the contention that this is a thoroughly up-to-date volume.

NOTE

1. Greater detail on the measures set forth above may be obtained from two papers: "The Rated Importance, Scientific Validity, and Practical Usefulness of Organizational Behavior Theories: A Quantitative Review" published in the 2003 *Academy of Management Learning and Education*, Volume 2, 250–68; and "The Institutionalization of Organizational Behavior Theories: An Empirical Investigation" to be published subsequently in this book series and available from the author. The nineteen theories not selected for inclusion in this book are discussed in *Organizational Behavior: Foundations, Theories, and Analyses* (2002). All of these sources are authored by myself.

John B. Miner
Eugene, Oregon
April 2004

ACKNOWLEDGMENTS

My major debt in preparing this book is acknowledged in the dedication. Without the efforts of the various theorists of motivation and leadership, there would have been nothing to write about. They have not only proved themselves to be very good theorists, but they have served in large part to carry the young field of organizational behavior through its formative years.

I am also indebted to Oxford University Press for giving me permission to use material from my *Organizational Behavior: Foundations, Theories, and Analyses* wherever in the present volume it proved appropriate. Harry Briggs at M.E. Sharpe has shown himself to be both a very helpful person and a highly proficient editor; it has been a pleasure to work with him. Susan Rescigno, my project editor, has been equally helpful.

Finally, in the absence of any university support, my wife, Barbara, has taken on all of the tasks involved in the preparation of this book, other than writing it. I thank her not only for her dedication and efficiency, but for her support and love.

PART I

SCIENTIFIC INTRODUCTION

CHAPTER 1

SCIENCE AND ITS THEORY

Theory and Practice
Science Defined
The Role of Theory in Science
　　Theory Defined
　　How Theory Works
Assumptions of Science
Rules of Scientific Inquiry
Theory Building
Defining a Good or Strong Theory
Kinds of Theories
　　Micro, Macro, and Meso
　　Typologies as Theory
　　Grounded Theory
Conclusions

What is *organizational behavior?* It is a social science discipline—much like cultural anthropology, economics, political science, psychology, and sociology. This means that it utilizes the scientific method to establish truth and to validate its theories. It is a discipline that historically has had its intellectual home in business schools. It is a new discipline relative to the other social sciences, having its origins in the middle twentieth century. The key points are that it is a science and that it has a history, which, though short, has been quite turbulent.

Although the exact boundaries of the discipline are somewhat fuzzy (see Blood 1994), organizational behavior's focus is clearly on the world of organizations. The concern is first with the behavior and nature of people within organizations, and second with the behavior and nature of organizations within their environments. The term *organizational behavior* initially made reference only to the behavior and nature of people in organizations. Given the fuzziness of its boundaries, the discipline always had a tendency to stretch beyond that domain, however. By the time it was approaching twenty-five years of age, it clearly had staked a claim to incorporating the behavior and nature of organizations as well. This is historically consistent in that both the study of the behavior and nature of people and the study of the behavior and nature of organizations emerged in the business schools in the same places at the same times. The focus of this volume, however, is on the former (i.e., the behavior and nature of people), with the usual caveat regarding fuzzy boundaries.

In line with its professional school origins, organizational behavior is an applied discipline, concerned with matters of practice and application. Despite this orientation, it has relatively few adherents who actually devote their primary professional efforts to the practice of organizational behavior in business and other organizational settings; rather, most are concentrated in academia—teaching, writing, and conducting research. In my opinion this is unfortunate; the field would be better off not by reducing its academic efforts, but by expanding its practitioner efforts. We will return to this theme in various ways throughout this book.

Several other terms have become intertwined with organizational behavior over the years, although none has achieved quite the same level of acceptance. One is *organization theory,* which has come to refer almost exclusively to the study of the behavior and nature of organizations in their environments. A second is *organization(al) science,* which appears to cover essentially the same ground as organizational behavior and which in many respects I prefer as a designation for our field (see Miner 1984). However, right now organizational behavior has won the day. Finally, there is the term *organization studies,* which also has a broad connotation extending at least in the recent period beyond the science of organizations to incorporate several different philosophic positions (see Clegg, Hardy, and Nord 1996).

Having explained what organizational behavior is, I need to say something about what it is not. It is not *strategic management,* a field that has emerged and achieved stature more recently than organizational behavior (see Schendel and Hofer 1979) and that has differentiated itself at the border that previously existed between organizational behavior and economics, borrowing from and overlapping with each. Also, organizational behavior is not *economics,* although in recent years there has been some confounding of the two fields, and some even foresee a possible future takeover of organizational behavior by economics (e.g., see Pfeffer 1995). However, economics was well established in business schools long before organizational behavior arrived, and organizational behavior was spawned, in large part at the behest of economists, as a separate and distinct discipline. Historically, the two are clearly different entities with very different origins.

Finally, organizational behavior is not *philosophy.* That, however, is a rather complex story. As a science our field is closely tied to, though separate from, the philosophy of science. In this respect it is like all other sciences, and the relationship can be expected to continue as long as organizational behavior defines itself as a social science. But from the very beginning, philosophy has been threaded into organizational behavior in other respects as well, not always to the benefit of either field. Sometimes, in the hands of certain individuals, organizational behavior and philosophy have become almost indistinguishable from one another. Understanding what is involved here requires a background in the nature of science, scientific theory, scientific research, and in the history of science—in short, in the scientific foundations of the field. It also requires a background in the ways in which philosophy has become threaded into organizational behavior at various points in time. These matters are considered in these introductory chapters of Part I.

The primary focus of this book, however, is on the major theories that have evolved within the broad field of organizational behavior that deal with the motivations of participants at all levels and in all positions, as well as with the leadership process operating within organizations. The goal is to provide an understanding of these theories and thus to determine what they can tell us that might prove useful to people who participate in organizations.

In point of fact, we all participate in various organizations such as schools, companies, and hospitals throughout our lives, and we devote a large percentage of our time to such participation. Most people would like to function more effectively in organizations and to contribute to more effective functioning of the organizations themselves. It seems logical that the more we know about organizations and the way they operate, the better our chances of coping with them adequately and of achieving our own goals within them and for them. Giving us this knowledge is what theories of organizational behavior attempt to do.

As a foundation for understanding these theories, it is important to know what scientific theory is and what it is not, as well as how theory relates to research and how research either supports or fails to support theory. These are the concerns of this Scientific Introduction. The intent is to provide a basic understanding that can be drawn on as specific theories are discussed in the remainder of the book.

THEORY AND PRACTICE

Theory is the cornerstone of any science. It provides the ideas that fuel research and practice. Theories of organizational behavior are as potentially useful when applied to organizations as theories of physics and chemistry are when used in developing new manufacturing technologies and consumer products, or theories of biology are in advancing medical practice. However, the relationship between theory and practice (or application, or usefulness) in organizational behavior is often misunderstood. For many people the term *theory* evokes images of a speculative, ivory-towered world, far removed from reality. Theories do not sound helpful in understanding the practical facts of organizational life. Yet one hears such statements as that of the eminent psychologist Kurt Lewin (1945), who said that "nothing is so practical as a good theory." And this dictum continues to receive widespread acceptance today (e.g., see Van de Ven 1989).

Confusion on this score is in fact widespread; the subject requires consideration here at the outset because a particular reader's preconceptions regarding the theory–practice relationship (or the lack thereof) can color that person's thinking about the entire field. The idea that theory is somehow "ivory tower" while practice is "real world"—and that the two are distinct and separate—permeates much current discussion of business school education and of the role of the organizational behavior discipline (Das 2003; Donaldson 2002).

What, then, is the state of the situation at the interface between academic theory and research and the world of application? What do studies tell us? One of the most comprehensive studies deals with the research knowledge, much of it theory-based, of human resource (HR) managers (Rynes, Brown, and Colbert 2002; Rynes, Colbert, and Brown 2002). This investigation indicated that these managers were not very knowledgeable regarding the research evidence, particularly in the areas of selection and motivation; they were only neutral on the value of research findings for practice; and most read very little in the research literature. Yet those few who were more conversant with the research worked for more financially successful companies. A difficulty appears to be that many HR managers rely almost entirely on the popular press for knowledge input (Mazza and Alvarez 2000), and they often receive wrong information from such sources.

Another study, focused on a specific theory, failed to find evidence of an understanding of this theory among managers, although MBA students were better informed (Priem and Rosenstein 2000). Thus, practicing managers could not go in the directions prescribed because they lacked the knowledge to do so. Although value and motivational differences are involved here (Brooks, Grauer, Thornbury, and Highhouse 2003; Miner 2004), this in itself would not logically account for the academic–managerial gap found; the problem appears to be in not going to appropriate sources of information (Roehling, Cavanaugh, Moynihan, and Boswell 2000).

The data thus seem to indicate a substantial gap between theory and perceived usefulness in practice. Yet there are reasons to believe that this gap can be reduced under appropriate circumstances (Rynes, Bartunek, and Daft 2001). One objective of this volume is to facilitate this process and accordingly to narrow the gap so that practitioners will come away with a greater appreciation of the value that organizational behavior theory can bring to practice. Examples of recent academic–practitioner collaborations on research studies (Ford, Duncan, Bedeian, Ginter, Rousculp, and Adams 2003; Rynes and McNatt 2001) and of increasing concern about linking theory to practice (Cooper and Locke 2000) give reason for optimism in this regard.

In this context, let me return to Lewin's (1945) dictum. What Lewin meant by a good theory is one that is validated by adequate research. To be truly useful, a theory must be intimately inter-twined with research, and to the extent that it is, it has the potential for moving beyond philo-sophic speculation to become a sound basis for action. Good theory is thus practical because it advances knowledge in a field, guides research to important questions, and enlightens practice in some manner (Van de Ven 1989).

Some theories are obviously more concerned with application than others. Some, at the time of inception, may fail to meet the test of usefulness, only to find their way to a juncture with practice later on. Some theories are never tested, or they fail the test of research and are not very good theories, at least as far as anyone can tell. In any event, a *good* theory has the potential for valid applications and thus can prove useful if correctly applied. A theory in an applied field, such as organizational behavior, that is so divorced from application (so ivory tower?) that is has no potential for speaking to practice is very unlikely to be a *good* theory. This is the viewpoint that guides the analyses and interpretations presented throughout this book.

SCIENCE DEFINED

Science is an enterprise by which a particular kind of ordered knowledge is obtained about natu-ral phenomena by means of controlled observations and theoretical interpretations. Ideally, this science, of which organizational behavior is a part, lives up to the following:

1. Definitions are precise.
2. Data-collecting is objective.
3. Findings are replicable.
4. Approach is systematic and cumulative.
5. Purposes are understanding and prediction, plus in the applied arena, control (Berelson and Steiner 1964).

The usually accepted goals of scientific effort are to increase understanding and to facili-tate prediction (Dubin 1978). At its best, science will achieve both of these goals. However, there are many instances in which prediction has been accomplished with considerable preci-sion, even though true understanding of the underlying phenomena is minimal; for example, this is characteristic of much of the forecasting that companies do as a basis for planning. Similarly, understanding can be far advanced, even though prediction lags behind. For in-stance, we know a great deal about the various factors that influence the level of people's work performance, but we do not know enough about the interaction of these factors in spe-cific instances to predict with high accuracy exactly how well a certain individual will do in a particular position.

In an applied field, such as organizational behavior, the objectives of understanding and pre-diction are joined by a third objective—influencing or managing the future, and thus achieving control. An economic science that explained business cycles fully and predicted fluctuations precisely would represent a long step toward holding unemployment at a desired level. Similarly, knowledge of the dynamics of organizations and the capacity to predict the occurrence of particu-lar structures and processes would seem to offer the possibility of engineering a situation to maximize organizational effectiveness. To the extent that limited unemployment or increased organizational effectiveness are desired, science then becomes a means to these goals. In fact, much scientific work is undertaken to influence the world around us. To the extent applied sci-ence meets such objectives, it achieves a major goal.

THE ROLE OF THEORY IN SCIENCE

Scientific method evolves in ascending levels of abstractions (Brown and Ghiselli 1955). At the most basic level, it portrays and retains experience in symbols. The symbols may be mathematical, but to date in organizational behavior they have been primarily linguistic.

Once converted to symbols, experience may be mentally manipulated, and relationships may be established.

Description utilizes symbols to classify, order, and correlate events. It remains at a low level of abstraction and is closely tied to observation and sensory experience. In essence, it is a matter of ordering symbols to make them adequately portray events. The objective is to answer "what" questions.

Explanation moves to a higher level of abstraction in that it attempts to establish meanings behind events. It attempts to identify causal, or at least concomitant, relationships so that observed phenomena make some logical sense.

Theory Defined

At its maximal point, explanation creates *theory*. Scientific theory is a patterning of logical constructs, or interrelated symbolic concepts, into which the known facts regarding a phenomenon, or theoretical domain, may be fitted. A theory is a generalization, applicable within stated boundaries, that specifies the relationships between factors. Thus, it is an attempt to make sense out of observations that in and of themselves do not contain any inherent and obvious logic (Dubin 1976). The objective is to answer "how," "when," and "why" questions.

Because theory is so central to science, a certain amount of repetition related to this topic may be forgiven. Campbell (1990) defines theory as a collection of assertions, both verbal and symbolic, that identifies what variables are important for what reasons, specifies how they are interrelated and why, and identifies the conditions under which they should be related or not. Sutton and Staw (1995) place their emphasis somewhat differently, but with much the same result. For them theory is about the connections among phenomena, a story about why acts, events, structure, and thoughts occur. It emphasizes the nature of causal relationships, identifying what comes first, as well as the timing of events. It is laced with a set of logically interconnected arguments. It can have implications that we have not previously seen and that run counter to our common sense.

How Theory Works

Figure 1.1 provides a picture of the components of a theory. A theory is thus a system of constructs and variables with the constructs related to one another by propositions and the variables by hypotheses. The whole is bounded by the assumptions, both implicit and explicit, that the theorist holds with regard to the theory (Bacharach 1989).

Constructs are "terms which, though not observational either directly or indirectly, may be applied or even defined on the basis of the observables" (Kaplan 1964, 55). They are abstractions created to facilitate understanding. Variables are observable, they have multiple values, and they derive from constructs. In essence, they are operationalizations of constructs created to permit testing of hypotheses. In contrast to the abstract constructs, variables are concrete. Propositions are statements of relationships among constructs. Hypotheses are similar statements involving variables. Research attempts to refute or confirm hypotheses, not propositions per se.

All theories occupy a domain within which they should prove effective and outside of which

Figure 1.1   **The Components of Theories and How They Function**

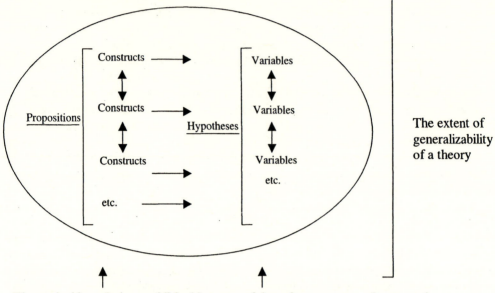

Theoretical boundaries established in terms of the values, spaces, cultures, and
times, etc. to which a theory applies.

they should not. These domain-defining, bounding assumptions (see Figure 1.1) are in part a
product of the implicit values held by the theorist relative to the theoretical content. These values
typically go unstated and if that is the case, they cannot be measured. Spatial boundaries restrict
the effective use of the theory to specific units, such as types of organizations or kinds of people.
Among these, cultural boundaries are particularly important for theory (Cheng, Sculli, and Chan
2001). Temporal boundaries restrict the effective use of the theory to specific time periods. To the
extent that they are explicitly stated, spatial and temporal boundaries can be measured and thus
made operational. Taken together they place some limitation on the generalizability of a theory.
These boundary-defining factors need not operate only to specify the domain of a theory, however; all may serve in stating propositions and hypotheses as well. For example, *time* has recently
received considerable attention as a variable that may enter into hypotheses (George and Jones
2000; Mitchell and James 2001).

   Organizational behavior has often been criticized for utilizing highly ambiguous theoretical constructs whose meaning is not at all clear (e.g., see Sandelands and Drazin 1989). This same ambiguity can extend to boundary definitions and domain statements. In a rather cynical vein, Astley and
Zammuto (1992) even argue that this ambiguity is functional for a theorist in that it increases the
conceptual appeal of a theory. Conflicting positions do not become readily apparent and the domain
of application may appear much greater than the empirical reality. Such purposeful ambiguity creation can cause the constructs and ideas of a theory to be extended into the world of practice to an
extent that is not empirically warranted. Not surprisingly, these views immediately met substantial
opposition (e.g., see Beyer 1992). The important point, however, is that science does not condone
this type of theoretical ambiguity. Precise definitions are needed to make science effective (Locke
2003), and a theory that resorts to ambiguity is to that extent a poor theory.

ASSUMPTIONS OF SCIENCE

Science must make certain assumptions about the world around us. These assumptions might not be factually true, and to the extent they are not, science will have less value. However, to the extent that science operates on these assumptions and produces a degree of valid understanding, prediction, and influence, it appears more worthwhile to utilize the assumptions.

Science assumes, first, that certain natural groupings of phenomena exist, so that classification can occur and generalization within a category is meaningful. For some years, for instance, the field then called business policy, operating from its origins in the case method, assumed that each company is essentially unique. This assumption effectively blocked the development of scientific theory and research in the field. Increasingly, however, the assumption of uniqueness has been disappearing, and generalizations applicable to classes of organizations have emerged (e.g., see Steiner and Miner 1986). As a result, scientific theory and research are burgeoning in the field of strategic management.

Second, science assumes some degree of constancy, stability, or permanence in the world. Science cannot operate in a context of complete random variation; the goal of valid prediction is totally unattainable under such circumstances. Thus, objects and events must retain some degree of similarity from one time to another. In a sense this is an extension of the first assumption, but now over time rather than across units (see McKelvey 1997 for a discussion of these premises). For instance, if organizational structures, once introduced, did not retain some stability, any scientific prediction of their impact on organizational performance would be impossible. Fortunately, they do have some constancy, but not always as much as might be desired.

Third, science assumes that events are determined and that causes exist. This is the essence of explanation and theorizing. It may not be possible to prove a specific causation with absolute certainty, but evidence can be adduced to support certain causal explanations and reject others. In any event, if one does not assume some kind of causation, there is little point in scientific investigation; the assumption of determinism is what sparks scientific effort. If, for instance, one assumes that organizational role prescriptions do not influence individual performance, then the whole area of organizational design moves outside the realm of scientific inquiry. Organizational behavior must assume some kind of causal impact of the organization on its members. It then becomes the task of science to determine the nature of this impact.

Finally, because science is firmly rooted in observation and experience, it is necessary to assume some degree of trustworthiness for the human processes of perceiving, remembering, and reasoning. This trustworthiness is always relative, but it must exist to some degree. The rules under which science operates are intended to increase the degree of reliability with which scientific observation and recording operate. The purpose is to achieve an objective, rational, replicable result that will be convincing to those who are knowledgeable in the area of study.

RULES OF SCIENTIFIC INQUIRY

First, if the findings of research are to be replicated, and the generalizations from research are to be valid, concepts must be clearly defined in terms of the procedures used to measure them. This has been a problem in the field of organizational behavior. On occasion theoretical concepts are stated in such an ambiguous manner, and the conditions for their measurement are left so uncertain, that the researcher is hard put to devise an adequate test of a theory.

Second, scientific observation must be controlled so that causation may be attributed correctly. The objective is to be certain that an outcome is in fact produced by what is believed to produce it and not by something else. Control of this kind is achieved through the use of various experimental designs, or through measurement and statistical adjustment as discussed in Chapter 2. In the complex world of organizational functioning, establishing controls sufficient to pin down causation often has proved to be difficult.

Third, because science is concerned with generalization to contexts that extend far beyond a given experiment, it is essential that research utilize samples that are adequate in both size and conditions of their selection. One must have confidence that the results obtained are generalizable and can be put to use outside the research situation. The field of statistics becomes important for organizational behavior because of its potential for determining how much confidence can be placed in a particular research outcome.

Fourth, and this bears repeating, science requires that its propositions, hypotheses, and theories be stated in terms that can be tested empirically. This is where philosophy and science part company. Unfortunately, organizational behavior has not always clearly separated scientific from philosophic statements. The result has been considerable confusion, and on occasion effort has been wasted on attempts to test theories that are not really testable as stated. Bacharach (1989) provides a good discussion of this falsifiability requirement.

THEORY BUILDING

A distinction is often made between deductive and inductive theory. In building a theory by deduction, one first establishes a set of premises. Then certain logical consequences of these premises are deduced, and subsidiary concepts are established. The starting point is rational thought, and logical consistency is a major concern in development of the theory. Often such theories are stated in mathematical terms.

Inductive theory, in contrast, builds up from observation, often from research, rather than down from a set of premises. Essentially, one puts together a theory that best seems to explain what is known in a given area at the present time. Then new tests of this theory, or of hypotheses derived from it, are carried out just as they would be if the theory were developed deductively.

Gottfredson (1983) points to three ways in which inductive theory may be developed from research findings. First, one may immerse oneself in the data generated by past research, but with a healthy skepticism regarding any interpretations by others found with these data. Second, one may pick one or more specific patterns of results to explain, thus narrowing the theory building task to a more limited domain than general theory. Finally, one may try to resolve inconsistencies, anomalies, puzzling results, and incompatible points of view in the literature and in the data reported there.

A major pitfall in the use of the inductive approach in theory building is that the research from which the theory is induced may tend to become confused with an adequate test of the theory. Thus, the same research is used twice for two different purposes, and a self-fulfilling prophecy results. In the case of truly deductive theories, this is not possible. When theories are developed inductively, it is crucial that they be tested on a new sample in a manner that is entirely independent of the pre-theory research. If one goes back to the prior sample or to data used in developing the theory, anything unique and ungeneralizable (attributable to chance fluctuation) in that particular situation is very likely to be confirmed. As a result, a theory that is erroneous—insofar as generalization and practical usefulness are concerned—may well be accepted.

It is actually more useful to think of theories as falling at points along a deductive–inductive continuum than as falling into distinct categories. Probably no theory is completely devoid of some inductive input. On the other hand, there are instances arising from entirely inductive processes. Such instances are often referred to as *dust-bowl empiricism*, implying that no theory is involved at all. However, the result may look very much like a theory.

An example of dust-bowl empiricism would be a study in which a great many measures, say several hundred, are obtained on a sample of organizations. These data are then put into a computer, and closely related measures are identified through the use of correlation techniques, factor analysis, or some similar procedure. What emerges is a set of hypothesized relationships among variables—a set of statements very much like an inductively derived theory. This "theory" is then tested on a new sample of organizations, using the appropriate measures to make sure that it does not incorporate relationships that represent mere chance fluctuations associated with the particular sample from which the theory was induced.

Any theory, irrespective of the method of construction and the extent of research confirmation, should always be treated as provisional in nature. Theories are constructed to be modified or replaced as new knowledge is developed; this is the way science advances. Furthermore, modification on the basis of research tends to be inductive rather than deductive. Findings emerge that do not quite fit the existing theory. Accordingly, the theory is changed so that these new data can be explained, and a test is then made of the revised theory. As a result of this kind of theoretical tinkering, even predominantly deductive theories may take on a strong inductive element over time; if they do not, they may well be replaced.

DEFINING A GOOD OR STRONG THEORY

In order to evaluate theories, science needs some criteria for deciding whether a theory is good or not so good. It is evident from what has been said already that some explanatory statements may not meet the requirements of scientific theory at all, and that what was good theory at one time may become not-so-good theory some years later.

First, theories should contribute to the goals of science. They should aid understanding, permit prediction, and facilitate influence. The more they do these things, the better they are. A theory that is comprehensive in its coverage of the phenomena that it explains is preferable to one that is limited in scope. However, broad scope alone is not enough. Many so-called grand theories attempt too much and fail simply because they do not really explain the wide range of phenomena they attempt to consider.

Second, there should be a clear delineation of the domain of the theory, as indicated in Figure 1.1. The boundaries of application should be specified so that the theory is not utilized in situations for which it was never intended and is therefore useless. Definition of the coverage of a theory often has been neglected in the social sciences generally (Dubin 1978), and the field of organizational behavior is no exception.

Third, theory should direct research efforts to important matters. The number of research studies that could be done in the world is almost infinite. Yet most of these studies, even if the time and effort to carry them out were available, would not yield significant results in a statistical sense, and many of those that did would be trivial in terms of their usefulness. Good theory helps us focus research efforts on salient variables, identify important relationships, and come up with truly *significant* findings in every sense of the word. Basically, then, good theory protects the researcher from wasting time.

Fourth, theories at their best yield a kind of added value to research efforts. If several key hypotheses derived from a theory are confirmed by research, then the whole body of the theory becomes available for use. Thus theory-based research has the potential for yielding not just a few isolated facts but powerful explanation and prediction across the whole domain of the theory.

This aspect of good theory is one of its most practical consequences. Unfortunately, many theories do not have this cumulative character.

Fifth, theories should be readily testable. It should be clear exactly what must be done to either confirm or disconfirm them. On occasion, experimenters will carry out studies that they believe to be adequate tests of a theory only to have the theorist say, "That is not what I meant." When a theory is well formulated, this situation should rarely arise. Ideally, the theorist will identify the variables of the theory in operational terms.

Sixth, good theory is not only confirmed by research derived from it, but is also logically consistent within itself and with other known facts. In the case of complex theories, it is entirely possible to develop propositions that would predict diametrically opposed outcomes in the same situation. This is particularly likely to happen when the theorist comes at the same subject matter from different directions, using different concepts and assumptions. Such internal, logical inconsistencies must be ironed out if the theory is to be of much use. Furthermore, theories do not exist in a vacuum; they are part of the total body of scientific knowledge. At any given time it may not be entirely clear how a particular theory fits into the larger scientific configuration, but a theory that from the outset quite obviously does not fit at all is to that degree deficient. Theories should build on what is known and fit consistently into the entire network of existing knowledge (Hartman 1988).

Seventh, the best theory is the one that is simplest in statement. If a given set of phenomena can be explained parsimoniously with a few variables, that theory should be preferred over one that achieves the same level of explanation with a much more complex set of variables and relationships. Science does not value complexity in its own right; there is enough of that all around us in nature. Highly complex and involved theories are often very difficult to put into practice. Thus, the ultimate objective must be to replace them with simpler explanations. Unfortunately, the process of inductive theory modification often demands that new constructs and variables be added continually as unanticipated findings emerge and need to be explained. Under such circumstances a theory may fall of its own weight, for it is just too cumbersome to be useful.

Theories that consistently fail to attain these criteria (and thus ultimately emerge as bad) can have negative consequences for science (Webster and Starbuck 1988). They can well sustain themselves for a considerable period of time and lead science in wrong directions. They can also produce confusion and conflict that block scientific progress. All this argues for immediate testing of new theories so that their status can be established quickly. Without this, the risk of impediment to scientific advance is substantial.

Writing in the *Harvard Business Review* under the title "Why Hard-Nosed Executives Should Care About Management Theory," Christensen and Raynor (2003) note that good theories are valuable in part because they help make predictions; because reliable data are available only from the past, using strong theories of causality is the only way a manager can peer into the future with confidence. In addition, sound theories help to interpret the present and thus to understand what is happening, and why. Good theories make it possible to differentiate the signals that portend significant changes in the future from the noise that means nothing.

At a very high level of abstraction, the ultimate goal of science, and its theory as well, is to discover truth. This involves a firm belief that there is a reality out there external to the observer within which this truth exists. The quest to know this truth based in reality is plagued with uncertainty. Science seeks truth with the full recognition that it never can be known with absolute certainty—only approximations to certainty are possible. This view has been categorized as "scientific realism" or "organizational realism" (McKelvey 1997). Such a view reflects the predominant position in organizational behavior at the present time.

However, a minority position also exists. Such a position emphasizes the socially constructed nature of organizational phenomena and espouses a subjectivity that seems to deny the existence of outside reality altogether (see Weiss 2000 for an extended discussion of this view). Accordingly, truth takes a backseat to novelty, provocativeness, and uniqueness. In this view the goal of theory construction and the basis for theory evaluation is not truth, but uniqueness (Mone and McKinley 1993). These are not the values of science, but they do reflect a current philosophic position. We will return to so-called "contra" views of this kind in Chapter 2, but for now it is sufficient to indicate that the fact that a theory is socially constructed does not make it incompatible with truth and objectivity and thus with the goals and methods of science (Meckler and Baillie 2003).

KINDS OF THEORIES

Theories can be good or bad, or more frequently somewhere in-between; they can seek truth or some other goal. Many additional ways to classify theories exist as well. Although the labels that result often are self-evident, several approaches require more discussion.

Micro, Macro, and Meso

Micro theory in organizational behavior deals with the behaviors and nature of individuals and small groups in organizations. It has been strongly influenced by psychology, and many of its theorists were originally trained in that field. A good understanding of the micro approach can be had from a reading of Staw (1991). Motivation and leadership are essentially micro subjects, although theories in both areas may contain variables that extend beyond that designation.

Macro theory focuses on the behavior and nature of organizations, not of individuals and groups. Parts of the organization may be of concern as well, and so may the environment surrounding the organization. Sociology has played a role in the development of macro theory very similar to that played by psychology in micro theory. In a companion piece to the Staw (1991) article, Pfeffer (1991) offers a good example of how macro theorizing works.

This distinction between micro and macro levels has been part of the organizational behavior field since its early years (for a recent example of this distinction, see Wright and Boswell 2002). A more recent arrival, at least in terms of terminology, is meso theory. House, Rousseau, and Thomas-Hunt (1995) define the meso approach as concerning the simultaneous study of at least two levels where one level deals with individual or group processes or variables, one level deals with organizational processes or variables, and bridging or linking propositions are set forth to relate the two levels. An example of meso theorizing is presented in a book by Tosi (1992).

Tosi's (1992) book contains a number of theoretical propositions that can be used to illustrate the macro-micro-meso distinctions:

> The relevant environment of an organization is defined as external organizations or institutions which have direct effects on decisions and processes in the focal organization (29)—*macro.*
>
> . . .
>
> The degree of volatility of the environmental sectors affects the structure of subsystem relationships in organizations (34)—*macro.*
>
> . . .
>
> When individual personality manifests itself it usually does so with respect to interactions with others or toward the organization, not in terms of work patterns or levels of performance (82)—*micro.*

. . .

A particular leader action is interpreted and attributions are made in the situational context. Different situations may result in different attributions about the same acts. It is the nature of the attribution, not the behavior itself, which is related to effectiveness (196)—*micro.*

. . .

The dominant form of conflict in organic organizations is rivalry. The bases for the rivalry will be

1. competition for resources for projects in process and/or
2. status-based competition between specialists from different disciplines.

There will be moderate to low levels of vertical conflict in organic organizations (110)—*meso.*

. . .

Power striving predispositions will lead to power striving and political behavior when organizations are loosely coupled (128)—*meso.*

Typologies as Theory

A number of theories set forth various categories of organizations, environments, people, or groups, usually in the range of two to five. These formulations may deal with ideal types—sets of intellectual, hypothetical constructs created purely to study variety and change, which are not necessarily found in their complete form in the real world at all (Lammers 1988). At the other extreme are formulations that utilize only empirically derived clusters, based on real world data, which are created using the techniques of dust-bowl empiricism (Ketchen and Shook 1996). There are variants between these two as well.

The terms *typology* and *taxonomy* may be applied to these formulations, but they have not been used in a consistent manner, and there is no universal agreement on either definitions or appropriate approaches (Rich 1992). There are even those who decry the use of such classification systems entirely, viewing them as inherently unsound (Donaldson 1996). Given this situation, a working approach to theories of this kind is needed. In what follows, I believe the discussion is consistent with the dominant position in the field of organizational behavior at the present time. If not, the position is at least a widely accepted one (Doty and Glick 1994; Miller 1996; Sanchez 1993).

The term *typology* is used to refer to a set of types developed on an a priori conceptual basis to operate as and serve the purposes of a theory. These constructs may be of an ideal nature or they may to varying degrees be intended to reflect the actual nature of the real world. These conceptual typologies are viewed as theories, and they may be good or not-so-good just like any other theory. Taxonomies, on the other hand, are empirically derived clusterings developed through multivariate analysis of existing data. As such they are data, not theories; description, not explanation. However, theoretical formulations may be developed inductively starting from taxonomies, thus folding a taxonomy into a more comprehensive theoretical system. Thus, a taxonomy alone does not constitute a theory, but each instance needs to be considered separately. For a more extended treatment of these matters, the reader is referred to Miner (1997).

Grounded Theory

Grounded theory focuses on qualitative data for the purpose of developing systematic, limited domain theories about observed phenomena. It derives its data from participant observation, direct observation, semi-structured or even unstructured interviews, and case studies in essentially the same manner that an anthropologist might use in studying a culture. Facets of these research data are sorted out of the mass of available qualitative information by means of consciously adopted strategies. These emerging concepts, grounded in the data, become the foundation of a growing theoretical understanding of the phenomena studied (Glaser and Strauss 1967; Turner 1983).

Such a theoretical approach is inductive, and the results are theoretical accounts of relatively small segments of reality. This process attempts to distill out the essence of these segments, and in doing so creates a theory that is rich in terms of the depth of its content, but not broad. These grounded theory accounts may be used to develop more formal theory, however, by focusing on a domain of more general interest, generalizing from the specific. Within organizational behavior one will find little by way of grounded theorizing in the original sense. On the other hand, more formal theories having their origins in such grounded theorizing are in evidence. In any event, it is important to keep in mind that the proper role of grounded theory is to generate theories, not to test them (Parry 1998).

CONCLUSIONS

The philosophy of science as set forth here places considerable emphasis on the role of theory. The reason is that although quantum leaps in science are very rare in any event, they are only possible if theory provides the opportunity. Organizational behavior has had its share of theories, and enough of these have proven useful to move the field forward quite rapidly. However, it is important to understand that further progress requires more good theories, and these will only be created if the field fully recognizes what theory is and how it operates. Yet theory only becomes useful if it is validated by research. Managers should not accept theories and apply them to their work unless there is reason to believe that the theories are empirically valid. At the same time, research results are the agents that determine whether theories are true or false. How good research is conducted is discussed in Chapter 2.

I noted in the Preface that the theories of motivation and leadership presented and explored in this volume are those that meet one or more of the requirements for being labeled as *essential*—important, institutionalized, valid, and/or useful—as determined by scholars and intellectual leaders of the field. It is interesting to compare this listing with one published in the *Harvard Business Review* (Prusak and Davenport 2003), which appears to have been influenced much more, though certainly not exclusively, by the popular press.

The latter listing contains forty-eight "gurus," many of whom in their writings deal with topics other than micro-organizational behavior. Yet the fact that only one person (Kurt Lewin) appears on both lists is revealing. The heroes of science and academe are clearly quite distinct from those one is likely to run across in the world of practice and the popular press. Accordingly, I think you will find some interesting, and very different, ideas in the chapters of this book that follow.

REFERENCES

Astley, W. Graham, and Zammuto, Raymond F. (1992). Organization Science, Managers, and Language Games. *Organization Science,* 3, 443–60.

Bacharach, Samuel B. (1989). Organizational Theories: Some Criteria for Evaluation. *Academy of Management Review,* 14, 496–515.

Berelson, Bernard, and Steiner, Gary (1964). *Human Behavior: An Inventory of Scientific Findings.* New York: Harcourt, Brace and World.

Beyer, Janice M. (1992). Metaphors, Misunderstandings, and Mischief: A Commentary. *Organization Science,* 3, 467–74.

Blood, Milton R. (1994). The Role of Organizational Behavior in the Business School Curriculum. In Jerald Greenberg (Ed.), *Organizational Behavior: The State of the Science*. Hillsdale, NJ: Lawrence Erlbaum Associates, 207–20.

Brooks, Margaret E., Grauer, Eyal, Thornbury, Erin E., and Highhouse, Scott (2003). Value Differences between Scientists and Practitioners: A Survey of SIOP Members. *The Industrial-Organizational Psychologist*, 40(4), 17–23.

Brown, Clarence W., and Ghiselli, Edwin E. (1955). *Scientific Method in Psychology*. New York: McGraw-Hill.

Campbell, John P. (1990). The Role of Theory in Industrial and Organizational Psychology. In Marvin D. Dunnette and Leatta M. Hough (Eds.), *Handbook of Industrial and Organizational Psychology*, Vol. 1. Palo Alto, CA: Consulting Psychologists Press, 39–73.

Cheng, Tsz-kit, Sculli, Domenic, and Chan, Fiona S. (2001). Relationship Dominance: Rethinking Management Theories from the Perspective of Methodological Relationalism. *Journal of Managerial Psychology*, 16, 97–105.

Christensen, Clayton M., and Raynor, Michael E. (2003). Why Hard-Nosed Executives Should Care about Management Theory. *Harvard Business Review*, 81(9), 67–74.

Clegg, Stewart R., Hardy, Cynthia, and Nord, Walter R. (1996). *Handbook of Organization Studies*. London: Sage.

Cooper, Cary L., and Locke, Edwin A. (2000). *Industrial and Organizational Psychology: Linking Theory with Practice*. Oxford, UK: Blackwell.

Das, T.K. (2003). Managerial Perceptions and the Essence of the Managerial World: What Is an Interloper Business Executive to Make of the Academic-Researcher Perceptions of Managers? *British Journal of Management*, 14, 23–32.

Donaldson, Lex (1996). *For Positivist Organization Theory*. London: Sage.

——— (2002). Damned by Our Own Theories: Contradictions between Theories and Management Education. *Academy of Management Learning and Education*, 1, 96–106.

Doty, D. Harold, and Glick, William H. (1994). Typologies as a Unique Form of Theory Building: Toward Improving Understanding and Modeling. *Academy of Management Review*, 19, 230–51.

Dubin, Robert (1976). Theory Building in Applied Areas. In Marvin D. Dunnette (Ed.), *Handbook of Industrial and Organizational Psychology*. Chicago, IL: Rand McNally, 17–39.

——— (1978). *Theory Building*. New York: Free Press.

Ford, Eric W., Duncan, W. Jack, Bedeian, Arthur G., Ginter, Peter M., Rousculp, Mathew D., and Adams, Alice M. (2003). Mitigating Risks, Visible Hands, Inevitable Disasters, and Soft Variables: Management Research that Matters to Managers. *Academy of Management Executive*, 17, 46–60.

George, Jennifer M., and Jones, Gareth R. (2000). The Role of Time in Theory and Theory Building. *Journal of Management*, 26, 657–84.

Glaser, Barney G., and Strauss, Anselm L. (1967). *The Discovery of Grounded Theory*. Chicago, IL: Aldine.

Gottfredson, Linda S. (1983). Creating and Criticizing Theory. *Journal of Vocational Behavior*, 23, 203–12.

Hartman, Edwin (1988). *Conceptual Foundations of Organization Theory*. Cambridge, MA: Ballinger.

House, Robert, Rousseau, Denise M., and Thomas-Hunt, Melissa (1995). The Meso Paradigm: A Framework for the Integration of Micro and Macro Organizational Behavior. *Research in Organizational Behavior*, 17, 71–114.

Kaplan, Abraham (1964). *The Conduct of Inquiry*. San Francisco, CA: Chandler.

Ketchen, David J., and Shook, Christopher, L. (1996). The Application of Cluster Analysis in Strategic Management Research: An Analysis and Critique. *Strategic Management Journal*, 17, 441–58.

Lammers, Cornelis (1988). Transience and Persistence of Ideal Types in Organizational Theory. *Research in the Sociology of Organizations*, 6, 203–24.

Lewin, Kurt (1945). The Research Center for Group Dynamics at Massachusetts Institute of Technology. *Sociometry*, 8, 126–35.

Locke, Edwin A. (2003). Good Definitions: The Epistemological Foundation of Scientific Progress. In Jerald Greenberg (Ed.), *Organizational Behavior: The State of the Science*. Mahwah, NJ: Lawrence Erlbaum, 415–44.

McKelvey, Bill (1997). Quasi-natural Organization Science. *Organization Science*, 8, 352–80.

Mazza, Carmelo, and Alvarez, José L. (2000). Haute Couture and Prêt-à-Porter: The Popular Press and the Diffusion of Management Practices. *Organization Studies*, 21, 567–88.

Meckler, Mark, and Baillie, James (2003). The Truth about Social Construction in Administrative Science. *Journal of Management Inquiry*, 12, 273–84.

Miller, Danny (1996). Configurations Revisited. *Strategic Management Journal*, 17, 505–12.

Miner, John B. (1984). The Validity and Usefulness of Theories in an Emerging Organizational Science. *Academy of Management Review,* 9, 297–306.

———— (1997). *A Psychological Typology of Successful Entrepreneurs.* Westport, CT: Quorum.

———— (2004). Congruence and the Significance of Careers in Testing Task Role Motivation Theory. Working paper, Eugene, Oregon, 1–49.

Mitchell, Terence R., and James, Lawrence R. (2001). Building Better Theory: Time and the Specification of When Things Happen. *Academy of Management Review,* 26, 530–47.

Mone, M.A., and McKinley, William (1993). The Uniqueness Value and Its Consequences for Organization Studies. *Journal of Management Inquiry,* 2, 284–96.

Parry, Ken W. (1998). Grounded Theory and Social Process: A New Direction for Leadership Research. *Leadership Quarterly,* 9, 85–105.

Pfeffer, Jeffrey (1991). Organization Theory and Structural Perspectives on Management. *Journal of Management,* 17, 789–803.

———— (1995). Mortality, Reproducibility, and the Persistence of Styles of Theory. *Organization Science,* 6, 681–86.

Priem, Richard L., and Rosenstein, J. (2000). Is Organization Theory Obvious to Practitioners? A Test of One Established Theory. *Organization Science,* 11, 509–24.

Prusak, Laurence, and Davenport, Thomas H. (2003). Who Are the Gurus' Gurus? *Harvard Business Review,* 81(12), 14–16.

Rich, Philip (1992). The Organizational Taxonomy: Definition and Design. *Academy of Management Review,* 17, 758–81.

Roehling, Mark V., Cavanaugh, Marcie A., Moynihan, Lisa M., and Boswell, Wendy R. (2000). The Nature of the New Employment Relationship: A Content Analysis of the Practitioner and Academic Literatures. *Human Resource Management,* 39, 305–20.

Rynes, Sara L., Bartunek, Jean M., and Daft, Richard L. (2001). Across the Great Divide: Knowledge Creation and Transfer between Practitioners and Academics. *Academy of Management Journal,* 44, 340–55.

Rynes, Sara L., Brown, Kenneth G., and Colbert, Amy L. (2002). Seven Common Misconceptions about Human Resource Practices: Resource Findings versus Practitioner Beliefs. *Academy of Management Executive,* 16, 92–102.

Rynes, Sara L., Colbert, Amy E., and Brown, Kenneth G. (2002). HR Professionals' Beliefs about Effective Human Resource Practices: Correspondence between Research and Practice. *Human Resource Management,* 41, 149–74.

Rynes, Sara L., and McNatt, D. Brian (2001). Bringing the Organization into Organizational Research: An Examination of Academic Research inside Organizations. *Journal of Business and Psychology,* 16, 3–19.

Sanchez, Julio C. (1993). The Long and Thorny Way to an Organizational Taxonomy. *Organization Studies,* 14, 73–92.

Sandelands, Lloyd, and Drazin, Robert (1989). On the Language of Organization Theory. *Organization Studies,* 10, 457–78.

Schendel, Dan E., and Hofer, Charles W. (1979). *Strategic Management: A New View of Business Policy and Planning.* Boston, MA: Little, Brown.

Staw, Barry M. (1991). Dressing Up Like an Organization: When Psychological Theories Can Explain Organizational Action. *Journal of Management,* 17, 805–19.

Steiner, George A., and Miner, John B. (1986). *Management Policy and Strategy.* New York: Macmillan.

Sutton, Robert I., and Staw, Barry M. (1995). What Theory Is Not. *Administrative Science Quarterly,* 40, 371–84.

Tosi, Henry L. (1992). *The Environment/Organization/Person Contingency Model: A Meso Approach to the Study of Organizations.* Greenwich, CT: JAI Press.

Turner, Barry A. (1983). The Use of Grounded Theory for the Qualitative Analysis of Organizational Behavior. *Journal of Management Studies,* 20, 333–48.

Van de Ven, Andrew H. (1989). Nothing Is Quite So Practical as a Good Theory. *Academy of Management Review,* 14, 486–89.

Webster, Jane, and Starbuck, William H. (1988). Theory Building in Industrial and Organizational Psychology. *International Review of Industrial and Organizational Psychology,* 3, 93–138.

Weiss, Richard M. (2000). Taking Science Out of Organization Science: How Would Postmodernism Reconstruct the Analysis of Organizations? *Organization Science,* 11, 709–31.

Wright, Patrick M., and Boswell, Wendy R. (2002). Desegregating HRM: A Review and Synthesis of Micro and Macro Human Resource Management Research. *Journal of Management,* 28, 247–76.

CHAPTER 2

THE CONDUCT OF RESEARCH AND THE DEVELOPMENT OF KNOWLEDGE

Measuring Variables
    Reliability
    Validity
Research Design
    Laboratory Experiments
    Field Experiments
    Quasi-Experimental Designs
    Common Method Variance and Bias
    Requirements for Conducting Experimental Research
Theoretical Knowledge of Organizational Behavior and Its Objections
    Objections to Scientific Dictates—Frontal Attacks
    Postmodernism and Siblings
    Threats from Within the United States
Values and Knowledge
    Values in Organizational Behavior
    Dispositions Versus Situations—A Value-Laden Controversy
    Positive Organizational Scholarship
The Role of Consensus
    The Consensus Problem
    The Inability to Compare Competing Theories
    The Road to Consensus
Conclusions

To a substantial degree, the value of a theory is inherent in the research it sparks and in the extent to which the theory is confirmed by this research. Research is only possible, however, to the extent that measures of the variables of the theory are developed, that is, to the extent that the constructs are made operational. These twin topics of measurement and research concern us here. The objective is not to provide a detailed treatment. However, in later chapters we will be asking questions such as "Does this measure really effectively represent the constructs of the theory?" and "Does this research provide an appropriate test of the theory?" The answers to these questions will draw on some knowledge of both measurement procedures and research design, and the ensuing discussion is intended to provide a basis for understanding in these areas.

MEASURING VARIABLES

Measures used in organizational research have often fallen short of what might be desired (Price and Mueller 1986). Many of organizational behavior's theories utilize constructs far removed from those previously measured in the social sciences. Thus, it has been necessary in many cases to develop reliable and valid measures to represent new constructs, which is a time-consuming process. Many organizational measures are still at a primitive stage of development. This situation can seriously hamper the interpretation of research results. For a number of years, for instance, expectancy theory (see Chapter 7) was thought to have limited value because the new measures used to test it were deficient. Only later, with greater attention to measurement problems, did the full value of the theory become apparent. This matter of effectively converting constructs into variables (see Figure 1.1) is what concerns us here.

Reliability

A major concern in research is the reliability of measurement. Measures that are sufficiently stable and unambiguous will not produce sizable differences in score values when applied to the same phenomenon on separate occasions. The reliability of a measure is usually established by a correlation coefficient. Different approaches are used to determine this reliability coefficient, but all approaches approximate the ideal procedure, which utilizes parallel forms of the same measure. Parallel forms exist when two indexes of the same construct contain the same number of items of each type, concentrate equally on the various aspects of the construct, and produce the same average scores and distributions of scores through the range of possible values. Once such parallel measures have been developed, reliability is determined by administering both measures in the same sample and correlating the scores on the two measures.

The value of a reliability coefficient fluctuates to some extent, depending on whether the parallel form or some other approach is used. However, if one wishes to use a measure in an individual situation—to measure the work motivation of a *particular* person, for instance, or to compute the average span of control in a *certain* company—reliability coefficients above 0.90 are required. If, on the other hand, one is dealing with group data such as mean work motivation scores in two units of a company or average span of control in relation to profitability in a number of companies, values down to about 0.70, and sometimes less, typically are acceptable. These standards represent what amount to "rules of thumb" or working conventions. Like many such conventions in science, they are enforced by gatekeepers such as journal editors and thesis or dissertation chairpersons.

The matter of reliability of measurement is important in research because it is impossible to interpret outcomes when unreliable measures are used, and results are not statistically significant. The failure to obtain evidence of a relationship between two variables could be due to the fact that there is no relationship. But if one or both measures of the two variables are unreliable, a relationship may well exist that has not been discovered because of inadequate measures. The only satisfactory way to resolve this uncertainty is to develop and use measures of high reliability. Then if relationships are not found, they are very unlikely to exist in the world of reality. For an example of how reliability estimates may be used to differentiate measures, see Loo (2002).

Validity

The variables of a theory need to be made operational in the form of specific measures. Accordingly, the measures must truly reflect the underlying constructs; they must provide valid data regarding the phenomena that they are supposed to represent. If, in fact, they measure constructs other than the ones they are intended to measure, the theory may well be assumed to be disconfirmed when it is actually correct. Worse still, a theory may be accepted when in fact its variables have been incorrectly stated (Edwards 2003).

I once developed an index intended to measure conformity to organizational norms (Miner 1962). Subsequent research revealed that the index was almost completely unrelated to any other measure of conformity that could be identified in the literature. However, moderate relationships were found with measures of intelligence. Apparently, if the measure did tap some tendency to conform, it was not the same construct that other researchers had in mind when they used the term. A likely interpretation was that we had developed a measure one of whose more pronounced components was intelligence, although there was evidence of a relationship to a desire to escape into a crowd as well. This clearly was a much more complex construct than we had originally envisioned, one that our underlying theory was ill equipped to handle.

This example demonstrates how one goes about determining the validity of a measure. If the measure is what it purports to be, there are certain phenomena to which it should be related and certain other phenomena to which it should not be related. In the case of conformity, there were other indexes of the construct available. Often, when a new and highly innovative theory is under test, other measures are not available. Nevertheless, it should be possible to identify certain relationships that would be expected to appear with a high degree of likelihood. In this process, however, it is important not to rely on *face validity* alone. The measure that looks to be appropriate as an index of a given variable on further investigation may or may not prove to tap that construct.

As we shall see later, establishing the validity of a particular construct measure is not easy. To some degree, the answer is always inferential (Cortina 2002). Yet there are organizational measures in which one can have considerable faith, while there are others that, even after long years of use, leave considerable doubt as to their construct validity. Certain statistical procedures have been developed to aid in construct validation (Bagozzi, Yi, and Phillips 1991), and these can be quite useful under appropriate circumstances. However, they do not circumvent the need for close reasoning and careful research design. In any event, in spite of occasional instances of confusion, reliability and validity need to be clearly differentiated (Schmidt, Viswesvaran, and Ones 2000).

A final point, however, should be noted with regard to this construct validity matter. There has been a tendency in recent years for reports of studies to neglect dealing with the validity of key measures (Scandura and Williams 2000). In fact, there are those who argue that the term *construct validity* is an invalid concept, in need of elimination from the language of organizational behavior (Locke 2003). This is not the position taken here. Research aimed at validation, and construct validation in particular, can have important implications for the inductive reconstruction of a theory, or for its abandonment. We need more of this type of research, not less.

RESEARCH DESIGN

Research conducted to test theories characteristically investigates hypothesized relationships between variables. Such research is first concerned with whether a relationship exists at all and then with the causal nature of that relationship. Research focused on the existence of a relationship is relatively easy to conduct; however, research into the causal problem is clearly much less tractable.

The study of causation typically requires the collection of data over time, on the premise that the cause must be shown to precede the effect. There are now techniques, however, known collectively as causal modeling approaches, that under appropriate circumstances can be used with data collected at one time, as well as longitudinally. These techniques have expanded in number, in complexity, and in explanatory power over the past twenty years. Their use is increasing rapidly, and they appear to offer considerable promise in evaluating causal hypotheses (Williams, Edwards, and Vandenberg 2003).

A second factor that makes identification of causal relationships difficult is the necessity for establishing adequate controls. Control may be accomplished statistically through the use of procedures that measure unwanted variables and then remove their effects from the relationship under study. However, these statistical techniques require that the data satisfy certain assumptions, and in many cases it is not at all clear that these assumptions can be met. The alternative is to control variables through the original design of the study. That is not always easy.

Laboratory Experiments

Much of the research on causal relationships has been done in the laboratory. An extreme instance of this laboratory research is computer simulation in which no real subjects are involved. More frequently, the experiment is of the small group or group dynamics type; experimental variables are introduced among subjects, often college sophomores, and the results are measured under highly controlled conditions. Because the study is conducted outside the real world of ongoing organizations, it is easier to use longitudinal measures and to control unwanted variables. Yet even here major difficulties in maintaining controls exist. Furthermore, the results are very much a function of the variables considered (this is particularly true of computer simulations). If the real world is not effectively modeled in the laboratory, or at least the key elements of that world, the results of laboratory experiments will not transfer.

This said, it appears that in many areas such transfers do occur (Locke 1986). Laboratory studies often appear to be well conducted, or conceivably field research is deficient in important areas, with the result that similar results are obtained. In any event, the evidence to date is that laboratory research, with its greater control, is much more valid than previously anticipated. There may be conditions under which this is not true. A degree of field research on laboratory findings still seems warranted. But, assuming initial confirmation, the need for extensive reiteration of these initial results does not seem as great as previously thought.

Field Experiments

The ideal situation is to take the techniques of sample selection, repetitive measurement, and variable control associated with laboratory research into the real world and conduct the same kind of research with ongoing organizations. In such a context the myriad variables that may be important do in fact operate, and any results obtained there can be expected to characterize the actual organizations to which any meaningful theory is addressed. The problem is that all the difficulties of designing and conducting good experiments that were so easily handled in the laboratory now become overwhelming. Real organizations have innumerable ways of resisting and undermining objective scientific research—not out of contrariness, but because the goals of the real world and the laboratory are different.

The difficulties of conducting causal research in organizations may be illustrated by a study by Belasco and Trice (1969) on the effects of a particular management development program. The study utilized 119 managers divided into four groups. Managers were assigned to each group on a random basis within sex, type of work supervised, and division groupings. In this manner, as many factors as possible were held constant across the four groups to control for spurious factors that might contaminate the findings and make causal attribution difficult.

One group of managers was pretested, trained, and posttested on knowledge, attitudes, and behavior. The objective was to see if a change occurred on any of these factors.

A second group took the pretest, received no training, and then took the posttest. If this group changed as much as the first, clearly the training was not the cause of change. If this group did not change as much as the first, the training remained a strong contender as a cause.

A third group underwent no pretest, received training, and took the posttest. By comparing the posttest result for the third group with that for the first group, it was possible to identify any apparent change due to a sensitizing effect of the pretest (the groups were similar in all other respects). The problem addressed here is control for any effects the pretest may have had in alerting the managers to what they were supposed to learn later in training.

The fourth group received no pretest, no training, and only the posttest. This group, in comparison with the others, yields a measure of the effects of the passage of time only, and therefore it isolates time from either repeated measurement or training as factors.

Clearly, this kind of research requires a large number of subjects, the opportunity to assign them to groups as desired for research purposes, and extensive collaboration from the sponsoring organization throughout the study. And, as elaborate as the research plan is, it could be argued that a fifth group, undergoing some training of a relatively neutral nature, should have been included to create a placebo situation and cancel out any so-called Hawthorne effect produced by receiving special attention. Thus, even this very complex experiment cannot be said to have achieved the ideal in terms of control. Such studies are very difficult to conduct, yet they continue to appear in the literature (e.g., see Probst 2003).

Quasi-Experimental Designs

Realistically elegant research designs with all possible controls are unlikely to be implemented in many organizations, and if an organization does decide to go this route, it may well be an atypical organization. Accordingly, certain variants have been proposed (Cook, Campbell, and Peracchio 1990; Evans 1999). These designs represent major advances over the noncausal, correlational analyses, but no one such study answers all questions. Basically, these studies utilize as many components of the ideal experimental design as possible, while recognizing that it is better to conduct some kind of research related to causes than to do nothing. Hopefully, the larger number of research investigations carried out will compensate for the relative relaxation of control requirements. Accordingly, several interlocking investigations should develop the same level of knowledge as one very elegant study. On the other hand, it is easy to relax scientific standards to the point where replication is not possible and thus not obtain scientific knowledge that can be substantiated. Some trends in qualitative research on organizations show this tendency. It is important to maintain a clear distinction between scientific research and personal narrative in testing organizational behavior theories.

A number of examples of well-conducted quasi-experiments exist in the recent literature. The typical design calls for some combination of the elements considered in the previous section (e.g., see Markham, Scott, and McKee 2002). A particularly good discussion of the limitations that may be inherent in the quasi-experimental design is contained in Morgeson and Campion (2002). Descriptions of how quasi-experimental designs may be utilized in studying promotion effects are presented in a series of studies conducted within an international bank based in Hong Kong (see in particular Lam and Schaubroeck 2000).

Common Method Variance and Bias

Common method problems can arise from having a common rater provide the measures of variables, a common measurement context, a common item context, or from characteristics of the items in a measure. Of these, obtaining measures of both the predictor and criterion within the same study from the same person produces the most pronounced such results; these biases can be quite substantial (Podsakoff, MacKenzie, Lee, and Podsakoff 2003). Thus, when the same person reports on the two types of variables, that person may change the correlations in an attempt to maintain logical consistency. The results are a function of the measurement method rather than of the underlying constructs.

In expectancy theory (Chapter 7), cross-sectional rather than longitudinal designs are often used. Accordingly, individuals' reports of their internal states (such as expectancies) are obtained at the same time and from the same person as reports of past behavior related to these internal states. As a result of a desire to maintain cognitive consistency, these correlations can be inflated substantially (Lindell and Whitney 2001). This bias is introduced because of the measurement approach taken and the failure to use more appropriate designs.

Solutions to this type of problem, as is typical in organizational behavior research, focus on designing the problem away or controlling it with statistics. In the past, however, many studies have been conducted that did neither of these, thus simply ignoring the problem. What is needed is to separate the measures of the variables involved by using different sources, and thus different research designs. An alternative is to use measures of variables that are not self-evident (such as projective techniques), so that the individual cannot mobilize attempts to attain cognitive consistency. Attempts to solve common method problems through the use of statistical approaches have been numerous, but as yet no widely accepted solution has emerged.

Requirements for Conducting Experimental Research

Blackburn (1987) has set forth a list of what he labels the ten commandments for conducting experimental research. These can serve as a guide in assessing research used to test theories in the organizational behavior field.

1. Thou shalt assess the extent to which the change actually took effect.
2. Whenever possible, thou shalt use multiple measures.
3. Whenever possible, thou shalt use unobtrusive measures.
4. Thou shalt seek to avoid changes in measurement procedures.
5. Thou shalt endeavor to use a randomized experimental design whenever possible.
6. In the absence of random assignment, thou shalt not select experimental or control groups on the basis of some characteristic that the group may possess to some unusual degree.
7. Thou shalt use appropriate statistical analyses to examine the differences between the experimental and control groups.
8. Whenever possible, thou shalt collect time-series data.
9. To the greatest extent possible, thou shalt protect the employee, the organization, and the experiment in that order.
10. Thou shalt report fully and honestly the procedures and results of the research.

Many of these points are illustrated in a book edited by Frost and Stablein (1992), which provides detailed descriptions of what actually happened in connection with seven research studies. This book is also a good source of information regarding ways in which qualitative research may be employed for purposes of inductive theory development.

THEORETICAL KNOWLEDGE OF ORGANIZATIONAL BEHAVIOR AND ITS OBJECTIONS

The high visibility of certain formulations that are clearly closer to philosophy than to scientific theory has led some to question whether or not organizational behavior truly possesses any theories at all. This negative position has received additional support from some individuals, a number of them scientists who place very little stock in theory building in any event, preferring the slow but solid pace of unswerving empiricism. Yet there does appear to be a number of real scientific theories dealing with organizations, or at least explanations so advanced that not to call them theories is something of a quibble. This is not to say that these theories are necessarily and entirely valid; some of them have not been fully tested. But overall they have contributed substantially to our knowledge of organizations.

On the other hand, there is a rather sizable body of literature that raises serious objections to the scientific concepts we have been considering. If one follows these views, quite a different picture of our theoretical knowledge of organizational behavior emerges.

Objections to Scientific Dictates—Frontal Attacks

A common method of dealing with antithetical positions is to simply ignore them, thus avoiding the need to cite them or to consider the views at all (Martin and Frost, 1996). I clearly could do this here. Yet the concept of science set forth in the preceding pages is what underlies the whole field of organizational behavior, and to simply ignore objections to it does not appear to be intellectually honest, nor does it truly reflect the reality of the times.

One "contra" position is that science as a whole, and certainly the organizational behavior part of it, has not proven convincing as a superior form of knowledge, that new narratives and new epistemologies are needed to supersede science, and that basically science has had its day and now has run out of steam (Burrell 1996). This is an across-the-board dismissal, and it applies to all aspects of science. In my opinion this line of assault requires an equally direct response. Given the realities of the world around us, such arguments for the demise of science make no sense, and they are best lumped with similar "end of the world" scenarios. Yet they persist (Alvesson 2003).

In addition to such blanket attacks, a number of more specific objections have been raised that typically focus on some aspect of scientific theory and/or research. One such approach is to challenge the various assumptions of science (Kilduff and Mehra 1997). For instance, the argument may be that natural groupings of organizations, groups, and individuals do not occur, that uniqueness is everywhere; and thus generalization from samples is not warranted. Another such argument is that things change so fast that the stability and constancy science requires is nonexistent; science thus gives way to journalism—the recording and explaining of fleeting phenomena. A third challenge asserts either that events are not determined, and thus cause–effect relationships do not exist, or that social science, as distinct from natural science, is concerned with meanings and significance, not causes. Finally, the trustworthiness of human processes of perception, memory, or reasoning may be questioned, thus introducing challenges to the observation and experience on which science is based. Advocates of these positions tend to give more credence to qualitative research than to quantitative (Kilduff and Kelemen 2003). Qualitative research is accordingly moved from its role as an adjunct to inductive theory building to a central role in theory testing.

Other objections are concerned with the objectivity and relevance of scientific research (see Ghate and Locke 2003). These views may emphasize the fact that people as the subjects of research react differently when they become aware of the researchers' hypotheses or experience a feeling of being controlled in the experimental situation; thus, the research process itself poses a threat to generalization. Alternatively, research studies, especially laboratory studies, may be viewed as lacking the realism required for generalization. Objections of these kinds seem to assert that all organizational behavior research is bad research and that researchers cannot overcome these threats to their findings through creative methodologies because objectivity is impossible to obtain. Data such as those summarized in Locke (1986) on the close proximity of laboratory and field research findings are totally ignored.

Postmodernism and Siblings

Some of the strongest attacks on social science, and inherently on organizational behavior, stem from a group of philosophies called critical theory, poststructuralism, and postmodernism (Agger 1991), or perhaps some combination of these terms (Voronov and Coleman 2003). These philosophies all had their origins outside the United States, and it is there that they originally had the greatest impact. In certain respects they have been influenced by Marxist ideology (see Barrett 2003). These views differ in a number of aspects, but the opposition to social science is pervasive, as reflected in the positions noted in the previous section. Science is portrayed as a source of authority and a perpetuator of the status quo. As such, it must be replaced. Objective analysis and a reliance on mathematics are rejected. In point of fact, this contra position operates to oppose anything that is institutionalized—that has achieved legitimacy and is taken for granted (Alvesson 2003; Clegg and Kornberger 2003). Thus, science, its theory, and the like are merely part and parcel of a much wider enemy.

The preferred approach to gaining knowledge in these philosophies is one that focuses on obtaining detailed understandings of specific situations at a point in time. This approach has much in common with that of grounded theory, although references to that specific procedure by name appear to be rare since Silverman (1971). Studies in this vein collect a great deal of information, and they often present much of the raw data to the reader in undigested form in lieu of statistical analyses. Typically, the studies are used to both create theory and confirm it at one and the same time. Literary methods and storytelling may be used to present the results of data collection (Jermier 1985). Indeed, the analysis of language and its usage has become pervasive within postmodernism (Alvesson and Kärreman 2000).

When grounded theory is used to create more formal theories, it parts company with postmodernism and its siblings to join company with science. This distinction is important. The qualitative approaches involved may serve to generate scientific theory, *or* they may yield the self-fulfilling prophesies of postmodernism.

Threats from Within the United States

Although critical theory, poststructuralism, and postmodernism have been slow in taking root in the United States, there have been manifestations of similar ways of thinking here for some time. This has been most characteristic of those in the organizational behavior field who espouse humanistic values with a substantial amount of passion (see Lawler, Mohrman, Mohrman, Ledford, and Cummings 1985; Tannenbaum, Margulies, and Massarik 1985). Argyris has attacked scientific research methodology on numerous occasions and proposes an anthropological approach, devoid of statistical analysis, to replace it (e.g., see Argyris 1980).

These attacks from within are described by Donaldson (1992), an Australian, as an outgrowth primarily of certain trends in organizational behavior in the United States. He summarizes this complex of ideas as follows. It:

1. stresses the empirical world as subjectively perceived and enacted rather than as brute fact,
2. asserts the superiority of qualitative over quantitative methods;
3. reveres paradox in both the content of theory and the formal expression of theory;
4. holds that scientific creativity is primarily linguistic inventiveness;
5. sees itself as championing creativity;
6. is counter cultural in the sense of being ever-ready to cock a snook at the establishment and established ideas; and
7. would also claim that practicing managers would be better aided not by plodding positivism but by taking a mind-trip. (Donaldson 1992, 462)

This description is presented in connection with a rebuttal to an article by Astley and Zammuto (1992), to place that article in context.

Many other rebuttals to the various objections to scientific dictates exist in the literature. Among these, Weiss (2000) is particularly impressive. Donaldson (2003) provides an analysis that points up the logical inconsistencies of postmodernism. McKelvey (2003) castigates postmodernism for ignoring research and the falsifiability of theories. Not infrequently the objections create a description of science that, although incorrect, makes it easy to mount an attack. In this process science may very well be redefined as art, with all the freedom to embody values and eliminate burdensome rules that art permits. Many of those who object to the standards and strictures of good theory and good research seem to be trying to remove what they perceive to be barriers that keep them from using the garb of science to advocate their values. Good science—whether in the form of theory construction or exemplary research—is very hard work. The rules of the game are onerous, and they make good science difficult. But that is as it should be; they are there for a reason.

Furthermore, as Pescosolido and Rubin (2000) note: "The fault of postmodernism is that even in its radical insistence on diversity, it insists that its practitioners 'line up'" (71). There is no freedom from rules of some kind, even in postmodernism.

VALUES AND KNOWLEDGE

Values are conceptions of good and bad that tend to carry with them a great deal of emotion. They attach to certain ideas and patterns of behavior, and they provoke behavior consistent with the values as well. For an in-depth treatment of this values construct, see Maierhofer, Kabanoff, and Griffin (2002).

Values in Organizational Behavior

Organizational behavior appears to have been influenced by two primary value dimensions throughout much of its history. One is the dimension extending from humanistic to scientific values. In recent years the humanistic pole increasingly has been joined by the often similar values of postmodernism and its siblings. The other dimension is essentially disciplinary in origin. At one end is psychology, while the other end is anchored primarily in sociology, joined on occasion by anthropology, political science, and economics. Basically, these are values related to micro and macro levels of analysis.

This second, disciplinary dimension has undergone some transformation over the years. In an earlier period, the dimension ranged from behavioral science (dominated in large part by psychology) to classical management theory. As classical theory has faded from the scene (see Miner 1995), the value differentiation involved has been replaced by one within the behavioral science designation itself. At present, it appears to be particularly concerned with variations in the value placed on the study of individuals in organizations (see House, Shane, and Herold 1996; Nord and Fox 1996).

Values of these kinds can play a useful role in theory construction, in part by focusing attention on specific areas of endeavor and in part by motivating concerted efforts to construct theories that end by fostering understanding and prediction. However, values other than those that foster objectivity have no place in the conduct of research and thus in testing theory. To the extent they might intervene at this stage, replications of initial studies should serve to identify them. Finally, values can reappear in the evaluation segment of the overall theory process, the part that involves reaching a consensus among knowledgeable scholars regarding the goodness of a theory and thus the contribution to knowledge involved (Miner 1990). The result is that those with different values may evaluate through different lenses, and as a consequence consensus may be hard to obtain.

Dispositions versus Situations—A Value-Laden Controversy

An example of how values may produce different views and impede consensus is provided by the dispute over the study of individuals in organizations noted previously. This dispute simmered over a period of ten years or more before bursting into flame (Davis-Blake and Pfeffer 1989).

The latter paper contained an attack on the dispositional approach that underlies the concept of individual differences and the application of personality theory in organizational behavior. Dispositions are defined as unobservable mental states (constructs) such as needs, values, attitudes, and personalities that are relatively stable over time and that to varying degrees serve as determinants of attitudes and behavior in organizations. The argument is that dispositions are a mirage and that the only significant determinants of individual organizational behavior are situational in nature. Thus, an antithesis is created pitting psychological constructs against sociological.

Later Nord and Fox (1996) authored a paper with the thesis that the individual (and individual personality) has disappeared from organizational behavior, being replaced by a contextual dimension consisting of attributes of the physical and social systems in which people exist (situations). The intent is to document the view that theories and research dealing with individual personality and dispositions have lost status to the point where organizational behavior is no longer interested in individual differences (and by implication *should* not be). There is reason to believe that this second attack from the sociological perspective may leave something to be desired in its coverage of the personality-related literature, but as an attack by *fait accompli*, it clearly reveals the values of the authors.

These position statements from the situationalist perspective have not gone unanswered. In defense of the dispositional view, George (1992) has offered a detailed consideration of much of the theory and research supporting an important role for personality in organizational behavior. House, Shane, and Herold (1996) also make a strong case for the retention of personality-based perspectives. The following quote appears to present a more balanced view of the issues and leaves the door open to both types of theory and research. It provides an instance of how extreme values may be reconciled and consensus thereby achieved.

> [P]ersonality is important for understanding at least certain classes of organizational phenomena. Obviously, this does not imply that situational factors are unimportant. Rather, it suggests that organizations do not stamp out all individual differences; being a member of an organization does not neutralize or negate one's own enduring predispositions to think, feel, and act in certain ways. An extreme situationalist perspective denies organizational

participants their individuality and exaggerates organizations' abilities to manipulate and control their members. Likewise, an extreme dispositional position credits too much power to the individual and ignores important situational influences on feelings, thoughts, and behaviors. Hence, personality and situational factors are needed to understand much of organizational life. (George 1992, 205–6)

Positive Organizational Scholarship

Positive organizational scholarship is a value orientation of very recent vintage—too recent to be able to say where it is going as far as organizational behavior is concerned (Bernstein 2003; Cameron, Dutton, and Quinn 2003). It had its origins in psychology, where it was in many respects a reaction to clinical psychology with its emphasis on illness, disorder, and thus the negative aspects of the human condition. Basically, it is a movement, unrelated to any specific theory, that values excellence, thriving, flourishing, abundance, resilience, and virtuousness—anything associated with positive human potential.

    Because scholarship here means science and scientific research, this is not another name for postmodernism. Certain ties to an earlier humanism and to the values of organization development are evident, but the coverage is broader than that. As noted, psychology is the discipline of origin, but the movement is interested in influencing any field that finds its values attractive. In short, it is a community of scholars, currently based in the School of Business at the University of Michigan, devoted to learning about positive aspects of the human condition, particularly as reflected in organizational functioning. The scope of the movement is as yet unclear; it may ultimately come to represent a reemergence of humanism in organizational behavior, or something else. But the appeal to strong values and the attempt to mobilize them in support of its aims is clear.

THE ROLE OF CONSENSUS

Threats to a unified science of organizational behavior take two major forms—those that relate specifically to science, including its theory and method, and those that impair unity by jeopardizing the creation of a stable and widely recognized body of knowledge that might be presented to practitioners as a basis for their actions. The latter is the concern of this discussion.

The Consensus Problem

A lack of consensus appears to exist in the field of organizational behavior, and as a result the field's limited amount of hard knowledge is often bemoaned. The evidence is there, but the consensus of knowledgeable scholars that makes it knowledge often is out of reach because conflicting values block the way. Testimony to this effect is not hard to find.

    In the introduction to his volume dealing with organizational behavior's conceptual base Hartman (1988) discusses this fragmentation using terms such as "disarray," "no consensus," "conflict," "disunity," "disagreements." The authors of a more recent handbook of the field (Clegg, Hardy, and Nord 1996) use their introduction to paint a picture that presents organizational behavior as infused with controversy and partisan politics; this latter volume appears in its own way to contribute to the fragmentation as well, even to extol it.

    A well-argued treatment of the consensus problem is that of Pfeffer (1993), which subsequently has sparked a great deal of debate pro and con. The thesis of his paper is that when sciences have developed shared theoretical structures and methodological approaches about which there is substantial consensus, these sciences and their members have experienced a number of positive consequences, including increased allocations of monetary and other resources. Organizational behavior, being fragmented as it is, holds a position low in the pecking order when rewards and resources are distributed among the sciences. In short, we are not viewed as doing a very good job, and this is true because of our lack of consensus. Pfeffer argues that consensus can be attained through the efforts of an elite network of individuals who utilize political positions and processes to impose a uniformity of view on a discipline. He seems to say that this should happen in organizational behavior. This appeal for consensus is reiterated in a later paper (Pfeffer 1995), but it is apparent that he prefers consensus around certain theoretical positions over others.

Not surprisingly, a number of organizational behaviorists jumped up to dispute Pfeffer on a variety of grounds. In general, the thrust of these views is that consensus is not really a desirable goal after all, and that enforced consensus is particularly undesirable. Tolerance for diverse approaches, theories, and methods should not be suppressed, and in any event there is no one best way that clearly deserves a dominant position. On occasion this rebuttal is mixed with a substantial dose of anti-science rhetoric (Van Maanen 1995).

All this having been said, it remains true that science relies on some degree of consensus among knowledgeable scholars, and that science has proved over and over again that its methods can advance understanding, prediction, and control to the benefit of human society. Certainly, some degree of disconsensus can be absorbed, and innovative, creative contributions should not only be tolerated, but supported. The questions are how much consensus is needed and in what areas; these are empirical questions as Pfeffer (1995) notes. Once the emotions that values arouse are activated, it is amazing how difficult it is to see the balanced, middle ground. For a balanced discussion of these issues from a perspective tempered by the passage of time, see Fabian (2000).

The Inability to Compare Competing Theories

One outgrowth of the consensus problem is a view that one cannot decide objectively between competing theories that use different languages, hold different assumptions, and utilize different constructs, thus reflecting totally disparate value systems. Under these circumstances, comparisons are impossible in the same sense that "comparing apples and oranges" is impossible. Science is said to be at a loss in such instances, and amongst the theory pluralism that we face at present, science becomes essentially useless (Scherer and Dowling 1995). Note that this argument requires a large number of very different theories coming together from different directions to offer contradictory solutions to common problems. This must be so if science is to be effectively neutralized. Thus, "create as many new and unique theories as you possibly can" becomes the rallying cry of proponents of this view; they are out to sink consensus (Clegg and Ross-Smith 2003). Practitioners in particular are left helpless to make decisions in the face of this barrage of competing theories and may be expected to eschew organizational behavior altogether.

The response to this line of reasoning is that it creates a pseudo-problem, a mirage, that is readily soluble in that science serves to test theories through research that is just as applicable to competing theories as to any others (McKinley 1995). Although valid, this position needs some amplification.

First, the theory pluralism that exists at present is not made up exclusively of scientific theories. There are a number of philosophic statements in existence that do not generate testable hypotheses and thus are not falsifiable. Subtracting this philosophic content reduces the degree of theory pluralism substantially. For example, many of the phenomena that exist in this world have multiple religious explanations and scientific explanations (confirmed by research) as well. To include the religious "theories," which are untestable, as part of the total count of scientific theories is unwarranted.

Second, a close study of existing organizational behavior theories reveals that the most frequent situation is one where the theories occupy different, nonoverlapping domains. There are instances of overlap and even some cases of competing positions, but this is not the norm by any means. Those who argue that an inability to compare competing theories is a major barrier to attaining consensus are simply wrong, at least insofar as organizational behavior is concerned; there are not that many competing theories, once theoretical domains are clearly drawn.

Third, competing theories can be compared using appropriate research designs. Differential experimentation that serves to determine the relative effectiveness of various approaches or hypotheses is commonly conducted. Any good theory contains clear specifications for operationalizing its variables, and these may be used in comparative research. For a good example of how research to deal with competing theoretical positions may be conducted, see Latham, Erez, and Locke (1988) and the more extended treatment of this research contained in Frost and Stablein (1992). What is clearly evident here is that with sufficient creative input into the research process, science can handle competing theoretical positions (see also McKinley 1995 on this point). Thus, a basis for achieving consensus, where it might otherwise appear to be lacking, does exist within science.

Fourth, a consensus of knowledgeable scholars can develop in the absence of full agreement among protagonists. Herzberg's motivation-hygiene theory (see Chapter 5) is generally assumed to be deficient in certain respects, based on extensive research conducted to test aspects of the theory. Yet to my knowledge Herzberg never repudiated his theory in any regard, and he continued to hold out against the growing consensus until his death. This is not unusual, and it does not matter. A few voices in opposition does not vitiate consensus.

Fifth, it is not correct to say consensus is totally lacking in organizational behavior; agreement among knowledgeable scholars in support of a theory occurs quite often. But the qualifier *among knowledgeable scholars* is important here. Organizational behavior has developed a breadth and depth of information that defies comprehension by a single person. There are specialties and subspecialties, and it is these that furnish the knowledgeable scholars whose judgment is at issue. To add in the many who know little or nothing about a particular theory and its research is bound to create an appearance of disconsensus as competing values become involved against an ambiguous (uncertain) background, but that is not the kind of consensus science seeks.

Sixth, practitioners (such as managers) do not require a consensus on the part of organizational behavior to utilize the tools, technology, and theories of that discipline. It would certainly be helpful if such a consensus existed, but managers in a particular area of a business, say human resources, are not necessarily uninformed consumers; they can make judgments as to the validity and usefulness of what comes to them from organizational behavior, and they do so all the time. Many of these inputs from organizational behavior prove useful and help to solve important practical problems. As a former practitioner of organizational behavior in the personnel research unit of a large corporation and a consultant in that area throughout my professional career, I can attest to the practical value of these inputs. In actuality, the freedom from political wars that the practitioner has may compensate for any lack of knowledge. Certainly errors are made, but low levels of consensus do not prevent practitioners from making choices among the potpourri of organizational behavior tools, technologies, and theories. And again, as Donaldson (1992) contends, the degree of consensus available to practitioners is probably greater than the critics have maintained.

The Road to Consensus

It becomes apparent from the above discussion that it would be very useful to have an operational measure of consensus on various matters within organizational behavior. With hard data on what knowledgeable scholars think, it would be possible to avoid much of the ambiguity that surrounds this treatment.

Actually, during the 1980s, a certain amount of data became available on the extent of consensus around first-generation organizational behavior theories that had achieved considerable visibility (Miner 1990). The correlations among data from different sources ranking these theories as to their validity ranged from 0.74 to 0.94. This is indicative of a considerable amount of consensus. More recent research of this nature provides evidence of increasing consensus around a number of theories in organizational behavior (Miner 2003). The field is still very young, and it is too early to expect high levels of agreement, but we are moving in that direction.

One might think that consensus could be obtained by noting the most frequently cited publications in the field and then building a picture of organizational behavior's knowledge base from the content of these publications. Unfortunately, however, evidence indicates that those publications that do particularly well in citation counts do so not because of the perceived quality of the publication or its usefulness to practitioners, but because of the usefulness to scholars of the field in carrying out their professional tasks (Shadish 1989). This is not the stuff out of which a picture of our knowledge base can be created.

Yet, there are multiple signs pointing to improving consensus as organizational behavior matures. One such sign is the increasing degree to which citations to other disciplines are appearing in the journals (Blackburn 1990). Discourse across disciplines is on the upswing; talking only with those people within the field who represent a reflection of one's own image is decreasing. When communication opens up in this way, at least the potential for consensus opens up as well.

A second encouraging sign is the relatively recent emergence not of meso theories per se, since such theories have in fact been in existence for some time, but of an explicit concern with the identification and creation of such theories, which bridge a major value-gap in the field. To the extent that they prove valid, meso theories can represent a major integrating force within organizational behavior.

In writing meso theory, one is forced to deal both with psychological and sociological variables as well as with the literatures that surround those variables. The result should be an integrated theory that not only ties together the two levels of analysis, but also commits the author to some type of synthesis of the two value positions. Accordingly, a strong commitment to a meso approach to theorizing could go a long way toward fostering consensus and firming up a stable knowledge base for organizational behavior.

In short, although it does seem that consensus is at a rather low level overall within organizational behavior, there are subfields and sectors where this is not the case. Thus, a body of accepted knowledge does exist within the field and is available to practitioners—a smaller body than many would desire, but still important. Furthermore, there are certain trends in evidence that seem to argue for improved consensus in the future.

CONCLUSIONS

This chapter has delved into the characteristics of research that can be used to test scientific theories. In all of this it should be understood that organizational behavior research may serve additional functions beyond merely testing theory. Hypotheses derived from practice may be evaluated through research to determine if what has been assumed to be true really is true. Areas that present particular problems may be studied to obtain a clearer picture of the landscape. The point is that scientific research in organizational behavior is not simply a matter of theory testing, yet theory testing is probably the most important function of organizational behavior research because a well-validated theory can establish a wide range of knowledge.

In the preceding discussion, certain terms that are to be found in the references, and that are often used in the literature, have been deliberately avoided. This is in part because these terms have taken on a variety of value-laden excess meanings that tend to stereotype the user. In some instances the terms are too ambiguous for most scientific purposes as well. Kuhn (1970), in introducing the term "paradigm," intentionally used it with a wide range of meanings (Astley and Zammuto 1992), and it continues to possess this same ambiguity today. In addition to paradigm I have avoided such terms as normal science, positivist theory, and incommensurability for the same reasons.

This is not to say that most of the concepts that appear to be covered by these terms are not treated—to the contrary, they are treated in detail, but using other words. Nor am I trying to avoid labeling my own position. The discussion here clearly identifies my commitment to science and spells out at considerable length the concept of science I have in mind. Terms such as *paradigm, normal science, positivist theory,* and *incommensurability* come to organizational behavior from philosophy, however. As a result, there is no commitment to make them precise and specific, in the mode of science. At the same time, there is no necessary commitment on the part of organizational behavior to make them part of our vocabulary—and we should not.

REFERENCES

Agger, Ben (1991). Critical Theory, Poststructuralism, Postmodernism: Their Sociological Relevance. *Annual Review of Sociology,* 17, 105–31.

Alvesson, Mats (2003). Interpretive Unpacking: Moderately Destabilizing Identities and Images in Organization Studies. In Edwin A. Locke (Ed.), *Postmodernism and Management: Pros, Cons, and the Alternative.* Oxford, UK: Elsevier Science, 3–27.

Alvesson, Mats, and Kärreman, Dan (2000). Taking the Linguistic Turn in Organizational Research—Challenges, Responses, Consequences. *Journal of Applied Behavioral Science,* 36, 136–58.

Argyris, Chris (1980). *Inner Contradictions of Rigorous Research.* New York: Academic Press.

Astley, W. Graham, and Zammuto, Raymond F. (1992). Organization Science, Managers, and Language Games. *Organization Science,* 3, 443–60.

Bagozzi, Richard P., Yi, Youjae, and Phillips, Lynn W. (1991). Assessing Construct Validity in Organizational Research. *Administrative Science Quarterly,* 36, 421–58.

Barrett, Edward (2003). Foucault, HRM and the Ethos of the Critical Management Scholar. *Journal of Management Studies,* 40, 1069–87.

Belasco, James A., and Trice, Harrison M. (1969). *The Assessment of Change in Training and Therapy.* New York: McGraw-Hill.

Bernstein, Susan D. (2003). Positive Organizational Scholarship: Meet the Movement—An Interview with Kim Cameron, Jane Dutton, and Robert Quinn. *Journal of Management Inquiry,* 12, 266–71.

Blackburn, Richard S. (1987). Experimental Design in Organizational Settings. In Jay W. Lorsch (Ed.), *Handbook of Organizational Behavior.* Englewood Cliffs, NJ: Prentice-Hall, 126–39.

——— (1990). Organizational Behavior: Whom Do We Talk to and Who Talks to Us? *Journal of Management,* 16, 279–305.

Burrell, Gibson (1996). Normal Science, Paradigms, Metaphors, Discourses, and Genealogies of Analysis. In Stewart R. Clegg, Cynthia Hardy, and Walter R. Nord (Eds.), *Handbook of Organization Studies.* London: Sage, 642–58.

Cameron, Kim S., Dutton, Jane E., and Quinn, Robert F. (2003). *Positive Organizational Scholarship: Foundations of a New Discipline.* San Francisco, CA: Berrett-Koehler.

Clegg, Stewart R., Hardy, Cynthia, and Nord, Walter R. (1996). *Handbook of Organization Studies*. London: Sage.

Clegg, Stewart R., and Kornberger, Martin (2003). Modernism, Postmodernism, Management and Organization Theory. In Edwin A. Locke (Ed.), *Postmodernism and Management: Pros, Cons, and the Alternative*. Oxford, UK: Elsevier Science, 57–88.

Clegg, Stewart R., and Ross-Smith, Anne (2003). Revising the Boundaries: Management Education and Learning in a Postpositivist World. *Academy of Management Learning and Education*, 2, 85–98.

Cook, Thomas D., Campbell, Donald T., and Peracchio, Laura (1990). Quasi Experimentation. In Marvin D. Dunnette and Leaetta M. Hough (Eds.), *Handbook of Industrial and Organizational Psychology*, Vol. 1. Palo Alto, CA: Consulting Psychologists Press, 491–576.

Cortina, José M. (2002). Big Things Have Small Beginnings: An Assortment of "Minor" Methodological Misunderstandings. *Journal of Management*, 28, 339–62.

Davis-Blake, Alison, and Pfeffer, Jeffrey (1989). Just a Mirage: The Search for Dispositional Effects in Organizational Research. *Academy of Management Review*, 14, 385–400.

Donaldson, Lex (1992). The Weick Stuff: Managing Beyond Games. *Organization Science*, 3, 461–66.

——— (2003). A Critique of Postmodernism in Organizational Studies. In Edwin A. Locke (Ed.), *Postmodernism and Management: Pros, Cons, and the Alternative*. Oxford, UK: Elsevier Science, 169–202.

Edwards, Jeffrey R. (2003). Construct Validation in Organizational Behavior Research. In Jerald Greenberg (Ed.), *Organizational Behavior: The State of the Science*. Mahwah, NJ: Lawrence Erlbaum, 327–71.

Evans, Martin G. (1999). Donald T. Campbell's Methodological Contributions to Organization Science. In Joel A.C. Baum and Bill McKelvey (Eds.), *Variations in Organization Science: In Honor of Donald T. Campbell*. Thousand Oaks, CA: Sage, 311–38.

Fabian, Frances H. (2000). Keeping the Tension: Pressures to Keep the Controversy In the Management Discipline. *Academy of Management Review*, 25, 350–71.

Frost, Peter J., and Stablein, Ralph E. (1992). *Doing Exemplary Research*. Newbury Park, CA: Sage.

George, Jennifer M. (1992). The Role of Personality in Organizational Life: Issues and Evidence. *Journal of Management*, 18, 185–213.

Ghate, Onkar, and Locke, Edwin A. (2003). Objectivism: The Proper Alternative to Postmodernism. In Edwin A. Locke (Ed.), *Postmodernism and Management: Pros, Cons, and the Alternative*. Oxford, UK: Elsevier Science, 249–78.

Hartman, Edwin (1988). *Conceptual Foundations of Organization Theory*. Cambridge, MA: Ballinger.

House, Robert J., Shane, Scott A., and Herold, David M. (1996). Rumors of the Death of Dispositional Research Are Vastly Exaggerated. *Academy of Management Review*, 21, 203–24.

Jermier, John M. (1985). "When the Sleeper Walks": A Short Story Extending Themes in Radical Organization Theory. *Journal of Management*, 11(2), 67–80.

Kilduff, Martin, and Kelemen, Michaela (2003). Bringing Ideas Back In: Eclecticism and Discovery in Organizational Studies. In Edwin A. Locke (Ed.), *Postmodernism and Management: Pros, Cons, and the Alternative*. Oxford, UK: Elsevier Science, 89–109.

Kilduff, Martin, and Mehra, Ajay (1997). Postmodernism and Organizational Research. *Academy of Management Review*, 22, 453–81.

Kuhn, Thomas (1970). *The Structure of Scientific Revolutions*. Chicago, IL: University of Chicago Press.

Lam, Simon S.K., and Schaubroeck, John (2000). The Role of Locus of Control in Reactions to Being Promoted and to Being Passed Over: A Quasi Experiment. *Academy of Management Journal*, 43, 66–78.

Latham, Gary P., Erez, Miriam, and Locke, Edwin A. (1988). Resolving Scientific Disputes by the Joint Design of Crucial Experiments by the Antagonists: Application to the Erez-Latham Dispute Regarding Participating in Goal Setting. *Journal of Applied Psychology*, 73, 753–72.

Lawler, Edward E., Mohrman, Alan M., Mohrman, Susan A., Ledford, Gerald E., and Cummings, Thomas G. (1985). *Doing Research That Is Useful for Theory and Practice*. San Francisco, CA: Jossey-Bass.

Lindell, Michael K., and Whitney, David J. (2001). Accounting for Common Method Variance in Cross-sectional Research Designs. *Journal of Applied Psychology*, 86, 114–21.

Locke, Edwin A. (1986). *Generalizing from Laboratory to Field Settings*. Lexington, MA: Lexington Books.

——— (2003). Good Definitions: The Epistemological Foundation of Scientific Progress. In Jerald Greenberg (Ed.), *Organizational Behavior: The State of the Science*. Mahwah, NJ: Lawrence Erlbaum, 415–44.

Loo, Robert (2002). A Caveat on Using Single-item Versus Multiple-item Scales. *Journal of Managerial Psychology*, 17, 68–75.

McKelvey, Bill (2003). Postmodernism versus Truth in Management Theory. In Edwin A. Locke (Ed.),

Postmodernism and Management: Pros, Cons, and the Alternative. Oxford, UK: Elsevier Science, 113–68.

McKinley, William (1995). Commentary on Scherer and Dowling. *Advances in Strategic Management,* 12A, 249–60.

Maierhofer, Naomi I., Kabanoff, Boris, and Griffin, Mark A. (2002). The Influence of Values in Organizations: Linking Values and Outcomes at Multiple Levels of Analysis. *International Review of Industrial and Organizational Psychology,* 17, 217–63.

Markham, Steven E., Scott, K. Dow, and McKee, Gail H. (2002). Recognizing Good Attendance: A Longitudinal, Quasi-experimental Field Study. *Personnel Psychology,* 55, 639–60.

Martin, Joanne, and Frost, Peter (1996). The Organizational Culture War Games: A Struggle for Intellectual Dominance. In Stewart R. Clegg, Cynthia Hardy, and Walter R. Nord (Eds.), *Handbook of Organization Studies.* London: Sage, 599–621.

Miner, John B. (1962). Conformity among University Professors and Business Executives. *Administrative Science Quarterly,* 7, 96–109.

——— (1990). The Role of Values in Defining the "Goodness" of Theories in Organizational Science. *Organization Studies,* 11, 161–78.

——— (1995). *Administrative and Management Theory.* Aldershot, UK: Dartmouth.

——— (2003). The Rated Importance, Scientific Validity, and Practical Usefulness of Organizational Behavior Theories: A Quantitative Review. *Academy of Management Learning and Education,* 2, 250–68.

Morgeson, Frederick P., and Campion, Michael A. (2002). Minimizing Tradeoffs When Redesigning Work: Evidence from a Longitudinal Quasi-experiment. *Personnel Psychology,* 55, 589–612.

Nord, Walter R., and Fox, Suzy (1996). The Individual in Organizational Studies: The Great Disappearing Act? In Stuart R. Clegg, Cynthia Hardy, and Walter R. Nord (Eds.), *Handbook of Organization Studies.* London: Sage, 148–74.

Pescosolido, Bernice A., and Rubin, Beth A. (2000). The Web of Group Affiliations Revisited: Social Life, Postmodernism, and Sociology. *American Sociological Review,* 65, 52–76.

Pfeffer, Jeffrey (1993). Barriers to the Advance of Organizational Science: Paradigm Development as a Dependent Variable. *Academy of Management Review,* 18, 599–620.

——— (1995). Mortality, Reproducibility, and the Persistence of Styles of Theory. *Organization Science,* 6, 681–86.

Podsakoff, Philip M., MacKenzie, Scott B., Lee, Jeong-Yeon, and Podsakoff, Nathan P. (2003). Common Method Biases in Behavioral Research: A Critical Review of the Literature and Recommended Remedies. *Journal of Applied Psychology,* 88, 879–903.

Price, James L., and Mueller, Charles W. (1986). *Handbook of Organizational Measurement.* Marshfield, MA: Pitman.

Probst, Tahira M. (2003). Exploring Employee Outcomes of Organizational Restructuring: A Solomon Four-group Study. *Group and Organizational Management,* 28, 416–39.

Scandura, Terri A., and Williams, Ethlyn A. (2000). Research Methodology in Management: Current Practices, Trends, and Implications for Future Research. *Academy of Management Journal,* 43, 1248–64.

Scherer, Andreas G., and Dowling, Michael J. (1995). Towards a Reconciliation of the Theory-Pluralism in Strategic Management—Incommensurability and the Constructivist Approach of the Erlangen School. *Advances in Strategic Management,* 12A, 195–247.

Schmidt, Frank L., Viswesvaran, Chockalingam, and Ones, Deniz S. (2000). Reliability Is Not Validity and Validity Is Not Reliability. *Personnel Psychology,* 53, 901–24.

Shadish, William R. (1989). The Perception and Evaluation of Quality in Science. In Barry Gholson, William R. Shadish, Robert A. Neimeyer, and Arthur C. Houts (Eds.), *Psychology of Science: Contributions to Metascience.* Cambridge, UK: Cambridge University Press, 383–426.

Silverman, David (1971). *The Theory of Organizations.* New York: Basic Books.

Tannenbaum, Robert, Margulies, Newton, and Massarik, Fred (1985). *Human Systems Development.* San Francisco, CA: Jossey-Bass.

Van Maanen, John (1995). Style as Theory. *Organization Science,* 6, 133–43.

Voronov, Maxim, and Coleman, Peter T. (2003). Beyond the Ivory Towers: Organizational Power Practices and a "Practical" Critical Postmodernism. *Journal of Applied Behavioral Science,* 39, 169–85.

Weiss, Richard M. (2000). Taking Science Out of Organization Science: How Would Postmodernism Reconstruct the Analysis of Organizations? *Organization Science,* 11, 709–31.

Williams, Larry J., Edwards, Jeffrey R., and Vandenberg, Robert J. (2003). Recent Advances in Causal Modeling Methods for Organizational and Management Research. *Journal of Management,* 29, 903–36.

PART II

THEORIES OF MOTIVATION

CHAPTER 3

FROM SOCIAL PSYCHOLOGY AND PERSONALITY THEORY

KURT LEWIN

Background
    Germany
    United States
Contributions Relevant for Organizational
    Behavior
        Leadership Climates
        Change Processes
        Expansion of Agenda
        Level of Aspiration
Evaluation and Impact
Conclusions

Importance rating	★ ★ ★ ★ ★
	Institutionalized
Estimated validity	★ ★ ★
Estimated usefulness	★ ★ ★
Decade of origin	1930s

Kurt Lewin was trained as a psychologist; he was a researcher as well as a theorist. His contributions to psychology were eclectic in terms of area, and it was only toward the end of his life that he concentrated on the social psychological studies and ideas that make him particularly relevant for organizational behavior. Because his theories were developed prior to the emergence of organizational behavior as a field (see Miner 2002 for a discussion), they are labeled in the title of this chapter in terms of the disciplines from which they had their origins.

Early in his career Lewin's major contributions were in the area of personality theory. He wrote several books on that subject during this period and established himself as a major theorist. However, his interest in personality theory gradually gave way to social psychology and in particular to group dynamics and action research. He was a man of broad humanist sympathies and democratic values. In the late 1930s and 1940s, when his writings of most relevance for organizational behavior appeared, Lewin wrote primarily in the form of journal articles and papers in edited volumes.

BACKGROUND

Kurt Lewin's life was split into two distinct phases. The early period, spread over forty-three years (1890–1933), was spent based in Germany. From 1933 to 1947, when he died from a heart attack, Lewin lived and worked in the United States. Lewin was Jewish, and he moved to this country because he foresaw the persecution that was to come under Hitler and the Nazis.

Germany

Lewin was born in Prussia and attended the Universities of Freiberg and Munich before receiving his doctorate from the University of Berlin in 1914. He served for four years in the German army during World War I and then returned to Berlin where he rose to professor in 1926. He was strongly influenced during the German years by the Gestalt psychologists with whom he worked, including Max Wertheimer and Wolfgang Köhler. Over time he developed a group around himself at the Psychological Institute of the University of Berlin, consisting of a number of like-minded scholars.

During this German period, Lewin published some articles that presaged his later social psychology (Papanek 1973). One paper dealt with job design in farm work, while another focused on humanizing the activities of factory workers employed under Taylor's scientific management. There was a theme of job enrichment in these papers and also in several additional studies of the field of forces operating on individual textile workers. These early papers illustrated Lewin's use of field theoretic concepts, linked laboratory experiments to applied problems (action research), and focused on individuals as opposed to groups.

Early in the 1930s, Lewin was invited to Stanford University by Lewis Terman, originator of the Stanford-Binet tests. He returned to Germany, but apparently the visit to Stanford set in motion a process that shortly resulted in a permanent move to the United States.

United States

Presumably as a consequence of his association with Terman and of some research he had conducted in the area, Lewin came to the United States perceived as a specialist in child development. He first joined the School of Home Economics at Cornell University as a child psychologist and after two years moved to the Child Welfare Research Station at the University of Iowa. Both of these positions were generously funded by the Rockefeller Foundation. At Iowa, Lewin began to concentrate more on groups rather than individuals, and again, as in Berlin, he surrounded himself with a group of scholars, many of whom joined him in his research (Ash 1992).

At Iowa, Lewin increasingly moved toward a kind of industrial social psychology focused on groups and actions research. To further his objective, he ultimately moved to the Massachusetts Instittue of Technology in Cambridge, where he became director of the Research Center for Group Dynamics, whose funding was arranged primarily by Lewin himself. Again, he created a group of young scholars interested in the topics that he found interesting. After Lewin's death, the center moved briefly to Syracuse University and then on to the University of Michigan, where it became part of the Institute for Social Research (Cannell and Kahn 1984). The center served over the years to foster Lewin's early work on sensitivity training and T-groups through the development of the National Training Laboratories (NTL), and the center also established a long informal exchange with the Tavistock Institute of Human Relations in England. An outgrowth of this relationship was joint publication of the journal *Human Relations*. Thus, Lewin's influence was extended in many directions.

CONTRIBUTIONS RELEVANT FOR ORGANIZATIONAL BEHAVIOR

Lewin typically formulated many of his field theoretic ideas in terms of mathematical symbols and spatial diagrams. The most widely cited of his mathematical formulations is $B = f(P,E)$—

that is, behavior is a functional interaction of person and environment. However, many such formulas are sprinkled throughout his works, as are life-space diagrams and force-field pictures (e.g., see Lewin 1943).

How important these accoutrements really are to Lewin's theorizing is a serious question. They appear to represent a personal language that serves to describe what is already known much more than to predict experimental results. Although they may foster understanding, and many who have struggled with them may have major doubts even on that score, these after-the-fact formulas and diagrams in and of themselves clearly are not predictive theoretical statements or hypotheses. Lewin's field theory is not a mathematical theory in spite of the symbolic nomenclature used to present it. Thus, in the following I will utilize only the verbal language.

As indicated, Lewin directed his theorizing, and his research, to multiple fields. This was true even within organizational behavior. Thus, it is not surprising that although his major concern was within the field of motivation, he started out by testing certain ideas regarding leadership and the effects of leadership climates. This breadth of application was typical of the early theorizing leading up to the actual creation of organizational behavior (Miner 2002). However, the leadership theory fed into the later motivation theory.

Leadership Climates

Conclusions on the effects of varying leadership climates were derived from experimental research conducted at the University of Iowa (Lewin, Lippitt, and White 1939; Lippitt and White 1958). This research served to establish Lewin's reputation in the United States. In it the effects of authoritarian (German) and democratic (American) leadership climates were contrasted. The research reflects in a microcosm the pattern of Lewin's own life and is a direct outgrowth of the juxtaposition of the two cultures. In addition, the study, apparently as a result of a misunderstanding among the researchers, came to include a laissez-faire condition or climate as well.

The ways in which these three climates were operationalized are set forth in Table 3.1. In the major study, the four groups experienced all three climates in succession; thus comparisons could be made across groups and also within groups (using a group as its own control). The subjects were eleven-year-old boys grouped into five-member clubs that met after school to participate in various activities—mask-making, mural-painting, soap-carving, model airplane construction, and so on—over an experimental period of five months.

Clubs were matched on patterns of interpersonal relationships; intellectual, physical, and socioeconomic status; and personality characteristics to control for these factors. The four adult leaders were systematically assigned across climate conditions and clubs. The behaviors and conversations of both leaders and club members were recorded in detail by four observers. These were then categorized for purposes of quantitative analysis. The interrater agreement of the observers was 0.84. Observations of leader behaviors, and reports obtained from the boys, indicated that the experimental conditions did in fact "take."

The findings with regard to aggression in the authoritarian groups were mixed—in some clubs manifestations of aggression were very frequent and in other clubs very infrequent (apathy). Democracy seemed to produce a mid-range frequency of aggressive expression and laissez-faire, a rather high level (presumably because there was no control on emotional expression from either the leader or the group). The democratic climate was much liked, the authoritarian much disliked, and on balance the laissez-faire context was more liked than disliked.

Achievement levels were much higher under the authoritarian and democratic climates than under laissez-faire. This failure of laissez-faire leadership has remained in evidence across many

Table 3.1

Methods Used to Create Leadership Climates

	Authoritarian climate	Democratic climate	Laissez-faire climate
Policy determination	By the leader	By group discussion and decision, assisted by the leader	Freedom for group or individual decision without leader participation
Task activities	Techniques and steps dictated by the leader one at a time	Perspective gained during first discussion; steps to goal sketched by group; technical advice provided by the leader in the form of multiple alternatives from which group made choices	Materials supplied by leader; leader indicated he would supply information if asked; leader not involved in work discussions
Division of labor and companions	Dictated by the leader	Members chose own work companions and group decided division of labor	No participation by the leader
Praise and criticism by leader	Personal by leader; aloof from group participation; friendly or impersonal, not hostile	Objective or fact-minded; a regular group member, but without doing a lot of the actual work	Very infrequent; only when questioned; no participation in course of the work

studies since (Eagly, Johannesen-Schmidt, and van Engen 2003). The lack of accomplishment in this instance was clearly evident to the boys and a source of dissatisfaction. They talked about doing better, but could not coordinate their efforts to do so under the laissez-faire conditions. The major difference between authoritarian and democratic groups was that in the first instance productivity dropped off when the leader left the room; in the democratic clubs it did not. The results as a whole seemed to offer strong confirmation of the hypothesis that democratic leadership climates are to be preferred, although the high performance in the authoritarian groups was not hypothesized.

Change Processes

Working from these findings on the value of group decision and democratic process, Lewin (1947, 1958) developed a theoretical structure to deal with change processes, and carried out a program of research on the motivation of change. The result was a good theory that has indeed turned out to be very practical. It has served for many years as a guide for organizational development practitioners (Goldstein 1993; Marshak 1993). Recent work suggests that Lewin's force-field analysis applies within a limited domain and that there are situations beyond the boundaries of that domain in which Lewin's views are less applicable. Nevertheless, this is a theory that has moved application a long way (Burke 2002).

The research on change was initially conducted to motivate changes in eating habits necessitated by World War II shortages. Housewives were identified as the gatekeepers

Figure 3.1   **Kurt Lewin's Force-field Analysis of the Change Process**

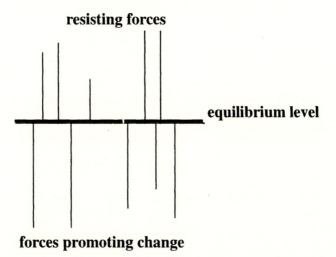

resisting forces

equilibrium level

forces promoting change

whose decisions would have to be altered if broader change were to occur. The research design involved exposing groups of housewives to attractive lectures linking nutrition to the war effort and attempting to persuade them to change the eating habits of their families. Another set of groups was given the same information, but the leader rapidly moved to a group discussion of how "housewives like ourselves" might react to the prospect of change. A group decision was reached in the sense that there was a show of hands as to who would commit to initiating the change.

This experimental approach was used to increase the use of beef hearts, sweetbreads, and kidneys; to expand home consumption of fresh and evaporated milk; and to foster giving cod liver oil and orange juice to their babies by new mothers. Other studies used similar designs to study changes in the productivity levels of factory sewing-machine operators and the decision to eat whole wheat rather than white bread by members of a students' eating cooperative. In all of these instances, the evidence provided strong support for the use of group decision techniques in motivating change.

The underlying theory states that before change the force field is in equilibrium between forces favorable to change and those resisting it; or, as Lewin preferred to say, a quasi-stationary social equilibrium exists. For change to occur this equilibrium must be disturbed, either by adding forces favoring the desired change or by diminishing opposing forces. Ultimately, a new equilibrium is established, but in the former case at a high-tension level and in the latter case at a low-tension level. Since high tension has the potential for aggressiveness, emotionality, and a lack of constructiveness, diminishing resistance to change is usually the preferred approach to change. Group decision appears to be such an approach. Figure 3.1 provides a picture of Lewin's force-field analysis.

Social habits represent inner resistances to change. The inner resistance must be unfrozen, usually by the action of some party external to the group, such as an environmental force. Groups hold to standards that can represent forces against change. If an individual varies widely from such a standard, that person will be ridiculed, punished, and ultimately rejected from group membership. Assuming a desire for group membership in good standing, members can be expected to hold closely to the standards of the group. However, if the group standards can be modified in some way, then the individual would be expected to change as well so as to stay close to them. This is what group decision is about—modifying group-based habits that serve to resist change.

This whole process may be conceptualized as one of first *unfreezing* the existing level, second *moving* to a new level, and then *freezing* group life on the new level so that a permanent and stable equilibrium that resists further change is established. Unfreezing is often difficult and may require different approaches under varying conditions. Accordingly, merely applying the group decision approach, for instance, to increase factory production standards without a thorough study of the circumstances, is unlikely to prove effective. Models of this unfreezing–moving–freezing kind have continued to be applied to motivate change. A recent example involves the process by which institutional change occurs (Greenwood, Suddaby, and Hinings 2002).

Lewin and Grabbe (1945) note that one way of changing an aspect of an individual is for that person to accept membership in a new group, a new culture, with different standards and values. New perceptions result from new identifications and memberships. However, in order for these changes to occur, the new group and culture cannot be forced upon the person; that only creates hostility. Belongingness to the new group must be experienced as an "in-group" feeling. To achieve this, the group must be voluntarily chosen. It has been noted that people who at one point in their lives identify with the far left end of the political spectrum (socialism, communism) may at another point come to identify with arch-conservative causes at the opposite pole. Lewin attributes these types of changes to shifting group identifications and memberships. New values are accepted as the individual comes to experience belongingness in a new in-group.

Expansion of Agenda

As his ideas regarding group decision making, democratic leadership, and change developed, Lewin expanded his activities into the national arena (Marrow 1969). He was instrumental in organizing the Society for the Psychological Study of Social Issues, which united various liberal groupings within the American Psychological Association and promoted action research beyond the universities. During World War II, he did morale research for the military, then community research for the American Jewish Committee. All this eventuated in his move to MIT and the Center for Group Dynamics. In this period he established a relationship with Alfred Marrow, a psychologist who also headed the family firm known as Harwood Manufacturing Company. Harwood, a textile firm, became the site for a number of well-known studies carried out by researchers from the Center for Group Dynamics, but it was Lewin who first developed the contact in order to extend his research into the industrial arena.

Another manifestation of action research was the development of sensitivity training and T-groups. This innovation is usually traced to a workshop conducted at New Britain, Connecticut's State Teachers College in 1946 by Lewin and others from the Center for Group Dynamics (Bradford, Gibb, and Benne 1964). However, it is apparent that Lewin was doing something very similar several years before at Iowa (Papanek 1973). T-groups are often very useful as a method of unfreezing resistances in a group. The lack of structure and ambiguity create a fertile ground for new learning and new values. Clearly, in the later years of his life, Lewin moved from theory- and university-based research to action research intended to produce changes in the world around him. He often advocated engaging the subjects of research in the design and conduct of the studies in which they participated, in order to foster a sense of "ownership" of the results and thus to facilitate change.

Level of Aspiration

Lewin's statements regarding level of aspiration are important as they relate to subsequent theory and research in the area of goal setting. They are thus somewhat separate from the work on leadership climates and change processes, although field theory continues to be employed. Lewin himself was primarily a theorist in this area, basing his formulations on the research of others (Lewin 1936; Lewin, Dembo, Festinger, and Sears 1944).

Goal levels within a person's goal structure may include a dream goal, a somewhat more realistic wish goal, the goal sought when an effort to be objective is involved, and a minimal goal should bad luck be operating. Somewhere on this scale is what the person really tries for at the time in a given situation—the action goal. Also, some ideal goals will be established above this. Knowledge of one's standing relative to a group will have an influence here, as will individual differences with respect to seeking success and avoiding failure.

Three variables appear to play a primary role in setting goals—the seeking of success, the avoiding of failure, and a cognitive factor representing a probability judgment. These factors operate in a context involving a choice of future objective. The strength (valence) of the success and failure variables and the value of the subjective probability estimate depend on numerous factors in the life space, particularly the way past experience with the task is viewed, the standards introduced by group and cultural comparisons, and the individual's personality.

An example of how these factors may operate in practice is given by Marrow (1972), who describes a situation at Harwood on which Lewin offered his advice. The company had moved its operations from New England to Virginia and as a consequence had to train a large number of new machine operators. The standard for acceptable production under the piece rate system was sixty units, brought with the company from New England. However, a number of apprentices were having difficulty reaching this standard during training, and turnover was unusually high. Lewin suggested that the company look into the circumstances under which people who quit experienced success and failure.

There was ample evidence that desire for success was consistently high, but fear of failure seemed to accelerate over the training period. Over time, doubts seemed to arise as to whether the sixty-unit goal was possible; progress slowed noticeably as that goal came in sight. The problem was not money, since the standard wage was guaranteed irrespective of production level. The closer they got to the goal, the less the apprentices expected to reach it. They saw how hard it was and their cognitive probabilities of goal attainment shifted accordingly. A check on turnover rates indicated that for those who reached thirty units the figure was 20 percent; at forty-five units it was up to 60 percent; at fifty-five units it was an unusually high 96 percent; over the goal of sixty units turnover dropped to 11 percent. As tension and frustrations spiraled upward more and more apprentices left the field and became turnover casualties.

The solution was to eliminate the sixty-unit goal and replace it with a series of short-range goals that rose slowly to the sixty-unit figure, thus permitting a continuing feeling of success. When this change was made, turnover decreased by more than half, and the escalating tension so apparent previously was no longer in evidence. Fear of failure had declined, and probability judgments regarding goal attainment were higher. There was no longer a reason to leave the field.

EVALUATION AND IMPACT

As Wolf (1973, 322) has noted, Lewin:

> has had a significant impact upon modern management. His concepts are widely used and his students are among the dominant contributors to human relations, personnel, and industrial psychology. Yet many students of management are completely unaware of Lewin and his contributions. His name is seldom mentioned in texts dealing with management or personnel relations. The failure to recognize Lewin's role in the evolving field of management is a serious neglect, for his philosophy of science, research methodology, and approach provide a potential for advancing the discipline of management. Kurt Lewin was an innovative researcher whose ingenuity in experimental design provides a scientific basis for many of our current concepts.

Within organizational behavior Lewin has had a major impact on organization development, on the various theories that serve to foster participative management, on work in the field of group dynamics, and on theorizing related to goal setting (see Chapter 10). Among those who contributed to the origins of organizational behavior, he is unique in that he was trained in the conduct of science and able to carry out significant research himself. Lewin brought science to the study of organizations, but he also brought humanistic and democratic values as well; in many respects his research supported his values.

CONCLUSIONS

Lewin's contributions were diverse, but they were all made in the name of psychology. Although he died before the field of organizational behavior came into existence, his theoretical thinking has been institutionalized by scholars of organizational behavior—an honor that has been applied to just two of the seven people who contributed most to the founding of organizational behavior (see Miner 2002) and to only eleven of organizational behavior's theories overall. It is based on an average importance rating of 5.31 on a 7-point scale.

Certainly Lewin was interested in applying his ideas to organizational practice, and he developed methods by which this could be accomplished, particularly in the areas of motivating change and fostering participative decision making. His theories were not totally valid on the evidence that exists at the present time, but they represented a solid beginning on which others could build (see in particular Chapter 12).

Lewin's theorizing overall was tied together by his field theory, with its mathematical formulas and force-field diagrams. As such, like most of the work of other contributors to the origins of organizational behavior, it approximated grand theory. On the other hand, David McClelland, whom we will meet in the next chapter, dealt with a substantially smaller theoretical domain, yet he too built his theory gradually over much of his professional lifetime.

REFERENCES

Ash, Mitchell G. (1992). Cultural Contexts and Scientific Change in Psychology. *American Psychologist,* 47, 198–207.

Bradford, Leland P., Gibb, Jack R., and Benne, Ken D. (1964). *T-Group Theory and Laboratory Method.* New York: John Wiley.

Burke, W. Warner (2002). *Organizational Change: Theory and Practice.* Thousand Oaks, CA: Sage.

Cannell, Charles F., and Kahn, Robert L. (1984). Some Factors in the Origins and Development of the Institute for Social Research, The University of Michigan. *American Psychologist,* 39, 1256–66.

Eagly, Alice H., Johannesen-Schmidt, Mary, and van Engen, Marloes L. (2003). Transformational, Transactional, and Laissez-Faire Leadership Styles: A Meta-Analysis Comparing Women and Men. *Psychological Bulletin,* 129, 569–91.

Goldstein, Jeffrey (1993). Beyond Lewin's Force Field: A New Model for Organizational Change Interventions. *Advances in Organization Development,* 2, 72–88.

Greenwood, Royston, Suddaby, Roy, and Hinings, C.R. (2002). Theorizing Change: The Role of Professional Associations in the Transformation of Institutionalized Fields. *Academy of Management Journal,* 45, 58–80.

Lewin, Kurt (1936). Psychology of Success and Failure. *Occupations,* 14, 926–30.

———— (1943). Defining the "Field at a Given Time." *Psychological Review,* 50, 292–310.

———— (1947). Frontiers in Group Dynamics: Concept, Method and Reality in Social Science; Social Equilibria and Social Change. *Human Relations,* 1, 5–41.

———— (1958). Group Decision and Social Change. In Eleanor E. Maccoby, Theodore M. Newcomb, and Eugene L. Hartley (Eds.), *Readings in Social Psychology.* New York: Henry Holt, 197–211.

Lewin, Kurt, Dembo, Tamara, Festinger, Leon, and Sears, Pauline S. (1944). Level of Aspiration. In J. McVicker Hunt (Ed.), *Personality and the Behavior Disorders.* New York: Ronald, 333–78.

Lewin, Kurt, and Grabbe, Paul (1945). Conduct, Knowledge, and Acceptance of New Values. *Journal of Social Issues,* 1(3), 56–64.

Lewin, Kurt, Lippitt, Ronald, and White, Ralph K. (1939). Patterns of Aggressive Behavior in Experimentally Created "Social Climates." *Journal of Social Psychology,* 10, 271–99.

Lippitt, Ronald, and White, Ralph K. (1958). An Experimental Study of Leadership and Group Life. In Eleanor E. Maccoby, Theodore M. Newcomb, and Eugene L. Hartley (Eds.), *Readings in Social Psychology.* New York: Henry Holt, 496–511.

Marrow, Alfred J. (1969). *The Practical Theorist: The Life and Work of Kurt Lewin.* New York: Basic Books.

———— (1972). *The Failure of Success.* New York: AMACOM.

Marshak, Robert J. (1993). Lewin Meets Confucius: A Re-view of the OD Model of Change. *Journal of Applied Behavioral Science,* 29, 393–415.

Miner, John B. (2002). *Organizational Behavior: Foundations, Theories, and Analyses.* New York: Oxford University Press.

Papanek, Miriam Lewin (1973). Kurt Lewin and His Contributions to Modern Management Theory. *Academy of Management Proceedings,* 33, 317–22.

Wolf, William B. (1973). The Impact of Kurt Lewin on Management Thought. *Academy of Management Proceedings,* 33, 322–25.

CHAPTER 4

ACHIEVEMENT MOTIVATION THEORY

DAVID McCLELLAND

Background
The Emergence and Development of the Theory
    Scope and Early Development
    Achievement Situations
    Economic Development
    Role of Power Motivation
    Adding in Affiliation Motivation
    Varying Concepts of Power
    Motivational Change and Development
    Other Innovations Including Competency
        Modeling
Evaluation and Impact
    Measurement Procedures
    Achievement Motivation and Entrepreneurship
    Achievement Motivation and Economic
        Development
    Power Motivation and Management
    Research Using Female Subjects
    Research on Motivational Development
    Evidence from Recent Reviews
Conclusions

Importance rating	★ ★ ★ ★ ★
Estimated validity	★ ★ ★ ★
Estimated usefulness	★ ★ ★ ★ ★
Decade of origin	1950s

Achievement motivation theory is among a group of theories rooted in formulations with regard to the human personality. Other organizational behavior theories of this type are Maslow's need hierarchy theory and Levinson's psychoanalytic theory applied to organizations. Need hierarchy theory has been largely discounted by subsequent research, and following Maslow's death, it has failed to develop further, although discussions of the theory still occur in the literature (see Payne 2000). Psychoanalytic theory as applied to organizations remains active (see Levinson and Wofford 2000; Meckler, Drake, and Levinson 2003), but it has never achieved the research attention it appears to warrant. In contrast, McClelland's theory has received substantial research support and remains an active contributor to the thinking of others, even subsequent to its author's recent death.

The primary input to the achievement motivation theorizing on McClelland's part came from Henry Murray, who was not himself a contributor to the organizational behavior literature. Murray was educated as a physician and came to personality theory after an early career devoted to medicine. His life spanned the years from 1893 to 1988, but his book describing research conducted at the Harvard Psychological Clinic (Murray 1938) had the greatest influence on McClelland. There Murray presents his theory of psychological needs, which he classifies or categorizes in various ways. Among the twenty-seven needs, those for achievement, affiliation, autonomy, dominance, harm avoidance, and understanding are particularly relevant for organizational behavior. These needs are used in analyzing stories given to the pictures of his Thematic Apperception Test.

BACKGROUND

Born in 1917, McClelland attended Wesleyan University and obtained a doctorate in experimental psychology from Yale in 1941. Not long afterward he returned to Wesleyan to chair the psychology department and begin the collaboration with Atkinson and others that led to achievement motivation theory. In 1956, he moved to Harvard and by that time had converted from experimental psychology to personality theory, a field in which he has remained throughout his career. Upon his retirement from Harvard in 1987, he joined the faculty of the psychology department at Boston University as a research professor of psychology, where he remained until his death in March, 1998 (Winter 2000).

McClelland was not a member of a business school faculty at any time (McClelland 1984). His business interests are reflected, however, in his founding of McBer and Company, a consulting and contract research firm, where he served as chairman of the board for many years. His theoretical ideas have been clearly relevant for organizational behavior since the publication of *The Achieving Society* in 1961. In addition, he wrote frequently for business school publications (e.g., see McClelland 1962, 1965a; McClelland and Burnham [1976] 2003; Miron and McClelland 1979). Thus, he is not a psychologist whose views found their way to organizational behavior through the efforts of others; he was an active participant in the literature of the field from the early 1960s on. At that time, however, he was in his mid-forties and well into his career. Most social scientists who made the move into business schools did so at a considerably younger age.

THE EMERGENCE AND DEVELOPMENT OF THE THEORY

Achievement motivation theory receives its name from the motive that has been the dominant focus of concern since the early 1950s. In a sense, the designation is a misnomer at present. The theory has been developmental, undergoing considerable branching and, on occasion, revision. The achievement motivation construct has been stretched to include not only hope of success, but also fear of failure and even fear of success. In addition, at least two other motives—those for power and affiliation—must now be considered part of the theory.

Scope and Early Development

The domain of achievement motivation theory is much more limited than that of Lewin's theory. It focuses on three motives (often broadly stated) and relates them to organizational behavior, or to behavior that appears to have relevance for organizations. The theory follows the three motives well beyond the organizational context into a great variety of aspects of daily life; however, our concern will be only with achievement motivation theory as related to organizations.

The theory was instigated by an investigation into the relationship between hunger needs and the degree to which food imagery dominates thought processes (Atkinson and McClelland 1948). It was found that the longer the subjects had gone without food, the more certain food-related words appeared in stories they wrote in response to various pictures. Subsequently, this arousal-based approach to studying motives was extended to affiliation, power, aggression, sex, fear, and achievement. However, in the early years achievement motivation saw the greatest theoretical development (McClelland, Atkinson, Clark, and Lowell 1953).

In McClelland' s view, all motives are learned, becoming arranged in a hierarchy of potential for influencing behavior that varies from individual to individual. As people develop, they learn to associate positive and negative feelings with certain things that happen to and around them. Thus, achievement situations such as a challenging task may elicit feelings of pleasure, and ulti-mately a person may be characterized by strong achievement motivation. For such a person, achievement is directed toward the top of the motive hierarchy; it takes only minimal achieve-ment cues to activate the expectation of pleasure and thus increase the likelihood of achievement striving. Under such circumstances, weaker motives are likely to give way to the achievement motive and assume a distinct secondary role in influencing behavior. Thus, if one asks such people to tell stories about a picture that contains potential achievement cues, their achievement motivations will be aroused, just as hunger was in the subjects deprived of food, and their stories will reflect what is on their minds—achievement.

Achievement Situations

McClelland (1961, 1962) specifies certain characteristics of the situations that are preferred by, and tend to elicit achievement striving from, people with a strong need for achievement. First and foremost, these situations permit people to attain success through their own efforts and abilities rather than through chance. Thus, these are situations in which it is possible to take personal responsibility and get personal credit for the outcome. The credit need not come from others. To such individuals, achieving through their own efforts is intrinsically satisfying.

Second, achievement situations are characterized by intermediate levels of difficulty and risk. Were the task to be too difficult, the chance of succeeding would be minimal and the probability of motive satisfaction low. In contrast, easy tasks represent things that anyone can do, thus there is little satisfaction in accomplishing them. Achievement-motivated people tend to calculate the risks involved in situations and pick those situations where they anticipate feeling slightly over-extended by the challenges but not too overextended.

Third, the situation must be one in which there is clear and unambiguous feedback on the success of one's efforts. There is little opportunity for achievement satisfaction when a person cannot tell success from failure. Thus, the situation must provide for knowledge of results within a reasonable time.

In addition to these three major features, McClelland posits two other aspects of achievement situations. They permit innovation and novel solutions, thus allowing a greater sense of satisfac-tion when solutions are attained, and they also require a distinct future orientation, thinking ahead and planning, or what McClelland calls "anticipation of future possibilities."

Quite apparently, these various situational characteristics are epitomized in the entrepreneur-ial role, and indeed McClelland did have this role in mind as he developed his theory. In his view it is the prospect of achievement satisfaction, not money, that drives the successful entrepreneur; money is important only as a source of feedback on how one is doing. To some extent then, the theory represents a deduction from a model of entrepreneurship, but also it is derived inductively from a wide range of research studies (McClelland 1961).

Economic Development

The theory as stated to this point is important for organizational behavior because it tells about the motivation of the key individual in the founding and development of business organizations—the successful entrepreneur. However, McClelland goes on to relate achievement motivation to the economic growth and decline of whole societies, thus considerably extending the applicable scope of the theory.

The starting point for this set of propositions is Max Weber's theory that modern capitalism arose out of the Protestant Reformation in Europe. It was Weber's view that Protestantism, in contrast with the existing Catholicism, fostered self-reliance and working hard to make the most of what one had, as well as the rationalization of life through attempting to improve oneself in every way. Weber formulated his theory in broad social terms:

Protestantism and the cultural values it produced → Economic development

McClelland accepts this formulation but adds a level of psychological explanation:

Protestantism and its values
↓
Independence and mastery training by parents
↓
Development of achievement motivation in sons → Economic development

As stated, this is a theory applicable to male children only. It assumes a generational lag (roughly fifty years) between the emergence of values fostering self-reliance and economic growth. Economic decline occurs with affluence, again with a generational lag. As parents become affluent, they turn over child rearing to others, such as slaves, and the conditions for developing strong achievement motivation are lost. Lacking the driving force of the achievement need and its associated entrepreneurship, the society goes into economic eclipse.

In his formulations of the early 1960s, McClelland does not clearly distinguish the domain of his theory, and he is not yet certain about the role of power motivation in the business world, although he does view it as important. These problems are related. At some points McClelland appears to equate entrepreneurship and the management of business organizations generally, making his theory of achievement motivation an overall theory of business development and management. Thus, little room is left for power motivation to play a significant role. At other times he sees some managerial jobs, such as those in marketing and sales, as more entrepreneurial than others, thus leaving a place for the power construct. In the end, the matter is left open— "Whether *n* Power is an essential ingredient in managerial success, as we have argued *n* Achievement is, or an accidental feature of the private enterprise system, cannot be settled" (McClelland 1961, 290). Later, the theory was filled out in this regard (McClelland 1975).

Role of Power Motivation

By the mid-1970s McClelland had moved to the position that achievement motivation was of organizational significance primarily within the limited domain of entrepreneurship, and that other constructs were needed to explain managerial effectiveness in large corporations. Thus, "A high need to achieve does not equip a man to deal effectively with managing human relationships.

For instance, a salesman with high n Achievement does not necessarily make a good sales manager" (McClelland 1975). And again, "The good manager in a large company does not have a high need for achievement" (McClelland and Burnham 1976).

McClelland (1975) views power motivation as the essential ingredient for understanding and predicting managerial success, although such power needs must be couched in an appropriate motivational context to yield the desired result.

The revised theory states that power motivation may be manifested in behavior in a variety of ways and that different individuals develop different characteristic modes of expression, one of which is managing. In part at least, the mode of expression is a function of the stage to which the power motive has developed in the individual; there is a hierarchy of growth or development, and people must experience one stage to reach the next. Adults may be at any one of the four stages at a point in time, and many never rise above the first level.

At Stage I power motivation involves seeking to derive strength from others. Such people tend to attach themselves to strong people and obtain a sense of strength and power from that relationship. At Stage II the source of strength shifts to the self, and a feeling of power is derived from being oneself and "doing one's own thing." Here power satisfaction does not involve influencing others at all. In contrast, Stage III power motivation does involve impact on other people, including dominating them and winning out over them in competitive endeavor. Also included at this stage is the satisfaction of power needs through helping behavior, which clearly establishes the weaker status of the person helped. At Stage IV the self moves into the background, and a feeling of power is derived from influencing others for the sake of some greater good, such as corporate success.

McClelland then distinguishes between what he calls personalized power and socialized power. The former is characterized by dominance–submission and win–lose. Satisfaction comes from conquering others. In an extensive series of studies, McClelland and his colleagues have shown that this kind of power motivation can be related to heavy drinking, and that people with strong personalized power motivation experience considerable satisfaction from fantasies of power elicited under alcohol (McClelland, Davis, Kalin, and Wanner 1972).

In contrast, socialized power involves a subtle mix of power motivation and inhibition, such that there is a "concern for group goals, for finding those goals that will move men, for helping the group to formulate them, for taking initiative in providing means of achieving them, and for giving group members the feeling of competence they need to work hard for them" (McClelland 1975, 265). Power motivation is mixed with a degree of altruism and of pragmatism; it is satisfied in many ways that will work and get results, not just in aggrandizing the self.

Adding in Affiliation Motivation

The theoretical relationships between the various types of power motivation and managerial performance are set forth in Table 4.1. The effective organizational manager begins to emerge in late Stage III with the advent of socialized power motivation (thus the addition of inhibitory tendencies). However, individuals at lower developmental stages may function effectively in some managerial roles.

It is important to note that affiliation motivation, which in earlier formulations had received relatively little attention insofar as theoretical statements involving the field of organizational behavior were concerned, now assumes a significant role. If affiliative needs are too strong, the consequences for managerial effectiveness are said to be negative. McClelland and Burnham (1976, 103) explain this proposition as follows: "For a bureaucracy to function effectively, those

Table 4.1

Development of the Power Motive and Managerial Performance

Maturity stage	Motivational pattern	Effect on management
I	Desire to influence others is low; in this sense power motivation is low	Generally not assertive enough to manage well
Ii	Power motivation expressed in ways having little to do with others	Not related to managing
III (early)	High power motivation coupled with low inhibition and low affiliation motivation	The conquistador pattern of the feudal lord
III (late)	High power motivation coupled with high inhibition and low affiliation motivation	The imperial pattern; personalized power shades into socialized power
IV	High power motivation of an altruistic type coupled with high inhibition and low affiliation motivation	Selfless leadership and efficient organizational management

Source: Adapted from McClelland (1975, 264).

who manage it must be universalistic in applying rules. That is, if they make exceptions for the particular needs of individuals, the whole system will break down. The manager with a high need for being liked is precisely the one who wants to stay on good terms with everybody, and, therefore, is the one most likely to make exceptions in terms of particular needs." In other words, strong affiliation motivation interferes with and subverts effective managerial performance. It may have similar effects on the relationship between achievement motivation and entrepreneurial success.

On the other hand, McClelland (1975) does accept a formulation originally put forth and documented by Litwin and Siebrecht (1967) that for managers who perform in an integrator role, such as project and product managers, a more balanced motivational pattern is desirable, perhaps even with affiliative needs stronger than power needs. Such individuals have little position power and need to work through personal relationships.

Varying Concepts of Power

Not all theorists associated with the achievement motivation viewpoint advocate stances identical to that of McClelland regarding the nature of power motivation. The positions taken by Veroff and Veroff (1972) and Winter (1973) vary at several points, even though both are generally aligned with the McClelland approach to motivation and its study.

The Veroffs take the position that power motivation is primarily a negative process involving the avoidance of feelings of weakness. Although McClelland would agree that such motivation exists, especially in the early stages of motivational development, it is certainly not his prevailing view of power needs in the organizational context.

Winter posits hope of power and fear of power as two distinct motivational processes, which appear to have much in common with the personalized and socialized categories but are not the same. Hope of power, for instance, is viewed as a source of excessive drinking *and* of organizational effectiveness. Fear of power is not entirely allied with altruistic power striving; it accounts for various kinds of emotional pathology as well. Thus, regarding the McClelland socialized/ personalized differentiation, Winter (1973, 163) says, "I do not think that power can be so neatly divided into 'good' and 'bad' . . . both aspects of the power motive are mixed."

Motivational Change and Development

An aspect of the McClelland theory relates to the acquisition of motives. Motives that are important for business development and effective continued operation, such as achievement needs and the socialized power motive, are said to be subject to the effects of appropriate educational processes (McClelland 1965b; McClelland and Winter 1969). What is proposed is that these motives can be moved to a more dominant position in the individual motive hierarchy and thus exert a more pervasive influence on behavior.

Educational efforts of this kind are considered most likely to "work" under certain circumstances:

1. when the person has numerous reasons to believe that he can, will, or should develop the motive;
2. when developing the motive appears to be rational in light of career and life situation considerations;
3. when the individual understands the meaning and various aspects of the motive;
4. when this understanding of the motive is linked to actions and behavior;
5. when the understanding is closely tied to everyday events;
6. when the motive is viewed positively as contributing to an improved self-image;
7. when the motive is viewed as consistent with prevailing cultural values;
8. when the individual commits himself to achieving concrete goals that are related to the motive;
9. when the individual maintains progress toward attaining these goals;
10. when the environment in which change occurs is one in which the person feels supported and respected as an individual who can guide his own future;
11. when the environment dramatizes the importance of self-study and makes it an important value of the group involved in the change effort; and
12. when the motive is viewed as an indication of membership in a new reference group.

Other Innovations Including Competency Modeling

Subsequent to when the preceding formulations were advanced, McClelland devoted his energies to integrating his views with others and thus into a more general theory of human motivation and behavior (e.g., see McClelland 1985). Although potentially useful for organizational behavior, these ideas were not cast in such a way as to focus on the issues of that field at the time.

A second thrust was concerned with the study of human competence at work (see McClelland 1973, 1994, 1998; Spencer and Spencer 1993). McClelland is credited with this work in launching the competency movement (Rodriguez, Patel, Bright, Gregory, and Gowing 2002). This approach folds the theory of achievement, power, and affiliation motives into a more comprehensive framework to determine what makes for higher levels of competence in various positions. It is not so much a theory of human competence or performance as a procedure for studying such factors as motives, traits, self-concepts, knowledge, and skills as they interact to produce superior as opposed to average performance. This competency framework has spawned a great many derivatives over the years and a substantial consulting industry as well (Shippmann, Ash, Carr, Hesketh, Pearlman, Battista, Eyde, Kehoe, Prien, and Sanchez 2000). In some cases these alternative approaches have moved to procedures that no longer include psychological testing of any kind (see Sandberg 2000).

EVALUATION AND IMPACT

Achievement motivation theory had its origins in research that measured the effects of motive-arousing stimuli through the analysis of stories told by the subjects after they saw appropriate pictures. Thus, measures of major variables were present from the beginning.

Measurement Procedures

The method of choice in measuring the various motives of achievement motivation theory has been to utilize derivatives of the Thematic Apperception Test (TAT) originally developed by Murray, relying on content scoring procedures that have their origins in clinical practice. Typically, from four to six pictures are used, selected to focus on the motive of greatest concern. Each picture is exposed briefly, from 10 to 20 seconds, and the subject is then asked to write a story about it within a specified time interval, usually 5 minutes. The story is to contain answers to the following questions:

1. What is happening? Who are the people?
2. What has led up to this situation? That is, what has happened in the past?
3. What is being thought? What is wanted? By whom?
4. What will happen? What will be done?

This procedure is much more structured than the traditional one used in clinical practice. There the pictures tend to be more ambiguous, there are no set time intervals for viewing the pictures and providing stories, the stories usually are given orally and recorded, and the instructions are not fully repeated for each picture. In addition, the original TAT contained twenty pictures (Morgan 2003). The achievement motivation theory TATs have the advantages of permitting group administration and greater manageability, but they lose something in the richness of fantasy content. Nevertheless, they remain projective in nature and thus do permit the measurement of unconscious motives.

Over the years a number of self-report measures that use a multiple choice format have been developed as substitutes for the TAT. Being less cumbersome to administer and score, these approaches are attractive. Considerable tension has become manifest between advocates of the projective TAT and advocates of the more objective self-report procedures. Only recently have answers begun to emerge as to the relative merits of the two.

Projective measurement places heavy demands on the scorer. A coding system must be developed, learned, and applied consistently. In developing a coding system for a particular motive, the preferred approach among achievement motivation theorists has been to compare stories produced in neutral and motive-arousal situations and generate a scoring system from the differences. An alternative occasionally used is to compare groups of known high and low characteristic motivational levels. In either case the coding systems are typically very detailed, and numerous examples are provided. When sufficient time is spent learning these coding systems, quite high levels of agreement can be achieved among different scorers.

Self-report procedures do not face this problem of scorer reliability. However, the items and the multiple choice alternatives must be developed based on a considerable understanding of what is to be measured and how to go about doing so. With regard to achievement motivation, at least, that understanding often has not been present. The result is that many self-report scales do not measure the totality of the achievement motivation construct (Kanfer and Heggestad 1997).

A major argument against the TAT approach has been that even with adequate scorer reliability, test reliability is inadequate. There are many problems inherent in determining the reliability of projective techniques, and consequently the correlations reported may have underestimated the reliability of the TAT measures. There is now good reason to believe this is the case (McClelland 1985). Accordingly, knowledgeable scholars have increasingly come to the conclusion that projective measures work at least as well as those of a self-report nature (Hogan 1991).

To test this conclusion, Spangler (1992) has carried out meta-analyses utilizing a large number of studies. His results support McClelland's contentions regarding the TAT. In fact, TAT-based correlations with outcome criteria were significantly higher than self-report correlations. Under the conditions specified by the theory, the TAT validities are sizable. Furthermore, a low but significant correlation was found between the two approaches to achievement motivation. This would appear to explain why both have on occasion proven useful in predicting performance indexes. An approach utilizing the sentence completion method (also projective in nature) has produced very promising results (Miner 2004), but it was not included in the Spangler (1992) analysis. The particular sentence completion scale involved measures the components of task role motivation theory—components that are almost identical to those of McClelland's achievement situation.

I should also note that there is clear evidence that projective and self-report measures tend to deal with somewhat different constructs, even when on their face they are treating similar variables. McClelland, Koestner, and Weinberger (1989) indicated this and presented evidence to this effect. The two constructs indicate different levels of awareness and involve different modes of information processing. The implicit motives measured by the TAT reflect "hot, affective experiences congruent with the implicit goal state"; explicit motives measured by self-report indexes reflect "events corresponding to self-descriptions and values" (Woike and McAdams 2001, 10). Apparently, these varying constructs can produce correlations with dependent variables that are in fact in opposite directions. This has been found to be true of risk-taking propensities among entrepreneurs (Miner and Raju 2004; Stewart and Roth 2001), where risk avoidance appears characteristic given projective measurement, and risk proneness is found with self-report measures. Thus, it is important to measure implicit motivation when testing McClelland's theory and to use a projective measure; this caveat is inherent in the theory.

Achievement Motivation and Entrepreneurship

Substantial evidence exists to the effect that individuals who start their own businesses and make them succeed tend to have high levels of achievement motivation. Furthermore, the growth and success of such entrepreneurial enterprises are closely related to the achievement needs of the founder. Thus, the prototype achievement situation (personal responsibility and credit, minimal risk taking, feedback, opportunity for innovation, and future orientation) turns out to provide fertile ground for the efforts of the highly achievement-motivated person.

A study conducted in Ecuador, Malawi, and India utilizing the competency approach consistently found that stronger achievement motivation differentiated superior entrepreneurs from those whose success was at the average level (Spencer and Spencer 1993). Baum, Locke, and Kirkpatrick (1998) indicate that vision attributes and content, involving planning and establishing goals, operate to cause growth of entrepreneurial firms. This reflects the operation of at least one component of achievement motivation.

Achievement Motivation and Economic Development

The primary source of data on achievement and economic development is McClelland's (1961) book *The Achieving Society*. This work contains a mass of data focused on the achievement motivation–economic development relationship.

Because TAT protocols on past societies were not available, various substitutes were used and scored in a manner as analogous to the TAT scoring procedure as possible. The objective was to utilize cultural products that represented distillations of the values and valued motives of the society, especially those related to transmitting the culture to future generations. Thus, indexes of achievement motivation were derived from folk tales, school readers for children, cultural artifacts, characteristic literature, and other sources.

This research indicated many relationships between achievement imagery and economic growth, often established in terms of electric power output. However, there is a lag of many years between cause and effect.

Data on the United States from 1800 to 1950 have been developed using fourth grade readers to generate achievement motivation scores and the rate of recorded patents as an index of economic activity (deCharms and Moeller 1962). The data show a steady rise in achievement imagery until 1890 and then a steady decline, which by 1950 had reached the 1850 level. A similar curve was found for the patent data, but the familiar lag between the two indexes was much less in evidence, perhaps because patents must precede actual production by a number of years.

Although the support for an achievement motivation theory of economic development is strong, there is reason to believe that other factors, and even other motives, may also be involved. For instance, low levels of affiliation motivation have consistently been found to be precursors of economic growth. Power motivation appears to be an important factor in the larger countries, particularly those already more industrialized. The role of affiliation motivation is also in evidence in the study of the United States (deCharms and Moeller 1962), with lower levels of motivation characterizing the period of greatest growth. McClelland himself (1966) has shown that educational level operates independently of achievement motivation, yet it contributes sizably to economic growth.

The net effect of findings such as these has been a decline in research along the lines that McClelland originally advocated. A quote from a review of the subject provides insight into what has happened:

> [C]onfronted by evidence that psychology probably accounts for a very small proportion of the variance in macroeconomic well being, by warnings that the encouragement of entrepreneurship in settings where the opportunity structure is deficient may produce frustration and domestic or international turmoil, and by evidence that in some societies achievement is defined explicitly in terms of group norms rather than individual accomplishment, interest in studying achievement motivation cross-culturally waned. (Segall 1986, 543)

There is also a problem in that the time span between rises in motivation and measured economic growth is quite variable in different studies. Factors affecting this lag need much more investigation. In general the theory appears to apply primarily to less developed countries rather than to growth in that sector of the world dominated by large multinational corporations. The concepts related to the Protestant ethic and independence training of sons receive only mixed support as well. It appears, for instance, that the most important factor in the development of achievement motivation is not independence training, but exposure to a parental role model of an entrepreneurial nature.

Table 4.2

Relationships Between Socialized Power and Promotion Among Nontechnical Managers

	Managers not having predictive pattern	Managers having predictive pattern
Level of management achieved after 8 years		
Lower management	64 percent	34 percent
Middle management	36 percent	66 percent
Level of management achieved after 16 years		
Lower management	43 percent	21 percent
Middle management	57 percent	79 percent

Source: Adapted from McClelland and Boyatzis (1982, 739).
Note: Socialized power here is viewed as reflected in high power motivation, low affiliation motivation, and high inhibition.

Power Motivation and Management

The theory as it relates to power motivation has been the subject of considerable confirmatory research in recent years. Particularly impressive is a long-term predictive study conducted at AT&T. The results given in Table 4.2 indicate that socialized power, reflecting a combination of high power, low affiliation, and high inhibition (see Table 4.1), leads to more promotions (McClelland and Boyatzis 1982). This does not hold for technical managers, however, where specialized skills other than the managerial may play a significant role in the work. Winter (1991) carried out an analysis of this same data set utilizing TAT measures of power and responsibility (rather than power, affiliation, and inhibition) and obtained essentially the same results. Note that in both instances power motivation played a key role in the prediction process.

In another major study, House, Spangler, and Woycke (1991) utilized this same predictive pattern involving power motivation to analyze the inaugural addresses of U.S. presidents. These data were then compared with various historical indexes of presidential performance. The power motivation pattern was quite effective as a predictor.

Enough is known now to make it clear that power motivation is a strong predictor of management success at least among males. Yet as McClelland (1975) notes, there are situations where achievement motivation emerges as a better predictor for managers. House and Aditya (1997), after reviewing the relevant literature, conclude that a need to specify the boundary conditions under which the theory holds remains a problem. Given the apparent convergence with hierarchic role motivation theory, which incorporates several measures of power motivation as well as of potential inhibitors, it may be that the best way of delimiting the theoretical domain would be in terms of bureaucratic theory (Miner 1993).

Research Using Female Subjects

As noted, achievement motivation theory is intended more for males than females, partly because of the independence training aspect and partly because the scoring system that operationalizes the theory was developed using male subjects. The result has been that when females have been studied, the results often have not been the same as those found with males; in fact, there frequently have been no results at all, where results might have been expected. Fear of success appears to be much more prevalent among females, thus lowering their achievement motivation scores. Yet achievement motivation has been found to play a significant role in the personality dynamics of many female entrepreneurs (Langan-Fox and Roth 1995). However, a study of female managers within AT&T did not yield the same results as for male managers. The type of power motivation that made for success was distinctly different and high inhibition did not operate in the same manner at all (Jacobs and McClelland 1994).

Research on Motivational Development

The hypothesis that motives can be moved up the individual hierarchy, and thus made to exert more extensive influence on behavior through exposure to appropriate training, has been generally confirmed. Although most of the research has been conducted with achievement motivation training, there are some data on the development of power motivation.

The major thrusts of achievement motivation training have been in the development of capitalism among black people in the United States, in stimulating economic growth in less developed countries, and in producing better performance from schoolchildren, especially disadvantaged children. A typical course lasts roughly a week and includes games and simulations, goal-setting and planning, lectures, TAT analysis, case discussions, films, action team discussions, and contests in achievement thinking. The objective is to induce the twelve conditions hypothesized to be conducive to motivational change.

There is considerable evidence now that such achievement motivation training does increase the target motive, and that given appropriate external circumstances, this increased motivation will yield expanded entrepreneurial behavior (McClelland and Winter 1969; Miron and McClelland 1979; Spencer and Spencer 1993). However, the training should not be used indiscriminately. Developing achievement motivation in an individual whose environment does not permit satisfaction of the motive can be self-defeating. In the past when this has been done, the people involved have either left the environment (quit to take more gratifying jobs) or attempted to change the existing environment through pressure tactics and other conflict-generating efforts.

On theoretical grounds, power motivation training should be equally effective, and there is some evidence to this effect. However, data for courses utilizing the McClelland format are not extensive. On the other hand, if managerial role motivation training, which appears to produce much the same motivational effects, is added to the McClelland evidence, the picture becomes much more positive (Miner 1993).

Evidence from Recent Reviews

A number of reviews dealing with achievement motivation theory have appeared in the last few years. Taken as a whole these reviews provide the most comprehensive evaluation of the research currently available. One of these evaluations (Rauch and Frese 2000) draws upon only a selected set of studies and incorporates self-report measures as well as projective measures. Nevertheless, it finds correlations averaging in the low 0.20s in support of the McClelland theory. Risk avoidance is found to be slightly positively correlated with success, but the average relationship is significant. These results provide overall support for the theory, but with the proviso that certain environmental conditions not specified by McClelland operate as well.

A review by Aditya, House, and Kerr (2000), which draws upon several unpublished sources and a rather wide range of studies, also reports validities in the low 0.20s for achievement motivation, but this effect occurs only in small firms. Power motivation was found to be similarly important but not always in large firms as hypothesized.

Shane, Locke, and Collins (2003) looked into a number of the same data sources as did Aditya, House, and Kerr (2000), plus information Locke (2000) accumulated on major wealth creators. Their overall conclusion with regard to achievement motivation was that it can play a very useful role in explaining entrepreneurial activity. Mean r's in the high 0.20s and 0.30s are noted.

These conclusions are uniformly supportive of the McClelland theory as far as they apply. However, an additional review (Vecchio 2003), although generally positive, notes that results have not always been supportive. Thus a longitudinal study over an eleven-year period found that the TAT measure of achievement motivation did not predict the subsequent start of a new business with any significance at all (Hansemark 2000).

Extending this evaluation process to McClelland's version of competency testing where tests (and sometimes interview data) for knowledge, skills, abilities, traits, and motives are set in opposition to the usual intelligence and scholastic aptitude measures, the overall evidence appears to be positive also (Shippmann et al. 2000). The personality measures do predict (Spencer and Spencer, 1993). On the other hand, it has become increasingly apparent that McClelland (1973) was incorrect in disparaging the predictive power of cognitive tests; they too can predict (Barrett and Depinet 1991). In fact, substantial evidence exists that psychological testing overall is quite effective and that the validity of psychological tests is comparable to what is obtained with medical tests (Meyer, Finn, Eyde, Kay, Moreland, Dies, Eisman, Kubiszyn, and Reed 2001).

CONCLUSIONS

McCelland's was a very fertile mind that took him in many directions, not unlike Lewin. Yet the broad brush that encompasses achievement motivation theory maintains a degree of connectedness. In some of his ideas, and his research designs as well, McClelland got somewhat ahead of himself and leaves some of the logical dots unconnected, but this is not the norm. As the stars in the box indicate, the ratings by peers of the importance attained by achievement motivation theory, as well as the other evaluation points, are all very high. The mean importance rating is 5.15 and, although the evidence is not sufficient to award the label of institutionalized, a trend in that direction does exist.

Validity is at a high level with a rating of 4 stars, but there are misses, as in the case of economic development, and the average correlations tend to be somewhat lower than might have been expected, simply because certain studies did not yield consistent support. How the theory applies to females is still not completely settled.

The usefulness of McClelland's theorizing is not possible to question, however. He founded a company to spread and develop his ideas, and he grew it to a point where it sold to a major player in the field (Hay Associates); he initiated competency modeling and began an approach that has provided considerable input to consulting practice; he created a variety of training and development programs to instill both achievement and power motivation, conducting evaluation research on these programs and doing this around the world. There is more, but this is sufficient—the 5 stars are clearly appropriate.

In Chapter 5 we will consider a theory that also is rooted in personality theory, but that focuses on job enrichment, a procedure intended to give employees a greater role in their work. Thus, the discussion of personality-oriented approaches to motivation continues in the next chapter, but the tack taken by Herzberg is quite different from McClelland's.

REFERENCES

Aditya, Ram N., House, Robert J., and Kerr, Steven (2000). Theory and Practice of Leadership: Into the New Millennium. In Cary L. Cooper and Edwin A. Locke (Eds.), *Industrial and Organizational Psychology: Linking Theory with Practice*. Oxford, UK: Blackwell, 130–65.

Atkinson, John W., and McClelland, David C. (1948). The Projective Expression of Needs. II. The Effect of Different Intensities of the Hunger Drive on Thematic Apperception. *Journal of Experimental Psychology*, 38, 643–58.

Barrett, Gerald V., and Depinet, Robert L. (1991). A Reconsideration of Testing for Competence Rather than Intelligence. *American Psychologist*, 46, 1012–24.

Baum, J. Robert, Locke, Edwin A., and Kirkpatrick, Shelley A. (1998). A Longitudinal Study of the Relation of Vision and Vision Communication to Venture Growth in Entrepreneurial Firms. *Journal of Applied Psychology*, 83, 43–54.

deCharms, Richard, and Moeller, Gerald H. (1962). Values Expressed in American Children's Readers: 1800–1950. *Journal of Abnormal and Social Psychology*, 64, 136–42.

Hansemark, Ove C. (2000). Predictive Validity of TAT and CMPS on the Entrepreneurial Activity, "Start of a New Business": A Longitudinal Study. *Journal of Managerial Psychology*, 15, 634–50.

Hogan, Robert T. (1991). Personality and Personality Measurement. In Marvin D. Dunnette and Leaetta M. Hough (Eds.), *Handbook of Industrial and Organizational Psychology*, Vol. 2. Palo Alto, CA: Consulting Psychologists Press, 873–919.

House, Robert J., and Aditya, Ram N. (1997). The Social Scientific Study of Leadership: Quo Vadis? *Journal of Management*, 23, 409–73.

House, Robert J., Spangler, William D., and Woycke, James (1991). Personality and Charisma in the U.S. Presidency: A Psychological Theory of Leader Effectiveness. *Administrative Science Quarterly*, 36, 364–96.

Jacobs, Ruth L., and McClelland, David C. (1994). Moving Up the Corporate Ladder: A Longitudinal Study of the Leadership Motive Pattern and Managerial Success in Women and Men. *Consulting Psychology Journal*, 46, 32–41.

Kanfer, Ruth, and Heggestad, Eric D. (1997). Motivational Traits and Skills: A Person-Centered Approach to Work Motivation. *Research in Organizational Behavior*, 19, 1–56.

Langan-Fox, Janice, and Roth, Susanna (1995). Achievement Motivation and Female Entrepreneurs. *Journal of Occupational and Organizational Psychology*, 68, 209–18.

Levinson, Harry, and Wofford, Jerry C. (2000). Approaching Retirement as the Flexibility Phase. *Academy of Management Executive*, 14(2), 84–95.

Litwin, George H., and Siebrecht, Adrienne (1967). Integrators and Entrepreneurs: Their Motivation and Effect on Management. *Hospital Progress*, 48(9), 67–71.

Locke, Edwin A. (2000). *The Prime Movers: Traits of the Great Wealth Creators*. New York: AMACOM.

McClelland, David C. (1961). *The Achieving Society*. Princeton, NJ: Van Nostrand.

——— (1962). Business Drive and National Achievement. *Harvard Business Review*, 40(4), 99–112.

——— (1965a). Achievement Motivation Can Be Developed. *Harvard Business Review*, 43(6), 3–20.

——— (1965b). Toward a Theory of Motive Acquisition. *American Psychologist*, 20, 321–33.

——— (1966). Does Education Accelerate Economic Growth? *Economic Development and Cultural Change*, 14, 257–78.

——— (1973). Testing for Competency Rather than Intelligence. *American Psychologist*, 28, 1–14.

——— (1975). *Power: The Inner Experience*. New York: Irvington.

——— (1984). *Motives, Personality, and Society: Selected Papers*. New York: Praeger.

——— (1985). How Motives, Skills, and Values Determine What People Do. *American Psychologist*, 40, 812–25.

——— (1994). The Knowledge-Testing–Educational Complex Strikes Back. *American Psychologist*, 49, 66–69.

——— (1998). Identifying Competence with Behavioral-Event Interviews. *Psychological Science*, 9, 331–39.

McClelland, David C., Atkinson, John W., Clark, Russell A., and Lowell, Edgar L. (1953). *The Achievement Motive*. New York: Appleton-Century-Crofts.

McClelland, David C., and Boyatzis, Richard E. (1982). Leadership Motive Pattern and Long-Term Success in Management. *Journal of Applied Psychology*, 67, 737–43.

McClelland, David C., and Burnham, David H. ([1976] 2003). Power Is the Great Motivator. *Harvard Business Review*, 81(1), 117–26.

McClelland, David C., Davis, William N., Kalin, Rudolph, and Wanner, Eric. (1972). *The Drinking Man: Alcohol and Human Motivation.* New York: Free Press.

McClelland, David C., Koestner, Richard, and Weinberger, Joel (1989). How Do Self-Attributed and Implicit Motives Differ? *Psychological Review,* 96, 690–702.

McClelland, David C., and Winter, David G. (1969). *Motivating Economic Achievement.* New York: Free Press.

Meckler, Mark, Drake, Bruce H., and Levinson, Harry (2003). Putting Psychology Back into Psychological Contracts. *Journal of Management Inquiry,* 12, 217–28.

Meyer, Gregory J., Finn, Stephen E., Eyde, Lorraine D., Kay, Gary G., Moreland, Kevin L., Dies, Robert R., Eisman, Elena J., Kubiszyn, Tom W., and Reed, Geoffrey M. (2001). Psychological Testing and Psychological Assessment: A Review of Evidence and Issues. *American Psychologist,* 56, 128–65.

Miner, John B. (1993). *Role Motivation Theories.* London: Routledge.

———— (2004). Congruence and the Significance of Careers in Testing Task Role Motivation Theory. Working paper, Eugene, Oregon, 1–49.

Miner, John B., and Raju, Nambury S. (2004). Risk Propensity Differences between Managers and Entrepreneurs and between Low- and High-Growth Entrepreneurs: A Reply in a More Conservative Vein. *Journal of Applied Psychology,* 89, 3–13.

Miron, David, and McClelland, David C. (1979). The Impact of Achievement Motivation Training on Small Business. *California Management Review,* 21(4), 13–28.

Morgan, Wesley G. (2003). Origin and History of the "Series B" and "Series C" TAT Pictures. *Journal of Personality Assessment,* 81, 133–48.

Murray, Henry A. (1938). *Explorations in Personality: A Clinical and Experimental Study of Fifty Men of College Age.* New York: Oxford University Press.

Payne, Roy L. (2000). Enpsychian Management and the Millennium. *Journal of Managerial Psychology,* 15, 219–26.

Rauch, Andreas, and Frese, Michael (2000). Psychological Approaches to Entrepreneurial Success: A General Model and an Overview of Findings. *International Review of Industrial and Organizational Psychology,* 15, 101–41.

Rodriguez, Donna, Patel, Rita, Bright, Andrea, Gregory, Donna, and Gowing, Marilyn K. (2002). Developing Competency Models to Promote Integrated Human Resource Practices. *Human Resource Management,* 41, 309–24.

Sandberg, Jörgen (2000). Understanding Human Competence at Work: An Interpretative Approach. *Academy of Management Journal,* 43, 9–25.

Segall, Marshall H. (1986). Culture and Behavior: Psychology in Global Perspective. *Annual Review of Psychology,* 37, 523–64.

Shane, Scott, Locke, Edwin A., and Collins, Christopher J. (2003). Entrepreneurial Motivation. *Human Resource Management Review,* 13, 257–79.

Shippmann, Jeffery S., Ash, Ronald A., Carr, Linda, Hesketh, Beryl, Pearlman, Kenneth, Battista, Mariangela, Eyde, Lorraine D., Kehoe, Jerry, Prien, Erich P., and Sanchez, Juan I. (2000). The Practice of Competency Modeling. *Personnel Psychology,* 53, 703–40.

Spangler, William D. (1992). Validity of Questionnaire and TAT Measures of Need for Achievement: Two Meta-Analyses. *Psychological Bulletin,* 112, 140–54.

Spencer, Lyle M. and Spencer, Signe M. (1993). *Competence at Work: Models for Superior Performance.* New York: Wiley.

Stewart, Wayne H., and Roth, Philip L. (2001). Risk Propensity Differences between Entrepreneurs and Managers: A Meta-Analytic Review. *Journal of Applied Psychology,* 86, 145–53.

Vecchio, Robert P. (2003). Entrepreneurship and Leadership: Common Trends and Common Threads. *Human Resource Management Review,* 13, 303–27.

Veroff, Joseph, and Veroff, Joanne B. (1972). Reconsideration of a Measure of Power Motivation. *Psychological Bulletin,* 78, 279–91.

Winter, David G. (1973). *The Power Motive.* New York: Free Press.

———— (1991). A Motivational Model of Leadership: Predicting Long-Term Management Success from TAT Measures of Power Motivation and Responsibility. *Leadership Quarterly,* 2, 67–80.

———— (2000). David C. McClelland (1917–1998). *American Psychologist,* 55, 540–41.

Woike, Barbara A., and McAdams, Dan P. (2001). TAT-based Personality Measures Have Considerable Validity. *APS Observer,* 14(5), 10.

CHAPTER 5

MOTIVATION-HYGIENE THEORY

FREDERICK HERZBERG

Background
Evolution of the Theory
    The Motivation to Work
    Work and the Nature of Man
    The Managerial Choice
Applications to Job Enrichment
    The Process of Orthodox Job Enrichment
    Results at AT&T
    Results in the U.S. Air Force
Evaluation and Impact
    The Original Study
    Closely Allied Research
    Using Alternative Methods
    Current State of the Theory
    Current State of Practice
Conclusions

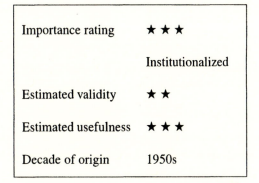

Importance rating	★ ★ ★
	Institutionalized
Estimated validity	★ ★
Estimated usefulness	★ ★ ★
Decade of origin	1950s

The theory to which we now turn often is referred to as the two-factor theory, a designation that has its rationale in the dual nature of its approach to the sources of job satisfaction, and ultimately job motivation. The prime generator of the theory, Frederick Herzberg, prefers the term motivation-hygiene; therefore, this designation is used here. The initial source of the theory was a comprehensive review of the literature on job attitudes and satisfaction undertaken by Herzberg and his associates at Psychological Service of Pittsburgh (Herzberg, Mausner, Peterson, and Capwell 1957). This review revealed often conflicting results, although with some slight overall tendency for job satisfaction to be positively correlated with job performance levels. To this finding Herzberg added an insight derived from his background in the field of mental health—the idea that mental health is not just the obverse of mental illness, but rather a totally separate process. He developed the hypothesis that a similar discontinuity exists in the field of job satisfaction (Herzberg 1976). Subsequent research produced a list of factors that contribute to satisfaction at work (motivation factors), and another separate list of factors that contribute to dissatisfaction (hygiene factors). Thus, the theory is an amalgam of deductive and inductive components so closely intertwined with the early research that the two cannot be separated effectively (Herzberg, Mausner, and Snyderman 1959). Out of this theoretical framework came a concept of job enrichment that proved to be particularly attractive to management (see Herzberg [1968] 2003).

Job enrichment as such appears to have begun with a project initiated at IBM in the mid-1940s (Walker 1962). At that time the approach was called job enlargement. However, it included both adding tasks to a job horizontally (strictly speaking, job enlargement) and adding requirements for greater skill and judgment, thus enriching the job vertically. The intent even at this early point was to introduce more interest, variety, and significance into the work.

This approach spread within IBM and eventually to other companies. It arose out of practical concerns and initially was devoid of theory. Scientific management had produced a simplification of many manufacturing jobs with the result that both the content and skills required shrank. It was only natural that the cycle would eventually swing back the other way. Yet theorists and advocates with strong humanist values flocked to job enrichment quickly. They saw their work as reversing what they regarded as the dysfunctional application of scientific management. During the 1960s, this groundswell built to the point where demonstration projects seemed to be everywhere. By the early 1970s, job enrichment was being endorsed as a solution to the country's productivity problems by the U.S. Department of Health, Education, and Welfare (1972).

BACKGROUND

Born in 1923, Frederick Herzberg grew up in New York City and went to college at City University there. After service during World War II in Europe, he completed his undergraduate degree in psychology and moved on to graduate work in the field at the University of Pittsburgh. There he obtained a Ph.D. in clinical psychology after an internship at Mayview State Hospital, and also a Master of Public Health degree (Herzberg 1993). He was awarded a doctorate in 1950 at the age of twenty-seven. In the early 1950s his publications were primarily in the clinical area (the Rorschach, electro-shock therapy, etc.), but during that decade he gradually came to write and work in industrial psychology.

For a while he was employed by John Flanagan, who developed the critical incident technique for job study and performance appraisal, at the American Institutes for Research; later he joined Psychological Service of Pittsburgh. In 1960 he accepted a joint appointment in psychology and in the medical school with Case Western Reserve University in Cleveland. There he wrote on his theory, published several related articles in the *Harvard Business Review,* became heavily involved in consulting and speaking on job enrichment, and headed a graduate program in industrial mental health. Clearly, Herzberg had been very close to the business school boundary for some time, but it was not until 1972 that he crossed it, becoming a professor of management at the University of Utah. He remained there throughout his career since that time. He died in January 2000.

EVOLUTION OF THE THEORY

Herzberg was a self-confessed humanist, as became increasingly evident as his thinking progressed. His motivation-hygiene theory is presented in three volumes (Herzberg, Mausner, and Snyderman 1959; Herzberg 1966, 1976). The most recent of these is primarily a compendium of articles previously published, the majority of them in the early 1970s. Although the basics of the theory established in 1959 have remained firm, Herzberg has elaborated considerably on them since then.

The Motivation to Work

The first volume promulgating the theory also contains a detailed report of the initial research. This research sought to explore two hypotheses:

1. The factors causing positive job attitudes and those causing negative attitudes are different.
2. The factors and the performance or personal effects associated with sequences of job events extending over long time periods differ from those associated with sequences of events of short duration.

Based on certain outcomes of this research, the factors leading to job satisfaction and to job dissatisfaction were specified and thus became part of the theory. Job satisfaction is viewed as an outgrowth of achievement, recognition (verbal), the work itself (challenging), responsibility, and advancement (promotion). These five factors are considered to be closely related both conceptually and empirically. When they are present in a job, the individual's basic needs will be satisfied and positive feelings as well as improved performance will result. The basic needs specified are those related to personal growth and self-actualization, and these are said to be satisfied by the five intrinsic aspects of the work itself.

In contrast, job dissatisfaction results from a different set of factors, all of which characterize the context in which the work is performed. These are company policy and administrative practices, supervision (technical quality), interpersonal relations (especially with supervision), physical working conditions, job security, benefits, and salary. These dissatisfiers, or hygiene factors, when appropriately provided, can serve to remove dissatisfaction and improve performance up to a point, but they cannot be relied upon to generate really positive job feelings or the high levels of performance that are potentially possible. To accomplish these outcomes, management must shift gears and move into motivation.

This means that good hygiene should be provided, but that it will yield benefits only up to a certain point. Beyond that, the focus needs to be on the intrinsic aspects of the work itself, not on its context: "[J]obs must be restructured to increase to the maximum the ability of workers to achieve goals meaningfully related to the doing of the job. . . . [T]he individual should have some measure of control over the way in which the job is done in order to realize a sense of achievement and of personal growth" (Herzberg, Mausner, and Snyderman 1959, 132).

Work and the Nature of Man

With this second book Herzberg (1966) began to add philosophical embellishments to what had been an eminently scientific and testable theory. Thus, the fringe benefits and other hygiene factors provided by large corporations were equated with the welfare state, and the motivation-hygiene distinction was extended beyond the work context through the use of extensive biblical analogies. More specifically, mankind was described as possessing two sets of basic needs—animal needs relating to environmental survival, and human needs relating to "the tasks with which he is uniquely involved." The former needs are allied with the notion of mankind as sinful and perpetually condemned to suffer and avoid suffering, as epitomized by Adam's fall. In addition, mankind may be characterized, like Abraham, as a capable being possessing innate potential and created in the image of God.

Herzberg (1966, 56) summarizes his expanded position regarding human motivation:

> [T]he human animal has two categories of needs. One set stems from his animal disposition, that side of him previously referred to as the Adam view of man; it is centered on the avoidance of loss of life, hunger, pain, sexual deprivation and in other primary drives, in addition to the infinite varieties of learned fears that become attached to these basic drives. The other segment of man's nature, according to the Abraham concept of the human being, is man's compelling urge to realize his own potentiality by continuous psychological growth. . . . [T]hese two characteristics must be constantly viewed as having separate biological, psychological and existential origins.

Although most people are best characterized in terms of both sets of needs, Herzberg also described individuals who are dominated by one set or the other. Thus, there are high growth–oriented people who actually experience what they interpret as unhappiness when deprived of motivators, and there are people who are fixated on hygiene-seeking, such as the mentally ill.

Hygiene seekers are generally considered to be poor risks for a company, because they tend to be motivated over short time periods and require constant doses of external reward; they cannot be relied upon in crisis. Furthermore, a lack of motivators in a job tends to sensitize people to any lack of hygiene factors, with the result that more and more hygiene must be provided to obtain the same level of performance. Herzberg emphasizes strongly the need for companies to build motivators into their jobs.

To facilitate this, he recommends that industrial relations departments be organized into two formal divisions, one to deal with hygiene matters and the other to deal with motivators. Assuming that most current departments are focused largely on hygiene, he devotes primary attention to what would be added with the division concerned with motivator needs. Among the tasks recommended are re-education of organization members to a motivator orientation (from the current welfare orientation), job enlargement, and remedial work in the areas of technological obsolescence, poor employee performance, and administrative failure.

The Managerial Choice

The third presentation of motivation-hygiene theory (Herzberg 1976) places much greater emphasis on job enrichment applications. However, it also extends the theory in several respects. One such extension utilizes the two-factor concept to develop typologies of workers. The normal types are described as follows:

1. The person who has both hygiene and motivator fulfillment, who is not unhappy (hygiene) and is also very happy (motivation).
2. The person who is on both need systems but has little fulfillment in the hygiene area even though motivator satisfaction is good. Such a "starving artist" is both unhappy and happy.
3. The person who is also on both need systems but whose satisfactions are reversed—hygienes are good but motivators are poor; such people are not unhappy but neither are they happy.
4. The down and out person who is lacking in fulfillment generally and is both unhappy and lacking in happiness.

To these four, Herzberg adds certain abnormal profiles that characterize people who are not actually on the motivator dimension at all and who attempt to substitute increased hygiene for this motivator deficiency. Such people may also resort to psychological mechanisms, such as denial of their hygiene needs and fantasized motivator satisfaction, which further compound their hygiene problems. In these pathological instances an inversion occurs in that fulfillment of hygiene needs may be viewed as satisfying, not merely as an avoidance of dissatisfaction.

A distinction is also made within the motivator factors. Achievement and recognition are described as preparatory in nature and as having, in common with hygiene factors, relatively short-term effects. The work itself, responsibility, and growth and advancement are generators that truly motivate people. In job redesign, these latter factors should be emphasized.

Throughout his writings Herzberg has wrestled with the role of salary. The most frequently stated position is that it is a hygiene factor. Yet there are contradictory statements in the 1976 book, which contains articles published at different times. A 1971 article clearly states, "Money is a hygiene factor" (Herzberg 1976, 305). But in 1974, the following statement appears, "Because of its ubiquitous nature, salary commonly shows up as a motivator as well as hygiene. Although primarily a hygiene factor, it also often takes on some of the properties of a motivator, with dynamics similar to those of recognition for achievement" (Herzberg 1976, 71). It appears that the motivation-hygiene problem created by compensation is very similar to the problem created by power motivation in the development of achievement motivation theory (see Chapter 4).

A final point that needs to be made is that Herzberg gradually became increasingly critical of his fellow social scientists and of alternative theories. His justification was that he was attacked first. Others may well view what he considers attacks as merely the presentation of objective scientific evidence. In any event, Herzberg (1976, 54–55) resorted to statements such as the following:

> Engrossed with their artificial measures and rarified statistics, social scientists have too long neglected the language and experience of people at work. . . . Their error is attempting to manipulate their instruments to produce a relationship that simply does not reflect the psychological and organizational realities in many companies.

Are such statements attempts to play to the stereotypes of management practitioners, as some have charged, or do they represent valid, scientific criticism? Certainly they reflect the existence of considerable controversy. The answers, though, must be found in an objective evaluation of the research evidence.

APPLICATIONS TO JOB ENRICHMENT

From the beginning, Herzberg advocated restructuring jobs to place greater reliance on motivators. The techniques of this kind that evolved over the years came to be designated by the term *orthodox job enrichment*, to differentiate them from similar approaches that do not have their origins in motivation-hygiene theory. Although Herzberg was a major influence in the development of job redesign procedures, a great deal has happened in this area that is not attributable either to him or his theory. Furthermore, his self-designation as "father of job enrichment" may be only partially correct, because efforts of this kind can be traced back many years, as noted previously.

The Process of Orthodox Job Enrichment

Herzberg (1976) makes a strong point that what he is *not* talking about is participative management, sociotechnical systems, industrial democracy, or organizational development. Yet there is a marked tendency for a great variety of activities to creep into and become part of a job enrichment effort. Orthodox job enrichment by definition involves only the introduction of motivators into a job, not hygienes. Yet, pay raises and various interpersonal factors have accompanied such efforts on occasion. Accordingly, it is important to understand clearly what is implied by the term.

Herzberg (1976, 114–116) has identified a number of factors that, although not limited to orthodox job enrichment alone, are primary to the approach:

1. Direct feedback of performance results to the employee in a nonevaluative manner and usually not through a superior. An example would be targets on a rifle range that fall down when hit.
2. The existence of a customer or client either within or outside the organization for whom work is performed. The unit assemblers who depend on the outcome of various prior manufacturing operations fit this designation; so do a salesperson's external customers.
3. The opportunity for individuals to feel that they are growing psychologically through new learning that is meaningful. For instance, a laboratory technician may be given a chance to learn many skills utilized by a research scientist.
4. Being able to schedule one's own work, with requirements set by realistic deadlines. Thus, work breaks might be taken when scheduled by the individual, not management.
5. Doing the job in one's own unique manner and utilizing time accordingly. As an example, individuals who finish their tasks ahead of time can be allowed to use the remaining work periods as they see fit.
6. Providing employees with mini-budgets that make them directly responsible for costs. In this way, cost and profit centers are pushed down to the lowest possible level, where employees may be authorized to approve expenditures within realistic limits.
7. Communication with the individuals needed to get the job done regardless of any possible hierarchic constraints. Accordingly, an employee whose work requires discussion with a supervisor in another department would be permitted to do so directly.
8. Maintaining individual accountability for results. For instance, responsibility for quality control may be taken away from a supervisor or external unit and built back into the job.

An indication of what these changes may involve is provided by a job enrichment program carried out within a sales unit:

1. Reports on each customer call were eliminated. Salespeople were to use their own discretion in passing on information to or making requests of management.
2. Salespeople determined their own calling frequencies and kept records only as might be needed for purposes such as staff reviews.
3. The technical service department agreed to provide service as needed by the individual salesperson. Communication between salesperson and technician was direct, with any needed paperwork cleared after the event.
4. If customers complained about product performance, salespeople could make settlements of up to $250 if they considered it appropriate.
5. When faulty material was delivered or customers proved to be overstocked, salespeople could deal with these issues directly, with no limit on sales value of material returned.
6. Salespeople were given a discretionary range of about 10 percent on quoted prices for most items, although quotations other than list did have to be reported to management (Herzberg 1976, 145).

Results at AT&T

One of the first applications of job enrichment in which Herzberg was directly involved occurred at AT&T (Ford 1969, 1973). The initial study was conducted in the treasury department among clerical personnel who answer inquiries from AT&T shareholders. Job changes were introduced for certain employees with the objective of providing greater opportunities for achievement, recognition, responsibility, advancement, and psychological growth. The jobs of other employees remained unchanged. The results are described as follows:

> The achieving or experimental group clearly exceeded the control and uncommitted groups on a variety of criteria, such as turnover, the quality of customer service, productivity, lowered costs, lower absence rates, and source of managerial upgrading. . . . [O]nly the experimental group members felt significantly better about the task at which they work. The upward change in this group is most striking. (Ford 1969, 39)

Because of this result, the program was expanded into a variety of departments—commercial, comptroller, plant, traffic, and engineering. In most cases the practice of comparing experimental (enriched jobs) and control (job not enriched) groups was continued. The overall results were very favorable, although there were instances when job enrichment did not have much effect. Some supervisors clearly resisted it, and 10 to 15 percent of the employees did not want the added responsibility. Blue-collar employees proved most resistant to enrichment.

Results in the U.S. Air Force

Another program of job enrichment was initiated at Hill Air Force Base in Utah after Herzberg arrived in the state but then spread to a number of other installations (Herzberg 1976, 1977; Herzberg and Zautra 1976). The enriched jobs vary from aircraft maintenance to routine clerical and from contract document preparation to foreign military sales. Results obtained with the initial eleven jobs that were changed indicated savings of over $250,000 in a ten-month period. The largest part of this saving occurred in two aircraft maintenance activities; several projects ran into considerable difficulty and did not yield tangible benefits. When tangible benefits were obtained, the return included reduced costs for materials, fuel, and personnel, and increased units of production.

When the program was subsequently expanded:

> The results were dramatic: a $1.75 million saving in 2 years on 29 projects that had matured to the point where careful auditing of savings was possible. The dollar benefits accrued from reduced sick leave, a lower rate of personnel turnover, less overtime and rework, a reduction in man-hours, and material savings. (Herzberg 1977, 25)

Table 5.1 contains data on reported increases in job satisfaction experienced over twelve months prior to job enrichment and again during the months of job change. It is apparent that job satisfaction did increase and that all motivators studied except recognition also showed an increase. Data on hygiene factors were not obtained.

EVALUATION AND IMPACT

It is to Herzberg's credit that he proposed measures of his theoretical variables when the theory was first presented, and that he has conducted research on the theory from the beginning. As

Table 5.1

Pre- and Post-Measures of Job Satisfaction for Job Enrichment Projects
(percentage experiencing increase)

Measure	Reported increase prior to enrichment (%)	Reported increase during enrichment (%)
Overall satisfaction factors	33	76
Recognition for achievement	15	20
Achievement	28	67
Work itself	10	70
Responsibility	15	80
Advancement	23	62
Growth	30	72

Source: Adapted from Herzberg and Zautra (1976, 66).

might be expected, these circumstances have served to stimulate considerable research by others. The result has been that both Herzberg's measures and his interpretation of his findings have been seriously challenged. To understand what has happened, it is necessary to start with the original research that spawned motivation-hygiene theory (Herzberg, Mausner, and Snyderman 1959).

The Original Study

The measurement procedure developed by Herzberg and his associates was a derivative of the critical incident technique that had been utilized previously by Flanagan (1954), primarily in the evaluation of job performance. However, while Flanagan asked his subjects to focus on good and bad performance, Herzberg asked for incidents describing "a time when you felt exceptionally good or a time when you felt exceptionally bad about your job, either a long-range sequence of events or a short-range incident" (Herzberg, Mausner, and Snyderman 1959, 35). Subjects were requested to provide several such incidents. In each instance a series of probing questions was asked regarding the incident to determine what factors were related to the job attitude expressed; these factors might be either antecedent objective occurrences (first level) or attributed internal reasons for the feelings (second level). Also, the perceived consequences or effects of the attitudes were explored with regard to such matters as job performance, tenure on the job, emotional adjustment, interpersonal relationships, and the like.

The outcome is a set of stories from each subject specifying a factors-attitudes-effects sequence. These stories are somewhat similar to those elicited using the Thematic Apperception Test. However, there is no standardized external stimulus such as that provided by the TAT pictures, and a story here is about the subject, rather than someone else. Both of these considerations reduce the psychological distance of the stories and thus increase the degree to which defensiveness may be manifested in them.

In the major study this procedure was applied to a large sample of accountants and engineers. The stories were content analyzed using thirty-nine scoring categories. Agreement between coders was at the 95 percent level.

The data indicate that recognition, achievement, responsibility, the work itself, and their related feelings are more commonly associated with job satisfaction than dissatisfaction. Advancement operates in a similar manner as a first-level factor but not at the second level. The remaining differences all occur on factors that cannot be measured at both levels. Within this context, group feeling is a satisfier, whereas interpersonal relations with supervisors and peers, technical super-vision, company policy and administration, working conditions, and factors in personal life are dissatisfiers. The data for second-level factors also indicate that feelings of fairness and unfair-ness is a dissatisfier.

The findings obtained are certainly consistent with the original hypotheses, and they largely fit the theory as it ultimately evolved based on interpretations of this study. On the other hand, the data yield several factors that emerge equally as satisfiers and dissatisfiers, among them the pos-sibility of growth, salary, and status, and feelings of pride and shame. Furthermore, although dissatisfiers rarely yield meaningful frequencies as satisfiers, the reverse is not true. At one level or another, recognition, achievement, advancement, and the work itself all operate as dissatisfiers as well as satisfiers more than 10 percent of the time.

Data on the factors associated with long- and short-term event sequences are not presented. The original hypothesis dealing with the differential causes and effects of sequences of job events extending over long and short time periods appears to have been dropped from the theory; it does not appear in later formulations.

The data on effects consequent upon feelings of satisfaction and dissatisfaction are introduced with appropriate qualifications, due to the lack of objective confirmation. Nevertheless, they are given considerable credence subsequently. Reports of satisfaction were associated with reports of positive effects, including improved performance, continued employment, improved attitude to-ward the company, improved mental health, better interpersonal relationships, and improved morale. In contrast, reports of dissatisfaction were associated with the reverse trends, although the overall results were less pronounced. These results "may be attributed to the unwillingness of some interviewees to admit to doing their jobs less well than usual" (Herzberg, Mausner, and Snyderman 1959, 87).

Whatever the merits of this original study and of the interpretation the authors place on it, it is best viewed as an inductive source from which the theory was, if not totally generated, at least specifically delineated in terms of its operative variables. Given this situation, it is best to look to subsequent research for adequate empirical tests.

Closely Allied Research

A number of studies utilizing the methods of the original research, or minor variants, were con-ducted in the years immediately following and are summarized by Herzberg (1966) as providing support for his theory. Most of these studies did not consider effects, and a number did not deal with second-level factors. Sequence duration was given practically no attention.

There is no question that when significant results are obtained in these studies, they are much more likely to support the theory than refute it. It is evident also that certain of the first-level factors are much more likely to receive support from the data than others. Among the motivators, achievement and recognition are strongly supported, but possibility of growth is not supported at all. Among the hygienes, company policy and administration and also technical supervision are supported, but not salary, status, and job security. The data also indicate that motivators fre-quently operate as dissatisfiers.

As research has continued using the techniques of the original study, the theory appears to continue to be supported on balance, but certain problems remain. The tendency for motivators to appear frequently as dissatisfiers, as well as satisfiers, represents a continuing difficulty. This tendency to appear in the wrong context is less characteristic of the hygienes, unless (and this clearly does occur) a true reversal is in evidence. Such reversals (or inversions) can apparently appear for salary and the various interpersonal relations factors, and there they can be sizable; they also may appear for status.

In view of Herzberg's own expressed concerns about the findings of the original study dealing with performance and personal effects, and the clear implications of these findings for the motivational as opposed to merely attitudinal hypotheses of the theory, it is surprising that so little research has focused on this area. A study conducted by Schwab, DeVitt, and Cummings (1971), utilizing essentially the same methods as the original research and dealing only with effects in the area of job performance, does serve to amplify the Herzberg findings. Favorable performance effects were reported often as an outgrowth of satisfying job experiences; to a lesser extent, unfavorable performance effects were associated with dissatisfying experiences. This pattern is consistent with the one originally reported.

One might assume from this result that the introduction of motivators is the key to improving employee performance. However, hygiene factors were occasionally reported as sources of satisfaction, and it was possible to determine in these instances that improved performance effects were reported to as great a degree as those for the motivators. Thus, it would appear that when hygiene factors operate as satisfiers, in this case interpersonal relations with a supervisor predominantly, they may be perceived as a source of performance stimulation just as much as motivators are. Furthermore, when there is dissatisfaction, motivators can have just as negative an effect as hygienes. It is the level of job satisfaction-dissatisfaction that yields the reported performance effect, not the presence of motivators or hygienes.

A study carried out by Herzberg, Mathapo, Wiener, and Wiesen (1974) bears upon the hypothesis that when hygienes are reported as sources of satisfaction, the inversions are characteristic of the mentally ill. Using the same method as in the previous research, hospitalized mental patients were found to attribute job satisfaction to hygiene factors 36 percent of the time, as contrasted with an average of 19 percent of the time for employed people who are not mentally ill. Furthermore, the evidence indicates that the frequency of inversions increases with the severity of the disorder. A second study of inversion percentages by the same investigators compared outpatients with varying degrees of diagnosed mental illness who were currently employed. Those with relatively minimal disturbances had an inversion percentage of 15; the more severely disturbed, 27.

The results of these studies are certainly consistent with motivation-hygiene theory, and the research was indeed stimulated by the theory. The research design does not rule out other interpretations of the data, such as the possibility that the mentally ill might easily tolerate and express certain kinds of logical inconsistencies.

Using Alternative Methods

In a number of its aspects, motivation-hygiene theory has received support from research utilizing the methods of the original study. Almost from the beginning, however, questions have been raised as to whether these methods might not somehow operate in and of themselves to determine the results; thus, the findings could be a direct consequence of the method per se, not the underlying attitudinal and motivational facts, and therefore might not be replicable when other methods are used.

Many of the early findings obtained when alternative methods were used were indeed negative for the theory. However, there were problems with these methods as well. As research progressed, many of these problems were overcome. Yet the failure to support motivation-hygiene theory continued. For instance, it appears that satisfaction tends to be more characteristic than dissatisfaction and that both are equally likely to be occasioned by motivators and hygienes. Also, defensiveness appears to be a major factor contributing to the results originally obtained with the critical incidents. Kahn (1961) suggested at an early point that these results were contaminated by the fact that respondents supplied information on job attitudes, factors that occasioned them, *and* their behavioral consequences; the components of the sequence could easily be coordinated to make the person look good. It now appears from research that measures defensiveness, as well as from studies that introduce more psychological distance into the measurement process, that Kahn was right; common method variance does operate.

Current State of the Theory

Motivation-hygiene theory has probably created as much controversy as any theory we will consider. There are several reasons for this, many having little relationship to either the scientific or the managerial usefulness of the theory. This controversy does make objective evaluation more difficult. It has been almost impossible not to be assigned an adversary position if one makes any kind of statement regarding the theory. Yet rational objective evaluation is crucial for both scientific advance and management practice.

The theory has been steadily losing components in subsequent tests and reformulations. Its focus has shifted, and even in the original study, data were collected without the results being reported. Concepts such as long- and short-term sequences, second-level factors, and behavioral outcome effects have virtually disappeared from consideration. Ratings of the strength of feelings (importance) were included in the original data collection, but only frequency data were reported. By no means can all of this lost concepts phenomenon be attributed to the major theorist. Yet somehow a great deal of the original theory has disappeared; it is no longer tested or mentioned. One gets the impression that this is by mutual consent.

This same phenomenon applies to the testing of the theory. The following statement is indicative:

> In an ideal world we would not only have been able to ask people about the times when they felt exceptionally good or bad about their jobs, but also to go out and find people who felt exceptionally good or bad about their job and watch them over long periods . . . such observation, especially when carried out by more than one observer to obtain measures of reliability, would be of great value. (Herzberg, Mausner, and Snyderman 1959, 19)

Similarly, Kahn (1961) called for independent measures of environmental factors, job attitudes, and performance criteria. Yet neither Herzberg nor his advocates nor his critics have conducted research of the kind these statements imply. Thus, we have to rely on less than ideal data.

The incident technique as used in the original study must be considered most predisposed toward the theory. Yet this technique does yield certain findings inconsistent with that theory. The problem, at this level, appears to be not in the overall trend of the data but in the findings for specific factors. Abstractions such as content and context, motivators and hygienes, and the like simply do not hold when one gets closer to specifics. Opportunity for growth, which should be the essence of a self-actualizing motivator, is no more a source of satisfaction than dissatisfaction. Salary, interpersonal relations, status, and security are not just sources of dissatisfaction; they are often equally likely to be sources of satisfaction, and in certain groups some of them may well be predominant sources of satisfaction. Ray Hackman's (1969) reanalysis of the original study data clearly supports these conclusions. Achievement and the work itself also are repeatedly found to be sources of dissatisfaction as well as satisfaction. Herzberg's categorization of pay as a hygiene factor appears now to be an artifact of the time in which he wrote (Rousseau and Ho 2000).

There is little question that motivation-hygiene theory is most vulnerable on the grounds that its support derives almost entirely from the critical incident method and that this method is subject to influence by defense mechanisms. Short of observational studies and entirely independent measures of variables, the weight of the evidence now clearly favors the defense mechanism interpretation insofar as the hygiene-dissatisfaction part of the theory is concerned. On theoretical grounds, given the very limited projective element in the incident measures and the reduction of psychological distance thus occasioned, one would expect defensiveness to manifest itself, as Kahn (1961) noted; the data from a number of studies utilizing quite varied research designs support this conclusion.

The self-report data on effects are particularly suspect on such logical grounds. And indeed the limited research that has been focused specifically on this matter raises serious questions as to whether the motivators do produce positive behavioral outcomes and the hygienes negative outcomes. The results of the job enrichment research have been invoked in support of the theory's hypotheses regarding performance effects (Herzberg 1976). However, it is clear that these results could well be occasioned by other factors and that they apply only to certain of the motivator variables. In a number of areas, the theory has great difficulty in dealing with hygiene-dissatisfaction relationships.

It seems that motivation-hygiene theory lacks the support needed to confirm it, in spite of an extended period of testing and a great deal of research. Rather surprisingly, the type of study recognized from the beginning as required to provide a definitive test has not been conducted. A new thrust in the research might, therefore, yield different conclusions.

The problem now is that researchers have lost interest in the theory, apparently assuming it is unlikely to yield valid predictions. In recent years the number of related studies has dropped off sharply, and the level of scientific concern is now low. Thus, more elegantly designed tests may simply never be conducted. One could have hoped that the author of the theory would conduct these studies, but he became more concerned with applications in the job enrichment area. It is as if the process of losing components has come to its ultimate conclusion. Now the applications may well have lost the entire theory.

In this vein, a quote from a major review of the job satisfaction area may provide a sense of what has happened:

> [T]hough the theory continues to be advocated by Herzberg and recommended for further study by others . . . , these attempts at resurrecting the theory run against considerable scientific evidence. . . . [D]isconfirming evidence has effectively laid the Herzberg theory to rest. . . . Given the virtual absence of tests of the two-factory theory since 1971, we find [this] a suitable epitaph. (Judge and Church 2000, 168)

The one possible rejoinder to this epitaph occurs as a result of recent reviews of research on the job satisfaction–performance relationship. At the beginning of this chapter, I noted that Herzberg found some positive correlation here; he tended to endorse the view that satisfaction and performance were positively related more than did other academics of the time. Now, however, the evidence that emerges from research seems to be more consistent with Herzberg's position (Judge, Thoresen, Bono, and Patton 2001). There is some support for the notion that in combining evidence from different measures of job satisfaction, this review may have been in error to some degree (Scarpello and Hayton 2001). However, a subsequent review focused on a single job satisfaction instrument (Kinicki, McKee-Ryan, Schriesheim, and Carson 2002) continues to uphold the Herzberg position.

Current State of Practice

The tremendous appeal motivation-hygiene theory has had for practitioners cannot be doubted. It appears simple, although Herzberg (1976, 323) admits to only partially understanding it himself. Its religious, ethical, and moral overtones may well fill a strong managerial need. Furthermore, the idea that investments in salary, fringe benefits, working conditions, and the like yield benefits only up to a point (and thus can be restricted on rational grounds) is bound to appeal to the cost-conscious manager. These appeals are probably reinforced for some by the antiacademic, anti-intellectual thrust of much of Herzberg's writing.

Yet it is well to avoid uncritical acceptance. Salary is not just a dissatisfier; it clearly operates as a source of satisfaction in many cases, as do status, security, and interpersonal relationships. To believe otherwise may well lead one far astray. Whether or not these factors yield satisfactions or not depends very much on the individual; in some cases those who derive satisfactions from such factors may be mentally ill, but one should not apply such a blanket designation to all.

The suggestion that industrial relations departments be divided into motivator and hygiene units is interesting, but its validity rests on that of the underlying theory. That such an approach has not been widely adopted may be a result of misgivings on the latter score. It would appear that many human resource functions such as selection, training, compensation, and appraisal are so concerned with all aspects of motivation that an artificial separation could only be self-defeating.

But these matters are not of crucial significance. The major applied outgrowth of motivation-hygiene theory has been the rejuvenation, if not the creation, of job enrichment. This is an important accomplishment, and it justifies the emergence of the theory, no matter what its deficiencies. Job enrichment as a motivational technique can work—with some people, under certain circumstances, for some period of time—and Herzberg said so for a long time.

Yet when one attempts to tie job enrichment back into motivation-hygiene theory, one encounters all kinds of difficulties. For example, job enrichment has nothing to do with hygienes at all; it involves adding only motivators to the job and thus relates at best to half of the theory. Furthermore, the motivators emphasized are those called generators—the work itself, responsibility, opportunity for growth, and advancement; achievement and recognition are downplayed. However, achievement and recognition are by far the most strongly supported motivators when the incident method is used to test the theory.

The research indicates that even in the most appropriate context, 10 to 15 percent of those exposed to job enrichment do not respond, and that in other contexts the total effect may be nil. Yet the theory provides no basis for predicting these failures and gives short shrift to the troublesome idea of individual differences.

Finally, one does not need motivation-hygiene theory to understand the job enrichment results. In fact, other theories may well better explain what happens in job enrichment, and indeed the theory set forth in Chapter 6 does just that.

CONCLUSIONS

The reason Herzberg's theory is included in this book is that it is institutionalized; a sizable number of organizational behavior scholars view it as legitimate and take it for granted. Yet its importance rating is only 3.81, well below average among the theories of motivation and leadership rated. Overall the raters do not consider motivation-hygiene theory very important, but a significant number dispute this labeling. The estimated validity is only 2 stars, consistent with the large number of deficiencies noted in the theory and the conclusion reached by Judge and Church

(2000). The estimated usefulness would have been higher than the 3 stars given were there not a more powerful theory available to explain job enrichment, and in particular to explain the failure to react to that intervention. Probably a major consideration leading to the institutionalization result was a positive evaluation of Herzberg's job enrichment results by the raters and the feeling that the generally positive view of the theory in management circles deserved recognition.

In any event, the theory that displaced Herzberg's by providing a more complete explanation of job enrichment needs to be considered, and that is what I do in Chapter 6.

REFERENCES

Flanagan, John (1954). The Critical Incident Technique. *Psychological Bulletin*, 51, 327–58.

Ford, Robert N. (1969). *Motivation Through the Work Itself.* New York: American Management Association.

——— (1973). Job Enrichment Lessons from AT&T. *Harvard Business Review*, 51(1), 96–106.

Hackman, Ray C. (1969). *The Motivated Working Adult.* New York: American Management Association.

Herzberg, Frederick (1966). *Work and the Nature of Man.* Cleveland, OH: World.

——— ([1968] 2003). One More Time: How Do You Motivate Employees? *Harvard Business Review*, 81(1), 87–96.

——— (1976). *The Managerial Choice: To Be Efficient and To Be Human.* Homewood, IL: Dow-Jones-Irwin.

——— (1977). Orthodox Job Enrichment: A Common Sense Approach to People at Work. *Defense Management Journal*, April, 21–27.

——— (1993). Happiness and Unhappiness: A Brief Autobiography. In Arthur G. Bedeian (Ed.), *Management Laureates: A Collection of Autobiographical Essays*, Vol. 2. Greenwich, CT: JAI Press, 1–37.

Herzberg, Frederick, Mathapo, J., Wiener, Yoash, and Wiesen, L. (1974). Motivation-Hygiene Correlates of Mental Health: An Examination of Motivational Inversion in a Clinical Population. *Journal of Consulting and Clinical Psychology*, 42, 411–19.

Herzberg, Frederick, Mausner, Bernard, Peterson, R.O., and Capwell, Dora F. (1957). *Job Attitudes: Review of Research and Opinion.* Pittsburgh, PA: Psychological Service of Pittsburgh.

Herzberg, Frederick, Mausner, Bernard, and Snyderman, Barbara S. (1959). *The Motivation to Work.* New York: Wiley.

Herzberg, Frederick, and Zautra, Alex (1976). Orthodox Job Enrichment: Measuring True Quality in Job Satisfaction. *Personnel*, 53(5), 54–68.

Judge, Timothy A., and Church, Allan H. (2000). Job Satisfaction: Research and Practice. In Cary L. Cooper and Edwin A. Locke (Eds.), *Industrial and Organizational Psychology: Linking Theory with Practice.* Oxford, UK: Blackwell, 166–98.

Judge, Timothy A., Thoresen, Carl J., Bono, Joyce E., and Patton, Gregory K. (2001). The Job Satisfaction–Job Performance Relationship: A Qualitative and Quantitative Review. *Psychological Bulletin*, 127, 376–407.

Kahn, Robert L. (1961). Review of *The Motivation to Work. Contemporary Psychology*, 6, 9–10.

Kinicki, Angelo J., McKee-Ryan, Frances M., Schriesheim, Chester A., and Carson, Kenneth P. (2002). Assessing the Construct Validity of the Job Descriptive Index: A Review and Meta-Analysis. *Journal of Applied Psychology*, 87, 14–32.

Rousseau, Denise M., and Ho, Violet T. (2000). Psychological Contract Issues in Compensation. In Sara L. Rynes and Barry Gerhart (Eds.), *Compensation in Organizations: Current Research and Practice.* San Francisco, CA: Jossey-Bass, 273–310.

Scarpello, Vida, and Hayton, James C. (2001). Identifying the Sources of Nonequivalence in Measures of Job Satisfaction. In Chester A. Schriesheim and Linda L. Neider (Eds.), *Equivalence in Measurement.* Greenwich, CT: Information Age, 131–60.

Schwab, Donald P., DeVitt, H. William, and Cummings, Larry L. (1971). A Test of the Adequacy of the Two-Factor Theory as a Predictor of Self-Report Performance Effects. *Personnel Psychology*, 24, 293–303.

U.S. Department of Health, Education and Welfare. (1972). *Work in America.* Cambridge, MA: MIT Press.

Walker, Charles R. (1962). *Modern Technology and Civilization: An Introduction to Human Problems in the Machine Age.* New York: McGraw-Hill.

CHAPTER 6

JOB CHARACTERISTICS THEORY

RICHARD HACKMAN, EDWARD LAWLER, AND GREG OLDHAM

Background
Development of the Theory
    The Original Hackman-Lawler Theory
    The Later Hackman-Oldham Theory
    Action Principles
    Group Tasks
    The Rural–Urban Moderator
    Recent Theoretical Additions
Evaluation and Impact
    Measurement and Operationalization
    Research by the Theory's Authors
    The State of the Theory by the Mid-1980s
    Recent Findings
    Critique from the Social Information
       Processing Perspective
    The Idea of Optimal Job Scope
An Aside on Personality Theory and Research
    Dispositional Effects as Mirage
    Dispositional Effects as Reality
Conclusions

Importance rating	★ ★ ★ ★ ★
Estimated validity	★ ★ ★ ★
Estimated usefulness	★ ★ ★ ★ ★
Decade of origin	1970s

Job enrichment has had intense appeal for organizational behavior, and it has attracted both theorists and researchers in substantial numbers. The approach to which we now turn, job characteristics theory, emerged originally out of the collaboration of Edward Lawler and Richard Hackman. Hackman has remained a steady contributor over the years, and he is the one who adopted the name *job characteristics theory*. Lawler, however, became increasingly interested in other issues and disappeared from the theory as it developed. He was replaced by Greg Oldham.

Both sociotechnical systems theory and organization development theory (in certain of its variations) also deal with job enrichment; both make job enrichment an important aspect of their applications in practice. However, these theories are directly concerned with many factors other than the motivating effects of jobs on incumbents. In both practice and the range of their primary variables, they extend far beyond the immediate job or even the work group context in which the job is performed. Thus, they are best treated separately from theories of job enrichment per se as being primarily theories of organizational process and structure.

BACKGROUND

Job characteristics theory arose out of a context in the School of Industrial Administration at Yale, which was strongly disposed toward theory and research dealing with personality variables. From the late 1960s into the 1970s, a group of people within this school made major contributions in this area. Job characteristics theory arose out of this orientation.

Lawler brought to this effort a strong predilection for, and research background in, expectancy theory (see Chapter 7) coming from his doctoral studies in psychology at Berkeley (Lawler 1969). Hackman had done research and written on the ways in which different types of tasks and task characteristics influence behavioral outcomes (Hackman 1968, 1969a, 1969b). In his writing on job enrichment independent of Lawler, Hackman, although not rejecting expectancy theory formulations, has given them a less central role.

Hackman was born in 1940 and received a Ph.D. in social psychology from the University of Illinois in 1966. From Illinois he went directly to Yale, where Lawler had already been on the faculty since 1964. Oldham, who was born in 1947, also came to Yale in this period and received his Ph.D. from the School of Industrial Administration in 1974. He left Yale a year earlier, however, to join the business school at the University of Illinois. Lawler, born in 1938, left Yale in 1972 to move to the University of Michigan. Hackman remained at Yale until 1986, when he returned to a psychology department at Harvard, where he has remained since. Oldham has continued at the University of Illinois in business. Thus, this group was together at Yale only very briefly, in part due to the financial pressures the university was experiencing at that time and in part due to negative pressures on the organizational behavior group emanating from the economics component of the school (Lawler 1993).

DEVELOPMENT OF THE THEORY

Like many theories, job characteristics theory has undergone considerable expansion since its first statement. In general this expansion has been devoted to achieving increased precision of predictions and to extending the boundaries within which the theory can operate. To place the theory in context, it first appeared at a point between Herzberg's second and third books when job enrichment was in its heyday.

The Original Hackman-Lawler Theory

The theory as originally stated rested on five propositions drawn from both Maslow's need hierarchy theory and from expectancy theory. These serve as a basis for the more specific hypotheses to follow:

1. To the extent that individuals believe they can obtain an outcome they value by engaging in some particular behavior or class of behaviors, the likelihood that they will actually engage in that behavior is enhanced.
2. Outcomes are valued by individuals to the extent that they satisfy the physiological or psychological needs of the individual, or to the extent that they lead to other outcomes that satisfy such needs or are expected by the individual to do so.
3. Thus, to the extent conditions at work can be arranged so that employees can satisfy their own needs best by working effectively toward organizational goals, employees will in fact tend to work hard toward the achievement of these goals.

4. Most lower-level needs (e.g., physical well-being, security) can be (and often are) reasonably well satisfied for individuals in contemporary society on a continuing basis and, therefore, will not serve as motivational incentives except under unusual circumstances. This is not the case, however, for certain higher-order needs (e.g., needs for personal growth and development or feelings of worthwhile accomplishment).

5. Individuals who are capable of higher-order need satisfaction will in fact experience such satisfaction when they learn that they have, as a result of their own efforts, accomplished something that they personally believe is worthwhile or meaningful. Specifically, individuals who desire higher-order need satisfactions should be most likely to obtain them when they work effectively on meaningful jobs that provide feedback on the adequacy of their personal work activities (Hackman and Lawler 1971, 262).

In this early version of the theory, four characteristics were proposed as essential to jobs constructed to engage higher-order needs. Essentially what was hypothesized is that these four elements must be introduced into a job to enrich it and thus make it motivating for individuals with strong higher-order needs. These four characteristics or task attributes are taken from earlier work by Turner and Lawrence (1965). The first is *autonomy*, defined as an indication of the degree to which individuals feel personally responsible for their work, and thus that they own their work outcomes. The authors consider autonomy as a necessary but not sufficient condition for experiencing personal responsibility for work or attributing performance to one's own efforts.

Second, there must be a high degree of *task identity,* defined as including a distinct sense of a beginning and an ending, as well as high visibility of the intervening transformation process itself, the manifestation of the transformation process in the final product, and a transformation process of considerable magnitude. As a subcomponent of this characteristic, the opportunity to use skills and abilities that are personally valued (and use them effectively) is noted.

In addition to task identity, another factor contributing to the meaningfulness of work is sufficient *variety,* the third task attribute specified by the theory. It is, however, only truly challenging variety that is included, variety that taps a number of different skills of importance to the worker.

Finally, the job must provide *feedback* on the level of accomplishment. Such feedback may be built into the task itself or it may stem from external sources (e.g., supervisors and coworkers). In any case it is the perception of feedback, just as it is the perception of autonomy, task identity, and variety, that makes the difference.

The theory anticipates that satisfaction, performance, and attendance should be higher when the four core characteristics are present in a job. The theory specifies that all four must be present for these consequences to accrue. Furthermore, these relationships are moderated by the level of higher-order need strength in the individual. When higher-order need strength is pronounced, the four core job dimensions should yield particularly high satisfaction, performance, and attendance levels. The implication is that many jobs in many organizations lack the core dimensions and that they should be redesigned (enriched) to provide them. Essentially this is the version of the theory to which Lawler remained committed (Lawler 1973).

The Later Hackman-Oldham Theory

Job characteristics theory as such was explicated initially by Hackman and Oldham (1976), and then in what has become its complete form in a 1980 book (see also Oldham 1996). This complete model is set forth in Figure 6.1. The number of core job characteristics is now extended to five with the inclusion of *task significance* as a third contributor to the meaningfulness of work. This

Figure 6.1   **The Complete Job Characteristics Model**

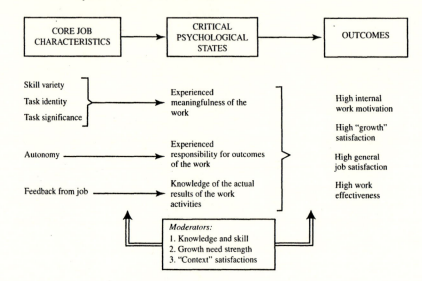

Source: Hackman and Oldham (1980, 90). Copyright © 1980 by Pearson Education, Inc. Reprinted with permission.

latter characteristic, which was in fact part of the early 1940s IBM formulations, is defined as involving the degree to which the job has a substantial impact on the lives or work of other people, either in the immediate organization or in the environment external to it.

The critical psychological states noted in Figure 6.1 are defined as follows:

1. Experienced meaningfulness of the work—the degree to which an individual experiences the job as one that is generally meaningful, valuable, and worthwhile.
2. Experienced responsibility for outcomes of the work—the degree to which an individual feels personally accountable for the results of the work done.
3. Knowledge of the actual results of the work activities—the degree to which an individual knows and understands, on a continuing basis, how effectively he or she is performing the job.

The model is explicitly employed to develop a formula to compute the motivating potential score (MPS) for a given job:

$$MPS = \frac{Skill\ variety + Task\ identity + Task\ significance}{3} \times Autonomy \times Feedback\ from\ job$$

It should be noted that this formula departs from the Hackman and Lawler (1971) view. There, all core characteristics had to be high; here, autonomy and feedback, as well as one or more of the three contributors to meaningfulness, must be high, but a zero on one of the latter three does not now have the potential for producing an overall zero MPS score.

The original higher-order need strength moderator has been respecified as growth need strength. The moderator process is also extended to include the knowledge and skill required to do the work well. Otherwise, as inadequate work causes negative consequences, there will be disillusionment with the enriched job and ultimately a tendency to avoid it. Finally, for enrichment to work, there must be a degree of overall satisfaction with the job context. If a person worries about job security, feels unfairly compensated, and encounters problems with co-workers and the boss, that person cannot give much attention to the challenge of job enrichment.

These moderator relationships have been summarized as follows:

> The worst possible circumstance for a job that is high in motivating potential would be when the job incumbent is only marginally competent to perform the work *and* has low needs for personal growth at work *and* is highly dissatisfied with one or more aspects of the work context. The job clearly would be too much for that individual, and negative personal and work outcomes would be predicted. It would be better, for the person as well as for the organization, for the individual to perform relatively more simple and routine work. On the other hand, if an individual is fully competent to carry out the work required by a complex, challenging task *and* has strong needs for personal growth *and* is well satisfied with the work context, then we would expect both high personal satisfaction and high work motivation and performance. (Hackman and Oldham 1980, 88)

At one point an additional moderator was espoused by both Lawler (1973) and Hackman (1977). This is the degree to which the organizational climate is of a mechanistic or organic type, following Burns and Stalker (1961). In general, an organic climate was considered favorable for job enrichment. This moderator has disappeared from the theory more recently. As in this instance, the matter of the precise nature of the moderator process has created many problems for the authors over the years. In characterizing the theory as involving person–environment fit, for instance, Kulik, Oldham, and Hackman (1987) say that job characteristics theory is a means of analyzing the fit between job characteristics (environment) and the abilities and needs (person) of jobholders. Although context satisfactions might be viewed as an aspect of the person, this moderator receives little attention when the theory is reformulated in fit terms.

Another area that has presented difficulties is that of outcomes. It follows from the theory that job enrichment that "takes" (is known to actually occur) should result in outcomes such as high internal work motivation, high growth satisfaction, and high general job satisfaction (not to include satisfaction with specific aspects of the job context such as security, pay, supervision, etc.). High work effectiveness is another matter, however; it includes the quality of output for certain, and it may include the quantity as well (but not always). It does not include low absenteeism and low turnover, although both have been considered likely outcomes of job enrichment in the past (but no longer are). The outcomes specified in Figure 6.1 represent the findings from research, much more than the theory's inherent logic; most are simply empirical generalizations. However, recently Oldham (2003) has specified that the core job characteristics operating through aroused emotions of a positive nature serve to generate creative ideas as an outcome.

Action Principles

A set of guidelines for enriching jobs, derived from the five core job characteristics of the theory, has been developed. These so-called action principles represent specific hypotheses regarding how enriched jobs may be achieved. The five such principles noted below should be prefaced with this statement: If enriched jobs and increased motivating potential are to be achieved, then:

Figure 6.2   **Links Between the Implementing Principles and the Core Job Characteristics**

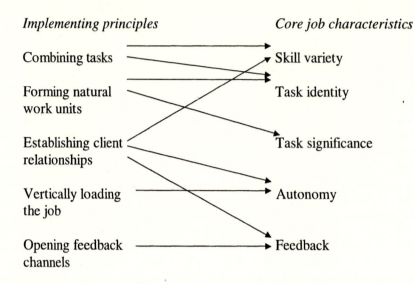

Implementing principles   *Core job characteristics*

Combining tasks   Skill variety

Forming natural
work units   Task identity

Establishing client   Task significance
relationships

Vertically loading   Autonomy
the job

Opening feedback   Feedback
channels

Source: Hackman and Oldham (1980, 135). Copyright © 1980 Pearson Education, Inc. Reprinted with permission.

1. Natural work units should be formed, in order to increase *task identity*, and *task significance.*
2. Tasks should be combined, in order to increase *skill variety* and *task identity.*
3. Client relationships with the ultimate user should be established, in order to increase *skill variety*, *autonomy*, and *feedback.*
4. The job should be vertically loaded with responsibilities and controls formerly reserved for management, in order to increase *autonomy.*
5. Feedback channels should be opened, especially channels flowing directly from the job itself, in order to increase *feedback.*

These guidelines have much in common with those set forth for orthodox job enrichment by Herzberg (Chapter 5). At the level of actual practice the two approaches have a good deal in common; at the level of theoretical origins, they are considerably more diverse.

What is different about the job characteristics approach is that it says job enrichment should not be attempted everywhere, with everyone. It is simply not appropriate in some work contexts and for some types of people. Thus, individual and organizational diagnosis should precede any attempt to enrich jobs.

The five action principles are diagrammed in Figure 6.2. There is no doubt that Hackman and Oldham have serious questions regarding the utility of these principles in many applications; their claims are quite conservative. They note that changes may be so small as to exert very little impact and that even when substantial changes are obtained, they may vanish quickly (Oldham and Hackman 1980). They attribute both of these sources of failure to negative properties built into certain organizations as social systems, properties that create resistances that simply cannot be overcome.

Group Tasks

Given Hackman's long-term interest in group processes, it is not surprising that job characteristics theory soon came to consider the design of group, as opposed to individual, tasks (Hackman 1978; Hackman and Morris 1975). The theorizing in this area is not as precise as that discussed to this point, but it does expand the boundaries of theoretical applications considerably.

Work group effectiveness is viewed as a consequence of the level of effort group members bring to the task, the amount of knowledge and skill relevant to task work the members have, and the appropriateness of the task performance strategies of the group. Thus group outcomes are considered to be a function of task factors. These so-called *interim criteria* are in turn hypothesized to result from group design factors such as the design of the group task, the composition of the group, and group norms about performance processes (Hackman and Oldham 1980; Hackman 1987).

In essence what is proposed is that the five core characteristics be applied at the work group rather than the individual level. This means that there must be two additional job characteristics: (1) task-required interdependence, in that the task itself requires members to work together and rely on each other, and (2) opportunities for social interaction, in that members are in social proximity, and conditions foster communication about the work. Group task performance, like individual task performance, assumes sufficient appropriate knowledge and skills to complete the task successfully.

The impacts of the group's effort, knowledge, and strategies are potentially constrained by the *technology*—a paced assembly line, for instance. They are also potentially constrained by imperfections in the *interpersonal processes* within the group, such as might be created by intense personal animosities, for instance. Thus, these two factors, technology and interpersonal processes, moderate the final impact of efforts, knowledge, and strategies emanating from the group on outcomes, including the overall quality of task performance.

Designing tasks on a group basis is recommended under the following conditions:

1. When the group can assume responsibility for a total product or service, but the nature of the work is such that individuals cannot. Thus, when the meaningful work potential of even the best possible individual job is low.
2. When the work is of such a nature that high interdependence among individual workers is essential.
3. When the workers involved have high social need strength, with the result that enrichment of individual jobs risks breaking up satisfying group relationships.
4. When the motivating potential of the job would be expected to be much higher if arranged as a group task rather than as a set of individual tasks.

In contrast, individual (as opposed to group) task design is recommended:

1. When the individuals have high needs for personal growth but weak needs for social relationships at work.
2. When the prospect of dysfunctional conflict within a group is high.
3. When there is no inherent interdependence in the work of the individuals.
4. When the expertise needed to design group tasks, an inherently difficult process, is lacking.

In many cases technological or interpersonal factors will make group task design infeasible. In any event, group task enrichment is a much more complex and less well understood process than individual job enrichment. It assumes the existence of self-managed, or autonomous, work groups whose work is enriched by taking over their own supervision (Hackman and Oldham 1980). There has, in fact, been little research dealing with this group task component of the theory. Overall, constituting groups to perform effectively on any task is described as a very difficult process (Hackman 2002).

The Rural–Urban Moderator

A full appreciation of job characteristics theory requires some understanding of a parallel theoretical thread that operated in the same time period, spawned its own research, and exerted a certain amount of influence as the Hackman-Oldham theory developed. Initially this approach involved a rural–urban moderator and was developed on an ad hoc basis to explain certain findings emerging from the Turner and Lawrence (1965) research. Since these findings were obtained only after an extensive search of the data, they may well have represented chance phenomena and thus had to be considered hypotheses for further testing.

In the primary analyses it was found that blue-collar workers in more enriched jobs were generally absent less than workers not experiencing job enrichment, but no clear relationships with job satisfaction were apparent. However, the secondary analyses revealed that the relationship with absenteeism characterized "town" workers only and that these same workers also exhibited the expected association between enriched jobs and satisfaction. For "city" workers, mostly of the Catholic religion, there was a negative relationship between enrichment and satisfaction.

Various possible explanations of these results are explored, although the Turner and Lawrence data do not permit reaching firm conclusions. Among the alternatives considered were the possibility that the town workers had stronger higher-order needs in accord with need hierarchy theory, that they had strong achievement needs (and the city workers stronger affiliation motivation) in accord with achievement motivation theory, and that the city workers were characterized by anomie (or normlessness) while the town workers were not, in accord with various sociological conceptions.

A number of studies bearing on this rural–urban factor subsequently emanated from the University of Illinois (Hulin 1971). Among the alternative Turner and Lawrence formulations regarding the moderator process, this research has come closest to emphasizing that of anomie (the third alternative). However, Hulin prefers to think in terms of alienation from middle-class norms. Urban workers are said to be so alienated; rural workers are not and, in fact, espouse these norms strongly. According to Hulin, the fact that writers and researchers in this area also come from middle-class backgrounds accounts for the historical tendency to generalize that what is true of rural workers applies to all workers and thus to prescribe job enrichment as a panacea for everyone.

The early evidence amassed by Hulin bearing on the rural–urban alienation hypothesis is generally favorable, as are the results of Hulin's own studies. However, there were, even in 1971, several conflicting findings. The data appear to support the idea of a moderator process, with job enrichment working for some people but not others. Hulin, like Turner and Lawrence before him, remains somewhat uncertain as to the exact nature of this process.

As research continued, the idea that some type of value or norm differential moderates the job characteristics–outcome relationship received increasing support. Subjects with strong intrinsic work values were more satisfied and showed more performance improvement when working on an enriched task than those with strong extrinsic work values. There was evidence for a similar kind of moderating effect using a measure of commitment to Protestant ethic values. In these studies, however, the relationships, although typically statistically significant, were not strong. One has the feeling that the moderators used are somehow hitting only the edges of the target and not the bull's eye.

Furthermore, as research continued, support for the type of gross rural–urban differential noted by Turner and Lawrence (1965) became more and more tenuous. A review by Pierce and Dunham (1976) questioned the value of the sociological explanations except as they served to point the way for more precise formulations such as those of job characteristics theory. Given the trend of the findings and known changes in population characteristics, it seems likely that although the rural–urban moderator concept may have possessed some validity at an earlier point in time, it no longer holds true. The increasing mobility of the population and changes in cultural values appear to have eliminated its explanatory power.

As these alternative formulations appeared, and then stumbled, job characteristics theory took on new strength, simply by virtue of its survival and its more compelling logic.

Recent Theoretical Additions

A burgeoning line of theoretical work building on job characteristics theory has come out of the United Kingdom and Australia recently. A major concern has been to add health outcomes to the existing list (Parker, Turner, and Griffin 2003). However, a more significant objective has been to expand the theory in numerous respects—antecedents, work characteristics, outcomes, mechanisms, and contingencies. The framework proposed links together a family of more specific concepts that might be applied, in one group or another, within particular domains or contexts. Thus the core job characteristics are expanded to include such factors as role conflict and opportunity for skill acquisition; outcomes now include not only creativity, but safety and outside-work activities (Parker, Wall, and Cordery 2001).

Because specific research on these propositions in the job enrichment context is lacking, I will not consider this line of theory development further here. However, these ideas appear to be the main alternative to job characteristics theory at the present time, thus replacing the rural–urban moderator formulations in that role.

EVALUATION AND IMPACT

One of the major strengths of job characteristics theory is that its variables are amenable to relatively easy operationalization. As a consequence, the measurement problem was tackled at an early date and considerable progress was made. Among other considerations this has meant that direct tests of the theory could be carried out; it has also facilitated research directed at determining the conditions under which job enrichment efforts actually "take" and thus serve to expand job scope.

Measurement and Operationalization

The first major effort at measurement of job enrichment was conducted by Turner and Lawrence (1965). The indexes thus created had a considerable impact on the Hackman and Lawler (1971) measures that in turn formed the basis for the current Job Diagnostic Survey (Hackman and Oldham 1980). Turner and Lawrence developed a number of scales to be used in rating jobs by those who have knowledge of them. Several of these scales were combined into a single overall measure called the Requisite Task Attribute Index. Included were items dealing with variety, autonomy, required interaction, optional interaction, knowledge and skill, and responsibility. An additional measure of task identity subsequently proved of considerable value, although it was not used in the composite index. All of these variables were intercorrelated at approximately the 0.50 level.

Hackman and Lawler (1971) drew items from the Turner and Lawrence measures to obtain their indexes of variety, autonomy, task identity, and feedback. They also developed measures of dealing with others (required interaction) and friendship opportunities (optional interaction) from the same source. The four job characteristics measures had reliabilities averaging 0.77, but the two social measures proved to be of unacceptable reliability. A measure of higher-order need strength based on an employee rating of how much the individual would like to have an opportunity for growth, variety, a feeling of worthwhile accomplishment, and the like had a reliability of 0.89.

The Job Diagnostic Survey (Hackman and Oldham 1980) represents a considerable refinement of these preliminary measures. It contains measures of job dimensions (the five core characteristics, plus the dealing-with-others factor, and an index of feedback from external agents, not the job itself), critical psychological states (the three specified by the theory), affective reactions to the job (general satisfaction, internal work motivation, and specific satisfactions with regard to security, pay, coworkers, supervision, and growth opportunity), and growth need strength (both the index of what the individual would like from a job and one in which choices are made between alternative jobs). With the exception of certain moderators and the variables introduced when the theory is extended to group tasks, the Job Diagnostic Survey provides a comprehensive coverage of the variables of the theory. The reported reliabilities for individual scales range from 0.56 to 0.88 with a median of 0.72. There is good evidence that the instrument does discriminate among different jobs.

Some question has been raised as to the psychometric soundness of the Job Diagnostic Survey on the grounds that factor analytic studies yield varied dimensionality under different circumstances and that the factor structure emerging may not match the five core theoretical variables. Yet overall measures, such as the motivating potential score, can be useful in spite of these findings. Furthermore, since the validity of the various measures has been established, the lack of a consistently supportive factor structure is not necessarily indicative of defects in either the measures or the theory (Kulik, Oldham, and Langner 1988).

Assessments of the psychometric properties of the Job Diagnostic Survey based on a considerable body of research certainly give it passing marks and probably much better (Taber and Taylor 1990). Furthermore, other measures of theoretical variables have been developed, freeing research from the need to rely on a single measure. Certainly these measures have facilitated the rapid emergence of research testing various aspects of job characteristics theory.

In addition, in various places the theorists have set forth a series of diagnostic steps to undertake and a list of guidelines for implementing job enrichment. These normative statements underline the practical value of the Job Diagnostic Survey:

Step 1. Check scores in the areas of motivation and satisfaction to see if problems exist in these areas. If they do, and job outcomes are deficient, then job enrichment may well be called for.

Step 2. Check the motivating potential scores of the jobs to see if they are low. If they are not, job enrichment is not likely to be the answer.

Step 3. Check scores for the five core dimensions to see what the basic strengths and weaknesses of the present job are. In this way it is possible to identify specific areas for change.

Step 4. Check to see what the growth need strength levels of job incumbents are. One can proceed with more confidence in enriching the jobs of high growth need employees because they are ready for the change.

Step 5. Check the scores for various aspects of job satisfaction and other information sources for roadblocks that might obstruct change or special opportunities that might facilitate it.

The prescriptive guidelines for implementation are as follows:

Guide 1. Diagnose the work system in terms of some theory of work redesign prior to introducing any change, to see what is possible and what kinds of changes are most likely to work.

Guide 2. Keep the focus of the change effort on the work itself, rather than the other aspects of the work context, so that real job enrichment does occur.

Guide 3. Prepare in advance for any possible problems and side effects, especially among employees whose jobs are not directly affected by the change; develop appropriate contingency plans.

Guide 4. Evaluate the project on a continuing basis to see if anticipated changes actually are occurring, and use as many and as objective measures as possible.

Guide 5. Confront difficult problems as early in the project as possible.

Guide 6. Design change processes in such a way as to fit the objectives of the job enrichment. Thus if autonomy in work is to be an objective, autonomy should be respected in designing the new jobs in the first place; in other words, be consistent with the theory guiding the change effort throughout.

Research by the Theory's Authors

In the early period, much of the research related to job characteristics theory came from the authors. This research tested the theory at points, but it also contributed inductive generalizations that changed the theory. The research contributions in this period included Hackman and Lawler (1971), Lawler, Hackman, and Kaufman (1973), Frank and Hackman (1975), Hackman and Oldham (1976), Oldham, Hackman, and Pearce (1976), and Oldham (1976). Certainly these studies contributed support for the theory more often than not, but they cannot be said to be definitive on that score. There were instances in which nothing seems to have happened, simply because the job enrichment interventions did not take. An important contribution of this research was that it was possible to show that common method variance of the kind that plagued the Herzberg studies could not be invoked to explain away the job characteristics theory findings. Also, there was some quite consistent support for certain of the moderator hypotheses (see Table 6.1). Note that although only 6 of the correlation differences are significant, 19 of 21 differences are in the predicated direction.

Since the early 1980s, research of this kind by the theory's authors has largely dried up, with the occasional exception of a study involving Oldham. Noteworthy, however, are a study by Oldham and Hackman (1981) that introduced certain macro, structural factors into the theory and another that dealt with the referents employees use in evaluating and reacting to the complexity of their jobs (Oldham, Nottenburg, Kassner, Ferris, Fedor, and Masters 1982). Although seemingly important, neither extension of the basic theory has elicited further investigation.

Table 6.1

Correlation Between Motivating Potential Score and Outcome Variables Moderated by Growth Need Strength and Context Satisfactions

Outcome variable	All Subjects	Growth need strength		Pay satisfaction		Security satisfaction	
		High	Low	High	Low	High	Low
Related performance	0.16	0.25	0.00	0.21	0.10	0.25	0.08
Salary	0.22	(0.44	0.03)	0.20	0.24	0.23	0.20
Intrinsic motivation	0.36	0.36	0.21	(0.47	0.25)	0.32	0.33

	Coworker satisfaction		Supervisory satisfaction		Combined satisfaction		Growth need strength and combined satisfaction	
	High	Low	High	Low	High	Low	High	Low
Related performance	(0.33	0.02)	0.29	0.08	0.26	0.13	(0.32	−0.19)
Salary	(0.3i	0.05)	0.29	0.17	0.30	0.13	(0.50	−0.06)
Intrinsic motivation	0.33	0.26	0.34	0.26	0.36	0.25	0.24	0.15

Source: Adapted from Oldham, Hackman, and Pearce (1976, 398–401).
Note: ( ) = Difference between correlations statistically significant.

The State of the Theory by the Mid-1980s

Shortly after the middle 1980s, sufficient research had accumulated, from the theory's authors and from others, so that a major stock-taking occurred. This most frequently took the form of a quantitative meta-analysis (Spector 1985; Loher, Noe, Moeller, and Fitzgerald 1985; Fried and Ferris 1987). Overall, these analyses provided considerable support for the theory. Because the research included varied somewhat, the results were not always the same. In particular the outcomes predicted tended to vary, yet all analyses indicate prediction of some outcomes. The core job characteristics and critical psychological states are important features of the model. Among the moderators, only growth need strength had been studied enough to warrant a conclusion, but evidence for its effect was obtained. A comparison of the results of laboratory and field studies indicates that, where sufficient research is available to reach a conclusion, the findings are favorable for the theory independent of which approach is utilized (Stone 1986).

In this body of research from the 1970s and early 1980s, it is evident that any given study may fail to support some core characteristic or the way a given psychological state operates or the impact upon a particular outcome. Such failures to obtain statistical significance may reflect sample fluctuations or the realities of specific situations. As long as certain positive results are obtained, assuming that some type of job enrichment was present (did take), there is no need for a study to support every tenet of the theory.

Recent Findings

In spite of the limited activity by its authors on the job characteristics theory front, research has continued up to the present. Several studies have now been conducted that consider job enrichment effects over extended periods of time. These multi-year investigations have shown positive effects both on performance (Griffin 1991) and on absenteeism (Rentsch and Steel 1998). Although job enrichment studies may appropriately utilize either experimental interventions or existing variations in the degree of enrichment across a range of jobs, longitudinal analyses of the impacts of interventions are more elegant. One such study showed an effect of enrichment in a field setting on actual observed performance (Luthans, Kemmerer, Paul, and Taylor 1987). A study that introduces long-standing personality characteristics into the mix of job characteristics and job satisfaction finds an important role for longitudinally measured positive self-evaluations (Judge, Bono, and Locke 2000).

The important role of the critical psychological states in the model (see Figure 6.1) has been supported, although they may not operate in exactly the same manner vis-à-vis core characteristics and outcomes as originally hypothesized (Renn and Vandenberg 1995). Calculating the motivating potential score using any multiplicative relationship between core characteristics does not appear to be optimal (e.g., see Hinton and Biderman 1995). Simply adding the five scores works best. In addition, empirical support exists for the directional hypothesis that job characteristics influence work-related psychological well-being including job satisfaction (deJonge, Dormann, Janssen, Dollard, Landeweerd, and Nijhuis 2001).

Not all of the more recent findings are positive for the theory, although the positive results far outweigh the negative. A study by Johns, Xie, and Fang (1992), for instance, is generally supportive of the theory, but it provides only minimal evidence of growth need moderator effects and no evidence for the operation of other moderators. Tiegs, Tetrick, and Fried (1992) also failed to support the various moderator hypotheses.

These studies, however, raise certain questions that future research needs to address. The original idea of job enrichment was to overcome the de-motivating effects of job fragmentation, brought about by scientific management, in low-level positions; job enrichment was to take from higher-level jobs, particularly those of managers, and add this component to make routine, highly specialized jobs more stimulating. Yet increasingly one finds managerial and professional jobs used to study job enrichment. Are we talking about the same thing? Also, it is now evident that some outcomes may be predicted in a given study, but not others (and that absenteeism and turnover are legitimate outcomes for the theory). Should not any test of the theory, then, consider all potential outcomes before reaching negative conclusions regarding the theory's tenability?

Critique from the Social Information Processing Perspective

As part of a more general attack on need-based views of motivation, which would appear to encompass the theories considered in this and the preceding two chapters, Salancik and Pfeffer (1977, 1978) proposed an alternative interpretation of the job characteristics theory findings. Their critique is entirely conceptual in that they do not back it up with any of their own research on job enrichment. Yet, at least for a period of time, this critique had substantial impact, and it may well still make a contribution to the development of an expanded theory.

The critique operates from the position that, as adaptive organisms, individuals adapt their attitudes, behavior, and beliefs to their social context and to the realities of their past and present behaviors and situations. This is the essence of the social information processing perspective.

Characteristics of a job, for instance, are not given, but constructed out of an individual's percep-tions. The behavior of a person can serve as information out of which that person constructs attitudes; other features of the social context can produce similar effects.

Out of this line of argument, Salancik and Pfeffer develop a number of reinterpretations of job characteristics research:

1. The distribution of a questionnaire can focus attention on particular aspects of a job, thus priming the respondent to pay attention to certain information and to a large degree predetermining the response. This is what has elsewhere been labeled pretest sensitization.
2. Individuals are aware of their own responses to questions and in an effort to be consis-tent in the pattern of their responses may generate many of the results found in job enrichment research. This is what elsewhere has been called common method variance; it is the problem discussed with regard to the Herzberg data in Chapter 5.
3. Cooptation of job dimensions and criteria constructed by the organization and its man-agers may cause employees to define their work situations in certain predetermined ways. This may include coopting the values and consequences of a job design program in which they have agreed to participate.

Processes of a social information type clearly can operate in job enrichment research contexts. This has been demonstrated on numerous occasions and with reference to the introduction of a variety of artifacts (e.g., see Glick, Jenkins, and Gupta 1986). The difficulty for the Salancik and Pfeffer hypotheses, however, is that there is also ample evidence that social information process-ing factors cannot be used to explain away the results of job characteristics theory research. The theory simply has not been refuted by this line of attack (Griffin and McMahon 1994), although it did undergo a few growing pains. Thus, at present, job characteristics theory remains a viable approach that, in spite of the loss of its authors to other endeavors, and some diminution of the rate of related research, continues to offer considerable promise.

The Idea of Optimal Job Scope

In many cases the desires of a company's work force for enriched work can be met simply through the traditional practices of upgrading and promotion, particularly if the company is growing and has a limited number of employees for whom enrichment is appropriate. However, there are many circumstances where work force composition and promotional opportunities make this an insuf-ficient solution. With the downsizing of U.S. corporations, promotions have become fewer, and job enrichment via this route is less available. On the other hand, downsizing may compel the combining of previously existing jobs to create a type of forced job enlargement and enrichment (Evangelista and Burke 2003). If this opportunity is grasped, and job enrichment occurs, research suggests that one consequence can be greater employee loyalty (Niehoff, Moorman, Blakely, and Fuller 2001). However, there is also the very real possibility that the scope of certain jobs might be pushed upward to a point where their positive potential is exhausted.

There has been discussion in the literature for a number of years regarding the idea that indi-viduals at a particular time have what amounts to an optimal task scope that is ideal for their particular capabilities and personality makeup (e.g., see Miner and Dachler 1973). In this view individual differences are pronounced and important. Jobs can be too enriched for a particular person, just as people can be promoted "over their head" and fail because of an inability to cope emotionally or intellectually. Similarly, jobs can be insufficiently enriched, and in such cases job characteristics theory or some modification of it becomes valuable as a guide. Studies indicate that supervisors may in fact modify job scope to adjust to the needs of specific employees in this regard (Klieman, Quinn, and Harris 2000).

AN ASIDE ON PERSONALITY THEORY AND RESEARCH

It is a fact of life that those who dabble in personality-based theories and research will eventually find themselves under attack. This is not a phenomenon that is limited to the scholarly world; it extends to the popular literature and to the legislative halls as well. It has a long history. Within organizational behavior the tendency has been to establish an antithesis between the individual and the external situation, with the attacks often coming from those who espouse a situational view of the causation of human experience and behavior. This often has meant scholars with a sociological perspective (e.g., see Salancik and Pfeffer 1977, 1978), but this has not necessarily been the case.

For those who have a strong commitment to the importance of individual differences, it would be appealing if this pattern of attacks could be written off as a product of some propensity to react against the study of human personality (probing into the private soul). It is not that easy. Certainly something of this kind is involved in some instances. But the attacks are not all bias; many have been appropriate, have contributed useful ideas, and have identified problems in research design and measurement. The problem is to separate the wheat from the chaff.

Dispositional Effects as Mirage

It is important first to distinguish generalized attacks from criticisms focused on specific theories. The Salancik and Pfeffer papers took job characteristics theory as their primary target, but the arguments were extended to include need theories in general. The first of these critiques, the 1977 paper, elicited a reasoned response from Alderfer (1977), who presented counterarguments to a number of the Salancik and Pfeffer statements regarding need theories. The latter were apparently aware of the Alderfer arguments at the time they wrote their 1978 paper, as they cite his critique. Yet the 1978 paper includes no reasoned response to Alderfer at all, only several brief comments that appear to be in the nature of asides.

This same tendency to shun direct debate occurs again in the context of a study by Stone and Gueutal (1984), which appeared to show that the priming and consistency artifacts proposed by Salancik and Pfeffer were not an important consideration in need satisfaction research. Salancik (1985) replied, attacking the research and defending his original position. Yet when Stone (1984) vigorously, and apparently effectively, took issue with Salancik and presented arguments for the validity of his research, Salancik declined to reply even when given an opportunity to do so by the journal's editor.

Five years later, Davis-Blake and Pfeffer (1989) published a paper, still without research data of its own, containing a major attack not on job characteristics theory per se, or need theories overall, but on what they call the dispositional approach. This controversy is discussed briefly in Chapter 2. Dispositions are defined as unobservable mental states (needs, values, attitudes, or personalities) that are relatively stable over time and that to some extent act as determinants of attitudes and behavior in organizations. The argument is that dispositions so defined are a mirage, and that the truly important determinants of organizational behavior are situational in nature. Thus, the arena is extended to include all theories of motivation rooted in personality theory. There is no mention in this paper of either Alderfer (1977) or Stone (1984). Subsequently, Pfeffer (1991) wrote a well-reasoned argument for the study of situational influences in organizations, now specified in terms of the constraints and opportunities for social interaction and comparison deriving from existing structural realities. Here the tone is much more balanced in nature; negative attacks on dispositions are downplayed, and in fact there is no mention of the 1989 paper at all.

Another publication in much the same vein as Davis-Blake and Pfeffer (1989) was authored by Nord and Fox (1996). Nord has a background in social psychology and sociology. The thesis of the paper is that the individual has disappeared from the field of organizational behavior, having been replaced by the contextual dimension consisting of attributes of the physical and social systems in which individuals exist. The authors attempt to document that theories and research dealing with individual personality and dispositions have lost status to a more situational concern, to the point where organizational behavior is no longer interested in individual differences.

In connection with this documentation, Nord and Fox (1996) give considerable attention to the papers variously authored by Salancik, Pfeffer, and Davis-Blake. Yet their attention to the major theories of the field, and the research that surrounds them, is minimal to nonexistent. These omissions inevitably raise questions regarding the objectivity of this attack.

Dispositional Effects as Reality

As might be expected, these attacks on the role and significance of personality factors have not gone unanswered. In addition to the Alderfer (1977) and Stone (1984) replies, there is a detailed presentation by George (1992) that considers much of the theory and research supporting an important role for personality in understanding, predicting, and influencing human experience and behavior in organizations.

Another line of argument to the same effect developed into a detailed critique of Davis-Blake and Pfeffer (see House, Shane, and Herold 1996). Taken together, these various replies seem to make a strong case for the retention of personality-based perspectives in organizational behavior, and for the position that theory and research of this kind remain vibrant within the field, even though under attack. The quote from George (1992) given in Chapter 2 of this volume provides a good summing-up of the current state of affairs. It calls for a live-and-let-live approach in the future and suggests that the pseudo-dichotomy between personality and situation be left to die a natural death. Both personality and situational constructs are important components of theory.

CONCLUSIONS

Judge and Church, in a brief review, say of job characteristics theory that "[t]hough the theory has its imperfections, the empirical data suggest that intrinsic job characteristics are the most consistent situational predictor of job satisfaction" (2000, 170). Judge says elsewhere that "[t]he Job Characteristics Model has amassed a great deal of support in the research literature" (Judge 2000, 82). He also notes that across a wide range of studies the correlation between core job characteristics and job satisfaction is consistently positive and averages 0.48. For individuals with high growth need strength this correlation is 0.68 on the average, and for those with low growth need strength it is 0.38, still significant. These findings are important for practice. Job satisfaction matters in that employees who are satisfied tend to perform better (see Chapter 5), withdraw less, and lead happier and healthier lives.

In this latter connection, however, a study of the health implications of job enrichment concludes that:

> [P]rograms designed to enrich the content of jobs in order to promote satisfaction and motivation among workers should be carefully considered when these interventions are conceived and adopted. It is important, from both an employee health and skill-level perspective, to make sure that the employees experiencing increased scope are ready and able to benefit. (Dwyer and Fox 2000, 1095)

Turning now to the evaluative ratings, the importance rating given by peers is 5.61, yet not institutionalized. The estimated validity is rated at 4 stars; this occurs because of certain shortcomings in the theory, with regard to the calculation of the motivating potential score (MPS), for instance, and the specification of outcomes as well as moderators. These limited defects do not undermine the usefulness of the theory, but as noted by Judge, defects do occur. Because this is a theory intended specifically for practice, and it is largely valid as well, the estimated usefulness value of 5 stars is not a particular surprise. During the 1970s, job characteristics theory displaced the motivation hygiene theory discussed in Chapter 5 as a guide for job enrichment; it remains the dominant position in that regard today.

REFERENCES

Alderfer, Clayton P. (1977). A Critique of Salancik and Pfeffer's Examination of Need Satisfaction Theories. *Administrative Science Quarterly*, 22, 658–69.

Burns, Tom, and Stalker, G.M. (1961). *The Management of Innovation.* New York: Oxford University Press.

Davis-Blake, Alison, and Pfeffer, Jeffrey (1989). Just a Mirage: The Search for Dispositional Effects in Organizational Research. *Academy of Management Review*, 14, 385–400.

deJonge, Jan, Dormann, Christian, Janssen, Peter P.M., Dollard, Maureen F., Landeweerd, Jan A., and Nijhuis, Frans J.N. (2001). Testing Reciprocal Relationships between Job Characteristics and Psychological Well-Being: A Cross-lagged Structural Equation Model. *Journal of Occupational and Organizational Psychology*, 74, 29–46.

Dwyer, Deborah J., and Fox, Marilyn L. (2000). The Moderating Role of Hostility in the Relationship between Enriched Jobs and Health. *Academy of Management Journal*, 43, 1086–96.

Evangelista, A.S., and Burke, Lisa A. (2003). Work Redesign and Performance Management in Times of Downsizing. *Business Horizons*, 46(2), 71–76.

Frank, Linda L., and Hackman, J. Richard (1975). A Failure of Job Enrichment: The Case of the Change That Wasn't. *Journal of Applied Behavioral Science*, 11, 413–36.

Fried, Yitzhak, and Ferris, Gerald R. (1987). The Validity of the Job Characteristics Model: A Review and Meta-Analysis. *Personnel Psychology*, 40, 287–322.

George, Jennifer M. (1992). The Role of Personality in Organizational Life: Issues and Evidence. *Journal of Management*, 18, 185–213.

Glick, William H., Jenkins, G. Douglas, and Gupta, Nina (1986). Method Versus Substance: How Strong Are Underlying Relationships between Job Characteristics and Attitudinal Outcomes? *Academy of Management Journal*, 29, 441–64.

Griffin, Ricky W. (1991). Effects of Work Redesign on Employee Perceptions, Attitudes, and Behaviors: A Long-Term Investigation. *Academy of Management Journal*, 34, 425–35.

Griffin, Ricky W., and McMahon, Gary C. (1994). Motivation through Job Design. In Jerald Greenberg (Ed.), *Organizational Behavior: The State of the Science.* Hillsdale, NJ: Lawrence Erlbaum, 23–43.

Hackman, J. Richard (1968). Effects of Task Characteristics on Group Products. *Journal of Experimental Social Psychology*, 4, 162–87.

——— (1969a). Toward Understanding the Role of Tasks in Behavioral Research. *Acta Psychologica*, 31, 97–128.

——— (1969b). Nature of the Task as a Determiner of Job Behavior. *Personnel Psychology*, 22, 435–44.

——— (1977). Work Design. In J. Richard Hackman and J. Lloyd Suttle (Eds.), *Improving Life at Work: Behavioral Science Approaches to Organizational Change.* Santa Monica, CA: Goodyear, 96–162.

——— (1978). The Design of Self-Managing Work Groups. In Bert T. King, Siegfried S. Streufert, and Fred E. Fiedler (Eds.), *Managerial Control and Organizational Democracy.* Washington, DC: Winston, 61–91.

——— (1987). The Design of Work Teams. In Jay W. Lorsch (Ed.), *Handbook of Organizational Behavior.* Englewood Cliffs, NJ: Prentice-Hall, 315–42.

——— (2002). *Leading Teams: Setting the Stage for Great Performances.* Boston, MA: Harvard Business School Press.

Hackman, J. Richard, and Lawler, Edward E. (1971). Employee Reactions to Job Characteristics. *Journal of Applied Psychology*, 55, 259–86.

Hackman, J. Richard, and Morris, Charles G. (1975). Group Tasks, Group Interaction Processes, and Group Performance Effectiveness: A Review and Proposed Integration. In Leonard Berkowitz (Ed.), *Advances in Experimental Psychology*, Vol. 8. New York: Academic Press.

Hackman, J. Richard, and Oldham, Greg R. (1976). Motivation through the Design of Work: Test of a Theory. *Organizational Behavior and Human Performance*, 16, 250–79.

——— (1980). *Work Redesign.* Reading, MA: Addison-Wesley.

Hinton, Michelle, and Biderman, Michael (1995). Empirically Derived Job Characteristics Measures and the Motivating Potential Score. *Journal of Business and Psychology*, 9, 355–64.

House, Robert J., Shane, Scott A., and Herold, David M. (1996). Rumors of the Death of Dispositional Research Are Vastly Exaggerated. *Academy of Management Review*, 21, 203–24.

Hulin, Charles L. (1971). Individual Differences and Job Enrichment—The Case against General Treatments. In John R. Maher (Ed.), *New Perspectives in Job Enrichment.* New York: Van Nostrand Reinhold, 159–91.

Johns, Gary, Xie, Jia Lin, and Fang, Yongqing (1992). Mediating and Moderating Effects in Job Design. *Journal of Management*, 18, 657–76.

Judge, Timothy A. (2000). Promote Job Satisfaction through Mental Challenge. In Edwin A. Locke (Ed.), *Handbook of Principles of Organizational Behavior.* Oxford, UK: Blackwell, 75–89.

Judge, Timothy A., Bono, Joyce E., and Locke, Edwin A. (2000). Personality and Job Satisfaction: The Mediating Role of Job Characteristics. *Journal of Applied Psychology*, 85, 237–49.

Judge, Timothy A., and Church, Allan H. (2000). Job Satisfaction: Research and Practice. In Cary L. Cooper and Edwin A. Locke (Eds.), *Industrial and Organizational Psychology: Linking Theory with Practice.* Oxford, UK: Blackwell, 166–98.

Klieman, Rhonda S., Quinn, Julie A., and Harris, Karen L. (2000). The Influence of Employee–Supervisor Interactions upon Job Breadth. *Journal of Managerial Psychology*, 15, 587–601.

Kulik, Carol T., Oldham, Greg R., and Hackman, J. Richard (1987). Work Design as an Approach to Person–Environment Fit. *Journal of Vocational Behavior*, 31, 278–96.

Kulik, Carol T., Oldham, Greg R., and Langner, Paul H. (1988). Measurement of Job Characteristics: Comparison of the Original and the Revised Job Diagnostic Survey. *Journal of Applied Psychology*, 73, 462–66.

Lawler, Edward E. (1969). Job Design and Employee Motivation. *Personnel Psychology*, 22, 426–35.

——— (1973). *Motivation in Work Organizations.* Monterey, CA: Brooks/Cole.

——— (1993). Understanding Work Motivation and Organizational Effectiveness: A Career-long Journey. In Arthur G. Bedeian (Ed.), *Management Laureates: A Collection of Autobiographical Essays*, Vol. 2. Greenwich, CT: JAI Press, 81–109.

Lawler, Edward E., Hackman, J. Richard, and Kaufman, Stanley (1973). Effects of Job Redesign: A Field Experiment. *Journal of Applied Social Psychology*, 3, 49–62.

Loher, Brian T., Noe, Raymond A., Moeller, Nancy L., and Fitzgerald, Michael P. (1985). A Meta-Analysis of the Relation of Job Characteristics to Job Satisfaction. *Journal of Applied Psychology*, 70, 280–89.

Luthans, Fred, Kemmerer, Barbara, Paul, Robert, and Taylor, Lew (1987). Impact of a Job Redesign Intervention on Salesperson's Observed Performance Behaviors. *Group and Organization Studies*, 12, 55–72.

Miner, John B., and Dachler, H. Peter (1973). Personnel Attitudes and Motivation. *Annual Review of Psychology*, 24, 379–402.

Niehoff, Brian P., Moorman, Robert H., Blakely, Gerald, and Fuller, Jack (2001). The Influence of Empowerment and Job Enrichment on Employee Loyalty in a Downsizing Environment. *Group and Organization Management*, 26, 93–113.

Nord, Walter R., and Fox, Suzy (1996). The Individual in Organizational Studies: The Great Disappearing Act? In Stuart R. Clegg, Cynthia Hardy, and Walter R. Nord (Eds.), *Handbook of Organization Studies*. London: Sage, 148–74.

Oldham, Greg R. (1976). Job Characteristics and Internal Motivation: The Moderating Effect of Interpersonal and Individual Variables. *Human Relations*, 29, 559–69.

——— (1996). Job Design. *International Review of Industrial and Organizational Psychology*, 11, 33–60.

——— (2003). Stimulating and Supporting Creativity in Organizations. In Susan E. Jackson, Michael A. Hitt, and Angelo S. DeNisi (Eds.), *Managing Knowledge for Sustained Competitive Advantage: Designing Strategies for Effective Human Resource Management*. San Francisco, CA: Jossey-Bass, 243–73.

Oldham, Greg R., and Hackman, J. Richard (1980). Work Design in the Organizational Context. *Research in Organizational Behavior*, 2, 247–78.

——— (1981). Relationships between Organizational Structure and Employee Reactions: Comparing Alternative Frameworks. *Administrative Science Quarterly*, 26, 66–83.

Oldham, Greg R., Hackman, J. Richard, and Pearce, Jone L. (1976). Conditions under Which Employees Respond Positively to Enriched Work. *Journal of Applied Psychology*, 61, 395–403.

Oldham, Greg R., Nottenburg, Gail, Kassner, Marcia W., Ferris, Gerald, Fedor, Donald, and Masters, Marick (1982). The Selection and Consequences of Job Comparisons. *Organizational Behavior and Human Performance*, 29, 84–111.

Parker, Sharon K., Turner, Nick, and Griffin, Mark A. (2003). Designing Healthy Work. In David A. Hofmann and Lois E. Tetrick (Eds.), *Health and Safety in Organizations: A Multilevel Perspective*. San Francisco, CA: Jossey-Bass, 91–130.

Parker, Sharon K., Wall, Toby D., and Cordery, John L. (2001). Future Work Design Research and Practice: Towards an Elaborated Model of Work Design. *Journal of Occupational and Organizational Psychology*, 74, 413–40.

Pfeffer, Jeffrey (1991). Organization Theory and Structural Perspectives on Management. *Journal of Management*, 17, 789–803.

Pierce, Jon L., and Dunham, Randall B. (1976). Task Design: A Literature Review. *Academy of Management Review*, 1, 83–97.

Renn, Robert W., and Vandenberg, Robert J. (1995). The Critical Psychological States: An Underrepresented Component in Job Characteristics Research. *Journal of Management*, 21, 279–303.

Rentsch, Joan R., and Steel, Robert P. (1998). Testing the Durability of Job Characteristics as Predictors of Absenteeism over a Six-Year Period. *Personnel Psychology*, 51, 165–90.

Salancik, Gerald R. (1984). On Priming, Consistency, and Order Effects in Job Attitude Assessment: With a Note on Current Research. *Journal of Management*, 10, 250–54.

Salancik, Gerald R., and Pfeffer, Jeffrey (1977). An Examination of Need-satisfaction Models of Job Attitudes. *Administrative Science Quarterly*, 22, 427–56.

——— (1978). A Social Information Processing Approach to Job Attitudes and Task Design. *Administrative Science Quarterly*, 23, 224–53.

Spector, Paul E. (1985). Higher-order Need Strength as a Moderator of the Job Scope–Employee Outcome Relationship: A Meta-Analysis. *Journal of Occupational Psychology*, 58, 119–27.

Stone, Eugene F. (1984). Misperceiving and/or Misrepresenting the Facts: A Reply to Salancik. *Journal of Management*, 10, 255–58.

——— (1986). Job Scope–Job Satisfaction and Job Scope–Job Performance Relationships. In Edwin A. Locke (Ed.), *Generalizing from Laboratory to Field Settings*. Lexington, MA: Lexington Books, 189–206.

Stone, Eugene F., and Gueutal, Hal G. (1984). On the Premature Death of Need-Satisfaction Models: An Investigation of Salancik and Pfeffer's Views on Priming and Consistency Artifacts. *Journal of Management*, 10, 237–49.

Taber, Tom D., and Taylor, Elisabeth (1990). A Review and Evaluation of the Psychometric Properties of the Job Diagnostic Survey. *Personnel Psychology*, 43, 467–500.

Tiegs, Robert B., Tetrick, Lois E., and Fried, Yitzhak (1992). Growth Need Strength and Context Satisfactions as Moderators of the Relations of the Job Characteristics Model. *Journal of Management*, 18, 575–93.

Turner, Arthur N., and Lawrence, Paul R. (1965). *Industrial Jobs and the Worker: An Investigation of Response to Task Attributes*. Boston, MA: Harvard Graduate School of Business Administration.

CHAPTER 7

EXPECTANCY THEORIES

VICTOR VROOM, AND LYMAN PORTER AND EDWARD LAWLER

Background
Variants on the Expectancy Theory Theme
    The Georgopoulos, Mahoney, and Jones
      (1957) Hypotheses
    Vroom's Theory of Work and Motivation
    The Porter-Lawler Model
    Lawler's Subsequent Statements
Evaluation and Impact
    The Georgopoulos, Mahoney, and Jones
      (1957) Research on Productivity
    Vroom's Research on Organizational Choice
    The Porter-Lawler Studies
    Philosophical and Logical Questions
    Applications
    The Research Evidence
    Intrinsic and Extrinsic Motivation
    Current Emphases
Conclusions

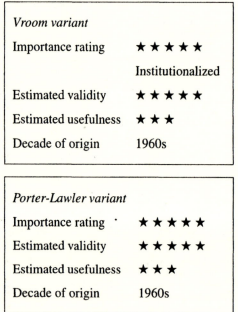

Vroom variant

Importance rating	★ ★ ★ ★ ★
	Institutionalized
Estimated validity	★ ★ ★ ★ ★
Estimated usefulness	★ ★ ★
Decade of origin	1960s

Porter-Lawler variant

Importance rating	★ ★ ★ ★ ★
Estimated validity	★ ★ ★ ★ ★
Estimated usefulness	★ ★ ★
Decade of origin	1960s

Just as personality theory contributed to the development of certain organizational behavior theories of motivation, learning theory has contributed in a similar manner. For learning to occur it must be energized in some manner, and that is where motivation comes in. Thus, learning theory and motivation have long been intertwined and they are in expectancy theory.

The theories considered in this chapter have multiple contributors. The formulations of Vroom, and Porter and Lawler, setting forth their concepts of expectancy theory appear to predominate, but there have been other contributors as well. Behind these major theorists, further back in the lineage of learning theory, lie certain early theorists whose influences were important even though they made no direct contribution to organizational behavior in this regard. These people are Edward Tolman, whose theories on learning sparked expectancy theory, and Kurt Lewin, who made certain contributions to learning theory.

Tolman was born in 1886 and obtained his doctorate in psychology from Harvard in 1915. After three years at Northwestern University, he moved to the University of California at

Berkeley where he remained throughout his career. There, Tolman Hall, which houses the psychology department, is named for him. Much of his research was with animals, and out of this he developed his sign-gestalt theory of learning. His major contributions insofar as providing underpinnings for expectancy theory were Tolman (1932) and (1959); Tolman died in the latter year.

Lewin's views on motivation were in many respects similar to Tolman's and their publication occurred in the same time period (Lewin 1938, 1951). As we saw in Chapter 3, Lewin was eclectic in his work, touching upon many areas within psychology. Although not a learning theorist per se, his topological and vector psychology was relevant for learning theory, and it is this aspect of his work that influenced expectancy theory.

During the 1960s, a number of variants on expectancy theory were proposed and a sizable body of research began to develop. Actually, the first such research within organizational behavior was conducted by Georgopoulos, Mahoney, and Jones (1957) as part of a research program of the Survey Research Center at the University of Michigan. However, no formal theory of motivation was formulated in connection with that research. That task remained for Vroom (1964), who was at Michigan at the time this early research was done. Several years later Porter and Lawler (1968), collaborating initially at the University of California at Berkeley not long after Tolman's death, expanded and extended these statements. These two versions of expectancy theory have stood the test of time and historical scrutiny, and they are generally recognized as representing the major contributions.

BACKGROUND

Victor Vroom grew up in Montreal and received both his undergraduate degree in psychology and his masters in industrial psychology from McGill University, the latter in 1955 at the age of twenty-three. From there he moved to the United States where he received a Ph.D. in industrial psychology from the University of Michigan. His doctoral dissertation (Vroom 1960) was a 1959 award winner in the Ford Foundation Doctoral Dissertation Series. In 1960 he joined the psychology faculty at the University of Pennsylvania, and it was during his three years there that he did much of the writing for *Work and Motivation* (Vroom 1964), presenting his version of expectancy theory. His entry into the business school world came with an appointment to the Graduate School of Industrial Administration at Carnegie just as the conflict between the economists and the organizational behaviorists was at its peak there. In 1972 Vroom moved to the Yale School of Industrial Administration at a time when, as it turned out, that school too was immersed in many of the same problems that had existed at Carnegie (Vroom 1993). Yet he has remained at Yale over the many years since.

Lyman Porter was born in 1930 and grew up in Indiana. His undergraduate work was in psychology at Northwestern. From there he went to Yale in experimental psychology, but in his final year he shifted informally to industrial psychology. Upon receiving his doctorate in 1956, he took a position in industrial psychology at Berkeley. Although he had several publications related to aspects of learning, consistent with his background in experimental psychology, Porter did not publish in the industrial area until after his arrival in California.

Lawler was born in 1938 and came to Berkeley in 1960 via an undergraduate major in psychology at Brown University. Shortly afterward the Porter-Lawler collaboration that led to the second version of expectancy theory began. This collaboration was one of many involving Porter and a graduate student who went on to achieve considerable success (see Nielson and Eisenbach 2001; Stephens and Sommer 2001). The Porter-Lawler effort was highly influenced by the publication of Vroom's 1964 book. Later in that same year, Lawler completed his degree and joined the School of Industrial Administration at Yale. He then went back to a psychology department at Michigan (see Chapter 6). His major appointment at Michigan, however, was in the Institute for Social Research. He subsequently moved to the business school at the University of Southern California, where he became involved in conducting large-scale research projects not unlike those in which he had been involved at Michigan (Lawler 1993), but now with primarily corporate funding. He has remained at USC over the subsequent years.

Porter left Berkeley in 1967 (after a visiting year working with Lawler at Yale) to join the University of California at Irvine's Graduate School of Administration. There he subsequently served as dean of the school for a number of years and remained there until his recent retirement (Porter 1993).

These are the primary authors of expectancy theory, but there were others who made theoretical and research contributions in the 1960s. Among these, Galbraith and Cummings (1967) and Graen (1969) deserve special mention. Graen's formulations in particular are noteworthy because they lead into his vertical dyad linkage theory of leadership; we will consider this theory in Chapter 14.

VARIANTS ON THE EXPECTANCY THEORY THEME

All versions of expectancy theory have been proposed by authors who conducted research on the subject as well. As has been the practice previously, consideration will be given to theoretical statements first and then to the authors' research.

The Georgopoulos, Mahoney, and Jones (1957) Hypotheses

This study aimed at identifying factors associated with high and low levels of productivity. The Survey Research Center program, of which the study was a part, was focused primarily on the role of supervisory practices but in the present instance dealt only with the motivation–productivity relationship. The theoretical hypotheses were formulated as derivations from prior work in the field of psychology and guided the conduct of the research. They were intended to deal only with the conscious, rational aspects of employee motivation.

The major variables considered are:

1. Individual needs as reflected in the goals sought. Examples of these goals would be making more money or getting along well in the work group.
2. Individual perceptions of the relative usefulness of productivity behavior (high or low) as a means of attaining desired goals (in theoretical terms, the instrumentality of various productivity levels or the extent to which they are seen as providing a path to a goal).
3. The amount of freedom from restraining factors the individual has in following the desired path. Examples of restraining factors might be supervisory and work group pressures or limitations of ability and knowledge.

The basic hypothesis is as follows:

If a worker sees high productivity as a path leading to the attainment of one or more of his personal goals, he will tend to be a high producer. Conversely, if he sees low productivity as a path to the achievement of his goals, he will tend to be a low producer. (Georgopoulos, Mahoney, and Jones 1957, 346)

This relationship between motivation and performance is moderated by the amount of freedom to act. When freedom is high, motivation will readily appear in productivity levels. When barriers operate, the hypothesized relationships will be disrupted and the motivation–performance correlation reduced. Path–goal perceptions are conceived as expectancies or estimated probabilities that there will be a given amount of payoff as a consequence of certain types of job behavior. Accordingly, high productivity may be viewed as likely to produce a desired goal (thus having a positive valence) or to impede goal attainment (thus having a negative valence).

Vroom's Theory of Work and Motivation

The initial preliminary statements of Vroom's expectancy theory appear in the published version of his doctoral dissertation (Vroom 1960). These statements have much in common with the views of his University of Michigan colleagues in the Georgopoulos, Mahoney, and Jones article. Subsequently, Vroom expanded his ideas into a more formally stated expectancy theory of work and motivation (Vroom 1964). Thus, all of the original thinking regarding applications of expectancy theory to employee motivation emanated from the University of Michigan.

Vroom's theory starts with the idea that people tend to prefer certain goals or outcomes over others. They thus anticipate experiencing feelings of satisfaction should such a preferred outcome be achieved. The term *valence* is applied to this feeling about specific outcomes. If there is positive valence, having the outcome is preferred to not having it. If negative valence exists, not having the outcome is preferred. Outcomes may acquire valence either in their own right or because they are expected to lead to other outcomes that are anticipated sources of satisfaction or dissatisfaction. Thus the accumulation of earnings per se might be viewed as inherently satisfying to one person, but to another it is important as a means to the end of buying a sports car.

As a basis for establishing the valence of a specific outcome, Vroom sets forth the following proposition:

> The valence of an outcome to a person is a monotonically increasing function of the algebraic sum of the products of the valences of all other outcomes and his conceptions of its instrumentality for the attainment of these other outcomes. (Vroom 1964, 17)

Thus, the size of the valence of an outcome is dependent on the extent to which it is viewed as a means to various other outcomes and the valence of the other outcomes. Because the proposition calls for the multiplication of the perceived instrumentality by the valence of each other outcome, any such outcome that has no valence for a person or that has no instrumental relationship to the outcome whose valence is being computed takes on a zero value, adding nothing to the final sum. An outcome with a large valence would tend to be one that is linked to many other outcomes, one that is considered highly instrumental to the attainment of a large number of these other outcomes, and one that is linked to other outcomes having large valences. Vroom specifically applies this first proposition to the topics of occupational choice (calculation of the valence of an occupation), job satisfaction (calculation of the valence of a job held), and job performance (calculation of the valence of effective performance in a job held). The latter was the single concern of Georgopoulos and his associates.

An additional and central variable in the theory is *expectancy*. People develop varying conceptions of the probability or degree of certainty that the choice of a particular alternative action will indeed lead to a desired outcome. In contrast to instrumentality, which is an outcome–outcome link, expectancy involves an action–outcome linkage. Expectancies combine with total valence to yield a person's aroused motivation or potential for a given course of action. Vroom uses the term *force* to describe this combination and offers the following proposition:

> The force on a person to perform an act is a monotonically increasing function of the algebraic sum of the products of all the valences of all outcomes and the strength of his expectancies that the act will be followed by the attainment of these outcomes. (Vroom 1964, 18)

The total force for an action is uninfluenced by outcomes that have no valence and also by outcomes that are viewed as totally unlikely to result from the actions, since again a multiplicative relationship between the two variables is posited. People are expected to choose among action alternatives in a rational manner to maximize force (in a positive direction). When an action is linked to many very positively valent outcomes by strong expectations that it will yield these outcomes, the force can be sizable. The theory makes specific statements with regard to the implications of the second proposition for occupational choice (calculation of the force on a person to enter an occupation), job satisfaction (calculation of the force on a person to remain in a job held), and job performance (calculation of the force on a person to exert a given amount of effort in the performance of a job held). Because the last of these statements has been the subject of considerable further theorizing and research, it is given in full:

> The force on a person to exert a given amount of effort in performance of his job is a monotonically increasing function of the algebraic sum of the products of the valences of different levels of performance and his expectancies that this amount of effort will be followed by their attainment. (Vroom 1964, 284)

The Porter-Lawler Model

Porter and Lawler (1968) present a model that draws heavily on Vroom but goes beyond the limited concept of motivational force to performance as a whole. Vroom (1964) himself moves in this direction by stating that ability and motivation relate to performance in a multiplicative manner:

Performance = f (Ability × Motivation)

The variables of the Porter-Lawler theory are as follows:

1. Value of reward—how attractive or desirable an outcome is (valence).
2. Effort–reward probability—a perception of whether differential rewards are based on differential effort. This breaks down into effort–performance (expectancy) and performance–reward (instrumentality) components.
3. Effort—the energy expended to perform a task (force).
4. Abilities and traits—the long-term characteristics of a person.

Figure 7.1 **The Original Porter-Lawler Model**

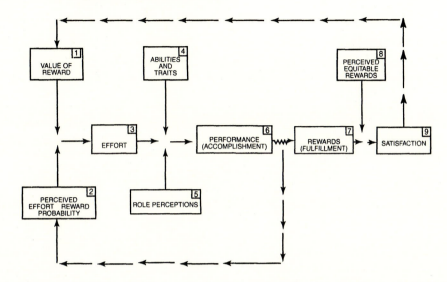

Source: Porter and Lawler (1968, 17). Copyright © 1968 McGraw-Hill. Reprinted with permission.

5. Role perceptions—the types of effort a person considers necessary to effective job performance.
6. Performance—a person's accomplishment on tasks that comprise the job.
7. Rewards—desirable states of affairs received from either one's own thinking or the actions of others (intrinsic and extrinsic outcomes).
8. Perceived equitable rewards—the quantity of rewards a person considers fair.
9. Satisfaction—the extent to which rewards received meet or exceed the perceived equitable level (dissatisfaction results from under-reward inequity only).

In line with prior formulations, the first two variables (value of reward and effort–reward probability), when multiplied together, are said to produce the third variable (effort). Following Vroom, abilities and traits also have a multiplicative relationship to effort in determining performance. A similar relation to effort (in establishing performance level) holds for role perceptions. Because of the intervention of such factors between effort and performance, these latter two cannot be expected to be perfectly related.

Porter and Lawler also posit certain feedback loops that make their theory more dynamic over time than Vroom's. First, to the extent that performance does result in reward, the perceived effort–reward probability is increased. Second, when satisfaction is experienced after receiving a reward, it tends to influence the future value (valence) of that reward. The nature of this effect varies with the particular reward (outcome).

Figure 7.1 sets forth these interrelationships as they were originally conceived. Since this initial statement, Porter has moved on to other endeavors and has made no significant contributions to the development of expectancy theory. However, one gets the impression that were he to return to this subject, he would focus his efforts on integrating macro variables into the model (Luthans 1990; Porter 1996).

Lawler's Subsequent Statements

We have seen (Chapter 6) that Lawler introduced expectancy thinking into the initial version of job characteristics theory. He also modified the theory in several respects, although the overall change is not marked. He elaborated certain factors that may influence effort–reward probabilities and thus continued the tendency to make the model dynamic over time, in contrast to Vroom's static approach (Lawler 1971, 1973). The most important change is an additional feedback loop from performance to effort–reward expectancy to the effect that within normal limits, heightened performance will yield greater self-esteem and thus subsequently higher expectancy. In addition, a much clearer distinction is made between intrinsic and extrinsic rewards.

Figure 7.2 depicts the central motivational chain of expectancy theory, devoid of feedback loops and ancillary forces. This is the basic model as set forth by Lawler (1981), and it is the model that he continues to endorse (Lawler 1994). Although more recently (Lawler 2000) he has written about expectancy theory, he has not changed this basic model. In this model, *effort-to-performance expectancy* refers to the expectation (assessed probability) that if effort is exerted, the result will be successful performance (though successful performance may fail to result because the job is too difficult, the evaluation process is deficient, or the individual lacks the needed skills). *Performance-to-outcome expectancy* refers to the expectation (assessed probability) that should effort be successfully exerted, something that is desired will result, such as a financial reward. An incentive system may be in effect that specifies a certain pay level for so many units produced. The person believes this and expects to be paid the designated amount upon completing the specified number of units. This is a performance-to-outcome expectancy. But it makes a difference only if the outcome, such as pay, has *valence*—that is, value or attractiveness. If the person has just inherited a fortune and does not care about the relatively small amount of pay involved, then additional pay as an outcome will not work as well in the motivational calculus as, say, an improvement in working conditions.

The distinction between first- and second-level outcomes goes back to Vroom (1964) who used the terms focal and "other"; Galbraith and Cummings (1967) were explicit in using the terminology of Figure 7.2 to apply to this distinction. The concepts involved are important. A person may value pay in its own right, as for instance an entrepreneur who views the business's earnings and his own as feedback on how well he has achieved through his own efforts—an index of performance. But pay may also be a means to second-level outcomes. A person may want the money in order to achieve an affluent life-style and impress others who are viewed as important. Then pay must be considered in terms of its *instrumentality* for gaining the second-level outcome of a more affluent life-style. If the pay involved is not enough to gain what is desired, then it lacks instrumentality—and motivational impact. *Intrinsic outcomes* are those that come from within a person—feelings of accomplishment, of doing important work, of freedom. *Extrinsic outcomes* are provided or mediated by external forces—a superior, the organization, other work-group members. This too is an important distinction.

The level of motivation in a given job situation is expressed in expectancy theory terms by a formula. Questionnaires are used to measure the components of this formula, and the scores obtained are inserted in it. The formula is as follows:

Motivation = Effort-to-performance expectancy x the sum of all operating factors
(performance-to-outcome expectancies x their valences).

Figure 7.2 **Lawler's Portrayal of the Basic Expectancy Theory Model**

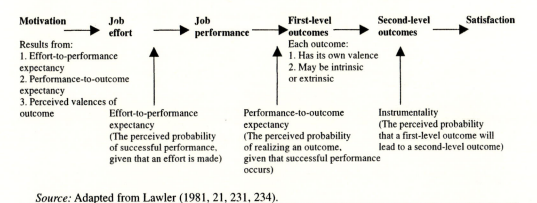

Source: Adapted from Lawler (1981, 21, 231, 234).

Inherent in this formula are the following ideas:

1. A person's motivation to perform is determined by the performance-to-outcome expectancy multiplied by the valence of the outcome. The valence of the first-level outcome subsumes the instrumentalities and valences of the related second-level outcomes. The relationship is multiplicative; no motivation exists when either performance-to-outcome expectancy or valence is 0.
2. Since a level of performance has multiple outcomes associated with it, the products of all performance-to-outcome expectancies x valence combinations are added together for all the outcomes seen as relevant to the specific performance.
3. The summed performance-to-outcome expectancies x valences is then multiplied by the effort-to-performance expectancy. Again, the multiplicative relationship indicates that if either effort-to-performance expectancy or the summed performance-to-outcome expectancies times their valences is 0, motivation is 0.
4. Summarizing, the strength of a person's motivation to perform effectively is influenced by:
    a) the person's belief that effort can be converted into performance, and
    b) the net attractiveness of the events that are perceived to stem from good performance. (Lawler 1981, 232–33)

EVALUATION AND IMPACT

Most versions of expectancy theory were introduced preliminary to a research study testing the theoretical formulation. These seminal studies are important not only because they bear directly on matters of theoretical validity, but also because they have tended to set the scene (particularly in experimental design and measurement) for almost all of the research that has followed.

The Georgopoulos, Mahoney, and Jones (1957) Research on Productivity

As noted, the hypotheses of this study were formulated as part of a study of motivation-performance relationships. The sample consisted of production workers for a household appliances

Table 7.1

Percentage of Those with Various Instrumental Perceptions Who Are High Performers

	Instrumental perceptions			
Goal involved	High productivity helps to achieve the goal	High productivity hinders achieving the goal	Low productivity hinders achieving the goal	Low productivity helps to achieve the goal
More money in the long run	(38	21)	(30	22)
Getting along well with the work group	32	23	33	28
Promotion to a higher base rate	26	23	(32	12)

Source: Adapted from Georgopoulos, Mahoney, and Jones (1957, 349).
Note: ( ) = Differences within parentheses are significant.

company. The measures used were all derived from a questionnaire and thus constitute entirely conscious self-reports of the variables.

The goals studied were the three ranked as most important by all the subjects out of a list of ten. These same rankings were used to determine whether each of the three was important to an individual subject. The three goals were:

1. making more money in the long run;
2. getting along well with the work group; and
3. promotion to a higher base rate of pay.

The instrumentality of either high or low productivity for attaining these goals was established through a rating scale extending from "helping," through a neutral value, to "hurting." For instance, high productivity might be rated as helping a great deal to make more money and low productivity as hurting a little in achieving the same goal.

Productivity was reported as a percentage of the standard usually achieved, on the basis of the standard hour incentive system in effect in the company. Freedom from restraining factors was established according to both reported freedom and amount of job experience.

As indicated in Table 7.1, the data tend to confirm the basic instrumentality hypothesis in that those who view performance levels as instrumentally related to goals in a positive sense are more likely to be high producers. However, the differences are not pronounced, and only three of the six differences attain accepted levels of statistical significance. Other data indicate that the presence of a stronger need to achieve a goal tends to be associated with an increase in relationship between instrumentality and productivity; freedom from restraining factors also tends to have the same facilitating effect. Again the differences are often small, and consistent statistical significance occurs only for the "making more money in the long run" goal. Overall, the results do support expectancy theory, but not strongly.

Vroom's Research on Organizational Choice

Although Vroom does not present research of his own on expectancy theory in his 1964 volume, he did publish an article two years later that bears on the subject (Vroom 1966). This research is related only to the first of his basic propositions, since it does not concern itself with expectancies and deals only with the occupational choice question, not with job satisfaction or job performance.

The subjects were business students about to obtain masters degrees from Carnegie-Mellon University. The objective was to predict the attractiveness of various potential employing organizations (and ultimately the choice itself) from a knowledge of what goals were important to the individual and how instrumental membership in each organization was perceived to be as a means of achieving each goal. Questionnaire ratings on a number of variables were obtained prior to choice. Job goals or outcomes such as a chance to benefit society, freedom from supervision, high salary, and the like were rated in terms of their importance to the person. The three organizations in which the subject was most interested were then evaluated to establish the degree to which the student thought each might provide an opportunity to satisfy each type of goal. Combining these two variables, an instrumentality–goal index was calculated for each organization and related both to the attractiveness rating given the organization and to the subsequent choice.

The results indicate clearly that organizations viewed as providing a means to achieving important goals were considered more attractive. Eliminating organizations that ultimately did not make an offer, 76 percent of the students subsequently chose the organization with the highest instrumentality–goal score. Although providing only a partial test of the theory, Vroom's research results are entirely consistent with it. Similar support of the theory was obtained in a follow-up study conducted several years after actual employment (Vroom and Deci 1971).

The Porter-Lawler Studies

The most extensive investigation by Porter and Lawler, and the one that is presented immediately after the major elaboration of their theory, was conducted among the managers of seven different organizations—three state government departments (employment, conservation, retail liquor) and four private firms (a large processor of canned goods, a large chemical firm, an aerospace company, and a utility). In all, some 563 managers below the officer level were included (Porter and Lawler 1968).

The study focuses primarily on pay as an outcome. Questionnaire measures of a number of theoretical variables were obtained from the managers, including measures of value of reward, effort–reward probability, effort, role perceptions, performance, rewards, perceived equitable rewards, and satisfaction. Ratings of effort and performance also were obtained from the managers' immediate supervisors.

Insofar as pay is concerned, the data do support the hypothesis that value of reward and perceived effort–reward probability combine to influence effort. Those who view pay as important and who consider pay to be tied to their efforts put more effort into their work, and this is true whether self or superior perceptions of effort are used. The same relationship also holds for performance but to a somewhat lesser degree. This, too, is what the theory predicts, because additional factors intervene between effort and performance in the model. Among these are role perceptions; data are presented indicating that certain kinds of role perceptions (when combined with the effort measures) do increase the precision with which performance level is predicted.

In another study of 154 managers in five organizations, the authors collected and analyzed data using several outcomes in addition to pay, such as promotion, friendship, and opportunity to use skills and abilities (Lawler and Porter 1967). There were seven outcomes in all. Basically the approach was the same as that used in the preceding research except that data for more outcomes were combined in the predictors. As indicated in Table 7.2, including value of reward (valence) in the

Table 7.2

Multiple Correlations for Seven Outcomes of Effort–Reward Probabilities Alone and in Combination with Value of Reward (Valence) as Predictors of Job Effort and Performance

Ratings	Effort–reward probability alone	Effort–reward probability multiplied by value of reward
By the manager's superior		
Job effort	0.22	0.27
Job performance	0.17	0.18
By the manager's peers		
Job effort	0.25	0.30*
Job performance	0.21	0.21
By the manager himself		
Job effort	0.32*	0.44*
Job performance	0.25	0.38*

Source: Adapted from Lawler and Porter (1967, 136).
*Correlations are significant.

prediction formula did make a difference; the correlations are consistently higher than without it. Job effort was consistently predicted more accurately than the further removed job performance. Yet the overall level of the coefficients is quite low for multiple correlation analyses. Considering that three of the four significant correlations involve self-ratings, where independence of the measures can be questioned, the overall results do not offer strong support for the theory.

In a later study Lawler (1968) used some of the same managers and obtained his measures twice, with a one-year interval between measurements. This time the multiple correlations were higher, and statistical significance was much more frequently attained. The data over time are consistent with the hypothesis that pre-existing perceived probabilities and valences of outcomes tend to exert a causal influence on subsequent performance.

A final early study related to the Porter-Lawler version of expectancy theory was conducted by Hackman and Porter (1968) with telephone company service representatives as subjects. A variety of performance criteria were predicted using effort–reward probability multiplied by value of reward as the predictor. In this instance, the rewards (or outcomes) considered were generated directly by the service representatives themselves in interviews; thus, they were the rewards the subjects perceived to be actually present. The correlations with performance criteria are significant in almost all instances. On the other hand, the median value is only 0.27.

Overall these various studies by Porter and Lawler do provide considerable support for the expectancy theories. Yet, given that this theoretical approach has identified an important way of looking at motivation at work, even Porter and Lawler appear puzzled by the low correlations found in many of the investigations.

Philosophical and Logical Questions

Certain questions were raised regarding the philosophical underpinnings and basic assumptions of expectancy theory at an early point (e.g., see Locke 1975), especially as they relate to decision theory. One such question is whether the concept of hedonism, as incorporated in the expected satisfaction definition of the valence variable, is tenable. The essence of the argument here is that much human behavior is in fact self-punitive. The difficulty of dealing with behavior of this kind, and with reactions to guilt, casts doubt on the strictly hedonistic formulations. Furthermore, there is reason to believe that many people do not attempt to maximize, even when they do strive for satisfaction, but rather accept some lesser level of effort. Issues like this have not really been faced by expectancy theorists. At the very least they suggest that there are behaviors, and perhaps people, to whom the theory may apply in a very limited way.

Questions may also be raised as to whether people can engage in the cognitive processes implied by the theory, such as weighting all possible outcomes as they contribute to other outcomes, and then others, to the point of infinite regress, or multiplying valences and instrumentalities in a manner that, according to the theory, assumes very complex internalized measurement processes. The theory assumes common tendencies to project one's thoughts into a future time span and to search for alternatives for all human beings, since it is silent on individual differences in these respects. Yet it is apparent that people do differ in both time perspective and the proclivity for search. Finally, individuals do act on occasion out of unconscious motives and in ways that cannot be based on the calculative, highly rational processes that expectancy theory specifies; impulsive behavior, the repetition compulsions of neurotic individuals, and the like are examples.

These questions do not void expectancy theories as useful methods of predicting and understanding work behavior. They do suggest that the theories may deal with only part of organizational behavior and that their propositions may well represent only approximations of human motivational processes (perhaps overly complex in certain respects and overly simplistic in others). Under these circumstances the theories could still work quite well in the theoretical domains to which they apply.

Another line of questioning has to do with the extent to which expectancy theories must meet the various rationality assumptions that have been developed for formal decision theory. Vroom (1964) notes certain similarities between his formulations and those of subjective, expected utility theory. Others have drawn out these parallels more fully, even to the point of considering expectancy theories of motivation as special cases within the broader context of decision theory.

Attempts to relate expectancy theories to rationality assumptions or postulates taken from decision theory have not always come to identical conclusions. However, if such assumptions are to be considered part of the theory or implicit in its basic propositions, then the range of empirical support required to validate these propositions is greatly expanded. Furthermore, those who have compared expectancy theories to criteria derived from decision theory clearly imply that expectancy theories are wanting in these respects.

On the other hand, strong arguments have been advanced that expectancy theories need not meet all of the tests derived from decision theory. For instance, it has been contended that the theory presupposes a lack of correlation (independence) between expectancy and valence and that such independence probably does not exist in reality. Regardless of the empirical facts, there is reason to conclude that independence is not necessary for the propositions of expectancy theory to prove valid.

Another assumption, transitivity, is generally conceded to be necessary for expectancy theories. Accordingly, if an outcome A is preferred to another outcome B, and B in turn is preferred to C, then A must be preferred to C. If this is not the case and C has greater valence than A, then intransitivity exists. To the extent that people actually think in intransitive terms, expectancy theory, with its strong reliance on rationality, is in trouble. Luckily for the theory, the evidence currently available suggests that intransitivity is a relatively uncommon phenomenon.

It seems appropriate to conclude that a number of rationality assumptions derived from decision theory do not represent necessary conditions for expectancy theories. If the theory works in the prediction of performance, effort expenditure, job satisfaction, occupational choice, and the like, then it is not necessary to give major attention to these considerations. To the extent that it fails to predict such factors, they become likely causes that require exploration. In this connection Locke, an early critic of expectancy theory, now holds that it is valid, especially in highly structured situations (Bartol and Locke 2000).

Applications

Most of the literature on expectancy theory gives only fleeting attention, if any, to practical applications. The major exception to this generally nonpractice-oriented approach is a series of statements about the administration of compensation and other reward systems initiated in the Porter and Lawler (1968) volume and continuing through a number of subsequent publications by Lawler.

Four recommendations for practice grew out of the original Porter and Lawler research, although the fourth is not a direct derivative of the theory per se:

1. Companies should collect systematic information as to what employees want from their jobs (value of rewards or valence) and their perceived probabilities of obtaining rewards relative to the effort they put out. This information could then be used in designing reward systems.
2. Companies should make sure that employees understand the role prescriptions for their jobs so that efforts are not misdirected and thus wasted.
3. Companies should take steps to tie rewards to performance in the minds of employees (to establish perceived contingencies). This argues against giving pay increases across the board, cost-of-living raises, and also against incentive raises that are kept secret, thus preventing any relative evaluation of their value. It argues for:
   a) tailoring rewards to what the individual wants;
   b) giving more extrinsic rewards and more opportunities to obtain intrinsic rewards to superior performers than to inferior performers; and
   c) permitting employees to see and believe that high performance results in high reward; thus, for example, secrecy about pay should be removed so that contingencies can be observed, and the best and most credible source of information should be used to evaluate performance, even to the point of obtaining peer- and self-ratings.
4. Continuously measure and monitor employee attitudes.

In his subsequent writings, Lawler has placed particular emphasis on procedures that create performance–outcome contingencies and on individualized approaches that, among other things, adjust rewards to valent outcomes. His most unique contributions in these respects have been the emphasis on eliminating pay secrecy and a call for the use of "cafeteria" compensation systems, which permit employees to structure their own compensation (pay and benefits) packages to place the greatest relative emphasis on what they desire the most. In recent years Lawler has expanded his idea of individualizing the organization to include other approaches, although these are not necessarily derived from expectancy theory (Lawler and Finegold 2000). The term *line of sight* has been applied to the expectancy theory view that, in order to be motivators, rewards must be seen as important and obtainable by the individual involved (Lawler 1994). I should note, however, that line of sight is not always defined in this manner in the literature (see Boswell 2000).

A point worth noting with regard to Lawler's concept of line of sight is the following:

Expectancy beliefs may be more difficult to achieve at team and organizational levels because of line-of-sight difficulties. Employees may question whether their efforts will in fact lead to the desired level of group or organizational performance because there are likely to be many factors other than their own efforts that are influencing performance as well. (Bartol and Durham 2000, 6)

Thus team-based rewards and organizational rewards such as stock options face motivational difficulties that extend well beyond pay for performance procedures at the individual level.

In certain respects, the highly rationalized organization that expectancy theory demands seems comparable to the ideal bureaucracy of organizational theory. Yet some people have allied expectancy theory with participative management. Either form can probably be compatible with expectancy theory, provided decisions are made in some manner, and those decisions emphasize performance–reward contingencies. It would appear that such decisions might be somewhat easier to obtain in the hierarchic context of a bureaucracy, but that if such contingencies do emerge from participative processes, the latter will facilitate the kind of information exchange that causes the contingencies to be widely recognized.

In any event, the theory argues for selecting employees who are likely to have high scores on the various expectancy theory measures and who thus will bring a maximal amount of effort or force to the work context. Such individuals should be most responsive to a situation within the domain of expectancy theory and least susceptible to any detrimental side effects.

A rather sizable body of research indicates that the people who bring the most motivational energy to their work (as that energy is determined from expectancy theory) are those generally referred to as *internals*. These people believe that events in their lives are largely subject to their own influence; in contrast, *externals* see themselves as largely at the mercy of fate, luck, and more powerful individuals. Given the rational, hedonistic emphasis of expectancy theory, it is not surprising that internals tend to emerge as strongly motivated in these terms. Furthermore, the idea of selecting people to fit an expectancy theory context has received research support as well (Miller and Grush 1988).

The Research Evidence

Research tests have yielded sufficient theoretical support so that it seems safe to conclude that expectancy theories are on the right track. They certainly do not explain all motivated behavior in all types of work organizations, but they do explain enough to be worth pursuing. The early research was far from conclusive in that the theory often emerged as invalid in a specific context and even when validity was established, the correlations tended to be low. Now enough is known so that studies can be designed that will yield not only significant results, but also correlations well above those that plagued the early research.

As Graen (1969) has indicated, expectancy theory works best when contingencies can be established in a concrete manner between effective job performance and attaining favorable role outcomes. In other words, people have to see that putting out effort to do what the job requires will give them what they want. When rewards are not so structured or existing performance–reward relationships are so ambiguous that they are not readily perceived, the theory appears to predict very little.

In addition to observing this boundary condition for the theory, a test also must utilize measures that are not only reliable but valid operationalizations of the theoretical variables. In the past these measurement requirements have not always been met, but it has become apparent that they can be met if sufficient attention is given to the selection or initial development of the measures (Ilgen, Nebeker, and Pritchard 1981).

Most of the early studies utilized lists of outcomes developed by those conducting the research. However, it has become evident that expectancy theory predictions derived from a limited set of outcomes specified by each subject outperform predictions made from a longer, entirely researcher established, standard list. These and other findings in the studies argue for the use of an individualized approach to outcome generation. However, one may wish to focus research attention on specific types of motivation, as Porter and Lawler (1968) did with pay as an outcome. In such cases, researcher designation of outcomes is entirely appropriate.

Vroom (1964, 19) states that "people choose from among alternative acts, the one corresponding to the strongest positive (or weakest negative) force." The implication is that force values for various alternative acts should be computed for each subject; the highest would then be predicted to result in behavior. Yet the approach used in all of the early research was to develop only one force prediction per subject and then run correlations with criterion measures across a number of subjects. In contrast to this typical across-subjects approach, the within-subjects procedure yields separate correlations between predicted force and criterion values for each subject. These correlations may then be averaged to get a composite measure. Using this latter approach does in fact yield a higher level of theoretical confirmation.

It is apparent also that correlations can often be raised by including measures of variables that are extraneous to the basic expectancy theory formulations—for instance, the family and peer pressure indexes utilized in certain of the occupational choice studies. To do this certainly contributes to our overall understanding of human motivation; however, extending the research in this manner contributes little to our understanding of expectancy theory and of how and why its component variables work. There is a real risk that the expectancy concepts may become lost in a mélange of other constructs so that true understanding of the basic theory is impaired.

Without question, research on expectancy theory has come a long way, and predictions have improved accordingly, as problems in the early studies have been unearthed, dealt with, and solved. Yet, there are remaining issues. One involves the use of multiplicative compositives such as expectancy x valence in correlational analyses. There are inherent problems in doing this, and these problems are present in expectancy theory research (Evans 1991). However, many people do not employ multiplicative information processing, as the expectancy model implies, but rather utilize additive processes. This situation is similar to that noted in Chapter 6 for job characteristics theory. Thus, ideally multiplicative and additive information processors would be identified in advance and appropriate procedures applied in analyzing data from each. Individual differences continue to force their way into a theory that originally gave little attention to them.

A recent meta-analytic review of the research (Van Eerde and Thierry 1996) confirms certain earlier conclusions and identifies some new ones. Within subjects, as opposed to between subjects, analyses continue to produce higher validity coefficients. When the total expectancy theory model (see Figure 7.1) is utilized in the analysis, results are consistently supportive of the theory, but similar results are often reported for components of the theory. Thus expectancy x valence and valence x instrumentality seemed to work just as well as the full valence-instrumentality-expectancy model (although a number of the studies used a multiplicative approach incorrectly). The highest correlations were obtained with preference (the attractiveness of preference ratings of jobs, occupations, or organizations), intention (either to apply for a job or to turn over in a job), and effort (including measures of effort expenditure on a task such as time spent, effort ratings by supervisors, self-reports of effort spent on a task or applying for a job, and intended effort). Performance (including measures of productivity, gain in performance, task performance, grades, performance ratings by supervisors, and self-ratings) and choice (the actual voluntary turnover, job choice, and organizational choice) produced lower validities.

The results suggest that common method variance may have inflated some of the findings. However, it is also true that roughly a third of the studies were conducted in the 1960s and early 1970s when methodological problems were frequent, thus depressing correlations overall. Other evidence indicates that expectancy theory is particularly suited to occupation/organizational choice situations (Wanous, Keon, and Latack 1983). In this context validity coefficients in the 0.70s are not uncommon.

Intrinsic and Extrinsic Motivation

Expectancy theory formulations have in general distinguished between extrinsic and intrinsic motivation, but they have viewed the two as additive, so that the distinction is of no special importance. There is, however, a line of reasoning and research that challenges this additive assumption. Statements of this position (see Deci and Ryan 1985) pose a clear threat to expectancy theory in this regard.

Intrinsic motivation is defined as based on the desire for competence and self-determination. Among those who challenge expectancy theory, it is measured almost exclusively by observing the amount of time spent on a task during a period when the subjects have a free choice as to what to do with their time. Intrinsic motivation is said to be facilitated by enhancing the subject's sense of self-determination, for instance by providing a choice of what to work on or what order to work on tasks, and by enhancing a sense of competence through the use of positive feedback. Extrinsic rewards, among which money is the most often cited, have a controlling aspect and an informational aspect. If the controlling aspect is salient, intrinsic motivation is decreased. If the informational or feedback aspect is salient and positive, intrinsic motivation is increased.

Many organizational behavior scholars have found it difficult to accept the view that extrinsic motivation often operates to reduce intrinsic motivation. The results of research testing expectancy theory do not seem to be consistent with such an interpretation. Furthermore, incentive pay systems repeatedly have been found to increase performance levels. It is hard to believe they should be abandoned because they control intrinsic motivation and reduce it. It seems unlikely that the phenomenon described by Deci and Ryan (1985) has practical relevance. Many jobs, such as those of a managerial, professional, and entrepreneurial nature, frequently appear to engage such high levels of intrinsic motivation that performance is impervious to any possible negative extrinsic impact. Also, some kind of explicit or implicit inducement–contribution contract involving extrinsic inducements including pay is the prevailing norm in the world of work, and under such circumstances the phenomenon described by Deci on the current evidence does not appear to operate.

As a result of these and other considerations reviewers have generally come to reject the idea of a subtractive relationship as inherent in what has been called cognitive evaluation theory (Bartol and Locke 2000), or they have concluded that more study is required before accepting the theory is warranted. There is some evidence that intrinsic motivation should be conceptualized as episodic and temporally bounded, and this too has led to reviewer concerns. Particularly significant are the results of a meta-analysis that used the nature of the research design employed as a contingency variable. These results are described as follows:

> Multiple measures are necessary to determine the convergent validity of a construct to avoid methodological weaknesses inherent in a particular measure. Free-time and performance measures, two different operationalizations of intrinsic motivation, do not converge, i.e. react similarly under similar experimental treatments. The lack of convergence suggests that different constructs may be being measured and that the two measures should not be used interchangeably as operationalizations of intrinsic motivation. Subsequent research should specify the domain of observables for the construct of intrinsic motivation more clearly. (Wiersma 1992, 112)

This lack of construct validity is inherent in the fact that 88 percent of the free time study results operate in a manner consistent with predictions from cognitive evaluation theory, but only 15 percent of the results produced from studies using performance results support that theory. Combining the two sets of findings, which to be entirely proper one should not do, gives a value of –0.136, in the direction posited by cognitive evaluation theory, but far from significantly different from 0. Clearly there is something going on here that needs explaining, but Deci's theory does not provide a full explanation.

More recent analyses unfortunately have not resolved this puzzle. At last count there were something like eight meta-analyses of the literature bearing in one way or another on the issue at hand. Furthermore, unlike what has been the case in most other literatures, the results obtained do not always coincide; in fact, a substantial controversy now exists as to what the literature really says, and whose approach to aggregating it is most valid (or least flawed). It is quite possible now to find a meta-analysis that supports almost any position one wishes to espouse.

Out of all this have come several conclusions that, although they do not solve the problems, may point the way (see Deci, Koestner, and Ryan 1999):

- An undermining effect can be demonstrated with considerable consistency and the free-time condition is particularly likely to elicit this effect.
- There are conditions where rewards such as money do not necessarily undermine intrinsic motivation; undermining is less pronounced in the case of performance-contingent rewards than otherwise.
- Meta-analysis may well not be the method of choice for combining literatures that are procedurally diverse, theoretically derived, and empirically complex—like the cognitive evaluation literature.
- When one focuses only on more applied studies, the results indicate a positive or null (not negative) relationship between reward and intrinsic motivation.
- The undermining effect is particularly pronounced among children.

The hope is that these conclusions might point to findings that undermining does not operate with adults, in employing organizations, where performance-contingent rewards are used. Perhaps there are more areas of exclusion as well. However, the research breakthroughs to provide definitive answers in this regard are still off in the future.

We do have data of the kind placed in the boxes at the beginning of each chapter in this volume for Deci and Ryan's cognitive evaluation theory. These ratings reflect the conclusions stated here. The importance rating is at the 4-star level (4.27), estimated validity is at 3, and estimated usefulness is at 1. None of these values is particularly high and the usefulness figure is quite low, primarily because the Deci and Ryan theory directly contradicts the evidence from applied contexts.

Current Emphases

Treatments of expectancy theory have declined since the early period of excitement, but they are far from being gone from the literature. One factor contributing to the decline is that utilizing these ideas directly in practice has proved to be difficult.

On the research front, a major emerging emphasis is that individual differences are receiving increased attention in contrast with the long-standing view that expectancy theory was not concerned with such matters. The within-subjects approach to research began to move the theory in that direction, but recently there has been much more. Tang, Singer, and Roberts (2000) find a wide variation on expectancy theory variables, including outcomes, among the employees of a single company. Van Eerde and Thierry (2001) conducted several laboratory studies that suggest that different motivation theories may be appropriate to different groups of people. They also find that self-efficacy is an important factor in expectancy theory results and that other individual differences operate as well. Judge and Ilies (2002) performed a meta-analysis on relationships between the so-called "big five" personality traits and expectancy motivation; they obtained significant findings in all five instances, but the negative correlation with neuroticism and the positive correlation with conscientiousness were most pronounced.

A set of laboratory studies indicated that arousing positive emotional states, or moods, influenced cognitive processes of the kind involved in expectancy theory so that motivation and performance were facilitated (Erez and Isen 2002). Also, it has proven possible to develop a measure of test-taking motivation based on expectancy theory (Sanchez, Truxillo, and Bauer 2000). All in all, the research being published indicates that expectancy theory is very much alive and well.

The expectancy theory framework taken in a general sense, and including the Vroom as well as the Porter-Lawler variants, seems at the present time to have achieved a position where it is widely supported by a diverse array of reviewers (Bartol and Locke 2000; Ambrose and Kulik 1999; Pinder 1998). We do not know as much as might be desired about how it works in a cognitive sense, but we do believe it works. The domain of the theory is limited to structured, rational, and conscious thought processes, however.

CONCLUSIONS

The evaluations of the Vroom and the Porter-Lawler variants on expectancy theory are identical except that the Vroom version is institutionalized; the stars themselves are the same. However, the Vroom variant has an average importance rating of 5.96, one of the highest values obtained. The Porter-Lawler importance rating is at 5.41. Also, the two variants, although both originating in the decade of the 1960s, differ somewhat on this score as well—Vroom's theory arrived in the first part of the decade and the Porter-Lawler theory in the latter part. Presumably both of these factors have contributed to the institutionalization difference. The Porter-Lawler variant appears to be close to achieving institutional status.

As indicated within this chapter, there is ample evidence, once the measurement problems got resolved, that expectancy theory is highly valid (5 stars), no matter whose variant one uses. The reviewers agree fully; as Bartol and Locke say, "the expectancy model is true" (2000, 112). However, the theory has much less value for practice, where the rating is 3 stars. Lawler has contributed the most in this regard, and he continues to write on these matters. Yet not all of the approaches he champions had their origins completely in expectancy theory.

Expectancy theory and the theoretical approaches to be considered in the next chapter have a great deal in common. Both derive from some version of learning theory, both rely heavily on contingent reinforcement, and both have demonstrated considerable validity in predicting a wide range of outcomes. Presumably they account for much common variance in these outcomes as well.

REFERENCES

Ambrose, Maureen L., and Kulik, Carol T. (1999). Old Friends, New Faces: Motivation Research in the 1990s. *Journal of Management*, 25, 231–92.

Bartol, Kathryn M., and Durham, Cathy C. (2000). Incentives: Theory and Practice. In Cary L. Cooper and Edwin A. Locke (Eds.), *Industrial and Organizational Psychology: Linking Theory with Practice*. Oxford, UK: Blackwell, 1–33.

Bartol, Kathryn M., and Locke, Edwin A. (2000). Incentives and Motivation. In Sara L. Rynes and Barry Gerhart (Eds.), *Compensation in Organizations: Current Research and Practice*. San Francisco, CA: Jossey-Bass, 104–47.

Boswell, Wendy R. (2000). Employee Alignment and the Role of "Line of Sight." *Human Resource Planning*, 23(4), 48–49.

Deci, Edward L., Koestner, Richard, and Ryan, Richard M. (1999). A Meta-Analytic Review of Experiments Examining the Effects of Extrinsic Rewards on Intrinsic Motivation. *Psychological Bulletin*, 125, 627–68.

Deci, Edward L., and Ryan, Richard M. (1985). *Intrinsic Motivation and Self-Determination in Human Behavior*. New York: Plenum.

Erez, Amir, and Isen, Alice M. (2002). The Influence of Positive Affect on the Components of Expectancy Motivation. *Journal of Applied Psychology*, 87, 1055–67.

Evans, Martin G. (1991). The Problem of Analyzing Multiplicative Composites. *American Psychologist*, 46, 6–15.

Galbraith, Jay, and Cummings, Larry L. (1967). An Empirical Investigation of the Motivational Determinants of Task Performance: Interactive Effects between Instrumentality–Valence and Motivation–Ability. *Organizational Behavior and Human Performance*, 2, 237–57.

Georgopoulos, Basil S., Mahoney, Gerald M., and Jones, Nyle W. (1957). A Path–Goal Approach to Productivity. *Journal of Applied Psychology*, 41, 345–53.

Graen, George (1969). Instrumentality Theory of Work Motivation: Some Experimental Results and Suggested Modifications. *Journal of Applied Psychology Monograph*, 53(2).

Hackman, L. Richard, and Porter, Lyman W. (1968). Expectancy Theory Predictions of Work Effectiveness. *Organizational Behavior and Human Performance*, 3, 417–26.

Ilgen, Daniel R., Nebeker, Delbert M., and Pritchard, Robert D. (1981). Expectancy Theory Measures: An Empirical Comparison in an Experimental Simulation. *Organizational Behavior and Human Performance*, 28, 189–223.

Judge, Timothy A., and Ilies, Remus (2002). Relationship of Personality to Performance Motivation: A Meta-Analytic Review. *Journal of Applied Psychology*, 87, 797–807.

Lawler, Edward E. (1968). A Correlational–Causal Analysis of the Relationship between Expectancy Attitudes and Job Performance. *Journal of Applied Psychology*, 52, 462–68.

——— (1971). *Pay and Organizational Effectiveness: A Psychological View*. New York: McGraw-Hill.

——— (1973, 1994). *Motivation in Work Organizations*. Monterey and San Francisco, CA: Brooks/Cole and Jossey-Bass.

——— (1981). *Pay and Organization Development*. Reading, MA: Addison-Wesley.

——— (1993). Understanding Work Motivation and Organizational Effectiveness: A Career-long Journey. In Arthur G. Bedeian (Ed.), *Management Laureates: A Collection of Autobiographical Essays*, Vol. 2. Greenwich, CT: JAI Press, 81–109.

——— (2000). *Rewarding Excellence: Pay Strategies for the New Economy*. San Francisco, CA: Jossey-Bass.

Lawler, Edward E., and Finegold, David (2000). Individualizing the Organization: Past, Present, and Future. *Organizational Dynamics*, 29, 1–15.

Lawler, Edward E., and Porter, Lyman W. (1967). Antecedent Attitudes of Effective Managerial Performance. *Organizational Behavior and Human Performance*, 2, 122–42.

Lewin, Kurt (1938). The Conceptual Representation and the Measurement of Psychological Forces. *Contributions to Psychological Theory*, 1(4).

——— (1951). *Field Theory in Social Science.* New York: Harper.

Locke, Edwin A. (1975). Personnel Attitudes and Motivation. *Annual Review of Psychology*, 26, 457–80.

Luthans, Fred (1990). Conversation with Lyman W. Porter. *Organizational Dynamics*, 18(3), 69–79.

Miller, Lynn E., and Grush, Joseph E. (1988). Improving Predictions in Expectancy Theory Research: Effects of Personality, Expectancies, and Norms. *Academy of Management Journal*, 31, 107–22.

Nielson, Troy R., and Eisenbach, Regina J. (2001). Mentoring in Academia: A Conversation with Lyman Porter. *Journal of Management Inquiry*, 10, 183–89.

Pinder, Craig C. (1998). *Work Motivation in Organizational Behavior.* Upper Saddle River, NJ: Prentice-Hall.

Porter, Lyman W. (1993). An Unmanaged Pursuit of Management. In Arthur G. Bedeian (Ed.), *Management Laureates: A Collection of Autobiographical Essays*, Vol. 3. Greenwich, CT: JAI Press, 1–29.

——— (1996). Forty Years of Organization Studies: Reflections from a Micro Perspective. *Administrative Science Quarterly*, 41, 262–69.

Porter, Lyman W., and Lawler, Edward E. (1968). *Managerial Attitudes and Performance.* Homewood, IL: Irwin.

Sanchez, Rudolph J., Truxillo, Donald M., and Bauer, Talya N. (2000). Development and Examination of an Expectancy-based Measure of Test-taking motivation. *Journal of Applied Psychology*, 85, 739–50.

Stephens, Gregory K., and Sommer, Steven M. (2001). Lyman Porter: A Celebration of Excellence in Mentoring. *Journal of Management Inquiry*, 10, 190–96.

Tang, Thomas L., Singer, Marc G., and Roberts, Sharon (2000). Employees' Perceived Organizational Instrumentality: An Examination of the Gender Differences. *Journal of Managerial Psychology*, 15, 378–402.

Tolman, Edward C. (1932). *Purposive Behavior in Animals and Men.* New York: Appleton-Century.

——— (1959). Principles of Purposive Behavior. In Sigmund Koch (Ed.), *Psychology: A Study of a Science*, Vol. 2. New York: McGraw-Hill, 92–157.

Van Eerde, Wendelien, and Thierry, Henk (1996). Vroom's Expectancy Models and Work-Related Criteria: A Meta-Analysis. *Journal of Applied Psychology*, 81, 575–86.

——— (2001). VIE Functions, Self-Set Goals, and Performance: An Experiment. In Miriam Erez, Uwe Kleinbeck, and Henk Thierry (Eds.), *Work Motivation in the Context of a Globalizing Economy*. Mahwah, NJ: Lawrence Erlbaum, 131–47.

Vroom, Victor H. (1960). *Some Personality Determinants of the Effects of Participation.* Englewood Cliffs, NJ: Prentice-Hall.

——— (1964). *Work and Motivation.* New York: Wiley.

——— (1966). Organizational Choice: A Study of Pre- and Post-decision Processes. *Organizational Behavior and Human Performance*, 1, 212–25.

——— (1993). Improvising and Muddling Through. In Arthur G. Bedeian (Ed.), *Management Laureates: A Collection of Autobiographical Essays*, Vol. 3. Greenwich, CT: JAI Press, 259–84.

Vroom, Victor H., and Deci, Edward L. (1971). The Stability of Post-decision Dissonance: A Follow-up Study of the Job Attitudes of Business School Graduates. *Organizational Behavior and Human Performance*, 6, 36–49.

Wanous, John P., Keon, Thomas L., and Latack, Janina C. (1983). Expectancy Theory and Occupational/Organizational Choices: A Review and Test. *Organizational Behavior and Human Performance*, 32, 66–86.

Wiersma, Uco J. (1992). The Effects of Extrinsic Rewards in Intrinsic Motivation: A Meta-Analysis. *Journal of Occupational and Organizational Psychology*, 65, 101–14.

Chapter 8

OPERANT BEHAVIOR AND ORGANIZATIONAL BEHAVIOR MODIFICATION

CLAY HAMNER, AND FRED LUTHANS AND ROBERT KRIETNER

Background
Formulations Regarding Operant Behavior Set
    Forth by Hamner
    Types of Contingencies
    Schedules of Reinforcement
    Stages in Developing a Positive Reinforcement
    Program
Organizational Behavior Modification Theory
    Rejection of Internal States as Causes
    Stages of the 1970s Behavioral Contingency
      Management Model
    Shaping, Modeling, and Self-Control in the 1970s
    The Status of Punishment
    Organizational Behavior Modification in the 1980s
    Reaching Out to Other Theories
Evaluation and Impact
    Research Involving Luthans
    Meta-Analysis of OB Mod Studies
    Does Behavior Modification Work?
    Does Behavior Modeling Work?
    Does Self-Control Work?
Conclusions

Hamner's Operant Behavior Formulations	
Importance rating	★ ★ ★ ★
Estimated validity	★ ★ ★ ★
Estimated usefulness	★ ★ ★
Decade of origin	1970s

Luthans and Kreitner's Organizational Behavior Modification	
Importance rating	★ ★ ★ ★
Estimated validity	★ ★ ★ ★
Estimated usefulness	★ ★ ★ ★·
Decade of origin	1970s

The theoretical positions to be considered in this chapter derive from the legacy that B.F. Skinner left organizational behavior. Skinner himself, however, wrote very little and conducted no research dealing directly with organizational topics; his concerns were either with individual behavior or with the broad spectrum of culture and societal functioning. Thus, it has fallen to others to extrapolate Skinner's ideas into the organizational setting and to conduct research related to those extrapolations. Skinner indicates his own relationship to the field of organizational study in the following quote from one of the interviews that represent his only specific published contributions to the field:

> I'm not a specialist in industrial psychology. I have only a casual acquaintance with the
> kinds of things done by Douglas McGregor and Abe Maslow. They do not strike me as

being particularly effective. You can classify motives and still neglect contingencies of reinforcement, and the contingencies are the important thing. Behavior modification is beginning to get into industry, and that may mean a change. Up to now it's been most effective in
psychotherapy, in handling disturbed and retarded children, in the design of classroom
management, and in programmed instruction. It is possible that we're going to see an entirely different kind of psychology in industry. Unfortunately there are not yet many people
who understand the principle. It is not something that can be taken over by the nonprofes-
sional to use as a rule of thumb. In the not-too-distant future, however, a new breed of
industrial manager may be able to apply the principles of operant conditioning effectively.
(Skinner and Dowling 1973, 40)

Skinner was born in 1904 and died in 1990. His contributions to psychology span a sixty-year
period, and his descriptive behaviorism has had a deep impact on psychological thinking (Lattal
1992). He obtained his doctorate in psychology from Harvard in 1931 and subsequently served
on the psychology faculties of the Universities of Minnesota and Indiana before returning to
Harvard in 1948. In the early years, Skinner's research focused on animals, and he gave little
attention to practical applications of his ideas in any form. Gradually, however, his horizons
expanded. Skinner subsequently wrote several books that provide statements regarding matters
that have possible relevance for the study of organizations, although none touches even tangentially on the field of organizational behavior.

BACKGROUND

A number of different individuals published extensions of Skinner's ideas to the organizational
domain during the late 1960s and early 1970s. The industrial *Zeitgeist* appears to have been
ripe for this kind of approach, since an earlier effort (Aldis 1961) had almost no impact. Some
of these extrapolations are presented as direct restatements of Skinner's previously published
views; others do not even acknowledge a debt to Skinner. But all are directly concerned with
the process of influencing employee behavior to desired ends using techniques of behavior
modification.

The initial statement in this period appears to be that of Nord (1969). This was soon followed
by articles by Luthans and White (1971), Sorcher (1971), and Adam and Scott (1971). Among
these early contributors, Luthans stands out on a number of grounds. His theoretical treatment is
more comprehensive, deals with a wider range of topics, and attempts a greater depth of explanation. He has written about a number of research applications and has continued to write on the
subject over a period of many years; the other early writers, on the other hand, have since turned
to other endeavors. Beginning in 1971 Luthans has conducted his research and set forth his theory
in conjunction with a number of doctoral students and former students, but throughout he has
remained the central figure in what he termed at an early point *organizational behavior modification*, or simply OB Mod (Luthans 1973).

Fred Luthans did his undergraduate work at the University of Iowa in engineering and mathematics. He entered the business school there in 1961 and after completing his MBA continued
on in the Ph.D. program. He received his doctorate from Iowa in 1965 at the young age of
twenty-five. From there he entered the military and taught at West Point for several years
before accepting a faculty position at the University of Nebraska, where he has remained throughout his career.

Luthans became interested in Skinner's ideas while doing training work with the Nebraska State Mental Health System during the late 1960s. There he learned about the successes being achieved with these ideas applying them to the treatment side of mental health. He set out to determine whether similar successes might be achieved applying operant-based learning approaches and techniques in human resource management (Luthans 1996). He has been studying the subject ever since.

As an introduction to OB Mod, I start with certain formulations set forth by W. Clay Hamner during the early to mid-1970s. These formulations provide a particularly useful bridge between Skinner and OB Mod. Hamner received his doctorate in organizational behavior from Indiana University and has taught there, at Michigan State University, at Northwestern, and at Duke—all in the business schools. During the 1980s, he began moving out of the field of organizational behavior and ultimately took up other endeavors. In many respects he was replaced in the literature of organizational behavior by Judith Komaki, who is now on the psychology faculty of the City University of New York.

FORMULATIONS REGARDING OPERANT BEHAVIOR
SET FORTH BY HAMNER

The basic concept of the theory is *learning*, defined as "a relatively permanent change in behavior potentiality that results from reinforced practice or experience" (Hamner1974a, 87). Performance is the translation of what is learned into practice. Through reinforcement certain behaviors are strengthened and intensified and thus occur more frequently.

Behavior may occur in a reflex manner in response to changes in the environment. This type of behavior is of little concern for the theory. What is important is *operant* behavior, behavior emitted by a person that influences or has an effect upon the individual's outside world. Operant behaviors are learned as consequences accrue in the form of rewards and punishments that are applied contingent upon whether certain behaviors do or do not occur. Thus, the role of the supervisor becomes one of orchestrating reinforcements to produce desired behaviors at a high frequency; this is how performance can be improved.

Operant learning involves a process whereby reinforcers are applied to initially randomly emitted behaviors. Accordingly, to understand a person's behavior one must know the situation in which the behavior occurs, the nature of the behavior, and the reinforcing consequences. To influence a person's behavior in a desired direction, one must know how to arrange correctly the contingencies of reinforcement. The major hypotheses of the theory relate to the relative effectiveness of manipulating the contingencies of reinforcement in different ways.

Types of Contingencies

Four different types of arrangements of contingencies are specified. Two serve to strengthen desired behavior (positive reinforcement and avoidance learning) and two serve to weaken undesired behavior (extinction and punishment). "A *positive reinforcer* is a stimulus which, when added to a situation, strengthens the probability of an operant response" (Skinner 1953, 73). Certain reinforcers such as food, water, and sex are innate and thus operate independent of past experiences. In the work context, however, the important reinforcers are learned, such as advancement, praise, recognition, and money. What is a reinforcer for one person may not be for another; it depends on the individual's past reinforcement history.

Hamner (1974a) describes three steps in the successful application of reinforcement theory in the work environment:

1. Select reinforcers that are powerful and durable for the individual.
2. Design contingencies so as to make the occurrence of reinforcing events contingent upon desired behavior.
3. Design contingencies so that a reliable procedure for eliciting the desired behavior is established.

The third point is important because if one cannot ever find the desired behavior to reward, learning cannot occur. Training thus becomes a method of *shaping* behavior so that it can be controlled by reinforcement procedures. Separate aspects and approximations of the total desired behavior are reinforced until finally the behavior as a whole is shaped; learning to drive a car might be an example.

Avoidance learning operates in a manner similar to positive reinforcement except that the desired behavior serves to prevent the onset of a noxious stimulus, or, in a variant, terminates such a stimulus that already exists. In the workplace, supervisory criticism is often such a noxious stimulus. Although avoidance learning is effective under certain circumstances, many behavior modification advocates, including Skinner, much prefer positive reinforcement.

Extinction occurs when a previously utilized positive reinforcer is withheld. Under such circumstances the behavior involved may continue for some time, but as the reward continually fails to appear, the behavior diminishes and ultimately is extinguished entirely. This approach is appropriate when an individual brings undesired behaviors to the job or when an undesired behavior has inadvertently been reinforced in the past.

Many behavior modification advocates prefer extinction to *punishment* as a method of influencing behavior, on the grounds that punishment may have certain negative side effects. Skinner himself does not favor the use of punishment. There are, however, many behavior modification approaches in use that draw heavily on the reinforcement effects of punishment. There is no unanimity on this matter.

Hamner (1974a) and Hamner and Hamner (1976) present several rules for using operant conditioning techniques, which might best be considered as hypotheses with regard to how desired behaviors may be obtained.

1. Do not give the same level of reward to all; differentiate based on some performance standard.
2. Failure to respond to behavior has reinforcing consequences; these consequences should be recognized, and nonaction as well as action should be adjusted to the desired ends.
3. Tell a person what behavior gets reinforced.
4. Tell a person what he or she is doing wrong.
5. Do not punish in front of others; there may be undesirable side effects not only for the person punished but for the others as well.
6. Make the consequences equal to the behavior.

Schedules of Reinforcement

Although a variety of different reinforcement schedules are possible, certain ones are of particular theoretical and practical relevance. *Continuous reinforcement* occurs when every instance of the desired behavior is followed by the reinforcer. This approach often is not practical in a complex work environment in which managers supervise many employees. Although continuous reinforcement fosters rapid learning, it also produces behavior that is subject to rapid extinction, should the reinforcer be removed for any reason. Overall, some kind of *partial reinforcement* schedule is recommended.

Partial reinforcement, when reinforcement does not occur after every emergence of an operant, is relatively slow but has the advantage of considerable permanence. Four such schedules require discussion:

- *Fixed interval*—reinforcement occurs when the desired behavior manifests itself after a set period of time has passed since the previous reinforcement.
- *Variable interval*—reinforcement occurs at some variable interval of time around an average.
- *Fixed ratio*—reinforcement occurs after a fixed number of desired behaviors are produced.
- *Variable ratio*—reinforcement occurs after a number of desired responses, with this number changing from one reinforcement to the next, varying around an average.

These schedules are presented in order of anticipated increasing effectiveness. Fixed interval procedures tend to yield cyclical fluctuations with desired behaviors maximized just prior to reinforcement. In general the variable approaches produce slower extinction and more stable performance levels. The variable ratio schedule is considered to be particularly attractive, although it may not be as easy to implement. In all instances it is important that the reinforcer follow the desired behavior as closely as possible.

Stages in Developing a Positive Reinforcement Program

Hamner (1974b) and Hamner and Hamner (1976) have set forth certain steps or stages that should be followed in introducing a positive reinforcement program in a company. In essence this is an applied theory of performance maximization. Underlying these statements is the view that positive reinforcement should be maximized and punishment minimized. Furthermore, worker attitudes as a cause of behavior are ignored on the grounds that behavior can be fully explained in terms of the work situation and the contingencies of reinforcement.

The *first* stage is to define performance in strictly behavioral terms and to conduct a performance audit with the objective of establishing a baseline for measuring future performance. This procedure makes it possible to determine what the current performance situation is, in as objective a manner as possible.

The *second* stage involves setting specific and reasonable performance goals for each worker, expressed in measurable terms. These goals, however they may be established, are external to the individual; there is no invoking of experiential concepts such as intentions, expectations, and the like.

The *third* stage is to have the employee maintain a continuing record of work, a schedule of reinforcements. This way it is possible for the individual to picture how current work contrasts with that of the performance audit stage and with the goals established in stage two. The objective is to create a situation in which behavior that will warrant positive reinforcement occurs. One way of doing this is to shorten the time intervals of measurement as much as possible.

The *fourth* stage is described as follows:

> The supervisor looks at the self-feedback report of the employee and/or other indications of performance (e.g., sales records) and then praises the positive aspects of the employee's performance (as determined by the performance audit and goals set). This extrinsic rein-

forcement should strengthen the desired performance, while the withholding of praise for the performance which falls below the goal should give the employee incentive to improve that level of performance. Since the worker already knows the areas of his or her deficiencies, there is no reason for the supervisor to criticize . . . use of positive reinforcement leads to a greater feeling of self-control, while the avoidance of negative reinforcement keeps the individual from feeling controlled or coerced. (Hamner 1974b, 285)

Although the above discussion focuses on reinforcement by praise, other approaches may be used as appropriate to the individual's reinforcement history, including money, freedom to choose one's activities, opportunity to see oneself achieving, higher status on some dimension, and power over others.

ORGANIZATIONAL BEHAVIOR MODIFICATION THEORY

Organizational behavior modification theory is set forth in two books and several articles. There is a 1970s version most fully presented in the book *Organizational Behavior Modification* (Luthans and Kreitner 1975) and then a 1980s version, which is different in important respects, presented in *Organizational Behavior Modification and Beyond* (Luthans and Kreitner 1985). We will start with the 1970s approach.

Rejection of Internal States as Causes

Luthans and Kreitner (1975) are explicit in following Skinner with regard to the rejection of internal states (attitudes, motives, feeling, and the like) as causes of behavior. Behavior is said to be strictly a function of its consequences, not of internal motives; thus the theory is really one of learning, not motivation, although the ultimate outcome remains performance, as in the preceding formulations. Unobservable internal states are irrelevant to understanding behavior and generally are mere concomitants of the behaviors themselves. Inner-state constructs such as achievement motivation, expectancy, intentions and goals, self-actualization, feelings of equity, and so on have no place in the theory. At least they are said not to. In this sense it represents a radical departure from previous theories (Luthans and Otteman 1973).

This 1970s theory, in contrast to others that generally espouse behaviorist principles but include internal variables in their formulations as well, fully accepts the following position (Skinner 1975, 43):

What we feel are conditions of our bodies, most of them closely associated with behavior and with the circumstances in which we behave. We both strike *and* feel angry for a common reason, and that reason lies in the environment. In short, the bodily conditions we feel are *collateral products* of our genetic and environmental histories. They have no explanatory force; they are simply additional facts to be taken into account.

Stages of the 1970s Behavioral Contingency Management Model

Luthans and Kreitner (1975) present an approach to identifying and managing the critical performance-related behaviors of employees in organizations. They call this approach the behavioral contingency management model for OB Mod. This model presents a series of stages not unlike those suggested by Hamner:

1. Identify performance-related behaviors using the following questions as guidelines:
    a) Can the behavior be reduced to *observable* behavioral events?
    b) Can one *count* how often each behavior occurs?
    c) *Exactly* what must the person do before a behavior is recorded?
    d) Is a key *performance-related* behavior involved?
2. Measure to establish frequencies of behaviors using such procedures as tally sheets and time sampling.
3. Identify existing contingencies of reinforcement to determine where the behavior takes place and what its consequences are by:
    a) analyzing histories of reinforcement;
    b) using self-report measures; and
    c) resorting to systematic trial and error to identify reinforcers.
4. Carry out the intervention process as follows:
    a) Develop an intervention strategy considering such environmental variables as structures, processes, technologies, groups, and tasks.
    b) Apply the appropriate strategy using suitable types of contingencies.
    c) Measure to establish the frequencies of behaviors after intervention.
    d) Maintain desired behaviors through the use of appropriate schedules of reinforcement.
5. Evaluate the overall performance impacts.

Obviously there are differences in this approach from that of Hamner, such as with regard to establishing goals and the techniques of measurement used. But overall the similarities are greater than the differences. The two together provide a reasonably good picture of how behavior modification theory can reduce to practice.

Shaping, Modeling, and Self-Control in the 1970s

Shaping, which is considered only relatively briefly by Hamner, is described in a step-by-step manner in Table 8.1. The following quote serves to amplify that statement:

> Closer approximations to the target response are emitted and contingently reinforced. The less desirable approximations, including those reinforced earlier in the shaping process, are put on extinction. In this manner, behavior may actually be shaped into what is desired. Shaping solves the problem of waiting for the opportunity to reinforce a desired response. It is a particularly important technique in behavior modification if a desired response is not currently in a person's behavior repertoire. (Luthans and Kreitner 1975, 55)

Table 8.1 also sets forth the steps in modeling, a type of learning that has a somewhat uncertain status in behavior modification. Note that phrases such as attention, participation, and demonstration of positive consequences come into the discussion—implying internal causal states that a true behaviorist should consider irrelevant to theory construction. It is difficult to deal with modeling or imitation without resort to such constructs; yet complex behaviors do become learned rather quickly, obviously too quickly to be a result of shaping. Luthans and Kreitner (1975) follow Bandura (1971) in making this kind of learning part of their theory even though it is almost impossible to handle it without resort to internal constructs such as imagination, memory, and the like. At this point a certain amount of logical inconsistency is introduced into their theory.

Table 8.1

Strategies for Shaping and Modeling

Shaping	Modeling
1. Define the performance-related target behavior.	1. Identify the target behavior desired.
2. If the target behavior is a complex chain, reduce it to a discrete, observable, and measurable sequence of steps.	2. Select the appropriate model and its medium, such as in-person demonstration, training film.
3. Be sure the individual is able to meet the skill and ability requirements of each step.	3. Be sure the individual is capable of meeting the skill requirements of the target behavior.
4. Select appropriate positive reinforcers based on the individual's history of reinforcement.	4. Structure a favorable learning context with regard to attention, participation, and the target behavior.
5. Structure the contingent environment so that antecedent conditions will foster desired behavior.	5. Model the target behavior and support it by activities such as role playing; demonstrate the positive consequences of the modeled behavior.
6. Make all positive reinforcements contingent on increasingly close approximations to the target behavior so that the behavioral chain is built gradually.	6. Reinforce all progress of the modeled behavior.
7. Once the target behavior is achieved, reinforce it at first continuously and then on a variable basis.	7. Once the target behavior is achieved, reinforce it at first continuously and then on a variable basis.

Source: Adapted from Luthans and Kreitner (1975, 132–33, 140–41).

This same problem plagues the discussion of *self-control* as well, another concept of somewhat uncertain status in behavior modification theory. In the strict behavioral sense, self-control involves the manipulation of environmental consequences by the individual to determine his own behavior. However, most who try to put the idea in the employment context, including Luthans and Kreitner (1975), find it impossible not to invoke internal constructs.

The Status of Punishment

Hamner notes that punishment as a type of contingency can have certain negative side effects that make it relatively unattractive. In contrast, Luthans is more accepting of the use of punishment, while recognizing its limitations. Four such side effects are noted:

1. Punishment serves to suppress behavior temporarily rather than to change it permanently, with the result that a method of continued punitive reinforcement must be devised; often this requires a manager's continued presence.
2. Punishment generates emotional behavior, often against the punisher.
3. Punishment may serve not to suppress behavior temporarily, but to stifle it permanently under any and all circumstances, thus producing a degree of behavioral inflexibility.
4. A frequently punishing individual may assume the role of a conditioned aversive stimulus, with the result that he or she disrupts self-control efforts and cannot effectively administer positive reinforcers.

These considerations are generally consistent with those discussed by Nord (1969), who also indicates that punishment does not necessarily produce the desired behavior, only the cessation of the punished behavior. Another undesired behavior may be next in the response hierarchy, replacing the one punished. Yet, given all these arguments punishment is still widely used in managing organizations and in behavior modification (Luthans and Kreitner 1973).

Organizational Behavior Modification in the 1980s

By the early 1980s, two versions of the theory were clearly in evidence. There was first the *Antecedent* (Environmental Context) → *Behavior* → *Consequences* of Behavior (A-B-C) model that characterized the 1970s (e.g., see Thompson and Luthans 1983). There was also a new model labeled S-O-B-C —*Situation* (the stimulus and the broader antecedent environment, overt or covert) ↔ *Organism* (the cognitive processes that play a mediating role; the person) ↔ *Behavior* (the response or pattern of behavior, overt or covert) ↔ *Consequences* (the contingent consequence which can be reinforcing or punishing, overt or covert) (e.g., see Davis and Luthans 1980). This new model adds *social learning* to the earlier view, whereby people learn by observing other people. This is manifest in the "organism" component and in the use of the term "covert" to imply a process within the person. By the middle of the 1980s these two models, or theoretical versions, had been combined so that social learning now had been made explicit, and internal states as causes were no longer rejected (Kreitner and Luthans 1984; Luthans and Kreitner 1985). Thus the logical inconsistency previously noted is cleared up.

Luthans draws heavily on the social learning theory of Bandura (1977) for this new version of his theory. The processes inherent in social learning are depicted in Figure 8.1. Here people influence their environment, which in turn influences their thoughts and behavior. Social learning extends the operant, A-B-C model of learning, with its entirely external emphasis, by explaining how individuals process environmental stimuli. Accordingly, it becomes much easier to explain why similar people in similar situations often behave in very different ways.

Figure 8.2 presents the revised and integrated model (the S-O-B-C approach). Under *situation,* cues do not actually cause subsequent behavior, but they do set the occasion for the behavior to be emitted in an operant manner. Under *organism,* the role that cognitive mediating and self-control processes play, as influenced by personal characteristics, is depicted. Note that *expectations* are explicitly included, bringing the revised theory much closer to expectancy theory. Under *behavior,* a number of dimensions are introduced including subvocalization (thought). Under *consequences,* self-reinforcement (self-control) is noted and a feedback loop is introduced indicating that consequences influence mediating cognitions, self-management processes, and personal moderators, and give power to situational cues.

Consonant with the introduction of social learning, the theory now says that much learning occurs through modeling one's behavior on the actions of others. People select, organize, and change stimuli around them as they learn new behaviors; they also anticipate consequences of their acts—rewards and punishments, for instance—and their behaviors are motivated accordingly. In contrast to radical behaviorists, social learning theorists believe that cognitive processes play an important role in learning (see Bandura 2001).

With the incorporation of social learning concepts, OB Mod can deal with approaches such as *self-management,* whereby people regulate their own actions. Self-management requires the deliberate manipulation of stimuli, internal processes, and responses to achieve personally identified behavioral outcomes. In Figure 8.2 note the frequent reference to internal thought processes—planning, personal goals, self-contracts, mental rehearsal, expectations, and the like— and the important causal role given these processes in the creation of self-controlled behavior.

Figure 8.1   **A Model of Social Learning Process**

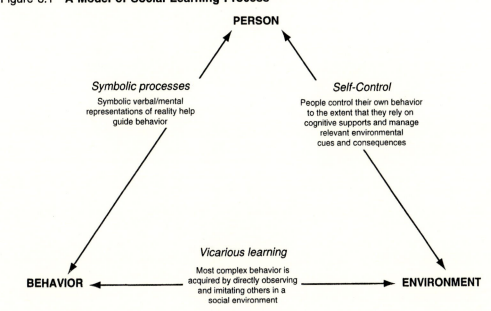

Figure 8.2   **The 1980s Expanded Model of Organizational Behavior Modification**

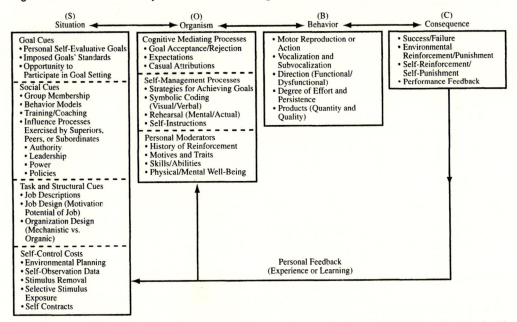

Self-management is much more important in organizations than has generally been recognized, although it is not sufficient in and of itself to produce a coordinated organizational effort. Self-management has the advantage that it reduces the chance of criticism on grounds of unethical manipulation of others for one's own benefit, as when a manager "uses" a subordinate. Self-management has the quality of self-determination and self-control, as opposed to being controlled by others.

Luthans (1996) is not entirely comfortable with the S-O-B-C model; he really prefers the radical A-B-C version with its much greater parsimony, and he considers the empirical support to be greater there as well. Yet he views the extension as necessary to handling a wider range of phenomena.

Reaching Out to Other Theories

Since the mid-1980s, Luthans on several occasions has proposed further extensions of OB Mod theory beyond the integration with social learning theory. The objective in each instance appears to be to expand the theoretical domain covered and to widen the number of phenomena explained. Examples are ties to goal-setting theory, attribution theory, and macro-oriented organizational perspectives (Luthans and Martinko 1987). More recently, ties have been proposed with social cognitive theory and with the self-efficiency construct (Stajkovic and Luthans 1998). An example here is the advocacy of managerial social recognition, contingent upon individual employees' desired behaviors, as a basic principle for organizational behavior (Luthans and Stajkovic 2000). This approach again brings Luthans together with Bandura (1997). Consonant with this reaching out, Luthans has joined forces with the positive organizational scholarship movement (see Chapter 2) emphasizing such concepts as confidence, self-efficacy, hope, optimism, subjective well-being, emotional intelligence, and resiliency (Luthans 2002; Luthans and Avolio 2003), as well as his agreement with various leadership concepts.

These extensions have not been worked out in the same degree of theoretical detail as with the social learning theory integration, and accordingly at present they cannot be considered components in full standing of OB Mod theory. It appears that Luthans is attempting to draft a comprehensive general theory of human motivation and behavior in organizational contexts, but the theoretical links necessary to achieve this objective have not been established as yet.

EVALUATION AND IMPACT

Starting in the late 1960s and continuing to the present, a number of organizations have undertaken sizable, continuing applications of behavior modification with the objective of reducing absenteeism, increasing output, achieving cost savings, and the like. These applications typically involve specific, relatively large components within the organization. In most instances they do not represent controlled experiments so much as demonstrations of behavior modification's feasibility. Frequently, hard data on successes and failures are lacking, and one must rely on testimonials. Yet there have been a sizable number of well-controlled studies as well. We will focus on the latter because it is there that any meaningful evaluation of OB Mod must obtain its data. The research in which Luthans has been involved is particularly relevant.

Research Involving Luthans

Although Luthans in collaboration with various students and former students has published considerable research testing his theory, certain studies stand out. A test using salespeople in a department store, for instance, is described by Luthans (1996) as his strongest methodologically, and his most comprehensive study on the impact of OB Mod. The design used experimental and control groups constituted from the membership of randomly selected departments (Luthans, Paul, and Baker 1981). There was also a feature whereby subjects served as their own controls using a baseline period, intervention, and then a return to baseline conditions. Criterion data were derived from periodic observations of behavior that yielded from 93 to 98 percent agreement depending on the reliability measure used. The intervention made available contingent rewards consisting of time off with pay, equivalent cash, and eligibility for a company-paid vacation for performance above standard. Engaging in selling and other performance-related behavior was very similar during the first baseline period for both experimental and control groups. These behaviors increased dramatically in the experimental (but not control) group during the intervention. This pattern of increase carried over into the return to baseline period, although the difference between experimentals and controls was less pronounced. When nonwork behavior was used as a criterion, these results were repeated except that, of course, the measure dropped with the intervention. That the measures post-intervention did not return to baseline levels is not totally unexpected, but it does invoke post-hoc explanation.

A later study conducted in a manufacturing context using an ABAB design, but without a control group, yields a more typical result (Luthans, Maciag, and Rosenkrantz 1983). In such a study the steps are as follows:

A. *The baseline period.* Establish a baseline measure of behavior prior to learning.
B. *The period of intervention.* Introduce the learning intervention while continuing to measure.
A. *The period of no intervention.* When the behavior has stabilized at a new level, withdraw the learning intervention and reestablish baseline conditions. This reversal should cause the behavior to revert to the baseline level.
B. *The period when intervention is reintroduced.* When the behavior has stabilized back at the baseline level, reintroduce the same learning intervention and see if the behavior frequency changes once again.

If withdrawing the intervention (the second A step) does not cause the behavior to shift back toward the baseline level (as it does in Figure 8.3), it is possible that some external factor, such as a pay raise, produced the initial results.

Another research effort that occasions special mention from Luthans (1996) was carried out in a Russian factory (Welsh, Luthans, and Sommer 1993). A within-subjects experimental design similar to that used in the department store was employed, but without control groups. Three different experimental interventions were compared: (1) provision of extrinsic rewards consisting of American goods rarely available in Russia contingent upon performance improvement, (2) provision of social rewards (praise and recognition) by supervisors trained to contingently administer these rewards, (3) initiation of participative decision making whereby the workers came up with suggestions for job enrichment and were empowered to carry them out. There is no specific evidence as to whether job enrichment per se actually "took" as an intervention. The first intervention increased production levels, and then there was a partial reversion to baseline levels subsequent to the withdrawal of the intervention. The second intervention produced a similar effect except that the decline after withdrawal was significant. The third intervention actually produced a decline in production levels. This latter result is attributed to culturally based mistrust of participative procedures. The Russian study is portrayed as representing the use of high-performance work practices in that country (Luthans, Luthans, Hodgetts, and Luthans 2000).

A recent study tested the following hypotheses using two locations, both of which were responsible for processing and mailing credit card bills:

Figure 8.3   **Reversal Analysis of the Effects of Organizational Behavior Modification Intervention on the Number of Defective Products Produced**

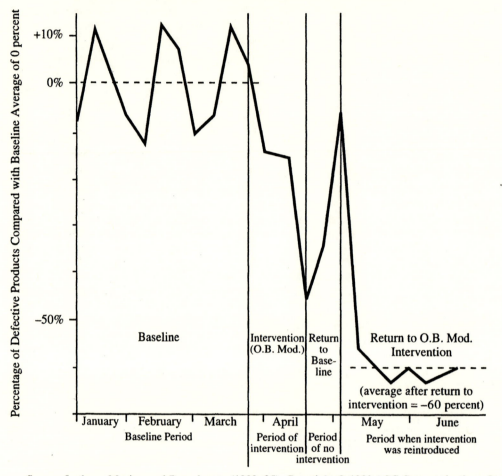

Source: Luthans, Maciag, and Rosenkrantz (1983, 35). Copyright © 1983 ACC Communications, Inc. Reprinted with permission.

1. Money, systematically administered using the OB Mod model, will have a greater impact on employee performance than will pay for performance routinely administered with no systematic application steps.
2. When all three incentive motivators are applied in the same way through the OB Mod model, money produces the strongest effect on performance, followed by social recognition, and then by performance feedback (Stajkovic and Luthans 2001, 582, 584).

The first hypothesis received support in that OB Mod increased performance 32 percent, and regular pay for performance did so at the 11 percent level; both represented significant increases, but OB Mod had a greater impact. When, in accordance with hypothesis 2, the motivators were compared, money proved to be most effective, while social recognition and feedback did not differ significantly.

Taken as a whole these studies demonstrate considerable validity for OB Mod, using not only varied experimental designs but varied research contexts and types of subjects as well.

Meta-Analysis of Organizational Behavior Modification Studies

A meta-analysis conducted by Stajkovic and Luthans (1997) draws upon a much larger research base, but it also reaches a very favorable conclusion for OB Mod. The inclusion requirements for the meta-analysis were established in such a way that over 60 percent of the studies used involved Luthans as a coauthor, and most of the remaining studies were authored by a person with ties to the University of Nebraska. Thus, this represents essentially a test of the theory proposed by Luthans. Although Luthans has endorsed single-subject studies (Luthans and Davis 1982), such studies were excluded from the analysis on the grounds that generalization is not warranted. However, the average effect size is based on only twenty-five subjects, a typical situation in behavior modification research.

Across the 19 studies and 115 effect sizes, there was a significant increase in performance, which amounted to a 17 percent improvement with the introduction of an OB Mod intervention. This increase existed for both manufacturing and service organizations, but it was greater in the manufacturing context. Financial, nonfinancial, and social reinforcers all demonstrated significant effects.

Does Behavior Modification Work?

There is considerable evidence that a theory that ignores cognitive variables does not work very well in explaining behavior when it moves into the realm of complex organizations. Extrapolators consistently have felt compelled to repudiate the radical behaviorism of Skinner and to introduce internal, cognitive factors. One reason for this is that under Skinnerian assumptions the only true way to understand and predict behavior, taking into account individual differences, is to comprehend the person's full reinforcement history. But this is a practical impossibility for mature working adults. Cognitively based theories typically view present thoughts, feelings, attitudes, and the like as providing an adequate representation of past experience and learning; accordingly, they offer a feasible method of dealing with factors that radical behaviorism cannot deal with practically.

Behaviorists argue that their theoretical approach has the advantage of parsimony. But in science, parsimony is a positive value only "all else being equal." In this case all is not equal; cognitive theories add something above and beyond the strict behaviorist approach in the areas of understanding, prediction, and managing the future. That is why when behavior modification moves into organizations, cognitive variables tend to emerge even when the theorists do their best to avoid them. This appears to be particularly true in dealing with such clearly important phenomena as modeling or imitation and self-control. But the question then becomes whether behavior modification and operant learning theory are needed at all. As a number of writers have indicated, expectancy theory and goal-setting theory, perhaps even equity theory, may be more suitable (e.g., see Locke 1980).

The question thus becomes—how well does behavior modification work, if at all? We have already seen from the Stajkovic and Luthans (1997) meta-analysis that one version of it works quite well. A review reported by Komaki, Coombs, and Schepman (1996) covering a much larger number of studies (fifty-one) finds that 92 percent of these resulted in substantial improvements in performance. These positive results extend across a variety of target behaviors, a variety of different consequences, a range of subjects and settings, and in some cases have been shown to operate over periods of many years. Many examples of the diversity of successful research applications, including a study by Komaki, may be found in O'Brien, Dickinson, and Rosow (1982). A review that updated their prior analysis, and as a result substantially increased the number of studies, reported a similar 93 percent success rate (Komaki, Coombs, Redding, and Schepman 2000).

A key aspect of the theory, noted by Hamner, Luthans, and many others, relates to the use of various schedules of reinforcement. In general the research strongly supports the application of contingent reinforcement, but beyond this things become more cloudy. Continuous reinforcement appears to be much more effective, in contrast to partial reinforcement schedules, than theory predicts. There is some evidence that the predicted superiority of variable ratio schedules can be anticipated among very experienced workers. However, there are numerous circumstances under which it is not superior. At present it is not at all clear which reinforcement schedule or how much reinforcement is best (Mitchell 1997). There appear to be major variations with the particular people involved.

Organizational behavior modification in some variant has been used widely and apparently successfully in practice. The unique practical contribution that this theory provides in contrast to other theories is captured in the following quote:

> Where then lies the distinctiveness of the OB Mod approach? Its major characteristic may be the mental set with which the manager approaches a situation. OB Mod requires the manager to observe quantifiable behaviors, to establish base rates in order to determine the extent of the problem, to determine what reinforcers are supporting the undesirable behaviors, to estimate what stimulus will reinforce the desired behavior, and to chart the frequency of the desired behavior after the reinforcement intervention. It is this critical look at behaviors and contingencies that promises to provide a refreshing addition to the organizational behavior literature. (Korman, Greenhaus, and Badin 1977, 189)

Given that a manager has developed the mental set implied by OB Mod, where is the approach likely to work best? One requirement is that precise behavioral measures of the central performance variables in the work be possible. This is much more feasible for manual work than for managerial and professional positions. In any job there is always the risk that one will measure and reinforce behavior that is easily measured but contributes little if anything to actual performance. This said, recently developed approaches suggest that managerial behaviors can be assessed appropriately using videotaping procedures (Komaki and Minnich 2002).

Another requirement is that it be possible to control the contingencies of reinforcement. Much of the success of behavior modification has been achieved with children, often in schools, with hospitalized mental patients, with prisoners, and of course originally with animals. In these cases control is relatively easy. In many jobs it is not; for instance, in cases where reinforcements administered by coworkers have long been a primary influence on individual performance. This need for control capability is closely related to a need for simplicity and independence. Developing an appropriate reinforcement approach becomes increasingly difficult as jobs become more complex, involving interacting performance dimensions, and relate to other jobs as subsystems of a larger whole. Behavior modification risks producing sufficient behavior rigidity so that the individual follows one particular course at the expense of other important goals. In interactive situations calling for coordinated effort, it can well yield something less than an optimal overall result. This is an area to which research is now beginning to move.

Does Behavior Modeling Work?

Other than in the area of self-management, OB Mod has been used primarily in dealing with nonmanagers in hierarchic organizations. Below the managerial level, it is much easier to prevent unintended environmental factors from intervening and disrupting the learning process. In contrast, *behavior modeling*, which like self-management is closely allied to social learning theory, has been used much more frequently at the managerial level. The approach is outlined in Table 8.1. It received its initial impetus from a book on the subject by Goldstein and Sorcher (1974).

There is good evidence that modeling one's own actions on the behaviors of superiors perceived as effective is an important method by which managers develop their own leadership styles. Thus the underlying premise of the approach is upheld. In addition, the studies that have been undertaken to evaluate the approach in terms of its impact on performance are generally favorable. A problem arises, however, because in actual practice wide variations in the techniques employed exist, and little knowledge is available as to which of these techniques are the most effective. Furthermore, like most OB Mod programs, behavior modeling can prove to be expensive. Accordingly, training in this area needs to be evaluated on a cost-benefit basis to determine how well it stacks up against alternative management development procedures. In this connection it should be noted that behavior modeling seems to have relatively little impact on long-term values and attitudes, with the result that training effects may dissipate if not reinforced in the actual continuing work situation.

Practical experience indicates that teaching managers to utilize behavior modification techniques effectively is not easy. At a minimum it requires a sizable investment in management development procedures. Although behavior modeling appears to have considerable promise, it is not clear that as utilized in the role-play component of the training it is a necessary condition for behavioral change. Considerable evidence of the type noted in Chapter 4 in connection with the discussion of achievement motivation training indicates that mental modeling in a person's mind alone can achieve similar results. Thinking one's way into a role initially, based on lectures, discussions, examples, and the like, may be less threatening and thus even more effective. Such an approach is inconsistent with the basic tenets of radical behaviorism and thus is less likely to be used by behavior modification advocates.

Does Self-Control Work?

A second offshoot of behavior modification that has received increased attention in recent years, and that, like behavior modeling, has an uncertain status among radical behaviorists because of its reliance on internal constructs, is self-control. I use the term self-control to include concepts such as self-regulation, self-management, and self-leadership, which have appeared to designate variations in technique of the same type as found in behavior modeling (Williams 1997).

Self-control in some form has an extended history in clinical psychology where it has a great deal of support. Labeled *self-management,* there is no outside role model and a person is taught to control and manipulate aspects of the environment so as to reward and punish behaviors that do and do not lead to intended results. The process may be described as follows:

> Self-management is an effort by an individual to control his or her behavior. Self-management involves goal setting, establishing a contract, monitoring the ways in which the environment is hindering the attainment of the goals, and administering reinforcement or

punishment based on self-evaluation. The first step in effective self-management is for the individual to set and commit to specific goals. Otherwise, self-monitoring—a precondition for self-evaluation—has no effect on behavior. Written contracts increase commitment by spelling out the reinforcing conditions for accepting the goal. (Frayne 1991, 3)

Training that teaches people how to train themselves in this manner has been found very effective in reducing absenteeism (Frayne 1991; Frayne and Geringer 2000) and in facilitating reemployment (Millman and Latham 2001). Clearly this is a very promising extension of OB Mod. To the extent that it incorporates goal-setting theory, it provides another instance of reaching out to other theories.

As previously noted, self-control procedures of any kind tend to relieve behavior modification of some of the ethical pressure it has been under, and this is another major plus for self-control. The reasoning here needs some explanation.

One of the reasons that behavior modification's organizational advocates often do not mention Skinner and attempt to disassociate themselves from his views is that certain of Skinner's writing, such as *Beyond Freedom and Dignity* (1971), have elicited strong negative reactions on strictly ethical grounds. There has been a distinct tendency to avoid this "bad press" by using terms other than behaviorism and operant conditioning. Yet it is important to understand and evaluate these ethical considerations wherever they may be involved. Court decisions related to the use of behavior modification procedures in the treatment of the emotionally ill have appeared with some frequency.

The primary ethical issue has been manipulation (Luthans and Kreitner 1985). The argument is that behavior modification techniques put too much power in the hands of management, create debilitating dependencies on superiors, are essentially totalitarian rather than democratic in concept, and ignore the rights of the individual as well as the principle of individual consent. Behavior modification thus becomes a method of using others for one's own purposes at their expense. It is particularly unethical when techniques of punishment and avoidance learning are employed, because individual suffering is added to the manipulation.

The purpose here is not to debate these issues but to provide an awareness of reactions that may follow the introduction of an OB Mod effort. Militant union officials, social activists, and dedicated liberals often have been at the forefront of the opposition. However, it is important to recognize that any valid theory of the kind discussed in this book could well elicit the same reactions. The reason that the other theories typically have not, and behavior modification has, is that the latter creates an explicit image of mindless obedience to the will of others, devoid of any voluntary component. The cognitive theories imply a greater degree of control over one's own behavior. In practice, however, when some people understand the theory fully and others are totally unaware of it, this difference may be misleading. Thus, as our knowledge of organizational behavior advances, the potential for misuse and manipulation for personal gain can become a basic social issue with regard to any theory.

CONCLUSIONS

Expectancy theory and OB Mod differ in their terminology, their focus on internal as opposed to external factors, and the extent to which useful applications have been developed. One might think that telescoping the two theories would produce a much more powerful composite, giving expectancy theory a set of applications to practice and OB Mod a set of processes to go in the black box that has been the organism or person. This would still leave unconscious motivation outside the composite theory, but it would go a long way toward handling individual motivational differences. Indeed, the way in which Luthans has been reaching out to other theories appears to be consistent with this scenario, although his focus appears to be more on theories that are closest to behavior modification, such as social learning theory and social cognitive theory.

One major barrier to integration of the two theoretical approaches is that two completely different sets of terminologies are involved. Yet theories, almost by definition, inevitably develop their own terminologies. In all likelihood a composite of expectancy and behavior modification theories would have to develop its own new terminology as well. Perhaps a greater barrier is that expectancy theory is not the only claimant to filling in the black box that radical behaviorism leaves. Two other such claimants are equity theory and goal-setting theory. These theories concern us in the next two chapters.

In many respects the evaluations of Hamner's operant formulations and OB Mod are the same, largely because they are both based on Skinner's theories. The importance ratings are 4.25 and 4.31, respectively; neither achieves institutional status. Both approaches have considerable validity, but fail in certain limited respects—the uncertainties about schedules of reinforcement and about the handling of internal states, as well as regarding the position of punishment in the theories. Thus, both receive a rating of 4 stars on validity. As to usefulness, OB Mod is clearly the more precise in its delineation of the processes involved and in reporting on studies that show the effectiveness of these processes. Hamner provides little evidence of the actual effectiveness in practice of the steps he recommends, although he does draw on related research conducted by others; thus the award of 3 stars, in contrast with OB Mod's 4, seems warranted.

REFERENCES

Adam, Everett E., and Scott, William E. (1971). The Application of Behavioral Conditioning Procedures to the Problems of Quality Control. *Academy of Management Journal*, 14, 175–93.

Aldis, Owen (1961). Of Pigeons and Men. *Harvard Business Review*, 39(4), 59–63.

Bandura, Albert (1971). *Psychological Modeling: Conflicting Theories.* Chicago, IL: Aldine-Atherton.

——— (1977). *Social Learning Theory.* Englewood Cliffs, NJ: Prentice-Hall.

——— (1997). *Self-Efficacy: The Exercise of Control.* New York: W. H. Freeman.

——— (2001). Social Cognitive Theory: An Agentic Perspective. *Annual Review of Psychology*, 52, 1–26.

Davis, Tim R.V., and Luthans, Fred (1980). A Social Learning Approach to Organizational Behavior. *Academy of Management Review*, 5, 281–90.

Frayne, Colette A. (1991). *Reducing Absenteeism Through Self-Management Training: A Research-Based Analysis and Guide.* Westport, CT: Quorum.

Frayne, Colette A., and Geringer, J. Michael (2000). Self-Management Training for Improving Job Performance: A Field Experiment Involving Salespeople. *Journal of Applied Psychology*, 85, 361–72.

Goldstein, Arnold P., and Sorcher, Melvin (1974). *Changing Supervisor Behavior.* New York: Pergamon.

Hamner, W. Clay (1974a). Reinforcement Theory and Contingency Management in Organizational Settings. In Henry L. Tosi and W. Clay Hamner (Eds.), *Organizational Behavior and Management: A Contingency Approach.* Chicago, IL: St. Clair Press, 86–112.

——— (1974b). Worker Motivation Programs: Importance of Climate, Structure, and Performance Consequences. In W. Clay Hamner and Frank L. Schmidt (Eds.), *Contemporary Problems in Personnel: Readings for the Seventies.* Chicago, IL: St. Clair Press, 280–308.

Hamner, W. Clay, and Hamner, Ellen P. (1976). Behavior Modification on the Bottom Line. *Organizational Dynamics*, 4(4), 3–21.

Komaki, Judith L., Coombs, Timothy, Redding, Thomas P., and Schepman, Stephen (2000). A Rich and Rigorous Examination of Applied Behavior Analysis Research in the World of Work. *International Review of Industrial and Organizational Psychology*, 15, 265–367.

Komaki, Judith L., Coombs, Timothy, and Schepman, Stephen (1996). Motivational Implications of Reinforcement Theory. In Richard M. Steers, Lyman W. Porter, and Gregory A. Bigley (Eds.), *Motivation and Leadership at Work.* New York: McGraw-Hill, 34–52.

Komaki, Judith L., and Minnich, Michelle R. (2002). Crosscurrents at Sea: The Ebb and Flow of Leaders in

Response to the Shifting Demands of Racing Sailboats. *Group and Organization Management*, 27, 113–41.

Korman, Abraham K., Greenhaus, Jeffrey H., and Badin, Irwin J. (1977). Personnel Attitudes and Motivation. *Annual Review of Psychology*, 28, 175–96.

Kreitner, Robert, and Luthans, Fred (1984). A Social Learning Approach to Behavioral Management: Radical Behaviorists "Mellowing Out." *Organizational Dynamics*, 13(2), 47–65.

Lattal, Kennon A. (1992). B.F. Skinner and Psychology. *American Psychologist*, 47, 1269–72.

Locke, Edwin A. (1980). Latham versus Komaki: A Tale of Two Paradigms. *Journal of Applied Psychology*, 65, 16–23.

Luthans, Fred (1973). *Organizational Behavior.* New York: McGraw-Hill.

——— (1996). A Common Man Travels "Back to the Future." In Arthur G. Bedeian (Ed.), *Management Laureates: A Collection of Autobiographical Essays*, Vol. 4. Greenwich, CT: JAI Press, 153–199.

——— (2002). Positive Organizational Behavior: Developing and Managing Psychological Strengths. *Academy of Management Executive*, 16, 57–72.

Luthans, Fred, and Avolio, Bruce (2003). Authentic Leadership Development. In Kim S. Cameron, Jane E. Dutton, and Robert E. Quinn (Eds.), *Positive Organizational Scholarship: Foundations of a New Discipline.* San Francisco, CA: Berrett-Koehler, 241–61.

Luthans, Fred, and Davis, Tim R.V. (1982). An Idiographic Approach to Organizational Behavior Research: The Use of Single Case Experimental Designs and Direct Measures. *Academy of Management Review*, 7, 380–91.

Luthans, Fred, and Kreitner, Robert (1973). The Role of Punishment in Organizational Behavior Modification (O.B. Mod.). *Public Personnel Management*, 2(3), 156–61.

——— (1975). *Organizational Behavior Modification.* Glenview, IL: Scott, Foresman.

——— (1985). *Organizational Behavior Modification and Beyond: An Operant and Social Learning Approach.* Glenview, IL: Scott, Foresman.

Luthans, Fred, Luthans, Kyle W., Hodgetts, Richard M., and Luthans, Brett C. (2000). Can High Performance Work Practices Help in the Former Soviet Union? *Business Horizons*, 43(5), 53–60.

Luthans, Fred, Maciag, Walter S., and Rosenkrantz, Stuart A. (1983). O.B. Mod.: Meeting the Productivity Challenge with Human Resources Management. *Personnel*, 60(2), 28–36.

Luthans, Fred, and Martinko, Mark (1987). Behavioral Approaches to Organizations. *International Review of Industrial and Organizational Psychology*, 2, 35–60.

Luthans, Fred, and Otteman, Robert (1973). Motivation vs. Learning Approaches to Organizational Behavior. *Business Horizons*, 16(6), 55–62.

Luthans, Fred, Paul, Robert, and Baker, Douglas (1981). An Experimental Analysis of the Impact of Contingent Reinforcement on Salespersons' Performance Behavior. *Journal of Applied Psychology*, 66, 314–23.

Luthans, Fred, and Stajkovic, Alexander D. (2000). Provide Recognition for Performance Improvement. In Edwin A. Locke (Ed.), *Handbook of Principles of Organizational Behavior.* Oxford, UK: Blackwell, 166–80.

Luthans, Fred, and White, Donald D. (1971). Behavior Modification: Application to Manpower Management. *Personnel Administration*, 34(4), 41–47.

Millman, Zeeva, and Latham, Gary (2001). Increasing Reemployment through Training in Verbal Self-Guidance. In Miriam Erez, Uwe Kleinbeck, and Henk Thierry (Eds.), *Work Motivation in the Context of a Globalizing Economy.* Mahway, NJ: Lawrence Erlbaum, 87–97.

Mitchell, Terence R. (1997). Matching Motivational Strategies with Organizational Contexts. *Research in Organizational Behavior*, 19, 57–149.

Nord, Walter R. (1969). Beyond the Teaching Machine: The Neglected Area of Operant Conditioning in the Theory and Practice of Management. *Organizational Behavior and Human Performance*, 4, 375–401.

O'Brien, Richard M., Dickinson, Alyce M., and Rosow, Michael P. (1982). *Industrial Behavior Modification: A Management Handbook.* New York: Pergamon.

Skinner, B.F. (1953). *Science and Human Behavior.* New York: Macmillan.

——— (1971). *Beyond Freedom and Dignity.* New York: Knopf.

——— (1975). The Steep and Thorny Way to a Science of Behavior. *American Psychologist*, 30, 42–49.

Skinner, B.F., and Dowling, William F. (1973). Conversation with B.F. Skinner. *Organizational Dynamics*, 1(3), 31–40.

Sorcher, Melvin (1971). A Behavior Modification Approach to Supervisory Training. *Professional Psychology*, 2, 401–2.

Stajkovic, Alexander D., and Luthans, Fred (1997). A Meta-Analysis of the Effects of Organizational Behavior Modification on Task Performance, 1975–95. *Academy of Management Journal*, 40, 1122–49.

——— (1998). Social Cognitive Theory and Self-Efficacy: Going Beyond Traditional Motivational and Behavioral Approaches. *Organizational Dynamics*, 26(4), 62–74.

——— (2001). Differential Effects of Incentive Motivators on Work Performance. *Academy of Management Journal*, 44, 580–90.

Thompson, Kenneth R., and Luthans, Fred (1983). A Behavioral Interpretation of Power. In Robert W. Allen and Lyman W. Porter (Eds.), *Organizational Influence Processes*. Glenview, IL: Scott, Foresman, 72–86.

Welsh, Dianne H.B., Luthans, Fred, and Sommer, Steven M. (1993). Managing Russian Factory Workers: The Impact of U.S.-Based Behavioral and Participative Techniques. *Academy of Management Journal*, 36, 58–79.

Williams, Scott (1997). Personality and Self-Leadership. *Human Resource Management Review*, 7, 139–55.

CHAPTER 9

EQUITY THEORY

J. STACY ADAMS

Background
Statement of the Theory
    Antecedents of Inequity
    Definition of Inequity
    Reactions to Inequity
    Choices Among Reactions to Inequity
    Extensions and Restatements
Basic Research on Pay
    Experiment I
    Experiment II
    Experiment III
    Experiment IV
    Experiment V
Evaluation and Impact
    Research on Overreward
    Underreward Research
    Referent Selection
    Situational and Individual Differences
    Equity and Expectancy
    Equity Theory in Practice
Expanding into Organizational Justice
    Types of Organizational Justice
    Research Findings
    Applications
Conclusions

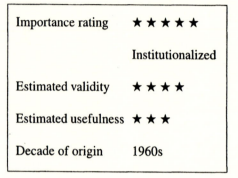

Importance rating	★ ★ ★ ★ ★
	Institutionalized
Estimated validity	★ ★ ★ ★
Estimated usefulness	★ ★ ★
Decade of origin	1960s

J. Stacy Adams, who introduced equity theory to organizational behavior, has indicated a wide range of influences on his thinking, including a number of social psychologists, industrial social psychologists, and sociologists. However, his equity theory per se, as distinct from his work in other areas, appears to have been influenced largely by two individuals whose contributions were proximate in time to those of Adams (1963a). Foremost among these was the social psychologist Leon Festinger (1957), who served on the psychology faculties of several universities including in this period Stanford University, where Adams was also employed. Festinger's cognitive dissonance theory had a strong impact. So, too, did other proponents of social exchange theories, including primarily the sociologist George Homans (1961), who set forth his ideas on distributive justice during a long career at Harvard.

Feelings of unfairness were the most frequently reported source of job dissatisfaction in the original Herzberg research (see Chapter 5). Although motivation-hygiene theory gave relatively little attention to this finding, other theories have made this desire or need for fairness, justice, or equity their focus.

Theories of this kind have been articulated by a number of individuals in a variety of forms. Basically, they are concerned with exchange relationships among individuals and groups, and the motivating effects of a perceived imbalance in the exchange. Applications of this type of theory were extended beyond the organizational relationships that are of primary interest here to other areas, notably exploitative relationships, helping relationships, and intimate relationships (Walster, Berscheid, and Walster 1973).

The theory developed by Adams (1963a, 1965) appears to be not only the most relevant for an understanding of employee motivation, but also the most fully articulated. It has been the source of a sizable body of research designed to test its various propositions and has been given considerable attention by wage and salary administrators.

BACKGROUND

Adams was born in 1925; he received all his degrees in psychology—at the undergraduate level from the University of Mississippi and as a graduate student from the University of North Carolina. After receiving his doctorate in 1957, he went to the psychology department at Stanford for three years and then served as a research psychologist with the General Electric Company in Crotonville, New York. This was as part of an effort to establish a basic social science program within the company, modeled on a small scale after the Bell Labs organization in the physical sciences. The Crotonville program did not last beyond the 1960s, but while there, Adams developed his theory and carried out the initial test studies.

After General Electric, Adams returned to the University of North Carolina, this time with an appointment in the business school, where he remained for the rest of his life. There he continued to publish on equity theory, but a long-standing interest in boundary spanning roles in organizations (Adams 1976) absorbed much of his attention in the 1970s and 1980s. At the time of his death in 1984, he had largely turned to more macro issues far removed from motivation.

STATEMENT OF THE THEORY

Although the term *equity* is usually used to describe the theory, it is at least as appropriate to describe it as *inequity* theory. The major motivating force considered is a striving for equity, but some degree of inequity must be perceived before this force can be mobilized.

Antecedents of Inequity

The theory starts with an exchange whereby the individual gives something and gets something in return. What the individual gives may be viewed as inputs to, or investments in, the relationship; examples are noted in Table 9.1. For such inputs to function, they must be recognized as existing by the individual and must be considered relevant to the relationship. They may or may not be recognized and perceived as relevant by the other party, for instance an employer. If they are not, a potential for inequity exists.

On the other side of the exchange are various things the individual may receive, the outcomes

Table 9.1

Possible Inputs to and Outcomes from an Employment Exchange
(noted by Adams in various writings)

Inputs	Outcomes
Education	Pay
Intelligence	Intrinsic rewards
Experience	Satisfying supervision
Training	Seniority benefits
Skill	Fringe benefits
Seniority	Job status
Age	Status symbols
Sex	Job perquisites
Ethnic background	Poor working conditions
Social status	Monotony
Job effort	Fate uncertainty
Personal appearance	Herzberg's dissatisfiers
Health	
Possession of tools	
Spouse's characteristics	

of the exchange relationship. As with inputs, these must be recognized by the individual who receives them and considered relevant to the exchange if they are to function effectively. Shared concepts of what are fair relationships between these outcomes and various inputs are learned as part of the overall socialization process.

The third type of theoretical variable, in addition to inputs provided and outcomes received, is the reference person or group used in evaluating the equity of one's own exchange relationship. This reference source may be a coworker, relative, neighbor, group of coworkers, craft group, industry pattern, profession, and so on. It may even be the focal person involved in another job or another social role. For an individual or group to operate in this capacity there must be one or more attributes that are comparable to those of the comparer. The theory is not more precise in specifying how the appropriate reference source may be identified, although it is assumed that coworkers are commonly used.

Definition of Inequity

Inequity is said to exist when the ratio of an individual's outcomes to inputs departs to a significant degree from the ratio perceived for the reference source. Thus, people may feel that they are underrewarded in terms of what they put into a job in comparison with what other workers are getting for their contributions. This might happen when people consider themselves much harder workers than other employees, but are paid the same as everyone else.

The theory is not limited to inequities that are unfavorable to the individual. Equity, balance, or reciprocity exists when outcome–input ratios for the individual and the reference source are equal, and the motivating force of inequity can arise when there is a departure either way from this steady state. Accordingly, people might consider themselves overrewarded, given their inputs, in comparison with others. This could be so should people perceive themselves as working as hard as their coworkers but, for reasons they consider irrelevant, were in fact being paid much more.

Table 9.2

The Amount of Inequity Experienced Under Various Input and Outcome Conditions

Perception of oneself	Perception of the reference source			
	Inputs low— outcomes high	Inputs high— outcomes low	Inputs low— outcomes low	Inputs high— outcomes high
Inputs low— outcomes high	No inequity	Much inequity	Some inequity	Some inequity
Inputs high— outcomes low	Much inequity	No inequity	Some inequity	Some inequity
Inputs low— outcomes low	Some inequity	Some inequity	No inequity	No inequity
Inputs high— outcomes high	Some inequity	Some inequity	No inequity	No inequity

Because most exchanges involve multiple inputs and outcomes, these must be summed across all factors perceived to be relevant to arrive at operative ratios. The various components of those outcome and input totals also may not have the same utilities or valence for the person; in the mind of a given individual, education may predominate among the inputs noted in Table 9.1, and pay may predominate among the outcomes. In such a case education and pay would be given disproportionate weight in their respective totals. Finally, "the thresholds for equity are different (in absolute terms from a base of equity) in cases of under- and overreward. The threshold presumably would be higher in cases of overreward, for a certain amount of incongruity in these cases can be acceptably rationalized as 'good fortune' without attendant discomfort" (Adams 1965, 282). Thus, the motivational effects of a favorable inequity may remain immobilized at a degree of disparity that would be motivating if the disparity were unfavorable.

This is an important consideration when testing the theory; overrewards must be sizable in order to have an effect.

The schema in Table 9.2 indicating the relative amount of inequity experienced by an individual under varying conditions of total inputs and outcomes may prove helpful in understanding the definition of inequity.

Reactions to Inequity

Inequity, when perceived, results in dissatisfaction either in the form of anger (underreward) or guilt (overreward). A tension is created in proportion to the amount of inequity. This tension, in turn, serves as a motivating force to reduce the inequity and move it to zero. A number of methods for reducing inequity tension are posited.

Altering inputs involves changing inputs either upward or downward to what might be an appropriately equitable level. In the employment context this means altering either the quantity or quality of work to align them with reference source ratios. Certain inputs such as age cannot be modified in this manner, while others such as effort expansion or restriction can be.

Input alteration is likely to occur when there is a variation from the perceived inputs of the reference source, as opposed to discrepancies in outcomes. Lowering inputs can also be anticipated when the inequity is unfavorable to oneself; when the inequity is favorable, the inputs are likely to be increased. Restrictive production practices, as elaborated by the early human relations writers, then become a means of reducing inequity.

Another approach to reducing felt inequity is to attempt to shift outcomes. Increasing outcomes, if achieved, will serve to reduce unfavorable inequities. Theoretically, attempts to decrease outcomes would be expected in cases involving favorable inequities. Charitable contributions often reflect this type of motivation, which, however, does not appear to be very common. The predominant mode in this instance appears to be the use of increased outcomes to reduce unfavorable inequity, as when union or other types of pressure are brought to bear to shift outcomes into balance with expectations.

As opposed to actually altering inputs and outcomes, a person may cognitively distort them to achieve the same results. To the degree that reality is important to an individual, distortions of this kind become difficult. Thus, the absolute level of one's education as an input, or the amount of one's pay as an outcome, may be hard to distort perceptually. Yet even in these cases distortion can occur, though less objective inputs and outcomes are much more easily perverted. Furthermore, shifts in the relative weighting of inputs and outcomes can be used to achieve the same result, as when the value of one's education is exaggerated or the personal utility of pay is misrepresented.

Leaving the field represents a way of dealing with inequity by reducing or entirely eliminating it through minimizing exposure to the inequity-producing context. This can occur through transfer, absenteeism, or even separation. Such responses are assumed to be relatively extreme and to occur only when the magnitude of inequity is sizable, or when the individual cannot deal with the inequity easily and flexibly.

Distortion may be applied not only to one's own inputs and outcomes but also to those attributed to a reference individual or group. Similarly, attempts may be made to eliminate a reference source from one's environment, as when a coworker who has been used as a reference person is harassed out of a job. Or the actual inputs or outcomes of the reference source may be altered, as when "rate busters" are induced to lower their efforts and productivity in response to strong individual and group pressure. Attempts to influence a reference source along these lines will vary considerably in their feasibility, but all are theoretically appropriate methods of reducing inequity.

It is also possible to shift to a new reference source to reduce inequity. Thus, a person who previously compared himself or herself to other similar professionals nationally may change from this cosmopolitan comparison to a local comparison utilizing only professionals within the company. This strategy may be least viable when a prior reference source has been used for a considerable time.

Choices Among Reactions to Inequity

The theory is not as explicit as it might be about the circumstances under which the different reactions to inequity will emerge. However, Adams (1965) is well aware of the need for theoretical statements of this kind. He offers the following propositions:

1. Generally, an individual will attempt to maximize highly valued outcomes and the overall value of outcomes.
2. Inputs that are effortful and costly to change can be expected to increase only minimally.
3. Real and cognitively distorted changes in inputs that are central to one's self-concept and self-esteem will tend to be resisted. The same applies to the outcomes for a person when they have high relevance for the self.

4. The inputs and outcomes attributed to a reference source are much more easily distorted than those attributed to oneself.
5. Leaving the field will be utilized only when the inequity is sizable and other means of reducing it are unfavorable. Partial withdrawals such as absenteeism will occur at lower inequity levels than full withdrawals such as separation.
6. Changing the object of comparison, or reference source, will be strongly resisted once such a comparison has been stabilized over time.

Adams (1968a) also indicates that when the inequity tension is sizable, the probability increases that more than one method of reducing that tension will be utilized. However, individuals tend to differ in tolerances for tension. A person with a high tolerance level might not yet resort to multiple modes of inequity reduction at a point where a person with a low tolerance level would long before have mobilized more than one reaction. Adams notes further that these extensions to the theory remain speculative as long as direct measures of inequity thresholds, tolerance for inequity tension, and the tension itself are not available.

Extensions and Restatements

The nature and rationale of equity theory are expanded upon in a series of four propositions set forth by Walster, Berscheid, and Walster (1973). Because these propositions subsequently have been endorsed by Adams (Adams and Freedman 1976), it seems appropriate to consider them part of the theory.

Proposition I. Individuals will try to maximize their outcomes (where outcomes equal rewards minus costs). The term *reward* refers to positive outcomes, and the term *cost* refers to negative outcomes.

Proposition IIA. Groups can maximize collective reward by evolving accepted systems for "equitably" apportioning rewards and costs among members. Thus, members will evolve such systems of equity and will attempt to induce members to accept and adhere to these systems.

Proposition IIB. Groups will generally reward members who treat others equitably and generally punish (increase the costs for) members who treat others inequitably.

Proposition III. When individuals find themselves participating in inequitable relationships, they become distressed (the more inequitable the relationship, the more distress). Anger and guilt are two of the major forms of distress.

Proposition IV. Individuals who discover that they are in an inequitable relationship attempt to eliminate distress by restoring equity. The greater the inequity, the more distress, and the harder they try to restore equity. There are two ways equity may be restored. People can restore actual equity by appropriately altering their own outcomes or inputs or the outcomes or inputs of others. People can restore psychological equity by appropriately distorting the perceptions of their own or others' outcomes or inputs.

BASIC RESEARCH ON PAY

Studies conducted by and in association with Adams in the early 1960s have had a major influence on subsequent research intended to test his theory. Although the theory is not restricted to matters of compensation, this early research did tend to establish such a focus. Furthermore, the type of experimental design utilized by the theory's author has had a strong influence on the designs used in subsequent investigations. There were five basic studies that tested the theory in the early period, and Adams did not publish any additional research in this area subsequently.

All five studies deal with the most controversial aspect of the theory, the predicted effects of overreward inequity.

Experiment I

Adams and Rosenbaum (1962) reported a study conducted at New York University in which students referred by the university placement office were hired to conduct market research interviews. The advertised rate for the work was $3.50 per hour, and the initial implication was that the work would continue for several months.

The twenty-two students hired were split into two equal groups, and all were actually paid at the $3.50 per hour figure. At the time of hiring, the experimental subjects were exposed to treatment intended to make them feel inequitably overcompensated for their work. They were told, "You don't have nearly enough experience in interviewing or survey work of the kind we're engaged in," but nevertheless, after some agonizing, they were hired. In contrast, the control subjects were led to believe that their inputs were entirely appropriate to the pay and that they met all the qualifications. Thus, a condition of equity was established vis-à-vis "interviewers in general" as a reference source.

The interviewing job was terminated after roughly 2.5 hours. Productivity in the experimental group, where presumably guilt had been induced, was significantly higher than that in the controls. This is what the theory predicts—in order to justify their inequitably high outcomes (pay), the experimental subjects should exert more effort to compensate for their lack of experience as an input, thus conducting more interviews in the allotted time.

Experiment II

A subsequent study conducted by Arrowood and reported by Adams (1963a) was designed to deal with a possible confounding effect in Experiment I. It is possible that the experimental subjects worked harder, not to correct an inequity, but to protect their jobs. The talk about their lack of qualifications may have made them feel insecure, with the result that they worked very hard to convince the experimenter to retain them.

To test this hypothesis, a study was conducted in Minneapolis using much the same approach as that used in Experiment I, except that half of the subjects mailed their completed work in a pre-addressed envelope to New York rather than merely turning it over to the experimenter. It was made clear that under these circumstances the experimenter never would know how many interviews had been produced; accordingly, he would be in no position to fire anyone, and there would be no need to feel insecure.

Under the insecurity hypothesis, eliminating job insecurity should eliminate the difference between the experimental (inequity) and control (equity) groups. It did not. The tendency for experimental subjects to conduct more interviews than controls remained regardless of whether the completed forms were returned to New York. Thus, the results of Experiment I do not appear to be attributable to insecurity; they are more likely to have been caused by attempts to reduce inequity tension.

Experiment III

Whereas the preceding studies utilized an hourly compensation rate, another investigation explored the effects of paying on a piece rate basis (Adams and Rosenbaum 1962). In most respects the procedure was the same as that in Experiment I. However, four groups were used, each containing nine subjects:

Group 1. Overreward inequity; paid $3.50 per hour.
Group 2. Equity; paid $3.50 per hour.
Group 3. Overreward inequity; paid 30 cents per interview.
Group 4. Equity; paid 30 cents per interview.

The use of piece rate payments adds a complicating factor in that exerting more effort to resolve the inequity will not solve the problem. Inputs do increase, but so do outcomes; thus the inequity remains and is exacerbated. As expected, the introduction of piece rate payment did have a markedly dampening effect on the tendency to produce more to eliminate inequity. In fact, the overrewarded piece rate workers completed the fewest interviews of any group; increasing their outcomes was apparently the last thing they wanted to do.

Experiment IV

The results of Experiment III tell much more about how people do not reduce inequity tension than about how they do. One hypothesis is that under this kind of inequity condition, effort is increased but is put into improved quality of work that will not increase outcomes rather than into improved quantity that under piece rate payment will increase outcomes. Experiment IV attempts to test this hypothesis (Adams 1963b). In this case, procedures were introduced to permit measurement of interview quality, something that was not possible in Experiment III.

To do this, interviewers were encouraged to obtain as much information as possible from respondents in reply to several open-ended questions. Because lengthy responses (quality) inevitably limited the number of interviews obtained (quantity), following the directive to obtain more information should be an attractive approach to restoring equity. The results were indeed in accord with this expectation. Subjects in the overrewarded inequity condition obtained longer interviews on average than those working under equitable payment, and they also completed fewer interviews.

Experiment V

The final study (Adams and Jacobsen 1964) was conducted to provide a further check on the insecurity hypothesis considered in Experiment II. Sixty students from Columbia University who answered an advertisement for part-time summer work were hired to perform a proofreading task. Quantity of work was determined by the number of pages proofed; and quality, by the number of errors detected. Three different conditions related to equity were introduced:

1. Inequity was produced by such statements as, "you don't have nearly enough experience" and "your score on the proofreading test isn't really satisfactory," but payment was given at the full 30-cent-per-page rate initially quoted.
2. The same reduction of inputs noted above was combined with a compensating reduction of outcomes—"I can't pay you at the regular rate of 30 cents per page. I can pay you only 20 cents per page because your qualifications aren't sufficient."
3. Full equity was produced at the 30 cents per page figure—"You're just what we're looking for. You meet all the qualifications."

Within each of these three conditions, two alternatives related to prospects for continued employment were introduced as follows:

Table 9.3

Errors Detected per Page and Number of Pages Proofed Under Varying Conditions of Equity

Conditions	Quality (errors detected)	Quantity (pages proofed)
1A. Inequity and insecure	7.9	8.7
1B. Inequity and secure	8.0	7.7
2A. Equity (at low pay) and insecure	4.7	11.3
2B. Equity (at low pay) and secure	4.9	11.8
3A. Equity and perhaps insecure	4.9	11.7
3B. Equity and secure	4.0	12.8

Source: Adapted from Adams and Jacobsen (1964, 22–23).

    a) "The book is only one of a series. . . . There is a lot of work ahead. . . . You may be able to help us in the future."

    b) "Usually it isn't necessary to hire someone to proofread for us, but . . . we've got to get this particular book out . . . the job will take a short time only."

Thus, there were six different conditions with ten people in each. Equity theory predicts better quality work and lower quantity for both conditions 1a and 1b. The insecurity hypothesis predicts that conditions 1a and 2b, where there was a job to be lost and every reason to believe it might be lost, would produce the high quality, lower productivity response.

After one hour of work the study was terminated, and the results reported in Table 9.3 were obtained. Questions asked of the subjects at that point indicated that the desired perceptions regarding qualifications, pay levels, and opportunity for continued employment had in fact been induced by the various treatments. The data are fully in line with equity theory predictions; they do not support the insecurity hypothesis.

However, Adams (1968a) notes that under the inequity conditions there were a few subjects who produced large quantities of relatively low-quality work. These individuals were found to be economically deprived, needing the money badly. As a result, they maximized their outcomes even though they were aware of the inequity. Adams interprets these data as indicating that for some people economic motivation may be dominant over equity motivation. It is apparent that equity theory is not an all-encompassing motivational theory but rather deals with one particular type of motivation that has major implications for behavior in the workplace. In this connection, Adams and Jacobsen (1964, 24) note:

> [O]verpayment by an employer need not necessarily increase his labor costs, provided he is primarily interested in quality, as opposed to production volume. If on the other hand the employer's objective is production volume, piecework overpayment may be very costly, especially for such work as inspection, quality control, finishing and other jobs that inherently permit considerable latitude in work quality.

EVALUATION AND IMPACT

A comprehensive review of the equity theory research indicates considerable support for the theory. This is not only my opinion, but the view of other scholars of the field as well (Greenberg

1990; Mowday 1996). In recent years the work on equity theory, which deals with what is called distributive justice (the fairness of outcome distributions), has been joined by a sizable outburst of research activity in the area of procedural justice, where the major concern is with the fairness of policies and procedures used to make decisions. This has led some to describe distributive justice research as on the decline. Yet research on equity theory in many of its aspects continues to be robust; activity dealing with *both* distributive and procedural issues is currently quite strong, and the distinction between the two is well established (Konovsky 2000).

Research on Overreward

By no means has all of the research dealing with the effects of overreward inequity produced the same type of favorable results that Adams obtained originally. However, the theory itself posits a high threshold for overreward inequity, and there are data to support this. Thus, there is always the possibility (in a given study) that overreward thresholds were not consistently breached. Furthermore, a treatment or experimental manipulation might not be perceived as producing inequity at all, even though the researcher believed it should. Such could be the case, for instance, if what was thought to be an input manipulation (say, changing the degree of job involvement) turned out to be an outcome manipulation (job involvement is considered a desirable opportunity for self-expression) for a sizable number of subjects. This kind of interchangeability among individual inputs and outcomes of the type noted in Table 9.1 has been clearly established. Given the variety of possible mitigating circumstances, it is important to consider the overall weight of the evidence in evaluating the theory rather than relying on any individual study.

When this is done, there turns out to be considerable support for the overreward inequity proposition. In cases where the motivational effects of overreward inequity are not demonstrated, strong feelings of inequity often appear not to have been mobilized.

Questions have been raised in some of the reviews as to whether it was inequity motivation that was aroused in the overreward studies; other motives have been suggested. There has been considerable wrestling with the issue over the years, and a number of studies have been conducted in an attempt to settle it. Adams (1968b) was quite critical of the approaches taken in some of this research. The upshot now appears to be that overreward inequity can be and has been aroused in many studies (Greenberg 1990).

Another set of questions regarding overreward inequity has revolved around the time dimension. Given that the research has demonstrated the effects predicted by equity theory, it is still posited that these effects are transitory and have no real meaning in understanding ongoing motivation in organizations (Lawler 1968).

Without question, much overreward research has been of short duration (under a week), and there is a distinct need for longitudinal studies. The possibility that in actual on-the-job practice overpayment only costs more and does not yield better performance is real. Initial improvements in performance may give way to cognitive adjustments that rationalize the overpayment into acceptability. Alternatively, the revised inputs provided by an employee may be in the form of good working relationships, friendliness, exemplary citizenship behavior, commitments to long-term employment, and the like (rather than direct performance-related effort), thus justifying the high pay on this basis. This appears to be a very likely reaction, and changes of this nature could be important enough to a company to warrant the overpayment. The problem is that for lack of appropriate research and precise theory, we have no idea exactly what happens under circumstances of long-term overreward; performance effects can hold up as long as a week or so, however.

Evidence also exists that some people are more sensitive to overreward inequity effects than others (Vecchio 1981). Those who are more morally mature and principled (with a greater propensity for experiencing guilt) are the ones who are particularly responsive to overpayment. The less morally mature do not exhibit the inequity reaction to nearly the same extent. This type of research begins to get directly at the underlying constructs of guilt and anger that account for equity tension; more such studies are needed.

Underreward Research

Although Adams did not create an underreward condition in his studies, other researchers have since conducted similar experiments that have extended the analysis to this condition. In addition to such pay–performance studies, there have been other research efforts relating underreward to such inequity reduction strategies as absenteeism and job separation.

With piece rate pay conditions, underrewarded individuals would be expected to increase the quantity of work in order to move total outcomes upward. At the same time, however, equity can only be achieved if inputs are not raised commensurate to the increase in outcomes. The most likely strategy for holding inputs down is to decrease the effort put into quality. The research data are entirely consistent with these expectations.

On an hourly pay schedule, underreward would be expected to result in less effort devoted to the work. Primarily this reduced input should yield a reduced quantity of work. On certain tasks, however, when quality is a major consideration, the reduced effort may well cause poorer quality work.

In general, the available research tends to support these equity theory predictions for the pay underreward condition. Reviewers have consistently indicated that this conclusion is well justified based on the research findings.

Another more extreme way of dealing with underreward inequity noted by Adams is to leave the field. This response could theoretically occur under any inequity condition, but given the differential thresholds involved, it might be expected to appear more widely in the underreward context. There, a common response is to achieve balance by increasing absenteeism. However, the turnover response represented by leaving the field is often in evidence as well (Summers and Hendrix 1991). Organizations with undesirably high turnover would do well to look into perceptions of pay equity and into the equitability of other aspects of the reward system. Thus, it appears that underreward inequity produces dissatisfaction, which, in turn, produces a number of possible consequences in addition to diminished performance (Bartol and Durham 2000).

Interestingly, and adding credence to the laboratory research, findings comparable to those obtained in the field have been obtained in simulated work studies dealing with pay and performance. It is not uncommon for some subjects in these studies to refuse further participation when faced with underreward inequity. Furthermore, if sizable inequities are made obvious and compelling through continued exposure to reference individuals known to be receiving greater compensation for the same work, expressions of anger and highly disruptive behavior may well occur. When these more extreme methods of responding to perceived inequity are mobilized, they appear to supersede any performance effects.

Another line of research has tested the proposition that an individual will allocate rewards (outcomes) in a manner proportional to the inputs of the various parties. Designs call for some demonstration of actual inputs, usually for two people, and then as a dependent variable, an allocation decision in accordance with perceptions of appropriate reward. The person making the allocation may be a third party or a person who has actually contributed inputs. The test of equity theory comes when the subject is given a chance to reallocate rewards. If an inequity has been created, will the subjects now act to restore equity? The answer appears to be that subjects will. Research of this kind has yielded strong support for equity theory for some time (Leventhal, Weiss, and Long 1969).

This raises a question as to how responsive people are to reports of injustice experienced by others vis-à-vis their own personal experiences in this regard. Clearly, people do take into account the experiences of others, but it takes a great deal of the reported injustice of others to equal even a little personally experienced injustice (Lind, Kray, and Thompson 1998).

A very important application of equity theory in instances of underreward has emerged as a result of a research program initiated by Jerald Greenberg starting in the late 1980s (Giacalone and Greenberg 1997). This research is important because the problem of theft by employees is widespread and represents a major cost to many businesses (Miner and Capps 1996). For small firms it often results in business failure. In many such instances theft of one kind or another turns out to be motivated by a desire to redress perceived grievances.

In equity theory terms, what the research shows is that theft represents an attempt to increase income to a point where an equitable balance is achieved relative to perceived input. Employees steal to pay themselves what they think is justly theirs for what they put into their work; thus, underreward tension is reduced and a source of dissatisfaction is alleviated. The greater the pre-existing inequity tension, the more the stealing. However, the research also indicates that to the extent adequate explanations are provided for the inequity state, reflecting a degree of compassion and social sensitivity in dealing with the issue, theft tends to be less in evidence. Thus a procedural justice factor is added to the purely distributive. Also, high-status job titles and office locations can represent increased outcomes in the equity formula, thus reducing inequity tension and any proclivity for theft.

Referent Selection

Certain problems inherent in equity theory have been recognized for some time, going back to Adams and Freedman (1976); yet to a large extent they remain with us today. Mitchell (1997, 91) has this to say on this score:

> [I]t is still difficult to be precise about what constitutes an input and an outcome, or the standard being used for comparison . . . standards and referents change over time and contexts. Kulik and Ambrose (1992) have elaborated on the importance of accurately determining the referent that people use. Also, it is still hard to predict exactly what will change as a result of inequity perceptions. One can change perceptions, comparisons, and actions and any combination of the three as a result of feeling unfairly treated. While theoretical work has helped to grapple with some of these issues . . . they still present problems.

This indictment of the theory on grounds of lack of precision is entirely justified. Adams simply did not know how to be more precise, and for the most part neither has anyone else since. Some of these issues have been considered previously. The matter of referent selection, how people choose among those with whom their own inputs and outcomes may be compared, concerns us here. This is one issue on which some progress has been made.

Research indicates that people do make a wide range of comparisons, extending from self-evaluations, to others in the company, to those in the same job outside, to those of the same educational level or age, to what is expected from the company (Scholl, Cooper, and McKenna 1987). All of these comparisons can contribute to pay dissatisfaction. Turnover, however, is par-

Figure 9.1   **Model of the Psychological Processes Involved in Referent Selection**

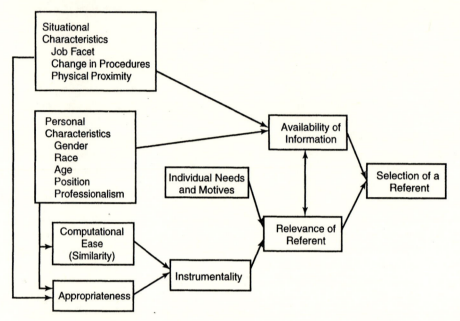

Source: Kulik and Ambrose (1992, 216). Copyright © 1992 Academy of Management. Reprinted with permission.

ticularly tied to perceived inequity in relation to external comparisons—people in the same job in other organizations and having similar education—as well as to self-evaluations. Investing extra effort in the job declines in the face of perceived inequity relative to others in the same job within the company. Thus, the nature of the comparisons made does have some differential impact; it matters which ones are chosen. A study conducted in Australia indicated that the market external to the organization when used as a referent, served as a particularly important source of dissatis-faction (Brown 2001).

Another approach seeks to specify which referent choices will in fact be made. The model given in Figure 9.1 is suggested for this purpose; it is theoretical in nature but induced from available research. This research indicates that most employees use one or two referent types, and that choices tend to be fairly stable over time (Kulik and Ambrose 1992). The key intervening constructs for choice are the availability of information regarding a referent and the relevance or acceptability of the referent for the person. In the latter instance similarity is a major consideration.

Propositions regarding the ways in which the variables of the model operate are set forth as follows:

1.   Individuals in integrated fields will make more cross-sex comparisons than those in sex-segregated fields.
2.   Individuals in desegregated conditions will make more cross-race comparisons than those in segregated conditions.
3.   Individuals under the age of sixty-five will make more other comparisons than individuals over the age of sixty-five.
4.   Individuals with longer tenure will make more other-external comparisons than individuals with less tenure.

5. Upper-level individuals will make more other-external comparisons than lower level individuals.
6. Professionals will make more other-external comparisons than nonprofessionals.
7. Individuals comparing extrinsic facets will make more other-comparisons than individuals comparing intrinsic facets.
8. Individuals experiencing a procedural change will choose more self-past referents than individuals who do not experience a procedural change.
9. Individuals who are physically proximate to other-internal referents will make more comparisons to these referents than to individuals who are not physically proximate.

The authors also note that although similar referents are likely to be most relevant in the sense that they provide directly interpretable comparison data, dissimilar referents can well be preferred when the comparer perceives those referents as at least minimally relevant and also has access to information about those referents.

Situational and Individual Differences

One issue that Adams did not envisage is that people from different backgrounds and operating in different contexts may develop different norms with regard to the appropriate distribution of rewards. The equity rule, and equity theory, are most appropriate to work situations where maximizing productivity and pay-for-performance are the norm. Historically this has been the situation in many companies in the United States. Yet cases exist where other distribution rules are supported by existing norms and internalized by organization members. Among these, equality, where outcomes should be distributed equally to all participants with the objective of minimizing conflict, has been considered the most; here the extent of a person's inputs does not matter. Another similar possibility is the use of a need-based distribution rule, with outcomes allocated in terms of a person's perceived need for them; thus a type of social responsibility enters into the allocation process (Mowday 1996). Where either equality or need-based norms dominate, equity theory will be less applicable.

Situations of the kind thus envisaged do exist. Different cultures at different points in time tend to adopt norms of one kind or another, at least with regard to certain aspects of the work process, and some cultures clearly do espouse equality and need-based norms. Chen (1995) has compared China and the United States at different points in time and finds evidence for an equality norm in both cultures. In Israel, need as a justice principle, although not a dominant factor, does serve as a guiding rule in the fairness evaluations of received pay (Dornstein 1989). Other such national cultural variations have been noted. Mannix, Neale, and Northcraft (1995) have shown that variations in organizational cultures with regard to equity, equality, and need-based norms significantly influence which group members are perceived to be more powerful and thus most entitled and what distribution principles do in fact operate to determine resource allocations among members.

The point is that for whatever reasons some people do not behave in accordance with equity norms, and their actions are not predictable from equity theory. Vecchio (1981) found essentially the same thing in his study of the effects of overreward inequity on those who lack moral judgment and have little predisposition to experience guilt. People who gamble frequently are less committed to equity in allocations and appear more prone to accept reward distributions unrelated to norms of equity (Larwood, Kavanagh, and Levine 1978). In these cases there appear to be individuals and groups of individuals who operate outside the boundaries of equity theory's domain.

Other studies identify wide individual and group variations among employees who nevertheless seem to be still operating within the domain of equity theory (e.g., see Dulebohn and Martocchio 1998). These individual differences do pose a major problem for equity theory (Bartol and Locke 2000). Adams clearly recognizes the role of individual differences, but specific propositions about them are lacking in the theory. Individuals differ not only in the utilities or valences they impute to various potential inputs and outcomes, but also in their inequity thresholds, tolerances for inequity tension, and the strength of their equity motivation relative to other types of motivation. It is not possible to predict from the theory who will respond to a particular inequality induction and who will not, although it is apparent that such individual differences exist.

In response to this need for theory and research dealing with individual differences in inequity tension levels, thresholds, and tolerances, the concept of equity sensitivity has been advanced (Huseman, Hatfield, and Miles 1987), and a measure has been developed. This theoretical extension posits three general types of individuals:

- Benevolents—those who prefer their outcome–input ratios to be less than the outcome–input ratios of the comparison other; they are givers, and distress occurs with a departure from this preferred situation (equitable or overreward).
- Equity sensitives—those who, conforming to the traditional norm of equity, prefer their outcome–input ratios to equal those of comparison others; distress occurs with both underreward and overreward.
- Entitleds—those who prefer their outcome–input ratios to exceed the comparison other's; they are getters, and experience distress in the face of equitable or underreward where they are not getting a better deal than others.

These formulations and others are expressed in a set of propositions:

   1A. Benevolents prefer situations of high inputs for self compared to low inputs for self.
   1B. Entitleds prefer situations of high outcomes for self compared to low outcomes for self.
   2A. Benvolents prefer that their own inputs exceed their own outcomes.
   2B. Entitleds prefer that their own outcomes exceed their own inputs.
   2C. Equity sensitives prefer that their own inputs equal their own outcomes.
   3A. Benevolents prefer that their outcome–input ratios be less those of the comparison other.
   3B. Entitleds prefer that their outcome–input ratios exceed those of the comparison other.
   3C. Equity sensitives prefer that their outcome–input ratios be equal to those of the comparison other.
   4. A negative, linear relationship should exist between Benevolents' perceptions of equity and job satisfaction.
   5. An inverted U-shaped relationship should exist between Equity sensitives' perceptions of equity and job satisfaction.
   6. A positive, linear relationship should exist between Entitleds' perception of equity and job satisfaction.

With regard to the question of when factors that are ambiguous on this score will be considered inputs and when they will be considered outcomes:

- Benevolents are more likely to perceive ambiguous elements as outcomes.
- Entitleds are more likely to perceive them as inputs.

Research indicates that even in identical situations individuals do in fact choose different distribution norms and in accordance with the expectations of equity sensitivity theorizing (King and Hinson 1994). Also, comparisons of business students in the United States and the Czech Republic indicate that the likelihood of having an entitled orientation was consistently higher among the European students, the mean difference being on the order of one-half a standard deviation or more (Mueller and Clarke 1998). To date at least, the equity sensitivity concept appears to be real, to yield valid results, and to provide useful information (Kickul and Lester 2001), but it is also complex and may demonstrate a wide range of ties to personality characteristics (Yamaguchi 2003) and to cultural values (Wheeler 2002).

As research on equity sensitivity has progressed, certain deficiencies in the original measure have become evident—not of sufficient magnitude to invalidate the prior findings, but of a kind that indicates a need for more precise measurement. Sauley and Bedeian (2000) accordingly have developed a new procedure and demonstrated its construct validity, as well as its validity for predicting satisfaction with different reward conditions. An acceptable level of test-retest reliability has been shown. This measure may well make it possible to establish relationships that could not have been effectively assessed with the previous instrument.

Equity and Expectancy

It would certainly appear that some of the concepts and research from equity theory, especially in the area of overreward inequity, are distinctly in conflict with expectancy theory. Under certain circumstances, equity theory predicts (and the research seems to substantiate) that people do not strive to maximize rewards.

This problem has been given some attention by expectancy theorists. Their position is that the equity theory results can be incorporated within the larger framework of expectancy theory if certain assumptions are made regarding the way valences are formed or operate. In discussing this matter, Lawler (1968, 609) says:

> There are two ways in which equity can come into play as a determinant of the valence of certain rewards. One way concerns the possibility that increasingly large piece-rate rewards could have a decreasing valence for subjects. That is, rewards that are seen as too large, and therefore inequitable, may have a lower valence than rewards which are perceived as equitable. A second point concerns the effect of the amount of a reward that has been received on the valence of additional amounts of the reward. It seems reasonable that once a perceived equitable level of rewards has been achieved future rewards will have lower valences.

Formulations of this kind, whatever their attractiveness, are clearly post hoc. Expectancy theory is completely silent on what effects of this kind would be predicted, while equity theory is quite explicit. That certain phenomena can possibly be explained within a certain theoretical orientation does not mean that they are best explained in that manner. It would seem most appropriate to view the two theories as separate and distinct but with partially overlapping domains. This conclusion is reinforced by the fact that when equity and expectancy theories are tested together, they tend to emerge as complementary, with each expanding the predictive power of the other. In fact, there is a possibility that the behavior of certain kinds of people may be predicted from expectancy theory, and that of others from equity theory. Vecchio's (1981) study of the effects of moral maturity is certainly consistent with this formulation, with equity theory clearly operating for the more mature and perhaps expectancy theory for the less so.

The majority of the research comparing equity and expectancy approaches recently has been carried out with major league baseball and basketball players who are approaching free-agency (see Harder 1991; Bretz and Thomas 1992). This research indicates that underreward performance effects will occur to the extent that they do not jeopardize future rewards, but if they do, then avenues other than performance will be utilized to achieve equity. Overreward clearly has its effects, and over an extended period of time. Perceived inequities lead to discontent, can influence performance, and can result in both trades and leaving the field (literally). But expectations of future rewards exert a motivational influence as well. The two theories seem to complement each other.

Equity Theory in Practice

Specifying what the impact of equity theory has been and is on practice is a difficult task. The theory is widely known among compensation specialists, and equity considerations typically are given major attention in setting pay scales, usually with a view to maintaining equity. Yet it is hard to determine cause-and-effect relationships, and there is no generally established or widely publicized procedure that can be directly linked to Adams or to equity theory. It would appear that compensation practitioners have been well aware of the importance of equity considerations for their work for many years. The more recent and precise formulations of Adams and those who have followed his lead have had an uncertain impact on existing practice. However, this situation says nothing about the *potential* utility of the theory in the future.

In view of the level of research support for equity theory, one could hope that it might provide the basis for major breakthroughs in management practice. This expectation is further increased because the two motives involved, guilt and anger reduction, are major influences on what people do. There can be little doubt that the theory deals with motivational processes that relate to large segments of human behavior, not only in the organizational context, but also outside it.

One obvious application is to use the theory as a guide in introducing changed circumstances in the workplace, so that improved quality or quantity of work will result. This was Adams's objective when as an employee of the General Electric Company, he undertook the early research on pay–performance relationships, and his writing clearly indicates his belief that this is feasible. Yet there appear to be no accounts of this type of application in the literature. As far as can be determined, feasibility studies have not been conducted even though they could move us out of the laboratory and short-term simulation contexts into the ongoing work environment.

Thus, we can only guess at the results of such feasibility studies. It is doubtful that overreward inequity could produce major performance changes. The amount of inequity would have to be sizable in order to exceed threshold, and thus the cost would be considerable; many businessmen would question this initial outlay.

Many of the research results have been obtained under highly structured circumstances with clearly established reference sources, input and outcome specifications, and rankings of inputs and outcomes. The experimenter has been free to adjust a wide range of factors and has chosen to hold many constant. In the ongoing organizational world, these circumstances often do not exist because of union and competitive pressures. The ambiguity and uncertainty may be so great that it is very difficult to focus the inequity reaction on a performance-related response.

The conceptual leap from existing knowledge to practical application is sizable, and existing constraints may rule it out completely in many contexts. Without full knowledge of individual differences and their implications, it is doubtful whether inequities should be introduced to spark performance improvements. However, influences on citizenship behavior seem to be more easily achieved, and knowledge of individual differences can be obtained.

In contrast to attempts to introduce inequities through variations in pay plans, compensation levels, input perceptions, and the like, traditional compensation administration has sought to achieve equity through an adjustment of outcomes to perceived inputs, thus reducing the probability of absenteeism, turnover, disruptive behavior, and the like. The major concern has been to avoid underreward inequity. In addition, equity theory can be of considerable value in understanding the behavior that follows unintentional inequities. Full comprehension of equity theory can be useful to a manager and can help to deal with individual circumstances. In particular, recent evidence regarding the influence equity considerations exert on theft, and the ways in which procedural justice may operate in conjunction with distributive justice in this context, has major implications for cost reduction.

The procedures developed by Jaques (see Jaques and Cason 1994), although incorporating an equity standard, do not assume an implicit motivational process. Jaques posits a single input, capacity, that is channeled through the amount of individual discretion that the person is allowed to exercise in the job. The longer the period of time a person is expected to exercise independent judgment in the work, the higher the pay level should be to be perceived as equitable. In general, this time span of discretion increases with occupational level.

Although Jaques's views have received criticism, and the measurement of time spans of discretion has proved difficult, the approach has much in common with equity theory and receives support from research. The major advance provided is the emphasis on time span of discretion, or freedom to act independently as a major factor conditioning input perceptions. In this respect, the theory has contributed a concept of considerable value for compensation administration. It is widely utilized in Europe and is deserving of more attention than it has received in U.S. practice.

EXPANDING INTO ORGANIZATIONAL JUSTICE

At various points in the preceding discussion, evaluations and research findings were noted that extend beyond equity theory but still have implications for it. Now we need to consider this expanding literature in much more detail. It is a literature that overlaps with equity theory in time and subject matter but in the past few decades has come to take a rapidly escalating, even dominant position. These are the various theories, and emerging theories, of organizational justice, some of which are well researched, while others have a very short history.

However, the major point is that this burgeoning field of organizational justice has spawned a plethora of theories, no one of which as yet has the standing that equity theory has attained. Figure 9.2 provides an overview of these theories including a specification of equity theory's position. These are primarily categories of theories, and in a number of instances, there are multiple theories within a category (see Cropanzano, Rupp, Mohler, and Schminke 2001 for details). It is not important to understand what these various category titles mean; the intent of Figure 9.2 is to demonstrate the large number and diversity of theories currently operating, to provide an understanding of aspects of organizational justice. Other less comprehensive statements regarding the theories of the field involve some overlapping authorship (Cropanzano, Byrne, Bobocel, and Rupp 2001; Folger and Cropanzano 2001).

The various theories may conflict with each other, they may complement one another, or they may stand alone to cover a specific domain. Yet overlaying these theories is a template consisting of various types of organizational justice; some theories address several types while others consider all, but there is little consistency in how the types are viewed as relating to one another. In any event, understanding what these organizational justice types are is important (Colquitt and Greenberg 2003).

Figure 9.2   **Theoretical Roads to Understanding Organizational Justice**

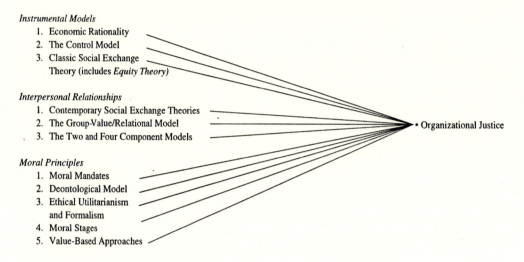

Instrumental Models
   1. Economic Rationality
   2. The Control Model
   3. Classic Social Exchange
       Theory (includes *Equity Theory)*

Interpersonal Relationships
   1. Contemporary Social Exchange Theories
   2. The Group-Value/Relational Model
   3. The Two and Four Component Models

Moral Principles
   1. Moral Mandates
   2. Deontological Model
   3. Ethical Utilitarianism
       and Formalism
   4. Moral Stages
   5. Value-Based Approaches

• Organizational Justice

Source: Adapted from Cropanzano, Rupp, Mohler, and Schminke (2001, 9–95).

Types of Organizational Justice

Distributive justice is the perceived fairness of decision outcomes—in particular, pay. It is promoted by following appropriate norms such as equity for allocating resources. Equity theory deals with distributive justice. Examples of items operationalizing this construct derived from Colquitt (2001) are:

- Does your pay reflect the effort you have put into your work?
- Is your pay justified, given your performance?

Procedural justice is the perceived fairness of the procedures used to make decisions. It is fostered by the use of certain procedural rules, such as granting an opportunity for input to the decision-making process and making decisions so as to be consistent, correctable, and to suppress bias. In many respects procedural justice parallels procedural due process in the legal domain, although the latter is more fully developed (Posthuma 2003). A good discussion of procedural justice is contained in Konovsky (2000). Items operationalizing this construct are:

- Have the procedures applied been free of bias?
- Have you been able to express your views and feelings during these procedures?
- Have the procedures applied upheld ethical and moral standards?

Interactional justice is the perceived fairness of how decisions are enacted by authority figures. It includes as a component *interpersonal justice* that is fostered by dignified and respectful treatment, and also *informational justice* that is fostered by adequate and honest explanations. These components, and indeed the separate existence of interactional justice, have been the subject of much controversy (see Bies 2001). Items operationalizing interpersonal justice are:

- To what extent has the authority figure who enacted the procedure treated you with dignity?
- To what extent has the authority figure who enacted the procedure refrained from improper remarks or comments?

Items operationalizing informational justice are:

- To what extent has the authority figure who enacted the procedure been candid in his communications with you?
- To what extent has the authority figure who enacted the procedure explained the procedure thoroughly?

In contrast to other areas of organizational justice, where approaches to consensus have not yet been attained, these four types appear to have been established as distinct entities (Colquitt and Greenberg 2003). The research that has accomplished this is reviewed in the next section.

Research Findings

The one investigation that has done the most to establish the four types noted above is in fact two studies, one using students and the other using manufacturing employees (Colquitt 2001). The items given previously to illustrate the four types, plus other similar items, were used to establish the types. In the student study the types were highly intercorrelated, with values ranging from 0.22 to 0.64 and a median of 0.46. One would expect this to work against distinguishing types, but each of the four justice dimensions was related strongly to a different outcome, and the best fitting model to describe the data proved to be the four-factor solution. Thus, using all four types added something above and beyond any other combination. The results from the manufacturing study were similar, with intercorrelations ranging from 0.14 to 0.74; the median was at 0.43. Both studies supported the four types. A limitation of this research overall, however, was that common source bias may well have operated to inflate the correlations.

Other evidence comes from two meta-analyses published in 2001. The first by Colquitt, Conlon, Wesson, Porter, and Ng (2001) covered studies published after 1975 and thus did not include the early equity theory studies, but it did deal with all four types of fairness. The intercorrelations ranged from 0.38 to 0.57 with a median of 0.50. Distributive justice had high correlations with satisfaction, commitment, trust, evaluation of authority, and withdrawal (negatively). Procedural justice had similar high relationships but with withdrawal somewhat less in evidence. Interpersonal justice was at a high level only in relation to evaluation of authority. Informational justice was similar but added trust to the list of high relationships The results indicate that all four types contribute incremental variance to fairness perceptions, although this is true to a lesser extent for informational justice. Again, common method bias seems to have been a problem in a number of the base studies that were utilized.

The meta-analysis by Cohen-Charnash and Spector (2001) appears to have been similarly restricted to studies published since the late 1970s, but it examined only three types, thus combining the interpersonal and informational varieties into a single interactional justice type. Also, this second analysis was somewhat more restrictive in the studies it included, and it utilized a different meta-analytic procedure, as well as breaking out laboratory studies for separate analysis. The mean correlations were once again highly interrelated (0.45 to 0.62; median 0.55). Outcome relationships were varied, but in many respects they followed those noted previously. The three justice types did not always predict the same outcomes, and they emerged as distinct constructs. Thus, once again the findings support the need to have separate operationalizations of justice types.

Several other conclusions emerge from the research that are worth noting, beyond the meta-analytic results (Greenberg 2001). One of these relates to when justice considerations become salient; this occurs when people receive negative outcomes, when change is introduced, when resources are scarce, and when power differentials are present as a result of role differences within an organization. Also, outcomes perceived as fair are not always favorable to the perceiver. We have already noted the effects of overreward inequity. Furthermore, fair procedures may elicit perceptions that lead to the acceptance of even undesirable outcomes, and research indicates that people do not necessarily choose groups for comparison purposes so as to maximize their own outcomes, thus choosing those who clearly fare worse.

Theory and research have not as yet combined to predict which reactions to injustice will manifest themselves in every instance. Even the best studies identify some individuals who do not follow the overall pattern, yielding off-quadrant cases or outliers. Why this occurs is not clear. Also, predicting cultural variations in reaction patterns presents many difficulties.

Applications

Potential applications of organizational justice theories and research findings of the kind that we have been considering abound. Yet actual applications to practice are few in number, presumably because the field of organizational justice has only just begun to accelerate its output in recent years (Greenberg and Lind 2000). Perhaps some understanding of what the future may hold can be achieved by describing some of the findings that appear to have a potential for application.

A study of incidents of sabotage as reported by those involved to a disinterested third party yields results that could help to control sabotage (Ambrose, Seabright, and Schminke 2002). Injustice was the most common cause noted. Interactional injustices seemed to elicit retaliation, while distributive injustice was more likely to yield equity restoration. An additive effect existed so that the more the different types of injustice activated, the greater the severity of the sabotage. The implication is that sabotage in large part can be managed by taking steps to minimize the various types of inequity, but the study does not provide guidance on exactly how to accomplish this.

A study of almost 1,000 ex-employees who had been fired or laid off dealt with the potential to file a legal claim for wrongful termination (Lind, Greenberg, Scott, and Welchans 2000), something one would expect a company to wish to avoid if at all possible given the costs involved. Filing status was strongly associated with feelings of unfair and insensitive treatment, especially at the time of termination; interpersonal injustice seemed to be involved. Legal action can be avoided if effective human relations practices are employed, and the person is treated with respect and dignity. Along the same lines, giving several weeks' notice of termination, helping to find reemployment, taking steps to alleviate any financial hardships, offering counseling, and anything else that can be done to bolster positive self-identity are recommended. But research has not been done actually evaluating these specific actions.

A study in Canada using employees of three different organizations was carried out to determine how justice types relate to satisfaction with pay and benefits (Tremblay, Sire, and Balkin 2000). The findings indicated that distributive justice was the better predictor of pay satisfaction (in accord with equity theory), while procedural justice provided a better explanation of benefits satisfaction. Thus, distinguishing the types of organizational justice, and dealing with each, is important to any firm that wishes to maintain high levels of satisfaction. This does not say exactly what to do to raise satisfaction, but it does say where to look.

A study conducted in two widely separated offices of a company, using customer service representatives, compared the actual theft behavior of people exposed to an ethics program and people who were not (Greenberg 2002). The ethics program included defining and admonishing theft by employees, as well as:

1. a formal code of ethics setting forth company expectations in that regard;
2. an ethics committee to develop and evaluate company policy;
3. an ethics training program designed to facilitate employee understanding of ethical issues; and
4. disciplinary practices established to punish unethical behavior.

The training noted in number 3 above included no less than ten hours over the nine months preceding the research; it contained role playing and case studies, and involved behavioral expectations, analyzing ethical decisions, plus summarizing company procedures in the ethics area. There was clear evidence that those who were involved in this ethics program, including the training, were less likely to engage in theft subsequently. Similar results have been obtained with training applied to managers (Greenberg and Lind 2000). Thus justice-related training does appear to have the desired effects in reducing outcomes of a negative nature.

Without question there are instances of negative organizational consequences, or organizational misbehavior, that occur without justice considerations being involved (Vardi and Weitz 2004). Yet organizational justice is at the heart of a great many such instances. Among the technologies that have been developed to date to deal with violations of the various types of organizational justice, some kind of ethical training for managers or employees has been taken to the most advanced level. Yet other potential applications are in the wings and may well be on center stage before long.

CONCLUSIONS

Returning now to the distributive justice agenda of equity theory, that theory seems to be moving increasingly to incorporate personality characteristics in its repertoire. If Adams had lived, it might well have incorporated macro organizational factors as well. In any event, equity theory remains quite active, but primarily in a broader organizational justice context.

The ratings on equity theory are impressive. Peers rate the theory at 5.93 and analyses of these data result in a conclusion that it has become institutionalized. The estimated validity of the theory is 4 stars, down slightly because matters within the theory's domain such as referent selection are not adequately handled. However, overreward inequity was predicted correctly and that is quite an accomplishment. As to application to practice, the rating of 3 stars is indicative of the fact that Adams never was able to develop a precise technology for putting his theory into practice. Like the other organizational justice approaches, equity theory has shown tremendous potential for contributing many useful applications, but this potential still remains to be fully developed. Justice theorizing is on the verge of reaching operational status, but equity theory has been sitting in that same status for many years. It will take something dramatic to kick this line of theorizing over the edge.

Next we turn to goal-setting theory, which has achieved somewhat greater success in moving into the applied area. This theory is closely intermingled with a number of theories that we have considered already, including organizational behavior modification and equity theory.

REFERENCES

Adams, J. Stacy (1963a). Toward an Understanding of Inequity. *Journal of Abnormal and Social Psychology*, 67, 422–36.

——— (1963b). Wage Inequities, Productivity, and Work Quality. *Industrial Relations*, 3, 9–16.

——— (1965). Inequity in Social Exchange. In Leonard Berkowitz (Ed.), *Advances in Experimental Social Psychology*, Vol. 2. New York: Academic Press, 267–99.

——— (1968a). A Framework for the Study of Modes of Resolving Inconsistency. In Robert P. Abelson et al. (Eds.), *Theories of Cognitive Inconsistency: A Sourcebook*. Chicago, IL: Rand, McNally, 655–60.

——— (1968b). Effects of Overpayment: Two Comments on Lawler's Paper. *Journal of Personality and Social Psychology*, 10, 315–16.

——— (1976). The Structure and Dynamics of Behavior in Organizational Boundary Roles. In Marvin D. Dunnette (Ed.), *Handbook of Industrial and Organizational Psychology*. Chicago, IL: Rand, McNally, 1175–99.

Adams, J. Stacy, and Freedman, Sara (1976). Equity Theory Revisited: Comments and Annotated Bibliography. In Leonard Berkowitz and Elaine Walster (Eds.), *Advances in Experimental Social Psychology*, Vol. 9. New York: Academic Press, 43–90.

Adams, J. Stacy, and Jacobsen, Patricia R. (1964). Effects of Wage Inequities on Work Quality. *Journal of Abnormal and Social Psychology*, 69, 19–25.

Adams, J. Stacy, and Rosenbaum, William B. (1962). The Relationship of Worker Productivity to Cognitive Dissonance about Wage Inequities. *Journal of Applied Psychology*, 46, 161–64.

Ambrose, Maureen L., Seabright, Mark A., and Schminke, Marshall (2002). Sabotage in the Workplace: The Role of Organizational Justice. *Organizational Behavior and Human Decision Processes*, 89, 947–65.

Bartol, Kathryn M., and Durham, Cathy C. (2000). Incentives: Theory and Practice. In Cary L. Cooper and Edwin A. Locke (Eds.), *Industrial and Organizational Psychology: Linking Theory with Practice*. Oxford, UK: Blackwell, 1–33.

Bartol, Kathryn M., and Locke, Edwin A. (2000). Incentives and Motivation. In Sara L. Rynes and Barry Gerhart (Eds.), *Compensation in Organizations: Current Research and Practice*. San Francisco, CA: Jossey-Bass, 104–47.

Bies, Robert J. (2001). Interactional (In)Justice: The Sacred and the Profane. In Gerald Greenberg and Russell Cropanzano (Eds.), *Advances in Organizational Justice*. Stanford, CA: Stanford University Press, 89–118.

Bretz, Robert D., and Thomas, Steven L. (1992). Perceived Equity, Motivation, and Final-offer Arbitration in Major League Baseball. *Journal of Applied Psychology*, 77, 280–87.

Brown, Michelle (2001). Unequal Pay, Unequal Responses? Pay Referents and Their Implications for Pay Level Satisfaction. *Journal of Management Studies*, 38, 879–96.

Chen, Chao C. (1995). New Trends in Rewards Allocation Preferences: A Sino–U.S. Comparison. *Academy of Management Journal*, 38, 408–28.

Cohen-Charnash, Yochi, and Spector, Paul E. (2001). The Role of Justice in Organizations: A Meta-alysis. *Organizational Behavior and Human Decision Processes*, 86, 278–321.

Colquitt, Jason A. (2001). On the Dimensionality of Organizational Justice: A Construct Validation of a Measure. *Journal of Applied Psychology*, 86, 386–400.

Colquitt, Jason A., Conlon, Donald E., Wesson, Michael J., Porter, Christopher O.L.H., and Ng, K. Yee (2001). Justice at the Millennium: A Meta-Analytic Review of 25 Years of Organizational Justice Research. *Journal of Applied Psychology*, 86, 425–45.

Colquitt, Jason A., and Greenberg, Jerald (2003). Organizational Justice: A Fair Assessment of the State of the Literature. In Jerald Greenberg (Ed.), *Organizational Behavior: The State of the Science*. Mahwah, NJ: Lawrence Erlbaum, 165–210.

Cropanzano, Russell, Byrne, Zinta S., Bobocel, D. Ramona, and Rupp, Deborah E. (2001). Moral Virtues, Fairness Heuristics, Social Entities, and Other Denizens of Organizational Justice. *Journal of Vocational Behavior*, 58, 164–209.

Cropanzano, Russell, Rupp, Deborah E., Mohler, Carolyn J., and Schminke, Marshall (2001). Three Roads to Organizational Justice. *Research in Personnel and Human Resources Management*, 20, 1–113.

Dornstein, Miriam (1989). The Fairness Judgments of Received Pay and Their Determinants. *Journal of Occupational Psychology*, 62, 287–99.

Dulebohn, James, and Martocchio, Joseph J. (1998). Employee's Perceptions of the Distributive Justice of

Pay Raise Decisions: A Policy Capturing Approach. *Journal of Business and Psychology*, 13, 41–64.

Festinger, Leon (1957). *A Theory of Cognitive Dissonance.* Evanston, IL: Row, Peterson.

Folger, Robert, and Cropanzano, Russell (2001). Fairness Theory: Justice as Accountability. In Jerald Greenberg and Russell Cropanzano (Eds.), *Advances in Organizational Justice.* Stanford, CA: Stanford University Press, 1–55.

Giacalone, Robert A., and Greenberg, Jerald (1997). *Antisocial Behavior in Organizations.* Thousand Oaks, CA: Sage.

Greenberg, Jerald (1990). Organizational Justice: Yesterday, Today, and Tomorrow. *Journal of Management*, 16, 399–432.

——— (2001). The Seven Loose Can(n)ons of Organizational Justice. In Jerald Greenberg and Russell Cropanzano (Eds.), *Advances in Organizational Justice.* Stanford, CA: Stanford University Press, 245–71.

——— (2002). Who Stole the Money, and When? Individual and Situational Determinants of Employer Theft. *Organizational Behavior and Human Decision Processes*, 89, 985–1003.

Greenberg, Jerald, and Lind, E. Allan (2000). The Pursuit of Organizational Justice: From Conceptualization to Implication to Application. In Cary L. Cooper and Edwin A. Locke (Eds.), *Industrial and Organizational Psychology: Linking Theory and Practice.* Oxford, UK: Blackwell, 72–108.

Harder, Joseph W. (1991). Equity Theory versus Expectancy Theory: The Case of Major League Baseball Free Agents. *Journal of Applied Psychology*, 76, 458–64.

Homans, George C. (1961). *Social Behavior: Its Elementary Forms.* New York: Harcourt, Brace, and World.

Huseman, Richard C., Hatfield, John D., and Miles, Edward W. (1987). A New Perspective on Equity Theory: The Equity Sensitivity Construct. *Academy of Management Review*, 12, 222–34.

Jaques, Elliott, and Cason, Kathryn (1994). *Human Capability.* Rockville, MD: Cason Hall.

Kickul, Jill, and Lester, Scott W. (2001). Broken Promises: Equity Sensitivity as a Moderator between Psychological Contract Breach and Employee Attitudes and Behavior. *Journal of Business and Psychology*, 16, 191–217.

King, Wesley C., and Hinson, Thomas, D. (1994). The Influence of Sex and Equity Sensitivity on Relationship Preferences, Assessment of Opponent, and Outcomes in a Negotiation Experiment. *Journal of Management*, 20, 605–24.

Konovsky, Mary A. (2000). Understanding Procedural Justice and Its Impact on Business Organizations. *Journal of Management*, 26, 489–511.

Kulik, Carol T., and Ambrose, Maureen L. (1992). Personal and Situational Determinants of Referent Choice. *Academy of Management Review*, 17, 212–37.

Larwood, Laurie, Kavanagh, Michael, and Levine, Richard (1978). Perceptions of Fairness with Three Different Economic Exchanges. *Academy of Management Journal*, 21, 69–83.

Lawler, Edward E. (1968). Equity Theory as a Predictor of Productivity and Work Quality. *Psychological Bulletin*, 70, 596–610.

Leventhal, Gerald S., Weiss, Thomas, and Long, Gary (1969). Equity, Reciprocity, and Reallocating Rewards in the Dyad. *Journal of Personality and Social Psychology*, 13, 300–5.

Lind, E. Allan, Greenberg, Jerald, Scott, Kimberly S., and Welchans, Thomas D. (2000). The Winding Road from Employee to Complainant: Situational and Psychological Determinants of Wrongful-Termination Claims. *Administrative Science Quarterly*, 45, 557–90.

Lind, E. Allan, Kray, Laura, and Thompson, Leigh (1998). The Social Construction of Injustice: Fairness Judgments in Response to Own and Others' Unfair Treatment by Authorities. *Organizational Behavior and Human Decision Processes*, 75, 1–22.

Mannix, Elizabeth A., Neale, Margaret A., and Northcraft, Gregory B. (1995). Equity, Equality, or Need? The Effects of Organizational Culture on the Allocation of Benefits and Burdens. *Organizational Behavior and Human Decision Processes*, 63, 276–86.

Miner, John B., and Capps, Michael H. (1996). *How Honesty Testing Works.* Westport, CT: Quorum.

Mitchell, Terence R. (1997). Matching Motivational Strategies with Organizational Contexts. *Research in Organizational Behavior*, 19, 57–149.

Mowday, Richard T. (1996). Equity Theory Predictions of Behavior in Organizations. In Richard M. Steers, Lyman W. Porter, and Gregory A. Bigley (Eds.), *Motivation and Leadership at Work.* New York: McGraw-Hill, 53–71.

Mueller, Stephen L., and Clarke, Linda D. (1998). Political–Economic Context and Sensitivity to Equity: Differences Between the United States and the Transition Economies of Central and Eastern Europe. *Academy of Management Journal*, 41, 319–29.

Posthuma, Richard A. (2003). Procedural Due Process and Procedural Justice in the Workplace: A Comparison and Analysis. *Public Personnel Management*, 32, 181–95.

Sauley, Kerry S., and Bedeian, Arthur G. (2000). Equity Sensitivity: Construction of a Measure and Examination of Its Psychometric Properties. *Journal of Management*, 26, 885–910.

Scholl, Richard W., Cooper, Elizabeth A., and McKenna, Jack F. (1987). Referent Selection in Determining Equity Perceptions: Differential Effects on Behavioral and Attitudinal Outcomes. *Personnel Psychology*, 40, 113–24.

Summers, Timothy P., and Hendrix, William H. (1991). Modeling the Role of Pay Equity Perceptions: A Field Study. *Journal of Occupational Psychology*, 64, 145–57.

Tremblay, Michel, Sire, Bruno, and Balkin, David B. (2000). The Role of Organizational Justice in Pay and Employee Benefit Satisfaction, and Its Effects on Work Attitudes. *Group and Organization Management*, 25, 269–90.

Vardi, Yoav, and Weitz, Ely (2004). *Misbehavior in Organizations: Theory, Research, and Management*. Mahwah, NJ: Lawrence Erlbaum.

Vecchio, Robert P. (1981). An Individual-Differences Interpretation of the Conflicting Predictions Generated by an Equity and Expectancy Theory. *Journal of Applied Psychology*, 66, 470–81.

Walster, Elaine, Berscheid, Ellen, and Walster, G. William (1973). New Directions in Equity Research. *Journal of Personality and Social Psychology*, 25, 151–76.

Wheeler, Kenneth G. (2002). Cultural Values in Relation to Equity Sensitivity within and across Cultures. *Journal of Managerial Psychology*, 17, 612–27.

Yamaguchi, Ikushi (2003). The Relationships among Individual Differences, Needs, and Equity Sensitivity. *Journal of Managerial Psychology*, 18, 324–44.

CHAPTER 10

GOAL-SETTING THEORY

EDWIN LOCKE AND GARY LATHAM

Background
Phase I Theory
    Research-guiding Hypotheses
    More Comprehensive Formulations
    The Job Satisfaction Model
The Theory in Maturity
    Goals, Expectancies, Self-Efficacy, and
        Performance
    Goal Mechanisms
    Determinants of Goal Choice
    Goal Commitment
    Further on Feedback
    Goals and Ability, Task Complexity,
        Personality, Affect
    The High Performance Cycle
    Goal Setting and Strategy Effects on Complex Tasks
    Phase III Developments
Applications
    The Management by Objectives Approach
    The Goal-setting Theory Approach
Evaluation and Impact
    Examples of Research by the Theory's Authors
    Findings from Meta-Analytic Studies
    Proposition-specific Evaluations
    Questions Raised from the Perceptual Control Theory Perspective
    Implications of the Motivation Sequence Model
Conclusions

Importance rating	★ ★ ★ ★ ★
	Institutionalized
Estimated validity	★ ★ ★ ★ ★
Estimated usefulness	★ ★ ★ ★
Decade of origin	1960s

Edwin Locke has been influenced throughout his career by the philosophy of objectivism as set forth by Ayn Rand (see Ghate and Locke 2003). However, his theory of goal setting owes its primary debts to Thomas Ryan (1970), an experimental psychologist who became an industrial psychologist as well during an extended career on the faculty of Cornell University, and to Kurt Lewin, the personality theorist and social psychologist whose work in the areas of level of aspiration and group decision making had a major impact on him. Locke traces goal-setting theory to other roots in psychology and in management (including management by objectives), but it is apparent that Ryan and Lewin exerted the major direct effects on his thinking. Starting in the latter 1970s, Locke was increasingly joined by Gary Latham as the two further developed goal-setting theory.

Modern goal-setting theory, although it has multiple historical origins, owes much to the formulations of Kurt Lewin. Lewin's views resulted in a sizable amount of research on the determinants of the level of aspiration (or goal setting) as a dependent variable (Lewin, Dembo, Festinger, and Sears 1944). The current resurgence of interest in this area (dating from the mid-1960s), however, delves primarily into the *effects* of goal setting on performance (Locke and Latham 1990a).

BACKGROUND

Edwin Locke was born in 1938 and attended Harvard University where he majored in psychology, graduating in 1960. His graduate work was done at Cornell in industrial psychology with Patricia Cain Smith as his mentor. Upon receiving his doctorate in 1964, he joined the American Institutes for Research (AIR), a nonprofit research organization in Washington, DC. There he continued the research on goal setting, which he had begun in connection with his dissertation, under a grant from the U.S. Office of Naval Research (Locke 1993).

At Cornell, Locke was exposed to the views of Thomas Ryan on the significant role that intentions play in human behavior. Although these views were not formally published until 1970, they were available in an early mimeographed version in 1964, and Locke was exposed to them well before that time. This debt to Ryan is acknowledged in numerous publications. Although the two never published together, Locke has continued the same line of work up to the present.

After three years at AIR, Locke joined the psychology faculty at the University of Maryland. In 1970 he moved to the business school there, retaining only a limited appointment in psychology. Ultimately the business school appointment became full time; he remained in this position until his recent retirement in 2001.

Gary Latham first published with Locke in 1975, but it was not until almost five years later that the collaboration began in earnest. Initially, Latham's role involved testing goal-setting theory in the field after many years during which the theory had been exposed only to laboratory testing. Later this role expanded considerably, but Latham's practical experience has always been a major contribution to the partnership. Latham was born in Halifax, Nova Scotia, in 1945 and received his Bachelor of Arts from Dalhousie University in Nova Scotia, his masters in industrial psychology from Georgia Tech, and his doctorate in the same field from the University of Akron in 1974. His business experience has included work as a psychologist with the American Pulpwood Association, with the Weyerhaeuser Company, and as an independent consultant. His faculty employment began at the business school of the University of Washington in 1976. In 1990 he returned to Canada with an appointment in the business school at the University of Toronto, where he remains.

PHASE I THEORY

The first theoretical statements regarding goal setting appear in published versions of Locke's doctoral dissertation. Initially, the research objective was merely to determine "how the level of intended achievement is related to actual level of achievement" (Locke 1966, 60), although there was an implicit hypothesis that higher levels of intended achievement would contribute to higher levels of performance. Soon thereafter this hypothesis was made explicit, with the added proviso that when an individual had specific goals or standards of performance to meet, the performance effects would be more pronounced than when specific goals were lacking (as with the instruction "do your best") (Locke and Bryan 1966a).

Research-Guiding Hypotheses

Subsequently this hypothesis regarding the superiority of specific over ambiguous goals was extended to task interest. "It was hypothesized . . . that working toward a determinate goal would lead to a higher level of task interest than would be the case with an abstract goal such as do your best" (Locke and Bryan 1967, 121). Thus, the presence of specific hard goals should reduce boredom at work.

This emphasis on the significant motivational effects of specific goals that are difficult to achieve was extended to explain various other motivational phenomena. The first such extrapolation was to the area of knowledge of results or feedback on the effectiveness of performance. More specifically, it was hypothesized that knowledge of results achieves its motivational effects through the incorporating of goal setting and that in the absence of such performance intentions, knowledge of results does not contribute to the level of work output (Locke and Bryan 1966b).

The popular Parkinson's Law is also explained as a goal-setting phenomenon (Bryan and Locke 1967). This law indicates that work expands to fill the time available for its completion; more generally it can be hypothesized that "effort (or work pace) is adjusted to the perceived difficulty of the task undertaken." This process is said to be mediated by goal setting, and accordingly a goal-setting process is assumed to intervene between task perception and actual performance. The following quote not only explains how this might occur, but also provides a first glimpse of the broader theoretical framework that emerged later:

> [A]djustment (of effort to difficulty level) requires first that the subject perceive the task, that he be conscious of the fact that there is a task to be performed, and that he have some idea or knowledge of what the task requires of him. Then, depending upon the situation and the individual's perception of it in relation to his own values, he will set himself a goal or standard in terms of which he will regulate and evaluate his performance. . . . This goal-setting procedure can vary widely in the degree to which it is conscious or subconscious, explicit or implicit . . . but once the goal is set, it is argued that effort and performance level will be regulated by and with reference to this goal. (Bryan and Locke 1967, 260)

A similar explanation in terms of goal setting is applied to the relationships between monetary incentives and work performance. The specific hypotheses are:

1. Goals and intentions will be related to behavior regardless of incentive conditions; that is, goals and intentions will be related to behavior both within and across different incentive conditions.
2. When incentive differences do correlate with behavior differences, these differences will be accompanied by corresponding differences in goals and intentions.
3. When goal or intention differences are controlled or partialed out, there will be no relationship between incentive condition and behavior (Locke, Bryan, and Kendall 1968, 106).

More Comprehensive Formulations

The theoretical statements considered to this point were all presented as hypotheses that were tested immediately in research. However, beginning in 1968 Locke began a series of attempts to pull his ideas together within a more comprehensive framework. That seven years later he still had serious doubts as to whether these efforts had amounted to a true theory does not deny the fact that something more than a set of loosely related first-order hypotheses was achieved.

Clearly, the formulations Locke presents are limited in various respects (Locke 1968). Little attention is given to the developmental causes of particular goals and why people consciously try to do what they do. Furthermore, goals are viewed as having significance for performance only to the extent that they are actually accepted by the individual, so the theory is one of accepted or internalized goals. Very difficult goals might well fail to achieve acceptance, and if this were the case, the positive relationship between goal difficulty and performance would no longer be expected to hold. On almost any task there is a hypothetical level of difficulty beyond which goal acceptance will not occur. At this point a boundary condition of the theory has been reached. One of the key reasons monetary incentives work with regard to performance levels is that they contribute to task and goal acceptance, or commitment.

In the early statements, goal setting was introduced as an explanation not only of the effects of monetary incentives, but also of knowledge of results and variations in available time. Later this list was expanded to several additional areas (Locke 1968, 1970b). The performance effects of participative management are attributed in part to explicit or implicit goal setting. Competition is viewed as a case in which the performance of others serves to establish goals that arouse individuals to higher levels of performance. Praise and reproof may well induce people to set hard performance goals, although it is apparent also that this need not necessarily occur; the theory is not specific as to when, under such circumstances, hard or easy goals will emerge.

Goals have two major attributes—content and intensity. Content refers to the nature of the activity or end sought. Intensity relates to the level of importance of the goal to the person. Goal content exerts a primarily directive influence, and it also serves to regulate energy expenditure because different goals require different amounts of effort. Goal intensity can also influence both the direction and level of effort. Important goals are more likely to be accepted, to elicit commitment, and thus to foster persistent striving.

The Job Satisfaction Model

The theory treats job satisfaction in the short range as a function of the size of the perceived discrepancy between intended and actual performance. Goal achievement leads to the pleasurable emotional state we call satisfaction; failure to achieve a goal leads to the unpleasurable state of dissatisfaction (Locke 1969, 1970a).

However, job satisfaction is usually viewed in a wider context than individual goal accomplishment. In this broader context, abstract job values serve in the manner of goals. "Job satisfaction and dissatisfaction are a function of the perceived relationship between what one wants from one's job and what one perceives it as offering or entailing" (Locke 1969, 316). Values establish what one wants. Like the more immediate goals, they are characterized by content and intensity (importance). Thus the achievement of more important values (financial security, for instance) will yield greater satisfaction, and the same value-percept discrepancy will produce more dissatisfaction if the value is important than if it is not. Beyond these directional hypotheses, the theory does not indicate in specific detail the relationships involving values, discrepancies, importance, and satisfaction-dissatisfaction. It does, however, view job satisfaction as primarily a product or outcome of goal or value-directed effort, and thus a consequence of performance.

Locke, Cartledge, and Knerr (1970) have proposed a theoretical model to explain how the various types of variables specified in Locke's theoretical formulations interact:

existents (such as incentives or previous outcomes) → cognition (evaluation against values)
→ emotional reactions → goal setting → action

The most immediate determinant of action is the individual's goal. External incentives influence action through their impact on the individual's goal. Emotional reactions result from evaluations in which the person cognitively compares the existents against standards established by relevant values.

As an example of how these processes work, let us take an examination situation:

existent: grade of C+ → cognition: C+ evaluated as too low relative to B value
standard → emotion: dissatisfaction → goal: improve on next examination → action:
improved examination performance

Improved performance should result ultimately in greater satisfaction.

Locke, Cartledge, and Knerr (1970) also extend this basic model to include anticipated existents and emotions as well as the judged instrumentality of anticipated goals. Subgoal attainment is valued to the extent it is seen as instrumental for an overall goal. Although these formulations regarding anticipatory states and subgoals add a degree of complexity to the model, they are nevertheless handled within the basic framework discussed above.

THE THEORY IN MATURITY

Throughout most of the 1970s, goal-setting theory was largely in hiatus. However, during this period Latham published a number of studies that moved goal-setting research from the laboratory out into the field. Then gradually activity on the theory front accelerated, culminating in Locke and Latham's *A Theory of Goal Setting and Task Performance* (1990a); this was phase II.

Goals, Expectancies, Self-Efficacy, and Performance

A problem that arose early on was that because difficult goals are harder to reach, expectancy of success should show a negative linear relationship to performance; goal theory posits a positive linear relationship between goal difficulty and performance. In contrast, expectancy theory asserts a positive linear relationship between expectancy of success and performance level. The conflicting predictions involved here have elicited a number of proposed solutions.

In the 1990 version of their theory, Locke and Latham introduce the concept of self-efficacy from Bandura (1982) to yield their most recent solution (see also Bandura 1997). Self-efficacy is a person's judgment of how well one can execute courses of action required to deal with prospective situations; it is positively related to future performance. It has a lot in common with the expectancy concept, but it is much broader in scope. In summarizing this solution they state:

> Goal-setting theory is in full agreement, rather than conflict, with expectancy theory regarding the relationship of expectancy to performance. Expectancy is positively related to performance within any given goal group; self-efficacy and/or overall expectancy of performing well across the full range of possible performance levels is positively associated with goal level and performance, both within and across goal groups. Assigned goals facilitate performance because they influence both self-efficacy and personal goals. Self-efficacy affects goal choice, and both self-efficacy and personal goals affect performance. (Locke and Latham 1990a, 85)

The means to the resolution is self-efficacy, and in fact this integration of goal-setting theory with Bandura's views has become increasingly evident since that time (Bartol and Locke 2000).

Goal Mechanisms

Why might goal setting work? On this score, phase II theory represents a major advance over the early formulations. The basic propositions are that (1) goals energize performance by motivating people to exert effort in line with the difficulty or demands of the goal or task (thus, they affect arousal by regulating intensity of effort); (2) goals motivate people to persist in activities through time; and (3) goals direct people's attention to relevant behaviors or outcomes and away from nongoal-relevant activities (thus, they orient people toward goal-relevant activities and they activate knowledge and skills perceived to be relevant to the task). If task strategies are held constant, and the goal mechanisms of effort, persistence, and direction are controlled or partialed out, goals should not affect task performance.

This raises the question of what are task strategies. They are directional mechanisms that entail methods of performing a task extending beyond the relatively automatic mechanisms inherent in effort, persistence, and direction, as just discussed, to conscious problem solving and creative innovation. They are an especially crucial link between goals and performance on complex tasks.

Why and how, then, are specific challenging goals hypothesized to lead to higher levels of performance? For the following reasons:

> They are associated with higher self-efficacy (whether the goals are assigned or self-set).
> They require higher performance in order for the individual to feel a sense of self-satisfaction.
> They entail less ambiguity about what constitutes high or good performance.
> They are typically more instrumental in bringing about valued outcomes.
> They lead individuals to expend more effort.
> They stimulate individuals to persist longer.
> They direct attention and action better and activate previously automatized skills.
> They motivate individuals to search for suitable task strategies, to plan, and to utilize strategies that they have been taught. (Locke and Latham 1990a, 108)

Determinants of Goal Choice

Although goal-setting theory has been primarily concerned with goals as independent variables, the earlier concern with goals as dependent variables (Lewin et al. 1944) has also been incorporated in the phase II theory. In this connection it should be recognized that although assigned goals typically are accepted, even then the relationship between the assigned goal and a person's personal goal level is far from perfect. Thus, the determinants of goal choice remain important even when goals are assigned.

In this connection the theory posits that people will typically raise their goals after failure as a compensation strategy; the operative motive is a desire to make up for past failure by dramatically increasing future performance. In this context, goal choice is a function of what a person thinks can be achieved (perceived performance capability given previous performance, ability levels, self-efficacy, and the like) and what a person would like to achieve or feels should be achieved (perceived desirability or appropriateness of performance given group norms, competition, goal assignments, any money incentives, dissatisfaction occasioned by previous performance, and other such factors). The goal actually chosen represents a compromise between these two types of factors.

Goal Commitment

Commitment is expected to relate to performance as a direct positive effect. In addition, it should serve to moderate the effects of goals on performance—goal level should be more highly (and positively) related to performance under conditions where the individuals involved have high commitment than where commitment is at a low level.

A number of factors are expected to influence commitment levels, some of which are the same as those previously noted for goal choice. One set of factors affects the perceived desirability or appropriateness (the valence) of trying for a given goal or goal level (such factors as authority, peer groups, publicness of goal statement, incentives, punishments, satisfaction, and goal intensity). Another set of factors affect the perceived ability of attaining (the expectancy) of a given goal or goal level (authority and goal intensity again, plus competition, attributions, and the like).

A commitment-related issue has to do with the relative effectiveness of assigned, participatively set, and self-set goals. Although there have been numerous positions taken on this score, goal-setting theory makes no a priori assumptions regarding the relative effectiveness of the different ways used to set goals. The importance of the matter from both practical and theoretical perspectives is recognized, however. The theory basically states that insofar as the motivational mechanism of commitment is concerned, the differences among the various methods of setting goals are negligible—it does not matter. This is a topic that has spawned considerable research; we will consider this research shortly.

Further on Feedback

The phase I theory dealt with feedback. Phase II theory extends that treatment. With respect to feedback, goals are said to act as *mediators*—they are one of the key mechanisms by which feedback becomes translated into action. (This is a restatement of the phase I position.) With respect to goals, however, feedback is now designated as a moderator—goals regulate performance far more reliably when there is feedback present than when feedback is absent. Figure 10.1 sets forth a tentative model of how goal setting mediates feedback into performance under the phase II formulations. The net effects involved here should be that when goal setting is withheld, feedback should not work; and when feedback is withheld, goal setting should not work, but when goal setting plus feedback are explicitly invoked, the result should be more effective performance than with either one alone.

In this and other contexts, Locke has been quite critical of classical behaviorist interpretations on the grounds that they do not recognize the effects of the goal setting implicit in their studies:

> The probable reason why goal setting has been de-emphasized and feedback emphasized in the behavior modification literature is that goal setting is frankly an embarrassment to behavior modification theory. Behaviorism asserts that the key events controlling human action are *consequents,* things that occur after behavior. However, goals are things that occur before behavior; thus they are antecedents, . . . [T]he key fallacy here is that a consequent cannot affect *action unless it becomes an antecedent.* How else can the past affect the future? Feedback does not result in anything unless the recipients do something with it, such as decide that they will try to improve their performance the next time they act.

Figure 10.1 **Model of How Feedback Leads to Action**

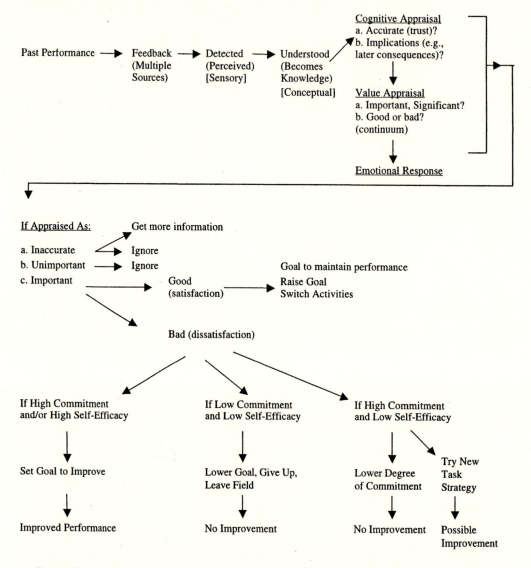

If consequent information is incorrectly interpreted or cannot be interpreted, it does not lead to any increase in the desired actions. . . . Nuttin (1984) identifies the fundamental behaviorist error as follows: "Human behavior does not consist of [automatically] repeating previously reinforced responses; it involves setting immediate or distant goals, elaborating behavioral projects or plans, and working toward their realization by means of learned and readapted behavioral techniques and experiences" (41). (Locke and Latham 1990a, 187)

Goals and Ability, Task Complexity, Personality, Affect

If goals set in a situation are not within the ability level of the person they will not be attained, irrespective of other considerations. The same is true if situational constraints block goal attainment. Essentially these are factors that set boundaries on the domain of goal-setting theory.

Complex tasks introduce demands that are expected to mute goal-setting effects to a degree and thus reduce the extent of the goal–performance relationship; thus performance will be less effective on complex tasks than simple tasks given the same goal input. At the same time, the relationship between task strategies and performance should be greater on complex tasks.

The phase I theory essentially held that individual differences in personality were not of concern for goal-setting theory; these factors should introduce only marginal amounts of variance into the components of the theory. At phase II this position has been modified. The current view is that a syndrome associated with achievement motivation (including need achievement, type A behavior, and internal locus of control) serves to characterize those who tend to set difficult goals. These are all characteristics found among the personal achiever type of successful entrepreneur (Miner 1997). Also self-esteem, a close cousin to self-efficacy, should operate in the same manner. The hypothesis is that these factors affect the extent to which people take steps to increase their ability, find ways to overcome situational constraints, and deal effectively with complex tasks.

Job satisfaction or affect represents a major factor in the phase I theory. Beyond this, phase II theory concerns itself with the aspects of the goal-setting process that should lead to positive appraisals (and satisfaction) or negative appraisals (dissatisfaction or anxiety). In the former category are success, the engagement of values, cognitive focus, and role clarity. In the latter category are failure, feelings of pressure, role conflict, and feelings of inequity.

The High Performance Cycle

The ideas and concepts that we have been considering in the phase II theory are combined in the model set forth in Figure 10.2. This version (Locke and Latham 1990b) differs somewhat from another published in the same year (Locke and Latham 1990a). In the latter instance, self-efficacy is moved from the moderator category to the demands category, giving it somewhat higher billing; there it is designated "high self-efficacy." At the same time expectancy is dropped from the model and situational constraints is added as a moderator. These two versions appear to have been produced at roughly the same time, although the paper in the edited volume (1990b) must have been written first. There is another slightly different version as well (Locke and Latham 1990c), and another that integrates the essential elements of goal-setting theory into the high performance cycle more fully (Locke and Latham 2002). Clearly, goal-setting theory is still undergoing development.

In none of these versions of the model is personality given any billing at all. The theory still has not fully overcome the antipathy toward personality factors that characterized the phase I formulations, although it is gradually moving to incorporate some such variables (Locke 2001).

In describing the high performance cycle, the authors consider applications of their theory, a matter that will concern us in much greater detail in a subsequent section:

> The high performance model has important implications for the management of organizations. Effective organizations must expect a lot from their employees and must try to insure that they gain a sense of satisfaction in return for their efforts. Employee satisfaction will derive, in part, from giving employees personally meaningful work that they are capable of

Figure 10.2   **Model of the High Performance Cycle**

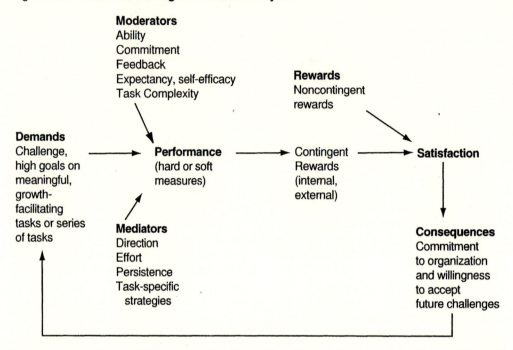

Source: Locke and Latham (1990b, 4). Copyright © 1990 Lawrence Erlbaum Associates. Reprinted with permission.

handling and, in part, from taking pains to reward good performance. Peters and Waterman (1982) have argued, consistent with this model, that the best American organizations in the private sector have organizational philosophies that place a high premium on excellence in performance and on respect for employees. (Locke and Latham 1990b, 18)

Goal Setting and Strategy Effects on Complex Tasks

Previously in connection with the discussion of goal mechanisms, task strategies, especially as they are utilized on complex tasks, were considered. These ideas are developed more fully in the model of Figure 10.3 dealing with the relationships among goals, plans (task strategies), and performance.

Again, there are two somewhat different versions of the theory in existence—the Wood and Locke (1990) version of Figure 10.3 and the version contained in Locke and Latham (1990a). The theoretical tinkering continues. In the latter instance the feedback loop at the bottom of the figure extending beyond (4a') to (1) is eliminated; thus this loop extends only to developing new task-specific plans. A link is also added running from these plans to (2a).

Phase III Developments

In the period since 1990, goal-setting theory has had relatively little new to say about its content but a great deal to say about its domain. The focus has been on extending that domain in many

Figure 10.3 **Model of the Relationships Among Goals, Plans (Task Strategies), and Performance**

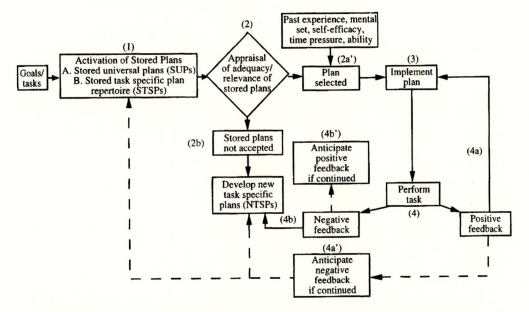

Source: Wood and Locke (1990, 76). Copyright © 1990 Elsevier Science. Reprinted with permission.

directions. First was a concern with applying the theory to organization goals and business strategies, thus making an essentially micro theory into a macro one as well (Chesney and Locke 1991; Audia, Locke, and Smith 2000). In addition, the theory entered the field of entrepreneurship with hypotheses about the effects of growth-oriented vision statements (read difficult goals) on business performance indexes (Baum, Locke, and Kirkpatrick 1998) and other similar formulations with regard to venture growth (Baum, Locke, and Smith 2001).

In addition to these macro emphases, the theory has moved in an exactly opposite direction, extending its domain to focus on self-set goals and self-management. Historically, goal setting has been primarily a social process consistent with the theory's origins in social psychology; assigned goals were set with the aid of an authority figure, and participative goal setting was an even more distinctly social process. More recently, however, the theory has joined forces with organizational behavior modification (see Chapter 8) to concentrate on the cognitive processes involved in self-management and the role that self-set goals can play in the self-regulation of behavior (Latham and Locke 1991). In this context, training for self-management, to set goals without the aid of others, becomes an important concern.

Finally, goal-setting theory has been extended in order to attempt a joining together with other motivation theories and thus achieve a degree of integration within the field. Figure 10.4 depicts this effort. The motivation hub and what happens thereafter represent a restatement of the high performance cycle (see Figure 10.2); this is where prediction of performance is said to be best achieved because it is closest to the action. However, Figure 10.4 also contains the motivation core (values and motives) and needs. These represent extensions of the theory's domain and the incorporation of previously separate ideas about motivation, most of which are discussed in the chapters of this book.

Figure 10.4 **Model of the Motivation Sequence**

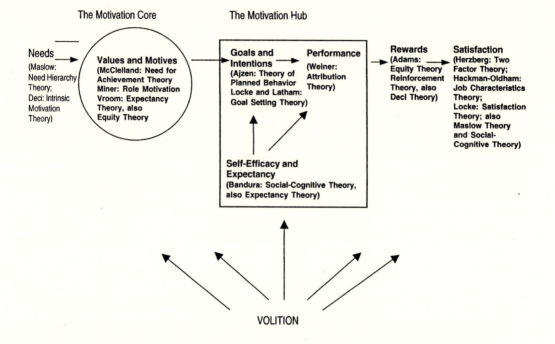

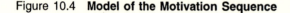

Source: Locke (1991, 289). Copyright © 1991 Academic Press. Reprinted with permission.

APPLICATIONS

Gary Latham is primarily responsible for bringing goal-setting theory into the world of practice. He has done so through his work as a psychologist in various companies both as an employee and as a consultant. However, goal setting existed in industry long before Latham arrived, in the form of management by objectives. We need to look at this phenomenon first.

The Management by Objectives Approach

Management by objectives (MBO) dates its popularity to Drucker's (1954) writings. Its historical antecedents, however, may be traced back through the classical and scientific management literature and through management practice to the early 1900s, especially as the literature and practice deal with planning and its related activities. The term *management by objectives* itself appears to have been coined around 1950. This approach is identified strongly with General Electric and with Harold Smiddy, a long-time vice-president of that company. Goal-setting theory appeared in the mid-1960s and had its origins in the research laboratory.

Management by objectives involves a joint determination by subordinate and superior of common goals, major areas of responsibility, and results expected; these measures are used as guides for operating the unit and assessing contributions of members. Usually a series of steps must be carried out, but the steps noted by different writers and used in different companies can vary widely. The key steps appear to be:

1. Setting objectives.
2. Working toward the goals.
3. Reviewing performance.

Beyond this basic goal setting–feedback nexus, a tremendous amount of diversity emerges. Among the components of MBO are strategic planning, performance appraisal, management development, compensation administration, career planning, organization planning, job design, and coaching. A review of individual company programs suggests that the following should also be included: control systems design, organization development, human resource planning, job enrichment, leadership style change, and changes in organizational climate. It is clear that beyond its core elements, management by objectives is many things to many people. The degree to which goals are participatively set can vary considerably and so too can the extent of formalization in the sense of documentation or paperwork requirements.

This diversity can be a strength in that it is possible to tailor a program to the needs of a specific company. But from the point of view of evaluation, it creates major problems. Even if an MBO program is shown to yield positive results, it is very difficult to know what factors were responsible, or to compare one study with others. In any given instance it may be goal setting that is the cause of a motivational effect, but it also may be any one of the other aspects of the program. Thus research on MBO must be viewed with some caution; variables are typically confounded, and implications for goal-setting theory tend to be indirect at best.

A problem for MBO is that the motivating effects of difficult goals appear to be particularly susceptible to dissipation over time, even among the particular kinds of individuals who are most responsive to them. To counteract this tendency, goal setting must be reinforced frequently. Thus, if the need is for an immediate burst of energy due to declining profits or shrinking markets, MBO can prove very valuable. For the long term it is less likely to maintain effort levels unless it is possible to reactivate goals frequently and perhaps to shift the actual content of certain goals (and thus introduce new jobs) at periodic intervals.

These considerations suggest that goal setting for particular, relatively isolated operations is most likely to yield favorable results. In contrast, a comprehensive companywide program can run into difficulties that will hamper its operations. Locke (1970b) has noted the value that goal setting may have when an individual supervisor deals with subordinates. In this limited context it can be adjusted to the individual characteristics of the subordinate to stay within the boundaries of theoretical application and establish appropriate priorities. An overall MBO program for a company, however, may well miss the mark with so many people that it ultimately loses its legitimacy, goal importance, and motivational impact for almost everyone. Many may feel they have been duped into setting certain goals only to have them "thrown in their face" months later (when they are almost forgotten) as justification for a denied promotion or salary raise.

Locke and Latham (1990a) evaluate a number of reviews of research studies that attempted to determine MBO effectiveness. They conclude: "By every reasonable method of counting, the overall MBO success rate hovers around the 90% success rate obtained for micro- and group-level studies" (45). However, this does not mean success was achieved in all units or at all points in time considered in a given study or on all indexes of success. There are many contingencies involved. A meta-analysis of evaluation studies indicates that a key contingency is the support of top management (Rodgers and Hunter 1991); without this support the effects of MBO are negligible. Furthermore, it is often unclear what caused the success—goal setting may or may not be the key factor. For an example of how goal setting of an organizational nature may go awry, see Humphreys (2003).

One thing, however, is clear and that is that MBO and goal-setting theory now have converged, to their mutual benefit, with the former thus acquiring a theoretical base and the latter getting a popular arena of application.

The Goal-setting Theory Approach

In their book, Locke and Latham (1990a) note a number of applications of goal setting in human resource management. It may be used in job analysis to get people to contribute their knowledge of the work. It may be used to develop interview formats in connection with the situational interview approach that is described as grounded in goal-setting theory. It may be used in connection with training, as for instance training in self-management, where goal setting is viewed as a core element. It may be used to establish mutual goals between management and labor as part of a relations by objectives program. It may be used as part of performance appraisal when feedback on performance is combined with setting specific improvement goals. Through goal setting managers may facilitate the operation of a superordinate goal to guide those who work for them (Latham 2003).

These are important applications. However, the most important use of goal setting in organizations is as a stand-alone procedure for improving performance—much like MBO, but without the formalization that has come to characterize that approach. As with MBO, there are certain steps that should be followed. Locke and Latham (1984, 40) outline these steps as follows:

1. Specify the nature of the task(s) to be accomplished (i.e., write a job description). This may be done in terms of work outcomes and/or in terms of work actions or behaviors.
2. Specify how performance is to be measured.
3. Specify the standard or target to be aimed for in quantitative terms based either on directly measured output or on a Behavioral Observation Scale. Make the goal challenging, that is, difficult but attainable.
4. Specify the time span involved.
5. If there are multiple goals, rank them in terms of importance or priority. Get a consensus on this ranking.
6. If necessary, rate each goal quantitatively as to importance (priority) and difficulty. To measure overall performance, multiply importance by difficulty by degree of goal attainment, and then sum the products.
7. Determine the coordination requirements (especially lateral) for goal achievement. If the tasks are highly interdependent, use group goals. If group goals are used, be sure to develop a means of measuring each individual's contribution to the group's product. The goals should be modified only if employees clearly lack the ability or knowledge needed to reach them or when substantial changes in the job situation have occurred.

Whether goals should be assigned by a superior or set participatively is an individual matter. Assigned goals appear to achieve much the same level of impact in hierarchic organizations as in the laboratory context, presumably because legitimate authority and the demand character of experiments operate in much the same manner. As with other human resource and organizational behavior approaches, findings with regard to goal setting seem to generalize from the research laboratory to the field rather well (Locke 1986). Assigned goals work best with those who are already intrinsically motivated and who thus find the assigned goals less onerous. Participative goal setting works best if people are accustomed to and comfortable with it, and when intrinsic motivation to perform is at a low level, thus requiring an added inducement.

Overall, goal-setting procedures appear to have considerable motivational potential with the right people under the right circumstances. Difficulty, specificity, and acceptance of goals are important. Goal setting within the context of a comprehensive MBO program is a more uncertain matter, especially over the long term. The ideal approach seems to be to train individual supervisors of relatively independent jobs in the techniques of goal setting, as well as when to use them.

An idea of what the goal-setting theory approach can accomplish is provided by a study of the relationship between goal-setting activity and organizational profits (Terpstra and Rozell 1994). A survey was sent to firms averaging approximately 6,000 employees inquiring about their use of goal-setting theory (61 percent used it) and also about firm profit levels and profit growth. Significant relationships were found. This does not establish causality, but the authors believe that the causal arrow runs from practice to profitability. Yet these findings are not always replicated. In one instance, within a single company, when goal setting was compared with indexes of performance, the two clearly were not positively related (Yearta, Maitlis, and Briner 1995). Yet problems inherent in both the goal-setting program and the conduct of the research serve to emphasize not only the difficulties of doing goal setting right, but also of doing research on goal setting right. In his analysis of prime movers in the business world, Locke (2000) documents many instances of the successful use of personal goal setting. When used correctly, goal setting can be a highly effective motivating force for performance whether the goals are self-set, set participatively, or assigned (Latham 2000).

EVALUATION AND IMPACT

Goal-setting theory's formal statements emerged gradually and were intertwined closely with the research. This might represent a major problem in evaluating the theory against these research results were it not for several considerations. One is that Locke appears to have operated from an implicit theory that influenced the design of his research and the selection of research topics from the beginning, long before he made this theory explicit; this implicit theory clearly owes much to Ryan. Second, Locke, and also Latham, typically have conducted many studies in each area they have investigated, thus replicating their results several times. Accordingly the theoretical hypotheses cannot be dismissed on the grounds that they incorporate empirical fluctuations attributable to chance on an ad hoc basis.

Examples of Research by the Theory's Authors

Both Locke and Latham have been involved in a large number of studies testing aspects of their theory. Describing all of these would be impossible, but it is possible to provide examples of the approaches taken. The highly inductive nature of the theory construction, going back and forth from research to theory to more research to theoretical refinement and so on, means that most theoretical statements were well established before they became true theory. Providing the full flavor of this process would carry us well beyond the space limitations of this chapter, but the following examples should help.

An initial series of studies utilized brainstorming tasks in which subjects were to list objects or things that could be described by a given adjective, or to give possible uses for certain objects (Locke 1966). Goal levels (easy or hard) typically were set by the experimenter, and performance was measured in terms of numbers of objects or uses noted in a given time period over a number of trials. The subjects were all college students.

Performance was consistently higher when harder goals existed. This was true even when the goals were set so high that they could actually be reached less than 10 percent of the time. In the one instance when subjects were permitted to set their own goals, they chose relatively easy ones, and their performance reflected this.

A similar experiment was conducted later using a complex psychomotor task involving adjusting certain controls to produce a pattern of lights to match a standard. The more matches achieved in a set time period, the better the performance (Locke and Bryan 1966a). Comparisons were made between the results achieved when specific, hard goals were set by the experimenter and those achieved when the student subjects were merely told to do their best. The results provided strong support for the hypothesis that specific hard goals improve performance.

These results were extended to various clerical tasks of a numerical nature in another series of studies (Locke and Bryan 1967). In this instance, subject acceptance of goals was essential for goal-setting effects to occur. In certain instances when post-experimental questions indicated that subjects had not accepted the specific, hard goals assigned, performance was not superior. The introduction of a monetary incentive appears to have been effective in gaining the necessary commitment in one study, although other studies were able to produce similar results without incentives. Data obtained with an interest questionnaire indicated that subjects working for hard goals were significantly less bored than subjects working without specific goals.

This is the laboratory approach to goal setting. It has been used in one form or another in many, many studies by the theory's authors and others. Usually, after substantial research, a theoretical synthesis is developed. Thus, the research on feedback effects resulted in the following theoretical statement:

> The present review found none of the evidence to be inconsistent with the notion that the effects of motivational knowledge of results depend upon the goals a subject sets in response to such knowledge. Most previous studies failed to separate the effects of knowledge qua knowledge from those of goal setting. . . . When the two effects are separated, there is no effect of knowledge of results over and above that which can be attributed to differential goal setting. (Locke, Cartledge, and Koeppel 1968, 482)

The field research involving Latham started in the logging operations of wood products companies. In the first study, productivity (mean cords per day) was found to be highest not only when specific production goals were assigned, but also when the crew supervisor stayed at the work site to encourage goal acceptance (Ronan, Latham, and Kinne 1973).

In a second study, ten matched pairs of logging crews were compared over a fourteen-week period. One of each pair was exposed to preliminary training in goal setting, and the other was not. Appropriate specific production goals were established for all crews each week, but only in the case of the previously trained crews were these goals communicated; thus, only one of each pair was actively engaged in goal setting, although the performance of both crews could be measured relative to goals (Latham and Kinne 1974). It is evident that the goal-setting crews exceeded their goals more often and usually outperformed the non–goal-setting crews in terms of a cords per man-hour criterion:

Matched pair no.	Goal-setting crew	Nongoal-setting crew
1	+2.3	+0.09
2	−0.9	−0.09
3	+0.05	−0.08

4	+0.05	−0.07
5	+0.04	+0.01
6	+0.13	−0.02
7	+0.08	−0.16
8	+0.22	+0.24
9	+0.08	−0.07
10	+0.11	+0.13
Mean	+0.09	−0.002

A similar approach was utilized in a study by Latham and Baldes (1975) to induce logging truck drivers to carry heavier loads to the mill. A goal of 94 percent of the legal weight limit was assigned. At the beginning of the period the trucks were averaging 60 percent. With the introduction of the goal, performance improved sharply, and by the end of nine months had stabilized at over 90 percent. "Without the increase in efficiency due to goal setting it would have cost the company a quarter of a million dollars for the purchase of additional trucks in order to deliver the same quantity of logs to the mills" (124).

Results such as these led to the conclusion that the goal-setting results obtained in the laboratory applied in the field as well.

Findings from Meta-Analytic Studies

I am aware of more than fifteen meta-analyses of studies related to goal setting that have been published to date. Six of these appeared in the 1983–87 period and were given attention in the Locke and Latham (1990a) volume. The early reviews tended to look at goal setting in conjunction with other approaches. However, beginning in 1986 meta-analyses focused specifically on goal setting became a feature of the major journals; included here was an early effort involving the author of the theory (Wood, Mento, and Locke 1987). This burst of activity was in part occasioned by the fact that meta-analysis was just finding its way into organizational behavior at this time. More significant was the fact that goal-setting theory had by then spawned sufficient research to justify separate meta-analyses. Over time, extending to the present, this output of related research has been tremendous; without the quantitative and qualitative reviews, comprehending and synthesizing this research becomes almost impossible.

The conclusion from these early meta-analyses is that goal difficulty and specificity do operate as the theory predicts in influencing performance, and that feedback combines with goal setting as hypothesized. Participation per se does not exhibit any special advantage in setting goals, again in line with theoretical expectations. Goal-setting effects are most pronounced on relatively simple tasks; they decline on complex tasks such as business game simulations and scientific work.

Later meta-analyses have typically looked at more specific issues. Thus, Wright (1990) found that goal difficulty has in fact been operationalized in a number of different ways and that how it is operationalized has a substantial effect on performance outcomes. Nevertheless, the expected results are consistently obtained irrespective of the operationalization. Klein (1991) identified similar problems in the measurement of expectancy theory variables; large variations were noted in different studies. When appropriate operationalization occurs, however, expectancy theory variables are significantly related to goal choice, goal commitment, and performance. These results confirm the compatibility of the two theories.

We have already noted the Rodgers and Hunter (1991) meta-analysis of management by objectives research. The key finding here was that MBO requires top management support and participation to work well.

Wofford, Goodwin, and Premack (1992) were able to identify prior performance, ability, and, with somewhat less certainty, knowledge of results as antecedents of personal goals. Self-efficacy, expectancy of goal attainment, task difficulty, and task complexity (with a negative sign) were identified as antecedents of goal commitment. Goal commitment appeared to affect goal achievement. That certain hypothesized relationships did not emerge as expected seems to be due to the lack of a sufficient number of studies that often plagued this meta-analysis.

This dearth of research appears not to have been a problem in a meta-analysis of group goal-setting effects (O'Leary-Kelly, Martocchio, and Frink 1994). There, group goals were found to strongly influence performance with an effect size exceeding that typically found for individual goal setting. Recently, the theory's author has been conducting research in this area and finds strong support for the role of goal difficulty in team performance (Knight, Durham, and Locke 2001).

A meta-analysis conducted by Stajkovic and Luthans (1998) dealt specifically with self-efficacy, not goal setting, but is relevant because of the affinity that has developed between the two theoretical approaches. Self-efficacy is strongly related to performance, at a level that appears to exceed that often found for goal setting. As has been noted with goal setting, self-efficacy–performance relationships decline as tasks move from simple to complex; yet significance does not disappear.

Another article provides the only meta-analytic results that bring any aspect of goal-setting theory into question (Donovan and Radosevich 1998). Here, although goal commitment served to moderate the goal difficulty–performance relationship significantly, it did not emerge as the powerful factor that theory would anticipate. This finding may in fact reflect a shortcoming of the theory, but it may also reflect problems of definition and operationalization or limitations of the laboratory context used primarily to study the phenomenon. Research that identifies or introduces wide variations in goal commitment appears to be needed. Yet, as occasionally happens with meta-analytic studies, a later investigation of this same literature incorporating somewhat different studies produced results more supportive of theory that are interpreted as refuting the Donovan and Radosevich (1998) conclusions (Klein, Wesson, Hollenbeck, and Alge 1999). Also, Klein, Wesson, Hollenbeck, Wright, and DeShon (2001) were able to develop a measure of goal commitment using meta-analytic procedures that overcome many of the difficulties inherent in previous measures.

With regard to personality factors, Judge and Ilies (2002) used meta-analysis to evaluate the relationship between the so-called "big five" model and motivation as specified by goal-setting theory. The personality characteristics having the most marked relation were neuroticism (negative), conscientiousness, and agreeableness (negative). The latter finding was hypothesized to result from the fact that "agreeable individuals set less ambitious performance goals because they are motivated more by communion (desire to be part of a larger spiritual or social community) than by agency (desire to achieve mastery or power)" (Judge and Ilies 2002, 803). However, this finding is based on a rather small number of studies and accordingly may be unstable.

Self-efficacy motivation was also studied in this meta-analysis with results that differed from those for goal setting, emphasizing that the two types of motivation do not contribute to performance outcomes in the same manner. Once again, neuroticism related to motivation in a negative manner, but in the case of self-efficacy, the only other major personality factor was extroversion.

Proposition-specific Evaluations

The meta-analyses overall provide very strong support for goal-setting theory. Yet there are aspects of the theory that they do not consider, often because there is insufficient research available as yet to use the approach.

As Locke and Latham (1990a) note, the theory suffers from ambiguity as regards the definition of its constructs, including goal difficulty and goal commitment, as well as in establishing certain boundary definitions, such as in the area of complex tasks. Nevertheless, a great deal of research of respectable quality has been conducted.

In general, the theoretical expectations of the phase I rubric have received strong support. There is reason to believe, however, that monetary incentives can involve motivational forces above and beyond goal setting (Locke and Latham 1990a). Also, research on the job satisfaction formulations has not been as extensive as might be desired. However, confirmatory findings do exist (McFarlin and Rice 1991).

The early concerns about conflicts between expectancy theory and goal-setting theory seem to have evaporated, and in fact expectancy concepts have been incorporated widely in goal-setting models. Self-efficacy represents a powerful addition to the goal-setting formulations as well, although there clearly is much common variance between the expectancy and self-efficacy concepts incorporated.

The elaboration of goal mechanisms in phase II has proved helpful in a number of respects. It fills a theoretical void that needed filling. The same can be said for the formulations regarding the determinants of goal choice. The recent Donovan and Radosevich (1998) review raises questions regarding the role of goal commitment, but there is previous support for this construct, and variance restrictions inherent in the laboratory research may have limited the effectiveness of the tests utilized. Measurement advances offer promise with regard to goal commitment as well (e.g., see Renn, Danehower, Swiercz, and Icenogle 1999). The research on the ways in which goals are set—assigned, self, participative—for a while seemed to support motivational superiority for a participative approach. With the collaborative research of Latham, Erez, and Locke (1988), it became evident that assigned goals do as well as participative goals if properly sold to those doing the goal setting. The theory's position that motivational differences are negligible appears to have been upheld. However, a recent study found that low power distance individuals are particularly responsive to the participative approach (Sue-Chan and Ong 2002), thus raising once again the issue regarding the role of personality factors in goal setting.

Feedback is considered in both the phase I and phase II theory. These hypotheses have considerable research support, although not all aspects of Figure 10.1 have been the subject of study (Locke and Latham 1990a). Ability and situational constraints also appear to operate as hypothesized. The theory recognizes the problems inherent in complex tasks, and the research supports the view that the basic theory works less well in this domain. Strategies exert a greater effect on performance in this context than goals (Chesney and Locke 1991). Personality factors have not been consistently incorporated in the theory, although there is increasing evidence that they should be (e.g., see Lee, Sheldon, and Turban 2003). The strong demand character of the laboratory setting no doubt minimizes personality influences, but as complex problem solving, plans, and strategies become of increasing interest, this is no longer true.

With regard to the different versions of the high-performance cycle model (Figure 10.2), it now appears that self-efficacy (and expectancy) should be treated both as moderators *and* as demands, with direct effects on performance. Presumably the alternating versions represented attempts to find simpler presentations of the model, which in the end did not fully reflect the reality.

The phase III domain extensions are clearly incomplete. There is going to be a need for some new theory if such matters as real and stated organizational goals, business strategies, and the like are to be a major concern of the theory. Nevertheless, some progress has been made. For instance, the vision statements of entrepreneurs (as goals) do affect organizational performance and growth (Baum, Locke, and Kirkpatrick 1998). Also, the movement into the realm of self-management has struck a chord within organizational behavior (see Rousseau 1997); it is still unclear as to how much new theory or cooptation of existing theory will be required by this thrust.

Mitchell, Thompson, and George-Falvy (2000) note that goal-setting theory has given insufficient attention to the context of goals, including multiple goals and goal priorities. Also lacking is concern with the actual process of setting goals—the political aspects of goal setting by managers, for instance. Multiple goals appear to increase the level of tension experienced, and to create at least the perception that performance decreases (Emsley 2003). Dealing with these multiple goal situations has for a considerable time been envisaged as involving some type of hierarchic representation of the motives operating, as held in an individual's cognitive schemas. This hierarchic view continues to spark research up to the present (Bagozzi, Bergami, and Leone 2003), and with a good deal of success. Concerns related to issues of these kinds are not merely reflective of research needs; they require theoretical extensions as well. Goal-setting theory now faces the problem that it has been so successful, and sparked so much research, that the research is in danger of overflowing the vessel that is its theory. It may no longer be possible to follow the inductive theory–research lockstep that Locke initiated in the 1960s. The problems unearthed seem to call for more expansive theorizing (Pinder 1998).

Questions Raised from the Perceptual Control Theory Perspective

Perceptual control theory uses a cybernetic model where perceptions are matched against a comparator (similar to a thermostat) to gain an understanding of goal striving. The theory is parsimonious, perhaps to a fault, and focuses on negative feedback loop structures. It is particularly concerned with the dynamic nature of these structures over time and thus introduces measurement requirements above and beyond what has been involved in goal-setting research previously (Vancouver and Putka 2000).

The questions that control theory has raised for goal-setting theory deal essentially with the self-efficacy concept. Control theory anticipates that self-efficacy can decrease, rather than increase, the amount of resources devoted to performance, and that the positive relationship between self-efficacy and performance often results from the impact of performance on self-efficacy, not the reverse, as goal-setting theory would have it. In the goal-setting view, self-efficacy raises the level of self-set goals, reinforces commitment to these goals, and thus enhances the level of performance. Control theory says that:

1. the positive correlation of self-efficacy with performance may be largely an effect of past performance on self-efficacy;
2. self-efficacy can negatively affect subsequent performance by rendering a person complacent; and
3. self-efficacy can positively affect subsequent performance by affecting choices like the adoption of a difficult goal (Vancouver, Thompson, and Williams 2001, 617).

When a research design that permitted the dynamic study of an individual's goal striving was brought to bear, the control theory formulations appear to have been supported.

A subsequent study (Vancouver, Thompson, Tischner, and Putka 2002) established further that the negative effect exists. Self-efficacy leads to overconfidence and thus an increased propensity to commit logic errors in these cases. Although self-efficacy was not necessarily detrimental, when it was, the result was a negative relationship to performance and a positive correlation with errors.

In response to these questions posed from the perceptual control theory perspective, Bandura and Locke (2003) offer a thoughtful rebuttal in an article that contains no new original research. The authors base their argument on the results of nine meta-analyses that consistently indicate that efficacy beliefs contribute significantly to the level of both motivation and performance. To the extent, however, that prior studies were of a kind that minimized the possibility that results similar to those of Vancouver and his associates would be obtained, these meta-analyses are not entirely to the point. Vancouver and his coworkers did draw upon some novel design approaches, thus bringing something new to the table. Also, Bandura and Locke (2003) offer some convincing criticisms of perceptual control theory, but that does not negate the research results obtained; they can stand alone, calling for the development of some future theory that brings this all together.

I do not see the Vancouver et al. findings as representing a serious threat to goal-setting theory overall, but they do call for a sizable extension of the theory, especially in relation to the functioning of self-efficacy. Such an extension should also consider a proposal put forth by Erez and Isen (2002, 1065): "In the same way in which positive affect influences the cognitive processes involved in expectancy motivation, it may also be integrated into other cognitive motivation theories such as goal setting." Is positive emotion per se a major force driving difficult and specific goals and thus improved performance?

Implications of the Motivation Sequence Model

Figure 10.4 sets forth goal-setting theory within a larger theoretical picture. Deci (1992) has criticized goal theory as representing only a partial theory of motivation in organizations, and adds that it fails to address many of the most interesting and important questions. The motivation sequence represents an attempt to open up goal theory and integrate it with other theories of a similar nature. In doing so it introduces needs, values, and motives not specifically tied to goals for consideration; Deci (1992) advocates this.

Consider the following findings from research:

- On complex tasks, specific challenging goals work to improve performance *only* if there is some type of help in searching for strategies (Earley, Connolly, and Lee 1989).
- On complex tasks, commitment to planning, and even to in-process planning, plays an important role in mediating the effects of goals on performance (Weingart 1992).
- On a complex task, individuals given a creative goal have lower productivity than those with *no goal,* presumably due to the fact that they are concentrating on creativity, not productivity (Shalley 1995).

These findings beg for information on the personality characteristics of the subjects; needs, values, and motive patterns become crucial as goal-setting theory moves to complex tasks of one kind or another. How would such characteristics as independence-dependence, the desire to plan, and a propensity for creative thought operate within the confines of the above studies? The motivation sequence makes such questions of legitimate concern for goal-setting theory and research.

It is evident that such factors as goal specificity, goal difficulty, and participation in setting goals affect various individuals differently. This finding could well be mediated by variations in the importance certain people attach to particular goals, or at a more abstract level, values. In any event there are some distinct variations in the kinds of individuals who react differently to aspects of the goal-setting process. A thorough study of these variations in the context of adequate theoretical perspectives could in fact move goal-setting theory out of its current status, firmly constrained within the motivation hub of Figure 10.4, to incorporate the motivation core, and beyond. There is indeed a glimmer here of the overarching motivation theory that Locke envisages.

CONCLUSIONS

Equity theory and goal setting do not appear to have much in common, other than a vaguely similar source of origin through ties to social psychology, but some commonalties can be noted. For one thing, both have survived over a considerable period of time and are still active today, goal-setting theory probably more so, presumably because Locke and Latham are still alive and professionally involved, but equity theory clearly did not die with its author.

Second, both the two theories have moved, or seem to be moving, in similar directions. Personality considerations have become more important for both theories, although neither can be said to be truly personality-based at present. Yet as these theories become more closely integrated with other theories of motivation, they inevitably acquire constructs of a personality nature. Furthermore, the theorists, although not necessarily their theories, have moved in a macro direction—not away from their definitely micro base, but to study or incorporate certain macro variables. We do not know what this might have meant for equity theory, but for goal-setting theory it has meant a concern with complex organizational tasks and strategies.

Goal-setting theory's ratings are exceptionally high. The importance rating of 5.97 is at the very top, and the theory is institutionalized as well. Estimated validity is at 5 stars; the research support is strong, and although I have noted a number of instances where theoretical extensions seem called for, this does not refute the validity of the existing theory. Locke has worked back and forth from research to inductively derived theory, and this strategy has served him well. The possibility that its potential for future theory development may have been exhausted is quite high, however. As to estimated usefulness, the score of 4 stars is down only slightly. Overall, Latham has demonstrated the practical utility of goal-setting theory across a wide range of applications. The major departure that has not worked out as well is the marriage with MBO. Also, there has been some question as to whether Latham's use of goal setting within companies may not be overly dependent on his own personal skill in such matters. There is some doubt as to whether the approaches he uses are fully generalizable to other contexts.

The last chapter on motivation theories, which is coming up, has a somewhat different perspective than the theories we have been considering. The focus in this instance is on motivated perceptions, rather than on motives per se, and in particular on the motivated perceptions of managers. This introduces the subject of attribution theory.

REFERENCES

Audia, Pino G., Locke, Edwin A., and Smith, Ken G. (2000). The Paradox of Success: An Archival and Laboratory Study of Strategic Persistence Following Radical Environmental Change. *Academy of Management Journal*, 43, 837–953.

Bagozzi, Richard P., Bergami, Massimo, and Leone, Luigi (2003). Hierarchical Representation of Motives in Goal Setting. *Journal of Applied Psychology*, 88, 925–43.

Bandura, Albert (1982). Self-Efficacy Mechanism in Human Agency. *American Psychologist*, 37, 122–47.

——— (1997). *Self-Efficacy: The Exercise of Control*. New York: Freeman.

Bandura, Albert, and Locke, Edwin A. (2003). Negative Self-Efficacy and Goal Effects Revisited. *Journal of Applied Psychology*, 88, 87–99.

Bartol, Kathryn M., and Locke, Edwin A. (2000). Incentives and Motivation. In Sara L. Rynes and Barry Gerhart (Eds.), *Compensation in Organizations: Current Research and Practice*. San Francisco, CA: Jossey-Bass, 104–47.

Baum, J. Robert, Locke, Edwin A., and Kirkpatrick, Shelley A. (1998). A Longitudinal Study of the Relation of Vision and Vision Communication to Venture Growth in Entrepreneurial Firms. *Journal of Applied Psychology*, 83, 43–54.

Baum, J. Robert, Locke, Edwin A., and Smith, Ken G. (2001). A Multidimensional Model of Venture Growth. *Academy of Management Journal*, 44, 292–303.

Bryan, Judith F.,and Locke, Edwin A. (1967). Parkinson's Law as a Goal Setting Phenomenon. *Organizational Behavior and Human Performance*, 2, 258–75.

Chesney, Amelia A., and Locke, Edwin A. (1991). Relationships among Goal Difficulty, Business Strategies, and Performance on a Complex Management Simulation Task. *Academy of Management Journal*, 34, 400–24.

Deci, Edward L. (1992). On the Nature and Functions of Motivation Theories. *Psychological Science*, 3, 167–71.

Donovan, John J., and Radosevich, David J. (1998). The Moderating Role of Goal Commitment on the Goal Difficulty–Performance Relationship: A Meta-Analytic Review and Critical Reanalysis. *Journal of Applied Psychology*, 83, 308–15.

Drucker, Peter F. (1954). *The Practice of Management*. New York: Harper.

Earley, P. Christopher, Connolly, Terry, and Lee, Cynthia (1989). Task Strategy Interventions in Goal Setting: The Importance of Search in Strategy Development. *Journal of Management*, 15, 589–602.

Emsley, David (2003). Multiple Goals and Managers? Job-related Tension and Performance. *Journal of Managerial Psychology*, 18, 345–56.

Erez, Amir, and Isen, Alice M. (2002). The Influence of Positive Affect on the Components of Expectancy Motivation. *Journal of Applied Psychology*, 87, 1055–67.

Ghate, Onkar, and Locke, Edwin A. (2003). Objectivism: The Proper Alternative to Postmodernism. In Edwin A. Locke (Ed.), *Postmodernism and Management: Pros, Cons, and the Alternative*. Oxford, UK: Elsevier Science, 249–78.

Humphreys, John (2003). The Dysfunctional Evolution of Goal Setting. *MIT Sloan Management Review*, 44(4), 95.

Judge, Timothy A., and Ilies, Remus (2002). Relationship of Personality to Performance Motivation: A Meta-Analytic Review. *Journal of Applied Psychology*, 87, 797–807.

Klein, Howard J. (1991). Further Evidence on the Relationship between Goal Setting and Expectancy Theories. *Organizational Behavior and Human Decision Processes*, 49, 230–57.

Klein, Howard J., Wesson, Michael J., Hollenbeck, John R., and Alge, Bradley, J. (1999). Goal Commitment and the Goal-Setting Process: Conceptual Clarification and Empirical Synthesis. *Journal of Applied Psychology*, 84, 885–96.

Klein, Howard J., Wesson, Michael J., Hollenbeck, John R., Wright, Patrick M., and DeShon, Richard P. (2001). The Assessment of Goal Commitment: A Measurement Model Meta-Analysis. *Organizational Behavior and Human Decision Processes*, 85, 32–55.

Knight, Don, Durham, Cathy C., and Locke, Edwin A. (2001). The Relationship of Team Goals, Incentives, and Efficacy to Strategic Risk, Tactical Implementation, and Performance. *Academy of Management Journal*, 44, 326–38.

Latham, Gary P. (2000). Motivate Employee Performance through Goal Setting. In Edwin A. Locke (Ed.), *Handbook of Principles of Organizational Behavior*. Oxford, UK: Blackwell, 107–19.

——— (2003). Goal Setting: A Five-Step Approach to Behavior Change. *Organizational Dynamics*, 32, 309–18.

Latham, Gary P., and Baldes, J. James (1975). The Practical Significance of Locke's Theory of Goal Setting. *Journal of Applied Psychology*, 60, 122–24.

Latham, Gary P., Erez, Miriam, and Locke, Edwin A. (1988). Resolving Scientific Disputes by the Joint

Design of Crucial Experiments by the Antagonists: Application to the Erez-Latham Dispute Regarding Participation in Goal Setting. *Journal of Applied Psychology,* 73, 753–72.

Latham, Gary P., and Kinne, Sydney B. (1974). Improving Job Performance through Training in Goal Setting. *Journal of Applied Psychology,* 59, 187–91.

Latham, Gary P., and Locke, Edwin A. (1991). Self-Regulation through Goal Setting. *Organizational Behavior and Human Decision Processes,* 50, 212–47.

Lee, Felissa K., Sheldon, Kennon M., and Turban, Daniel B. (2003). Personality and the Goal-striving Process: The Influence of Achievement Goal Patterns, Goal Level, and Mental Focus on Performance and Enjoyment. *Journal of Applied Psychology,* 88, 256–65.

Lewin, Kurt, Dembo, Tamara, Festinger, Leon, and Sears, Pauline S. (1944). Level of Aspiration. In J. McVicker Hunt (Ed.), *Personality and the Behavior Disorders,* Vol. I. New York: Ronald, 333–78.

Locke, Edwin A. (1966). The Relationship of Intentions to Level of Performance. *Journal of Applied Psychology,* 50, 60–66.

——— (1968). Toward a Theory of Task Motivation and Incentives. *Organizational Behavior and Human Performance,* 3, 157–89.

——— (1969). What is Job Satisfaction? *Organizational Behavior and Human Performance,* 4, 309–36.

——— (1970a). Job Satisfaction and Job Performance: A Theoretical Analysis. *Organizational Behavior and Human Performance,* 5, 484–500.

——— (1970b). The Supervisor as Motivator: His Influence on Employee Performance and Satisfaction. In Bernard M. Bass, R. Cooper, and J. A. Haas (Eds.), *Managing for Task Accomplishment.* Lexington, MA: Heath, 57–67.

——— (1986). *Generalizing from Laboratory to Field Settings.* Lexington, MA: Lexington Books.

——— (1991). The Motivation Sequence, the Motivation Hub, and the Motivation Core. *Organizational Behavior and Human Decision Processes,* 50, 288–99.

——— (1993). Principled Ambition. In Arthur G. Bedeian (Ed.), *Management Laureates: A Collection of Autobiographical Essays,* Vol. II. Greenwich, CT: JAI Press, 217–48.

——— (2000). *The Prime Movers: Traits of the Great Wealth Creators.* New York: AMACOM.

——— (2001). Self-Set Goals and Self-Efficacy as Mediators of Incentives and Personality. In Miriam Erez, Uwe Kleinbeck, and Henk Thierry (Eds.), *Work Motivation in the Context of a Globalizing Economy.* Mahwah, NJ: Lawrence Erlbaum, 13–26.

Locke, Edwin A., and Bryan, Judith F. (1966a). Cognitive Aspects of Psychomotor Performance: The Effects of Performance Goals on Level of Performance. *Journal of Applied Psychology,* 50, 286–91.

——— (1966b). The Effects of Goal Setting, Rule Learning, and Knowledge of Score on Performance. *American Journal of Psychology,* 79, 451–57.

——— (1967). Performance Goals as Determinants of Level of Performance and Boredom. *Journal of Applied Psychology,* 51, 120–30.

Locke, Edwin A., Bryan, Judith F., and Kendall, Lorne M. (1968). Goals and Intentions as Mediators of the Effects of Monetary Incentives on Behavior. *Journal of Applied Psychology,* 52, 104–21.

Locke, Edwin A., Cartledge, Norman, and Knerr, Claramae S. (1970). Studies of the Relationship Between Satisfaction, Goal Setting, and Performance. *Organizational Behavior and Human Performance,* 5, 135–38.

Locke, Edwin A., Cartledge, Norman, and Koeppel, Jeffrey (1968). Motivational Effects of Knowledge of Results: A Goal-Setting Phenomenon. *Psychological Bulletin,* 70, 474–85.

Locke, Edwin A., and Latham, Gary P. (1984). *Goal Setting: A Motivational Technique that Works.* Englewood Cliffs, NJ: Prentice-Hall.

——— (1990a). *A Theory of Goal Setting and Task Performance.* Englewood Cliffs, NJ: Prentice-Hall.

——— (1990b). Work Performance: The High Performance Cycle. In Uwe Kleinbeck, Hans-Henning Quast, Henk Thierry, and Hartmut Häcker (Eds.), *Work Motivation.* Hillsdale, NJ: Lawrence Erlbaum, 3–25.

——— (1990c). Work Motivation and Satisfaction: Light at the End of the Tunnel. *Psychological Science,* 1, 240–46.

——— (2002). Building a Practically Useful Theory of Goal Setting and Task Motivation. *American Psychologist,* 57, 705–17.

McFarlin, Dean B., and Rice, Robert W. (1991). Determinants of Satisfaction with Specific Job Facets: A Test of Locke's Model. *Journal of Business and Psychology,* 6, 25–38.

Miner, John B. (1997). *A Psychological Typology of Successful Entrepreneurs.* Westport, CT: Quorum.

Mitchell, Terence R., Thompson, Kenneth R., and George-Falvy, Jane (2000). Goal Setting: Theory and

Practice. In Cary L. Cooper and Edwin A. Locke (Eds.), *Industrial and Organizational Psychology: Linking Theory and Practice.* Oxford, UK: Blackwell, 216–49.

Nuttin, J.R. (1984). *Motivation, Planning and Action: A Relational Theory of Behavioral Dynamics.* Hillsdale, NJ: Lawrence Erlbaum.

O'Leary-Kelly, Anne M., Martocchio, Joseph J., and Frink, Dwight D. (1994). A Review of the Influence of Group Goals on Group Performance. *Academy of Management Journal,* 37, 1285–1301.

Peters, Thomas J., and Waterman, Robert H. (1982). *In Search of Excellence: Lessons from America's Best-Run Companies.* New York: Harper and Row.

Pinder, Craig C. (1998). *Work Motivation in Organizational Behavior.* Upper Saddle River, NJ: Prentice-Hall.

Renn, Robert W., Danehower, Carol, Swiercz, Paul M., and Icenogle, Marjorie L. (1999). Further Examination of the Measurement Properties of Leifer and McGannon's (1986) Goal Acceptance and Goal Commitment Scales. *Journal of Occupational and Organizational Psychology,* 72, 107–13.

Rodgers, Robert, and Hunter, John E. (1991). Impact of Management by Objectives on Organizational Productivity. *Journal of Applied Psychology,* 76, 322–35.

Ronan, W.W., Latham, Gary P., and Kinne, Sydney B. (1973). Effects of Goal Setting and Supervision on Worker Behavior in an Industrial Situation. *Journal of Applied Psychology,* 58, 302–7.

Rousseau, Denise M. (1997). Organizational Behavior in the New Organizational Era. *Annual Review of Psychology,* 48, 515–46.

Ryan, Thomas A. (1970). *Intentional Behavior: An Approach to Human Motivation.* New York: Ronald.

Shalley, Christina E. (1995). Effects of Coaction, Expected Evaluation, and Goal Setting on Creativity and Productivity. *Academy of Management Journal,* 38, 483–503.

Stajkovic, Alexander D., and Luthans, Fred (1998). Self-Efficacy and Work-Related Performance: A Meta-Analysis. *Psychological Bulletin,* 124, 240–61.

Sue-Chan, Christina, and Ong, Mark (2002). Goal Assignment and Performance: Assessing the Mediating Roles of Goal Commitment and Self-efficacy and the Moderating Role of Power Distance. *Organizational Behavior and Human Decision Processes,* 89, 1140–61.

Terpstra, David E., and Rozell, Elizabeth J. (1994). The Relationship of Goal Setting to Organizational Profitability. *Group and Organization Management,* 19, 285–94.

Vancouver, Jeffrey B., and Putka, Dan J. (2000). Analyzing Goal-striving Processes and a Test of the Generalizability of Perceptual Control Theory. *Organizational Behavior and Human Decision Processes,* 82, 334–62.

Vancouver, Jeffrey B., Thompson, Charles M., Tischner, E. Casey, and Putka, Dan J. (2002). Two Studies Examining the Negative Effect of Self-Efficacy on Performance. *Journal of Applied Psychology,* 87, 506–16.

Vancouver, Jeffrey B., Thompson, Charles M., and Williams, Amy A. (2001). The Changing Signs in the Relationship Among Self-Efficacy, Personal Goals, and Performance. *Journal of Applied Psychology,* 86, 605–20.

Weingart, Laurie R. (1992). Impact of Group Goals, Task Component Complexity, Effort, and Planning on Group Performance. *Journal of Applied Psychology,* 77, 682–93.

Wofford, J.C., Goodwin, Vicki L., and Premack, Steven (1992). Meta-Analysis of the Antecedents of Personal Goal Level and Antecedents and Consequences of Goal Commitment. *Journal of Management,* 18, 595–615.

Wood, Robert E., and Locke, Edwin A. (1990). Goal Setting and Strategy Effects on Complex Tasks. *Research in Organizational Behavior,* 12, 73–109.

Wood, Robert E., Mento, Anthony, and Locke, Edwin A. (1987). Task Complexity as a Moderator of Goal Effects: A Meta-Analysis. *Journal of Applied Psychology,* 72, 416–25.

Wright, Patrick M. (1990). Operationalization of Goal Difficulty as a Moderator of the Goal Difficulty–Performance Relationship. *Journal of Applied Psychology,* 75, 227–34.

Yearta, Shawn K., Maitlis, Sally, and Briner, Rob B. (1995). An Exploratory Study of Goal Setting in Theory and Practice: A Motivational Technique that Works. *Journal of Occupational and Organizational Psychology,* 68, 237–52.

CHAPTER 11

ATTRIBUTION THEORY— MANAGERIAL PERCEPTIONS OF THE POOR PERFORMING SUBORDINATE

TERENCE MITCHELL AND STEPHEN GREEN

Background
    Attribution Theory in Psychology
    The Management of Ineffective Performance
Theoretical Statements
    Attributional Processes in Leader–Member
        Interactions
    The Attributional Model of Leader Response to
        Poor Performance
    Impression Management
    Group Poor Performance
    Introducing Ingratiation into the Theory
    Attributional Effects of Group Performance
        and Leader Power
Evaluation and Impact
    Early Mitchell Studies
    Mitchell's Expanded Research Agenda
    Closely Related Research
    Outside Research on the Basic Theory
    Outside Research Related to Psychological Distance
    Outside Research Related to Accounts
    Concerns Regarding Attributional Approaches
Conclusions

Importance rating	★ ★ ★ ★
Estimated validity	★ ★ ★ ★
Estimated usefulness	★ ★
Decade of origin	1970s

Attribution theory had a long history in psychology, particularly social psychology, before it found its way into organizational behavior. Theorists who make attributions the core constructs of their thinking are concerned with the perceived causes of events and the consequences of the particular types of perceptions involved. There is no one attribution theory; many different forms have emerged. Within organizational behavior, however, responsibility assignment approaches have prevailed; these approaches are concerned with how people make attributions for the behavior and outcomes of other individuals (Martinko 1995). The most widely known and extensively researched of these theories is the approach developed by Mitchell and others to indicate how leaders perceive and explain the poor performance of subordinates. This is an interpersonal attribution model concerned with explanations for the actions of others. Within psychology there has been much more concern with intrapersonal attributions—explanations of and for one's own behavior. Thus in organizational behavior, attribution processes tend to be viewed as perceptual in nature, not entirely motivational, although elements of both are involved. The Mitchell theory adds a leadership component as well.

Attributions are to be viewed in the wider context of person perception (London 2001). The basic cognitive model for person perception is that people tend to have rather fixed views of the way that things should be as they enter into interpersonal relationships. These views, in the form of schemas or prototypes, serve as filters to assist in processing information about the characteristics and behaviors of others. In this manner, people are able to eliminate or ignore information that fails to fit their initial views and make the input to their perceptual processes more manageable. Heuristics are formed to help perceivers make decisions in the face of sizable data inputs. This information-processing formulation is elaborated in more detail later in this volume (see Chapter 15).

Person perception includes the processes through which individuals form impressions and draw inferences regarding other people (Klimoski and Donahue 2001). Within this process, the specific procedures that people use to establish the assumed causes of another person's behavior are labeled as attributions. Perceiver inputs in such instances include traits and other characteristics, motives, abilities and skills, and values, beliefs, or attitudes. Understanding how this motivated perceptual process operates is the domain of attribution theory.

BACKGROUND

Born in 1942, Terence Mitchell obtained his undergraduate degree in psychology from Duke University in 1964 and completed subsequent work in public administration at the University of Exeter in England. His graduate study was in social psychology at the University of Illinois, but with a minor in public administration. He received the Ph.D. in 1969. Immediately thereafter he took a position at the University of Washington with a joint appointment in organizational behavior (in the business school) and in psychology.

In 1969 Fred Fiedler moved from Illinois to Washington also (see Chapter 13), and it is no coincidence that both he and Mitchell had a major interest in interpersonal perception: They conducted research and published together for several years, although their interests have taken them in different directions since the early 1970s. Mitchell was promoted to full professor at Washington in 1977 and has remained there since.

Consistent with his wide range of scholarly activities, Mitchell has published with many different individuals. This is also true of his contributions to attribution theory. His major coauthor in the early period was Stephen Green, who was then with him at the University of Washington and subsequently spent many years on the faculty of the business school at the University of Cincinnati. Green now holds a similar appointment at Purdue University. He became increasingly involved in the study of poor and ineffective performance, as distinct from its fusion with attribution processes, and did not continue to publish with Mitchell after the early 1980s.

Attribution Theory in Psychology

Mitchell's theory has its roots in a fusion of work in two areas—attribution theory and the management of ineffective performance. The attribution theory component is the most extensive and goes back further in time. The beginning is generally considered to be the work of Fritz Heider

(1958). The subsequent names are Edward Jones, Harold Kelley, and Julian Rotter (Martinko 1995). Mitchell cites all of these as sources of his own thinking. Jones contributed in particular to the distinction between actors and observers. Kelley provided views of the attribution process that were later formally built into Mitchell's theory, as we will see. Rotter was primarily an input to Mitchell's early research, which was on the developmental path leading up to the actual creation of the attribution theory of poor performance.

In addition to these formulations, Mitchell drew upon certain ideas related to achievement motivation (see Chapter 4) put forth by Bernard Weiner. In relating achievement motivation to attribution processes, Weiner at that time was attempting to enlarge upon McClelland's view that achievement-motivated people prefer to attribute credit for outcomes to their own efforts rather than to chance or luck.

Weiner's (1972, 356) theory deals with the degree to which people ascribe their successes and failures to:

1. their own ability—viewed as a stable characteristic and inside oneself;
2. their effort level—viewed as a variable factor, also inside oneself;
3. the difficulty of the task—viewed as stable and given, but external to the self; and
4. luck—viewed as variable and unstable, also external to the self.

Wide individual differences are postulated in the tendency to attribute what happens to a person to each of these factors. In particular, achievement-motivated people are expected to attribute their successes to their own efforts and their failures to not trying hard enough. If they fail they are likely to try again because they tend to believe that with greater effort they can succeed. Thus, they consistently perceive their ability levels as being quite high. When they do succeed it is because they tried hard and used their abilities.

In contrast, those with a low need for achievement view effort as irrelevant. They attribute failure to other factors, in particular lack of ability, a condition that they believe is generally characteristic of themselves. Success is viewed as primarily a consequence of the external factors of easy tasks and luck.

Obviously, if one is interested in motivating a person to do something, what will work in dealing with an achievement-oriented person may be absolutely useless in dealing with a person lacking achievement motivation. This suggests, as Weiner has indicated, that educational programs attempting to bring about motivational change and development in the achievement area should focus first on teaching the participants that effort does make a difference and that internal causation is a key factor mediating between a task and the level of performance on that task.

Although relevant research at the time was not extensive, there was a degree of support for an explanation of the dynamics of achievement motivation in terms of attribution mechanisms (Weiner 1972; Weiner and Sierad 1975). These findings, if nothing else, served to demonstrate to Mitchell that attribution theory was a useful vehicle for explaining many phenomena within organizational behavior. An essay by Calder (1977) served to demonstrate more directly the ways in which attributional thinking could contribute to an understanding of leadership processes.

The Management of Ineffective Performance

The second line of development leading to Mitchell's theory of attribution and poor performance harks back to my own personal experiences in developing a diagnostic scheme to aid managers in determining the causes of (making attributions regarding) the ineffective performance of subordinates. The key writings here that appear to have influenced Mitchell are Miner (1963), Steinmetz (1969), and Miner and Brewer (1976). The idea in these early statements was that faced with an instance of poor performance, managers should try to figure out (diagnose) the various causes contributing to failure. Only with this knowledge could a suitable treatment or corrective action be determined that could establish effective performance where failure had existed before. What Mitchell's theory added to this is that it viewed the diagnostic process as one of making attributions, with all the potential for error inherent in perceptions of this type.

THEORETICAL STATEMENTS

Before actually moving to the presentation of the basic theory, Mitchell participated in several studies that dealt with attributional subject matter but in a manner somewhat tangential to the theory that finally evolved. These studies considered Rotter's locus of control construct (Mitchell, Smyser, and Weed 1975) and attributional biases in ratings of leader behavior (Mitchell, Larson, and Green 1977). In his *Annual Review* article, Mitchell (1979, 251) concludes: "While the work on applying attribution theory to the organizational context is rather recent, what has been done seems promising." Shortly thereafter he began the presentation of his own theory (with Green).

Attributional Processes in Leader–Member Interactions

In the first presentation of the theory (Green and Mitchell 1979), leaders are considered to be information processors where the naïve causal attributions serve as mediators between the behaviors of subordinates and the leaders' behaviors. Following Kelley, these attributions may be categorized as grounded in a perception (1) of the employee (person) as cause, (2) of the task (entity) as cause, or (3) of the external circumstances surrounding the event (context) as cause. The cause of an event (behavior of subordinate) will in all likelihood be found in something that varies during and after the event occurs, rather than remaining stable—the principle of covariation. The information sought by the leader (and this too follows Kelley) is of three kinds:

Distinctiveness—did the behavior occur on this task but not others?
Consistency—how consistent is this behavior with the other behavior of the person?
Consensus—is the behavior unique to this particular person as opposed to being widespread among others?

These and other factors are brought together in the model of the attributional process set forth in Figure 11.1. This identical model appears in a later publication as well (Mitchell, Green, and Wood 1981). The organizational and/or personal policy loop refers to mechanisms that circumvent the attributional process so that if it occurs at all, it has no impact on leader behavior. A variety of hypotheses related to factors in Figure 11.1 are sprinkled through the Green and Mitchell (1979) essay and brought together toward the end. These represent the essential original contribution of the theory:

(I)   Leaders can be seen as scientists engaging in a process of hypothesis testing by gathering information and seeking causal explanations about the behavior and performance of their group members.

Figure 11.1 . **The Basic Attributional Model**

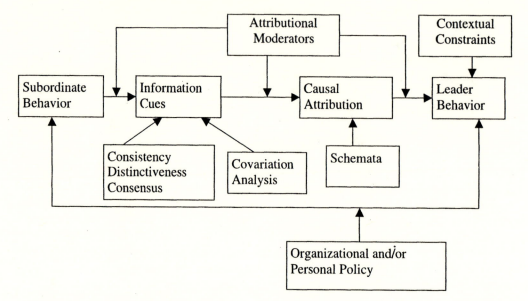

Source: Green and Mitchell (1979, 450). Copyright © 1979 Academic Press. Reprinted with permission.

(II)   A leader's behavior is likely to depend more on consistency and distinctiveness information about a member's performance than on consensus information.

    (a) When consensus information is used, it is likely to be self-based consensus.

(III)   Because a leader is more likely to explain member performance with internal causes than external causes, leader behavior is more likely to be directed at the member than at situational factors.

    (a) Since a member is more likely to explain his or her own performance with external causes, this basic difference in causal explanations and the resultant leader behavior serves as a major source of leader–member conflict and miscommunication.

(IV)   Locus of control and stability are two critical dimensions of causal attributions which mediate leaders' responses to member performance.

    (a) A leader is likely to focus his or her actions on the member when performance is seen as due to internal causes (e.g., suggest training when performance is seen as due to lack of knowledge).

    (b) A leader is likely to focus his or her actions on situational factors when the member's performance is seen as due to external causes (e.g., changing a job procedure if it is too difficult for most employees).

    (c) A leader's evaluations of a member's present performance are heavily influenced by effort (internal, unstable) attributions.

    (d) A leader will be both more rewarding and more punishing of present performance which is attributed to effort.

    (e) A leader's expectancies about a member's future performance are heavily influenced by the stability of attributions; the more stable the cause is seen to be (e.g., ability) the more future performance of the member is expected to be consistent with present performance.

(V)   Attributional processes are directly related to how much uncertainty a leader experiences in attempting to manage subordinates.

      (a) Multiple causation tends to result in leader uncertainty. This uncertainty may intensify the testing of the member by the leader and result in less extreme actions by the leader.

      (b) Unstable causal explanations create uncertainty, with unstable, external attributions presenting the most uncertainty for the leader.

(VI)   The relationship between leader and member is a critical moderator of the leader's attributions and subsequent behavior.

      (a) The more a leader is empathetic with the member, sees the member as similar, respects and/or likes the member, the more likely the leader is to form "favorable" causal attributions for the member's performance (e.g., attributing success to internal causes and failure to external causes).

      (b) The more removed the leader (e.g., the greater the power), the more likely the leader is to make "unfavorable" causal attributions about the member's performance.

      (c) Favorable attributions will enhance rewarding behavior and reduce punishing behavior on the part of the leader. Unfavorable attributions will result in the opposite type of behavior on the part of the leader.

(VII)   Leader expectations about member performance interact with actual performance to determine the leader's attributions.

      (a) The leader will attribute member performance to internal causes (e.g., effort) when expectations and performance are consistent.

      (b) The leader will attribute member performance to external causes (e.g., luck) when expectations and performance are inconsistent.

(VIII) The effects of the subordinate's behavior and the degree of responsibility inferred by the leader will influence the action selected.

      (a) The more extreme the effect, the more extreme the response.

      (b) The greater the perceived responsibility of the member, the more likely the leader is to take action concerning the member and the more extreme the response. (Green and Mitchell 1979, 451–52)

The Attributional Model of Leader Response to Poor Performance

The next theoretical statement was the presentation of the model of Figure 11.2. In conjunction with this model, which is more theoretically focused than Figure 11.1, certain propositions are set forth:

- At link #1 high distinctiveness, low consistency, and high consensus should result in internal attributions.
- The more severe the consequences of the poor performance, the greater the probability that the leader will make internal attributions and respond with punishment.
- When an internal attribution is made, the leader should respond by attempting to change the subordinate's behavior through feedback, punishment, or training; when the attribution is external, the response should be directed at changing the situation or task.
- Leaders in general will attribute poor performance in subordinates to internal rather than external causes (based on Mitchell and Wood 1980, 125).

Figure 11.2   **The Attributional Model of Leader Response to Subordinate Poor Performance**

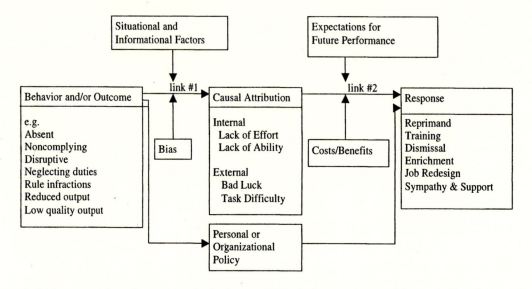

Source: Mitchell and Wood (1980, 124). Copyright © 1980 Academic Press. Reprinted with permission.

In a subsequent publication the model of Figure 11.1 is presented, but the discussion suggests that Figure 11.2 was actually in mind (see Mitchell, Green, and Wood 1981). Here attention is focused on moderators of the attributional process:

> [A] number of factors other than the classical attributional factors (e.g., Kelley or Weiner's work) may moderate the informational processes. Some of these moderators such as individual characteristics seem likely to alter or distort the causal explanation the leader believes. Other moderators such as the effects of the subordinate's behavior seem likely to alter the leader's behavior so it does not follow directly from prior attributions. In either case, it is clear that factors outside of the classical information processing models have real implications for the extent to which attributions affect leader behavior toward the member. (Mitchell, Green, and Wood 1981, 209)

The moderators noted are:

At link #1—
Self-serving attributions by the leader (taking responsibility for positive outcomes, but not for negative).

Relationship of leader and member (whatever decreases psychological distance between the two, increases the leader's tendency to make attributions similar to the subordinate's self-attributions).

Personal characteristics (race and sex, among other personal factors, can serve to increase biases inherent in the attributional process).

Leader expectations (behavior consistent with leader expectations tends to elicit internal attributions, while behavior that is inconsistent with expectations tends to elicit external attributions—i.e., difficult task).

At link #2—
Leader's perceptions of responsibility (the more a subordinate is judged responsible for an outcome, the greater the likelihood that the leader will take action toward the subordinate and the greater the degree of that action).

The effects of behavior (the effects or impact of the behavior will be taken into account in determining the leader response).

Accounts (the subordinate's explanation of the event can exert an influence on the leader response).

Ease of change (believing that the behavior of people is easier to change than the environment, a leader faced with uncertainty will opt for changing the subordinate). (Mitchell, Green, and Wood 1981, 205–9)

Certain of these moderators were considered in the 1979 paper, but others are new. In addition, various boundary conditions for the attribution process are noted. These include restrictions on leader behaviors, replacing attributional processes with organizational policy, and the use of rigid personal policy decision rules. The eventual goal of the theorizing and research is not only to establish sources of error that influence practice, but to determine ways of reducing these errors as well; training may be a means to this latter end.

Variants of the model set forth in Figure 11.2 have been published since, although the basic structure remains the same (Mitchell 1982; Mitchell and O'Reilly 1983). The major changes appear to be an emphasis on the fact that biases may enter at both links #1 and #2 and on the fact that at these same points rational inputs occur as well (the terminology of situational and informational factors and expectations for future performance is replaced by rational inputs).

Impression Management

An article by Wood and Mitchell (1981) picks up on the matter of accounts noted previously and elaborates the theory more fully in this regard. This is an area that was not adequately considered in initial presentations of the model. The hypotheses read:

[A]ccounts of external causes, when given by the subordinate, will lead a supervisor to discount internal causes as explanations for poor performance.

[A]ccounts of external causes will reduce the likelihood of the manager directing a disciplinary action at the subordinate and the punitiveness of any disciplinary action chosen.

[A]ccounts of prior external causes should lead the manager to have lower expectations of future failure by the subordinate and to be less likely to closely supervise the subordinate after the event.

Also, with regard to apologies, which are statements of remorse and thus are self-punitive in nature:

Apologies by the subordinate should . . . reduce the likelihood of the manager directing a disciplinary action at the subordinate and, in particular, should reduce the punitiveness of disciplinary action. (Wood and Mitchell 1981, 359–60)

Table 11.1

Managerial Attributions Regarding Poor Group and Individual Performance Hypothesized from Theory at Link #1 of the Attributional Model

Attributions about poor group performance	Attributions about poor individual performance
External attributions are made about the work environment.	Internal attributions are made about the poorly performing subordinate.
Internal attributions are made about employees' poor attitudes. These attitudes are viewed as having developed because of the negative influence of one or more "bad apples" in a cohesive or interdependent group.	External attributions are made about the work environment. Attitude problems are viewed as being more likely as causes of group poor performance and less likely as causes of individual poor performance.
Internal attributions are made by upper-level managers, regardless of whether poor performance is associated with one individual or an entire group. This results from a lack of task experience and direct contact and also from the fact that these upper-level managers take a broader system perspective and compare groups rather than individuals in assessing performance.	
Attributions are made that remove blame from the supervisor. These can include internal attributions about employees and external attributions about system factors that are outside of the supervisor's control.	External attributions are more likely here because individual poor performance is less relevant to the supervisor and, therefore, less likely to elicit a defensive or self-protecting diagnosis.
Internal attributions about group members escalate over time when poor performance persists, particularly when group failure is viewed as a personal failure by the supervisor.	External attributions about system or supervisory factors may be more comfortably made because the accumulated failures of one employee are less likely to be viewed as personal failures for the supervisor.

Source: Adapted from Brown (1984, 58).

Group Poor Performance

The development work on the theory in the area of group poor performance was done by Karen Brown (1984) at the University of Washington, with Mitchell's assistance and using funds from a research grant awarded to Mitchell. Thus, this extension legitimately may be considered a part of the Mitchell theory, especially since Mitchell and Brown subsequently published research on the subject together (Brown and Mitchell 1986).

The essence of the theory is contained in the propositions listed in the left column of Table 11.1. The propositions at the right involve individual performance failure, and are provided to facilitate contrasting the two concepts. It is apparent that dealing with poor performance at the group level introduces some new considerations.

Introducing Ingratiation into the Theory

Ingratiation represents an attempt by a person to increase his or her attractiveness in the eyes of others. It is a social influence process that comes to organizational behavior from social psychology, where it has previously been integrated with attribution processes (Jones and Wortman 1973). Liden and Mitchell (1988) attempt to extend this integration of ingratiation and attribution theories to create a more comprehensive theory of leader reactions to poor performance.

The article in which this theory is presented contains eighteen propositions dealing with ingratiation, a number of these with multiple variants. Most of these are rather general in nature, and only a limited set deal directly with the application of the ingratiation concept to attribution theory as applied to poor performance. Within this set some propositions deal with strategies to defend oneself against criticism and others with strategies to promote or assert oneself. The propositions that are clearly relevant for prior theory read as follows:

> Ingratiation strategies used to defend oneself following poor performance will tend to be short-term, reactive, and designed to manipulate target attributions concerning the poor performance.
>
> Assertive strategies used to promote oneself will tend to be long-term, proactive, and either designed to manipulate target attributions, or to simply be liked by the target.
>
> Targets will be less likely to alter their attributions for the ingratiator's poor performance when the ingratiator has a history of poor performance and/or if the outcome of the poor performance is serious.
>
> . . .
>
> The more frequent and serious a performance problem, the more likely a leader will have a policy for handling the problem; leaders who have chosen to bypass the attributional process by developing policies for handling performance problems will ignore apologies, accounts, and excuses. (Liden and Mitchell 1988, 577–78, 580)

From these propositions it becomes apparent that the extension of the theory into the realm of ingratiation builds upon the prior work in the area of impression management.

Attributional Effects of Group Performance and Leader Power

A recent extension to the basic theory builds upon the group level work by Brown (1984) and also on a program of research by Kipnis (1987) dealing with the consequences of leader power. The hypotheses involved are as follows:

> 1a. Individuals (members and leaders) in high-performing groups will make more internal attributions for performance than will individuals in low-performing groups.
> 1b. Individuals (members and leaders) in low-performing groups will make more external attributions for performance than will individuals in high-performing groups.
> 2a. High-power leaders will make more internal attributions for *success* than will low-power leaders.
> 2b. High-power leaders will make more external attributions for *failure* than will low-power leaders.
> 3a. Leaders who experience a gain in power will increase their level of internal attributions for *success*; leaders who experience a loss in power will decrease their level of internal attributions for *success*.
> 3b. Leaders who experience a gain in power will increase their level of external attributions for *failure*; leaders who experience a loss in power will decrease their level of external attributions for failure. (Ferrier, Smith, Rediker and Mitchell 1995, 318)

There are several other hypotheses dealing with power, but these do not relate to the basic attributional theory.

EVALUATION AND IMPACT

Statements of the theory consist essentially of a few models showing relationships among constructs and a long list of propositions and hypotheses spread over a period extending from 1979 to 1995. This does not represent a parsimonious theoretical formulation, but to date it is the best we have. Mitchell has not written a book containing a distillation of his theory, perhaps because he views the theory as still developing. However, we do have the advantage of a large number of research studies that Mitchell has conducted with a diverse array of coauthors, many of them students and colleagues at the University of Washington.

Early Mitchell Studies

Not all of the hypotheses of the theory have been subjected to research test by Mitchell, and some of the tests that have been conducted offer rather indirect evidence, primarily because nontheory variables and relationships were incorporated. Nevertheless, operationalizations of the major constructs are available, and a good deal of information has accumulated regarding the conduct of research into the attributional aspects of the analysis of ineffective performance—primarily via laboratory study.

Biases are clearly evident in that when performance is held constant, performance evaluations are influenced by whether attributions are made to effort or ability (Knowlton and Mitchell 1980). There is also a bias toward attributing causality for poor performance to internal factors generally, and this bias is accentuated when a history of poor performance exists and the outcome is serious (Mitchell and Wood 1980). Furthermore, attributions play a role in determining leader responses; internal attributions make for responses directed at the poor performer, not the context. Low, as compared to high, performing subordinates elicit more negative attributions, more negative attitudes, a preference for closer supervision, less feedback, and reduced financial compensation (Ilgen, Mitchell, and Fredrickson 1981). However, these consistently negative reactions were mitigated somewhat when the leader's rewards were dependent upon the performance level of the subordinate. While leaders tend to focus on internal attributions, subordinates see their poor performance as externally caused, thus creating conditions for conflict (Mitchell, Green, and Wood 1981).

These early findings lend considerable support to the basic theory. There is a problem, however, in that the results stem from research that is consistently of a laboratory nature and uses reactions to cases and simulations. The subjects are mostly students, playing both leader and subordinate roles. We know little from this research about how attributions operate in the world of practice. Furthermore, Mitchell (1982, 71) interjects certain concerns of his own:

> Not only are attributions only one contributor to action . . . according to our findings attributions play a *minor* role. . . . there are many settings where actions may be simply determined by personal, social or organizational policies. Attributions would be completely bypassed. In many other settings it appears that contextual, task, social, and cost/benefit type factors are as important or more important than attributions. Therefore, in many settings attributions may be weakly related to action at best.

This suggests that attributional biases may be counteracted in many instances, or simply replaced by other biases.

Mitchell's Expanded Research Agenda

Studies since the early ones on the basic theory cover considerable ground, including some looks back at the initial hypotheses. The Wood and Mitchell (1981) studies dealing with impression management are generally supportive of the theory. Subordinate accounts do operate as hypothesized to reduce leader negative reactions. However, expectations of future failure did not operate consistently as hypothesized, and apologies appeared to have a minimal effect. Research on the specific hypotheses dealing with ingratiation, beyond what is reported above, has not been reported.

Research conducted to determine how prior experience in the same job as the poor performer, and thus less psychological distance, influences attributions indicates that the result is a greater resort to external causes (Mitchell and Kalb 1982). Field data tend to support this laboratory finding. Evidence also indicates that subjects will react more positively to feedback when the feedback implies that an external cause for performance problems exists (Liden and Mitchell 1985).

Studies bearing on the group theory indicate that multiple poor performers, as opposed to a single one, do have an effect on the diagnosis of reasons for poor performance (Brown and Mitchell 1986), tending to shift attributions away from internal causes and toward external ones. In another study (Ferrier, Smith, Rediker, and Mitchell 1995), it was found that members from high-performing groups tend to resort to more internal attributions than do those from low-performing groups. External attributions follow the reverse pattern. This result is as hypothesized. However, attempts to test hypotheses regarding leader power did not provide consistent support and suggest a need for theoretical revisions. Gain and loss of power did not have the expected consequences, and the theory proved defective with regard to power use in other respects as well. Perhaps adding in the power variable served to overextend the basic theory.

Research dealing with a resort to company policy, as opposed to personal diagnosis, in handling instances of poor performance indicates that even when an appropriate policy is available, there is a 50–50 chance that the policy will not govern. Following policy has the benefit of saving time, and when managers feel judged and pressured they are more likely to opt for this approach. Concern with matters of fairness prompts individual diagnosis and thus the use of attributions. Staying with company policy tends to foster more severe actions (Liden, Mitchell, and Maslyn 1998). Faced with large numbers of subordinates and many instances of performance problems, it appears that the balance often shifts sharply toward a manager holding closely to policy.

Closely Related Research

What I have in mind here is research on either attributions or ineffective performances conducted by people who have at one time or another been closely allied to the theory. My intent is to merely note these contributions rather than treat them in detail when they do not provide evidence for the theory's evaluation. In general, however, they do say something regarding the network that has evolved around Mitchell's work, and thus its impact.

Green, after participating in the early theoretical efforts, has devoted himself to the study of ineffective performance largely independent of ties to attribution theory. There was an early, and only partially successful, effort to relate the causes of performance failure set forth by Miner (1963) and Steinmetz (1969) to the attribution framework (in Mitchell and O'Reilly 1983). And Green and Liden (1980) carried out a study looking into attributional and company policy factors in leader responses (control decisions):

As hypothesized when the subordinate was seen as causal, vis-à-vis situational factors, control responses were directed at the subordinate, were more punitive, and included more change to his/her job. Also, as expected, the supervisors complied with policy least when it disagreed with their causal beliefs or was severe. (Green and Liden 1980, 457)

More recently, however, Green has been concerned with poor performance extending over a period of time as it occurs in actual field situations rather than with the single episodes and laboratory conditions that have been the focus of Mitchell's work. These efforts (Green, Fairhurst, and Snavely 1986; Gavin, Green, and Fairhurst 1995) raise questions about some of the practical implications of the basic theory, especially as related to the development of leader responses at link #2. However, they do not deal with the attributional formulations that represent the core of the theory.

Liden has cooperated with a number of others to study the disciplinary process applied to poor performance and the role of group decision making in this regard (Liden, Wayne, Judge, Sparrowe, Kraimer, and Franz 1999). Mitchell himself has joined forces with others at the University of Washington with a primary interest in the self-efficacy concept to study the relationships among attributions, self-efficacy, and performance (Silver, Mitchell, and Gist 1995). This work considers self-attributions rather than the attributions to others that characterize almost all of Mitchell's prior theorizing and research; it finds sizable interrelationships.

Finally, mention should be made of a study conducted with Judith Heerwagen (Heerwagen, Beach, and Mitchell 1985) that attempted to utilize a film to sensitize people to internal and external causes of poor performances and thus remove biases. However, when the costs and benefits associated with different leader responses were introduced as a factor, these nonattributional aspects came to dominate the situation and the responses. Mitchell (1983, 55) concludes: "More research is clearly needed on how the social and situational factors influence appraisal and how errors or biases can be removed."

Outside Research on the Basic Theory

Probably the most extensive research program on the theory, besides those involving Mitchell or those closely allied with him, has been carried out by Ashkanasy in Australia (see Ashkanasy and Gallois 1994; Ashkanasy 1995). This research has studied the role of distinctiveness, consistency, and consensus in relation to attributions for performance failure and success. The results indicate that poor performance does foster complex cognitive processes aimed at developing causal explanations. Furthermore, these processes tend to follow the pattern established by the Mitchell theory, although the findings from field research are more consistently supportive than those obtained in the laboratory. The use of varied designs and samples in this program yields considerable confidence in the conclusions.

Another field study indicates that at link #2 leader responses tend to be tied to the attributions made at link #1 (Judge and Martocchio 1995). When the attributions for poor performance are of an external nature, disciplinary responses tend to be less severe than when an internal attribution is made. This study also looked into the moderating role of an individual difference variable (fairness orientation), thus moving beyond what Mitchell and colleagues have considered in their theorizing. The findings indicate that a strong sense of fairness serves to make for the use of more severe punishment, although this factor accounts for only a modest effect on disciplinary decisions. Tjosvold (1985) also finds a tie between attributions and leader responses, in that superiors who make internal attributions to effort respond to poor performance with threats, assertions of

Table 11.2

**Significant Correlations Between Attributions for Performance and
Corrective Actions Recommended**

Corrective response	Attributed cause of poor performance				
	Effort	Ability	Task difficulty	Working conditions	Quality of supervision
Additional training	—	0.24	—	—	0.21
Transfer to less difficult task	—	0.31	0.16	—	—
Disciplinary warning	0.31	—	—	−0.22	—
Modified work environment	—	—	0.19	0.30	—
Encouragement and support from supervisor	—	−0.19	—	0.16	0.21
Hiring people with more ability	0.23	0.20	—	—	—

Source: Adapted from Smither, Skov, and Adler (1986, 129, 134).

power, dislike, increased social distance, and dissatisfaction, while attributions to ability yield more encouragement and favorable conclusions. As hypothesized, the existence of an interdependent relationship between superior and subordinate, where the superior receives rewards based on the subordinate's behavior, serves to produce more assistance and open-mindedness toward the subordinate. Pence, Pendleton, Dobbins, and Sgro (1982) provide evidence to support the idea that the specific causal attribution involved, not merely whether it is internal or external, determines leader responses. A lack of effort elicits the most coercive corrective action.

These findings confirm the basic theory with a good deal of consistency and this support comes from both laboratory and field studies. However, some disparity from theoretical expectations is introduced by a study conducted in a casino setting (Smither, Skov, and Adler 1986). As the data of Table 11.2 indicate, relationships at link #2 were much what would be expected, but the correlations are rather low. Furthermore, the expected tendency for supervisors to pick internal attributions and performers to favor external ones was not clearly evident. Effort and task difficulty showed differential tendencies in the expected directions, but the two sources (supervisors and performers) did *not* differ significantly. Supervisors attributed causation to the quality of supervision (an *external* factor) more frequently than the performers. Control subjects without task experience attributed causation to the external factors of task difficulty and working conditions *more* than the performers did. The authors conclude that the attributions made often depend on the specific context and accordingly may deviate from theoretical expectations; biases may or may not operate depending on context.

Outside Research Related to Psychological Distance

A number of studies have been conducted dealing with some definition of psychological distance between leader and poor performer. Of particular interest has been the matter of the effects of gender and race differences when the leader is a white male and the performer a female, or black, or both. One expectation here is that attributions to ability will be less likely for women and blacks. Among women overall, however, this does not appear to be the case, although it does appear to be true when analyses are restricted to the most highly successful performers—a post hoc analysis (Greenhaus and Parasuraman 1993). Blacks did show the expected pattern, and in addition their performance was attributed less to effort and more to the effects of help. Taken as a whole, the effects of psychological distance were much more in evidence for blacks than for women. This tendency for differences in subordinate gender to exhibit minimal effects has been found in other studies as well.

Another aspect of psychological distance considered is the liking the leader has for the poor performer. Less liking (more distance) should result in attributions to internal factors and more punitive responses. Both of these expectations were supported in a field study, but only the latter in a laboratory study (Dobbins and Russell 1986). Certain deficiencies in the realism of the laboratory research appear to account for the failure to identify effects of liking on attributions in the laboratory context. A variant on the study of liking here is to consider ingroup and outgroup status as defined by leader–member exchange theory (see Chapter 14). When this approach to the psychological distance factor is invoked, the following results are obtained:

> Internal attributions were significantly higher for ingroup members than for outgroup members when performance was effective. Internal attributions were significantly higher for outgroup members than for ingroup members when performance was ineffective. Supervisors appear to be less consistent in assigning external attributions to ingroup and outgroup members than they are in making internal attributions. None of the mean differences in external attributions were significant. (Heneman, Greenberger, and Anonyuo 1989, 471)

Insofar as they go, these findings are consistent with theory, but the failure to find expected results for external attributions (luck and task difficulty) does give some pause.

Outside Research Related to Accounts

A body of research has developed that relates in one way or another to the accounts concept. Gioia and Sims (1986) studied performance-related conversations between managers and subordinates, finding that the subordinates tended to present self-serving arguments that apparently were heard. The face-to-face interactions resulted in considerable information seeking by the managers, and ultimately an attributional shift to greater leniency—less blame for failure and more credit for success.

Dugan (1989) reports a similar leniency shift, but only when the original attribution for poor performance was to lack of effort. Under such conditions more problem solving occurred, there was more attributional change, agreement was more common, and salary raises were more frequently granted. When lack of ability was at the core of attributions, leniency effects and attributional change were not in evidence. Thus the expected consequences of subordinate accounts were found only when effort was the attributional focus.

A more recent series of studies looked into the extent to which newness on the job might serve as an excuse for poor performance (Greenberg 1996). Using newness and lack of experience for impression management purposes did serve to evoke more positive evaluations as long as the observer was unaffected by the poor performance. However, if the observer bears some cost as a result of the poor performance, the use of newness for impression management purposes tends to backfire and actually reduces performance evaluations, as well as shifting attributions in an internal direction.

Thus it appears that accounts and related phenomena can well change attributions and raise evaluations through a leniency effect, but there are conditions under which these hypothesized consequences do not occur. The variable impact of accounts at link #2 would seem to be a factor in the relatively low correlations between attributions and leader response (see Table 11.2). Klaas and Wheeler (1990) also report substantial variations in the policies employed by managers in selecting corrective actions. All in all there appears to be somewhat more variability in the approaches taken to ineffective performance than attribution theory would anticipate.

Concerns Regarding Attributional Approaches

As we have seen, the attribution theory advanced by Mitchell and his colleagues has considerable research support, although there are certain departures from theoretical expectations. Biases of the kind hypothesized are inherent in perceptual processes and the major propositions of the theory have been confirmed to a large extent. These conclusions are now generally recognized. Yet certain concerns, and even disagreements, with the theory have been noted.

One such concern relates to the degree of convergence between leader and subordinate attributions. In general, it is assumed that the most likely occurrence in the face of subordinate poor performance is that the leader attribution will be internal, and somewhat biased in that regard, while the subordinate's self-attribution will be external and self-serving. The resulting disagreement can mean undesirable conflict with negative consequences for all involved. However, another possible consequence is that the supervisor's influence serves to bring about convergence, not conflict, with the internal attribution being adopted by both. This can happen because of the authority role the supervisor holds; it can mean reduced self-efficacy for the subordinate and worse, if the assessment is essentially inaccurate, which it may well be due to operative biases. Should inaccuracy be present in the now joint attribution, corrective actions are unlikely to work and the problem will escalate. This line of reasoning argues for accurate assessments, removal of biases, and actions fitted to real causes, whether attributions converge or not.

Another concern of a similar nature is that Mitchell's presentation of attribution theory in the leader–member dyad places too much emphasis on leader attributions at the expense of a full elaboration of member attributions (e.g., see LePine and Van Dyne 2001). In this approach an expanded theory of attribution processes is proposed, replete with its own models and propositions. Unfortunately, although these ideas have merit, they have not elicited much research attention. In this respect they are similar to the theoretical extension proposed by Brown (1984) dealing with group poor performance. Neither attempt to expand the domain of the theory has yielded the research response that appears warranted.

These concerns call for theoretical modifications and extensions, but they do not attack the basic formulations of attribution theory. In contrast, Lord (1995) has expressed what amount to core disagreements with the theory as developed by Mitchell and colleagues. In this view the highly rational, perceiver-as-scientist view of the attribution process should be reconsidered. The more likely process is one that is automatic, implicit, and so rapid that reasoning has not yet had time to occur. This perceiver-as-primitive-processor view is very different from that proposed by Mitchell. Explicit, rational problem solving may well occur only after implicit information processing, with its high potential for error, has already occurred. These implicit types of attributions are based on primitive categorizations, are prelinguistic, and are affect laden. As we will see in Chapter 15, they have been found to operate widely in the leadership domain, although those who use them often are not aware of what is happening. For this reason training is unlikely to influence these implicit processes.

Cronshaw and Lord (1987) present evidence in support of this alternative view of what happens at the point of attribution. However, a study by Gooding and Kinicki (1995) using practicing managers indicates that implicit categorizations are most likely to be mobilized when events have positive outcomes. The more explicit, reasoned, problem-solving approach envisioned by Mitchell is characteristic in the case of events with negative outcomes, such as poor performance. Implicit theories were not found to operate in the latter instance. Thus, insofar as the Mitchell theory remains one of attributions under conditions of ineffective performance, the evidence available to date seems to support it and to reject Lord's alternative interpretation. An expanded theory, however, which dealt in detail with effective performance, would have to give serious attention to implicit categorization processes.

Although the basic theory speaks to the matter of multiple causes in the sense that greater uncertainty is anticipated, most of the theory, and the research, assumes a single incident of poor performance and a single cause. Yet, as Green and his colleagues have shown, in actual practice poor performance is typically an ongoing affair. Furthermore, the causation of ineffective performance tends to be overdetermined with a number of different types of factors impinging at the same time. Evidence from clinical practice indicates that this number can range from one to eight with an average of four (Miner 1991). Rarely is it a matter of just effort, or ability, or task difficulty. The point is that attribution theory focuses on a small microcosm of the underlying reality, which is much more complex. This is cause for concern as well.

As Mitchell (1982) has indicated, attributions are only part of a much larger process. They are bypassed by personal and organizational policies, do not account for any substantial amount of variance in outcomes, and deal with only a limited aspect of the diagnosis and correction of ineffective performance. Yet because it serves to identify sources of bias and error, attribution theory remains important. Furthermore, from our knowledge of the nature of the process, it is apparent that training can intervene to change what happens at links #1 and #2. Quite possibly managerial role motivation training, as discussed in Chapter 17, serves to reduce bias in this manner. However, although motivation-increasing effects have been demonstrated for this training, bias-reducing effects have not been considered specifically. Mitchell's group has looked into other types of training, but without definitive conclusions. The need for further research on how training may be used to rid the diagnosis and correction of ineffective performance of attributional biases is apparent. Without such research, extensive application of the theory is unwarranted and seems unlikely. In fact, applications derived from person perception theory in general tend to be rather cursory and lacking in clarity or detail (Antonakis 2002).

The failure to elicit strong guides for practice is particularly noteworthy in the area of performance appraisal, where one would anticipate considerable input from attribution theory. Yet there has been little attention to aspects of the formal performance evaluation process, including design considerations, on the part of the attribution theory literature (see Barnes-Farrell 2001).

CONCLUSIONS

Mitchell has not published on attribution theory topics in the last few years, and Green left the theory some time ago. The broader field of decision making, which is allied to Mitchell's work on attribution theory and research, has occupied his efforts for some time; more recently he has turned this interest to the study of voluntary turnover decisions (Mitchell and Lee 2001) and to the matter of controlling turnover (Lee and Mitchell 2000). At the present time it remains unclear whether Mitchell will return to his work on attributions for poor performance, but he remains active in closely related areas. Should he choose to reenter the theoretical arena represented by this chapter, I can only hope that he will devote at least a part of his energies to the void that currently exists with regard to applications.

Attribution theory achieves somewhat uneven evaluations insofar as the ratings are concerned. The importance rating is four stars, but the mean value is 4.18, below average for the theories considered in this book. Yet, estimated validity is at the 4-star level. Overall the theory is supported by research on it, and by the context within psychology from which it derives, but there are departures from theory in the research findings as well. In particular, tests of the hypotheses involving the power factor fail to provide adequate validation. As to established usefulness (rated at 2 stars), there have been attempts to provide appropriate training applications, but these have failed to yield the necessary research support. Furthermore, as indicated, areas such as performance appraisal, which might well benefit from input from attribution theory, simply have not received it. As a result, clinical psychology approaches to the management of poor performance, which operate without benefit of attribution theory contributions, remain the preferred alternatives in this area of application (see Strassberg, 2001).

REFERENCES

Antonakis, John (2002). Review of Manuel London (Ed.), *How People Evaluate Others in Organizations. Contemporary Psychology*, 47, 381–83.

Ashkanasy, Neal M. (1995). Supervisory Attributions and Evaluative Judgments of Subordinate Performance: A Further Test of the Green and Mitchell Model. In Mark J. Martinko (Ed.), *Attribution Theory: An Organizational Perspective*. Delray Beach, FL: St. Lucie Press, 211–28.

Ashkanasy, Neal M., and Gallois, Cynthia (1994). Leader Attributions and Evaluations: Effects of Locus of Control, Supervisory Control, and Task Control. *Organizational Behavior and Human Decision Processes*, 59, 27–50.

Barnes-Farrell, Janet L. (2001). Performance Appraisal: Person Perception Processes and Challenges. In Manuel London (Ed.), *How People Evaluate Others in Organizations*. Mahwah, NJ: Lawrence Erlbaum, 135–53.

Brown, Karen A. (1984). Explaining Group Poor Performance: An Attributional Analysis. *Academy of Management Review*, 9, 54–63.

Brown, Karen A, and Mitchell, Terence R. (1986). Influence of Task Interdependence and Number of Poor Performers on Diagnoses of Causes of Poor Performance. *Academy of Management Journal*, 29, 412–24.

Calder, Bobby J. (1977). An Attributional Theory of Leadership. In Barry M. Staw and Gerald R. Salancik (Eds.), *New Directions in Organizational Behavior*. Chicago, IL: St. Clair Press, 179–204.

Cronshaw, Steven F., and Lord, Robert G. (1987). Effects of Categorization, Attribution, and Encoding Processes on Leadership Perceptions. *Journal of Applied Psychology*, 72, 97–106.

Dobbins, Gregory H., and Russell, Jeanne M. (1986). The Biasing Effects of Subordinate Likeableness on Leaders' Responses to Poor Performers: A Laboratory and Field Study. *Personnel Psychology*, 39, 759–77.

Dugan, Kathleen W. (1989). Ability and Effort Attributions: Do They Affect How Managers Communicate Performance Feedback Information? *Academy of Management Journal*, 32, 87–114.

Ferrier, Walter J., Smith, Ken G., Rediker, Kenneth J., and Mitchell, Terence R. (1995). Distributive Justice Norms and Attributions for Performance Outcomes as a Function of Power. In Mark J. Martinko (Ed.), *Attribution Theory: An Organizational Perspective*. Delray Beach, FL: St. Lucie Press, 315–30.

Gavin, Mark B., Green, Stephen G., and Fairhurst, Gail T. (1995). Managerial Control Strategies for Poor Performance over Time and the Impact on Subordinate Reactions. *Organizational Behavior and Human Decision Processes*, 63, 207–21.

Gioia, Dennis A., and Sims, Henry P. (1986). Cognition–Behavior Connections: Attribution and Verbal Behavior in Leader–Subordinate Interactions. *Organizational Behavior and Human Decision Processes*, 37, 197–229.

Gooding, Richard Z., and Kinicki, Angelo J. (1995). Interpreting Event Causes: The Complementary Role of Categorization and Attribution Processes. *Journal of Management Studies*, 32, 1–22.

Green, Stephen G., Fairhurst, Gail T., and Snavely, B. Kay (1986). Chains of Poor Performance and Supervisory Control. *Organizational Behavior and Human Decision Processes*, 38, 7–27.

Green, Stephen G., and Liden, Robert C. (1980). Contextual and Attributional Influences on Control Decisions. *Journal of Applied Psychology*, 65, 453–58.

Green, Stephen G., and Mitchell, Terence R. (1979). Attributional Processes of Leaders in Leader–Member Interactions. *Organizational Behavior and Human Performance*, 23, 429–58.

Greenberg, Jerald (1996). "Forgive Me, I'm New": Three Experimental Demonstrations of the Effects of Attempts to Excuse Poor Performance. *Organizational Behavior and Human Decision Processes*, 66, 165–78.

Greenhaus, Jeffrey H., and Parasuraman, Saroj (1993). Job Performance Attributions and Career Advancement Prospects: An Examination of Gender and Race Effects. *Organizational Behavior and Human Decision Processes*, 55, 273–97.

Heerwagen, Judith H., Beach, Lee Roy, and Mitchell, Terence R. (1985). Dealing with Poor Performance: Supervisor Attributions and the Cost of Responding. *Journal of Applied Social Psychology*, 15, 638–55.

Heider, Fritz (1958). *The Psychology of Interpersonal Relations*. New York: Wiley.

Heneman, Robert L., Greenberger, David B. and Anonyuo, Chigozie (1989). Attributions and Exchanges: The Effects of Interpersonal Factors on the Diagnosis of Employee Performance. *Academy of Management Journal*, 32, 466–76.

Ilgen, Daniel R., Mitchell, Terence R., and Fredrickson, James W. (1981). Poor Performers: Supervisors' and Subordinates' Responses. *Organizational Behavior and Human Performance*, 27, 386–410.

Jones, Edward E., and Wortman, Camille B. (1973). *Ingratiation: An Attributional Approach*. Morristown, NJ: General Learning Press.

Judge, Timothy A., and Martocchio, Joseph J. (1995). The Role of Fairness Orientation and Supervisor Attributions in Absence Disciplinary Decisions. *Journal of Business and Psychology*, 10, 115–37.

Kipnis, David (1987). Psychology and Behavior Technology. *American Psychologist*, 42, 30–36.

Klaas, Brian S., and Wheeler, Hoyt N. (1990). Managerial Decision Making about Employee Discipline: A Policy-Capturing Approach. *Personnel Psychology*, 43, 117–34.

Klimoski, Richard J., and Donahue, Lisa M. (2001). Person Perception in Organizations: An Overview of the Field. In Manuel London (Ed.), *How People Evaluate Others in Organizations*. Mahwah, NJ: Lawrence Erlbaum, 5–43.

Knowlton, William A., and Mitchell, Terence R. (1980). Effects of Causal Attributions on a Supervisor's Evaluation of Subordinate Performance. *Journal of Applied Psychology*, 65, 459–66.

Lee, Thomas W., and Mitchell, Terence R. (2000). Control Turnover by Understanding Its Causes. In Edwin A. Locke (Ed.), *Handbook of Principles of Organizational Behavior*. Oxford, UK: Blackwell, 90–104.

LePine, Jeffrey A., and Van Dyne, Linn (2001). Peer Responses to Low Performers: An Attributional Model of Helping in the Context of Groups. *Academy of Management Review*, 26, 67–84.

Liden, Robert C., and Mitchell, Terence R. (1985). Reactions to Feedback: The Role of Attributions. *Academy of Management Journal*, 28, 291–308.

——— (1988). Ingratiatory Behaviors in Organizational Settings. *Academy of Management Review*, 13, 572–87.

Liden, Robert C., Mitchell, Terence R., and Maslyn, John M. (1998). An Exploratory Investigation of Policy Use in the Management of Poor Performers. *Journal of Business and Psychology*, 13, 245–62.

Liden, Robert C., Wayne, Sandy J., Judge, Timothy A., Sparrowe, Raymond T., Kraimer, Maria L., and Franz, Timothy M. (1999). Management of Poor Performance: A Comparison of Manager, Group Member, and Group Disciplinary Decisions. *Journal of Applied Psychology*, 84, 835–50.

London, Manuel (Ed.) (2001). *How People Evaluate Others in Organizations*. Mahwah, NJ: Lawrence Erlbaum.

Lord, Robert G. (1995). An Alternative Perspective on Attributional Processes. In Mark J. Martinko (Ed.), *Attribution Theory: An Organizational Perspective*. Delray Beach, FL: St. Lucie Press, 333–50.

Martinko, Mark J. (Ed.) (1995). *Attribution Theory: An Organizational Perspective*. Delray Beach, FL: St. Lucie Press.

Miner, John B. (1963). *The Management of Ineffective Performance*. New York: McGraw-Hill.

——— (1991). Psychological Assessment in a Developmental Context. In Curtiss P. Hansen and Kelley A. Conrad (Eds.), *A Handbook of Psychological Assessment in Business*. New York: Quorum Books, 225–36.

Miner, John B., and Brewer, J. Frank (1976). The Management of Ineffective Performance. In Marvin D. Dunnette (Ed.), *Handbook of Industrial and Organizational Psychology*. Chicago, IL: Rand, McNally, 995–1030.

Mitchell, Terence R. (1979). Organizational Behavior. *Annual Review of Psychology*, 30, 243–81.

—— (1982). Attributions and Actions: A Note of Caution. *Journal of Management*, 8, 65–74.

—— (1983). The Effects of Social, Task, and Situational Factors on Motivation, Performance, and Appraisal. In Frank Landy, Sheldon Zedeck, and Jeanette Cleveland (Eds.), *Performance Measurement and Theory*. Mahwah, NJ: Lawrence Erlbaum Associates, 39–59.

Mitchell, Terence R., Green, Stephen G., and Wood, Robert E. (1981). An Attributional Model of Leadership and the Poor Performing Subordinate: Development and Validation. *Research in Organizational Behavior*, 3, 197–234.

Mitchell, Terence R., and Kalb, Laura S. (1982). Effects of Job Experience on Supervisor Attributions for a Subordinate's Poor Performance. *Journal of Applied Psychology*, 67, 181–88.

Mitchell, Terence R., Larson, J., and Green, Stephen G. (1977). Leader Behavior, Situational Moderators, and Group Performance: An Attributional Analysis. *Organizational Behavior and Human Performance*, 18, 254–68.

Mitchell, Terence R., and Lee, Thomas W. (2001). The Unfolding Model of Voluntary Turnover and Job Embeddedness: Foundations for a Comprehensive Theory of Attachment. *Research in Organizational Behavior*, 23, 189–246.

Mitchell, Terence R., and O'Reilly, Charles (1983). Managing Poor Performance and Productivity in Organization. *Research in Personnel and Human Resources Management*, 1, 201–34.

Mitchell, Terence R., Smyser, Charles M., and Weed, Stan E. (1975). Locus of Control: Supervision and Work Satisfaction. *Academy of Management Journal*, 18, 623–31.

Mitchell, Terence R., and Wood, Robert E. (1980). Supervisor's Responses to Subordinate Poor Performance: A Test of an Attributional Model. *Organizational Behavior and Human Performance*, 25, 123–38.

Pence, Earl C., Pendleton, William C., Dobbins, Greg H., and Sgro, Joseph A. (1982). Effects of Causal Explanations and Sex Variations on Recommendations for Corrective Actions Following Employee Failure. *Organizational Behavior and Human Performance*, 29, 227–40.

Silver, William S., Mitchell, Terence R., and Gist, Marilyn E. (1995). Responses to Successful and Unsuccessful Performance: The Moderating Effect of Self-Efficacy on the Relationship between Performance and Attributions. *Organizational Behavior and Human Decision Processes*, 62, 286–99.

Smither, James W., Skov, Richard B., and Adler, Seymour (1986). Attributions for the Poorly Performing Blackjack Dealer: In the Cards or Inability? *Personnel Psychology*, 39, 123–39.

Steinmetz, Lawrence L. (1969). *Managing the Marginal and Unsatisfactory Employee*. Reading, MA: Addison-Wesley.

Strassberg, Zvi (2001). Understanding, Assessing, and Intervening with Problem Employees. In Manuel London (Ed.), *How People Evaluate Others in Organizations*. Mahwah, NJ: Lawrence Erlbaum, 253–73.

Tjosvold, Dean (1985). The Effects of Arbitration and Social Context on Superiors' Influence and Interaction with Low Performing Subordinates. *Personnel Psychology*, 38, 361–76.

Weiner, Bernard (1972). *Theories of Motivation: From Mechanism to Cognition*. Chicago, IL: Markham.

Weiner, Bernard, and Sierad, Jack (1975). Misattribution for Failure and Enhancement of Achievement Strivings. *Journal of Personality and Social Psychology*, 31, 415–21.

Wood, Robert E., and Mitchell, Terence R. (1981). Manager Behavior in a Social Context: The Impact of Impression Management on Attributions and Disciplinary Actions. *Organizational Behavior and Human Performance*, 28, 356–78.

PART III

THEORIES OF LEADERSHIP

CHAPTER 12

NORMATIVE DECISION PROCESS THEORY

VICTOR VROOM, PHILIP YETTON, AND ARTHUR JAGO

Background
    How to Choose a Leadership Pattern
    Evaluation and Impact of Tannenbaum
        and Schmidt (1958)
The Initial Group Decision-Sharing Theory
    Decision Rules
    Decision Trees
The Initial Individual Decision-Sharing Theory
    Decision Rules
    Decision Trees
The Later Decision-Sharing Theory
    Reasons for Revision
    Nature of the Revisions
    Mathematical Functions
Evaluation and Impact
    Early Descriptive Research
    Normative Tests
    Validity of Component Rules
    Construct Validity Issues
    Research on the Revised Theory
    Does Participative Management Work?
    Reviewer Reactions
    Applications
Conclusions

Importance rating	★ ★ ★
Estimated validity	★ ★ ★ ★ ★
Estimated usefulness	★ ★ ★
Decade of origin	1970s

What initially came to be called the decision tree approach in leadership theory took its lead from an article published by Tannenbaum and Schmidt in 1958. That article examines how managers select or decide upon the behaviors they will use in different situations and with different subordinates. It also focuses on the degree to which these behaviors are boss-centered or subordinate-centered, that is, participative. These same concerns, the choice of leader behaviors and the degree of participativeness, also have characterized several theories that have followed.

The most comprehensive of these theories has been proposed by Victor Vroom and various colleagues. The original work was done while Vroom was on the faculty at Carnegie-Mellon University (Vroom and Yetton 1973); it was expanded upon following Vroom's move to Yale.

Over much the same time period, starting in the late 1960s, another theoretical framework emerged with a quite similar orientation. This is Frank Heller's influence–power continuum theory (Heller 1971), which is not considered in detail here because it fails to meet the criteria as an essential theory.

As with his concern with motivation and expectancy theory (see Chapter 7), Vroom's interest in leadership, and particularly participative leadership, extends back to the period of his doctoral study at the University of Michigan (Vroom 1960). During this early period and subsequently in his formulation of a theory of leadership, Vroom was influenced strongly by the thinking of Norman Maier. This influence is manifest in the distinction between sharing decisions with individual subordinates and with the subordinate group as a whole, for instance, and in the differentiation between decision quality and decision acceptance (Maier 1970). Yet Maier's formulations did not meld into a formal, cohesive theory of leadership of the kind Vroom and his coworkers have achieved.

BACKGROUND

In view of the fact that Vroom also gave us his version of expectancy theory, Chapter 7 contains information on his career. There have been two major statements of normative decision process theory, both written by Vroom with two different former doctoral students. The first version was written with Philip Yetton, who received his doctorate in 1972 from Carnegie-Mellon in industrial administration, having come to the United States from Great Britain. Yetton subsequently returned to England as a research fellow at the Manchester Business School. Most of his professional career, however, has been spent at the University of New South Wales in Australia on the faculty of the Graduate School of Management.

The second version of the theory was written with Arthur Jago, who received his Ph.D. in administrative science from Yale University in 1977. At about the same time that he received his doctorate, he moved to the University of Houston, where he has remained since. This version of the theory had a long gestation period, as the two authors began working on related matters while they were together at Yale; the final product, however, was published much later (Vroom and Jago 1988).

The present presentation of normative decision process theory is introduced with a consideration of the related article that served as a base for Vroom's thinking and was a product of a long-standing group at the University of California at Los Angeles. This group was active in promoting sensitivity training in the 1950s and later. Robert Tannenbaum headed up the group for many years (see Culbert 2003). Warren Schmidt was director of Conferences and Community Services for the University Extension.

How to Choose a Leadership Pattern

Vroom and Yetton (1973, 18) comment as follows on the Tannenbaum and Schmidt (1958) article:

> The most comprehensive treatment of situational factors as determinants of the effectiveness and efficiency of participation in decision making is found in the work of Tannenbaum and Schmidt (1958). They discuss a large number of variables, including attitudes of the manager, his subordinates, and the situation, which ought to enter into the manager's decision about the degree to which he should share his power with his subordinates. But they

stop at this inventory of variables and do not show how these might be combined and translated into different forms of action.

Because the Vroom and Yetton theory and the extensions that have followed build upon these views and attempt to combine the variables and translate them into action, it is instructive to begin with the Tannenbaum and Schmidt formulations. In essence, these formulations deal with a range of leadership behaviors that a manager may draw upon:

1. The manager makes and announces the decision.
2. The manager sells his decision to subordinates.
3. The manager presents ideas and invites questions.
4. The manager presents a tentative decision subject to change.
5. The manager presents a problem, invites suggestions, and then decides.
6. The manager defines the limits of a decision the group makes.
7. The manager permits his subordinates to function within the same limits imposed on him.

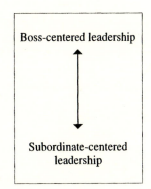

The particular type of leadership behavior that a manager chooses to employ in a given situation depends on a variety of factors in the manager, the subordinates, and the situation itself:

1. Manager factors
   a) manager's value system, including the value placed on decision sharing
   b) manager's confidence and trust in subordinates
   c) manager's basic inclination toward directive or team leadership
   d) manager's security in the face of the uncertainty produced by delegation
2. Subordinate factors
   a) level of independence needs among subordinates
   b) readiness to assume responsibility of subordinates
   c) degree of tolerance for ambiguity possessed by subordinates
   d) extent to which subordinates are interested in problem and believe it to be important
   e) subordinates' understanding of and identification with organizational goals
   f) knowledge and experience subordinates bring to problem
   g) extent to which subordinates expect to share in decision making
3. Situation factors
   a) type of organization (including, in particular, its values vis-à-vis participation) and size and geographical dispersion of units
   b) effectiveness of work group as a smoothly functioning team
   c) nature of problem relative to capabilities of manager and group
   d) degree to which time pressure exists, thus limiting subordinate involvement

Successful managers are defined as those who accurately and flexibly adjust their behavior to these various situational constraints on the choice of a leadership pattern.

Vroom (2000) continues to emphasize the important role these views have played in the development of normative decision process theory.

Evaluation and Impact of Tannenbaum and Schmidt (1958)

Data of the kind noted in the boxes at the beginning of each chapter are available for the Tannenbaum and Schmidt (1958) formulations. The importance rating is 3.02, while estimated validity and estimated usefulness both are at 2 stars. These are relatively low values. The problem is that neither of the authors did any research on their views, nor did anyone else until Vroom. Yet Vroom's research was on a different version of the theory, which was much more precisely stated. Thus, the Tannenbaum and Schmidt (1958) views are best considered as a now outdated precursor of the Vroom theory; they are too incomplete to permit adequate testing and are insufficient to provide guidance for practice either. However, this article did have considerable impact at the time it was published, and it did spark a major theoretical thrust that has spanned many years since.

THE INITIAL GROUP DECISION-SHARING THEORY

In its original version, normative decision-process theory differentiates between instances when, if decision sharing occurs, it will be with two or more subordinates and thus of a group nature, and instances when only a single subordinate would be involved (Vroom and Yetton 1973, 13). Under the group condition, the following leader behaviors are specified:

- The manager solves the problem or makes the decision himself, using information available at the time (A1).
- The manager obtains the necessary information from subordinates, then decides the solution to the problem himself (A2).
- The manager shares the problem with relevant subordinates individually, getting their ideas and suggestions without bringing them together as a group, and then makes the decision himself (C1).
- The manager shares the problem with subordinates as a group, obtaining their collective ideas and suggestions, and then makes the decision himself (C2).
- The manager shares the problem with subordinates as a group, serves in a role much like that of a chairman in attempting to reach a consensus on a solution, and is willing to accept any solution that has the support of the group (G2).

Decision Rules

A number of decision rules have been developed to guide the use of these leadership behaviors. The first three rules are intended to protect the quality of decisions and the last four, their acceptance.

The information rule: If the quality of the decision is important, and if the leader does not possess enough information or expertise to solve the problem by himself, A1 behavior is eliminated.

The goal congruence (or trust) rule: If the quality of the decision is important and if the subordinates do not share the organizational goals to be obtained in solving the problem (cannot be trusted to base their efforts to solve the problem on organizational goals), G2 behavior is eliminated.

The unstructured problem rule: When the quality of the decision is important, the leader lacks the necessary information or expertise, and the problem is unstructured, A1, A2, and C1 behaviors are eliminated.

The acceptance rule: If acceptance of the decision by subordinates is critical to effective imple-

Figure 12.1   **Decision Tree for Arriving at Feasible Sets of Leader Behaviors for Different Group Problem Types**

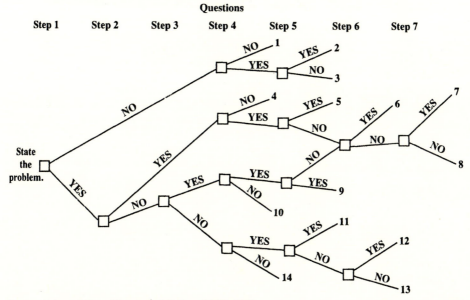

Source: Adapted from Vroom and Yetton (1973, 188).

mentation, and if it is not certain that an autocratic decision made by the leader would receive acceptance, A1 and A2 behaviors are eliminated.

The conflict rule: If acceptance of the decision is critical, an autocratic decision is not certain to be accepted, and subordinates are likely to be in conflict or disagreement, A1, A2 and C1 behaviors are eliminated.

The fairness rule: If the quality of decision is unimportant and if acceptance is critical and not certain to result from an autocratic decision, A1, A2, C1, and C2 behaviors are eliminated.

The acceptance priority rule: If acceptance is critical, not assured by an autocratic decision, and if subordinates can be trusted, A1, A2, C1, and C2 behaviors are eliminated.

These decision rules incorporate certain of the factors noted by Tannenbaum and Schmidt, although by no means all of them; included are the importance of decision quality, the manager's level of information, the extent to which the problem is structured, the criticalness of subordinate acceptance, the probability of subordinate acceptance of an autocratic decision, the degree to which subordinates are motivated to attain organizational goals, and the amount of subordinate conflict.

Decision Trees

When the decision rules are applied, they yield a feasible set of acceptable behaviors for different types of problems. To arrive at the feasible set for a given type of problem, one answers a series of questions either yes or no. The process involved can be depicted as a decision tree. Several variants of this tree for the group situation may be found in the literature (Vroom 1973, 1974, 1975, 1976a; Vroom and Yetton 1973). The version given in Figure 12.1 is somewhat easier to follow than some of the others. It yields fourteen problem types and requires that answers be provided for seven questions:

Table 12.1

Feasible Sets of Leader Behaviors for Each of Fourteen Group Problem Types

Problem type	Behavior calculated to minimize man hours spent	Total feasible set — Behaviors providing for increasing amounts of team development ⟶			
1	A1	A2	C1	C2	G2
2	A1	A2	C1	C2	G2
3	G2				
4	A1	A2	C1	C2	G2[a]
5	A1	A2	C1	C2	G2[a]
6	G2				
7	C2				
8	C1	C2			
9	A2	C1	C2	G2[a]	
10	A2	C1	C2	G2[a]	
11	C2	G2[a]			
12	G2				
13	C2				
14	C2	G2[a]			

Source: Adapted from Vroom and Yetton (1973, 37).
[a]Within the feasible set only when the answer to the Step 6 question is "yes."

Step 1: Is there a quality requirement such that one solution is likely to be more rational than another?

Step 2: Do I have sufficient information to make a high quality decision?

Step 3: Is the problem structured?

Step 4: Is acceptance of decision by subordinates critical to effective implementation?

Step 5: If I were to make the decision by myself, is it reasonably certain that it would be accepted by my subordinates?

Step 6: Do subordinates share the organizational goals to be attained in solving the problem?

Step 7: Is conflict among subordinates likely in preferred solutions?

The feasible sets of behaviors remaining after the decision rules are applied are noted in Table 12.1 for each of the problem types, indicated by the numbers to the right of Figure 12.1. The behaviors specified in the second column of Table 12.1 are those that should be used to minimize the number of man-hours devoted to the problem. As one moves to the right across the third column, time minimization is increasingly traded off against subordinate team development.

THE INITIAL INDIVIDUAL DECISION-SHARING THEORY

Like the group theory, the theory for dealing with individual subordinates specifies what kinds of manager behaviors are feasible in different problem situations; it, too, states what a manager should and should not do in a normative sense, but specifically when the problem would affect only one subordinate.

The A1, A2, and C1 behaviors considered in the group theory are equally applicable to the individual situation. However, C2 and G2 are no longer appropriate, and two new behaviors become possible (Vroom and Jago 1974; Vroom and Yetton 1973, 13):

- The manager shares the problem with the subordinate, and together they analyze it and arrive at a mutually agreeable solution (G1).
- The manager delegates the problem to the subordinate, providing him with relevant information but giving him responsibility for solving the problem (D1).

Decision Rules

With the change in relevant behaviors, certain changes in decision rules also become necessary. The goal congruence rule now serves to eliminate D1 and G1 behaviors. The unstructured problem rule eliminates A1 and A2 behaviors. The conflict rule is no longer relevant. A new rule, *the subordinate information rule*, indicates that if the quality of the decision is important and the subordinate lacks the information to solve the problem, D1 behavior is eliminated.

Decision Trees

The individual situation has not been depicted in a separate decision tree. However, various combined group and individual versions are available. Figure 12.2 presents a decision tree of this kind. In this instance, Step 7 is not relevant for individual problems because it relates to conflict among subordinates and only one subordinate exists for the individual case. A new question is added at the end:

Step 8: Do subordinates have sufficient information to make a high-quality decision?

The feasible sets for the eighteen problem types noted in Figure 12.2 for individual problems only are:

A1	D1	A2	C1	G1
D1	G1			
A1	D1	A2	C1	G1
A1	A2	C1	G1	
A1	A2	C1		
D1	G1			
G1				
C1				
C1				
A2	C1			
D1	A2	C1	G1	
A2	C1	G1		
C1				
D1	C1	G1		
C1	G1			
D1	G1			
G1				
C1				

Note: The behaviors specified by A1, D1, A2, C1, and G1 provide for increasing amounts of individual behavior.

Figure 12.2   **Decision Tree for Arriving at Feasible Sets of Leader Behaviors for Different Group and Individual Problem Types**

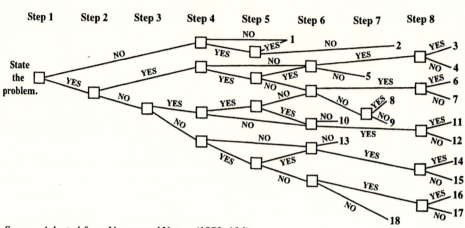

Source: Adapted from Vroom and Yetton (1973, 194).

In the above listing the minimum man-hour solution is given first and the most participative behavior is given last. Although Figure 12.2 may be used with group problems, it is more cumbersome than Figure 12.1 for that purpose.

THE LATER DECISION-SHARING THEORY

The revision of the theory was available in some form in the mid-1980s, although it was not published until 1988. This new version is considerably more complex than the original, and it is claimed to be more valid as well.

Reasons for Revision

In Vroom and Jago (1988), a number of shortcomings of the original theory are stated that served to guide the revision. The identification of these shortcomings is said to derive from prior research and from the experience of the authors in teaching the theory in management development programs. However, it appears that the latter has had more impact than the former. The shortcomings are as follows:

1. The original theory is not sufficiently specific on how to handle different situations, given that the feasible set can contain as many as five decision processes.
2. Also, there is no differentiation among behaviors outside the feasible set, even though the rules violated can vary in importance and number, and thus behaviors outside the set are not ineffective to the same degree.
3. The yes and no answers of a decision tree do not capture the shades of gray and degrees of uncertainty that exist in reality.
4. Although the decision trees ask managers if they possess the information needed for a good quality decision, they do not ask the same question as regards subordinate information (in the group theory).

5. The original theory had difficulty dealing with situations in which time to reach a decision is short.
6. The original theory could not handle circumstances where subordinates are geographically dispersed, making meetings impractical at best.
7. In its original version the theory fails to grasp the multiple complexities of organizational life; it is too primitive, too much an oversimplification.

Nature of the Revisions

The two models are the same in the decision processes specified (all seven of them) and in the criteria against which the effects of participation are evaluated (quality, commitment, time, and development). These latter, however, are combined in two equations:

$$D_{Eff} = D_{Qual} + D_{Comm} - D_{TP}$$
where D_{Eff} = *decision effectiveness*

D_{Qual} = *decision quality*

D_{Comm} = *decision commitment*

D_{TP} = *decision time penalty*
and

$$O_{Eff} = D_{Eff} - Cost + Development$$
where O_{Eff} = *overall effectiveness*

Cost = the time and energy used up in decision making

Development = the value added to human capital by a decision-making process

The prior decision rules are replaced by twelve problem attributes. Each of these is now stated initially as a question to be answered on a scale extending over five points. The first eight of these attributes are essentially the same as noted previously, but the yes–no dichotomy has been replaced by the five-point scale. However, the conflict question now has both group and individual versions:

- Is conflict among subordinates over preferred solutions likely (group)?
- Is conflict between you and your subordinate over a preferred solution likely (individual)?

The time and development factors are now handled as problem attributes as well:

- Does a critically severe time constraint limit your ability to involve subordinates?
- How important is it to you to minimize the time it takes to make the decision?
- How important is it to you to maximize the opportunities for subordinate development?

The remaining question is entirely new: Are the costs involved in bringing together geographically dispersed subordinates prohibitive?

Mathematical Functions

The function of the decision rules is also taken up by a number of equations. The two basic equations have already been stated. There are additional equations to provide input to the basic two; these provide values for D_{Qual}, D_{Comm}, D_{TP}, Cost, and Development. The equations for group decisions and individual decisions are different. The formulas for D_{Comm} for instance are:

$$\textit{Group: } D_{Comm} = CR - CR/2 \, [(f_1)(CP) - (f_3 + f_4 + 1)(CO)(CP)/2]$$
$$\textit{Individual: } D_{Comm} = CR - CR \, [(f_1)(CP)]$$

where CR = the value for the rescaled problem attribute—commitment requirement;
CP = the value for the rescaled problem attribute—commitment probability; and
CO = the value for the rescaled problem attribute—conflict.

The rescaling of the problem attribute scores designated by the manager on the five point scales is carried out using a table provided. The function values (f_3, f_4, f_1) vary with the decision process and are also derivable from a table; these latter have their origins in multiple regression analysis.

The equations (all of them) are applied five times in any given situation, once for each possible decision process. The theory's normative recommendation is the decision process, out of the five for either group or individual decision sharing, that yields the highest score for O_{Eff}. O_{Eff} is said to be a prediction of the overall effectiveness of a decision process, including its consequences on decision costs and subordinate development.

For a group problem these scores might be as follows:

Decision process	A1	A2	C1	C2	G2
Overall effectiveness	1.19	2.82	3.36	5.75	5.50

C2 has the highest score and is recommended. (You share the problem with your subordinates in a group meeting. In this meeting you obtain their ideas and suggestions. Then *you* make the decision, which may or may not reflect your subordinates' influence.)

For an individual problem the scores might be as follows:

Decision process	A1	A2	C1	G1	D1
Overall effectiveness	2.00	1.83	1.73	1.58	1.97

A1 has the highest score and is recommended. (You solve the problem or make the decision yourself using the information available to you at the present time.)

The process involved here involving rescaling, determining functions, and calculating numerous values using multiple equations is a complex one. It benefits substantially from computer support (Vroom 2000). Decision trees have been developed that remove much of the complexity, but still draw upon the new theory. However, their simplicity eliminates much of the discriminating power from the theory as well.

EVALUATION AND IMPACT

Vroom and Jago (1995, 179) indicate their rejection of participative leadership, when applied across the board, as follows:

Participation cannot be studied without explicit attention to the context in which it is displayed. Leadership measures that try to capture a leader's style by asking a few questions about typical or average behavior are simply of little value. Certainly, there are those of us who are predisposed to be more autocratic or participative than another. However, the circumstances a person faces often dictate behavior other than that to which he or she is predisposed. And those situational forces have the larger effect when pitted against the person's inclinations or desires.

These are the assumptions that guide normative decision process theory. We now turn to the evidence on how valid they are and to the related issue of the validity of the theory overall.

Early Descriptive Research

Much of the early research conducted by Vroom and his colleagues utilized managers participating in management development programs (Vroom and Yetton 1973). These managers typically report how they would deal with a particular problem or how they have dealt with it in the past. The data are thus of a self-report nature; how a manager actually behaves in different problem situations is not known with certainty.

In one variant of the descriptive research procedure, managers were asked to select a problem from their experience that affected at least two subordinates. Data were then obtained about which of the leader behaviors specified by the theory was utilized and about the various aspects of the problem situation that go into the decision tree. The results from a comprehensive study of all theoretical variables and from an earlier, less complete study conducted as the theory was being developed are given in Table 12.2.

The findings provide rather strong support for the view that the perceived locus of information is related to the degree of participation in the decision; to a lesser degree, decision sharing appears to be a function of the extent to which subordinates can be trusted. The other findings tend to be equivocal except for some evidence indicating that when it appears probable that an autocratic decision will be accepted, participation is less likely. Subordinate conflict does not appear to be a relevant consideration.

A second research procedure early on utilized a set of standardized problem situations, and the managers were asked to place themselves in these situations. The various aspects of problem situations considered by the theory and built into the decision trees were incorporated deliberately in the problems, and the managers indicated for each problem which of the leader behaviors they would choose.

One important finding was that differences in the nature of the problem situations accounted for nearly three times as much variation in responses as differences between individuals. There was a tendency for managers to choose a more or less participative style with some consistency, but the tendency to vary one's style depending on the situation was much more pronounced. In all probability this situational effect was inflated in the research over what would be found in any one actual managerial situation, because the case problems covered an atypically large range of situations. Nevertheless, the theoretical expectation that situational factors do matter is supported. The problem or situation faced is a much better predictor of managerial behavior than the manager's basic style. People do vary their behavior to match the demands of the problems they face, and they do so over a wide range.

The research using standardized problems also indicates that the various situational attributes of the theory are related to level of participation in the expected manner across eight different managerial samples. Among the variables of the theory, only the quality requirement failed to

Table 12.2

Correlations Between Aspects of the Problem Situation and the Degree of Participativeness of the Reported Leader Behavior

Aspects of the problem situation	Level of participation	
	Comprehensive study	Partial study
Importance of a quality decision	(0.12)	−0.02
Amount of leader information	(−0.36)	(−0.34)
Amount of subordinate information	(0.43)	not measured
Degree to which the problem is structured	(−0.15)	not measured
Importance of subordinate acceptance	(0.24)	0.02
Probability of an autocratic decision being accepted	(−0.23)	not measured
Extent to which subordinates can be trusted to accept organizational goals	(0.21)	(0.18)
Amount of subordinate conflict	0.08	−0.01

Source: Adapted from Vroom and Yetton (1973, 81–82).
Note: ( ) = Statistically significant.

yield a significant relationship sufficiently often to bring the theoretical hypothesis into question. These latter results are in general agreement with other data obtained using a somewhat improved set of standardized problems as a measure (Jago 1978). In this study the quality requirement also failed to show the predicted relationship on occasion, as did subordinate conflict.

Direct comparisons between what managers indicate as their behavior and what the theory recommends may be made using both the recalled and standardized data. When this is done, the managers portray themselves as somewhat more participative and less variable in their behavior than the theory would prescribe. There is a strong tendency to avoid A1 behavior when it would be theoretically appropriate, and to a somewhat lesser extent G2 behavior; C1 behavior is clearly overstressed and so also is C2. In these comparisons, the most time-conserving behavior alternative is taken as the ideal.

When the single most theoretically appropriate behavior is used in the comparison, agreement occurs in something over one-third of the cases; when the whole feasible set is used, this proportion is doubled. Violation of the various decision rules is much more likely to occur with regard to acceptance than quality. The fairness rule, the acceptance priority rule, and the conflict rule are often violated; the goal congruence rule and the information rule practically never are. Thus, it appears managers are much more likely to risk implementation of a decision by subordinates than the basic quality of the decision itself.

While the initial studies dealt entirely with group situations (Vroom and Yetton 1973), another study used standardized problems of both a group and an individual nature (Vroom and Jago 1974). The results from this study indicate that the individual situation elicits less participative behavior than the group. Once again situational differences were found to account for about three times as much variation on group problems as individual differences, but on individual problems this ratio jumped to 5 to 1, a much greater situational impact.

In general, the findings with regard to the effects of the various problem aspects are consistent with the theory for both group and individual problems. There are, however, certain departures from theoretical expectations in the case of the importance of a quality decision on individual problems (a low quality requirement yields *more* participation) and subordinate conflict on group problems (more conflict yields *more* participation).

Agreement with the feasible set occurred 68 percent of the time on group problems, thus replicating prior findings. It rose to 83 percent for individual problems, wherein decision rule violation occurs predominantly with regard to the acceptance priority rule; it is quite rare for the rules designed to protect decision quality. On group problems the fairness and acceptance priority rules are again frequently violated, and the leader information rule is not. The most pronounced finding, however, is the much greater agreement with the theoretical model obtained with the individual problems.

A very likely problem with the methodology used in the descriptive research is that the reports of managers as to what they would do in the case situations might have little relationship to what they actually do in such situations. To investigate this hypothesis, responses to the cases were obtained from a group of managers and also from their subordinates (Jago and Vroom 1975).

When the subordinates were asked to indicate how their superiors would respond in each situation, substantial agreement was found among subordinates of the same superior. However, the expected agreement between subordinates and superiors was not obtained. Further analysis suggested that several sources of bias existed in the subordinate descriptions, in particular a tendency to attribute behaviors to the superior that the subordinates also attributed to themselves. There was consistent underestimation of the variability of superior behavior and overestimation of the degree of autocratic behavior on the part of superiors, in comparison with the superior's own self-descriptions. A similar "autocratic shift" also has been noted by Vroom and Yetton (1973) and by Jago and Vroom (1977). On the evidence this shift appears to be a function of perceptual error rather than behavioral fact.

The results of this study indicate that obtaining attributed descriptions of superiors from subordinates is a highly questionable method of determining the validity of the standardized case procedure. It may be that the problem is inherent in the use of situations not typically observed as such by the superiors or the subordinates. This line of research has neither proved nor disproved the value of the methodology used in the descriptive studies. Standardized observation of ongoing manager behavior appears to be needed.

The same problems with the use of subordinate data noted above have continued to be found (e.g., see Field and House 1990). Data of this kind do not mirror what is obtained from the managers themselves, nor do they provide the same high level of support for the theory.

Normative Tests

The real need in validating the theory (or theories) is not for descriptive findings, although these can prove useful in an inferential sense, but for normative findings that tie the theoretical variables to indexes of managerial success and failure. A preliminary effort of this kind is reported by Vroom and Yetton (1973, 183). In this instance managers were asked to describe a situation using the recalled problems design and then to rate both the quality and the acceptance of the decision. The expectation was that decisions outside the feasible set for the problem would be rated less effective.

The results indicated a tendency for decisions within feasible sets to be viewed as more effective. However, their superiority over decisions outside the feasible set was minimal and not statistically significant. A problem in interpreting these data is that the number of decision rule violations was minimal, and the rated effectiveness level was consistently high. Thus, there was sufficient

Table 12.3

Validity Evidence from Six Studies Representing Normative Tests

	Decision effectiveness	
	Unsuccessful (%)	Successful (%)
Choice was within the feasible set		
Vroom and Jago (1978)	32	68
Zimmer (unpublished)	33	67
Tjosvold, Wedley, and Field (1986)	39	61
Field (1982)	51	49
Liddell (unpublished)	46	54
Böhnisch, Jago, and Reber (1987)	33	67
Average	**39**	**61**
Choice was outside the feasible set		
Vroom and Jago	78	22
Zimmer	59	41
Tjosvold et al.	62	38
Field	64	36
Liddell	71	29
Böhnisch et al.	56	44
Average	**65**	**35**

Source: Adapted from Vroom and Jago (1988, 80).

restriction of range on the criteria to make the lack of significant findings difficult to interpret. The study does not yield clear evidence one way or another. Subsequent research has attempted to overcome these difficulties.

Vroom and Jago (1988) report on six studies in which successful and unsuccessful decisions were identified and then the leader's behavior established under each of these conditions. Table 12.3 summarizes the results of these studies. In the first three studies all of the information came from the manager subjects, thus permitting common method bias. This was not true of the next two, which were laboratory studies. The downside here, however, is that the situations were of no real consequence to the subjects. The final study was like the first three, but used small groups of managers to actually classify a decision (thus intervening in the common method sequence). Overall these results are strongly supportive of the theory.

A study by Margerison and Glube (1979) used franchisees to classify standardized problems, and related the results to franchise performance and employee satisfaction. Those whose decisions more closely approximated the theory were more likely to have ventures that did well on both criteria. Similar findings were obtained in another study of retail sales people and their managers (Paul and Ebadi, 1989). Managers who conformed closely to theoretical prescriptions had more productive sales personnel and these people were more satisfied with their supervision and their work (but not with their pay or coworkers).

Validity of Component Rules

A number of the studies noted previously provide information not only on the validity of the seven group decision rules in the aggregate, but individually as well. The results would seem to provide convincing support for all rules except the conflict rule (Vroom and Jago 1988). This rule exhibited difficulties in the descriptive studies as well.

The problems identified in this area have served to stimulate more intensive research on the issue. One study (Ettling and Jago 1988) seems to indicate that no problems exist with the conflict rule, that managers should resort to group participation when conflict among subordinates exists. The authors argue that previous failures to support the rule resulted from a lack of sufficient instances to adequately test the rule.

An additional study (Crouch and Yetton 1987) finds that although the rule holds for managers with conflict management skills sufficient to deal with the conflict within the group, it does not hold for managers who lack conflict management skills. Such managers resort to participation at their own peril and may find themselves in the middle of a heated and escalating controversy. These authors argue that the Ettling and Jago (1988) study turned out as it did because the problems considered required very low levels of conflict management skills and did not challenge the managers in that regard. Crouch and Yetton's (1987) findings would seem to say that managers who are lacking in conflict management skills should undergo training in this regard before utilizing the conflict rule. However, this assumes that the training would achieve its goal, a not altogether certain eventuality. In any event, this line of research places increased emphasis on individual differences as moderators for the theory. There may be room for more moderators of this type as the theory continues to develop. Past mentoring experience, for instance, has been found to influence the decision-making processes of the theory when protégés are involved (Horgan and Simeon 1990).

Construct Validity Issues

One approach to validation asks whether the constructs of a theory behave in ways that might be expected in their relationships with other variables. Vroom and Jago (1988, 1995) report data on this issue. Here, responses to standardized problems are collapsed across situations to yield an individual difference measure of disposition toward autocratic versus participative decisions.

The data indicate that more autocratic predispositions characterize the military, and that participative tendencies are more likely in academic settings and in government. Differences across industries in the private sector are minimal, but individual firms do vary in their characteristic approaches. Also, higher-level managers are more participative than those at lower levels, perhaps because they are in a position to be. Sales/marketing and finance/accounting managers tend to be more autocratic, especially as compared with human resource managers, who are the most participative.

Cultural variations do exist. Within Europe managers in Germany, Austria, and Switzerland are the more participative, while those from Poland and Czechoslovakia are the more autocratic. France is in-between, along with the United States. Managers from less developed countries tend to be on the autocratic side.

Managers in their twenties are the most autocratic, with participativeness increasing up to a maximum during the forties, where it levels off. Women are considerably more predisposed to participation, and this appears to be true of both managers and business students (Jago and Vroom 1982). Thus the predisposition seems to antedate managerial experience. Yet other findings indicate that no gender differences exist, either in the desire for participation or in asking for such involvement (Kahnweiler and Thompson 2000). This disparity in results is not easily explained.

Correlational analyses indicate that participativeness as determined from the normative decision process theory measures is positively related to other indexes of an employee-centered orientation; it is negatively correlated with authoritarianism.

These findings overall provide good evidence for construct validity. Not all of the findings noted are equally supportive, but in general the data can be said to offer no serious threats to construct validity, and several instances of clear substantiation.

Research on the Revised Theory

Several years before the 1988 publication of the later version of normative decision process theory, a laboratory study was conducted to provide a partial comparison of the new theory with the original (Jago, Ettling, and Vroom, 1985). The results are as follows, expressed in terms of the validity coefficients obtained:

	Initial theory	Later theory
Decision quality criterion	0.24	0.38
Decision commitment criterion	0.53	0.84
Decision effectiveness	0.29	0.75

All of these validity coefficients are significant, but the major finding is the substantial improvement achieved with the new theory. Also, irrespective of the theory used, commitment is predicted much better than decision quality. One real possibility is that the resort to participation has its major impact in facilitating acceptance of the decision. Quality may be changed less because the decision actually resulting is not very participative; the expert power of the managers often prevails in spite of efforts to do otherwise. Thus, the theory deals more with perceived participation than actual; accordingly, the main effect is on commitment.

Another study obtained solid evidence that the addition of the new decision attributes did bring about changes in the decision process; subjects did consider them (Field, Read, and Louviere 1990), and they did so in a way that agreed with the theory. In this study the conflict rule once again presented difficulty. Also, we have no data on the situation of manager–subordinate conflict posited in the individual model. Clearly, the theoretical statements regarding conflict require more study.

Yet this and other research needs involving the new theory are not being satisfied at present. In part, of course, research answers provided previously for the initial theory—and there has been an abundance of these—are equally applicable to the later theory. But a research void seems to have set in now, to the disadvantage of a full evaluation of the new theory (which on the limited evidence available appears to represent a major advance) and to the detriment of the theory's overall testing and development. There is a definite problem when one compares the amount of research done on the two theoretical versions issued fifteen years apart. Not only are the theories' authors conducting little research now, but others are equally remiss in this regard.

As far as Vroom and Jago are concerned, the lack of research appears to be attributable to several factors—a marked escalation in long-simmering conflicts at Yale, which affected Vroom, and conflicts of a legal nature with the firm that has marketed a training program based on the theory for many years, which has affected both Vroom and Jago (Vroom 1993). A more widespread concern, however, may be the impact of converting the theory into equations and burying it in a computer. From the viewpoint of scientific precision, this appears highly laudable, but from the viewpoint of user-friendliness for researchers, it may be far less attractive. In this connection a new program now has been created that is described as being "simple and very easy to use" (Vroom 1999). Whether this will overcome the previously stated problem remains to be determined. Certain limited changes in the A1 taxonomy have been introduced as well.

Does Participative Management Work?

At this point we need to determine how effective across the board participative management is, although this is not what Vroom advocates, and whether participation is more effective with certain kinds of people than others, something that Vroom has not considered in any depth. Normative decision process theory is a theory of participation limited to specific situations, but it competes with formulations that take a more general approach to participation and with other views that consider participation to be effective only for certain people (the individual difference approach).

In Chapter 10, research on different approaches to goal setting, including participation, was discussed. The evidence indicates that when other considerations are held constant, differences attributable to participative procedures are negligible; they have no special motivational value in goal setting. However, we need to look beyond goal setting to the wide array of organizational issues that might be subject to a participative approach.

There has been a substantial amount of research on this topic going back to the early research by Kurt Lewin (see Chapter 3). These early investigations proved to be less than definitive, but they did provide the spark needed to initiate research of a more theoretically focused nature. The consequence at present is that meta-analyses, qualitative reviews, and even reviews of the reviews abound.

Correlations between participation and both performance and job satisfaction tend to be significant but low. The most comprehensive data are those utilized by Wagner (1994), who reports that the average value for performance is in the 0.15 to 0.25 range and for job satisfaction, in the 0.08 to 0.16 range. Subsequently, based on a consideration of all factors involved, these figures were revised downward somewhat to a value of 0.11 for both performance and satisfaction (Locke, Alavi, and Wagner 1997). Yet these analyses do not include all forms of participation, including in many instances the use of delegation (Heller, Pusic, Strauss, and Wilpert 1998). A number of studies are plagued by common methods variance, whereby measures of both the extent of participation and outcomes are obtained from the same source, thus potentially inflating the correlations. One meta-analysis yields a correlation of 0.14 for all studies, using performance as a criterion (Sagie 1994). In contrast to these figures of 0.20 or below, and by way of providing a benchmark for comparison, a meta-analysis of studies investigating the impact of financial incentives on the quantity of performance produced a value of 0.32 (Jenkins, Gupta, Mitra, and Shaw 1998). Clearly, if one wants to improve performance levels, incentive compensation appears to have more potential than participative management. Yet combining the two could well do even better.

There seems to be little question that across the board the research on participative management has produced the kinds of results noted. However, there has been some controversy over how participative management should be defined for research purposes. Liden and Arad (1996, 217) make the point that "one explanation for the lack of strong effects uncovered by literature reviews and meta-analyses is that the forms of participation studied did not include cases in which employees had full control over decision making." Yet the fact that participation occurs within the confines of hierarchic, bureaucratic organizations places limits on what is possible. Probably the research merely samples the types of participation that can be carried out in such organizations. Higher levels of participation might well produce stronger relationships, but they would also result in almost complete abdication of managerial authority, thus making hierarchic systems incapable of functioning.

The results obtained from participative management research in general do not yield support for across-the-board prescriptions, or for the extent to which empowerment has become a key ingredient of the current business scene; the relationships to performance and satisfaction are not sufficiently strong. However, the data do support a view that under appropriate circumstances participative management can work quite well, and under other circumstances it can have profoundly negative effects (Sagie 1994). Research on normative decision process theory certainly confirms that situational factors can make a big difference. There is even evidence that both positive and negative effects of participation can occur in the same study. This occurred in a laboratory investigation with electronic groups, where participation was associated positively with performance level and negatively with satisfaction level; these results appear to be a function of the electronic interaction situation (Kahai, Sosik, and Avolio 2004).

The issue of whether participative management functions more successfully with certain kinds of people as opposed to others has also been the subject of research. Vroom contends, based on his data, that situational factors account for much more variance than do individual difference factors, but this does not mean there is no room for such considerations as personality characteristics and values to operate. In fact, a search of recent research in this area indicates that individual differences do contribute to outcomes from participation.

By no means does this research permit a full mapping of how personality variables function in this regard. What we do have is bits and pieces of such a map. Thus, efficacy (both self and group) and individualism-collectivism were found to operate as moderators of the participation–performance relationship in one investigation (Lam, Chen, and Schaubroeck 2002). Similarly, in a study also noted in Chapter 10, low power distance was found to enhance the effects of participation in a goal-setting context (Sue-Chan and Ong 2002). Findings such as these raise the possibility that normative decision process theory might well be expanded to incorporate individual difference variables.

Reviewer Reactions

At least relative to many theories, this one is free of ambiguities and stated with considerable precision. Much of it has been tested by both the authors and others with positive results. The 1988 book was written with three audiences in mind—managers, professional colleagues, and practitioners in the field of executive education and organizational development. This is a difficult balancing act to accomplish, perhaps an impossible one. In this instance it has been only partially successful, with insufficient detail on the research for organizational behavior professionals and in addition a degree of overselling that on occasion amounts to exaggeration. Yet the book is an important one, if only it were longer and more detailed and somewhat more objective.

But what do others have to say about the theory? Two sources already considered come out in support of normative decision process theory (Wagner 1994; Locke, Alavi, and Wagner 1997). They are favorably disposed to the way in which moderator variables are used, as opposed to a pursuit of the main effects of participation, and they find the research evidence convincing.

Yukl (2002) considers this to be one of the best-supported theories of leadership, but he also notes that it deals with only a small part of leadership, assumes that managers have the needed skills to put the theory into action, fails to consider decisions that extend over long periods of time while invoking multiple processes, and lacks the parsimony needed in a good theory. Much of this is a matter of domain definition. Vroom and colleagues are not trying to deal with many of the matters Yukl mentions, and the theory makes that clear. Theorists are justified in defining their domain as they see fit, but in doing so they risk the possibility that their theory will be considered trivial (because its domain is too small). Yukl does say the theory covers a small part of leadership, but neither he, nor anyone else to my knowledge, has accused it of being trivial.

A possibly more telling criticism involves the parsimony issue. Without question, normative decision process theory is complex, and it became more complex with the 1988 version. Yet concluding that a theory lacks parsimony requires that making it simpler does not sacrifice understanding, prediction, and control. It is parsimony with all else being equal that is the criterion. Several more parsimonious approaches to the theory's domain have been proposed. However, when put to the test, these alternatives both were found to achieve parsimony only at the expense of predictive power (Jago and Vroom 1980). Until a less complex formulation can be developed that achieves the same effectiveness as the Vroom/Jago theory, we will have to accept the complexity that currently exists.

A review by Chemers (1997) is more critical of the research evidence than the other reviews we have been considering, and it does not accept that the ability of managers to change behaviors at will has been proved. As to the former, the charge is that the validity of the theory rests on studies that utilize relatively weak methodologies. This criticism was entirely justified when all that was available was the descriptive research, but as more studies have accumulated using a diverse array of methodologies, that situation has changed. It is hard to accept Chemers's (1997) negative views given the nature of the evidence. The reader should know also that Chemers is strongly identified with an alternative theoretical position to be discussed in the next chapter. This does not mean that his arguments should be discounted, but they should be carefully evaluated relative to the evidence. On this score, and considering the research discussed in the previous pages, I have to disagree with Chemers's evaluation of the evidence.

A final review by Aditya, House, and Kerr (2000, 137) is also rather critical. The position here is that research on normative decision process theory vastly overestimates support for the theory. These authors have proposed alternative theories also (see Chapters 16 and 18). But we need to consider their observations:

1. The theory assumes that the decision maker's goals are always congruent with the goal of the organization.
2. Because training is required in order to use the theory reliably, the population that may use it prescriptively is limited.
3. The theory ignores the discussion and conference skills required of the manager to actually solve problems on a group decision.
4. The theory is excessively complex.
5. Because the theory allows 1.5 million combinations of possible relevant attributes, it appears to be virtually untestable.

Several of these criticisms deal with domain issues, taking normative decision process theory into areas that it was not designed to consider. Other criticisms deal with parsimony and complexity. Here we should note that no theory needs to be tested in the totality of its aspects. Because of the interconnectedness of most theories, there is added value in each test. If a number of tests are conducted across the full range of the theory, and they turn out to be supportive, then one can be increasingly convinced of the validity of the whole theory, even though many specific propositions have never been tested. Given the research that has been conducted to date, it seems realistic to conclude that normative decision process theory is rapidly approaching a point where it can be considered valid in most of its aspects.

Applications

There are two related types of applications that have received attention in the literature. One is merely the use of the theory to guide managerial decisions in the hope of improving both their quality and acceptance. The second involves training in the use of the theory.

The 1988 theory was devised to be used in the former manner to guide on-the-job decisions. Although a method for that theory's use in training has been devised (Vroom and Jago 1988), little information on that method is available. What research has been done on training, and almost all of the descriptions of use in both training and on-the-job decision making, involve the earlier version (Vroom and Yetton 1973).

The essential argument for applying the theory in actual managerial decision making is that in doing so, a manager will achieve more effective decisions and thus better leadership. With regard to this point, the authors conclude the following:

> Using the data collected in this investigation, we can estimate that agreement with the model in all cases would have increased the number of successful decisions from 52 percent to 68 percent in our sample and increased the overall effectiveness of decisions from 4.45 to 5.19 (on a 7-point scale). The latter effect is due more to the usefulness of the model in enhancing decision acceptance (where the expected increase would be from 4.62 to 5.41) as opposed to decision quality (from 4.56 to 4.97). It is of course difficult to translate these estimates into economic terms. . . . Although the use of the model is no guarantee of an effective decision and evidence obtained has already suggested avenues for its improvement, its use even in the present form can be expected to reduce many of the errors to be found in current managerial practice. (Vroom and Jago 1978, 162)

To use the theory, a manager would answer the questions at steps 1 through 7 or steps 1 through 8 in a yes or no manner with reference to a particular problem faced. The selection of the particular decision tree to use would depend on whether a single subordinate or more than one was affected. Ultimately, this process yields a single problem type number. Using this number, a feasible set of decisions for the particular problem can be identified; these are the decisions that do not violate one or more decision rules. If minimizing the man-hours spent on the problem (and thus the time to decision implementation) is important, one selects the first alternative in the feasible set. To the extent participation is desired and time constraints are less important, one moves to the right in the feasible set.

The training program based on the initial theory has been described widely (Vroom 1973, 1974, 1975, 1976b; Vroom and Yetton 1973; see also Smith 1979; Vroom and Jago 1988). As provided by the consulting firm with which the theory's authors contracted it was called "TELOS," and more recently Managing Involvement; it lasts from two to four days.

Although the procedures used have varied somewhat over time, the following description provides an example of how the training may be conducted. It starts with a general familiarization with basic components of the theory and practice in using this information to describe oneself and others. Films are used in this phase. The participants then describe their own leadership behavior using one or another set of standardized cases. Next comes a certain amount of practice in simulated contexts in the use of different leadership behaviors, particularly G2, which is likely to be unfamiliar. Standard human-relations exercises are used to demonstrate the effects of participation on decision quality and acceptance. The normative model is then presented (including decision trees and feasible sets) and practice in using it is provided through application to another set of standardized cases.

Probably the key aspect of the training is the feedback of information on each manager's leadership style via computer printout, utilizing data from responses to the standardized cases. A manual is provided to help in interpreting these data. The computer feedback provides answers to the following questions:

1. How autocratic or participative am I in my dealings with subordinates in comparison with other participants in the program?
2. What decision processes do I use more or less frequently than the average?
3. How close does my behavior come to that of the model? How frequently does my behavior agree with the feasible set? What evidence is there that my leadership style reflects the pressure of time as opposed to a concern with the development of my subordinates? How do I compare in these respects with other participants in the class?
4. What rules do I violate most frequently and least frequently? How does this compare with other participants? On what cases did I violate these rules? Does my leadership style reflect more concern with getting decisions that are high in quality or with getting decisions that are accepted?
5. What circumstances cause me to behave in an autocratic fashion; what circumstances cause me to behave participatively? In what respects is the way in which I attempt to vary my behavior with the demands of the situation similar to that of the model? (Vroom 1973, 79–80)

The results from the printout typically cause considerable soul searching and re-analysis of the cases. Small group discussions often are used to facilitate this process. Presumably this is the point at which change occurs, if it does occur, since the manager is inevitably under some pressure to shift behavior toward that of others and toward the normative model.

Evaluations of this training continue to present a problem, especially in view of the skepticism in the field regarding the effectiveness of such efforts (see Doh, 2003). Vroom and Jago (1988) address this problem and present some evidence, but it is not adequate to the need. Numerous testimonials, and post-training evaluations from participants, indicate generally favorable reactions. Also, there is good evidence that the training moves managers in a participative direction, and that this change is maintained over time. Violations of decision rules decrease across the training.

However, we do not know whether the training actually makes participants better managers. What is needed is a design that compares trained and untrained managers on pre-test/post-test measures of managerial performance. That kind of study has not been conducted and it should be.

The theory has been criticized on the grounds that it stops at the level of the decision and does not proceed to skill development and application. Accordingly, a manager might learn how to make the right decision regarding leadership behavior without being able to execute that decision effectively, whether the intended behavior was autocratic or participative. Certainly this is an important problem in application, although not an insurmountable one, as Maier (1970) has shown. Skill training, in both autocratic and participative modes, should be introduced along with cognitive training.

A more difficult problem relates to whether under the stress of day-to-day activities managers actually can and will carry out the very complex rational, conscious processes the theory requires (see Schriesheim 2003). Doing so with hypothetical cases, stripped of personal emotional impact in an educational context far removed from the job is one thing; doing it in reality is another. Clearly there is a great deal of research that needs to be done, especially with regard to the management development applications.

Aditya, House, and Kerr (2000) add to this certain practitioner reactions. They note that the training is widely used in corporate leadership development centers. It is appealing because it legitimates *both* autocratic and democratic managerial behavior, thus reinforcing the values of a wide range of organizational cultures. For this and other reasons the training seems to resonate well in the corporate world, as companies are increasingly resorting to team operations and empowerment values.

Yet the following cautions from a practitioner point of view should be noted:

1. While the model permits and legitimates democratic leadership, it is always *the leader* who decides which style to use in each situation.
2. The model has no memory. It considers each decision in terms of its situational characteristics, but does not factor in what the leader did last time or the time before. Thus [the model] tends to recommend rather drastic swings from autocratic to democratic leadership. However, most managers have learned that if their behavior does vary so drastically, they will be perceived as acting inconsistently and unpredictably. (Aditya, House, and Kerr 2000, 151–52)

Such concerns only serve to point up further the need for training evaluation studies that measure actual behavior on the job using control groups as appropriate (see Chapter 2).

CONCLUSIONS

It is instructive to compare Heller's (1971) theory of decision sharing, mentioned at the beginning of this chapter, with decision process theory. Although Heller's theoretical statements lack the precision achieved by Vroom, they have served to guide an extensive program of research. The Heller theory utilizes a decision-sharing continuum very similar to Vroom's, but the contingency variables are only partially overlapping. Furthermore, the theory is primarily, although not entirely, descriptive rather than normative.

Both sets of research provide strong support for the view that participation is not a stable leadership style that characterizes certain managers but rather that it is a variable behavior that managers may or may not use depending on the situation. There are many other similarities between the two sets of results as well. Both seem to support the idea of a prevailing organizational character or culture with regard to participation, for instance.

The matter of conflict among subordinates, how it relates to participativeness and its importance as a contingency variable, raises concerns for both theories. Clearly skill in handling conflict is needed and it may well be absent. This is an area that requires further study and perhaps theoretical elaboration as well.

Time pressures emerge as of differing significance for the two theories. Heller's research found no evidence that time pressure is related to the use of participation. Vroom makes this of central concern. The difference may be attributable to the measures used, but this is an area that needs study, especially since time pressure and a desire to foster subordinate development would appear to introduce conflicting demands.

Heller finds that judgments of the degree of participation attributed to a person may in fact be influenced by the status power of the position held by that person; this offers an approach to the problems the Vroom theory has had with conflicting ratings from managers themselves and their subordinates. Again this is an area that requires new research.

Finally, there is the question of decision quality. This is rapidly becoming a key, if not *the* key, rationale for engaging in participative behavior. Yet acceptance of the decision is achieved at a much higher level than decision quality, given the same input of participativeness. Both the Vroom and the Heller research raises questions about the extent to which major improvements in quality can be expected from decision sharing. This, too, is a subject that needs further study.

The frequent similarities between findings related to Vroom's normative decision process theory and the research on Heller's influence power continuum theory gives considerable credence to the Vroom formulations. Thus, the evaluations for decision process theory reported at the beginning of this chapter are consistently favorable. The importance rating is 4.44, certainly not at the level of the expectancy or goal-setting theories, but still quite respectable. There are issues that await further research, but these usually are not as central to theory as those that have been successfully addressed. Thus, a rating of 5 stars on validity seems warranted. As to estimated usefulness, the complexity of the theory and the lack of research on outcomes from the training in the long term raises concerns, and they result in the award of only 4 stars. Yet this is a theory that can and has contributed to practice, especially if one has ongoing access to the necessary computer software.

In Chapter 13 we take up what has come to be designated as *the* contingency theory of leadership, even though this is in fact a misnomer, since currently normative decision process theory, and several other theories as well, are just as aptly given this name.

REFERENCES

Aditya, Ram N., House, Robert J., and Kerr, Steven (2000). Theory and Practice of Leadership: Into the New Millennium. In Cary L. Cooper and Edwin A. Locke (Eds.), *Industrial and Organizational Psychology: Linking Theory with Practice*. Oxford, UK: Blackwell, 130–65.

Böhnisch, W., Jago, Arthur, G., and Reber, G. (1987). Zur interkulturellen Validität des Vroom/Yetton Modells. *Die Betreibswirtschaft*, 47, 85–93.

Chemers, Martin M. (1997). *An Integrative Theory of Leadership*. Mahwah, NJ: Lawrence Erlbaum.

Crouch, Andrew, and Yetton, Philip (1987). Manager Behavior, Leadership Style, and Subordinate Performance: An Empirical Extension of the Vroom-Yetton Conflict Rule. *Organizational Behavior and Human Decision Processes*, 39, 384–96.

Culbert, Samuel A. (2003). Biography of Robert Tannenbaum—In Memorial. *Journal of Applied Behavioral Science*, 39, 361–63.

Doh, Jonathan P. (2003). Can Leadership Be Taught? Perspectives from Management Educators. *Academy of Management Learning and Education*, 2, 54–67.

Ettling, Jennifer T., and Jago, Arthur G. (1988). Participation under Conditions of Conflict: More on the Validity of the Vroom-Yetton Model. *Journal of Management Studies*, 25, 73–83.

Field, Richard H.G. (1982). A Test of the Vroom-Yetton Normative Model of Leadership. *Journal of Applied Psychology*, 67, 523–32.

Field, Richard H.G., and House, Robert J. (1990). A Test of the Vroom-Yetton Model Using Manager and Subordinate Reports. *Journal of Applied Psychology*, 75, 362–66.

Field, Richard H.G., Read, Peter C., and Louviere, Jordan J. (1990). The Effect of Situation Attributes on Decision Method Choice in the Vroom-Jago Model of Participation in Decision Making. *Leadership Quarterly*, 1, 165–76.

Heller, Frank A. (1971). *Managerial Decision-Making: A Study of Leadership Styles and Power-Sharing among Senior Managers*. London: Tavistock.

Heller, Frank A., Pusic, Eugen, Strauss, George, and Wilpert, Bernhard (1998). *Organizational Participation: Myth and Reality*. Oxford, UK: Oxford University Press.

Horgan, Dianne D., and Simeon, Rebecca J. (1990). Mentoring and Participation: An Application of the Vroom-Yetton Model. *Journal of Business and Psychology*, 5, 63–84.

Jago, Arthur G. (1978). A Test of Spuriousness in Descriptive Models of Participative Leader Behavior. *Journal of Applied Psychology*, 63, 383–87.

Jago, Arthur G., Ettling, Jennifer T., and Vroom, Victor H. (1985). Validating a Revision to the Vroom/Yetton Model: First Evidence. *Academy of Management Proceedings*, 45, 220–23.

Jago, Arthur G., and Vroom, Victor H. (1975). Perceptions of Leadership Style: Superior and Subordinate Descriptions of Decision-Making Behavior. In James G. Hunt and Lars L. Larson (Eds.), *Leadership Frontiers*. Kent, OH: Kent State University Press, 103–39.

——— (1977). Hierarchical Level and Leadership Style. *Organizational Behavior and Human Performance*, 18, 131–45.

——— (1980). An Evaluation of Two Alternatives to the Vroom/Yetton Normative Model. *Academy of Management Journal*, 23, 347–55.

——— (1982). Sex Differences in the Incidence and Evaluation of Participative Leader Behavior. *Journal of Applied Psychology*, 67, 776–83.

Jenkins, G. Douglas, Gupta, Nina, Mitra, Atul, and Shaw, Jason D. (1998). Are Financial Incentives Related to Performance? A Meta-Analytic Review of Empirical Research. *Journal of Applied Psychology*, 83, 777–87.

Kahai, Surinder S., Sosik, John J., and Avolio, Bruce J. (2004). Effects of Participative and Directive Leadership in Electronic Groups. *Group and Organization Management*, 29, 67–105.

Kahnweiler, William M., and Thompson, Margaret A. (2000). Levels of Desired, Actual, and Perceived Control of Employee Involvement in Decision Making: An Empirical Investigation. *Journal of Business and Psychology*, 14, 407–27.

Lam, Simon S.K., Chen, Xiao-ping, and Schaubroeck, John (2002). Participative Decision Making and Employee Performance in Different Cultures: The Moderating Effects of Allocentrism/Idiocentrism and Efficacy. *Academy of Management Journal*, 45, 905–14.

Liden, Robert C., and Arad, Sharon (1996). A Power Perspective of Empowerment and Work Groups: Implications for Human Resource Management Research. *Research in Personnel and Human Resources Management*, 14, 205–51.

Locke, Edwin A., Alavi, Maryam, and Wagner, John A. (1997). Participation in Decision Making: An Information Exchange Perspective. *Research in Personnel and Human Resources Management*, 15, 293–331.

Maier, Norman R.F. (1970). *Problem Solving and Creativity—In Groups and Individuals.* Belmont, CA: Brooks/Cole.

Margerison, Charles, and Glube, R. (1979). Leadership Decision Making: An Empirical Test of the Vroom and Yetton Model. *Journal of Management Studies*, 16, 45–55.

Paul, Robert J., and Ebadi, Yar M. (1989). Leadership Decision Making in a Service Organization: A Field Test of the Vroom-Yetton Model. *Journal of Occupational Psychology*, 62, 202–11.

Sagie, Abraham (1994). Participative Decision Making and Performance: A Moderator Analysis. *Journal of Applied Behavioral Science*, 30, 227–46.

Schriesheim, Chester A. (2003). Why Leadership Research Is Generally Irrelevant for Leadership Development. In Susan E. Murphy and Ronald E. Riggio (Eds.), *The Future of Leadership Development*. Mahwah, NJ: Lawrence Erlbaum, 181–97.

Smith, Blanchard B. (1979). The TELOS Program and the Vroom-Yetton Model. In James G. Hunt and Lars L. Larson (Eds.), *Crosscurrents in Leadership*. Carbondale: Southern Illinois University Press, 39–45.

Sue-Chan, Christina, and Ong, Mark (2002). Goal Assignment and Performance: Assessing the Mediating Roles of Goal Commitment and Self-Efficacy and the Moderating Role of Power Distance. *Organizational Behavior and Human Decision Processes*, 89, 1140–61.

Tannenbaum, Robert, and Schmidt, Warren H. (1958). How to Choose a Leadership Pattern. *Harvard Business Review*, 36(2), 95–101.

Tjosvold, Dean, Wedley, W.C., and Field, Richard H.G. (1986). Constructive Controversy, the Vroom-Yetton Model, and Managerial Decision Making. *Journal of Occupational Behavior*, 7, 125–38.

Vroom, Victor H. (1960). *Some Personality Determinants of the Effects of Participation.* Englewood Cliffs, NJ: Prentice-Hall.

——— (1973). A New Look at Managerial Decision Making. *Organizational Dynamics*, 1(4), 66–80.

——— (1974). Decision Making and the Leadership Process. *Journal of Contemporary Business*, 3, 47–64.

——— (1975). Leadership Revisited. In Eugene L. Cass and Frederick G. Zimmer (Eds.), *Man and Work in Society.* New York: Van Nostrand, 220–34.

——— (1976a). Leadership. In Marvin D. Dunnette (Ed.), *Handbook of Industrial and Organizational Psychology.* Chicago, IL: Rand, McNally, 1527–51.

——— (1976b). Can Leaders Learn to Lead? *Organizational Dynamics*, 4(3), 17–28.

——— (1993). Improvising and Muddling Through. In Arthur G. Bedeian (Ed.), *Management Laureates: A Collection of Autobiographical Essays*, Vol. III. Greenwich, CT: JAI Press, 259–84.

——— (1999). New Developments in Leadership and Decision Making. *OB News*, Spring, 4–5.

——— (2000). Leadership and the Decision-Making Process. *Organizational Dynamics*, 28(4), 82–94.

Vroom, Victor H., and Jago, Arthur G. (1974). Decision Making as a Social Process: Normative and Descriptive Models of Leader Behavior. *Decision Sciences*, 5, 743–69.

——— (1978). On the Validity of the Vroom/Yetton Model. *Journal of Applied Psychology*, 63, 151–62.

——— (1988). *The New Leadership: Managing Participation in Organizations*. Englewood Cliffs, NJ: Prentice-Hall.

——— (1995). Situation Effects and Levels of Participation. *Leadership Quarterly*, 6, 169–81.

Vroom, Victor H., and Yetton, Philip W. (1973). *Leadership and Decision-Making*. Pittsburgh, PA: University of Pittsburgh Press.

Wagner, John A. (1994). Participation's Effects on Performance and Satisfaction: A Reconsideration of Research Evidence. *Academy of Management Review*, 19, 312–30.

Yukl, Gary (2002). *Leadership in Organizations*. Upper Saddle River, NJ: Prentice-Hall.

CHAPTER 13

CONTINGENCY THEORY OF LEADERSHIP

FRED FIEDLER

Background
Evolution of Contingency Theory
    The Exploratory Stage
    The Move to Formal Theory
    Classification of Interacting Task Groups
    Types of Groups, Leadership, and Effectiveness
    Changes in the Basic Model
    The Changing Meaning of LPC
    Extensions to Leadership Dynamics
    Multilevel and Multiple Sources
Evaluation and Impact
    The Status of Contingency Theory
    The Problem with LPC
    Fiedler's Own Evaluation of Contingency Theory
Applications–Leader Match
    The Nature of Leader Match
    Leader Match: Pro and Con
Cognitive Resource Theory—Addendum to Contingency Theory?
    Pre-theory Views and Research
    Formal Theory
    Theory-forming and Theory-testing Research
    The Status of Cognitive Resource Theory
Conclusions

Importance rating	★ ★ ★ ★
Estimated validity	★ ★ ★
Estimated usefulness	★ ★ ★
Decade of origin	1950s

In this chapter the discussion focuses on a theoretical approach that once again follows the contingency path that has prevailed in leadership for many years. Fred Fiedler's initial views were called contingency theory, reflecting the fact that his was the only such approach around at the time, and thus had the contingency field all to itself. Although direct concern with participation and power sharing in the beginning was minimal, such matters were ultimately considered as the theorizing progressed.

Contingency theory has had a long history, extending back to 1951, and has evolved slowly. Fiedler has been extremely responsive to research results, both those generated by him and those of others. As a consequence, it is very difficult to separate research and theory as we have done in discussing other theories; there is a constant interplay back and forth. The theory is almost entirely inductive in nature, and in fact some have questioned whether it should be labeled a theory at all. At least in the early period, contingency theory was a set of continually changing empirical generalizations.

Another distinguishing characteristic is that contingency theory has evolved around a measurement process. In fact, there was a measure before there was a theory. As a result, the usual procedures of theory construction have been reversed. Instead of proposing a set of theoretical constructs and then devising measures to match, Fiedler started with the measurement process and then sought to develop theoretical constructs to go with the measures and the research results obtained with them.

BACKGROUND

Fred Fiedler was born in Vienna in 1922 and moved to the United States shortly after Hitler invaded Austria in 1938. He ended up at the University of Chicago, from which he received both his undergraduate degree and his Ph.D. in clinical psychology, replete with a personal psycho-analysis (Fiedler 1992a). In 1951 he moved to the University of Illinois, where he eventually became a member of the psychology faculty. In this early period he spent a great deal of time working on funded research projects, an exposure that served him well later in obtaining his own research funding.

A major area of interest for many years was interpersonal perception, a subject he pursued first in terms of therapeutic relationships and later in leadership. By the middle 1950s, Fiedler's publications had shifted largely from clinical psychology to leadership and leader–follower relations. After his move from Illinois to the University of Washington in 1969, he began to work more closely with the business school, where he held an adjunct appointment, but his primary base has remained in psychology. He has worked extensively with graduate students and other faculty members throughout his career, thus generating a very large amount of research (see Hooijberg and Choi 1999). Consistent with his international origins, he has remained interested in cross-cultural research and has held a number of visiting appointments at foreign universities. He retired from the University of Washington in 1992, although he has continued to publish since then (e.g, see Fiedler 2002).

EVOLUTION OF CONTINGENCY THEORY

There have been two major stages in the development of contingency theory. The first, extending from the early 1950s to the early 1960s, was essentially exploratory. A sizable body of research data was collected, and various hypotheses were tried out in an attempt to explain the findings. During this period it is totally impossible to separate research from theory. The second stage began with the statement of contingency theory in a form much the same as that currently existing. This stage has continued to the present with the testing of these early propositions and of others that have emerged since.

The Exploratory Stage

Fiedler's original research interests involved the relationship between psychotherapist and patient, and the ways in which similarities and differences in ascribed self-concepts were related to effectiveness in such relationships (Fiedler 1951). Self-concepts were measured originally using the Q-technique methodology, in which descriptive statements are sorted into categories in terms of the degree of approximation to perceived reality. This rather cumbersome approach was modified later as Fiedler's interests shifted to leader–member relationships in small task groups, but the concern with assumed similarities and differences among people remained.

Through a series of gradual transformations, the measurement process moved from the Q-technique to an approach of a semantic differential type (Fiedler 1958). In this latter procedure the subject is asked to "think of the person with whom you can work best" and later to "think of the person with whom you can work least well." In both cases a description of that person is then obtained by having the subject place a mark on a six-point graphic scale between two polar adjectives such as careless–careful, gloomy–cheerful, efficient–inefficient, and the like. The differences between the numerical descriptions applied to the most and least preferred coworkers are then used to compute an Assumed Similarity Between Opposites Score (ASo) by summing over all the adjective pairs.

When the difference score is large, it means that the least and most preferred coworkers are seen as quite disparate, and thus assumed similarity is minimal; when it is small, the two are perceived as much the same. Essentially what is involved is that when ASo is low, the person strongly rejects the least preferred coworker; job performance makes considerable difference in how people are judged.

The true meaning of the construct or constructs thus measured has presented difficulties from the beginning:

> One of the main problems in the research program has been in finding an adequate interpretation of Assumed Similarity scores, especially Aso. While we have no difficulty in designating the operations which define these scores, we have encountered considerable problems in attempting to anchor their meaning within a more general framework of psychological theory. (Fiedler 1958, 17)

The early resolution of this problem was as follows:

> The Assumed Similarity Between Opposites Score measures an attitude toward others which may best be described as emotional or psychological distance. A person with high ASo tends to be concerned about his interpersonal relations, and he feels the need for the approval and support of his associates. In contrast, the low ASo person is relatively independent of others, less concerned with their feelings, and willing to reject a person with whom he cannot accomplish an assigned task. (Fiedler 1958, 22)

The studies conducted during the 1950s utilized a variety of different approaches to the measurement of ASo, and thus it cannot be assumed that the findings are entirely comparable. The measures were related to indexes of group effectiveness using basketball teams, surveying parties, bomber crews, tank crews, open hearth steel shops, farm supply cooperatives, and others (Fiedler 1958; Godfrey, Fiedler, and Hall 1959). The results indicated that ASo tends to relate to group performance only when moderated by some additional factor. These additional factors varied from study to study and were usually identified afterward. In some cases they were aspects of the task; in other cases they were aspects of the group's informal structure and sociometric choices or of the relationship between a leader and a key subordinate.

Also, although generally the tendency was for the more psychologically distant, low ASo leader to be associated with success, there were occasions when this was reversed. Thus, in the open hearth steel shops ASo was negatively correlated with effectiveness under certain task conditions (Cleven and Fiedler 1956), and in the farm supply cooperatives the ASo of the general manager was negatively related to success under certain sociometric conditions (Godfrey, Fiedler, and Hall 1959). However, in this latter study the ASo of the informal leader of the board of directors was positively related to organizational success, again when appropriate sociometric moderators operated.

After reading the reports of this early research, one comes away with a feeling that there is something there, but with no clear conception of what that "something" is. The lack of comparability across studies, the variations in moderators, many of them identified after an extensive empirical search of possible alternatives, and the uncertainty as to whether ASo might not be subject to considerable influence by environmental circumstances including management development, all contribute to a sense of uneasiness. There is a clear need for a theoretical structure to guide research, rather than continuing to permit the research to generate a procession of short-lived theories.

The Move to Formal Theory

In recognition of the need for a more stable theoretical structure, Fiedler articulated the major outlines of a contingency theory of leadership in the mid-1960s, drawing heavily on the research of the earlier, exploratory period. Fiedler's theory thus developed was first published in 1964, and its practical applications were elaborated in his 1965 work. The most comprehensive statement of this period appears in a subsequent book (Fiedler 1967).

One change that occurred at this point is that ASo was dropped as a central theoretical variable and one component of ASo, the least preferred coworker (LPC) rating, was substituted; descriptions of the most preferred coworker were no longer employed. The semantic differential approach to measurement had been utilized exclusively, but the actual adjective pairs incorporated tended to vary from study to study. The graphic scale now was extended from six to eight points, and LPC was obtained by summing the values marked for each adjective pair in describing "the person with whom you can work least well." LPC and ASo are reported to correlate in the 0.80 to 0.90 range (Fiedler 1967).

The struggle with the meaning of the central constructs appears not to have been affected by the shift from ASo to LPC.

> [I]t has been extremely difficult to develop an adequate and readily supportable interpretation of ASo and LPC scores. These scores do not measure attributes which correlate with the usual personality and ability tests or with attitude scales. Nor is there a one-to-one relationship between these scales and behaviors.
>
> . . .
>
> [W]e visualize the high-LPC individual (who perceives his least-preferred coworker in a relatively favorable manner) as a person who derives his major satisfaction from successful interpersonal relationships, while the low-LPC person (who describes his LPC in very unfavorable terms) derives his major satisfaction from task performance. (Fiedler 1967, 45)

Classification of Interacting Task Groups

Fiedler's theory is initially presented as applying within the domain of groups that have a task to perform or a goal to achieve and in which this task accomplishment requires interaction among members, not a series of entirely independent efforts. Within this domain groups may be classi-

Table 13.1

Fiedler's Early Classification of Interactive Task Groups

Group category	Leader–member relations	Task structure	Position power
1	Good	High	Strong
2	Good	High	Weak
3	Good	Low	Strong
4	Good	Low	Weak
5	Moderately poor	High	Strong
6	Moderately poor	High	Weak
7	Moderately poor	Low	Strong
8	Moderately poor	Low	Weak
8-A	Very poor	High	Strong

fied with reference to three major factors—the leader's position power, the structure of the task, and the interpersonal relationship between leader and members.

Position power is a function of such considerations as legitimate authority and the degree to which positive and negative sanctions are available to the leader. It appears to assume the existence of an organization surrounding the group and a hierarchic means of conveying the power. The existence of position power makes the leader's job easier.

Task structure refers to the extent to which rules, regulations, job descriptions, policies—role prescriptions—are clearly and unambiguously specified. It is easier to lead in highly structured situations because structured tasks are enforceable. Task structure is presumed to exist when decisions are subject to clear-cut verifiability in terms of correctness, goals are clearly stated and understood, multiple paths to attaining the goals are not present, and only one correct answer or solution exists. Like position power, task structure is derived from the organization.

The relationship between the leader and group members is much more an internal matter. It is reflected in the degree to which the leader is accepted and members are loyal to that person, and in the affective reactions of members to the leader. When leader–member relations are good, the leadership job is much easier. Good leader–member relations are reflected in a highly positive group atmosphere.

Using this set of classification factors, Fiedler developed a taxonomy for interacting task groups. The taxonomy does not deal with all possible alternatives. In keeping with the tendency to empirical generalization, it applies to groups of the kind that have been actually studied. The results are presented in Table 13.1.

The theoretical assumption is that these groups require different approaches to the leadership process to be effective. Subsequent analyses indicate that the degree of favorableness of the situation for the leader declines steadily from category 1 down. Actually, category 8-A was first labeled 5-A (Fiedler 1964). However, it was later changed to 8-A to reflect its relative position on the favorableness scale (Fiedler 1967).

Types of Groups, Leadership, and Effectiveness

Leader–member relations are the most important consideration in classifying groups, task structure is next, and position power is least important. Empirically based predictions regarding LPC–group effectiveness relationships are generated for each group using the degree of favorableness of the group situation for the leader as a moderator or contingency variable as follows:

Group category	Relationship of LPC to performance
1	Negative
2	Negative
3	Negative
4	Positive
5	Positive
6	Positive
7	Positive (but lower)
8	Negative
8-A	Negative

In presenting this contingency model, Fiedler (1967) repeatedly refers to research data rather than to theoretical logic. Qualifications and uncertainties are numerous, again because findings from research raise questions regarding the influence of additional variables. There is no point at which Fiedler states exactly what his theory is, why it makes sense on logical grounds, and what its delimiting boundary statements are. In concluding his book, he cites the need for:

1. A better method of measuring the favorableness of the leadership situation.
2. A method of weighting leader–member relations, task structure, and position power.
3. Knowledge of what really causes good or poor leader–member relations.
4. Information on the role of leader and member intelligence and ability.
5. Relating leader consideration, initiating structure, supportiveness, and so forth, to performance under varying degrees of situational favorableness.
6. Data on how task characteristics other than structure may operate.
7. Research on co-acting groups in which the members work independently.
8. Research on counteracting groups in which the members bargain with one another.
9. An understanding of individuals whose LPC scores fall in the middle range.
10. Specification of the influences of managers above the first level, line-staff status, and differing leadership styles among interacting managers.
11. Studies of the effects of training in diagnosing the favorableness of a leadership situation and in modifying it.

In none of these instances is a specific hypothesis stated, although hypotheses have been developed in some of the areas since. There is little attempt to posit a logically coherent theoretical system independent of the appeal to empirical data. The ambiguities surrounding the meaning of LPC make it almost impossible to do so.

Changes in the Basic Model

After the early statements of the theory in the mid-1960s there were a number of further developments, almost invariably as a result of subsequent research results. This continuing proliferation of both research findings and theoretical changes and extensions makes it difficult to determine which came first, and thus what is ad hoc theorizing and what is a test of theory. The following discussion will focus on what at one time or another have been statements of theory; in later discussions an effort is made to identify true tests of these theoretical statements.

In subsequent presentations of the model, group category 8-A has typically been eliminated, and leader–member relations in categories 5 through 8 often have been referred to as poor rather than as moderately poor (Mitchell, Biglan, Oncken, and Fiedler 1970). However, there are subsequent statements that the situation can be even less favorable for the leader than octant 8 indicates. There is some ambiguity on this whole matter of extreme unfavorableness.

In addition, there is some inconsistency as to which octants are predicted and which are not. Negative LPC–performance relations are anticipated for octants 1, 2, and 8, and positive relationships for octants 4 and 5. The other octants are variously ignored or even specifically not predicted, or they are predicted. When predictions are made, octant 3 is expected to yield a negative correlation and octants 6 and 7 positive correlations (Fiedler 1971; Fiedler and Chemers 1974).

The original domain of the theory was that of interacting task groups. This subsequently has been extended to co-acting task groups but not to co-acting training groups that are said not to follow the contingency model (Fiedler 1971; Fiedler and Chemers 1974). The training groups referred to are those created to assist individuals to achieve their own goals, and in such groups a tentative suggestion is advanced that high LPC leaders consistently are more effective.

The situational favorableness dimension has been renamed *situation control and influence* in order to eliminate misunderstandings (Fiedler 1978b). Also, a specific formula for weighting the three aspects of this dimension has been proposed. This formula calls for multiplying the leader–member relations score by four, the task structure score by two, and then adding these values to the position power score (Fiedler 1978a, 1978b). Yet, it has been apparent for some time that situational control (or favorableness) is not simply a matter of the three basic factors:

> It must be pointed out, of course, that the three major subscales of leader–member relations, task structure, and position power by no means represent the only factors which determine the leader's situational control and influence. Other studies have pointed to situational stress as affecting the leader's control; cross-cultural studies have shown that linguistic and cultural heterogeneity also play a major role in determining leader control. And leader experience and training also increase control. In unusual cases this formula may thus require appropriate modification, and specific rules governing these modifications still need to be developed. (Fiedler 1978b, 66)

Thus, in one study, the following hypothesis was tested:

> As environmental stress increases, the relationship-oriented leader will become relatively more effective in promoting member adjustment than task-oriented leaders. Hence, under conditions of high stress, high LPC leaders should have better adjusted groups than low LPC leaders, while under conditions of low stress, low LPC leaders should have better adjusted groups than high LPC leaders. (Fiedler, O'Brien, and Ilgen, 1969)

As noted, the role of these additional factors is not stated specifically.

Furthermore, there is ambiguity regarding the theoretical status of the middle LPC group, then estimated to be some 15 to 20 percent of the population. These individuals are considered to be different from either the high or low LPC groups and are labeled socioindependent without a clear picture of their actual characteristics (Fiedler 1978b). As in other areas where the theory lacks clarity, the problem is that no inherent theoretical logic exists, and therefore hypotheses await empirical findings. Each step of theory development must depend upon the inductive theory generating processes of empiricism, or it does not occur.

The Changing Meaning of LPC

In the early writings LPC (or ASo) was variously described as measuring psychological distance (Fiedler 1958), controlling versus permissive attitudes in the leadership role (Fiedler 1964), and task versus relationship orientations (Fiedler 1967). Later these categories were described as over-simplifications, although not necessarily totally incorrect, and two additional construct definitions were proposed.

Of these two, Fiedler most consistently has supported what he calls the motivational hierarchy view (Fiedler 1972a, 1973, 1978b; Fiedler and Chemers 1974). Essentially, this view states that leaders will manifest their primary motives under conditions over which they have little control and influence, but that when control and influence are assured (favorableness is high), primary motives are easily satisfied and it is possible to move down the hierarchy and seek to satisfy motives of secondary importance. Thus, high LPC leaders seek relatedness under unfavorable circumstances and seek to satisfy more task-related motives as conditions become more favorable. Low LPC leaders will manifest their primary task orientation in unfavorable situations but can be expected to shift to a more considerate, interpersonal relations–oriented pattern of behavior as their control and influence increase. In this view it is only under conditions of stress that the basic personality, or primary motive structure, reveals itself.

Sometimes, however, Fiedler is hesitant about the motivation hierarchy view:

> These findings favor a motivational hierarchy interpretation, although other interpretations, consistent with these findings, are also tenable. Whatever the precise and final interpretation of the LPC score might turn out to be, there is very little question that it measures a personality attribute which has very important consequences for organizational behavior. (Fiedler, 1978b, 103)

Consistent with this hesitancy is the fact that another formulation remains viable and is in fact frequently mentioned in favorable terms by Fiedler. This second view is considered to be "quite compatible with the interpretation of LPC as an index of motivational hierarchy" (Fiedler and Chemers 1974, 77). It is stated in the greatest detail in Foa, Mitchell, and Fiedler (1971).

This second formulation is a cognitive interpretation. The LPC scale contains a variety of adjective pairs. Some are task oriented, some are interpersonal in nature, and some are mixed, although the majority are interpersonal. The cognitively complex individuals who differentiate among these types of adjectives are very likely to have high LPC scores because they describe their least preferred coworker positively on interpersonal adjectives and negatively on task adjectives. The low LPC, nondifferentiating people will describe their least preferred coworker negatively not only with regard to task performance but in interpersonal terms as well—as inefficient, cold, rejecting, and the like. Thus, the degree of differentiation among types of adjective pairs is the key to interpreting LPC.

A moderately favorable leadership situation is characterized by considerable differentiation among the various aspects—some are positive and some are negative insofar as leader control and influence are concerned. Thus, a high LPC leader who is cognitively complex would provide a good match for the moderately favorable situation and do well. Very favorable or very unfavorable situations are much less differentiated in terms of the three major classification variables, and the low cognitive complexity of the low LPC leader should be a positive value. In fact, greater differentiation might well introduce problems. The key to success is a matching of differentiation levels in the leader and the task situation.

Figure 13.1   **Effects of Leadership Training on Subsequent Performance as Moderated by Situational Favorableness**[a]

Perception of situation		Effective performer	
Before training	After training	Before training	After training
1. Octant 4 ──────▶Octant 1 (Moderately favorable) (Very favorable)		High LPC	Low LPC
2. Octant 8 ──────▶Octant 4 (Unfavorable) (Moderately favorable)		Low LPC	High LPC
3. Beyond Octant 8──▶Octant 8 (Extremely (Unfavorable) unfavorable)		High LPC (speculative)	Low LPC

Source: Adapted from Fiedler, Bons, and Hastings (1975, 237).

[a]Predicated on the hypothesis that training changes favorability as perceived by the leader to whatever next higher degree will reverse the leader effectiveness level.

Extensions to Leadership Dynamics

The first extensions of contingency theory into the domain of leadership dynamics involved changes introduced by training and increasing experience. Fiedler (1972b) starts with the assumption that both leadership training and experience in the leadership role have not been shown to improve performance. He then uses an argument of the kind outlined in Figure 13.1 for training to show why this might be expected (Fiedler, Bons, and Hastings 1975).

The primary consequence of the training is to increase leader influence and control through improved leader–member relations, task structuring, and position power. Such changes are equally likely to shift an individual into a good LPC–situation match or out of it, assuming that LPC itself is not changed. On the average, therefore, leadership performance will not be altered; an improvement in one person will be canceled out by the decreased effectiveness of another. In Figure 13.1 the extremely unfavorable situation beyond octant 8 is assumed to be rare but might occur with racially divided groups or when extreme stress is present; it appears to have much in common with the original category 8-A, although the hypothesized LPC relationship to performance is reversed.

One approach suggested to achieve effective results from training is to teach managers how to modify the favorableness of a situation to match their LPC scores—how to engage in situational engineering. Another approach is to select for training only those individuals whose performance can be expected to improve because they will move into a good LPC–situation match, not out of it. Alternatively, all might be trained, but the training must be selectively combined with job rotation so that some return to more challenging jobs, thus offsetting the increased favorableness induced by the training for these particular individuals. Rotation of some kind, including promotion, may be the only way of offsetting the automatic increases in situational favorableness that come with increased managerial experience.

What the dynamic theory posits is that as leader control and influence (favorability) increase, for whatever reason, the performance level of the *high* LPC leader, will change as follows:

Octant	8 →	7 →	6 →	5 →	4 →	3 →	2 →	1
Performance	Low	Low	High Medium	High	High	Low	Low	Low

For the *low* LPC leader this pattern is reversed:

Octant	8 →	7 →	6 →	5 →	4 →	3 →	2 →	1
Performance	High	High	Low Medium	Low	Low	High	High	High

It should be noted that these statements (Fiedler 1978a, 1978b) are not consistent with other statements of the theory insofar as octant 7 is concerned. Also, octant 6 is labeled as unfavorable (low control), although from the theory one would expect it to be included in the moderate range (with octant 7). These inconsistencies appear in schematic representations of the theory and are not discussed in the texts; thus the reasons for them are unclear.

The dynamic theory indicates that in selecting individuals for leadership positions, a decision should be made as to whether high initial performance is needed, or whether it is desirable to wait and permit training and experience to shift favorableness and performance levels. Also, as experience in a given job accumulates, there comes a point at which rotation into a new, less familiar position is advisable. The theory is not specific in any general sense as to exactly how much experience is required before these hypothesized performance changes can be anticipated, although the degree of structure and complexity of the work and the intelligence of the leader are viewed as relevant (Fiedler 1978a).

There is also some ambiguity regarding the effects of different kinds of training programs. Fiedler (1972b) describes human relations training as improving the leader–member relations factor and thus increasing favorableness, yet later (Fiedler 1978b) he notes that training in participative management (which human relations training certainly is) reduces position power and accordingly decreases favorableness.

The theory also deals with changes in the degree of turbulence and instability in the organizational environment. With greater turbulence there is greater uncertainty and thus less leader control and influence. Personnel shakeups, reorganizations, new product lines, and the like introduce turbulence. Under continuing turbulent conditions the downward shift in favorableness can be expected ultimately to bring about a situation in which low LPC leaders are needed.

Multilevel and Multiple Sources

Ayman, Chemers, and Fiedler (1995) have advanced the position that the strength of contingency theory is in its use of a multilevel and multiple-sources approach to defining leadership effectiveness. They note that measures of the leader's motivational orientation derive from leader responses (individual level), aspects of the situation have been determined by leader reports as well as reports from subordinates and researchers (multilevel, multiple sources), and outcomes have been established primarily based on group performance (group level). Detailed evidence in support of this contention is set forth in Table 13.2.

EVALUATION AND IMPACT

Fiedler's theories have in one way or another been a source of a great deal of research. He has had substantial funding at the universities of both Illinois and Washington, and this made it possible to

Table 13.2

Contingency Theory Variables, Level of Analysis, Measures Used, and Sources of Data

Variables	Level	Measure	Source
Leader's motivational orientation	Individual	Least Preferred Coworker (LPC) scale	Leader
Situational control			
Group climate	Group	Group Atmosphere; (GA); Leader–member relation; Sociometric method	Leader or averaged group score
Task structure	Individual	Task structure; Scale or type of job	Leader or experimenter
Authority	Individual	Position power scale	Leader; Experimenter; Superior
Effectiveness			
Satisfaction	Group or dyadic	Job Descriptor Index (JDI)	Subordinate
Performance	Group	Supervisory rating archival data	Superior; Experimenter organization's records
Stress	Individual	Fiedler's job stress scale	Leader

Source: Ayman, Chemers, and Fiedler (1995, 149). Copyright © 1995 Elsevier Science. Reprinted with permission.

produce a continuing stream of studies; there have been a number of studies done on the outside as well, often initiated because someone did not believe Fiedler was correct. As might be anticipated, this situation has sparked a great deal of controversy in the literature; commentaries, rejoinders, replies, and the like occur frequently, and Fiedler has almost invariably been in the midst of each such debate.

The Status of Contingency Theory

In the early years all this controversy, the frequent changes in theoretical position, and the uncertainty as to what was theory-forming and what was theory-testing research created a rather negative climate for contingency theory. The ideas were different (creative?) and intriguing. Yet organizational behavior as a whole was far from reaching a consensus, except perhaps to the effect that it was next to impossible to say what was going on, and that thus the most prudent approach was to delay a decision, or perhaps not to express any views at all. This milieu of uncertainty prevailed up to the early 1980s, when meta-analysis first came to the rescue. Figure 13.2 is presented to clarify the discussion as we now turn to these comprehensive, quantitative reviews.

The first meta-analysis was carried out by Strube and Garcia (1981). This was very early in the application of the technique within organizational behavior, and the procedures used were not entirely up to the standards that have developed since. Nevertheless, the results produced sub-

Figure 13.2 **The Octants of Contingency Theory**

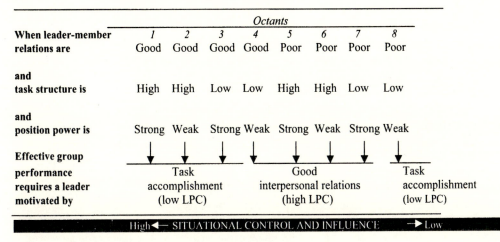

	Octants							
When leader-member relations are	1	2	3	4	5	6	7	8
	Good	Good	Good	Good	Poor	Poor	Poor	Poor
and task structure is	High	High	Low	Low	High	High	Low	Low
and position power is	Strong	Weak	Strong	Weak	Strong	Weak	Strong	Weak

Effective group performance requires a leader motivated by

Task accomplishment (low LPC)	Good interpersonal relations (high LPC)	Task accomplishment (low LPC)

High ← SITUATIONAL CONTROL AND INFLUENCE → Low

Source: Adapted from Fiedler and Chemers (1974, 80).

stantial support for contingency theory overall and for all octants except 2. There was a tendency for studies conducted by researchers affiliated with Fiedler to yield more positive results for the theory.

A subsequent meta-analysis reported by Peters, Hartke, and Pohlman (1985) appears to be somewhat more procedurally defensible. The results, although generally supportive, indicated that the octant-specific findings in a number of cases required additional moderators beyond those of contingency theory to explain the data. Thus the theory appears to be to some degree incomplete. Octant 2 again presents problems. Support for the theory is considerably stronger when laboratory studies are used than from field studies.

Later Schriesheim, Tepper, and Tetrault (1994) utilized meta-analysis to study the performance means in the various octants. Although the data obtained are not entirely consistent with expectations, the problems unearthed are most troublesome for the leader match application to be considered shortly. In conjunction with the two previous meta-analyses, the findings from this study are interpreted as providing "more than sufficient evidence to conclude that the contingency model warrants further investigation and exploration (rather than abandonment)" (Schriesheim, Tepper, and Tetrault 1994, 572). I take this to mean that the theory is more right than wrong, but that further adjustments and elaborations are needed.

Bass (1990), in reviewing the research on contingency theory including the meta-analyses, notes that although outnumbered by the positive findings, a number of unsupportive studies exist as well. In some of the latter, Fiedler has pointed to design problems that he feels invalidate the results. On the evidence these criticisms appear justified in some cases, but not always. Nevertheless, there remain a goodly number of studies, usually of a field nature and not conducted by Fiedler's group, that do not support the theory. Bass also points to evidence indicating that the variability of validity coefficients within each octant is extremely large, presumably in part at least as a result of the inclusion of nonsupportive studies. The chance that a particular study will not produce the theoretically anticipated results in a given octant is substantial. Yet only the octant 2 data fail completely to support the theory. Fiedler contends, in the latter instance, that the theory is really one of three zones as specified in Figure 13.2, not eight octants. Thus, the results for octant 2 would average with those for octants 1 and 3, and obliterate the departure from theory. This appears, however, to represent a post hoc adjustment in the theory to make it fit the data.

On the positive side, Chemers (2002, 152), a frequent coauthor with Fiedler, is consistently favorable toward contingency theory. The following quote summarizes his main argument:

> [L]eaders with a good match between leadership orientation and situational characteristics tended to perform more effectively, express greater job satisfaction, report less job stress and stress-related illness, and most interestingly, describe themselves as upbeat, confident, and in control of the leadership situation compared to leaders who are "out of match."

The latter reaction is said to be comparable to self-efficacy.

Ayman (2002), in connection with a comprehensive overview of contingency theory, reviews a number of criticisms that have been leveled at the theory, and rebuts each in turn. Yukl (2002), on the other hand, seems to accept many of the criticisms that have been advanced in the past, and accordingly ends with an evaluation of contingency theory that is lukewarm at best. Aditya, House, and Kerr (2002), in their most recent review, appear to be closely aligned with Yukl (2002).

Overall, despite the evident support for contingency theory's validity, there are remaining problems. Yet attempts to develop alternative approaches to explain the findings generated around the theory have not produced anything better (Schriesheim, Tepper, and Tetrault 1994). The alternatives considered to date do not predict the pattern of the data as well as contingency theory.

The Problem with LPC

LPC still represents a source of difficulties. Having a theory depend upon one measure whose meaning is not clearly established cannot be a plus for any theory. Although Fielder now appears to have settled on the motivational hierarchy interpretation, there continues to be some disagreement within his camp (Ayman, Chemers, and Fiedler 1995). In the early years there were serious questions regarding the psychometric properties of LPC, but these have been largely resolved; the remaining problem is one of construct validity.

Perhaps the best evidence for an LPC problem is a study by Kennedy (1982) that focused on the middle 25 percent of the population and the scores covered by this group. Fiedler has typically identified such a group, although recently specifying it as smaller, at 10 percent or less of the population, and essentially has excluded it from contingency theory's domain. Kennedy finds, however, that his middle LPC group performs well in all leadership situations, and that in five of the eight octants, these were the best-performing leaders. In octants 1, 5, and 7, the relationship between LPC and performance was significantly curvilinear. These results are not consistent with the linear hypothesis posited by contingency theory. A possibility exists that LPC measures two aspects of personality—a dimension from strong to weak work motivation at the low end and a dimension from sociophobia to sociophilia at the high end. Consistent with this view, Ayman (2002) notes that the LPC measure is at least semi-projective in nature and may well measure different needs (thus achievement motivation at the low end and affiliation motivation at the high end—see Chapter 4) at different points. Ayman concludes that "the LPC measure is clearly not without considerable merit" (205).

Fiedler's Own Evaluation of Contingency Theory

For many years Fiedler's personal view of what he had wrought was primarily manifest in his replies to attacks. He consistently defended his theory, and he did so by referring to research that he believed supported his positions. More recently, beginning in the 1990s, Fiedler has become somewhat more reflective and in the process provided more insight into the underpinnings of his theory. He believes that the greatest contribution is "the conceptualization of leadership effectiveness as the product of an interaction between personality and situational factors and empirical support for this proposition" (Fiedler 1991, 503). The criticism that he feels is particularly justified is that the contingency model itself is something of a "black box" that does not immediately reveal the reasons for the relationships it describes and predicts. As a result, true understanding is at a minimum.

Although he indicates an appreciation for deductive theorizing, Fiedler notes that this is impossible for him because he is constantly distracted by data—"For me, developing hypotheses has always been an inductive, messy, a posteriori process" (Fiedler 1995, 453). Further to this point he says:

> The model's greatest weaknesses arise from its inductive development. The LPC construct has little face or concurrent validity, and even evidence for its construct validity requires some faith. The lack of process-based explanations for performance effects makes both the understanding and application of the model more difficult. (Ayman, Chemers, and Fiedler 1995, 162)

Yet major strengths are emphasized as well:

1. The conceptual and statistical independence of the theory's central constructs.
2. The theory's emphasis on independent and, where possible, objective measures of important organizational outcomes such as group productivity.
3. The theory's relatively lesser vulnerability to the invalidation of its constructs and findings as a result of information-processing biases and methodological weaknesses.
4. The theory's proven predictive validity (162).

APPLICATIONS–LEADER MATCH

For some time contingency theorists have advocated a process of situational engineering whereby an individual leader is placed in a situation appropriate to his or her LPC score (Fiedler 1965). For this approach to work for a given organization, LPC would have to be stable over time, and performance levels would have to be essentially the same across octants. In other words, with LPC appropriate to the situation, it should not matter whether octant 1, or 5, or 8, or whatever, was used. Furthermore, this approach assumes that it is easier to change aspects of the situation, either by reengineering the job itself or by transfer to a different position, than it is to change the person, and in particular those aspects of the person that LPC measures. All of these assumptions and expectations are built into the leader match procedure whereby individuals learn to modify their leadership situations so as to provide a degree of situational favorableness or control appropriate to their LPC.

The Nature of Leader Match

Leader match training utilizes a programmed learning text. The process starts with a self-measurement of LPC and then with measures of the various aspects of the leadership situation—

leader–member relations, task structure, and position power—to obtain an index of situational favorableness. Next, the individual learns how to match leadership style (LPC level) with the situation and subsequently to influence or self-engineer it to his or her personality. This may be done through the use of a variety of techniques, from influencing one's superior to actually moving to a new position. There is also a section on how to engineer the leadership situations of subordinate managers for those at the second level of supervision and above.

The training is self-paced with appropriate measurement instruments incorporated in the text. It adheres closely to the theory and utilizes theoretical discussions, problems, questions, and feedback statements. As a programmed learning text, it appears to be conceptually adequate. The emphasis on self-awareness is consistent with much that is currently being advocated in the leadership field (Ayman, Adams, Fisher, and Hartman 2003). However, the real test is in the research.

There have been two editions of this training manual. The first was Fiedler, Chemers, and Mahar (1976). The second came eight years later (Fiedler and Chemers 1984) and is much the same as the first edition except that there is a technical note on the effectiveness of leader match evaluation studies; some new normative data; and a new chapter dealing with intelligence, boss stress, job intellectual demands, and the like. It is reported that leader match in one of these two forms has been widely used for management development purposes.

Leader Match: Pro and Con

The amount of research conducted by Fiedler and his coworker to evaluate the effects of leader match training is substantial (Fiedler and Mahar 1979; Fiedler and Garcia 1985; Fiedler and Chemers 1984). Typically this training has compared the subsequent performance of experimental (trained) and control leaders. The results quite consistently indicate that exposure to leader match does improve leader performance. In many instances these are little studies with small N's and marginal significance. Occasionally leader match is bundled in with some other training program so that it is impossible to separate the effects of each. But there are studies of leader match only with samples of respectable size. That the sum total of these results from studies both strong and weak adds up to an impressive endorsement of leader match training is attested to by a meta-analysis of management development evaluation research, which found leader match to be highly effective (Burke and Day 1986). The training costs little to conduct, being self-administered, although the use of a facilitator is claimed to be beneficial (Ayman 2002). At least in some quarters, it is viewed as being presented in a clear and understandable form (Schriesheim 2003). This is the pro side.

On the con side, however, are a number of disturbing findings. Leader match does not always follow the same procedures for operationalizing variables used in the research to validate contingency theory. A question arises as to whether these departures from past practice, presumably intended to make the approach more palatable to practitioners, introduce a real change in such aspects as the classification into octants. The answer is that the changes do make a difference (Jago and Ragan 1986). Leader match is not a direct offshoot of contingency theory, and thus cannot legitimately claim that body of theory and research in its support. There has been some arguing back and forth on this matter, but the evidence indicating that leader match and contingency theory differ is quite compelling.

Another problem for situational engineering and leader match is inherent in the following quote:

> [D]ata reported by Fiedler (1967, 259) show a steady decline in performance from favorable to unfavorable situations for an unstructured task and rather erratic variations for

two structured tasks. Yet Fiedler (1965) has suggested situational engineering as an alternative to leadership training. In other words change the situation—shift a group up or down on the favorableness dimension—to fit the leadership style. But if mean productivity is not constant across situations, one might find that a leader who has the wrong leadership style in one situation may become even less effective when his group is changed to a second situation where, according to the model, his leadership style is right. (Shiflett 1973, 435–36)

Recent evidence makes it apparent that, indeed, "mean productivity is not constant across situations" (Schriesheim, Tepper, and Tetrault 1994). Shifting people around across octants does not seem to be a very good idea.

Furthermore, there is reason to believe that those who experience leader match training often do not understand the material and thus are in no position to manipulate situational variables as the training prescribes. Also, the LPC score results may not be accepted, and accordingly adapting the situation to them may not even be attempted. All this means that the positive training results may well have nothing at all to do with contingency theory and situational engineering (Kabanoff 1981).

A more likely explanation, given what is now known, is that leader match training serves to increase personality factors such as the belief in one's ability to change things, self-confidence, self-efficacy, and managerial motivation, and that these in turn make for more effective managerial performance (Bass 1990). It seems very unlikely that contingency theory is the cause of the results.

We have previously considered the stability of LPC. Under normal circumstances it tends to remain stable, and it is based on this fact that Fiedler argues for the need to resort to situational engineering. But there clearly are conditions under which considerable variation can be expected (Rice 1978). This suggests the possibility that concerted efforts to change LPC in a consistent manner might prove successful. The lack of reports of results from such efforts in the literature does not demonstrate that situational engineering is more easily accomplished. The problem is that as long as the true nature of LPC remains an enigma, it is hard to develop training programs to change it.

Although Fiedler has considered other possible applications of his theories, beyond leader match, particularly with regard to the use of LPC in selection, nothing specific has been formulated in this regard. Even on the leader match front, things have been rather quiet since the 1980s. Aditya, House, and Kerr (2000) report that leader match has had relatively little influence in practitioner organizations in recent years.

COGNITIVE RESOURCE THEORY—ADDENDUM TO CONTINGENCY THEORY?

Throughout the preceding discussion, and thus the writings on contingency theory, there are references to intelligence, stress, and experience as variables that interested Fiedler and his coworkers; occasionally they are incorporated in research, but never made part of contingency theory. The references to intelligence go back at least to the 1967 book, references to stress to the Fiedler, O'Brien, and Ilgen (1969) article, and those to experience to Fiedler's (1972b) article. These three variables, however, ultimately came to serve as the core of cognitive resource theory. Although presented as a separate theory, a case can be made that this is really an addendum to the contingency theorizing.

Pre-theory Views and Research

As is typical with Fiedler, a period of research dabbling preceded any resort to theorizing. The first signs of formal hypotheses, but not of the full theory, appeared in the latter 1970s. At this point Fiedler (1979), often with coworkers (Fiedler, Potter, Zais, and Knowlton 1979), began to report on studies that dealt with the interrelations among intelligence, stress, and experience. These studies tested formally stated hypotheses in this regard, hypotheses developed out of induction derived from research extending back at least ten years.

The clearest statements of the two major hypotheses (other subsidiary hypotheses appeared to come and go) were the following:

1. The intelligence of staff personnel will be positively correlated with performance under stress-free conditions but uncorrelated or negatively correlated when stress with the immediate superior is high.
2. The experience of staff personnel will be uncorrelated with performance when stress with boss is low but positively correlated when stress with the immediate superior is high. (Potter and Fiedler 1981, 363)

Research to test these hypotheses was consistently supportive for leaders as well as staff personnel. However, there was evidence that stress from other sources, beyond stress with boss, could produce effects (Barnes, Potter, and Fiedler 1983). This core of tested hypotheses later provided the basis for cognitive resource theory (Fiedler and Garcia 1987). That theory added a number of variables to this core, variables that at the time did not have the same empirical standing as intelligence, stress, and experience.

Formal Theory

The primary assumptions and hypotheses of cognitive resource theory relate to the decision tree set forth in Figure 13.3. Once again, as with contingency theory, the hypotheses are stated in contingent form. The assumptions are as follows:

1. Intelligent and competent leaders make more effective plans, decisions, and action strategies than do leaders with less intelligence or competence.
2. Leaders of task groups communicate their plans, decisions, and action strategies primarily in the form of directive behavior.

These are followed by seven hypotheses dealing with the variables in Figure 13.3.

1. If the leader is under stress, the leader's intellectual abilities will be diverted from the task, and the leader will focus on problems not directly related, or counter to the performance of the group task. Hence, under stress, and especially interpersonal stress, measures of leader intelligence and competence will not correlate with group performance.
2. The intellectual abilities of directive leaders correlate more highly with group performance than do intellectual abilities of nondirective leaders.
3. Unless the group complies with the leader's directions, the leader's plans and decisions will not be implemented. Hence the correlation between leader intelligence and performance is higher when the group supports the leader than when the group does not support the leader.

Figure 13.3 **Decision Tree for Cognitive Resource Theory**

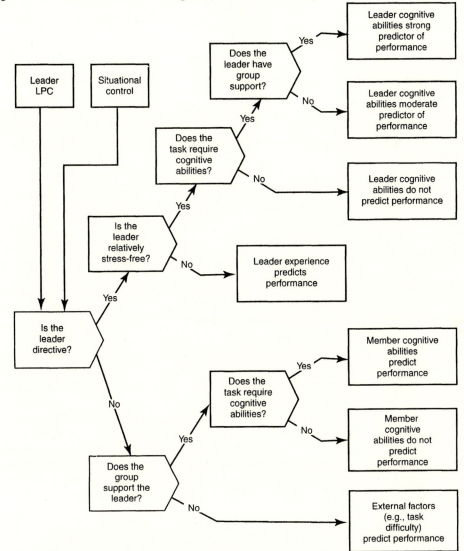

4. If the leader is nondirective and the group is supportive, the intellectual abilities of group members correlate with performance.
5. The leader's intellectual abilities will contribute to group performance to the degree to which the task requires these particular abilities (i.e., is intellectually demanding).
6. Under conditions of high stress, and especially interpersonal stress, the leader's job-relevant experience (rather than his or her intellectual abilities) will correlate with task performance.
7. Directive behavior of the leader is in part determined by the contingency model elements, the leader's task motivation or relationship-motivation (determined by the Least Preferred Coworker scale), and situational control. (Fiedler and Garcia 1987, 8)

Certain contingency theory variables provide the starting point, but the major goal is to identify links between leader personality (as indicated by LPC score), as well as situational control and influence, and group and organizational performance. The chain includes cognitive abilities (intelligence), stress, and experience, but directive behavior, group support, and external factors are added to this basic core.

Cognitive abilities may include measured creativity as well as intelligence test score. Stress is most frequently a self-report of boss-induced stress. Experience is the time served in an organization, position, or occupation; this type of index is generally unrelated to leadership performance. Directive behavior is observed behavior as reported by subordinates (often using initiating structure items from the Ohio State scales); considerate behavior, although measured, was not a powerful enough predictor to justify inclusion in the theory. Group support reflects a favorable group climate or atmosphere, and thus good leader–member relations.

The Fiedler and Garcia (1987) book contains, in addition to the theory just stated, descriptions of a large number of research studies. The amount of new theory presented is rather thin. However, in a later publication Fiedler (1993) attempts to remedy this problem by spelling out in more detail how LPC and situational control link to effective leader performance. The argument is as follows:

> The basis for contingent relations in leadership theories lies in the nature of the situational factors, namely uncertainty and stress, which arouse leader anxiety. A change in the interaction between LPC and situational control from one of being "in match" (when the leader's LPC and situational control are likely to result in good leadership performance) to one of being not "in match" (when low-LPC leaders are in moderate-control situations and high LPC leaders are in either high- or low-control conditions) causes the leader stress and anxiety, stemming . . . from a perceived inability to deal with situations of this nature.
>
> Anxiety-arousing conditions cause the leader to fall back on previous successful reinforced behavior patterns. On a cognitive level these behaviors reflect what was learned from experience. On the affective level these behaviors reflect an earlier model of coping with interpersonal problems. Thus anxiety is associated with changes in leader behavior and performance; anxiety induces behavior that is simpler or represents a regression to an earlier stage in the leader's personality development.
>
> The effectiveness of the leader's behavior and the resulting group and organizational performance depend on the degree to which the evoked leader reactions match the demands of the situation. (Fiedler 1993, 16, 19)

Theory-forming and Theory-testing Research

As noted previously, much of Fiedler and Garcia's (1987) book is devoted to descriptions of research. The status of this research in relation to the theory is at issue. The research is presented initially as an aid to theory construction. Elsewhere it is referred to as part of a fifteen-year research program that led to the *development* of cognitive resource theory (Fiedler and House 1988). Thus this research would appear to be theory forming in nature. Yet there are questions as to whether this is what the theory's authors really mean and believe.

There are nineteen citations in the Fiedler and Garcia (1987) book that are marshaled to support cognitive resource theory; these appear to have been an outgrowth of Fiedler's research program funded primarily by grants from the U.S. military and conducted there also. The citations start in 1961 and spread over the period through 1983; all are pre-theory. In a number of instances N's are small, statistical significance is often marginal, and psychometric properties of measures are on occasion unreported. Many of the studies were originally designed for completely different purposes. All this is fine for exploratory research used to induce theory, but it is not appropriate for theory testing. Yet the authors tend on occasion to treat it as of a theory-testing nature (see Fiedler and Garcia 1987, esp. 204). I do not accept this position; none of the research reported in the 1987 book is evidence for or against the comprehensive cognitive resource theory.

The Status of Cognitive Resource Theory

Cognitive resource theory has proved to be as diverse in the reactions it has elicited as contingency theory. Aditya, House, and Kerr (2000) feel that the empirical support for the theory is strong and that it has important implications for selection and situational management. Yukl (2002) feels that the research results have been inconsistent across studies, and that a number of methodological weaknesses plague the studies so that it is difficult to interpret them; he also points to various conceptual weaknesses.

The operationalization of experience and intelligence within the theory has produced particular problems. In the former instance research suggests that prior experience that is *relevant* for performance in the present job is the factor that should be used, rather than merely organizational tenure (see Quiñones 2004). With regard to intelligence, the argument is that relevant special abilities should be invoked rather than general intelligence. This has not been tested, but it is clear that Fiedler tends to underestimate the role of intelligence in managerial performance when he says that the relationship is low and weak overall. He draws upon various publications of Ghiselli's to support this interpretation, but in fact Ghiselli (1966) reports a highly significant correlation in the upper 0.20s and makes intelligence one of his more important indexes of managerial talent.

There are also conceptual problems in the theory's handling of the stress variable. Fiedler, Potter, and McGuire (1992) make the point, which is emphasized elsewhere also, that the stress that is central to cognitive resource theory is the type generated by the boss for the leader. First, this does not take into account the fact that stress in this dyad is often occasioned by anti-authority attitudes in the leader; the cause is not always the boss. Second, no logical rationale is provided for the use of this particular type of stress. One would think that any stress that produced anxiety would impede functioning in the same manner. This interpretation is reinforced by the reported finding that stress-reduction training produces a major increase in the performance of more intelligent subjects over less intelligent ones (Fiedler 1996). See also Fiedler's (2002) recent advocacy of such training.

Theory-testing research on cognitive resource theory has not been extensive and tends to deal with segments of the model rather than the whole. The early research on the intelligence-stress-experience relationships continues to be given considerable attention (Fiedler 1992b).

The importance of the directive behavior component of the model has also been demonstrated; this incidentally is entirely in line with Vroom's proposition from normative decision process theory (see Chapter 12). The leader's cognitive resources contribute to group performance when the leader is knowledgeable and directive in getting that knowledge put to use (Murphy, Blyth, and Fiedler 1992). On the other hand, group members' task-related knowledge is utilized only if the leader is nondirective and participative. Thus, bright leaders should be directive, because they have ideas to convey (under low stress). Less bright leaders should be participative because they need the ideas of the group. However, when bright leaders are under stress, they tend to impede group performance by talking a lot without contributing useful ideas (Gibson, Fiedler, and Barrett 1993). Training bright leaders in task-relevant knowledge—a form of cognitive skills training—

so as to make them the most knowledgeable in the group, appears to be beneficial in this context (Gist and McDonald-Mann 2000).

As indicated above, most of the research testing cognitive resource theory formulations has involved Fiedler (see also Fiedler and Macauley 1998). There is a need for data from other sources, and a study by Vecchio (1990) provides some of this. The major positive finding from this research once again involved the directive behavior variable. When directive and nondirective situations were compared, the former produced more positive correlations between intelligence and group performance than the latter. Other aspects of the theory either could not be tested adequately or leave many questions with regard to the procedures employed (see Fiedler, Murphy, and Gibson 1992).

Overall I believe that there is good support for the intelligence-stress component of the theory in some form, although the specific nature of the variables needs further work. Also, the role of the directive behavior segment appears to be well delineated. It would be desirable to see this role studied more, however, outside the military. It is possible that the military situation conditions people to be especially responsive to directive approaches. The ties to LPC and contingency theory have not been adequately studied, although cognitive resource theory could be cut loose from these ties with no great loss in understanding or prediction. Research that incorporates all of the theory's variables is lacking; not all of the theory's relationships have been investigated.

Furthermore, several alternative interpretations of the cognitive resource theory phenomena have been advanced, expanding the number of variables and/or the domain of the theory. One such approach seems to suggest that a variable of the nature of leadership self-efficacy, or ego resiliency, or ego strength may serve to mute the effects of stress (Murphy 2002). Another alternative advocates that something called interpersonal acumen be introduced to explain behavior in stress situations, and that cognitive resource theory phenomena may be generalized well beyond the current leadership domain (Aditya and House 2002).

Perhaps the best summary of cognitive resource theory's status is provided by my data on the theory. The importance rating from peers is 3.29, the estimated validity is 3 stars, reflecting the theory's inductive underpinnings coupled with the limited research since, and the estimated usefulness is 2 stars based on the rather sparse attention given to applications.

CONCLUSIONS

In contrast to the evaluations of cognitive resource theory, contingency theory itself performs rather well, as indicated by the data given in the box at the beginning of this chapter. The importance rating is 4.33, not high, but a whole point above cognitive resource theory and certainly respectable. Both estimated validity and estimated usefulness get 3 stars. In the former instance this reflects the abundance of research supporting contingency combined with the numerous criticisms that have been lodged against the theory and the research on it over the years. Perhaps the biggest problem here is understanding what happens within the "black box" that subsumes why contingency takes the form that it does. Empirically based inductive theorizing does not always work well in these situations. As to practical applications, leader match is clearly a major accomplishment, but it too has problems given the findings from research on it. In large part these are produced by the complexity of the underlying theory and the uncertainty regarding LPC. In any event, contingency theory, with the leader match application, is clearly superior to cognitive resource theory, with no distinctive application at all.

I should probably note that the evaluative ratings of contingency theory do not in any instance reach the high levels that other theories in this volume have attained. What is distinctive about contingency theory, and what justifies its inclusion here, is that all of the ratings are respectable; they add up to a positive assessment and thus a designation as an essential theory, even though no one dimension achieves that status.

In Chapter 14 we turn to another theory, one that has been as active as contingency theory over the years, although not quite as many years, but which had its origins in a disparate source within organizational behavior. This too is a contingency theory, although the contingency is of a somewhat different nature.

REFERENCES

Aditya, Ram N., and House, R.J. (2002). Interpersonal Acumen and Leadership across Cultures: Pointers from the GLOBE Study. In Ronald E. Riggio, Susan E. Murphy, and Francis J. Pirozzolo (Eds.), *Multiple Intelligences and Leadership*. Mahwah, NJ: Lawrence Erlbaum, 215–40.

Aditya, Ram N., House, Robert J., and Kerr, Steven (2000). Theory and Practice of Leadership: Into the New Millennium. In Cary L. Cooper and Edwin A. Locke (Eds.), *Industrial and Organizational Psychology: Linking Theory with Practice*. Oxford, UK: Blackwell, 130–65.

Ayman, Roya (2002). Contingency Model of Leadership Effectiveness: Challenges and Achievements. In Linda L. Neider and Chester A. Schriesheim (Eds.), *Leadership*. Greenwich, CT: Information Age Publishing, 197–228.

Ayman, Roya, Adams, Susan, Fisher, Bruce, and Hartman, Erica (2003). Leadership Development in Higher Education Institutions: A Present and Future Perspective. In Susan E. Murphy and Ronald E. Riggio (Eds.), *The Future of Leadership Development*. Mahwah, NJ: Lawrence Erlbaum, 201–36.

Ayman, Roya, Chemers, Martin M., and Fiedler, Fred E. (1995). The Contingency Model of Leadership Effectiveness: Its Levels of Analysis. *Leadership Quarterly*, 6, 147–67.

Barnes, Valerie, Potter, Earl H., and Fiedler, Fred E. (1983). Effect of Interpersonal Stress on the Prediction of Academic Performance. *Journal of Applied Psychology*, 68, 686–97.

Bass, Bernard M. (1990). *Bass and Stogdill's Handbook of Leadership: Theory, Research, and Managerial Applications*. New York: Free Press.

Burke, Michael J., and Day, Russell R. (1986). A Cumulative Study of the Effectiveness of Managerial Training. *Journal of Applied Psychology*, 71, 232–45.

Chemers, Martin M. (2002). Efficacy and Effectiveness: Integrating Models of Leadership and Intelligence. In Ronald E. Riggio, Susan E. Murphy, and Francis J. Pirozzolo (Eds.). *Multiple Intelligences and Leadership*. Mahwah, NJ: Lawrence Erlbaum, 139–60.

Cleven, Walter A., and Fiedler, Fred E. (1956). Interpersonal Perceptions of Open-Hearth Foremen and Steel Production. *Journal of Applied Psychology*, 40, 312–14.

Fiedler, Fred E. (1951). A Method of Objective Quantification of Certain Countertransference Attitudes. *Journal of Clinical Psychology*, 7, 101–7.

——— (1958). *Leader Attitudes and Group Effectiveness*. Urbana: University of Illinois Press.

——— (1964). A Contingency Model of Leadership Effectiveness. In Leonard Berkowitz (Ed.), *Advances in Experimental Social Psychology*, Vol. I. New York: Academic Press, 149–90.

——— (1965). Engineer the Job to Fit the Manager. *Harvard Business Review*, 43(5), 115–22.

——— (1967). *A Theory of Leadership Effectiveness*. New York: McGraw-Hill.

——— (1971). Validation and Extension of the Contingency Model of Leadership Effectiveness: A Review of Empirical Findings. *Psychological Bulletin*, 76, 128–48.

——— (1972a). Personality, Motivational Systems, and Behavior of High and Low LPC Persons. *Human Relations*, 25, 391–412.

——— (1972b). The Effects of Leadership Training and Experience: A Contingency Model Interpretation. *Administrative Science Quarterly*, 17, 453–70.

——— (1973). Personality and Situational Determinants of Leader Behavior. In Edwin A. Fleishman and James G. Hunt (Eds.), *Current Developments in the Study of Leadership*. Carbondale: Southern Illinois University Press, 41–61.

——— (1978a). Situational Control and a Dynamic Theory of Leadership. In Bert King, Siegfried Streufert, and Fred E. Fiedler (Eds.), *Managerial Control and Organizational Democracy*. New York: John Wiley, 107–31.

———— (1978b). The Contingency Model and the Dynamics of the Leadership Process. In Leonard Berkowitz (Ed.), *Advances in Experimental Social Psychology*, Vol. 11. New York: Academic Press, 59–112.

———— (1979). Organizational Determinants of Managerial Incompetence. In James E. Hunt and Lars L. Larson (Eds.), *Crosscurrents in Leadership*. Carbondale: Southern Illinois University Press, 11–22.

———— (1991). Review of *A Theory of Leadership Effectiveness* by Fred E. Fiedler. *Journal of Management*, 17, 501–3.

———— (1992a). Life in a Pretzel-shaped Universe. In Arthur G. Bedeian (Ed.), *Management Laureates: A Collection of Autobiographical Essays*, Vol. I. Greenwich, CT: JAI Press, 303–33.

———— (1992b). Time-based Measures of Leadership Experience and Organizational Performance: A Review of Research and a Preliminary Model. *Leadership Quarterly*, 3, 5–23.

———— (1993). The Leadership Situation and the Black Box in Contingency Theories. In Martin M. Chemers and Roya Ayman (Eds.), *Leadership Theory and Research: Perspectives and Directions*. San Diego, CA: Academic Press, 1–28.

———— (1995). Reflections by an Accidental Theorist. *Leadership Quarterly*, 6, 453–61.

———— (1996). Research on Leadership Selection and Training: One View of the Future. *Administrative Science Quarterly*, 41, 241–50.

———— (2002). The Curious Role of Cognitive Resources in Leadership. In Ronald E. Riggio, Susan E. Murphy, and Francis J. Pirozzolo (Eds.), *Multiple Intelligences and Leadership*. Mahwah, NJ: Lawrence Erlbaum, 91–104

Fiedler, Fred E., Bons, P.M., and Hastings, Limda L. (1975). New Strategies for Leadership Utilization. In W.T. Singleton and P. Spurgeon (Eds.), *Measurement of Human Resources*. New York: Halsted Press, 233–44.

Fiedler, Fred E., and Chemers, Martin M. (1974). *Leadership and Effective Management*. Glenview, IL: Scott, Foresman.

———— (1984). *Improving Leadership Effectiveness: The Leader Match Concept*. 2d ed. New York: John Wiley.

Fiedler, Fred E., Chemers, Martin M., and Mahar, Linda (1976). *Improving Leadership Effectiveness: The Leader Match Concept*. New York: John Wiley.

Fiedler, Fred E., and Garcia, Joseph E. (1985). Comparing Organization Development and Management Training. *Personnel Administrator*, 30(3), 35–47.

———— (1987). *New Approaches to Effective Leadership: Cognitive Resources and Organizational Performance*. New York: John Wiley.

Fiedler, Fred E., and House, Robert J. (1988). Leadership Theory and Research: A Report of Progress. *International Review of Industrial and Organizational Psychology*, 3, 73–92.

Fiedler, Fred E., and Macaulay, Jennifer L. (1998). The Leadership Situation: A Missing Factor in Selecting and Training Managers. *Human Resource Management Review*, 8, 335–50.

Fiedler, Fred E., and Mahar, Linda (1979). The Effectiveness of Contingency Model Training: A Review of the Validation of Leader Match. *Personnel Psychology*, 32, 45–62.

Fiedler, Fred E., Murphy, Susan E., and Gibson, Frederick W. (1992). Inaccurate Reporting and Inappropriate Variables: A Reply to Vecchio's (1990) Examination of Cognitive Resource Theory. *Journal of Applied Psychology* 77, 372–74.

Fiedler, Fred E., O'Brien, Gordon E., and Ilgen, Daniel R. (1969). The Effect of Leadership Style upon the Performance and Adjustment of Volunteer Teams Operating in a Stressful Foreign Environment. *Human Relations*, 22, 503–14.

Fiedler, Fred E., Potter, Earl H., and McGuire, Mark A. (1992). Stress and Effective Leadership Decisions. In Frank A. Heller (Ed.), *Decision-Making and Leadership*. Cambridge, UK: Cambridge University Press, 46–57.

Fiedler, Fred E., Potter, Earl H., Zais, Mitchell M., and Knowlton, William A. (1979). Organizational Stress and the Use and Misuse of Managerial Intelligence and Experience. *Journal of Applied Psychology*, 64, 635–47.

Foa, Uriel G., Mitchell, Terence R., and Fiedler, Fred E. (1971). Differentiation Matching. *Behavioral Science*, 16, 130–42.

Ghiselli, Edwin E. (1966). *Explorations in Managerial Talent*. Pacific Palisades, CA: Goodyear.

Gibson, Frederick W., Fiedler, Fred E., and Barrett, Kelley M. (1993). Stress, Babble, and the Utilization of the Leader's Intellectual Abilities. *Leadership Quarterly*, 4, 189–208.

Gist, Marilyn E., and McDonald-Mann, Dana (2000). Advances in Leadership Training and Development.

In Cary L. Cooper and Edwin A. Locke (Eds.), *Industrial and Organizational Psychology: Linking Theory with Practice*. Oxford, UK: Blackwell, 52–71.

Godfrey, Eleanor P., Fiedler, Fred E., and Hall, D.M. (1959). *Boards, Management, and Company Success*. Danville, IL: Interstate Press.

Hooijberg, Robert, and Choi, Jaepil (1999). From Austria to the United States and from Evaluating Therapists to Developing Cognitive Resources Theory: An Interview with Fred Fiedler. *Leadership Quarterly*, 10, 653–65.

Jago, Arthur G., and Ragan, James W. (1986). The Trouble with Leader Match Is That It Doesn't Match Fiedler's Contingency Model. *Journal of Applied Psychology*, 71, 555–59.

Kabanoff, Boris (1981). A Critique of Leader Match and Its Implications for Leadership Research. *Personnel Psychology*, 34, 749–64.

Kennedy, John K. (1982). Middle LPC Leaders and the Contingency Model of Leadership Effectiveness. *Organizational Behavior and Human Performance*, 30, 1–14.

Mitchell, Terence R., Biglan, Anthony, Oncken, Gerald R., and Fiedler, Fred E. (1970). The Contingency Model: Criticisms and Suggestions. *Academy of Management Journal*, 13, 253–67.

Murphy, Susan E. (2002). Leader Self-Regulation: The Role of Self-Efficacy and Multiple Intelligences. In Ronald E. Riggio, Susan E. Murphy, and Francis J. Pirozzolo (Eds.), *Multiple Intelligences and Leadership*. Mahwah, NJ: Lawrence Erlbaum, 163–86.

Murphy, Susan E., Blyth, Dewey, and Fiedler, Fred E. (1992). Cognitive Resource Theory and the Utilization of the Leader's and Group Members' Technical Competence. *Leadership Quarterly*, 3, 237–55.

Peters, Lawrence H., Hartke, Darrell D., and Pohlman, John T. (1985). Fiedler's Contingency Theory of Leadership: An Application of the Meta-Analysis Procedures of Schmidt and Hunter. *Psychological Bulletin*, 97, 274–85.

Potter, Earl H., and Fiedler, Fred E. (1981). The Utilization of Staff Member Intelligence and Experience under High and Low Stress. *Academy of Management Journal*, 24, 361–76.

Quiñones, Miguel A. (2004). Work Experience: A Review and Research Agenda. *International Review of Industrial and Organizational Psychology*, 19, 119–38.

Rice, Robert W. (1978). Psychometric Properties of the Esteem for Least Preferred Coworker (LPC) Scale. *Academy of Management Review*, 3, 106–17.

Schriesheim, Chester A. (2003). Why Leadership Research Is Generally Irrelevant for Leadership Development. In Susan E. Murphy and Ronald E. Riggio (Eds.), *The Future of Leadership Development*. Mahwah, NJ: Lawrence Erlbaum, 181–97.

Schriesheim, Chester A., Tepper, Bennett, J., and Tetrault, Linda A. (1994). Least Preferred Co-Worker Score, Situational Control, and Leadership Effectiveness: A Meta-Analysis of Contingency Model Performance Predictions. *Journal of Applied Psychology*, 79, 561–73.

Shiflett, Samuel C. (1973). The Contingency Model of Leadership Effectiveness: Some Implications for Its Statistical and Methodological Properties. *Behavioral Science*, 18, 429–40.

Strube, Michael J., and Garcia, Joseph E. (1981). A Meta-Analytic Investigation of Fiedler's Contingency Model of Leadership Effectiveness. *Psychological Bulletin*, 90, 307–21.

Vecchio, Robert P. (1990). Theoretical and Empirical Examination of Cognitive Resource Theory. *Journal of Applied Psychology*, 75, 141–47.

Yukl, Gary (2002). *Leadership in Organizations*. Upper Saddle River, NJ: Prentice-Hall.

CHAPTER 14

VERTICAL DYAD LINKAGE AND LEADER–MEMBER EXCHANGE THEORY

GEORGE GRAEN

Background
Theoretical Statements Regarding Vertical
   Dyad Linkages
     The Role of Dyadic Relationships
     Extensions to the Vertical Dyad Model
Theoretical Statements Regarding Leader–
   Member Exchanges
     The Relationship-Based Approach
     Dyadic Partnership Building
     Expansion to Larger Components
Theory-related Research in which Graen
   Has Participated
     Studies Using Indirect Criteria of Dyadic Relations
     Tests of Vertical Dyad Linkage Theory Propositions
     Research on the Extended Vertical Dyad Linkage Model
     Measurement of Leader–Member Exchange
     Research on Dyadic Partnership Building
     The Japanese Research
Evaluation and Impact
     Leader–Member Exchange and Outcome Relationships
     Other Meta-Analytic Results
     Research on Other Propositions of the Theory
     New Theoretical Directions and Their Prospects
     Applications for Organizations and Individuals
Conclusions

Importance rating	★ ★ ★ ★
Estimated validity	★ ★ ★ ★ ★
Estimated usefulness	★ ★ ★
Decade of origin	1970s

The formulations set forth by George Graen and his colleagues have focused on the dyad created by a superior and one subordinate, initially referred to as a vertical dyad linkage and later as a leader–member exchange. This is much like the individual situation considered in Vroom's normative decision process theory. It has in common with other leadership theories the fact that it, too, deals with differences in the way a manager behaves toward different subordinates and with the degree of participativeness characterizing this behavior. In large part Graen's ideas represent a reaction against the tendency to consider leader behaviors as averages that apply to all subordinates (or all subordinate perceptions), as was done in the Ohio State University research on consideration and initiating structure (see Miner 2002). For an evaluation of these empirically derived factors, see Judge, Piccolo, and Ilies (2004). In developing his own alternative views, Graen appears to have been influenced by the ideas of Katz and Kahn (1966) regarding the processes of role taking in organizations and later by Jacobs's (1971) conceptions of the various kinds of exchange occurring in the leadership context.

This line of theorizing is the product of George Graen, who has published with a number of different co-workers, primarily his doctoral students. In the very early period, Graen was concerned with the various roles people assume in organizations and with what he called the role-making process. As this approach increasingly began to focus on the superior–subordinate dyad, the term vertical dyad linkage (VDL) was adopted. Then in the early 1980s leader–member exchange (LMX) replaced VDL as more appropriately descriptive of the processes involved, although some publications of this period use the term vertical exchange as well, and some refer to dyadic career reality theory.

BACKGROUND

Born in 1937, Graen was schooled at the University of Minnesota and received his Ph.D. in industrial psychology from there in 1967 (Graen 2002). Subsequently, he took a faculty position in the psychology department at the University of Illinois. In 1977, he moved to the business school at the University of Cincinnati, where he remained for a number of years. In 1997, upon retirement from Cincinnati, he accepted a position at the University of Southwestern Louisiana, where he remains until now. In 1972, he held a visiting appointment at Keio University in Japan, and an interest in Japanese management kindled at that time has continued to exert an influence on his research.

Graen's initial research efforts involved expectancy theory (see Chapter 7). He extended the Vroom model, moving beyond motivation into leadership and taking the role perception aspect, also included in the Porter/Lawler theory, and developing it into a much more central theoretical concept (Graen 1969). His idea of work roles, and the effective performer work role, led to the role-making formulations and thus to the beginnings of vertical dyad linkage theory.

THEORETICAL STATEMENTS REGARDING VERTICAL DYAD LINKAGES

Graen's concept of the vertical dyad refers to the relationship between a supervisor and an individual subordinate. There are as many such dyads in a work group as there are immediate subordinates to the unit's manager. For theoretical purposes, two types of dyadic relationships are important. These are variously referred to as relationships with informal assistants and ordinary members (Graen 1976), leadership and supervisory relationships (Dansereau, Graen, and Haga 1975), in-group and out-group relationships (Graen and Cashman 1975), or high- and low-quality relationships (Graen and Schiemann 1978).

The Role of Dyadic Relationships

The essential concept is that when the relationship between manager and subordinate is of the informal assistant, leadership, in-group, or high-quality type, very different kinds of outcomes in terms of job performance ratings, job satisfaction (including turnover), and experienced problems are to be anticipated. Specifically, under these circumstances performance ratings will be higher, subordinate satisfaction greater (and turnover lower), and problems with supervision fewer.

The process involved has been summarized as follows:

> [T]he inputs to team development are the characteristics of each member and those of their leader. These characteristics are harnessed to outputs, such as member performance, satisfaction, and job problems, through their interactions with leader-member exchanges. Based on the compatibility of some combination of member's characteristics and some combination of leader's characteristics, a leader initiates either an in-group or an out-group exchange with his member early in the life of the dyadic relationship. (Graen and Cashman 1975, 154–55)

The major early indicator of what type of relationship will subsequently emerge is the degree to which negotiating latitude is extended by the manager. When the manager is relatively open in extending individualized assistance to work through job problems, an in-group relationship is likely. Such relationships

> involve interlocking different task behaviors and forming different working relationships than do out-group exchanges. Specifically, in-group exchanges will involve first, the interlocking of more responsible tasks accepted by members and higher levels of assistance provided by leaders; and second, working relationships will be characterized by greater support, sensitivity, and trust than occurs in outgroup exchanges. Furthermore, the mechanism of this interlocking of member and leader behaviors probably is reciprocal reinforcement . . . once these structures emerge, they demonstrate high stability over time. Thus, until the nature of the linkage becomes altered, both member and leader behavior can be both understood and predicted over time. (Graen and Cashman 1975, 155)

When an in-group relationship develops, leadership occurs in that behaviors depend upon the interpersonal exchange, not formal authority. The leader gives resources at his or her command and the member gives expanded effort and time. The leader loses control and becomes more dependent on the outcomes of negotiations with the member, while the member risks receiving less-than-equitable rewards and the unilateral institution of supervision. In contrast, under an out-group relationship supervision does exist, and the employment contract with its implicit acceptance of legitimate authority in exchange for pay and benefits governs.

The in-group relationship exhibits many of the characteristics of participative decision making and of job enrichment as well:

> The superior for his part can offer the outcomes of job latitude, influence in decision making, open and honest communications, support of the member's actions and confidence in and consideration for the member, among others. The member can reciprocate with greater than required expenditures of time and energy, the assumption of greater responsibility, and commitment to the success of the entire unit or organization, among others. (Dansereau, Graen, and Haga 1975)

Extensions to the Vertical Dyad Model

Subsequently the basic dyadic model was extended one level upward to include the manager's superior as well as subordinate (Cashman, Dansereau, Graen, and Haga 1976). The hypothesis is that the nature of this manager–superior relationship (in-group or out-group) will affect the extent to which the manager can bring resources to the manager–subordinate relationship and thus exert an indirect effect on subordinate outputs such as satisfaction, job problems, termination, and the like.

A second extension relates to the matter of agreement between the manager and the dyadic subordinate (Graen and Schiemann 1978). Two hypotheses are stated:

> If a leader and a member have a high-quality dyadic relationship, the leader should be more aware of the problems confronting the member on the job. Hence, their perceptions should be more alike regarding the severity of job problems than those of a leader and a member in a low-quality relationship.
>
> Another important set of variables . . . includes sensitivity of the leader to the member's job and attention, information, and support given the member by the leader. . . . If the quality of the interdependencies is high, leader and member should agree more accurately about these variables than those locked into lower quality relationships. (Graen and Schiemann 1978, 206–7)

THEORETICAL STATEMENTS REGARDING LEADER–MEMBER EXCHANGES

Initially at least, the shift to the LMX designation had relatively little meaning for the theory. However, it has come to have considerable significance in that the result has been to focus attention on the relationship in the dyad—the characteristics of that relationship and the ways in which the dyadic relationship is tied to organizational outcome variables (Graen and Uhl-Bien 1991). In contrast, the vertical dyad linkage theory dealt with differential in-group and out-group member types within the work group, as well as with differentiation that resulted from resource constraints on managers that forced them to develop one or more trusted assistants to aid in the functioning of the unit.

The Relationship-based Approach

One statement of the evolving theory introduces the concept of dyadic career reality (DCR) to focus on the dyadic relationship (Graen and Scandura 1986). This concept is defined as "a system of components and relationships; involving both members of a dyad; in interdependent patterns of behavior; sharing mutual outcome instrumentalities; and producing concepts of environments, cause maps, and value" (150). This is a restatement of the former in-group process. Table 14.1 outlines the procedures through which dyadic career realities develop. Role concepts once again become central to the theory.

Dyadic career realities often involve dyads of managers, and these managers exchange positional resources to their mutual benefit. Resources noted include information, influence, tasks, latitude, support, and sensitivity (concern). The theory now includes not only vertical dyads, but horizontal and diagonal dyads as well, although little is said with regard to these latter.

A companion piece develops these ideas further with special reference to the performance of unstructured tasks (Graen and Scandura 1987). The authors invoke Barnard's (1938) idea of an inducement–contributions balance to explain what happens within a vertical dyad. The exchange involved is depicted in Figure 14.1, which shows how the relationship solidifies as it moves from role taking to role making to what is now called role routinization. DCR in the figure means

---

Table 14.1

Normative Model for the Development of Dyadic Career Realities

Role finding—the discovery of (1) the functional definitions of official duties and responsibilities, (2) the instrumental value of resources, and (3) the utility of formal written procedures
    Procedure:
    1. Treat the official written role as problematic.
    2. Generate alternative definitions of duties and responsibilities, resources, and procedures.
    3. Reduce the alternative definitions to several multiple working hypotheses.

Role making—the enactment of interlocking behaviors
    Procedure:
    1. Treat dyadic working relationships as problematic.
    2. Generate alternative possibilities of task assignments, resource allocations, interdependencies, and inducements for contributions.
    3. Reduce the alternative possibilities to a feasible set.
    4. Enact interlocking behavior cycles.

Role implementation—the assembly of interlocked behavior cycles into systems according to rules
    Procedure:
    1. Treat systems as problematic.
    2. Generate alternative models of systems.
    3. Reduce the alternative models to a prioritized set.
    4. Construct the systems according to the model as prioritized.

Source: Graen and Scandura (1986, 153). Copyright © 1986 Elsevier Science. Reprinted with permission.

---

dyadic career reality and it implies an exchange of positional resources as stated previously. When routinized and thus stabilized, the dyadic relationship involves trust, respect, loyalty, liking, intimacy, support, openness, and honesty.

The total process depicted in Figure 14.1 may or may not move through to completion. If it does not, the leader–member exchange remains of low quality. When certain variables take high values, the role-emergence process is more likely to reach completion. For this to occur the superior should have:

1. adequate latitude in task assignment and a need to exercise it;
2. reasonably attractive positional and personal (power) resources and the imagination to employ them; and
3. some members possessing job growth potential (ability) and the motivation to accept challenges beyond their job description (Graen and Scandura 1987, 185).

Leaders tend to select members for dyadic relationships who are dependable in that they can be counted on to complete tasks as the leader would if necessary, and who collaborate effectively (Graen 1990). This selection may well eventuate in a productive leadership system that is said to expand the influence and commitment of a unit to capitalize on opportunities and available resources as well as member abilities and motives so as to integrate dyadic roles into cohesive, coordinated management teams and larger networks. Once engaged in such a productive leadership system, managers are hypothesized to attempt to replicate it in new job situations in the future throughout their careers.

Figure 14.1 **Description of the Role-making Process**

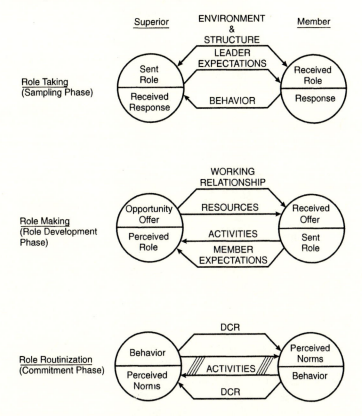

Source: Graen and Scandura (1987, 180). Copyright © 1987 Elsevier Science. Reprinted with permission.

More recently, in the 1990s, leader–member exchange theory has begun to consider the role-making process in terms of a stranger-acquaintance-maturity classification (Graen and Wakabayashi 1994). At the initial stranger stage the leader and member interact only on a limited basis and what interaction there is is of a strictly contractual nature. As the relationship moves to the acquaintance stage it becomes more involved, but trust and loyalty remain less than fully developed. At the mature stage a high degree of trust, respect, and obligation are achieved; now the potential for incremental influence is substantial, and members are encouraged to grow beyond the formal work contract and help redesign the unit. Role finding occurs at the stranger stage when LMX is low in the dyad. Role making occurs in the acquaintance stage when LMX is medium. Role implementation occurs at the mature leadership stage when LMX is high. Leadership making is said to occur as networks are built up one relationship at a time consisting of people both within and outside a team.

Dyadic Partnership Building

At this point leadership is defined as a partnership among dyadic members, a partnership that should (normatively) be developed if at all possible:

[R]ather than managers treating some employees more favorably than others (as the "differentiation" approach of VDL suggests), this stage states that managers should provide all employees access to the process of LMX by making the initial offer to develop LMX partnerships to each subordinate. Making the partnership offer to every subordinate has a two-fold effect: (1) the LMX process may be perceived as more equitable (and the model more palatable to practitioners and students who may have been uncomfortable with the inequity issue), and (2) the potential for more high-quality relationship development (partnerships) would increase the potential for more effective leadership and expanded organizational capability. (Graen and Uhl-Bien 1995, 229)

Increasing the number of high-quality relationships in this way should improve unit performance. Although the theoretical objective is to teach and motivate leaders to develop high quality partnerships with all group members, the reality that this may not in fact occur in every instance is recognized.

Expansion to Larger Components

Throughout the articles referenced in the prior section, there are relatively brief discussions of horizontal dyads, diagonal dyads, systems of interdependent dyads, combinations of dyads, network assemblies (of dyads), and the like. The idea is that one could map a complex interlocking leadership structure as an overlay on the task structure of an organization. Such a structure of multiple high-quality dyads should yield much added value in terms of organizational performance. Self-directed teams are said to function most effectively when contrived out of the dyadic processes we have been considering (Graen and Uhl-Bien 1991). This application to team dynamics continues to the present (see Graen and Hui 2001).

Expansion to the organizational level, although contemplated, has not been the subject of empirical investigation (Graen and Uhl-Bien 1995). This is the path down which leader–member exchange theory is headed, nevertheless, and the beginnings of a formal theory for this purpose have been proposed (Uhl-Bien, Graen, and Scandura 2000). The idea is that multiple high quality dyads offer a source of competitive advantage through the social capital thus created. This approach draws upon the literature dealing with social capital, strategic human resource management, social network theory, and of course LMX theory.

THEORY-RELATED RESEARCH IN WHICH GRAEN HAS PARTICIPATED

Initial research by Graen and his coworkers utilized the leader behavior description measures of consideration and initiating structure but employed an individual subordinate level of analysis rather than average data for each work group as in the original Ohio State studies. The nature of the analytical approach used in this research was highly consistent with the vertical dyad linkage model. However, the studies were not carried out as tests of that particular set of theoretical hypotheses; rather, they test certain hypotheses related to the relative predictive power of expectancy and equity theories (Dansereau, Cashman, and Graen 1973), to the validity of the man-in-the-middle interpretation of managerial role stress (Graen, Dansereau, and Minami 1972b), and to the nature of performance feedback (Graen, Dansereau, and Minami 1972a; Graen, Dansereau, Minami, and Cashman 1973). These studies are important, nevertheless, because they represent the empirical base from which vertical dyad linkage (VDL) theory subsequently developed.

Studies Using Indirect Criteria of Dyadic Relations

The next set of studies moved closer to actually testing vertical dyad linkage theory formulations without actually achieving this goal. In these cases actual measures of the quality of the dyadic relationships were not obtained, but other indexes that yielded results consistent with theoretical expectations were used to differentiate the groups studied.

Thus, in one case newly hired clerical employees at a university were differentiated into those who separated relatively quickly and those who did not. Analysis of data obtained over a period of sixteen weeks indicated that there was greater role conflict and ambiguity in relationships with superiors among those who subsequently left employment (Johnson and Graen 1973). The design of this study does not permit direct extrapolation to vertical dyad linkage hypotheses, but the relationships are consistent with them.

The same is true of another analysis of additional data obtained from the same subjects (Graen, Orris, and Johnson 1973). In this instance the group was differentiated not by job tenure but in terms of the extent to which the individual viewed the job as career relevant. Those who did not consider the job to be career relevant tended to have more turnover, but they also evidenced less communication with superiors, including less participation in decisions, as well as other responses consistent with an out-group status.

In another case, a group of university housing and food service managers was split in terms of their degree of professionalism and studied over a nine-month period subsequent to an extensive reorganization (Haga, Graen, and Dansereau 1974). The findings are consistent with an interpretation that describes the professionals as possessing in-group status. In particular, they appear to be engaged in a sizable amount of role-making or role-altering behavior that is entirely consistent with theoretical expectations under conditions of negotiated roles.

Tests of Vertical Dyad Linkage Theory Propositions

A subsequent analysis of data obtained from this same group of university managers is more directly supportive of the theory (Dansereau, Graen, and Haga 1975). In this case, a measure of negotiating latitude perceived by the dyadic subordinate early in the relationship was used as a basis for differentiation. This early index of negotiating latitude proved to be a good predictor of in-group and out-group status throughout the nine months of the study. In-group members received more supervisory attention and greater support, experienced fewer job problems, perceived their superior as more responsive to their needs and as communicating with them more, were evaluated as behaving in a manner closer to superior expectations, indicated more job satisfaction, and were less likely to separate. This pattern of results is quite congruent with the theory.

A replication study with a new sample that extended the measures to include communication frequency, bases of influence, and dyadic loyalty provides further support (Graen and Cashman 1975). Clearly the in-group members were more involved in all aspects of their work and expended greater time and effort; they influenced decisions more and were in a better position to do so. Outcomes such as rated performance, job satisfaction, and job problems were all more positive for in-group members, and as expected, dyadic loyalty and trust were greater in these exchanges.

In this study data were obtained on the use of various bases of influence or power. Referent and expert power characterize the in-group exchanges, consistent with their more participative, negotiated nature. There is also some basis for concluding that coercive or legitimate (bureaucratic) influence characterizes the out-group exchanges. In any event, these findings are consistent with the hypothesized leadership–supervision distinction.

A study by Graen and Ginsburgh (1977) partially replicates the earlier study involving the career relevance of the job (Graen, Orris, and Johnson 1973) and extends it by investigating the quality of the dyadic relationship, in this instance as perceived by the superior, not the subordinate, as in previous studies. Although university clerical employees also were used in this study, they were not new employees. The sample is essentially the same as that used in the Graen and Cashman (1975) research.

The findings indicate that in-group subordinates were given greater amounts of sensitivity and self-determination by their superiors. They also were rated as better performers. However, the anticipated job satisfaction differences did not emerge, even though turnover was greater among out-group subordinates. Taken as a whole, the data show that the quality of the dyadic relationship is associated with work outcomes but that the career relatedness of the work accounts for additional variance.

Research on the Extended Vertical Dyad Linkage Model

A re-analysis of the original data derived from university housing and food managers (Dansereau, Graen, and Haga 1975) extends those findings to the level of the superior's superior (Cashman, Dansereau, Graen, and Haga 1976). The data provide some support for the view that whether a superior has an in- or out-group relationship with the person above affects the outcomes from dyadic relationships with subordinates. In particular, when the upward exchange is of an out-group nature, subordinates tend to perceive job problems, especially problems in bringing about change. They are also less satisfied with their rewards and the technical competence of their superior. Although the findings with regard to the impacts of higher-level relationships are less pervasive than those for the immediate dyad, significant results do occur. This study did not yield the expected results for the turnover outcome, however.

A later study, also conducted within the administrative components of a university, yields similar support for the impact of the quality of the upper-level dyadic relationship at lower levels (Graen, Cashman, Ginsburgh, and Schiemann 1977). However, the specific types of job problems and other factors affected are frequently quite different. These differences in results in the two settings are attributed to variations in the organizational contexts of the studies—in flux in the first instance and stable in the second.

An investigation carried out to determine whether greater perceptual agreement within the dyad was to be anticipated as a function of the quality of the relationship provides generally supportive results (Graen and Schiemann 1978). In this case quality was measured at the subordinate level with a measure of known good reliability. Again the samples were obtained within the administrative contexts of universities and overlapped prior studies. The findings indicate that perceptual agreements are consistently less pronounced when out-group dyads are involved.

During the 1970s, research that did not involve Graen appears to be nonexistent. The existing research tended to draw on a very small number of subject pools, most of them apparently from one university. In many respects, the development of vertical dyad linkage theory seems to reflect the use of grounded theory in that the formulations emerged from concentrated study of a single context. Subsequently data to test the theory were obtained from a substantially different university setting, but still a university (Liden and Graen 1980). This study yielded strong support for vertical dyad theory, except in the case of satisfaction measures. Perceptual agreement was also found in accordance with the extended model.

Measurement of Leader–Member Exchange

Over the years the instrument used to determine the quality of a leader–member exchange as perceived by either member of a dyad has grown in length from two items to fourteen; there are at least seven versions. Most recommended is the seven-item measure, which correlates well with the longer versions (Graen and Uhl-Bien 1995). LMX appears to be constituted out of three dimensions: (1) mutual respect for the capabilities of the other, (2) anticipation of deepening trust with the other, (3) expectation that interacting obligation will grow over time. These dimensions are highly related so that development of separate measures does not appear justified. A core item reads, "How would you characterize your working relationship with your leader (your member)?" (rated on a five-point scale from ineffective to effective).

An example of the use of such a leader–member exchange scale involved a comparison of LMX with average leadership style in predicting the turnover criterion among computer personnel of a public utility. In this instance the five-item measure was used, and turnover was high. Leader–member exchange proved to be a much stronger predictor of turnover than average leadership style, accounting for three times more variance. The unique exchange between leader and member appears to be what influences a person to remain in the organization (Graen, Liden, and Hoel 1982).

Research on Dyadic Partnership Building

This research involved efforts to improve the quality of all dyad relationships with the objective of increasing performance levels; thus it is a test of the normative theory, not just the descriptive theory.

The first such effort was carried out in a department of a government installation where the employees processed case data at computer terminals (Graen, Novak, and Sommerkamp 1982). Managers in the department received training that included lectures, discussion, and role modeling. Topics covered were the leader–member exchange model, active listening, exchanging mutual expectations, exchanging resources, and practicing one-on-one sessions with subordinates. Actual treatment sessions followed this training and involved conversations between leaders and their members:

> During the training sessions the general structure of the conversations as well as the specific questions and techniques to facilitate the conversations were devised by the managers with the help, of the trainer: (1) the manager was to spend time asking about and discussing each person's gripes, concerns, and job expectations about (a) the member's job, (b) the supervisor's job, and (c) their working relationship; (2) using "active listening" skills learned in the training, the manager was to be particularly attentive and sensitive to what issues were raised and how they were formulated by each subordinate; (3) the manager was to refrain from imposing his/her frame of reference or management's frame of reference about the issues raised; and (4) the manager was to share some of his/her own job expectations about (a) his/her own job, (b) his/her member's job, and (c) their working relationship. Increasing the level of reciprocal understanding and helpfulness within dyads regarding job issues and behaviors was the goal of the treatment. (Graen, Novak, and Sommerkamp 1982, 114)

These sessions were conducted with all participants in the treatment group. Before–after results in terms of performance were compared for this group and for other groups from the department not exposed to the LMX treatment.

Productivity increases measured in terms of the quantity of cases handled showed a significant advantage in favor of the LMX-trained group. Furthermore, this gain was primarily a function of effects occurring in a high-growth-need group of subjects. This latter index was included in the study because a job enrichment treatment based on job characteristics theory was introduced along with the LMX treatment (see Chapter 6). Any job enrichment effects per se, however, were negated by certain policy changes introduced by the organization unknown to the experimenters; thus job characteristics theory was not in fact tested.

A subsequent publication (Scandura and Graen 1984) based on data from the same context was aimed at determining whether low or high initial LMX subjects were most responsive to the treatment effects. The results clearly indicated that the low LMX subjects responded most positively to the treatment in terms of both the quality of their leader–member exchanges and the quantity of their productivity. This analysis did not include any consideration of growth-need effects.

Another report on this project (Graen, Scandura, and Graen 1986) substantiates the moderator effects of growth need strength, but makes no mention of the finding that low-quality leader–member exchange translates into greater productivity with the appropriate training. This latter result is most consistent with theory in that it means that dyadic partnership building applied across the board should result in both low- and high-quality dyads initially moving with training to high-quality relationships. However, if growth need strength is a moderator of the training effect, one would anticipate that it would also moderate the initial dyadic choices as well. In such an event, low-quality dyads would not contain many high-growth-need-strength people and thus would offer little potential for upward movement. This seeming contradiction is neither explained nor even confronted. Growth-need strength is not a component of the theory as stated in comprehensive forms.

The Japanese Research

On his first visit to Japan in 1972, Graen began a research project with various Japanese corporations that, at least in the case of one company, extended for thirteen years (Wakabayashi and Graen 1989). The results of this longitudinal analysis indicate that the establishment of high-quality exchanges in the early period after joining a company was a strong predictor of promotion and subsequent career success as a manager. Those with initial low-quality relationships did not do nearly as well.

When leader–member exchanges, measured organizational commitment, potential as determined from assessment centers, and performance appraisals by supervisors were compared in terms of their capacity to predict promotions and success subsequently, the performance appraisals were most effective (Graen, Wakabayashi, Graen, and Graen 1990). However, LMX was almost as good and a better predictor of satisfaction measures. The assessment center predictions and organizational commitment were much less effective. Overall, the Japanese research provides a strong endorsement for the vertical dyad linkage/leader–member exchange theory.

EVALUATION AND IMPACT

Many of the criticisms and questions applied to the vertical dyad linkage model and the research on it no longer hold. Subjects outside of universities have been used extensively now. Research by others besides Graen and his coworkers has expanded rapidly in the 1980s and 1990s. Varied criterion measures have been utilized in research studies to a point where concerns about common method biases cannot be invoked to dismiss the theory's validity. The theory has become more normative in nature, thus supplementing its initial purely descriptive emphasis. The fact of in-group and out-group relationships (or high- and low-quality LMX) has been demonstrated with sufficient frequency so that the existence of such relationships is no longer in doubt; they appear to occur in roughly 90 percent of all groups. Yet criticisms do remain, especially on the grounds that theory statements have been inconsistent over time, measures have varied widely, and analyses have not adequately considered the levels at which phenomena occur (e.g., see Schriesheim, Castro, and Cogliser 1999).

Leader–Member Exchange and Outcome Relationships

Like a number of theories we have been considering, vertical dyad linkage theory has now grown to the point where the research generated by it is sufficient to justify meta-analysis. Up until recently only one such application had been undertaken (Gerstner and Day 1997), and in that instance the focus was primarily on the relationship between LMX indexes and a wide variety of outcome variables. The research considered extends up through 1996. The results obtained and the number of separate samples on which each correlation is based are given in Table 14.2.

From Table 14.2 it is apparent that LMX is more strongly related to subjective factors than to objective ones. The only outcome not predicted is actual turnover. Objective performance is predicted, but at a marginal level; it is doubtful that this finding has much practical significance. However, objective measures of performance and turnover were used as criteria in relatively few studies.

A review conducted by Liden, Sparrowe, and Wayne (1997) without benefit of the meta-analytic results reaches much the same conclusions as those indicated in Table 14.2. In this instance, however, the objective performance results were considered to be nonsignificant, thus placing them in the same category as actual turnover. In spite of the positive results found using a promotion criterion in Japan, it has not been possible to replicate these findings in the United States.

A thorough review by House and Aditya (1997), also without benefit of the meta-analytic findings, points to the fact that although studies involving Graen have found significant relations with turnover, a number of other studies have not. It appears likely that natural inclinations to separate among low-quality LMX employees are stifled by other considerations in many situations. House and Aditya (1997) also note the problems LMX has had in predicting performance, and they conclude that the theory can be most accurately viewed as one dealing with dyadic relationships and their subjective consequences, rather than being a true theory of leadership. A later review (Aditya, House, and Kerr 2000) reiterates these concerns regarding the prediction of objective measures of turnover and performance.

Yet other reports suggest it is too early to dismiss the idea that there are hard performance data consequences of high-quality leader–member exchanges. Two such reports post-date the meta-analytic review and thus were not included in it (Klein and Kim 1998; Vecchio 1998). Both studies yield correlations in the mid to upper 0.20s using performance criteria that are centrally focused on the specific work done, a matter that has been of concern in prior studies. Also, a meta-analysis concerned specifically with turnover reported average correlations in the low 0.20s (Griffeth, Hom, and Gaertner 2000). There is reason to believe that because greater opportunities for negotiating role latitude allow for a more pronounced association between LMX and performance, the LMX–performance relationship may be more likely to manifest itself in higher-level positions (Fernandez and Vecchio 1997).

Table 14.2

Relationships Between LMX and Outcome Variables

Outcome measure	Number of samples	Correlation (corrected for unreliability)
Performance		
Objective measure	8	0.11[a]
Rating: leader LMX	12	0.55[a]
member LMX	30	0.30[a]
Satisfaction		
Overall	33	0.50[a]
With supervision	27	0.71[a]
Turnover		
Actual	7	−0.04
Intention	8	−0.31[a]
Organizational commitment	17	0.42[a]

Source: Adapted from Gerstner and Day (1997, 832–33).
[a]Significant at the 0.05 level or better.

Other findings suggest that the LMX–performance relationship is likely to be facilitated under specific circumstances. Dunegan, Uhl-Bien, and Duchon (2002) found that low role conflict, high role ambiguity, and high intrinsic satisfaction with the work performed all serve to enhance the link between leader–member exchange and performance. Thus, where role conflict is high, role ambiguity is low, and intrinsic satisfaction is less, the chances of failing to obtain a significant LMX–performance correlation become more pronounced. It appears that studies in the past may well have tapped into these nonfacilitating situations quite often. Accordingly, it seems appropriate to conclude that leader–member exchange theory is not entirely subjective in nature.

Other Meta-Analytic Results

A number of meta-analyses have been conducted recently that deal with aspects of leader–member exchange theory other than the performance relationship. These tend to focus on limited aspects of the theory. Thus, the relationship between trust and LMX from eight studies turns out to be 0.69, a rather sizable correlation (Dirks and Ferrin 2002). Yet trust is often noted as a component of the definition of LMX, and in that context the *r* value is not unexpectedly high; indeed, aspects of various kinds of justice yield even higher correlations with trust.

Relationships between LMX and organizational citizenship behaviors have been the subject of considerable study and several meta-analyses. Organizational citizenship behaviors are individual behaviors that are discretionary—and thus not explicitly recognized by any formal reward system—yet they promote the effective functioning of an organization; they are not part of the employment contract and failure to perform them is not considered to be punishable.

One such meta-analysis found LMX to correlate at 0.30 with an overall index of organizational citizenship behavior and 0.36 with an aspect of the whole in six studies (Podsakoff, MacKenzie, Paine, and Bachrach 2000). A later analysis located eighteen studies on which to base its conclusions and reported a mean correlation for overall organizational citizenship behavior of 0.32 (Hackett, Farh, Song, and Lapierre 2003). The comparable correlation in a small set of Chinese studies was 0.28. These data are entirely consistent with predictions from leader–member exchange theory.

What the addition of organizational citizenship behaviors seems to accomplish is to create a job of considerably greater breadth for those involved in high-LMX relationships (Klieman, Quinn, and Harris 2000). It is not always clear, however, that this expansion of job breadth is viewed as entirely discretionary on the part of the members. Many may genuinely believe that these actions are requirements of their jobs; this is a factor that needs further research. A related phenomenon is that those operating in high-LMX relationships tend to experience a sense of substantial psychological empowerment (a type of job broadening). At the same time, and to the detriment of employee empowerment efforts, out-group members tend to experience much less actual empowerment (Gómez and Rosen 2001).

Research on Other Propositions of the Theory

A problem for leader–member exchange theory, as for certain other theoretical positions, is that the perceptions of subordinates do not match up well with those reported by their superiors. Gerstner and Day's (1997) meta-analysis finds a corrected correlation between the two LMX values of 0.37, significant but by no means sufficient to say the two are measuring the same thing. Chemers (1997) takes this disparity to mean that at least in some cases leader–member exchanges derive from perceptions and assumptions more than factual realities. It is possible that the problem reflects in part the fact that subordinates tend to report on their perceptions of the *position* and its status-based relationships as much as on their perceptions of the *person* (see Chapter 12).

Theory states that high-quality dyadic relationships tend to form based on similarities. Although the matter of demographic similarity has produced mixed results to date, perceived attitudinal similarity does characterize these dyads (Engle and Lord 1997), as does emotional similarity (Bauer and Green 1996). Liking for each other is also tied into this constellation, and agreement with leaders is stronger for those members in a high-quality LMX (Gerstner and Day 1997). Thus the similarity proposition receives considerable support, at least insofar as particular types of similarity are involved.

Several studies have considered the longitudinal development of dyadic relationships from their inception and thus the role-making process (Liden, Wayne, and Stilwell 1993; Bauer and Green 1996). It appears that as high-quality relationships emerge, and they do so very quickly, the leader grants considerable latitude to the member, and delegation occurs frequently. The importance of delegation in the exchange has been noted by Schriesheim, Neider, and Scandura (1998) as well. This pattern involving delegation is consistent with the trust-building and trust-testing features of the role-making component of leader–member exchange theory. In this manner role routinization occurs. However, it is also apparent that performance is not the only factor operating in high-quality dyadic relationships (Liden, Wayne, and Stilwell 1993; Liden, Sparrowe, and Wayne 1997). Affective reactions most frequently manifest in mutual liking are closely intertwined with the performance aspect; there may well be an ingratiatory feature. This nonperformance component of LMX appears to account for its multidimensional nature.

Graen's international research has focused on Japanese applications of the theory. Others, however, have found that the theory generalizes to China as well. In general, the theory appears to exhibit good validity with Chinese subjects. Another extension based on research has to do with the conceptually similar mentoring construct. It appears that as perceived by subordinates, mentoring and high-quality LMX relationships are indistinguishable. Yet the superiors involved react to the two differently and for them they appear to be empirically distinct (Scandura and Schriesheim 1994). Presumably the superiors are influenced by the fact that mentoring often occurs across the boundaries of the immediate work group.

Although certainly not part of leader–member exchange theory in its present form, there are findings that link that theory with goal-setting theory (Klein and Kim 1998). It has been found that LMX can operate to exert a strong positive influence on goal commitment (see Chapter 10). This influence occurs for high-LMX people, but it disappears completely when the LMX is low. A substantial goal commitment–performance correlation given high LMX occurs, which is non-existent with low LMX.

There are other findings: research into the dynamics of the *exchange* in leader–member relationships, and the positive role of reciprocity in that exchange, provides strong support for theory (Uhl-Bien and Maslyn 2003). One would expect that high communication frequencies would serve to facilitate more positive performance ratings in high-quality leader–member exchanges, and that is what was found, in accord with the theory (Kacmar, Witt, Zivnuska, and Gully 2003). At low levels of LMX, frequent communication within the exchange was associated with less favorable performance ratings, however.

The research considered in this section provides considerable support for the validity of leader–member exchange theory in a number of its component aspects. We have not as yet touched upon the extension of the theory beyond the within-group vertical dyadic relationship to networks of dyads, to horizontal and diagonal dyads, and to higher levels of aggregation within the focal organization and even across organizational boundaries, however. Graen and Uhl-Bien (1995) envisage such an extension beyond leadership, perhaps to create macro theory; House and Aditya (1997) view the prospects here as promising; and Uhl-Bien, Graen, and Scandura (2000) present one limited approach of this type tied to social capital formulations.

Nevertheless, the fact is that no really comprehensive theory of this kind exists, and the subject has been raised intermittently for a number of years. Is it likely that expanded, valid macro theory will emerge from leader–member exchange theory as it currently exists? I do not think so. The domain of the theory now is narrow and specifically delimited. The relationships involved have been shown to be almost entirely within-group in nature; they do not support the average leadership style or a between-groups model (Schriesheim, Neider, and Scandura 1998). The phenomenon is real enough, but using it to understand macro-organizational functioning represents a large theoretical leap. Dyadic linkages could well be part of such a theory, but that leader–member dyads actually drive organizational level processes and structure seems unlikely. A very limited body of research supports this conclusion. In general, macro-level variables that relate to other factors do not relate to LMX (e.g., see Wayne, Shore, Bommer, and Tetrick 2002). My belief is that if leader–member exchange theory is to move to the macro level, this will happen through an integration into some concept of relational wealth (see Leana and Rousseau 2000). Yet no movement in this direction by either party is currently in evidence.

New Theoretical Directions and Their Prospects

Leader–member exchange theory does not lack for alternative or supplementary theorizing, much of it serving the purpose of expanding the domain of the basic theory in some way, just as Graen has been trying to do. Thus, as is often noted, leaders do deal with all members of the group on occasion, and thus the concept of an average leader–group relationship does have meaning, as Fiedler's contingency theory posits (see Chapter 13). Leader–member exchange theory had its origins in the idea that there is more to within group functioning than average leadership style, and that is clearly true, but it does not mean that dyadic relationships are the whole story. A theory that goes beyond dyads simply at the group level, not into organization level phenomena and complex networks, would seem to offer the prospect of achieving greater understanding without requiring a major domain expansion. Such a theory would, however, need to add new constructs to those of leader–member exchange theory. Group goal commitment might be one such related construct.

As it has become evident that high-quality leader–member exchanges involve something more than a purely work-based relationship and that in this regard LMX is multidimensional, there has been increasing concern with affective considerations and the liking that develops between two people. This has eventuated in theory development dealing with how friendship relationships enter into leader–member exchanges (Boyd and Taylor, 1998). Propositions have been set forth and research questions proposed. The idea is that by utilizing the concept of a developing friendship, new insights into the nature of LMX may be obtained. This remains to be demonstrated. It gets into such matters as romances that develop at work, matters that Graen and his coworkers have avoided by emphasizing the work-based rather than friendship-based nature of the vertical dyad relationship.

Certainly, extensions of this kind are warranted, given the direction research findings have taken, and they may even prove quite fruitful in understanding how organizations operate. The propositions, which involve similarity, extent of contact, power distance, quality of reward levels, attribution processes, charismatic features, overly close or exploitive relationships, and their ties to LMX, appear promising and worthy of testing. But to date research tests have not been carried out, and without them we cannot determine how useful this line of theorizing really is.

A related extension to the theory involves diversity issues, specifically gender and race, but also perhaps age and disability. Graen (2003) has edited a volume on this issue, but little by way of original research is presented there. To date the theoretical position is that demographic similarity should foster high-quality LMX relationships; yet the research is decidedly mixed as to its support for this proposition. Similarity clearly operates in other respects to foster high-quality relationships but not necessarily demographic similarity (Erdogan and Liden 2002). The one exception is that studies indicate that same-sex dyads are characterized by higher LMX, particularly so for female–female dyads (see Varma and Stroh 2001).

Scandura and Lankau (1996) argue that because LMX is fundamentally based on the connectedness of one person to another, it should incorporate diversity variables reflecting the nature of today's workforce. It is not entirely clear whether this view stems from a value-based position or a scientific one. No formal theory on the matter is proposed, although suggestions along these lines are offered. Whether the specific inclusion of diversity issues in leader–member exchange theory might prove fruitful from a scientific perspective is inevitably dependent on how the issues are formulated, what variables are included and what relationships involving them are posited, and how the research tests turn out. At present we appear to be a long way from having answers in these areas.

Dansereau, a major participant in the early development of vertical dyad linkage theory, has proposed a theoretical position that is in a number of respects more an alternative to Graen's theorizing than an extension to it. The development of Dansereau's (1995) thinking is outlined in Table 14.3. The break with leader–member exchange theory appears to have occurred in late stage 2. The key concepts here are a view of leadership as individualized, operating differently with each other member of a dyad (consistent with a clinical approach to superior–subordinate relationships) and the emphasis on the leader's role in providing a sense of self-worth (consistent with the concept of self-efficacy). This approach takes a different direction from leader–member exchange theory, although it stems from the same origins, and the two are not necessarily fully contradictory. It appears to have very good prospects as a way to gaining a more complete understanding of a leader's relationships with others, although it represents only one aspect of leadership (Mumford, Dansereau, and Yammarino 2000).

Table 14.3

The Development of Dansereau's Dyadic Approach to Leadership

Phase 1. (1972–77) *Allowing for More than the Traditional (ALS) View*

Although an individual may be a leader, in part due to his or her individual style or individual difference, this is only one possible component of leadership. This traditional individual difference view is sometimes referred to as the average leadership style (ALS) approach.

Phase 2. (1978–83) *Development of the (VDL) Vertical Dyad Linkage (Dyad–Group) Approach*

An individual may be a leader for some individuals (in-group members) and not for others (out-group members). Leaders discriminate among individuals against the backdrop of the formal assignment of subordinates to leaders.

Phase 3. (1984–89) *Development of the Individualized Leadership Approach*

Individuals link with other individuals on a one-to-one independent dyadic basis. A leader may link with many other individuals, as well as with only a few individuals and not others. It depends on the two individuals: the leader and the other individual. It does not depend on the formal assignment of subordinates to groups or on the style or individual differences of the leader.

Phase 4. (1990 and beyond) *Source of Linkages in the Individualized Leadership Approach*

Individuals become leaders by providing a focal person with a sense of support for the focal person's self-worth as an individual. Individuals become followers from receiving a sense of self-worth from the leader and perform in ways that satisfy the leader and themselves; in the process, they validate their own sense of self-worth. For other individuals (nonfollowers), leaders do not provide a sense of self-worth. Nonfollowers may or may not be located in a formal supervisory unit (i.e., in-groups and out-groups are not required in each formal group).

Source: Adapted from Dansereau (1995, 481–86).

Another derivative theory is in part the product of another of Graen's coworkers, Robert Liden. The approach has been stated somewhat differently in various sources as it attempts to focus on somewhat different problems, but the key features remain the same (see Liden, Sparrowe, and Wayne 1997; Sparrowe and Liden 1997). The central idea is to put exchange theory back into leader–member exchanges and to use the concept of reciprocity to accomplish this. Furthermore, the context of these exchanges is viewed as important, and social network analysis is invoked to deal with this context. Roles are viewed as multidimensional, and affect, loyalty, contribution, and professional respect are considered to be the key dimensions of the roles inherent in the LMX relationship. A set of propositions that represent the latest extensions of this approach is contained in Erdogan and Liden (2002). Several of these propositions relate to the problem considered next.

A final derivative theoretical approach seeks to deal with the problem posed by the following quote:

[I]n order to effectively apply LMX theory it is necessary to understand what constitutes desired, acceptable, and effective relationships between superiors and subordinates. In collectivistic societies, group identification often defines individual self-concept. . . . Differences in interpretation of specific behaviors across cultures can lead to deviations from the predicted course of LMX development in multicultural environments, restricting its applicability. (Aditya, House, and Kerr 2000, 157)

This situation is comparable to that existing when equity norms are set against either equality or need-based norms (see Chapter 9). In both such cases there are contexts in which a theory simply does not work.

The social identity model of leadership (van Knippenberg and Hogg, 2003) takes the position that LMX theorizing is much less effective within groups that are highly salient and with which people identify strongly. In such contexts a collective spirit tends to dominate, and members may prefer to be treated equally by the leader; thus, depersonalized leader–member relations are perceived to be more effective. Research consistent with this position is presented, conducted with groups from organizations in the United Kingdom and India. But remember that LMX has been found to operate effectively in Japan and China. Thus, we are not dealing with a clear-cut United States versus the rest of the world dichotomy here. Considerable research is needed to sort all of this out.

Applications for Organizations and Individuals

We have already considered one type of intervention arising out of leader–member exchange theory. This intervention is described in three publications (Graen, Novak, and Sommerkamp 1982; Scandura and Graen 1984; Graen, Scandura, and Graen 1986). It appears to offer promise, but there has been little by way of follow-up to this work. The intent is to create as many dyadic relationships of a high-quality nature as possible, and the normative theory involved states that expanding the opportunity for high-quality exchanges to everyone should improve performance overall.

It is apparent that in the research reported, when high LMX formation was facilitated by the training and treatment, performance did improve. However, there are remaining uncertainties that have never been resolved. It appears that an initial increase in performance levels was followed by a return to base-line conditions, suggesting that the effects were short-lived. It is possible that the facilitated relationships were not maintained, although the data indicate that at least for a time, high-quality exchanges were induced on a widespread basis.

The problem discussed previously involving the apparent moderator effects of high growth-need strength coupled with the finding of improvements focused among those with former low-quality exchanges is perplexing. Furthermore, although an argument in favor of the approach is that it acts to deal with feelings of inequity by making high-quality exchanges available to all, it also serves to eliminate any elitist motivations that may have driven the behavior of high LMX people previously. These individuals may well have considered themselves winners before, but with the intervention this status is taken away from them.

All in all the value of an across-the-board high-quality exchange intervention must be considered promising but uncertain at present. It has not had widespread application, and it should not until the uncertainties are resolved. This area contains some of the greatest research needs surrounding LMX theory. In particular, studies should be conducted over considerable periods of time to resolve the questions involving continuing effects. Also, the role of growth-need strength needs to be established both in normal dyad formations and in facilitated relationships. Until these questions are resolved, applications of the training to practice on other than an experimental basis do not seem warranted (see Erdogan and Liden 2002).

A related application is concerned not with what organizations should do to improve their effectiveness, but with what individual members should do to achieve their personal ends (Graen 1989). The focus is on things a person should do to achieve fast-track status in management, what unwritten rules exist in organizations, and how to become an insider who understands these rules and follows them to move up the hierarchy. These unwritten rules are part of the informal organization and constitute the secrets of organizational politics.

There are fifteen such secrets of the fast track:

1. Find the hidden strategies of your organization and use them to achieve your objectives. (This involves forming working relationships—networks—with people who have access to special resources, skills, and abilities to do important work.)
2. Do your homework in order to pass the tests. (These tests can range from sample questions to command performances; you should test others, as well, to evaluate sources of information.)
3. Accept calculated risks by using appropriate contingency plans. (Thus, learn to improve your decision average by taking calculated career risks.)
4. Recognize that apparently complete and final plans are merely flexible guidelines to the actions necessary for implementation. (Thus, make your plans broad and open-ended so that you can adapt them as they are implemented.)
5. Expect to be financially undercompensated for the first half of your career and to be overcompensated for the second half. (People on the fast track inevitably grow out of their job descriptions and take on extra duties beyond what they are paid to do.)
6. Work to make your boss successful. (This is at the heart of the exchange between the two of you and involves a process of reciprocal promotion.)
7. Work to get your boss to promote your career. (This is the other side of the coin and involves grooming your replacement as well.)
8. Use reciprocal relationships to build supportive networks. (It is important that these be competence networks involving effective working relationships and competent people.)
9. Do not let your areas of competence become too narrowly specialized. (Avoid the specialists trap by continually taking on new challenges.)
10. Try to act with foresight more often than with hindsight. (Be proactive by identifying the right potential problem, choosing the right solution, and choosing the best implementation process.)
11. Develop cordial relationships with your competitors: Be courteous, considerate, and polite in all relationships. (You need not like all these people, but making unnecessary enemies is an expensive luxury.)
12. Seek out key expert insiders and learn from them. (Have numerous mentors and preserve these relationships of your reciprocal network.)
13. Make sure to acknowledge everyone's contribution. (Giving credit can be used as a tool to develop a network of working relationships.)
14. Prefer equivalent exchanges between peers instead of rewards and punishments between unequal partners. (Equivalent exchanges are those in which a resource, service, or behavior is given with the understanding that something of equivalent value will eventually be returned; this requires mutual trust.)
15. Never take unfair advantage of anyone, and avoid letting anyone take unfair advantage of you. (Networks cannot be maintained without a reputation for trustworthiness.)

To aid in achieving the goals of these secrets, there are discussions of reading the unwritten rules, finding out whether or not you are on the fast track, methods of getting on the fast track, outgrowing your present job, developing resources with superiors and competent peers, solving problems, obtaining inside information, developing fast-track leadership, and discovering the broader organizational picture. This is a comprehensive manual for moving quickly up the hierarchy, with many appealing ideas.

More recently, in another book, Graen (2003) has revisited this topic and set forth another partially overlapping list of thirteen actions that distinguish key players from others (i.e., high-quality LMX players from low-quality LMX others). These guidelines (based on Graen 2003, 17–20) for how to play the hierarchy and gain fast-track status are as follows:

1. *Demonstrate initiative* to get things done (i.e., engage in organizational citizenship behaviors).
2. *Exercise leadership* to make the unit more effective (i.e., become an informal group leader).
3. Show a willingness to *take risks* to accomplish assignments (i.e., go against group pressures in order to surface problems if necessary).
4. Strive to *add value* to the assignments (i.e., enrich your own job by making it more challenging and meaningful).
5. Actively seek out new job assignments for *self-improvement* (i.e., seek out opportunities for growth).
6. *Persist* on a valuable project after others give up (and learn not to make the same mistake twice).
7. *Build networks* to extend capability, especially among those responsible for getting work done.
8. *Influence others* by doing something extra (i.e., this means building credibility and adjusting your interpersonal style to match others).
9. *Resolve ambiguity* by dealing constructively to resolve ambiguity (i.e., gather as much information as possible and obtain frequent feedback).
10. *Seek wider exposure* to managers outside the home division, which helps in gathering information.
11. *Build on existing skills*. Apply technical training on the job and build on that training to develop broader expertise; be sure not to allow obsolescence to creep in.
12. *Develop a good working relationship with your boss*. Work to build and maintain a close working relationship with the immediate supervisor (Strive to build a high quality LMX, devote energy to this goal—see Maslyn and Uhl-Bien, 2001).
13. *Promote your boss*. Work to get the immediate supervisor promoted (i.e., try to make that person look good; as your boss goes up, so well may you).

Graen (2003) does not present this second list as a replacement for the first. In both instances there are frequent references to studies and the results of studies. Some of what is said is clearly research based, but there are normative statements that go beyond the research as well. The ideas are intriguing and they have the ring of truth. Not all are supported by research, nor does Graen claim that they are. All in all, efforts of this kind would seem to be a useful contribution to organizational behavior practice, although one could wish for a somewhat more solid empirical underpinning. For instance, is it the high-growth-need people who are most likely to take these ideas and run with them? Do we have here sets of guidelines that are applicable only to certain individuals (or to everyone, as Graen implies)?

CONCLUSIONS

Assessments of leader–member exchange theory and its applications in the literature reach somewhat varied conclusions. Yukl (2002) seems to feel that even more improvements are needed to overcome various conceptual weaknesses and that the research is still insufficient. Elkins and Keller (2003) focus on implication for research and development units and reach much more favorable conclusions, especially with regard to the propensity for high quality leader–member exchanges to foster innovation and creativity. Schriesheim (2003) is critical on the grounds that the theory is concerned with what happens at the level of the dyad, but empirical measurement at that level is rare if not nonexistent. Erdogan and Liden (2002) present a positive picture of the theory as developed to this point, while indicating a potential for significant extrapolation to deal with new issues that the theory has unearthed. Gerstner and Day (1997) draw upon their meta-analysis to indicate that the theory predicts a number of significant outcomes and does so quite well.

I would take issue with certain of the questions involving research findings on the evidence that other data refute many of these criticisms. In support of this interpretation, let me draw on a set of studies reported by Schriesheim, Castro, Zhou, and Yammarino (2001). They say, after describing their research, which they believe more correctly deals with the dyadic relationship within LMX:

> The results in both samples support a between-dyads perspective, suggesting the presence of differentiated dyads consistent with LMX theory. (541)
>
> . . .
>
> As a whole, then, these results show relatively good support for both the substantive hypothesis and the level of analysis predictions that are drawn concerning LMX theory. . . . [T]he results of this study support the LMX approach. (542)
>
> . . .
>
> With respect to LMX theory, our illustrative study supported a fundamental LMX prediction of multiple levels of analysis. . . . We believe that the LMX approach has merit. (543).

With these reviews in mind, I turn to the evaluations presented at the beginning of the chapter. The importance rating by peers is at 4 stars with an actual rating of 4.69, very good among leadership theories. The estimated validity is 5 stars based upon my assessment of the research, which is without question voluminous and in recent years at least has been of very high quality. There are many questions that the theory has unearthed that remain unanswered, but without the theory these questions would never have been asked. As to estimated usefulness, the applications that have been proposed, and it is to the theory's credit that they do exist, indeed show promise. Yet maximizing the number of high-quality leader–member exchanges in a group may well be self-defeating, and following the rules for achieving fast-track status has not been shown to work in all instances. Given the need for further research here, the 3-star rating seems warranted.

In the next chapter we take up a completely different type of theory, still, however, with its origins in the Ohio State leadership research. This theory derives much of its content from the information-processing approach and is of a thoroughly cognitive nature.

REFERENCES

Aditya, Ram N., House, Robert J., and Kerr, Steven (2000). Theory and Practice of Leadership: Into the New Millennium. In Cary L. Cooper and Edwin A. Locke (Eds.), *Industrial and Organizational Psychology: Linking Theory with Practice.* Oxford, UK: Blackwell, 130–65.

Barnard, Chester I. (1938). *The Functions of the Executive.* Cambridge, MA: Harvard University Press.

Bauer, Tayla N., and Green, Stephen G. (1996). Development of Leader–Member Exchange: A Longitudinal Test. *Academy of Management Journal,* 39, 1538–67.

Boyd, Nancy G., and Taylor, Robert R. (1998). A Developmental Approach to the Examination of Friendship in Leader–Follower Relationships. *Leadership Quarterly*, 9, 1–25.

Cashman, James, Dansereau, Fred, Graen, George, and Haga, William J. (1976). Organizational Understructure and Leadership: A Longitudinal Investigation of the Managerial Role-making Process. *Organizational Behavior and Human Performance*, 15, 278–96.

Chemers, Martin M. (1997). *An Integrative Theory of Leadership*. Mahwah, NJ: Lawrence Erlbaum.

Dansereau, Fred (1995). A Dyadic Approach to Leadership: Creating and Nurturing This Approach under Fire. *Leadership Quarterly*, 6, 479–90.

Dansereau, Fred, Cashman, James, and Graen, George (1973). Instrumentality Theory and Equity Theory as Complementary Approaches in Predicting the Relationship of Leadership and Turnover among Managers. *Organizational Behavior and Human Performance*, 10, 184–200.

Dansereau, Fred, Graen, George, and Haga, William J. (1975). A Vertical Dyad Linkage Approach to Leadership within Formal Organizations: A Longitudinal Investigation of the Role-Making Process. *Organizational Behavior and Human Performance*, 13, 46–78.

Dirks, Kurt T., and Ferrin, Donald L. (2002). Trust in Leadership: Meta-Analytic Findings and Implications for Research and Practice. *Journal of Applied Psychology*, 87, 611–28.

Dunegan, Kenneth J., Uhl-Bien, Mary, and Duchon, Dennis (2002). LMX and Subordinate Performance: The Moderating Effects of Task Characteristics. *Journal of Business and Psychology*, 17, 275–85.

Elkins, Teri, and Keller, Robert T. (2003). Leadership in Research and Development Organizations: A Literature Review and Conceptual Framework. *Leadership Quarterly*, 14, 587–606.

Engle, Elaine M., and Lord, Robert G. (1997). Implicit Theories, Self-Schemas, and Leader–Member Exchange. *Academy of Management Journal*, 40, 988–1010.

Erdogan, Berrin, and Liden, Robert C. (2002). Social Exchanges in the Workplace: A Review of Recent Developments and Future Research Directions in Leader–Member Exchange Theory. In Linda L. Neider and Chester A. Schriesheim (Eds.), *Leadership*. Greenwich, CT: Information Age Publishing, 65–114.

Fernandez, Carmen F., and Vecchio, Robert P. (1997). Situational Leadership Theory Revisited: A Test of an Across-Jobs Perspective. *Leadership Quarterly*, 8, 67–84.

Gerstner, Charlotte R., and Day, David V. (1997). Meta-Analytic Review of Leader–Member Exchange Theory: Correlates and Construct Issues. *Journal of Applied Psychology*, 82, 827–44.

Gómez, Carolina, and Rosen, Benson (2001). The Leader–Member Exchange as a Link between Managerial Trust and Employee Empowerment. *Group and Organization Management*, 26, 53–69.

Graen, George (1969). Instrumentality Theory of Work Motivation: Some Experimental Results and Suggested Modifications. *Journal of Applied Psychology Monograph*, 53(2), Part 2, 1–25.

——— (1976). Role-making Processes within Complex Organizations. In Marvin D. Dunnette (Ed.), *Handbook of Industrial and Organizational Psychology*. Chicago, IL: Rand, McNally, 1201–45.

——— (1989). *Unwritten Rules for Your Career: 15 Secrets for Fast-track Success*. New York: John Wiley.

——— (1990). Designing Productive Leadership Systems to Improve Both Work Motivation and Organizational Effectiveness. In Uwe Kleinbeck, Hans-Henning Quast, Henk Thierry, and Hartmut Häcker (Eds.), *Work Motivation*. Mahwah, NJ: Lawrence Erlbaum, 133–67.

——— (2002). "It's All about LMXs, Stupid": Collect High-quality Data, Follow It, Trust LMXs, and Always Seek Serendipity. In Arthur G. Bedeian (Ed.), *Management Laureates: A Collection of Autobiographical Essays*, Vol. 6. Oxford, UK: Elsevier Science, 53–81.

——— (2003). *Dealing with Diversity*. Greenwich, CT: Information Age Publishing.

Graen, George, and Cashman, James F. (1975). A Role-making Model of Leadership in Formal Organizations: A Developmental Approach. In James G. Hunt and Lars L. Larson (Eds.), *Leadership Frontiers*. Kent, OH: Kent State University Press, 143–65.

Graen, George, Cashman, James F., Ginsburgh, Steven, and Schiemann, William (1977). Effects of Linking-Pin Quality on the Quality of Working Life of Lower Participants. *Administrative Science Quarterly*, 22, 491–504.

Graen, George, Dansereau, Fred, and Minami, Takao (1972a). Dysfunctional Leadership Styles. *Organizational Behavior and Human Performance*, 7, 216–36.

——— (1972b). An Empirical Test of the Man-in-the-Middle Hypothesis among Executives in a Hierarchical Organization Employing a Unit-Set Analysis. *Organizational Behavior and Human Performance*, 8, 262–85.

Graen, George, Dansereau, Fred, Minami, Takao, and Cashman, James (1973). Leadership Behaviors as Cues to Performance Evaluation. *Academy of Management Journal*, 16, 611–23.

Graen, George, and Ginsburgh, Steven (1977). Job Resignation as a Function of Role Orientation and Leader Acceptance: A Longitudinal Investigation of Organizational Assimilation. *Organizational Behavior and Human Performance*, 19, 1–17.

Graen, George B., and Hui, Chun (2001). Approaches to Leadership: Toward a Complete Contingency Model of Face-to-Face Leadership. In Miriam Erez, Uwe Kleinbeck, and Henk Thierry (Eds.), *Work Motivation in the Context of a Globalizing Economy*. Mahwah, NJ: Lawrence Erlbaum, 211–25.

Graen, George B., Liden, Robert C., and Hoel, William (1982). Role of Leadership in the Employee Withdrawal Process. *Journal of Applied Psychology*, 67, 868–72.

Graen, George, Novak, Michael A., and Sommerkamp, Patricia (1982). The Effect of Leader–Member Exchange and Job Design on Productivity and Satisfaction: Testing a Dual Attachment Model. *Organizational Behavior and Human Performance*, 30, 109–31.

Graen, George, Orris, James B., and Johnson, Thomas W. (1973). Role Assimilation Processes in a Complex Organization. *Journal of Vocational Behavior*, 3, 395–420.

Graen, George B., and Scandura, Terri A. (1986). A Theory of Dyadic Career Reality. *Research in Personnel and Human Resources Management*, 4, 147–81.

——— (1987). Toward a Psychology of Dyadic Organizing. *Research in Organizational Behavior*, 9, 175–208.

Graen, George B., Scandura, Terri A., and Graen, Michael R. (1986). A Field Experimental Test of the Moderating Effects of Growth Need Strength on Productivity. *Journal of Applied Psychology*, 71, 484–91.

Graen, George, and Schiemann, William (1978). Leader–Member Agreement: A Vertical Dyad Linkage Approach. *Journal of Applied Psychology*, 63, 206–12.

Graen, George B., and Uhl-Bien, Mary (1991). The Transformation of Professionals into Self-Managing and Partially Self-Designing Contributors: Toward a Theory of Leadership Making. *Journal of Management Systems*, 3(3), 33–48.

——— (1995). Relationships-based Approach to Leadership: Development of Leader–Member Exchange (LMX) Theory of Leadership over 25 Years: Applying a Multi-level Multi-domain Perspective. *Leadership Quarterly*, 6, 219–47.

Graen, George B., and Wakabayashi, Mitsuru (1994). Cross-cultural Leadership Making: Bridging American and Japanese Diversity for Team Advantage. In Harry C. Triandis, Marvin D. Dunnette, and Leaetta M. Hough (Eds.), *Handbook of Industrial and Organizational Psychology*, Vol. 4. Palo Alto, CA: Consulting Psychologists Press, 415–46.

Graen, George B., Wakabayashi, Mitsuru, Graen, Michael R., and Graen, Martin G. (1990). International Generalizability of American Hypotheses about Japanese Management Progress: A Strong Inference Investigation. *Leadership Quarterly*, 1, 1–23.

Griffeth, Roger W., Hom, Peter W., and Gaertner, Stefan (2000). A Meta-Analysis of Antecedents and Correlates of Employee Turnover: Update, Moderator Tests, and Research Implications for the Next Millennium. *Journal of Management*, 26, 463–88.

Hackett, Rick D., Farh, Jiing-Lih, Song, Lynda J., and Lapierre, Laurent M. (2003). LMX and Organizational Citizenship Behavior—Examining the Links within and across Western and Chinese Samples. In George B. Graen (Ed.), *Dealing with Diversity*. Greenwich, CT: Information Age Publishing, 219–64.

Haga, William J., Graen, George, and Dansereau, Fred (1974). Professionalism and Role Making in a Service Organization: A Longitudinal Investigation. *American Sociological Review*, 39, 122–33.

House, Robert J., and Aditya, Ram N. (1997). The Social Scientific Study of Leadership: Quo Vadis? *Journal of Management*, 23, 409–73.

Jacobs, T.O. (1971). *Leadership and Exchange in Formal Organizations*. Alexandria, VA: Human Resources Research Organization.

Johnson, Thomas W., and Graen, George (1973). Organizational Assimilation and Role Rejection. *Organizational Behavior and Human Performance*, 10, 72–87.

Judge, Timothy A., Piccolo, Ronald F., and Ilies, Remus (2004). The Forgotten Ones? The Validity of Consideration and Initiating Structure in Leadership Research. *Journal of Applied Psychology*, 89, 36–51.

Kacmar, K. Michele, Witt, L.A., Zivnuska, Suzanne, and Gully, Stanley M. (2003). The Interactive Effect of Leader–Member Exchange and Communication Frequency on Performance Ratings. *Journal of Applied Psychology*, 88, 764–72.

Katz, Daniel N., and Kahn, Robert L. (1966). *The Social Psychology of Organizations*. New York: John Wiley.

Klein, Howard J., and Kim, Jay S. (1998). A Field Study of the Influence of Situational Constraints, Leader–Member Exchange, and Goal Commitment on Performance. *Academy of Management Journal*, 41, 88–95.

Klieman, Rhonda S., Quinn, Julie A., and Harris, Karen L. (2000). The Influence of Employee–Supervisor Interactions upon Job Breadth. *Journal of Managerial Psychology*, 15, 587–601.

Leana, Carrie R., and Rousseau, Denise M. (2000). *Relational Wealth: The Advantages of Stability in a Changing Economy.* New York: Oxford University Press.

Liden, Robert C., and Graen, George B. (1980). Generalizability of the Vertical Dyad Linkage Model of Leadership. *Academy of Management Journal*, 23, 451–65.

Liden, Robert C., Sparrowe, Raymond T., and Wayne, Sandy J. (1997). Leader–Member Exchange Theory: The Past and Potential for the Future. *Research in Personnel and Human Resources Management*, 15, 47–119.

Liden, Robert C., Wayne, Sandy J., and Stilwell, Dean (1993). A Longitudinal Study on the Early Development of Leader–Member Exchanges. *Journal of Applied Psychology*, 78, 662–74.

Maslyn, John M., and Uhl-Bien, Mary (2001). Leader–Member Exchange and Its Dimensions: Effects of Self-Effort and Other's Effort on Relationship Quality. *Journal of Applied Psychology*, 86, 697–708.

Miner, John B. (2002). *Organizational Behavior: Foundations, Theories, and Analyses.* New York: Oxford University Press.

Mumford, Michael D., Dansereau, Fred, and Yammarino, Francis J. (2000). Followers, Motivations, and Levels of Analysis: The Case of Individualized Leadership. *Leadership Quarterly*, 11, 313–40.

Podsakoff, Philip M., MacKenzie, Scott B., Paine, Julie Beth, and Bachrach, Daniel G. (2000). Organizational Citizenship Behaviors: A Critical Review of the Theoretical and Empirical Literature and Suggestions for Future Research. *Journal of Management*, 26, 513–63.

Scandura, Terri A., and Graen, George B. (1984). Moderating Effects of Initial Leader–Member Exchange Status on the Effects of a Leadership Intervention. *Journal of Applied Psychology*, 69, 428–36.

Scandura, Terri A., and Lankau, Melenie J. (1996). Developing Diverse Leaders: A Leader–Member Exchange Approach. *Leadership Quarterly*, 7, 243–63.

Scandura, Terri A., and Schriesheim, Chester A. (1994). Leader–Member Exchange and Supervisor Career Mentoring as Complementary Constructs in Leadership Research. *Academy of Management Journal*, 37, 1588–1602.

Schriesheim, Chester A. (2003). Why Leadership Research Is Generally Irrelevant for Leadership Developments. In Susan E. Murphy and Ronald E. Riggio (Eds.), *The Future of Leadership Development.* Mahwah, NJ: Lawrence Erlbaum, 181–97.

Schriesheim, Chester A., Castro, Stephanie L., and Cogliser, Claudia C. (1999). Leader–Member Exchange (LMX) Research: A Comprehensive Review of Theory, Measurement, and Data-Analytic Practices. *Leadership Quarterly*, 10, 63–113.

Schriesheim, Chester A., Castro, Stephanie L., Zhou, Xiaohua, and Yammarino, Francis J. (2001). The Folly of Theorizing "A" But Testing "B"—A Selective Level-of-Analysis Review of the Field and a Detailed Leader–Member Exchange Illustration. *Leadership Quarterly*, 12, 515–51.

Schriesheim, Chester A., Neider, Linda L., and Scandura, Terri A. (1998). Delegation and Leader–Member Exchange: Main Effects, Moderators, and Measurement Issues. *Academy of Management Journal*, 41, 298–318.

Sparrowe, Raymond T., and Liden, Robert C. (1997). Process and Structure in Leader–Member Exchange. *Academy of Management Review*, 22, 522–52.

Uhl-Bien, Mary, Graen, George B., and Scandura, Terri A. (2000). Implications of Leader–Member Exchange (LMX) for Strategic Human Resource Management Systems: Relationships as Social Capital for Competitive Advantage. *Research in Personnel and Human Resources Management*, 18, 137–85.

Uhl-Bien, Mary, and Maslyn, John M. (2003). Reciprocity in Manager–Subordinate Relationships: Components, Configurations, and Outcomes. *Journal of Management*, 29, 511–32.

van Knippenberg, Daan, and Hogg, Michael A. (2003). A Social Identity Model of Leadership Effectiveness in Organizations. *Research in Organizational Behavior*, 25, 243–95.

Varma, Arup, and Stroh, Linda K. (2001). The Impact of Same-Sex LMX Dyads on Performance Evaluations. *Human Resource Management*, 40, 309–20.

Vecchio, Robert P. (1998). Leader–Member Exchange, Objective Performance, Employment Duration, and Supervisor Ratings: Testing for Moderating and Mediation. *Journal of Business and Psychology*, 12, 327–41.

Wakabayashi, Mitsuru, and Graen, George (1989). Human Resource Development of Japanese Managers: Leadership and Career Investment. *Research in Personnel and Human Resources Management*, Suppl. 1, 235–56.

Wayne, Sandy J., Shore, Lynn M., Bommer, William H., and Tetrick, Lois E. (2002). The Role of Fair Treatment and Rewards in Perceptions of Organizational Support and Leader–Member Exchange. *Journal of Applied Psychology*, 87, 590–98.

Yukl, Gary (2002). *Leadership in Organizations.* Upper Saddle River, NJ: Prentice-Hall.

CHAPTER 15

INFORMATION PROCESSING THEORY OF LEADERSHIP

ROBERT LORD

Background
Developments Prior to the 1990s
Linking Perceptions and Performance
    Human Information Processing
    Recognition-based and Inferential Processes
    Information Processing and Change
    Culture, Information Processing, and Leadership
    Leadership Effects on Performance
    Applied Value
Developments Subsequent to the Initial Theory
    Organization of the Self
    Leadership Processes and Follower Self-Identity
Evaluation and Impact
    Research on the Perceptual Theory
    Perceptual Changes
    Research on Leadership and Performance
    The Use of Catastrophe Theory
    Decline in Research Support
    Individual and Cultural Differences
    Evaluation of the Subsequent Theorizing
Conclusions

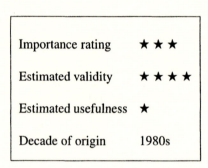

Importance rating	★ ★ ★
Estimated validity	★ ★ ★ ★
Estimated usefulness	★
Decade of origin	1980s

Robert Lord's views were developed over a period of roughly fifteen years during which he and his colleagues conducted a number of studies culminating in several theoretical articles and later still, a book (Lord and Maher 1991a). The version of the theory presented in this book is given primary attention here simply because it is more comprehensive than are the articles. However, the path followed in getting to *Leadership and Information Processing: Linking Perceptions and Performance* is outlined in order to provide insight into the sources of this more comprehensive presentation of the theory.

BACKGROUND

Born in 1946, Robert Lord received a Ph.D. in industrial/organizational psychology from Carnegie-Mellon University in 1975; his B.A. is in economics from the University of Michigan. At Carnegie he was strongly influenced by the thinking of Allen Newell and Herbert Simon (1972). At essentially the time of obtaining his doctorate, Lord accepted a faculty appointment in psychology at the University of Akron, where he has remained since.

In conducting his research and developing his publications, Lord has frequently been joined by various individuals who began as doctoral students in psychology at Akron. After these individuals moved on to their first professional positions at other universities, these collaborations continued in a number of instances. Karen Maher, Lord's coauthor in writing up the comprehensive theory and in several other scholarly endeavors as well, was one such individual. She took a position in the business school at the University of Missouri–St. Louis after completing her doctorate at Akron.

DEVELOPMENTS PRIOR TO THE 1990s

The initial impetus to Lord's research and theorizing on information processing and leadership came from laboratory investigations conducted at Carnegie in connection with his dissertation. This work dealt with relationships among task structure, leader behavior, and group performance; it extended to the matter of perceptions of leader behavior and the role of stereotypes in this process (Lord 1976, 1977).

This work was followed by a series of studies intended to explain much of the variance in leader behavior questionnaires, with particular reference to consideration and initiating structure (from the Ohio State studies), in terms of follower-implicit theories and biases. The focus was on demonstrating that leader behavior as such could not explain the results obtained, and that other factors of a primarily perceptual and cognitive nature within those providing the descriptions and ratings were heavily involved (Rush, Thomas, and Lord 1977; Lord, Binning, Rush, and Thomas 1978; Binning and Lord 1980; Lord, Phillips, and Rush 1980; Rush, Phillips, and Lord 1981). A similar approach was applied to attribution theory findings with the objective of demonstrating that causal attribution processes often stem from cognitive categorizations on the part of a perceiver. Some of this literature was discussed in Chapter 11, but there were earlier studies as well (Phillips and Lord 1981, 1982).

The studies noted to this point were all carried out with students in laboratory settings. A program of research involving perceptions of political leaders deviated somewhat from this model, but still faced similar limitations (Foti, Fraser, and Lord 1982). All of this research involved the testing of prestated hypotheses and in this sense involved theory, but the theory was not extensively developed and lacked integration. Beginning in 1982, however, Lord began to concentrate on the theoretical underpinnings of his research and to publish more extensively along theoretical lines (Lord, Foti, and Phillips 1982). Research now became more theoretically based (Lord, Foti, and DeVader 1984). This move from a primary concern with research controls and methodology to an emphasis on developing good theory continued up to and through the publication of the Lord and Maher (1991a) book. Examples include Lord (1985), Lord and Kernan (1987), and Day and Lord (1988).

Figure 15.1 provides a theoretical model developed in this period to indicate the steps involved in social perception. The following quote indicates what is involved:

> These steps were chosen because they represent the major points at which information is filtered or changed by social information processing. Information input involves a *selective attention/comprehension* step in which relevant information is selected from a

Figure 15.1   **Model of Information Processing Directed by Cognitive Schema**

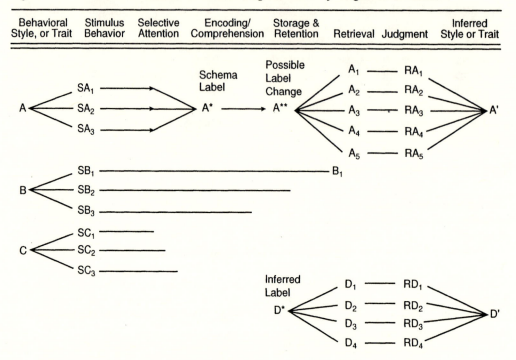

Behavioral Style, or Trait	Stimulus Behavior	Selective Attention	Encoding/ Comprehension	Storage & Retention	Retrieval	Judgment	Inferred Style or Trait

Source: Lord (1985, 90). Copyright © 1985 Elsevier Science. Reprinted with permission.

complex social environment, in part through the process by which it is comprehended or recognized; a step in which noticed information is *encoded and simplified* into a form more easily stored in long-term memory; and a *storage and retention* step during which information is frequently altered through integration with subsequent information concerning the stimulus person. Information output involves two conceptually distinct but highly related steps: the *retrieval* of relevant information and the translation of information into required *judgments* such as causal attributions or the selection of the appropriate response for each item on a questionnaire. (Lord 1985, 89, emphasis in original)

Figure 15.1 depicts these steps and shows that information processing is:

highly dependent on heuristic or automatic processes associated with cognitive schema . . . which reduce information processing demand while still yielding reasonable, albeit suboptimal, social judgments. That is, perceivers simplify perceptions of complex social stimuli by classifying them into already existing, contextually meaningful categories such as leader/ nonleader (A*). Once so classified subsequent information processing can rely primarily on these well learned schema (category prototypes) (A_1 to A_5) rather than the observed stimulus characteristics (SA_1 to SA_3). Though cognitively economical, reliance on prototypes as an information processing aid can result in systematic distortions of stimulus descriptions (e.g.,

RA_4 and RA_5) or social judgments. In addition, reliance on such automatic processes will reduce the relationship of "behavioral ratings" to the behaviors psychologists want to measure. Particularly troublesome is the possibility that "sensible" ratings (RD_1 and RD_5) can be produced for behaviors that were never seen. . . . Thus, clusters of "behavioral" items with high covariances may reflect rater effects rather than traits of the stimulus person being rated. (Lord 1985, 89–91)

Although there was a substantial development of theory during the 1980s, the intermixture of theory and research continued in this period (e.g., see Foti and Lord 1987). This is not a theory that lacks for either research tests or inductive stimulation from empirical sources.

LINKING PERCEPTIONS AND PERFORMANCE

From the preceding discussion it would seem that the theory developed deals only with perceptual processes and thus is more closely allied to the consideration of attribution processes in Chapter 11 than to the leadership focus of Part III. Certainly, perceptions of followers are given considerable attention. However, the theory also deals with how these perceptions influence the outcomes of the leadership process and more directly with leadership as a determinant of performance. The theory presented in Lord and Maher (1991a) is both one of leadership perception and of executive performance. Yet the authors define leadership as the process of being perceived by others as a leader. It involves "behaviors, traits, characteristics, and outcomes produced by leaders as these elements are interpreted by followers" (11).

Human Information Processing

The theory uses the term *knowledge structure* to refer to cognitive schemas that also may be called scripts, plans, categories, implicit theories, prototypes, or heuristics. There is considerable variation in usage among these terms. Categorization processes serve to group nonidentical stimuli into sets that are treated as equivalent, even though they are not.

Four models of information processing are distinguished. The first is *rational* and is illustrated by the "naïve scientists" of attribution theory. It assumes an optimizing process that is often not possible. The second is of *limited capacity* and includes satisficing. The third is *expert* and, although limited-capacity in nature, relies on well-organized or highly developed knowledge structures applied to a specific content domain. The fourth is *cybernetic* and relies heavily on feedback from a task or social environment. Humans are flexible in their information processing and tend to move back and forth across these models, although the limited-capacity form is the most frequent; leadership categorization theory is of this type.

These four models are described elsewhere as well (Lord and Maher 1990), and the distinctions involved are set forth in Table 15.1.

Recognition-based and Inferential Processes

Perceivers of leadership may utilize *automatic processes*, which operate outside awareness, devoid of intent, without interfering with other cognitive tasks, and with minimal effort. In contrast are *controlled processes*, which have antithetical features—awareness, intent, interference, and effort. At the same time, leadership may be *recognized* from qualities and behaviors evidenced in

Table 15.1

Comparison and Evaluation of Information Processing Models

Features	Rational	Limited capacity	Expert	Cybernetic
Information requirements	Knowledge of expectancies and utilities for many alternatives	Knowledge of expectancies and utilities for a few salient alternatives	Highly selective use of schema relevant information	Selective use of current information along with recall and evaluation of past actions
Choice process	Optimization by maximizing expected utility; evaluation of all alternatives	Simplified by heuristic evaluation procedures; and termination when satisfactory alternative is found	Very good alternative recognized by automatic match with information in long-term memory	Feedback guided use of recognition or heuristic processes
Perceptual requirements	Accurate perception of environment based on surface features	Accurate perception of limited environment based on surface features	Accurate perception of limited environment based on meaning	Perception of limited environment and ability to shift perspectives over time
Short-term memory requirements	Extensive capacity	Moderate capacity	Low capacity	Very low capacity
Long-term memory requirements	Extensive information accessed and transferred to short-term memory	Moderate amount of information accessed and transferred to short-term memory	Extensive, highly organized, and accessible long-term memory; minimal information transferred to short-term memory	Varies depending on task familiarity: new task—same as limited capacity; familiar task—same as expert
Type of process emphasized	Controlled, serial, analytic	Controlled or automatic use of heuristics; serial	Automatic parallel	Learning; controlled or automatic; serial
Timing of processing	Prior to choice or behavior	Prior to choice or behavior	Prior to or concurrent with choice or behavior	Intermixed with choice or behavior
Descriptive accuracy	Weak	Strong	Moderate	Strong
Prescriptive value	Strong	Weak	Strong	Strong

Source: Adapted from Lord and Maher (1990, 12, 17).

the course of normal interactions, or it can be *inferred* from the outcomes of relevant events. Using these ideas, a two-by-two classification may be developed to describe alternative processes involved in leadership perceptions:

- automatic, recognition-based—prototype matching with face-to-face contact
- automatic, inferential—perceptually guided involving simplified causal analyses
- controlled, recognition-based—prototype matching using socially communicated information
- controlled, inferential—logically based and comprehensive causal analyses

Category prototypes develop from experience and represent attributes that become associated with each other to form an abstract image in long-term memory; they are expected to vary across contexts. Due to the fact that substantial experience is required to build prototypes, recognition-based perceptions involve expert information processing. Much recognition-based perception of leaders is automatic, but the same categories, and prototype matching, can be used where the stimulus is socially communicated information, not face-to-face contact.

Inferential processes have an attributional aspect in that leadership is inferred from causal analyses related to successful task organizational performance in the past. While leadership at lower levels tends to be automatic and recognition-based, executive leadership may involve any of the other three processes (including both automatic and controlled inferential). Automatic inferential processing occurs when leadership is assumed because the person is salient for, or close to, favorable events. Controlled inferential processes reflect a more careful analysis of potential causal agents. Under conditions of information overload, the automatic version tends to prevail.

Information Processing and Change

Person-based processing into memory results in classifying people as to traits and related behaviors. *Event-based processing* yields analogous schema called scripts which are goal-based and help to make sense of perceived events or to generate actions to attain goals. Both may be updated and changed through cybernetic feedback, but there are differences between what happens when controlled processes are involved and automatic processes. Change via controlled processing tends to be gradual and incremental; automatic processing, on the other hand, produces discontinuous change, as there may well be a shift to an entirely different category.

Changes of the latter type can be quite dramatic. Linear relationship models are not adequate to the task involved, and Lord and Maher (1991a) invoke graphs based on catastrophe theory to depict what occurs. Essentially, with automatic processing, an initial categorization serves as a source of cognitive inertia that must be overcome before a shift occurs. This resistance to change produces bias, but "exactly what processes produce the sudden shift to another category requires further research" (84). A three-dimensional catastrophe theory graph with continuous change on the back surface and discontinuous change on the front is shown in Figure 15.2. This graph combines the change mechanisms of both controlled and automatic processing. The former is considered to be by far the more accurate (free of distortion). Although catastrophe theory allows for mathematical statements of theory, only the graphical presentations are utilized by Lord and Maher (1991a) in their leadership theory.

This approach to the subject of changing cognitive structures is applied to perceptions of women in management in a separate chapter with an added coauthor (Baumgardner, Lord, and Maher 1991). The essential idea is that female managers tend to be categorized as women, not as leaders, with a resulting bias that is a consequence of information-processing limitations, not intentional discrimination. Included here is the resistance to recategorization from woman to leader when automatic processing is involved, even as increased leader performance information is received.

Sex-related stereotypes are hypothesized to operate differently at different hierarchic levels. Within lower management, gender-related categories are particularly easily accessed; due to a lack of performance history, inferential processes tend to be weak. This is less true in middle management, and leadership categories are more readily accessed so that women in these positions are more able to establish leadership perceptions. However, at the upper executive levels, a scarcity of women and frequent resort to limited-capacity processes by external constituents can reverse this favorable trend.

Culture, Information Processing, and Leadership

The theory's handling of culture draws heavily on Schein's formulations (see Miner 2002). Culture perpetuation and change are a function of (1) values and beliefs, (2) schemas related to

Figure 15.2 **Catastrophe Model of Changing Social Perceptions**

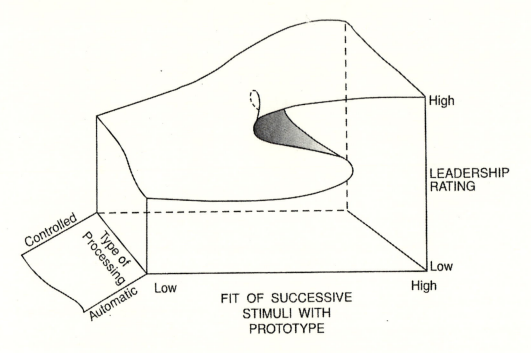

Source: Lord and Maher (1991a, 87). Reprinted with permission from Routledge.

problem solving and behavior or to social perceptions and interactions (both equivalent to Schein's assumptions), and (3) a factor not considered by Schein—the type of information processing (rational, limited-capacity, expert, cybernetic). With regard to the latter, different facets of culture may be generated by different types of information processing, although the limited-capacity type is the most frequent guiding process. Culture change is difficult simply because the rational processes that guide values do not operate often to generate cultural schemas.

Leaders can influence culture as Schein indicates, even if not easily. Change is most likely during periods of crisis, when leadership is defined so as to expand discretion (a type of perceptual credit-granting), and when the culture is weak. Cultures, especially strong cultures, constrain what leaders can do and thus the changes that are possible. The process of culture change may involve changing values, as many have proposed, but more frequently schemas must be changed (consistent with Schein), as when new leadership is installed or subcultures come to achieve dominance. One method of changing schemas is to shift from the limited-capacity or expert processing of an existing culture to cybernetic or rational modes, and then back to new schemas with automatic processing. In any event, changes in type of information processing are essential, along with schema changes, if substantially revised behavior is to be achieved.

Leadership Effects on Performance

To this point the theory has been concerned with the perception of leadership by others. However, there are also effects that leadership exerts on performance. Here the theory moves beyond the realm of perception. A distinction is made between direct and indirect means by which performance may be affected. In the *direct* case influence is exerted on subordinates, decisions, or policies. At lower levels this means leader behavior that shifts subordinate skills or motivation, thus impacting performance. At executive levels changes are made in aspects of the organization—technology, size of workforce—that are closely related to organizational performance.

Indirect means, on the other hand, involve influencing conditions that in turn affect subordinates, decisions, or policies. There is now an intervening mechanism in the linkage. At lower management levels this can be the socialization process or the nature of dyadic exchange. At executive levels it can be the organization's culture, as well as related cognitive schemas and the strategic thrust. Indirect leadership yields much slower feedback and has less impact on leadership perceptions than direct. The leadership literature in general has been less concerned with indirect means, but they are important nevertheless.

Lord and Maher's (1991a) theory advances a clear hypothesis that leadership can exert a causal impact on performance. The executive succession literature is reviewed and re-analyzed in this context. The conclusion, consistent with the dominant hypothesis, is that "if properly interpreted, these studies show that succession has a substantial impact on performance" (190). Leadership effects are most likely to be in evidence when executive discretion is high and during periods of reorientation (rather than convergence).

Catastrophe theory is again brought to bear to explain how these change processes are expected to operate. The graph that results is similar to Figure 15.2, but the three variables utilized are different. The nature of change (incremental to discontinuous) is substituted for the controlled-automatic variable in Figure 15.2. This nature of organizational change variable and environmental fit (instead of prototype fit) are the two control variables:

> Discontinuous (catastrophic) change is represented on the front surface . . . continuous (linear) change is represented on the back face.
>
> Discontinuous change involves shifts in schemas that guide leaders' perceptions of the environment; continuous change reflects incremental shifts within an existing schema. The type of change affects organizational performance.
>
> The degree of fit with the environment is also a factor incorporated into this model. Thus, the degree of environmental fit and the nature of organizational change processes (convergence or reorientation) affect organizational performance. The model also accounts for the history of evolutionary processes within an organization. Organizations at the same level of environmental fit but approaching it from different directions can have different levels of performance, based on their history.
>
> The impact of leadership is also different, depending on the location of the organization on the performance surface. On the back face, lower- and middle-level managers can maintain the organization's performance. Similarly, symbolic activities on the part of top leaders also serve to keep the organization operating on the back surface. Organizations on the front, or discontinuous, face of the cusp model (the crisis region) may require substantive activities on the part of top leaders to yield considerable improvements in an organization's performance. (Lord and Maher 1991a, 208–9)

The theory then turns to the types of activities executives at the top level may utilize to affect organizational performance. These may be broadly classified as those targeted at the internal environment of the organization, at adapting to external environments, and at influencing exter-

Table 15.2

Potential Means That Can Be Used by Executives to Influence Organizational Performance

| Target | Objective | Tactics | |
		Direct	Indirect
A. Adapting to and influencing internal environments			
1. Subsystem organization and management	Rationalization and integration	Define and specify function of roles	Shape top management's schemas; organizing; select those with similar schemas
	Coordination and appraisal	Design and implement management information systems	Use information as sign and symbol
2. Productivity	Increased organizational efficiency.	Reduce capital or personnel costs	Strengthen productivity norms
3. Quality	Increased product quality	Increase quality control	Strengthen quality norms
4. Organizational climate and culture	Increased employee motivation and commitment	Determine or influence organizational politics	Enhance participative decision making norms; symbolism of CEO
B. Adapting to external environments			
1. Choice of markets or environments	Increased stability and munificence	Improve strategic planning	Influence top management's schemas; select those with similar schemas
2. Management and production system	Fit with environment and strategy	Improve organizational design	Guide top management's labeling of environments
C. Influencing external environments			
1. Acquisition of resources and maintenance of boundaries	Increased stability and reduced competition	Integrate horizontally or vertically; promote entry barriers and noncompetitive pricing	Create favorable public opinion; enhance image of organization or product
2. Government policy (e.g., regulation, taxation, trade)	Policy change to reduce uncertainty or increase resources	Exercise direct political influence	Exercise political influence via other groups (e.g., unions, suppliers)

Source: Adapted from Day and Lord (1988, 461).

nal environments. The means proposed may be classified as direct or indirect following the definitions noted previously. Table 15.2 provides examples of these influence processes.

Toward the end, the book presenting the theory focuses primarily on organizational level phenomena. Both groups and organizations are viewed as collective information processors, operating with much the same dynamics as individual processors. The concern here shifts sharply to issues usually considered to lie within the domain of strategic management. The Miles and Snow (1978) theory and data receive considerable attention, but a number of other theories dealing with strategic phenomena are introduced as well. This discussion is much more speculative, and the tie to the basic body of laboratory research is often lost. Yet the stress on leadership at the top is an effective antidote to the group dynamics emphasis that characterizes most of the earlier leadership literature.

Applied Value

Only in the last two paragraphs of their book do the authors explicitly address the application issue. In this regard it seems best to let them speak for themselves:

> Our bias has been to stress theoretical and conceptual development and to ground ideas in the extant scientific literature. We think, however, the theory has applied value as well. Throughout this book, we discuss many practical issues, such as why females may not be perceived as leaders, how to expand discretion, and how context may limit leadership perceptions, to name just a few. We think that understanding such issues from a theoretical perspective is valuable. In addition, we have extended thinking about leadership by integrating it with theories of information processing and organizational evolution; such extensions are of practical value because they go beyond the experience and perspectives of most individual leaders or organizations.
>
> A widespread pragmatic issue is that real leaders address problems from a perspective that is too narrow. Our approach suggests ways of expanding leaders' perspectives by considering alternative types of information processing. . . . A key strategy for leaders to consider is first to diagnose the type of information processing they typically apply to problems and then to consider how the problems might be approached using alternative types of information processing. In doing so, leaders should focus both on processes related to social perceptions and on processes related to performance. (Lord and Maher 1991a, 308)

DEVELOPMENTS SUBSEQUENT TO THE INITIAL THEORY

Following the publication of the comprehensive theory in book form, the authors' major contribution was an overview of cognitive theory generally, although with little specific reference to leadership processes (Lord and Maher 1991b). In addition, Lord provided several commentaries on information processing as related to aspects of leadership, but without particularly significant new theoretical input to the field (Lord and Hall 1992; Lord 1995).

However, later in the decade of the 1990s, Lord began to develop ideas related to information processing at different levels of analysis, to affective considerations, and to self-identities, while writing with various coauthors, again primarily colleagues at Akron (Hall and Lord 1995; Engle and Lord 1997; Lord and Smith 1999). As with the progression of publications leading up to the book with Maher (1991a), these statements ultimately culminated in a comprehensive theoretical position (Lord, Brown, and Freiberg 1999). This latter represents a significant extension of the basic theory, an extension that is in fact more theoretically elegant than its predecessor, since the ideas are stated in propositional form.

Organization of the Self

The theory starts with the idea that follower self-concepts serve to influence follower behavior and that leaders can affect these self-concepts. The self is a system of self-schemas derived from experience, and possessing cognitive, affective, and behavioral consequences. At the core are highly stable schemas, but there are also more peripheral aspects whose accessibility depends upon motivational and social contexts. An individual's self-identity is made up of *personal* and *social identities*; the former is a self-categorization based on perceptions of similarities and differences from others (the sense of uniqueness), while the latter is based on how individuals define themselves in relation to the broader social world. There are two levels of social identities—*interpersonal* and *group* (or collective). It is assumed that followers are unable to focus on more than one of these three levels at the same time. Propositions then follow. I limit the presentation here to those that are perpetuated in a later version of the theory (Lord and Brown 2004).

> Proposition 1. The importance of many leadership and social processes will vary with iden-
>   tity level.

> 1a. When the self is defined at the individual level, leader expectancy effects, effects of performance feedback, effects of contingent rewards, and procedures related to distributive justice will have greater effects on subordinate behavior and attitudes.
> 1b. When the self is defined at the relational level, perceived and actual leader–subordinate congruence in attitudes and values, leader affective behaviors, and interactional justice will have greater effects on subordinate behavior and attitudes.
> 1c. When the self is defined at the group (or organizational) level, structural aspects of procedural justice, organizational identities, and team-based leadership will have greater effects on subordinate behavior and attitudes.

> Proposition 2.   The effectiveness of leadership activities will depend on whether they are
>   matched to appropriate identity levels. (Lord, Brown, and Freiberg 1999, 175)

Next came a series of propositions related to the *working self-concept,* which is the portion of the potentially accessible aspects of the self that because of limited attention capacity is actually activated to guide information processing and behavior at a point in time. There are three components—self-views, current goals, and possible selves (broader standards). Leaders' prophecies for their subordinates' performance influence self-views:

> Proposition 4. The relationship between leaders' self-fulfilling prophecies and subordinates'
>   expectancies is mediated by changes in subordinates' self-views. (178)

Possible selves specify who the individual could be, and these images can be nourished by leaders:

> Proposition 6. Linking goals to self-views will accentuate self-enhancement motivations
>   and affective reactions to task feedback, whereas linking goals to possible
>   selves will promote self-verification motivation and cognitive reactions to
>   task feedback.

> Proposition 7a. The relation of current goal-performance discrepancies to task satisfaction
>   will be highest when task goals are strongly linked to self-views.
> Proposition 7b. The relation of rate of change in goal-performance discrepancies (i.e., ve-
>   locity) to task satisfaction will be highest when task goals are strongly linked
>   to possible selves.

Proposition 8. The resiliency of task motivation when discrepancies are encountered will be higher when task goals are strongly linked to possible selves and lower when task goals are linked to self-views. (181)

The remaining propositions (there are fourteen in all) deal primarily with how leaders can influence subordinates, and they integrate leader–member exchange theory (see Chapter 14) into the propositions. These formulations are not replicated in a subsequent publication.

Taken as a whole these propositions appear to have something in common with Dansereau's (1995) views to the effect that the role of a leader is to support the follower's sense of self-worth and to participate in validating that self-worth (see Chapter 14).

Leadership Processes and Follower Self-Identity

Five years after the 1999 article, Lord and his former doctoral student published a book version of this subsequent theory under the title of the heading of this section (Lord and Brown 2004). In the interval there was relatively little by way of published research dealing with the theory, but considerable dabbling with the theory's constructs (e.g., see Lord, Brown, and Harvey 2001; Lord, Brown, Harvey, and Hall 2001; Brown and Lord 2001); there was even a new set of propositions (Lord and Emrich 2000), although not in quite the same vein as others. Apparently Lord and Brown were not yet entirely pleased with the theory they were developing. Not surprisingly, therefore, the book that ultimately eventuated contained 31 propositions, only 7 of which had a close resemblance to the propositions contained in the publication of five years earlier.

Although discussing all of these added propositions is not possible here, I will take up at least one of each type to give the flavor of Lord and Brown's (2004) current thinking.

Proposition 3.1. A leader's reflected appraisal [our perceptions of how others perceive us] will have a powerful impact on a subordinate's self-view. The appraisal will be communicated through both cognitive and affective channels and by both explicit and implicit processes. (44)

Proposition 4.2. Leaders can prime [make some schemas more accessible than others] subordinate identities through multiple means with the effectiveness of priming processes varying with
a) the strength and coherence of primes,
b) the salience of leaders,
c) subordinate sensitivity to leadership, and
d) follower differences in the ease with which different aspects of the self can be activated (85).

Proposition 4.4. Leaders can produce permanent changes in subordinate identities by
a) making peripheral aspects of self-identities chronically accessible, and
b) by creating new chronically accessible identities through subordinates' observation, experimentation, and evaluation of provisional selves. (97)

Proposition 5.4. Patterns of values mediate between leader behavior and working self-concept activation.

Proposition 5.5. Leader behavior has its greatest effect when it activates coherent patterns of values. (120)

Proposition 6.6. Behavior or attitudes toward leaders may be affectively or cognitively (attitudinally) driven. (134)

Proposition 7.1.   Identity will influence the dimension of justice that is salient, with individual level identity priming distributive justice, relational-level identity priming interactional justice, and collective-level identity priming procedural justice. (167)

These views utilize some of the constructs of the original information processing theory, while using many other constructs that are new. In many ways follower self-identity theory is a separate theory, but it still has ties back to information processing as its source.

EVALUATION AND IMPACT

The amount of published research dealing with implicit leadership theories was much greater during the late 1970s and 1980s than it was later. The earlier interest appears to have been sparked by the fact that a major research and theoretical thrust—the behavioral description of leadership styles—was in the process of being undermined. Yet research related to Lord's theorizing has continued to the present (e.g., see Weber, Camerer, Rottenstreich, and Knez 2001).

Research on the Perceptual Theory

The four information processing models proposed have not been considered in research that compares and contrasts them, but each model separately has been the subject of a substantial stream of research (Lord and Maher 1990, 1991a). It is apparent that people do use rational, limited-capacity, expert, and cybernetic approaches, although there is no certainty that other approaches are not possible as well.

Of the four, Lord and his colleagues have been concerned in their research primarily with the limited-capacity approach. In this context they have developed considerable evidence in support of the roles of implicit theories and categorization processes in yielding biases inherent in the perceptions of raters. The methodology in much of this research has been to hold actual leader behavior constant via written descriptions or videotapes, and then to vary the labels applied to this behavior. Other studies show that the factor structures of actual (real) and contrived (imaginary) leader behavior patterns look much the same. The studies, whether conducted by Lord or without his participation (see Larson 1982), consistently indicate that implicit theories and categorization processes account for a sizable proportion, though certainly not all, of the variance in perceptions of leadership. This has been demonstrated recently in the hierarchic context in a study conducted by Foti and Hauenstein (2004).

The theory is further supported by research showing that leaders displaying more prototypical leader behaviors evoke stronger impressions of leadership, and that observers must both register and encode prototypical behaviors before classifying individuals as leaders (Palich and Hom 1992). The automatic-controlled differentiation is clearly evident from the research, and automatic processes do occur more rapidly. Studies reported in Lord and Maher (1991a) demonstrate the validity of both recognition-based and inferential processes in leadership perceptions. Success enhances a perception of leadership while failure removes it.

As noted in the previous chapter, Lord has been critical of attribution theory on the grounds that it overemphasizes rational, controlled processing at the expense of more automatic information approaches. Lord and Maher (1991a, 121) say: "We suggest that attribution processes of the kind described by Green and Mitchell (1979) are rarely used; rather, attributional processes are linked to more schema-driven processes." Certainly the evidence supports a role for automatic processes in attributions, but as we saw in Chapter 11, less so when poor performance is involved. The comparative position of various approaches to information processing in attributions (and in other areas) does not appear to have been fully established by research as yet.

Also still to be established is the role that individual differences play in implicit theories. There is good evidence that they do have a role, but the extent of that role and exactly how they operate are uncertain (see Keller 1999, 2003). This uncertainty is confounded by the finding, reported by Lord and Maher (1991a), that the implicit theories of leadership held in the United States and in Japan are quite different; the two appear in fact to be totally uncorrelated, indicating that individual differences tied to cultures may be sizable.

Perceptual Changes

The ways in which perceptual changes operate vis-à-vis the theory are less well supported by research than are the information processing models and the fact of implicit theories. As Chemers (1997) notes in his review, there is good evidence to indicate that once categorization occurs, a significant inertia develops that holds back any shift to a new category. However, what triggers a change when it does occur remains unknown. Furthermore, there can be no certainty that controlled processing will inevitably result in incremental change; the possibility that reasoning can produce discontinuous changes must be entertained until clear evidence to the contrary is obtained.

The application of the perceptual change theory to the case of female managers makes sense in view of the literature. However, direct support from research is limited, especially for the view that hierarchic differences in perceptual biases, which operate most strongly at the bottom and top levels, serve to limit female managers at these levels in particular. We simply do not have the research to test the theory in this regard.

The theory as applied to culture and cultural change appears to provide a useful extension of Schein's thinking as described in Miner (2002). However, like that theory, and theories about culture in general, Lord and Maher's (1991a) formulations lack research support. This is one place where the almost total absorption with laboratory research has hurt information processing theory. It is difficult to study organizational culture in the laboratory.

Research on Leadership and Performance

The distinction between direct and indirect influences on performance appears useful, and to be consistent with what is known in the area of socialization, culture, strategy formulation, and the like. The contention that the leadership field has not given sufficient attention to indirect means is certainly justified, although a recent book by Zaccaro (2001) on executive leadership seems to represent a reversal of this trend.

Although the perceptual theory indicates that actual leadership behavior explains only part of what is perceived, it says nothing that negates the view that such behavior directly or indirectly influences performance outcomes. However, certain interpretations of the executive succession research do come to the conclusion that the interjection of new leadership behaviors into a situation has no effect on performance and thus that leadership does not make any difference. Lord and Maher (1991a) go a long way toward reversing this conclusion with their re-analysis of certain studies and their introduction of other findings. At top levels combinations of expert and cybernetic information processing seem to provide the key to organizational effectiveness. However, there has been further research which indicates that leadership, and succession, definitely can make a difference. According to the Lord theory, this occurs when leader discretion is high and during periods of reorientation and crisis. There is some evidence consistent with that view, but it would also seem that when leadership traits are appropriately aligned with existing needs, these traits may also be a contributing factor to effective performance. Personality factors are surely involved here (see Pitcher, Chreim, and Kisfalvi, 2000).

The Use of Catastrophe Theory

It is never entirely clear whether Lord and Maher (1991a) are using catastrophe theory as a vehicle for depicting their ideas or as a means of theory generation. Used in the former manner, the three-dimensional graphs do appear to have some explanatory value, although statements to the effect that this treatment is "hard work to get through" (Gioia 1993) do seem justified.

As a source of hypotheses, however, the catastrophe theory presentations fall short. They seem on occasion to lead to unintended conclusions, or at least counterintuitive ones, which are not well explained (Weick 1993). More typically the attempts at hypothesis generation resulting from the catastrophe theory presentations lack the crispness required to apply adequate research tests. Words such as "doubt," "may," "can," and the like serve to neutralize any specific commitment to hypotheses and leave the reader with a sense of equivocality. The authors simply do not seem to be convinced that catastrophe theory is a good source of leadership theory. The fact that it has not been mobilized to support more recent research or to contribute propositions for research testing adds to this impression.

Decline in Research Support

As one moves from the first two parts of *Leadership and Information Processing* to the last, there is a steady decline in the amount of research support adduced and a precipitous decline in relevant research conducted by Lord and those who worked with him. The work on perceptions of leadership and implicit theories is ingenious, significant and grounded in solid research evidence. This work has been described as a productive synthesis (Chemers 1997) and an important contribution (House and Aditya 1997).

The theory developed later in the book is often equally ingenious, but it does not reflect quite the same level of relevant literature knowledge, nor is it grounded in research by the authors or those of a similar orientation. And the research needed to test these more macro theoretical formulations has not been forthcoming since either. The difficulty appears to be that, like many of us, Lord has a particular type of research expertise—conducting tightly controlled laboratory studies to test very specific hypotheses using methods that exhibit a high degree of rigor. Lord is a very good scientist. But this approach is not applicable in the types of field situations that must be utilized in testing his expanding theory. The same type of experimental control is rarely possible, and multiple studies are needed to compensate for this fact. In all likelihood Lord has not extended his research to the more macro aspects of his theory because his preferred research approach is less applicable there, and he is not comfortable with those approaches that are applicable. Also, as I have noted previously, the research approach taken by a theory's author tends to establish a model for future researchers. Others may well have felt that they would be unable to uphold Lord's high standards in the field setting.

One possible way around the need for field studies here is to draw upon evidence that laboratory and field studies produce very similar results. There is some evidence that appears to be of this kind (DeVader, Bateson, and Lord 1986). A meta-analysis indicates strong support for attribution theory hypotheses across the fields of performance appraisal, motivation, and leadership. At the same time the data indicated that this same conclusion could be generalized from laboratory to field studies.

Many of the studies utilized dealt with matters extending well outside the domain of attribution theory applied to poor performance as discussed in Chapter 11, although a few studies within that domain were included. More significant for present purposes is the fact that there were only fourteen studies dealing with leadership at all (roughly 20 percent of the total); the number of field leadership studies was well below what would normally be required for meta-analysis. Furthermore, the field studies that were utilized relate to attributions at lower organizational levels, not at the executive level with which the Lord theory is concerned. All in all it does not seem appropriate to apply the DeVader, Bateson, and Lord (1986) findings to the later theory, and in fact Lord and Maher (1991a) do not attempt to do so.

Individual and Cultural Differences

In the early period implicit theories of leadership were considered to be very similar, at least within a single culture. Thus consideration and initiating structure ratings were seen as to a large extent reflections of implicit theories and categorizations held in common by a large number of followers, and indeed other perceivers of leadership as well. This does not mean that the results of all studies employing leader behavior ratings are totally invalidated as Chemers (1997) points out. But it does mean that implicit theories shared by many have now come to encroach upon the variance previously thought to be the province of leader behavior only.

A problem arises, however, with the finding that individual differences are related to the implicit theories held by followers. This suggests that implicit theories of leadership are, to some degree at least, an individual matter, rather than being held in common within a culture. At present it is not clear just how universal, versus individual, implicit theories of leadership are. That question can only be answered through research outside the laboratory, which remains to be done.

This problem is compounded by the finding that the cultures of the United States and Japan produce very different implicit theories of leadership. Theory proposes that these implicit theories are indeed culture bound, but what about the perceptual processes of Japanese Americans? The point is that cultural differences can merge into group and individual differences, and may well produce substantial variations from universality. House and Aditya (1997) call for a much wider investigation of cultural differences in leadership perceptions; this seems essential if the universality problem is to be unraveled. We need to know just how much the categorization processes of different cultures, groups, and individuals have in common.

A related question has to do with the frequency with which different information processing approaches are used. Lord and his colleagues put substantial stress on the role of automatic processes at the expense of reasoning, especially in their treatment of attributions. Yet in Chapter 11 evidence is considered indicating that controlled processes are more pervasive than Lord indicates. It is not surprising that a person who has identified a wholly new phenomenon in the leadership field (implicit theories) might overgeneralize the impact of that phenomenon, pushing the limits as far as they would go. But ultimately we need to know how people around the United States and around the world are predisposed to use one information processing approach or another. Knowledge of the demographics of information processing could prove immensely valuable. These issues, including such matters as how expert processing comes into being, are understood to be important by the theory's authors (Lord and Maher 1989).

Evaluation of the Subsequent Theorizing

A question remains as to the status of the subsequent theorizing dealing with follower self-identity. A certain amount of general research support related to these propositions is marshaled in connection with their presentation, enough research to make them plausible and palatable. However, this support is rarely focused on these specific formulations as tests; Lord and Brown (2004) repeatedly note gaps in the existing research findings and the speculative nature of their thinking. They indicate that "the theory that was developed was based on extensive social science research; nevertheless, it reflects our interpretation and our inferences from this research . . . it needs to be empirically tested" (210).

A check of the references in the Lord and Brown (2004) volume indicates that there are twenty-two authored by one or both of the authors in the period since 1999 when the theory was first proposed in some form. Most of these that have been published do not contain reports of original research. However, such reports are contained in citations noted as submitted, in preparation, unpublished, and the like; fourteen of these exist, 64 percent of the total. My point is that the research engine is indeed being revved up once again, but full reports of these studies are not yet part of the literature. Thus, it is too soon to make any kind of meaningful evaluation of follower self-identity theory; the needed information simply is not yet available. Furthermore, the relation between the 1999 and 2004 propositions needs clarification. Are all of these propositions still standing, or are those 1999 statements that were not retained now defunct?

Although an overall review of the subsequent theorizing does not seem warranted at this time, I do want to repeat a point that I have made in the past (Foti and Miner 2003) that applies to information processing theory as a whole. As Lowe and Gardner (2000) note, context in any form has been understudied in the leadership field. Context specified in terms of organizational forms, although considered occasionally (e.g., see Mumford, Zaccaro, Harding, Jacobs, and Fleishman 2000), has been given even less attention. In my view this is a great oversight. Leadership needs to be studied in the context of the type of organization or organizational component in which it occurs. Information processing theory would benefit from incorporating variables of this kind, and it is less effective to the extent that it neglects this aspect of theorizing.

As indicated previously, information processing theory has implications for leadership practice, but little has been done to cast these implications in usable form. Lord and Brown (2004) discuss this issue further, noting that "leaders face a rather daunting task in terms of understanding differences among subordinates in identity levels . . . the social perceptiveness requirement exceeds the capabilities of even the most sensitive individuals" (66). They go on to suggest systematic assessment of subordinates and leadership training as approaches to overcoming this problem, but they do not get specific. Elsewhere they say that "the direct application of our model remains a distant goal, one dependent on the outcomes of future empirical tests" (201), and that "our discussion of applied relevance was mainly to show how the theory could be useful, but suggestions should be carefully assessed with validation studies as part of their application" (210). I would agree with the authors that this is not a theory that is as yet ready for practical application. Consonant with this conclusion, Aditya, House, and Kerr (2000), while providing a generally favorable evaluation of information processing theory's validity, do not discuss the theory at all in their section on practice.

CONCLUSIONS

The evaluations presented at the beginning of the chapter depict a rather strange picture. The importance rating at 3 stars, 3.84 actually, is among the lowest of theories featured in this book. Of course, this is very good company indeed, so the value obtained is not really that low, but it does seem surprising. Perhaps the problem is that peers within organizational behaviors are reacting to the strangeness of this approach to theorizing, which breaks dramatically with the emphasis on leader behavior that has dominated the field for so long. In any event this importance rating is at variance with an estimated validity of 4 stars, which seems to be entirely justified based on the large body of research supporting the initial information processing formulations. This rating does not include any evaluation of the follower self-identity theorizing, one way or the other, on the grounds that insufficient time has elapsed to permit an assessment of this body of theory. The estimated usefulness figure, at 1 star, drops off to a very low value simply because no specific applications exist. The theories' authors recognize the need for practical implementations, and the potential is clearly there, but this is quite complex material, and to be used, it needs to be formatted specifically for that purpose.

In the chapter that follows we consider another theory that takes off in a different direction than the prevailing trend. Leadership substitutes accomplish this in a unique way, however. Yet along with information processing theory, the theory to which we now turn serves to expand the domain of leadership theory to a substantial degree.

REFERENCES

Aditya, Ram N., House, Robert J., and Kerr, Steven (2000). Theory and Practice of Leadership: Into the New Millennium. In Cary L. Cooper and Edwin A. Locke (Eds.), *Industrial and Organizational Psychology: Linking Theory with Practice*. Oxford, UK: Blackwell, 130–65.

Baumgardner, Terri L., Lord, Robert G., and Maher, Karen J. (1991). Perceptions of Women in Management. In Robert G. Lord and Karen J. Maher, *Leadership and Information Processing: Linking Perceptions and Performance*. Boston, MA: Unwin Hyman, 95–113.

Binning, John F., and Lord, Robert G. (1980). Boundary Conditions for Performance Cue Effects on Group Process Ratings: Familiarity versus Type of Feedback. *Organizational Behavior and Human Performance*, 26, 115–30.

Brown, Douglas J., and Lord, Robert J. (2001). Leadership and Perceiver Cognition: Moving Beyond First Order Constructs. In Manuel London (Ed.), *How People Evaluate Others in Organizations*. Mahwah, NJ: Lawrence Erlbaum, 181–202.

Chemers, Martin M. (1997). *An Integrative Theory of Leadership*. Mahwah, NJ: Lawrence Erlbaum.

Dansereau, Fred (1995). A Dyadic Approach to Leadership: Creating and Nurturing this Approach under Fire. *Leadership Quarterly*, 6, 479–90.

Day, David V., and Lord, Robert G. (1988). Executive Leadership and Organizational Performance: Suggestions for a New Theory and Methodology. *Journal of Management*, 14, 453–64.

DeVader, Christy L., Bateson, Allan G., and Lord, Robert G. (1986). Attribution Theory: A Meta-Analysis of Attributional Hypotheses. In Edwin A. Locke (Ed.), *Generalizing from Laboratory to Field Settings*. Lexington, MA: D.C. Heath, 63–81.

Engle, Elaine M., and Lord, Robert G. (1997). Implicit Theories, Self-Schemas, and Leader–Member Exchange. *Academy of Management Journal*, 40, 988–1010.

Foti, Roseanne J., Fraser, Scott L., and Lord, Robert G. (1982). Effects of Leadership Labels and Prototypes on Perceptions of Political Leaders. *Journal of Applied Psychology*, 67, 326–33.

Foti, Roseanne J., and Hauenstein, N. M. A. (2004). Linking Leadership Emergence to Leadership Effectiveness in a Military Context. Working paper, Virginia Polytechnic Institute and State University, Blacksburg, VA, 1–46.

Foti, Roseanne J., and Lord, Robert G. (1987). Prototypes and Scripts: The Effects of Alternative Methods of Processing Information on Rating Accuracy. *Organizational Behavior and Human Decision Processes*, 39, 318–40.

Foti, Roseanne J., and Miner, John B. (2003). Individual Differences and Organizational Forms in the Leadership Process. *Leadership Quarterly*, 14, 83–112.

Gioia, Dennis A. (1993). Review of *Leadership and Information Processing*. *Academy of Management Review*, 18, 153–56.

Green, Stephen G., and Mitchell, Terence R. (1979). Attributional Processes of Leaders in Leader–Member Interactions. *Organizational Behavior and Human Performance*, 23, 429–58.

Hall, Rosalie J., and Lord, Robert G. (1995). Multi-Level Information-Processing Explanations of Followers' Leadership Perceptions. *Leadership Quarterly*, 6, 265–87.

House, Robert J., and Aditya, Ram N. (1997). The Social Scientific Study of Leadership: Quo Vadis? *Journal of Management*, 23, 409–73.

Keller, Tiffany (1999). Images of the Familiar: Individual Differences and Implicit Leadership Theories. *Leadership Quarterly*, 10, 589–607.

——— (2003). Parental Images as a Guide to Leadership Sensemaking: An Attachment Perspective on Implicit Leadership Theories. *Leadership Quarterly*, 14, 141–60.

Larson, James R. (1982). Cognitive Mechanisms Mediating the Impact of Implicit Theories of Leader Behavior on Leader Behavior Ratings. *Organizational Behavior and Human Performance*, 29, 129–40.

Lord, Robert G. (1976). Group Performance as a Function of Leadership Behavior and Task Structure: Toward an Explanatory Theory. *Organizational Behavior and Human Performance*, 17, 76–96.

——— (1977). Functional Leadership Behavior: Measurement and Relation to Social Power and Leadership Perceptions. *Administrative Science Quarterly*, 22, 114–33.

——— (1985). An Information Processing Approach to Social Perceptions, Leadership and Behavioral Measurement in Organizations. *Research in Organizational Behavior*, 7, 87–128.

——— (1995). An Alternative Perspective on Attributional Processes. In Mark J. Martinko (Ed.), *Attribution Theory: An Organizational Perspective*. Delray Beach, FL: St. Lucie Press, 333–50.

Lord, Robert G., Binning, John F., Rush, Michael C., and Thomas, Jay C. (1978). The Effect of Performance Cues and Leader Behavior on Questionnaire Ratings of Leadership Behavior. *Organizational Behavior and Human Performance*, 21, 27–39.

Lord, Robert G., and Brown, Douglas J. (2004). *Leadership Processes and Follower Self-Identity*. Mahwah, NJ: Lawrence Erlbaum.

Lord, Robert G., Brown, Douglas J., and Freiberg, Steven J. (1999). Understanding the Dynamics of Leadership: The Role of Follower Self-Concepts in the Leader/Follower Relationship. *Organizational Behavior and Human Decision Processes*, 78, 167–203.

Lord, Robert G., Brown, Douglas J., and Harvey, Jennifer L. (2001). System Constraints on Leadership Perceptions, Behavior, and Influence: An Example of Connectionist Level Processes. In Michael A. Hogg and R. Scott Tindale (Eds.), *Blackwell Handbook of Social Psychology: Group Processes*. Oxford, UK: Blackwell, 283–310.

Lord, Robert G., Brown, Douglas J., Harvey, Jennifer L., and Hall, Rosalie J. (2001). Contextual Constraints on Prototype Generation and Their Multilevel Consequences for Leadership Perceptions. *Leadership Quarterly*, 12, 311–38.

Lord, Robert G., and Emrich, Cynthia G. (2000). Thinking Outside the Box by Looking Inside the Box: Extending the Cognitive Revolution in Leadership Research. *Leadership Quarterly*, 11, 551–79.

Lord, Robert G., Foti, Roseanne J., and DeVader, Christy L. (1984). A Test of Leadership Categorization Theory: Internal Structure, Information Processing, and Leadership Perceptions. *Organizational Behavior and Human Performance*, 34, 343–78.

Lord, Robert G., Foti, Roseanne J., and Phillips, James S. (1982). A Theory of Leadership Categorization. In James G. Hunt, Uma Sekaran, and Chester A. Schriesheim (Eds.), *Leadership—Beyond Establishment Views*. Carbondale, IL: Southern Illinois University Press, 104–21.

Lord, Robert G., and Hall, Rosalie J. (1992). Contemporary Views of Leadership and Individual Differences. *Leadership Quarterly*, 3, 137–57.

Lord, Robert G., and Kernan, Mary C. (1987). Scripts as Determinants of Purposeful Behavior in Organizations. *Academy of Management Review*, 12, 265–77.

Lord, Robert G., and Maher, Karen J. (1989). Cognitive Processes in Industrial and Organizational Psychology. *International Review of Industrial and Organizational Psychology*, 4, 49–91.

——— (1990). Alternative Information-Processing Models and Their Implications for Theory, Research, and Practice. *Academy of Management Review*, 15, 9–28.

——— (1991a). *Leadership and Information Processing: Linking Perceptions and Performance*. Boston, MA: Unwin Hyman.

——— (1991b). Cognitive Theory in Industrial and Organizational Psychology. In Marvin D. Dunnette and Leaette M. Hough (Eds.), *Handbook of Industrial and Organizational Psychology*, Vol. 2. Palo Alto, CA: Consulting Psychologists Press, 1–62.

Lord, Robert G., Phillips, James S., and Rush, Michael C. (1980). Effects of Sex and Personality on Perceptions of Emergent Leadership, Influence, and Social Power. *Journal of Applied Psychology*, 65, 176–82.

Lord, Robert G., and Smith, Wendy G. (1999). Leadership and the Changing Nature of Performance. In

Daniel R. Ilgen and Elaine D. Pulakos (Eds.), *The Changing Nature of Performance: Implications for Staffing, Motivation, and Development.* San Francisco, CA: Jossey-Bass, 192–239.

Lowe, Kevin B., and Gardner, William L. (2000). Ten Years of the *Leadership Quarterly:* Contributions and Challenges for the Future. *Leadership Quarterly*, 11, 459–514.

Miles, Raymond E., and Snow, Charles C. (1978). *Organizational Strategy, Structure, and Process.* New York: McGraw-Hill.

Miner, John B. (2002). *Organizational Behavior: Foundations, Theories, and Analyses.* New York: Oxford University Press.

Mumford, Michael D., Zaccaro, Stephen J., Harding, Francis D., Jacobs, T. Owen, and Fleishman, Edwin A. (2000). Leadership Skills for a Changing World: Solving Complex Social Problems. *Leadership Quarterly*, 11, 11–35.

Newell, Allen, and Simon, Herbert A. (1972). *Human Problem Solving.* Englewood Cliffs, NJ: Prentice-Hall.

Palich, Leslie E., and Hom, Peter W. (1992). The Impact of Leader Power and Behavior on Leadership Perceptions: A LISREL Test of an Expanded Categorization Theory of Leadership Model. *Group and Organization Management*, 17, 279–96.

Phillips, James S., and Lord, Robert G. (1981). Causal Attributions and Perceptions of Leadership. *Organizational Behavior and Human Performance*, 28, 143–63.

——— (1982). Schematic Information Processing and Perceptions of Leadership in Problem-Solving Groups. *Journal of Applied Psychology*, 67, 486–92.

Pitcher, Patricia, Chreim, Samia, and Kisfalvi, Veronika (2000). CEO Succession Research: Methodological Bridges over Troubled Waters. *Strategic Management Journal*, 21, 625–48.

Rush, Michael C., Phillips, James S., and Lord, Robert G. (1981). Effects of a Temporal Delay in Rating on Leader Behavior Descriptions: A Laboratory Investigation. *Journal of Applied Psychology*, 66, 442–50.

Rush, Michael C., Thomas, Jay C., and Lord, Robert G. (1977). Implicit Leadership Theory: A Potential Threat to the Internal Validity of Leader Behavior Questionnaires. *Organizational Behavior and Human Performance*, 20, 93–110.

Weber, Roberto, Camerer, Colin, Rottenstreich, Yuval, and Knez, Marc (2001). The Illusion of Leadership: Misattribution of Cause in Coordination Games. *Organization Science*, 12, 582–98.

Weick, Karl E. (1993). Review of *Leadership and Information Processing. Leadership Quarterly*, 4, 109–13.

Zaccaro, Stephen J. (2001). *The Nature of Executive Leadership: A Conceptual and Empirical Analysis of Success.* Washington, DC: American Psychological Association.

CHAPTER 16

SUBSTITUTES FOR LEADERSHIP

STEVEN KERR

Background
How the Substitutes Formulations Evolved
    Implications for Organizational Design
    Meaning and Measurement
    Controlling the Performance of People
    Moderator Variables
    Alternatives to Ineffective Leadership
    Later Observations
Evaluation and Impact
    Research at the Inception
    Psychometric Properties
    Moderator Analyses
    Main Effects
    Reactions Within the Field
    Repositioning the Theory
Conclusions

Importance rating	★ ★ ★ ★
Estimated validity	★ ★ ★
Estimated usefulness	★ ★ ★
Decade of origin	1970s

Substitutes for leadership theory is best considered in the context of the existing leadership theory of the period in which it emerged. The dominant thrust at that time was to emphasize the leader behaviors and styles used by lower-level leaders in hierarchic organizational systems. Thus "substitutes" meant something other than the behaviors of these first-level supervisors, and by implication the theory clearly rejected the idea that an understanding of these behaviors is the key to unraveling the enigma of organizational functioning. There is much more to it than that, and the theory set out to establish what exactly that "more" is.

BACKGROUND

Steven Kerr's career has extended back and forth across the academic and corporate worlds several times. Kerr was born in 1941. Educated at the Baruch School of the City University of New York, he began work on an MBA there while a programmer for Mobil Oil—part of some eight years spent in industry in the New York City area. He was recruited into the doctoral program at CUNY by Robert House, and House remained his mentor throughout his doctoral studies (Frost 1997). From there he moved to the business faculty at Ohio State for seven years. Next came a lengthy period at the University of Southern California, where Kerr held a variety of administrative appointments within the business school. This association tailed off into several years on leave doing consulting, primarily with General Electric; this was in 1992–93.

After a visiting appointment at the University of Michigan, which still permitted considerable consulting, Kerr ultimately moved to General Electric on a full-time basis where he became vice president of Corporate Leadership Development with responsibility for the company's management development operation at Crotonville, NY. In 2001 he moved back to New York City and became chief learning officer and a managing director of Goldman Sachs (Greiner 2002).

The full theory with which we are concerned here was published early in the University of Southern California years, after Kerr had left Ohio State, which had been the primary source of the behavior description thrust in the leadership field. However, much of the development work on the theory and some early formulations on the subject emanated from the Ohio State period. Kerr received his Ph.D. from CUNY in 1973, and the basic theory first appeared in print four years later. He was president of the Academy of Management in the late 1980s.

Kerr often has utilized a strategy of building upon an existing theory that had already become widely recognized and well established, a strategy employed by House as well. He joined House in preparing a second edition of a book grounded in classical management theory (Filley, House, and Kerr 1976). He wrote a very influential piece on the use of rewards to motivate behavior in organizations entitled "On the Folly of Rewarding A, While Hoping for B" (see Kerr 2003), which was grounded in Edward Thorndike's law of effect (circa 1900). His substitutes for leadership theory was built upon a structure of prior contributions of a related nature, including House's own path–goal theory (see Miner 2002).

There is certainly nothing wrong with this strategic approach to theorizing; in fact, it has the value of adding directly to the current body of knowledge in a field and keeping promising theories at the center of scientific attention. The only proviso is that the new theory must indeed add something new, and thus extend understanding in significant ways. There is no question that Kerr's theorizing, especially substitutes for leadership theory, has done this.

HOW THE SUBSTITUTES FORMULATIONS EVOLVED

I have indicated that the basic substitutes for leadership theory was a product of the 1977–78 time period. But Kerr had been using the terminology and providing examples of what he had in mind over several years prior to that. These early statements did not incorporate a truly systematic approach to theory development, however; they were typically appended to a treatment of some other leadership topic, and were brief in nature (Schriesheim 1997).

Implications for Organizational Design

Characteristically, Kerr (1977) presents the theory initially as if it were an adjunct to the topic of organizational design. However, it soon becomes apparent that this time the real topic of concern is substitutes for leadership whatever their nature. The latter are described as often serving to neutralize or substitute for a formal leader's ability to influence work group satisfaction and performance. Examples noted are:

1. In the subordinate—ability, experience, training, knowledge, professional orientation, need for independence, and indifference to organizational rewards.

2. In the task—repetitiveness and unambiguity, methodological invariance, intrinsic satisfaction, and task-provided feedback on accomplishments.
3. In the organization—formalization, inflexibility, highly specified and active advisory or staff functions, closely knit and cohesive work groups, rewards outside the leader's control, and spatial distance between the leader and the subordinates.

The thrust of the presentation is evident from the following quote—

> If the existence of substitutes for hierarchical leadership is ignored, then efforts at leadership training, organizational development, and task design may well result in ineffectiveness for the organization and frustration for its members, as they come to realize that inflexible policies, invariant work methodologies, or other barriers . . . are interfering with intended changes and preventing desired benefits. (Kerr 1977, 139)

In this view substitutes are seen primarily as barriers that prevent such measures as human relations training and organization development from actually changing the organization, even though they may change the leader. Yet Kerr (1977) was also influenced by certain other work in which he was involved dealing with professionals (Kerr, Von Glinow, and Schriesheim 1977). Thus, he recognized that many aspects of professionals and their training (norms, standards, knowledge, independence, etc.) could serve to substitute for leader influence and at the same time create opportunities. Substitutes and their nature need to be given more attention. They need not only to be clearly identified, but in certain instances need to be systematically created.

Meaning and Measurement

The next presentation of the theory (Kerr and Jermier 1978) included considerable research, which we will consider shortly. The theoretical statement applied the substitutes considered previously to two leader behaviors—consideration and initiating structure—thus creating what amount to hypotheses regarding specific neutralization effects. Table 16.1 is the result. Feedback on performance may derive from the task itself or from other people—primary work group members, staff personnel, the client. If these types of instances prevail, the formal leader's role in performance feedback may be trivial.

A distinction is made between substitutes and neutralizers. *Neutralizers* make it impossible for the leader behaviors noted to make any difference. They are a type of moderator variable when they are uncorrelated with either predictor or criterion. They act as suppressor variables when correlated with predictors, but not the criterion. *Substitutes* make the leader behaviors not only impossible but unnecessary. They "may be correlated with both predictors and the criterion, but tend to improve the validity coefficient when included in the predictor set. . . . [S]ubstitutes do, but neutralizers do not, provide a 'person or thing acting or used in place of' the formal leader's negated influence. The effect of neutralizers is therefore to create an 'influence vacuum' from which a variety of dysfunctions may emerge" (Kerr and Jermier 1978, 395). Strictly speaking, the characteristics of Table 16.1 are all neutralizers, but not all need be substitutes.

A further distinction is made between direct and indirect leader effects. A *direct effect* occurs when a subordinate is influenced by a leader behavior in and of itself. An *indirect effect* occurs when a subordinate is influenced by the implications of the leader behavior for some future con-

Table 16.1

Neutralization Effects of Substitutes for Leadership on Two Types of Leader Behavior

Characteristic	Will tend to neutralize	
	Relationship-oriented, supportive, people-centered leadership; consideration, support, and interaction facilitation	Task-oriented, instrumental, job-centered leadership; initiating structure, goal emphasis, and work facilitation
Of the subordinate		
1. ability, experience, training, knowledge		X
2. need for independence	X	X
3. "professional" orientation	X	X
4. indifference toward organizational rewards	X	X
Of the task		
5. unambiguous and routine		X
6. methodologically invariant		X
7. provides its own feedback concerning accomplishment		X
8. intrinsically satisfying	X	
Of the organization		
9. formalization (explicit plans, goals, and areas of responsibility)		X
10. inflexibility (rigid, unbending rules and procedures)		X
11. highly specified and active advisory and staff functions		X
12. closely knit, cohesive work groups	X	X
13. organizational rewards not within the leader's control	X	X
14. spatial distance between superior and subordinates	X	X

Source: Kerr and Jermier (1978, 378). Copyright © 1978 Academic Press. Reprinted with permission.

sequence such as rewards. A factor can substitute for one type of effect without substituting for the other. The direct-indirect differentiation made here is not the same as the one used in Lord and Maher's formulations (see Chapter 15).

The theory assumes, but does not specify, additional types of leader behaviors beyond consideration and initiating structure, each of which will have its own set of neutralizers and substitutes. Further extensions to the theory should also specify at what point a particular substitute becomes important (the threshold) and how substitutes combine to create a barrier to leader influence (interaction effects). The goal is to learn how things are accomplished in organizations, whether or not they are activated by hierarchical leadership.

Kerr's coauthor in this article, John Jermier, was a graduate student at Ohio State at the time, whose primary interests were of a macro nature and who identified more with sociology than with the prevailing psychological orientation of the Ohio State program. He saw the substitutes formulations as a means of dealing with the kinds of variables that held the greatest interest for him (Jermier and Kerr 1997).

Controlling the Performance of People

Kerr's next coauthor, in contrast, was an established contributor to the organizational behavior field who had been a visiting professor at Ohio State during Kerr's tenure there (Kerr and Slocum 1981). This piece deals with the topic of control in organizations in a general sense, but devotes considerable space to control via substitutes for leadership. Control by leaders is described as often time-consuming, detrimental to subordinate development, and weak. Thus, a case is made that control by substitutes can be the more effective mechanism.

The classification system used in this presentation to identify substitutes differs somewhat from that used previously. Substitutes for hierarchy used to obtain organizational control are specified as falling into four classes—task, professional orientation, work groups, and organizational development and training programs. Assuming that the latter efforts may indeed be parceled out among hierarchic, task, professional, and group types, this classification system looks much like the one specified by Miner (see Chapter 17). This classification approach is then applied to the mechanistic-organic differentiation as set forth by Burns and Stalker (see Miner 2002). Table 16.2 presents the results. Note that the list of leader behaviors considered is now expanded well beyond the original two. These leader behaviors, of whatever type, are a primary source of control in mechanistic (hierarchic) organizations; substitutes operate most strongly in organic (professional) organizations.

Moderator Variables

In an attempt to improve upon the original treatment of moderator variables within the theory, Kerr joined forces with two scholars at New Mexico State University who had been conducting research on substitutes theory (Howell, Dorfman, and Kerr 1986). The presentation attempts to focus on the mechanisms by which moderators operate and establishes a typology of moderators as follows:

1. Leadership neutralizers/enhancers
2. Leadership substitutes/supplements
3. Leadership mediators

Neutralizers interrupt the predictive relationship between the leader behavior and criteria; they remain much as previously defined. *Enhancers* serve to augment relationships between leader behaviors and criteria, but like neutralizers they have little if any influence on the criteria themselves. Enhancers represent a positive moderating influence, as opposed to neutralizers, which represent a negative moderating influence. This neutralizer/enhancer idea differs from the previous neutralizer concept as follows:

1. It acknowledges the existence of partial neutralizers, removing the need to completely eliminate a leader behavior's impact in order to identify a neutralizer variable.
2. By adding the enhancer dimension, it recognizes that some moderators . . . have the potential to augment as well as neutralize leader behavior-criterion relationships.
3. It recognizes the possibility that neutralizers/enhancers may have a main effect on the criterion as predictors in a multiple regression equation (Howell, Dorfman, and Kerr 1986, 91).

Table 16.2

Effects of Various Organizational Characteristics on Members' Task-relevant Information and Motivation in Mechanistic and Organic Organizations

	Sources of information or motivation	
	Mechanistic organizations	Organic organizations
Formal roles	Information, yes: functions, powers, methods, and responsibilities are explicit, though some ambiguity remains. Motivation, no.	No: position differentiation—based on expertise—exists, but the concept of responsibility as a limited field of rights and obligations does not exist.
Leadership behaviors		
Role clarification	Yes: mechanistic systems are characterized by superior-subordinate role making, in the form of instructions and decisions.	No: tasks are continually redefined through interactions with peers; however, role conflict and ambiguity are usually prevalent.
Goal setting	Yes: goal setting by superiors is a source of task-relevant information, and of motivation under certain conditions.	No: goals are set by each person in interaction with other people, possibly including, but certainly not primarily with, superiors.
Leader initiation of structure	Yes: task-relevant knowledge is assumed to increase with hierarchical level, and the superior's job is to reconcile subordinates' performances. Motivation can also be increased under certain conditions.	No: task-relevant knowledge is assumed to reside everywhere in the network.
Feedback	Yes: formal leaders provide task-relevant information through feedback, and motivation under certain conditions.	No: feedback stems primarily from peers.
Consideration and stroking	Information, no; motivation, sometimes: consideration by leaders is more necessary in mechanistic systems because jobs tend to be routine and uninteresting.	No.
Participative leadership	No: though exceptions exist, participative leadership is uncharacteristic of mechanistic systems.	Yes, under conditions such as those specified. Participative leadership is one of the principal ways that formal leaders exert influence in organic systems.
Charismatic leadership	Information, not usually; motivation, sometimes: charisma does not often exist but is most likely to be attributed to leaders who are physically and hierarchically distant.	No: day-to-day intimacy almost invariably destroys impressions of charisma.

(continued)

Table 16.2 (continued)

	Sources of information or motivation	
	Mechanistic organizations	Organic organizations
Administration of rewards and punishments	Information, no; motivation, yes, to the extent that rewards and punishments are linked to task-relevant behaviors.	Information, no; motivation, yes, to the extent that rewards and punishments are linked to task-relevant behaviors.
Substitutes for formal leadership behaviors		
Tasks	Information, yes, because tasks are likely to be highly predictable; motivation, no.	Information, not usually, because tasks tend to be unstructured. However, tasks in organic systems tend to be closely related to organizational ends, so task provided feedback is possible. Motivation, yes, because tasks tend to be high in identity, significance, and other aspects characteristic of enriched jobs.
Professional orientation	No, not in the sense of informal norms and values. If professional expertise is necessary, formal staff functions are usually created.	Yes: autonomy, commitment to calling, and the other attributes of a professional orientation are highly valued in organic organizations.
Work group	Information, no; motivation, sometimes, when conditions such as those specified exist. Differentiation of tasks, combined with emphasis upon vertical channels of communication, often prevent groups in mechanistic systems from contributing to members' motivation.	Yes, particularly when conditions such as those specified exist.
Organizational development and training	Yes: skills training is often emphasized.	Yes: conceptual, interpersonal, and team-building methods are often emphasized.

Source: Kerr and Slocum (1981, 130). Copyright © 1981 Oxford University Press. Reprinted with permission.

Figure 16.1   **Causal Model Showing the Roles of Leader Behaviors, Moderators, and Mediators**

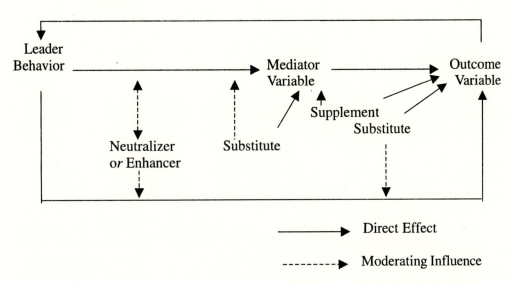

Source: Howell, Dorfman, and Kerr (1986, 97). Copyright © 1986 Academy of Management. Reprinted with permission.

Substitutes also remain as previously defined. However, three criteria must be met for a variable to qualify as a substitute:

1. There must be a logical reason why the leader behavior and the potential substitute should provide the guidance and/or good feeling indicated by the criterion measure.
2. The potential substitute must be a neutralizer-moderator; at certain levels of the moderator it must weaken the leader behavior's effect on the criterion.
3. The potential substitute must have an important impact on the criterion; increasing levels of the substitute result in higher criterion levels (Howell, Dorfman, and Kerr 1986, 92).

Supplements have the effect that they serve to supplement, rather than neutralize and replace, the leader's ability to influence a criterion. In contrast to substitutes, which produce low leader behavior impact and high criterion levels, supplements do not influence leader behavior, yet they do result in higher criterion levels.

Mediators represent an intermediate step between leader behavior and a criterion, a step that operates as part of a causal chain; as such mediators must be correlated with both the leader behavior and the criterion. This mediation process may be partial or complete, although the former is more typical.

The way in which these moderator concepts operate is depicted in Figure 16.1. Suppressor variables are not included there, or in the theory, because they are viewed as statistical artifacts with high conceptual ambiguity, which in any event are rarely found in the organizational behavior field.

Alternatives to Ineffective Leadership

Up until the early 1990s, Kerr limited his discussions of theoretical applications to urging companies to introduce and expand the use of substitutes. This changed with an article coauthored with a number of people who had been contributing research on the theory (Howell, Bowen, Dorfman, Kerr, and Podsakoff 1990). The thrust of this article was that substitutes should be used as remedies for problems created by ineffective and weak leadership. Special mention is made of the use of closely knit teams of highly trained individuals, of intrinsic satisfaction in the work, of computer technology especially as it provides immediate feedback, and of extensive professional education.

The treatment of what to do in dealing with specific problems is now quite detailed, as indicated by Table 16.3. The suggested solutions are presented as examples of the many possibilities that can be invoked to deal with the various leadership problems noted. Also, a decision tree is utilized to show when substitutes might be most appropriate. These circumstances are as follows:

- Create substitutes when the traits and/or personality of the problem leader are inadequate *and* replacement of that leader is for some reason not feasible.
- Create substitutes when the traits and/or personality of the problem leader are adequate, the skills and/or knowledge of that leader are inadequate, *and* training the leader is not feasible.
- Eliminate neutralizers but create enhancers when the traits/personality are adequate *and* the skills/knowledge are adequate.

A listing of creative substitutes for an emphasis on leader behavior includes developing collegial systems of guidance (peer appraisals, quality circles), improving performance-oriented formalization (commission payment, group management by objectives [MBO]), increasing administrative staff availability (training personnel, human relations troubleshooters), increasing the professionalism of subordinates (staffing with professionals, development planning), redesigning jobs to increase inherent performance feedback and ideological importance, and starting team-building activities to develop group self-management skills in solving work problems as well as resolving conflicts and providing support. A similar listing of creative enhancers includes increasing subordinate perception of leader influence and expertise, building organizational climate, increasing leader position power, and creating cohesive work groups with high-performance norms.

Later Observations

The final additions to the theory derive from a retrospective that appears to have been written primarily by John Jermier, the former graduate student at Ohio State with a macro perspective (Jermier and Kerr 1997). This piece is significant more for its shift in emphasis than for its original contribution of content.

The emphasis on moderators of the leader behavior-criterion relationships that had been developing steadily over the years is now downplayed. In contrast, the main effects from substitutes to criteria or outcomes are stressed. This view is epitomized in the following:

> It is not the study of interpersonal interactions between managerial leaders and subordinate followers that is the core of the substitutes for leadership framework, but the idea that managerial leadership works through technological, structural, and other impersonal processes

309

Table 16.3

Effective Coping Strategies That Might Be Used to Deal with Specific Leadership Problems

Leadership problems	Enhancer/Neutralizer	Substitutes
Leader doesn't keep on top of details in the department; coordination among subordinates is difficult.	Not useful.	Develop self-managed work teams; encourage team members to interact within and across departments.
Competent leadership is resisted through noncompliance or passive resistance.	*Enhancers:* Increase employees' dependence on leader through greater leader control of rewards/resources; increase their perception of leader's influence outside of work group.	Develop collegial systems of guidance for decision making.
Leader doesn't provide support or recognition for jobs well done.	Not useful.	Develop a reward system that operates independently of the leader. Enrich jobs to make them inherently satisfying.
Leader doesn't set targets or goals, or clarify roles for employees.	Not useful.	Emphasize experience and ability in selecting subordinates. Establish group goal setting. Develop an organizational culture that stresses high performance expectations.
A leader behaves inconsistently over time.	*Enhancers:* These are dysfunctional. *Neutralizers:* Remove rewards from leader's control	Develop group goal setting and group rewards.
An upper-level manager regularly bypasses a leader in dealing with employees, or countermands the leader's directions.	*Enhancers:* Increase leader's control over rewards and resources; build leader's image via in-house champion or visible "important" responsibilities. *Neutralizer:* Physically distance subordinates from upper-level manager.	Increase the professionalization of employees.
A unit is in disarray or out of control.	Not useful.	Develop highly formalized plans, goals, routines, and areas of responsibility.
Leadership is brutal, autocratic.	*Enhancers:* These are dysfunctional. *Neutralizers:* Physically distance subordinates; remove rewards from leader's control.	Establish group goal setting and peer performance appraisal.
There is inconsistency across different organizational units.	Not useful.	Increase formalization. Set up a behaviorally focused reward system.
Leadership is unstable over time; leaders are rotated and/or leave office frequently.	Not useful.	Establish competent advisory staff units. Increase professionalism of employees.
Incumbent management is poor; there's no heir apparent.	*Enhancers:* These are dysfunctional. *Neutralizers:* Assign nonleader duties to problem managers.	Emphasize experience and ability in selecting employees. Give employees more training.

Source: Howell, Bowen, Dorfman, Kerr, and Podsakoff (1990, 28–29). Copyright © 1990 Elsevier Science. Reprinted with permission.

in the organization to achieve its effects. That is, formal leaders do attempt to control the organization, but they do so by making decisions that minimize the need for the face-to-face exercise of power. (Jermier and Kerr 1997, 98–99)

In line with this position the paper argues that greater attention should be given to the study of the substitutes themselves—how they are created, how they influence outcomes, and how leadership interactions change as a result. The idea that substitutes for leadership theory is essentially a contingency theory is given a distinctly secondary role for the future. The ties between substitutes theory and classic group dynamics theory are downplayed in favor of a more macro, sociological emphasis.

EVALUATION AND IMPACT

From the beginning substitutes theory has been closely tied to research. Measures were constructed at an early point, and Kerr and Jermier (1978) present research findings along with their statement of the theory. This set the stage for others, and indeed others have followed, most notably a group of researchers associated with Indiana University headed by Philip Podsakoff and Scott MacKenzie. The research is not as extensive as might be desired, but it is sufficient to answer a number of questions.

Research at the Inception

The first reported study was conducted using college students who completed a questionnaire intended to measure substitutes for leadership. The students were asked to assume the role of a popular television character who had been widely portrayed as a subordinate working for a particular boss; the characters were Mary Richards, Hawkeye Pierce, and Archie Bunker. Each student was asked to pick one character, or if unfamiliar with any character, take the role of a low-level assembly line worker.

The measures were short, containing for most of the substitutes only three items, although a few measures had from six to nine items. Yet the internal consistency reliabilities were good, ranging from 0.74 to 0.85 with a median of 0.80. Correlations among scales were as often positive as negative and tended to be low, with 60 percent under 0.20. High scores on the various scales were taken to indicate negation of leader influence and thus provided evidence for construct validity. The best evidence of this kind came from the ability-experience-training-knowledge scale, and thus focused on individual characteristics. However, some other substitutes appeared to operate as hypothesized also.

Also reported in Kerr and Jermier (1978) were two field studies conducted in police departments using the same questionnaire measure of various substitutes. Reliabilities calculated as before ranged from 0.53 to 0.85 with a median of 0.81 in one department and from 0.63 to 0.85 with a median of 0.77 in the other. Correlations among characteristics were again under 0.20 in the majority of instances. Once again the mean scores for ability-experience-training-knowledge were highest, but spatial distance and several other factors also appeared to be strong substitutes.

In one of the police departments, data were also collected to determine how the various substitutes and leader behaviors (consideration and initiating structure) influence outcomes (organizational commitment and role ambiguity). These data indicate that leader behavior influences are minimal as contrasted with the effects of substitutes such as intrinsically satisfying work and task-provided feedback. Yet aspects of initiating structure did appear to hold up against the onslaught of the various substitutes, and they remain independent predictors of outcomes. This aspect of the study is interpreted as supportive of the role of substitutes, but it also indicates that in any given context only certain substitutes will be operative and that leader behaviors may well not be eclipsed.

A study published only slightly later than the initial presentation of substitutes for leadership theory (Jermier and Berkes 1979), although mentioning the theory, focuses primarily on other issues. It too utilizes police subjects, but substitutes from the theoretically specified set are considered only tangentially and the hypotheses tested are derived from path–goal theory primarily, not substitutes theory. This does not appear to represent a true test of the theory in any comprehensive sense, and the findings vis-à-vis the stated hypotheses are mixed in any event.

Research continued during the early 1980s, but with inconclusive results. Two studies conducted in hospitals are typical, one of which used the Kerr and Jermier (1978) scales. This latter study (Howell and Dorfman 1981) utilized a moderator design with organizational commitment and job satisfaction as criteria. The authors describe their findings as providing only mixed support for theory; only organizational formalization operated as hypothesized, although several other potential substitutes yielded evidence of weak or partial influence. The second study (Sheridan, Vredenburgh, and Abelson 1984) operationalized the substitutes differently, and both added to and deleted from the theoretically specified list. The results, using a performance criterion, provide some support for the theory, but with differential influences from the various substitutes appearing in different contexts. Given these inconsistent results and the extent to which this research test departed from theoretical specifications, it is inappropriate to view this study as providing conclusive evidence for or against the theory.

All in all the field entered the mid-1980s with a positive disposition toward substitutes for leadership theory, but without adequate research findings to fully support that disposition. This is the point at which the Indiana University researchers began to exert an influence.

Psychometric Properties

One possible cause of the less than striking findings often reported in various studies is that, in spite of the Kerr and Jermier (1978) data, the reliabilities of their substitutes scales appear to be sufficiently low so as to limit the possibility of obtaining significant results. This problem was considered by Williams, Podsakoff, Todor, Huber, Howell and Dorfman (1988). They present internal consistency reliability data for six samples in which all, or in one instance most, of the substitutes were measured. These samples vary, but in no instance do they contain either students or police. The data follow:

1. range 0.25–0.86—median 0.53
2. range 0.32–0.84—median 0.59
3. range 0.40–0.80—median 0.60
4. range 0.35–0.81—median 0.59
5. range 0.36–0.70—median 0.52
6. range 0.37–0.83—median 0.59

Only one scale (organizational formalization) appears to have a reliability in the 0.80s and two (closely knit, cohesive groups and spatial distance) are in the 0.70s. For the rest the data seem to suggest that respondents do not have a clear picture of what is being asked. This in turn raises questions about the findings, or lack of same, from studies that utilized the Kerr and Jermier (1978) measures. It also raises questions regarding why internal consistency coefficients across multiple samples would decline by over 0.20 on the average from the authors' original analyses to those reported by Williams et al. (1988). Time, subjects, perhaps methods of calculation may all be involved, but this is not the type of difference that one finds often in psychometric research. One might think that findings like this would have triggered a resort to other types of reliability analysis beyond the internal consistency approach that has prevailed. Yet there are no reports of test-retest or parallel form analyses.

Correlations among the various substitutes measures remain low, as previously reported, and there is little evidence of social desirability effects. Analyses to establish the factor structure of the measures indicated that the items of certain measures loaded on a single factor, while in other instances this was not the case. Such factor purity is not essential to the construct validity of a measure, however (see Streiner 2003). There are numerous indexes in use possessing conceptual integrity without statistically loading on a single factor, which have contributed substantially to both understanding and prediction in organizational behavior. On the evidence one would have to hold that although factor purity has its benefits, it is not essential.

In any event, the reliability data did seem to indicate a need for new and better scales if substitutes for leadership research was to progress. Accordingly, the Indiana researchers undertook the task of constructing such scales (Podsakoff and MacKenzie 1994). Initially this effort involved writing many more items, although ultimately it proved possible to select an abbreviated set of items that accomplished much the same results.

The best estimates of internal consistency reliability for the longer and shorter measures created were as follows:

Longer: range 0.73–0.92—median 0.82
Shorter: range 0.70–0.91—median 0.77

Other evidence on the psychometric properties of these scales appeared to support their use. Factor loadings were on the hypothesized factors and the different scales remained empirically distinct. Correlations with known, independent variables, which were hypothesized to be significant as evidence of construct validity, were indeed significant in over twenty-five comparisons. If previous research using the Kerr and Jermier (1978) scales had been damaged by the measures used, the scales now available should help to correct this problem in subsequent research.

Moderator Analyses

A study carried out to test moderator relationships by Podsakoff, Todor, Grover, and Huber (1984) used the original Kerr and Jermier (1978) scales and found only 2 percent of the interactions to be significant at the 0.05 level. This lack of moderating effects might, of course, have been anticipated given the unreliability of the scales. The leader behavior utilized in this study involved leader administration of rewards and punishments, not consideration or initiating structure, but since this variable had been noted previously by Kerr and Slocum (1981)—see Table 16.2—its use would not seem to be at variance with the theory.

Subsequent studies to be discussed here emanating from Indiana replaced the original substitutes measures with one of the new ones. The first of these dealt with both the traditional consideration and initiating structure leader behaviors and reward and punishment behavior. Eight different outcome criteria were measured, four of them based on ratings by supervisors (Podsakoff, Niehoff, MacKenzie, and Williams 1993). Moderator effects were determined using the substitutes as specified by Howell, Dorfman, and Kerr (1986), and thus in accordance with the most recent directives from theory. Of the over 700 possible interactions, less than 3 percent were consistent with these theoretical criteria; the proportion of outcome variance thus accounted for was quite small. Overall, moderator effects identified were minimal. However, the paper does raise a question as to whether certain substitutes, such as group cohesiveness, might not have been produced by direct efforts from a leader. Are such substitutes really replacing leadership?

Another difficulty with the previous study is that the sample studied did not include professionals to any meaningful extent and thus may have failed to identify a major set of moderators. To remedy this difficulty, a sample with a substantial number of professionals was considered (Podsakoff, MacKenzie, and Fetter 1993). In most respects this research followed the same procedures as its predecessor. Again, the amount of support for moderator effects as specified by the revised theory (Howell, Dorfman, and Kerr 1986) is minimal. Furthermore, those effects identified in this new, more professional, sample are not at all consistent with the ones found previously. Whether this lack of consistency is at variance with theory is a matter of some disagreement; probably it is not in this instance, because of the wide variation in professional representation in the samples.

The next step by the Indiana researchers was an extensive literature review focused on moderator effects as specified both by path–goal theory and by substitutes for leadership theory (Podsakoff, MacKenzie, Ahearne, and Bommer 1995). Focusing on the latter only, and insofar as possible holding to the dictates of the theory, something less than 9 percent of the moderator effects found proved to be significant. This is higher than chance expectancy but hardly overwhelming support for the theory; the authors interpret it as little support. Consistency in type of moderator effect across samples was low, suggesting a substantial chance component in the findings. On the other hand, many studies utilized rather small samples, thus bringing power levels down to a point where significance would be hard to detect. Not all studies were so limited, however. The authors' conclusions overall are worth noting:

> When we first began our research in this area, we firmly believed that there were a number of important situational factors that influenced a leader's effectiveness. . . . [T]he findings summarized in this study have raised some serious doubts. Quite frankly, we find the lack of support for the moderating effects predicted by the path goal and substitutes for leadership models both shocking and disappointing. (Podsakoff, MacKenzie, Ahearne, and Bommer 1995, 464–65)

One other study utilized much the same approach as that applied in previous Indiana studies, but focused on transformational leader behaviors (Podsakoff, MacKenzie, and Bommer 1996a). This is not a variable actually specified by the theory, but any such behavior is implicitly included, and there is no basis for excluding it. The results of this study are of primary interest for the concerns of Chapter 19, but it is important to note here that once again moderator findings consistent with the theory were minimal (some 2 percent). Also, support for the theory came only from self-report criteria where common method variance may have played a role. As in the other Indiana research, sample size was sufficiently large so that power considerations should not be a concern.

A more recent study (Dionne, Yammarino, Atwater, and James 2002) looked into certain moderating effects of substitutes for leadership, as well as the effects of treating substitutes as mediators, and the role of common source biases. The findings were generally nonsupportive of the theory as it relates to moderators in any form, and they raised serious questions with regard to the extent to which common source bias may have contaminated previous results. Thus, once again, substitutes for leadership theory appear to have come up short.

Main Effects

Although the research reviewed to this point has focused on moderator analyses and has found the theory wanting in this area, these same studies have consistently found sizable main effects extending from both substitutes and leader behaviors to criterion or outcome variables; both sets of factors tend to contribute to criterion variance. A study designed to look into these effects more fully was conducted using measures calculated at both the within-group or individual level and as averages for existing work groups (Podsakoff and MacKenzie 1995). Controlling for the leader behaviors and substitutes for leadership at both levels of analysis using multiple regression, the study found that:

1. The combination of leader behaviors and substitutes for leadership accounted for substantial amounts of variance in the subordinate's attitudes, role perceptions, and performance.
2. The leadership substitutes accounted for more variance in the subordinate criterion variables than did the leader behaviors.
3. Although the effects of within-group variation in leader behaviors and substitutes for leadership were substantially stronger than between-groups variation on subordinates' attitudes and role perceptions, both within-group and between-groups variation in the leader behaviors and leadership substitutes had important effects on . . . performance. (Podsakoff and MacKenzie 1995, 289)

Consideration, initiating structure, and leader reward and punishment behaviors were studied along with thirteen substitutes. Leader behaviors and substitutes were found to have quite a bit of variance in common, suggesting the need to include both in future research.

Subsequently, a meta-analysis of main effects from substitutes to criterion variables was carried out utilizing twenty-two studies in which data were reported (Podsakoff, MacKenzie, and Bommer 1996b). The substitutes clearly accounted uniquely for more criterion variance than the leader behaviors, but combined the two had a much greater impact. Task feedback, task routinization, group cohesiveness, organizational formalization, and organizational inflexibility were the substitutes having the most extensive ties to criteria. Both common method variance and implicit theories of leadership may have influenced some of the findings. However, this is least likely in the case of the substitutes–performance relationships, which nevertheless were found to be strong. All in all the evidence for the substitutes' main effects on criteria is quite convincing.

Elsewhere the Indiana researchers note that one might adopt the argument—

> that the variables identified by Kerr and Jermier (1978) "substitute" for leadership in the sense that when these variables are added to the model, they eliminate the main effects of the leader behaviors. . . . Although this position is not consistent with the statistical criteria established by Howell, Dorfman, and Kerr (1986) . . . , it is somewhat consistent with the original statistical tests of the model by Kerr and Jermier (1978). (Podsakoff, MacKenzie, and Fetter 1993, 40)

Although the data for the overall effects of combined substitutes and combined leader behaviors do not support such a conclusion, it is true that the theory as originally formulated did give more attention to main effects than did subsequent versions.

Reactions Within the Field

How has the field of organizational behavior reacted to the developing state of affairs? Schriesheim (1997) indicates a long-standing concern that substitutes theory is in fact no more than an elaboration of aspects of path goal theory. He finds certain of the theoretical arguments less than compelling, but recognizes the appeal the theory has had. At the present time he feels the need is for better construct definitions and better conceptualization overall. These views are reiterated, but with a special concern about level of analysis issues, in Schriesheim, Castro, Zhou, and Yammarino (2001). Yukl (2002) expresses similar views regarding the conceptual weaknesses of the theory; he feels that the theory in its present form represents an insufficient mapping of its domain.

Tosi and Kiker (1997) call for a theory that is more fully developed and elaborated. They believe that the effects of particular substitutes as they operate in certain types of organizations need specification.

Villa, Howell, Dorfman, and Daniel (2003) stress that substitute variables have been shown to play an important role in organizations. They argue that moderator tests have often incorporated relationships not hypothesized by theory, and have utilized extraneous predictor variables. If these errors are corrected, substitutes for leadership theory achieves a much higher batting average. Podsakoff and MacKenzie (1997), however, feel that the evidence regarding moderator effects is overwhelmingly negative. Yet they point to the main effects findings in endorsing continued study of the operation of substitutes for leadership variables. They, too, point up errors in design and method characterizing leadership research. (Podsakoff, MacKenzie, Podsakoff, and Lee 2003) Perhaps it is time for a major reassessment on this score, a reassessment that quite possibly could operate to produce a more favorable evaluation of substitutes for leadership theory.

Lord and Smith (1999) are particularly concerned that the theory does not incorporate the fact that so-called substitutes for leadership are in many cases indirect products of managerial action. They point to the similar main effects findings for substitutes and leader behaviors as evidence that leadership processes of a kind are involved in both instances. Yet professional characteristics, to cite an example, are influenced primarily by the profession, not by managers within a firm.

A line of, at least intended, endorsement comes from those who claim substitute status for variables not included in the original list of substitutes. An example is the Manz and Sims (1980) nomination of the capability of the follower for self-management as a substitute. Under self-management or self-control, individuals take responsibility for their own behaviors by setting their own standards, evaluating their performance against these standards, and administering consequences to themselves as appropriate. Yet the extent to which self-management in practice operates as a true substitute may be questioned. External leaders play an important role for self-managing work teams. These external leaders, or coordinators, serve to encourage self-reinforcement and self-evaluation primarily, but this is stroking behavior of a kind, and falls within the definition of leader behavior.

As with most other reactions to substitutes theory, the endorsers of new substitutes present a mixed picture; they like the theory and want to include something toward which they feel quite positively under its umbrella, but it is not at all clear that this "substitute" fits where they want to place it. Thus they may really be promoting something other than substitutes for leadership theory.

How then does Kerr feel about the theory now? In an interview, he reacted to a question regarding what he was proud of in his work as follows:

> I like very much my work on "Substitutes for Leadership." But it never had solid empirical support, and I've never wavered in my conviction that it's right. . . . I've never wavered that

there's something important there. And I could be flat out wrong, but I think there's probably something in there. So I like that a lot. (Frost 1997, 346)

Yet Kerr is not saying that he believes first-line leadership in hierarchic organizations will be replaced completely by other factors. That has never been his position (Kerr, Hill, and Broedling 1986). He simply holds that other factors in addition to leadership play an important role in controlling and influencing subordinates. Chemers (1997) criticizes substitutes theory on the ground that it gives too little attention to the interpersonal and emotional aspects of the leader–follower relationship. But it is entirely possible that this is indeed what accounts for the leader behavior–produced criterion variance that remains after the substitutes are deleted. Nothing that Kerr has said or written appears to contradict this conclusion.

Repositioning the Theory

That the substitutes play an important role in performance and other outcomes is clearly evident from the main effects data. What is not evident is that the substitutes truly act as substitutes for leadership. In some instances they appear to be part of overall leadership, and technically at least they involve processes other than substituting—neutralizing, enhancing, and supplementing. However, the major problem is that substituting for leadership implies some type of moderation of the leader behavior–outcome relationship, and research fails to establish conclusively that the substitute characteristics do operate as moderators. The sum total of the evidence from research is that although the "substitutes" should be retained in the revised theory that the critics are calling for, the substitute aspect itself probably should not.

I believe that the answer required to reposition the theory lies in the classification system proposed by Kerr and Slocum (1981) and inherent in role motivation theory (see Chapter 17). Some of the substitute characteristics are bureaucratic in nature extending beyond direct face-to-face leader behavior; they are hierarchic methods of control and influence, such as formalization, which achieve the same results as direct hierarchic leadership but in different ways. Some of the characteristics are primarily associated with professional systems operating to achieve control and influence in this type of system along the lines indicated in Table 16.2 for organic organizations. Some of the characteristics operate primarily within group systems; the cohesiveness of work groups achieves control and influence in this manner. Finally, some characteristics achieve control and influence within task or entrepreneurial systems through the impact of pushes and pulls that are inherent in the task itself—task-inherent feedback, for instance.

My point is that hierarchic leadership behavior has no special status that requires substituting for it. It is simply one among many mechanisms utilized in hierarchic systems to achieve control and influence. In this view it does not matter really whether a mechanism is classified as leader behavior (direct or indirect) or not. Hierarchic systems are managed systems, and all mechanisms for control and influence that are part of these systems derive from managerial behavior in some way.

Kerr's theory is a product of its times. The central role it gives to leadership was consistent with most thinking in the field at the time, and probably remains so even now (e.g., see Zaccaro 2001). It is doubtful that much attention would have been paid to the theory if it had not emphasized the salience of the leadership concept. Yet the research evidence that has accumulated over some thirty years seems to be telling us that what is really needed is a theory of organizational control and influence processes that merely includes direct leader behavior as one factor among many.

CONCLUSIONS

Substitutes for leadership theory is another example of an approach that fails to achieve really high ratings on any of the three variables, but which on average across all three proves worthy of the designation as essential. The importance rating of 4.46 is entirely respectable, certainly among leadership theories, most of which do not stand out in this regard. The estimated validity at 3 stars reflects the concern about moderators and conceptual adequacy, while still incorporating the positive findings, including those for main effects. The idea that substitutes should be utilized insofar as possible, especially to limit the negative impact of ineffective leaders, earns the theory a 3 star rating. However, the lack of a more comprehensive treatment of how to put the theory to use (perhaps in book form) keeps it at the 3 star level. One would think that based on his experience at General Electric and Goldman, Sachs, Kerr could do more in this regard.

REFERENCES

Chemers, Martin M. (1997). *An Integrative Theory of Leadership.* Mahwah, NJ: Lawrence Erlbaum.
Dionne, Shelley D., Yammarino, Francis J., Atwater, Leanne E., and James, Lawrence R. (2002). Neutralizing Substitutes for Leadership Theory: Leadership Effects and Common Source Bias. *Journal of Applied Psychology*, 87, 434–64.
Filley, Alan C., House, Robert J., and Kerr, Steven (1976). *Managerial Process and Organizational Behavior.* Glenview, IL: Scott, Foresman.
Frost, Peter J. (1997). Bridging Academia and Business: A Conversation with Steve Kerr. *Organization Science*, 8, 332–47.
Greiner, Larry (2002). Steve Kerr and His Years with Jack Welch at GE. *Journal of Management Inquiry*, 11, 343–50.
Howell, Jon P., Bowen, David E., Dorfman, Peter W., Kerr, Steven, and Podsakoff, Philip M. (1990). Substitutes for Leadership: Effective Alternatives to Ineffective Leadership. *Organizational Dynamics*, 19(1), 21–38.
Howell, Jon P., and Dorfman, Peter W. (1981). Substitutes for Leadership: Test of a Construct. *Academy of Management Journal*, 24, 714–28.
Howell, Jon P., Dorfman, Peter W., and Kerr, Steven (1986). Moderator Variables in Leadership Research. *Academy of Management Review*, 11, 88–102.
Jermier, John M., and Berkes, Leslie J. (1979). Leader Behavior in a Police Command Bureaucracy: A Closer Look at the Quasi-Military Model. *Administrative Science Quarterly*, 24, 1–23.
Jermier, John M., and Kerr, Steven (1997). "Substitutes for Leadership: Their Meaning and Measurement"—Contextual Recollections and Current Observations. *Leadership Quarterly*, 8, 95–101.
Kerr, Steven (1977). Substitutes for Leadership: Some Implications for Organizational Design. *Organization and Administrative Sciences*, 8, 135–46.
——— (2003). On the Folly of Rewarding A, While Hoping for B. In Lyman W. Porter, Harold L. Angle, and Robert W. Allen (Eds.), *Organizational Influence Processes*. Armonk, NY: M.E. Sharpe, 142–50.
Kerr, Steven, Hill, Kenneth D., and Broedling, Laurie (1986). The First-Line Supervisor: Phasing Out or Here to Stay? *Academy of Management Review*, 11, 103–17.
Kerr, Steven, and Jermier, John M. (1978). Substitutes for Leadership: Their Meaning and Measurement. *Organizational Behavior and Human Performance*, 22, 375–403.
Kerr, Steven, and Slocum, John W. (1981). Controlling the Performances of People in Organizations. In Paul C. Nystrom and William H. Starbuck (Eds.), *Handbook of Organizational Design*, Vol. 2. New York: Oxford University Press, 116–34.
Kerr, Steven, Von Glinow, Mary A., and Schriesheim, Janet (1977). Issues in the Study of "Professionals" in Organizations: The Case of Scientists and Engineers. *Organizational Behavior and Human Performance*, 18, 329–45.
Lord, Robert G., and Smith, Wendy G. (1999). Leadership and the Changing Nature of Performance. In Daniel R. Ilgen and Elaine D. Pulakos (Eds.), *The Changing Nature of Performance: Implications for Staffing, Motivation, and Development*. San Francisco, CA: Jossey-Bass, 192–239.

Manz, Charles C., and Sims, Henry P. (1980). Self-Management as a Substitute for Leadership: A Social Learning Theory Perspective. *Academy of Management Review*, 5, 361–67.

Miner, John B. (2002). *Organizational Behavior: Foundations, Theories, and Analyses.* New York: Oxford University Press.

Podsakoff, Philip M., and MacKenzie, Scott B. (1994). An Examination of the Psychometric Properties and Nomological Validity of Some Revised and Reduced Substitutes for Leadership Scales. *Journal of Applied Psychology*, 79, 702–13.

——— (1995). An Examination of Substitutes for Leadership within a Levels-of-Analysis Framework. *Leadership Quarterly*, 6, 289–328.

——— (1997). Kerr and Jermier's Substitutes for Leadership Model: Background, Empirical Assessment, and Suggestions for Future Research. *Leadership Quarterly*, 8, 117–25.

Podsakoff, Philip M., MacKenzie, Scott B., Ahearne, Mike, and Bommer, William H. (1995). Searching for a Needle in a Haystack: Trying to Identify the Illusive Moderators of Leadership Behaviors. *Journal of Management*, 21, 422–70.

Podsakoff, Philip M., MacKenzie, Scott B., and Bommer, William H. (1996a). Transformational Leader Behaviors and Substitutes for Leadership as Determinants of Employee Satisfaction, Commitment, Trust, and Organizational Citizenship Behaviors. *Journal of Management*, 22, 259–98.

——— (1996b). Meta-Analysis of the Relationships between Kerr and Jermier's Substitutes for Leadership and Employee Job Attitudes, Role Perceptions, and Performance. *Journal of Applied Psychology*, 81, 380–99.

Podsakoff, Philip M., MacKenzie, Scott, B., and Fetter, Richard (1993). Substitutes for Leadership and the Management of Professionals. *Leadership Quarterly*, 4, 1–44.

Podsakoff, Philip M., MacKenzie, Scott B., Podsakoff, Nathan P., and Lee, Jeong Yeon (2003). The Mismeasure of Man(agement) and its Implications for Leadership Research. *Leadership Quarterly*, 14, 615–56.

Podsakoff, Philip M., Niehoff, Brian P., MacKenzie, Scott B., and Williams, Margaret L. (1993). Do Substitutes for Leadership Really Substitute for Leadership? An Empirical Examination of Kerr and Jermier's Situational Leadership Model. *Organizational Behavior and Human Decision Processes*, 54, 1–44.

Podsakoff, Philip M., Todor, William D., Grover, Richard A., and Huber, Vandra L. (1984). Situational Moderators of Leader Reward and Punishment Behaviors: Fact or Fiction. *Organizational Behavior and Human Performance*, 34, 21–63.

Schriesheim, Chester A. (1997). Substitutes for Leadership Theory: Development and Basic Concepts. *Leadership Quarterly*, 8, 103–8.

Schriesheim, Chester A., Castro, Stephanie L., Zhou, Xiaohua, and Yammarino, Francis J. (2001). The Folly of Theorizing "A" but Testing "B"—A Selective Level-of-Analysis Review of the Field and a Detailed Leader–Member Exchange Illustration. *Leadership Quarterly*, 12, 515–51.

Sheridan, John E., Vredenburgh, Donald J., and Abelson, Michael A. (1984). Contextual Model of Leadership Influence in Hospital Units. *Academy of Management Journal*, 27, 57–78.

Streiner, David L. (2003). Being Inconsistent about Consistency: When Coefficient Alpha Does and Doesn't Matter. *Journal of Personality Assessment*, 80, 217–22.

Tosi, Henry L., and Kiker, Scott (1997). Commentary on "Substitutes for Leadership." *Leadership Quarterly*, 8, 109–12.

Villa, Jennifer R., Howell, Jon P., Dorfman, Peter W., and Daniel, David L. (2003). Problems with Detecting Moderators in Leadership Research Using Moderated Multiple Regression. *Leadership Quarterly*, 14, 3–23.

Williams, Margaret L., Podsakoff, Philip M., Todor, William D., Huber, Vandra L., Howell, Jon P., and Dorfman, Peter W. (1988). A Preliminary Analysis of the Construct Validity of Kerr and Jermier's Substitutes for Leadership Scales. *Journal of Occupational Psychology*, 61, 307–33.

Yukl, Gary (2002). *Leadership in Organizations.* Upper Saddle River, NJ: Prentice-Hall.

Zaccaro, Stephen J. (2001). *The Nature of Executive Leadership: A Conceptual and Empirical Analysis of Success.* Washington, DC: American Psychological Association.

CHAPTER 17

ROLE MOTIVATION THEORY

JOHN MINER

Background
The Theory Behind Managerial Role Motivation Training
    Role Motivation Training at Atlantic Refining
    Formulations Related to Ineffective Performance
Managerial (Hierarchic) Role Motivation Theory
    The Original Theory
    The Components of Managerial Motivation
    The Theory Applied to Bureaucracy
Subsequent Role Motivation Theory
    The Professional Theory
    The Task Theory
    The Group Theory
    Organizational Types
    Leadership as Career
Evaluation and Impact
    Positive Findings and Evaluations
    Negative Evaluations
    Applications
Conclusions

Importance rating	★ ★ ★ ★
Estimated validity	★ ★ ★ ★
Estimated usefulness	★ ★ ★ ★
Decade of origin	1960s

Role motivation theory was presented for many years as dealing essentially with motivational constructs, in much the same manner as achievement motivation theory (see Chapter 4). From its origin, however, it has focused on managers and leaders of various kinds without making this leadership orientation explicit. In recent years certain concepts of leadership have taken a dominant position within the theory as it has evolved. This, then, is the reason for moving this discussion from Part II to Part III.

In what follows I will attempt to treat role motivation theory as objectively as possible, and in the same manner as other theories we have been considering. This includes writing about myself in the third person. Nevertheless, the reader should recognize that a potential for subjective bias exists here that does not exist elsewhere.

BACKGROUND

Miner was born in 1926, and his education was all in psychology, both clinical psychology and personality theory. His graduate work was done at Clark and Princeton universities; the latter granted the doctorate in 1955. After briefly teaching industrial psychology in the psychology departments at Georgia Tech and Brooklyn College, he joined the research staff of the Conservation of Human Resources project in the Graduate School of Business at Columbia University. A personal psychoanalysis was completed at this time. Subsequently, Miner took a position as a psychologist in the corporate personnel research unit of The Atlantic Refining Company in Philadelphia. While employed at Atlantic, he began work on an MBA in industrial relations at the Wharton School of the University of Pennsylvania, thus entering a business school for the second time. Within a year, however, his status shifted from student to adjunct faculty member at Wharton. In 1960 he moved west to the University of Oregon. This third brush with a business school proved enduring. There have been moves—from Oregon to Maryland to Georgia State University, and ultimately to the State University of New York at Buffalo—but with the exception of a year each on leave with the psychology department at Berkeley and the New York office of McKinsey and Company, his career has been spent in business schools ever since joining the University of Oregon faculty. However, consulting to various business firms has been a major activity throughout, contributing both to a knowledge of business practice and to a research data base.

Throughout this diversified career, Miner (1993a) continued to work on the development of role motivation theory. In this regard he was influenced most by his early mentors at Princeton (Silvan Tomkins) and at Columbia (Eli Ginzberg).

THE THEORY BEHIND MANAGERIAL ROLE MOTIVATION TRAINING

One of Miner's activities with the research unit at Columbia was to help prepare a book describing the factors that caused World War II soldiers to be discharged prematurely. The group had army personnel records, Veteran's Administration records, military unit histories, and follow-up questionnaires on these men. From these a schema of the strategic factors that caused failure was developed, and also case histories to illustrate points. The schema that finally emerged (Ginzberg, Miner, Anderson, Ginsburg, and Herma 1959) looks like this:

Personality (physical condition, intelligence, emotional stability, motivation)

Family (separation, breakup)

Immediate group (cohesion, leadership)

Military organization (investment, planning and improvisation, discipline and overpermissiveness, assignment)

Conflict of cultural values (equity, religious and moral values)

Situational stress (location, combat)

Role Motivation Training at Atlantic Refining

While at Atlantic, Miner taught a course for managers in the Research and Development (R&D) Department with the objective of arousing their interest in managing. The rationale behind this course was that the manager/scientists would be cast directly in the role of manager, responsible for those assigned to them and for getting the work accomplished as well. The idea was to construct a role model for them, make that role model attractive, and give them the tools to perform in accordance with what the model prescribed. In the terminology of psychoanalysis, this meant helping the managers develop a particular type of ego ideal. On the possibility that some managers had avoided managing because it created anxiety, the Columbia model of ineffective performance and its causes was presented, and extended to them personally, with the objective of getting them involved in diagnosing and correcting their own performance failures. In particular, attention was focused on sources of phobic reactions to the managerial situation. By providing the managers with what amounted to psychoanalytic interpretations of their unconscious motives, and how these might yield anxiety on the job, a diminution in negative affect was hypothesized to result from the training. This theory drove the creation of the course administered to seventy-two R&D managers at Atlantic. Evaluations conducted on this course using control groups indicated that managerial motivation was in fact increased, and thus support for the theory was obtained (Miner 1960).

Formulations Related to Ineffective Performance

The schema of strategic determinants of ineffective performance first developed at Columbia has gone through several iterations. The course was initially written up in book form in Miner (1963). Table 17.1 presents the statement that stands at the present time. Also, based on a book by Jerome (1961), aspects of the control model were gradually incorporated into the developing theory. The approach that finally emerged is depicted in Figure 17.1.

MANAGERIAL (HIERARCHIC) ROLE MOTIVATION THEORY

The research proposal for the training at Atlantic created a need to develop a measure of managerial motivation, later called motivation to manage. A search of the literature of the time (1957) yielded little on the topic, and accordingly a measure was devised, validated, and applied to evaluate role motivation training to see if it raised levels of managerial motivation.

The Original Theory

This measure, a sentence completion instrument, employed stems and a scoring system that adhered closely to the definition of "the good manager" as held at the Atlantic Refining Company, particularly at corporate headquarters. Information was obtained partly through participant observation and partly via a close reading of a large number of management appraisal documents. The theory that resulted was in the grounded theory tradition.

The theory development process involved writing possible items for the test, paring these down through a "quick and dirty" item analysis, and then abstracting the implicit theory behind this measure after the fact. Thus, theory construction was a highly inductive process. Clearly, the items were all intended to relate to managerial motivation from the beginning, but the components of that motivation emerged from a conceptual grouping of these items after learning how people responded to them.

Furthermore, the idea behind the components was that managers were evaluated relative to informal role prescriptions inherent in the specific situation, prescriptions that managers either met (behaved in accordance with), and thus were highly valued (judged effective), or did not meet and thus were judged ineffective. This was a strictly psychological approach to role behavior predicated on individual differences. (See Ashforth 2001 for a treatment of the current status of role theory.)

Table 17.1

Schema of Strategic Factors That May Contribute to Ineffective Performance

Intelligence and job knowledge problems
  Insufficient verbal ability
  Insufficient special ability
  Insufficient job knowledge
  Defect of judgment or memory
Emotional problems
  Frequent disruptive emotion: anxiety, depression, anger, excitement, shame, guilt, jealousy
  Neurosis: with anxiety, depression, anger predominating
  Psychosis: with anxiety, depression, anger predominating
  Alcohol and drug problems
Motivational problems
  Strong motives frustrated at work: pleasure in success, fear of failure, avoidance motives, dominance, desire to be popular, social motivation, need for attention
  Unintegrated means used to satisfy strong motives
  Low personal work standards
  Generalized low work motivation
Physical problems
  Physical illness or handicap, including brain disorders
  Physical disorders of emotional origin
  Inappropriate physical characteristics
  Insufficient muscular or sensory ability or skill
Family-related problems
  Family crises: divorce, death, severe illness
  Separation from the family and isolation
  Predominance of family considerations over job demands
Work-group problems
  Negative consequences of group cohesion
  Ineffective management
  Inappropriate managerial standards or criteria
Organizational problems
  Insufficient organizational action
  Placement error
  Organizational overpermissiveness
  Excessive spans of control
  Inappropriate organizational standards and criteria
Society-related problems
  Application of legal sanctions
  Other enforcement of societal values, including the use of inappropriate value-based criteria
  Conflict between job demands and cultural values: equity, freedom, moral and religious values
Problems related to the work situation
  Negative consequences of economic forces
  Negative consequences of geographic location
  Detrimental conditions in the work setting
  Excessive danger
  Problems inherent in the work itself

Source: Miner (1985, 312–14).

Figure 17.1 **Steps in the Control Process as Applied to Instances of Ineffective Performance**

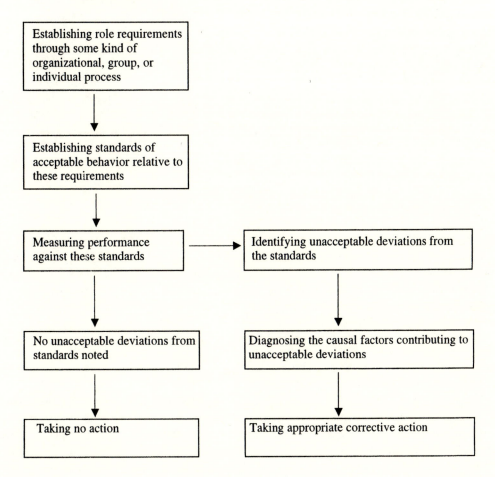

The Components of Managerial Motivation

The components of managerial motivation that were identified in the items is listed below:

- Favorable attitudes to superiors
- Desire to compete
- Desire to exercise power
- Desire to perform in the masculine role, and thus to assert oneself
- Desire to be distinct and different
- Desire to perform routine duties responsibly

To the extent that scores on the items in each grouping are consistently positive, the person was assumed to possess the motive (or motive constellation) involved. However, many people gave negative responses, often a number of them. This was not merely indicative of a lack of the particular type of motivation; it reflected a desire not to do these things, to avoid such behavior.

The theory was that this occurs because the type of motivation aroused by the role requirement had become associated with anxiety and guilt. Consequently, the motives are driven to the level of the unconscious in order to avoid recognizing them. Yet this attempt is only partially success-ful, and the negative emotion persists.

Thus, favorable attitudes to superiors can mean unnatural behavior, perhaps involving sexual activity with a parental figure. Competitiveness can mean out-of-control aggression and vio-lence, even murder. Power motivation can mean acting superior, authoritarianism, and dictato-rial. Masculinity can mean questioning one's sexual identity for women, and macho sexual arousal for men. Being distinct and different can mean showing off, phoniness, and even exhibitionism. Performing routine duties can carry implications of dishonesty, vindictiveness, and jealousy. The underlying dynamics involved here are described in detail in Miner (1975). The theory is that informal role requirements involved in managerial work thus can elicit phobic reactions to the managerial situation.

The Theory Applied to Bureaucracy

For some time the theory thus specified was not defined as to domain. With expanding research, however, (see Miner 1965, 1977), it became apparent that the domain was really bureaucracy as initially defined by Weber (see Miner 2002a). The theory then was expanded to state that manage-rial motivation would explain and predict the success of managers in bureaucratic organizations with multiple levels of hierarchy, but it would not work with nonmanagers, and it would not work in structures other than the bureaucratic ones.

Figure 17.2(a) sets forth the hierarchic role motivation theory as thus formulated.

SUBSEQUENT ROLE MOTIVATION THEORY

Sometime in the mid-1970s Miner began to theorize regarding the fact that the hierarchic views were restricted to the domain of bureaucratic organizations, and thus that other organizational forms might require similar theories. His efforts in this regard settled first on a concept of *control* hypothesized to operate broadly through various organizational systems (see Miner 1977). Later the idea of *inducement systems* was substituted (Miner 1980a), and specific role prescriptions and their motivational bases were identified. Finally, theoretical hypotheses were stated:

> *Hypothesis 1.* In hierarchic systems, managerial motivation should be at a high level in top management and it should be positively correlated with other managerial success in-dexes; managerial motivation should not differentiate in these ways within other types of systems.
>
> *Hypothesis 2.* In professional systems, professional motivation should be at a high level among senior professionals, and it should be positively correlated with other profes-sional success indexes; professional motivation should not differentiate in these ways within other types of systems.
>
> *Hypothesis 3.* In group systems, group motivation should be at a high level among emergent leaders, and it should be positively correlated with other group-determined success in-dexes; group motivation should not differentiate in these ways within other types of systems.
>
> *Hypothesis 4.* In task systems, task (achievement) motivation should be at a high level among task performers (entrepreneurs, for example), and it should be positively correlated with

Figure 17.2 **Outlines of the Four Forms of Role Motivation Theory**

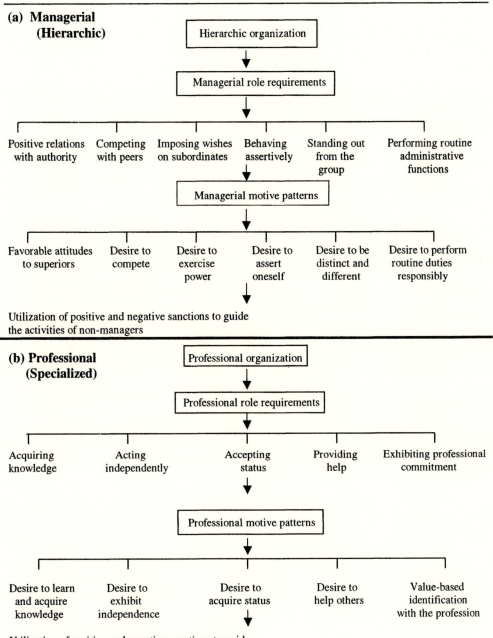

(a) **Managerial
    (Hierarchic)**

Hierarchic organization

Managerial role requirements

Positive relations with authority | Competing with peers | Imposing wishes on subordinates | Behaving assertively | Standing out from the group | Performing routine administrative functions

Managerial motive patterns

Favorable attitudes to superiors | Desire to compete | Desire to exercise power | Desire to assert oneself | Desire to be distinct and different | Desire to perform routine duties responsibly

Utilization of positive and negative sanctions to guide the activities of non-managers

(b) **Professional
    (Specialized)**

Professional organization

Professional role requirements

Acquiring knowledge | Acting independently | Accepting status | Providing help | Exhibiting professional commitment

Professional motive patterns

Desire to learn and acquire knowledge | Desire to exhibit independence | Desire to acquire status | Desire to help others | Value-based identification with the profession

Utilization of positive and negative sanctions to guide the activities of non-professionals

(Continued)

Figure 17.2 (continued)

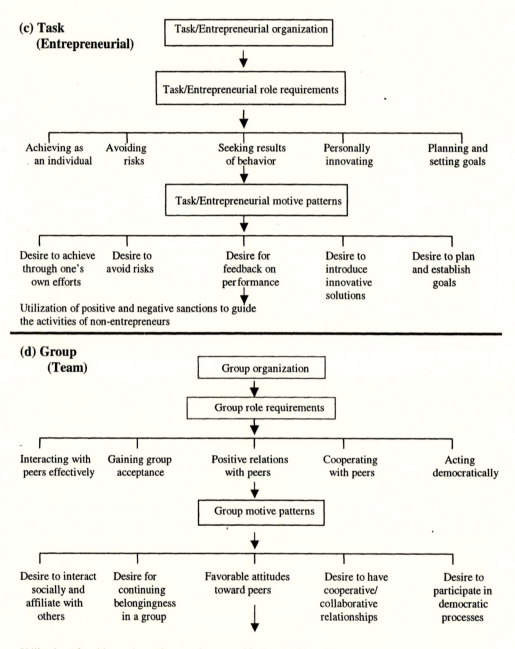

**(c) Task
(Entrepreneurial)**

Task/Entrepreneurial organization

Task/Entrepreneurial role requirements

| Achieving as an individual | Avoiding risks | Seeking results of behavior | Personally innovating | Planning and setting goals |

Task/Entrepreneurial motive patterns

| Desire to achieve through one's own efforts | Desire to avoid risks | Desire for feedback on performance | Desire to introduce innovative solutions | Desire to plan and establish goals |

Utilization of positive and negative sanctions to guide the activities of non-entrepreneurs

**(d) Group
(Team)**

Group organization

Group role requirements

| Interacting with peers effectively | Gaining group acceptance | Positive relations with peers | Cooperating with peers | Acting democratically |

Group motive patterns

| Desire to interact socially and affiliate with others | Desire for continuing belongingness in a group | Favorable attitudes toward peers | Desire to have cooperative/collaborative relationships | Desire to participate in democratic processes |

Utilization of positive and negative sanctions to guide the activities of non-group members and members temporarily or permanently not in good standing

Source: Miner (1993b, 11, 15, 18, and 22).

task success indexes; task motivation should not differentiate in these ways within other types of systems (Miner 1982, 298).

The Professional Theory

The professional system did not arise out of test items as the hierarchic theory did. Specific informal role prescriptions were developed and motivational patterns that fit them were then stated, using the literature and personal experience as a guide.

The components of professional motivation thus identified were as follows:

- Desire to learn and acquire knowledge
- Desire to exhibit independence
- Desire to acquire status
- Desire to help others
- Value-based identification with the profession

The way in which these patterns fit into the theory is indicated in Figure 17.2(b). A measure of the motives involved was constructed in much the same matter as for the hierarchic theory, except that the five motive patterns were known at the outset, and this fact guided the selection of items. The resulting instrument, the Miner Sentence Completion Scale (Form P), was used in a validation study conducted among members of the Academy of Management to test the theory thus constructed (Miner 1980b).

The Task Theory

Task theory is an adaptation of McClelland's work on achievement motivation (see Chapter 4). Initially Miner set out to test the hypothesis that entrepreneurs found companies to have something to manage, and thus managerial motivation should be the major source of entrepreneurial accomplishment. This hypothesis had only limited success at best (Smith and Miner 1983). Only then did he turn to task theory using achievement motivation theory as a guide.

The components of this theory are as follows:

- Desire to achieve through one's own efforts
- Desire to avoid risk
- Desire for feedback on performance
- Desire to introduce innovative solutions
- Desire to plan and establish goals

Of these, only the second (risk) departs to some degree from McClelland. The theory as a whole is outlined in Figure 17.2(c). A measure was constructed using the sentence completion format—the Miner Sentence Completion Scales (Form T). This in turn was employed in a study of high-tech entrepreneurs to provide an initial test (Miner, Smith, and Bracker 1989).

A related program of theory and research should be distinguished from the work on task theory. In this instance data were derived from an entrepreneurship development program and from an MBA course in entrepreneurship. The theory involved sets forth a typology of entrepreneurs consisting of personal achievers, real managers, expert idea generators, and empathic super salespeople (Miner 1997). Although the Miner Sentence Completion Scales are used in this research, the overall theory itself is not really a role motivation theory.

The Group Theory

Group role motivation theory exists as a theory, but the motives involved have not been operationalized, nor the theory tested, as of this writing. The theory is almost completely a consequence of the literature on autonomous work groups, sensitivity training, and organization development. The literature that appears to have exerted the most influence is in the tradition of Kurt Lewin (see Chapter 3)—from MIT, the University of Michigan, and the Tavistock organization in England.

The components of the theory thus derived are:

- Desire to interact socially and affiliate with others
- Desire for continuing belongingness in a group
- Favorable attitudes toward peers
- Desire to have cooperative/collaborative relationships
- Desire to participate in democratic processes

The way in which these components fit into the group organizational form is set forth in Figure 17.2(d).

Organizational Types

The previous discussion, and the research noted, have focused at the level of individual motivation utilizing primarily the various Miner Sentence Completion Scales (MSCS). Yet the theories are meso theories dealing as much with organizational forms, and the informal role requirements they posit, as with intrinsic motive patterns.

Given that the theories predict particular types of person–organization fit (see Tinsley 2000), if role behavior and role requirements are to mesh, there was a clear need for a measure of the four organization types. This became evident in the late 1970s as the three organizational forms beyond the hierarchic were developed. As a result, Oliver (1982) created an instrument, the Oliver Organization Description Questionnaire, to operationalize the four organizational forms. Oliver's questionnaire has been used extensively in research conducted since its development (e.g., see Wilderom and Miner 1991). It appears to be effective in differentiating the domains of the various role motivation theories.

Leadership as Career

The concept of leadership was first introduced into the role motivation literature by Miner (2000). Leaders within different organizational forms are said to be completely different types of people whose personalities must mesh with role requirements fitting the organization type in order to prosper.

Later this view is expressed in hypothesis form as follows:

> Leadership roles take different forms in different organizational contexts and require different types of people to perform in these roles effectively—people whose motives are strongly congruent with the particular organizational type involved; thus leadership careers vary in important ways with the organizational forms in which they occur. (Miner 2002b, 318)

Leadership in any such form is a developing process of career identification where a person increasingly takes on a set of institutionalized roles viewed as personally compatible. Within hierarchic organizations leaders are those in the upper reaches of the pyramid often referred to as top management; managers below this level are considered to be in a pre-leadership role. Within professional organizations leaders are those who are identified with the intellectual elite, in contrast with being rank-and-file practitioners; such intellectual leaders may achieve their status within a cosmopolitan or local context. Within task systems entrepreneurial leaders are characterized as being lead entrepreneurs who own a large share of the venture or hold a dominant position (as with corporate entrepreneurship—see Sathe 2003) *and* who are growth oriented; in the team context the lead entrepreneur concept is especially important, and the vision of that person plays a key strategic role (see Ensley, Carland, and Carland 2000). Within group systems leadership is emergent predicated on group norms; examples would be elected leaders of autonomous work groups and committee chairs within legislative bodies.

Leadership careers are much the same as any other type of career and they operate in the same manner. First of all leadership is established, then leadership persistence, and finally a leadership career (Foti and Miner 2003). Congruent careers, whether of the leader variety or of some other type, will be predicted at higher levels than the other criteria (outcomes) of role motivation theory. The role prescriptions against which leaders match their motivational patterns are viewed as organizational form-specific prototypes that observers (including followers) develop. This thinking follows that of Chapter 15. However, these prototypes are said to be institutionalized, and thus widely held, and also informal, rather than highly correlated with the formal roles established by the organization. Institutionalization is defined using Scott's (2001) formulations, and is then further specified as informal following Zenger, Lazzarini, and Poppo (2002).

A final point involves levels of analysis issues and the use of a projective technique such as the sentence completion method, which gets at unconscious or automatic processes. Miner holds that to measure the motives of role motivation theory one must use some index that taps into the unconscious, such as projectives. Self-report indexes and projectives dealing with the same construct do not produce the same results; in fact, they can produce directly opposite results (Miner and Raju 2004). Schriesheim, Castro, Zhou, and Yammarino (2001) make the point that theories that posit constructs at one level (individual, dyad, group, organizational) should be tested using those constructs at that same level. But they do not break the individual level down further. Miner indicates that a clear differentiation should be made between motives at the implicit level and at the self-attributed level, and that using a projective technique is appropriate, and indeed required, by the fact that the role motivation theory motives are stated at the implicit level.

EVALUATION AND IMPACT

Initially most of the research on role motivation theory was conducted by Miner, but gradually it spread to joint authorships, studies by doctoral students, and completely independent investigations. Because organizational form is the key to all that follows, it is important to determine first whether the four types do in fact reflect the present realities of organizational structuring. This may be accomplished by surveying the relevant literature.

The hierarchic organization type appears to be well supported (e.g., see Leavitt 2003; Russell 2001), as would be expected from the wide prevalence of bureaucracy. Professional organizations can be differentiated from bureaucracies as a distinct type as well (Golden, Dukerich, and Fabian 2000), and exhibit characteristic competencies (Jones and Lichtenstein 2000). A book by Schoonhoven and Romanelli (2001) differentiates the entrepreneurial type of organization, while a number of publications describe the role of growth orientation in entrepreneurial firms (e.g., see Wiklund and Shepherd 2003). Articles by Taggar, Hackett, and Saha (1999) and by Shaw, Duffy, and Stark (2000) serve to establish the identity of group systems. Quite possibly, as Miner recognizes, other types of organizations exist, or have existed, but the hypothesized four types seem well established now.

Positive Findings and Evaluations

The initial studies on each theory mentioned previously, including the Atlantic research within a hierarchy, the Academy of Management study within universities, and the analysis of high-tech entrepreneurs within task systems, all produced positive findings as to theoretical validity. Since then, these three theories have received much favorable attention. This is particularly true of the hierarchic theory (e.g., see the literature reviews of Cornelius 1983; Latham 1988; Adler and Weiss 1988; and the meta-analyses of Nathan and Alexander 1985; Carson and Gilliard 1993). A meta-analysis comparing the sexes on the hierarchic theory also provides support (Eagly, Karau, Miner, and Johnson 1994). The other three theories are newer, and there has been less time to evaluate them. The group theory is really nothing more than speculation at the moment for lack of measures and research tests. The task theory is so closely allied to achievement motivation theory that it can hardly be said to exist as a separate entity. Thus, the evidence in support of achievement motivation as a key ingredient of entrepreneurial success (see Chapter 4) can be mobilized to substantiate role motivation theory in this regard. Winter (2002) in fact specifies achievement motivation as an essential element of entrepreneurial leadership, while noting that power motivation plays the same role in bureaucratic leadership. The professional theory has received consistent support, but the research evidence to date is more limited. There is nothing from achievement motivation theory that is applicable in this instance.

Note should be made of the most recent tally of the results of research on role motivation theories (see Miner 1993b). Overall there are 57 studies to draw upon and these describe 92 criterion relationships. In 92 percent of the latter, the results are significant and consistent with theoretical predictions. When the analysis is conducted outside the appropriate domain (with 28 studies and 59 criterion relationships), 100 percent of the results prove to be nonsignificant or (in six cases) significant in a negative direction. The lowest number of criterion relationships involved in this tally for any of the theories is 13 (for the professional theory). To these results should be added more recent findings from China that consistently support the hierarchic theory (Chen, Yu, and Miner 1997; Ebrahimi 1999).

Miner (2002b) has begun to present evidence consistent with the leadership theorizing. He also has data that are relevant to the leadership career formulations. Thus, in an exchange of letters with Foti, he has the following to say:

> Not previously published are the results of eight separate analyses . . . which relate the MSCS total scores to congruent and noncongruent career data. The congruent correlations range from .41 to .75 with a median of .58. . . . The median of nine noncongruent values is .11. Given the similarity between leadership and career findings, it seems appropriate to view the two as overlapping constructs. (Foti and Miner 2003, 96)

A search of the recent literature dealing with role motivation theory indicates considerable support on the part of reviewers. Yukl (2002) notes that the hierarchic theory works well in predicting managerial criteria in large, bureaucratic organizations; it does not work well within small organizations (entrepreneurial firms). Other reviewers focus on the task theory and cite evidence that it effectively predicts various entrepreneurial outcome criteria (see Rauch and Frese 2000; Shane, Locke, and Collins 2003). Vecchio (2003) indicates that "the results for Miner's theory have been consistently supportive of the view that different types of people may be drawn to different types of organizational systems" (312), but he also suggests the possibility that occupying a given set of roles may serve to modify their motivation.

Negative Evaluations

Like Fiedler's contingency theory of leadership (Chapter 13), role motivation theory has been the subject of considerable controversy. Both theories utilize projective, or semi-projective, measures, and these measures appear to be at the center of the controversies. Projective techniques came to organizational behavior from clinical psychology; they are rarely taught in organizational behavior doctoral programs, and in fact they tend to elicit rather negative prototypes among many in the field. Many of the disputes surrounding projective techniques have come to organizational behavior from their original home in clinical psychology (for a recent example among a long line of similar cases, compare Lilienfeld, Wood, and Garb 2000 with Hibbard 2003).

Miner (1993b) contains a treatment of the controversies and criticisms leveled at role motivation theory (with reference to the hierarchic version) in the period from the late 1970s through the 1980s. This treatment also considers new evidence presented by Miner in response to these criticisms. The criticisms may be distilled down to five as follows, although most of these are put forth by only a few critics:

1. Construct validity is lacking.
2. Reliability is lacking.
3. Role motivation training teaches the theory.
4. The decline (in motivation to manage) is questionable.
5. Gender effects are widespread (Miner 1993b, 289–96).

With regard to the construct validity issue, the response by Miner, and other evidence that we have already considered, appears to have laid this matter to rest. Scorer unreliability has been charged, but on the evidence good reliability can be achieved at above the 0.90 level with adequate training and attention to detail. Internal consistency reliability has not been demonstrated, and does not appear to be present, but it is not needed with instruments of this type, which are not intended to be factor pure (for a discussion, see Streiner 2003). The average total score test-retest reliability for a MSCS is reported at 0.86; the subscales overall average 0.20 lower. To this should be appended the argument that if validity proves adequate (which it has), then reliability becomes a secondary issue.

The contention that role motivation training teaches the theory, and thus primes a rise in motivational score on the sentence completion measure, served to instigate research to test this hypothesis. As reported in Miner (1993b), the evidence provides no support for this hypothesis.

The decline criticism refers to a finding that managerial motivation scores decreased during the 1960s and early 1970s when activism on university campuses was at its height. This was based on a happenstance finding and thus not predicted by theory (see Miner 1974). In any event, the evidence presented to support it was felt to be inadequate. However, the contrary evidence offered to refute any decline proved to be faulty, and Miner in various publications provides rather convincing data that the decline did occur. Given that this finding does not derive from role motivation theory per se, the issue has no bearing on the validity of that theory in any event.

The gender criticism, in contrast to the other four, does appear to have some credibility insofar as the measure used to test the hierarchic theory is concerned. As a result of cultural changes, certain items that were entirely acceptable during the 1960s have come to elicit negative reactions from test takers forty years later. This effect does not appear to influence the validity of the instrument, but it can well have an impact on acceptability. The reader is referred to Miner (1993b) for an item-by-item analysis. Older test takers, having lived in the earlier culture, would not appear to be influenced by the content of the offending items.

Also, to provide an example of an instance that did not fully support role motivation theory, a predictive study over a two-year period can be noted (Schneider, Ehrhart, and Ehrhart 2002). This research was conducted with high school students and used the hierarchic theory to predict teacher and peer ratings related to leadership. Several of the predicted subscale findings were significant, but not as many as might have been expected; total score findings are not provided. Presumably the pre-career status of these students, with role prototypes not yet completely formed, accounts for the negligible results.

A very recent criticism (Stewart and Roth 2004) focuses primarily on the inclusion of various studies in meta-analyses. However, it also escalates the matter of the psychometric properties associated with the measurement of risk avoidance (a subscale) to a critique of role motivation theory measures overall. Of the five points noted in Miner (1993b), only the construct validity and reliability issues are grounds for criticism; in the latter instance scorer, internal consistency, and test–retest reliability are all questioned. However, in drawing upon previous criticisms, Stewart and Roth (2004) do not mention any of those discussed in Miner (1993b), nor do they cite any of the replies noted there or the appropriate chapter of that book. They do cite several reviews with a date of 1992, but these could not have been informed by Miner's 1993 book. Thus, given the issues raised in this critical statement, the implications for role motivation theory seem best addressed, as noted previously, in Miner (1993b). The reader who is interested in the details of such controversies should consider Stewart and Roth (2001), Miner and Raju (2004), and Stewart and Roth (2004) in that order.

APPLICATIONS

The most obvious application of role motivation theory is the training instituted at Atlantic Refining Company. This type of training, which is based on the hierarchic theory, has been given many times to both university students and managers (e.g., see Miner 1977). In a number of instances, it has been evaluated using various experimental designs—in some instances by Miner but as often by others. The results of these studies on managerial motivation are as follows:

> Among the 24 experimental group analyses 96 percent indicate an overall improvement subsequent to managerial role motivation training. Among the 11 control group analyses, none indicate a total score improvement, and in fact there is one instance of a significant decline. It is hard to argue with the conclusion that the training does have an impact on motivation. (Miner 1993b, 185)

As well, a study on promotion rates over a five-year period subsequent to training (using a control group) indicated that of those who stayed, 86 percent in the trained group were promoted, and 57 percent in the control group were promoted (and 10 percent were demoted). Of those who left, 69 percent in the trained group were recommended for rehire, and 30 percent in the control group were recommended for rehire. A number of reviews of these training evaluation studies have been published, with the overall reaction being "that it is soundly grounded in research, and does produce substantial change" (Miner 1993b, 198).

The task theory has not produced an application derived directly from it, largely because McClelland's achievement motivation training was available (see Chapter 4). Insofar as the professional theory is concerned, only one attempt at a training application is noted in the literature and that involved special education teachers who received ten hours of training. The primary orientation of this effort was along the lines discussed in Chapter 8. The only change identified as a result was an increase in the desire to acquire status.

Another application is to use the role motivation theory instruments to select leaders or potential leaders in the appropriate domain. In this connection the major use has been to assess candidates by consulting firms or companies, following the leads established by validity studies, many of which are longitudinal in nature. The decline in motivation to manage during the 1960s and 1970s and thereafter (Miner 1974) accelerated the need for this type of application. Given the somewhat cumbersome demands of learning to score projective techniques at present, it would have been desirable to develop alternative methods. However, attempts to do this have not proved fruitful, and Miner appears to have given up on such efforts. In this connection a recent attempt to promote a general measure of motivation to lead, which appears to represent hierarchic leadership primarily, lacks the capacity to tap implicit levels of motivation and thus is inappropriate for testing role motivation theory (Chan and Drasgow 2001).

CONCLUSIONS

The ratings provided for role motivation theory present a generally positive picture. The importance rating by peers, at 4.05, is on the low side for the essential theories discussed in this book, suggesting a degree of ambivalence perhaps associated with the widespread use of a projective measure in testing the theory. The 4 star evaluation of validity is consistent with the extensive research in this area, almost all of which is positive. However, problems exist in that alternative measures that work as well have not been developed. One could also hope for a more gender neutral measure for the hierarchic theory and for an instrument to assess the validity of the group theory, although Miner's strategic decision to focus on the measures currently available seems justified. The similar 4 star rating for applications to practice is based largely on the demonstrated value of role motivation training and of the various MSCS measures for assessment purposes. Yet the lack of a truly effective approach to professional training represents somewhat of a problem and so too does the failure to provide more precise guidance on the use of the motivational measure for selection and assessment. In the latter instance, however, an article by Miner, Ebrahimi, and Wachtel (1995) does offer some solutions.

In the next two chapters, I take up two of the most dominant approaches to leadership at the present time. Both have moved leadership a long way from its early origins in the Ohio State University scales for consideration and initiating structure.

REFERENCES

Adler, Seymour, and Weiss, Howard M. (1988). Recent Developments in the Study of Personality and Organizational Behavior. *International Review of Industrial and Organizational Psychology,* 3, 307–30.

Ashforth, Blake E. (2001). *Role Transitions in Organizational Life: An Identity-Based Perspective.* Mahwah, NJ: Lawrence Erlbaum.

Carson, Kenneth P., and Gilliard, Debora J. (1993). Construct Validity of the Miner Sentence Completion Scale. *Journal of Occupational and Organizational Psychology,* 66, 171–75.

Chan, Kim-Yin, and Drasgow, Fritz (2001). Toward a Theory of Individual Differences and Leadership: Understanding the Motivation to Lead. *Journal of Applied Psychology,* 86, 481–98.

Chen, Chao C., Yu, K.C., and Miner, John B. (1997). Motivation to Manage: A Study of Women in Chinese State-owned Enterprises. *Journal of Applied Behavioral Science,* 160–73.

Cornelius, Edwin T. (1983). The Use of Projective Techniques in Personnel Selection. *Research in Personnel and Human Resources Management,* 1, 127–68.

Eagly, Alice H., Karau, Steven J., Miner, John B., and Johnson, Blair T. (1994). Gender and Motivation to Manage in Hierarchic Organizations: A Meta-Analysis. *Leadership Quarterly,* 5, 135–59.

Ebrahimi, Bahman (1999). Motivation to Manage in China: Implications for Strategic HRM. *Asia Pacific Business Review.* Special Issue on Management Revolution in China, 5 (3/4), 204–22.

Ensley, Michael D., Carland, James W., and Carland, Jo Ann C. (2000). Investigating the Existence of the Lead Entrepreneur. *Journal of Small Business Management,* 38(4), 59–77.

Foti, Roseanne J., and Miner, John B. (2003). Individual Differences and Organizational Forms in the Leadership Process. *Leadership Quarterly,* 14, 83–112.

Ginzberg, Eli, Miner, John B., Anderson, James K., Ginsburg, Sol W., and Herma, John L. (1959). *Breakdown and Recovery.* New York: Columbia University Press.

Golden, Brian R., Dukerich, Janet M., and Fabian, Frances H. (2000). The Interpretation and Resolution of Resource Allocation Issues in Professional Organizations: A Critical Examination of the Professional–Manager Dichotomy. *Journal of Management Studies,* 37, 1157–87.

Hibbard, Stephen (2003). A Critique of Lilienfeld et al.'s (2000) "The Scientific Status of Projective Techniques." *Journal of Personality Assessment,* 80, 260–71.

Jerome, William T. (1961). *Executive Control—the Catalyst.* New York: Wiley.

Jones, Candace, and Lichtenstein, Benyamin M.B. (2000). The "Architecture" of Careers: How Career Competencies Reveal Firm Dominant Logic in Professional Services. In Maury A. Peiperl, Michael B. Arthur, Rob Goffee, and Timothy Morris (Eds.), *Career Frontiers: New Conceptions of Working Lives.* Oxford, UK: Oxford University Press, 153–76.

Latham, Gary P. (1988). Human Resource Training and Development. *Annual Review of Psychology,* 39, 545–82.

Leavitt, Harold J. (2003). Why Hierarchies Thrive. *Harvard Business Review,* 81(3), 96–102.

Lilienfeld, Scott O., Wood, James M., and Garb, Howard N. (2000). The Scientific Status of Projective Techniques. *Psychological Science in the Public Interest,* 1, 27–66.

Miner, John B. (1960). The Effect of a Course in Psychology on the Attitudes of Research and Development Supervisors. *Journal of Applied Psychology,* 44, 224–32.

——— (1963). *The Management of Ineffective Performance.* New York: McGraw-Hill.

——— (1965). *Studies in Management Education.* New York: Springer.

——— (1974). *The Human Constraint: The Coming Shortage of Managerial Talent.* Washington, DC: BNA Books.

——— (1975). *The Challenge of Managing.* Philadelphia, PA: W.B. Saunders.

——— (1977). *Motivation to Manage: A Ten Year Update on the "Studies in Management Education" Research.* Eugene, OR: Organizational Measurement Systems Press.

——— (1980a). Limited Domain Theories of Organizational Energy. In Craig C. Pinder and Larry F. Moore (Eds.), *Middle Range Theory and the Study of Organizations.* Boston, MA: Martinus Nijhoff, 273–86.

——— (1980b). The Role of Managerial and Professional Motivation in the Career Success of Management Professors. *Academy of Management Journal,* 23, 487–508.

——— (1982). The Uncertain Future of the Leadership Concept: Revisions and Clarifications. *Journal of Applied Behavioral Science,* 18, 293–307.

——— (1985). *People Problems: The Executive Answer Book.* New York: Random House.

—— (1993a). Pursuing Diversity in an Increasingly Specialized Organizational Science. In Arthur G. Bedeian (Ed.), *Management Laureates: A Collection of Autobiographical Essays*, Vol. 2. Greenwich, CT: JAI Press, 283–319.

—— (1993b). *Role Motivation Theories.* London: Routledge.

—— (1997). *A Psychological Typology of Successful Entrepreneurs.* Westport, CT: Quorum.

—— (2000). Testing a Psychological Typology of Entrepreneurship Using Business Founders. *Journal of Applied Behavioral Science, 36,* 43–69.

—— (2002a). *Organizational Behavior: Foundations, Theories, and Analyses.* New York: Oxford University Press.

—— (2002b). The Role Motivation Theories of Organizational Leadership. In Bruce J. Avolio and Francis J. Yammarino (Eds.), *Transformational and Charismatic Leadership: The Road Ahead.* Oxford, UK: Elsevier Science, 309–38.

Miner, John B., Ebrahimi, Bahman, and Wachtel, Jeffrey M. (1995). How Deficiencies in Motivation to Manage Contribute to the Untied States' Competitiveness Problem (and What Can Be Done about It). *Human Resource Management, 34,* 363–87.

Miner, John B., and Raju, Nambury S. (2004). Risk Propensity Differences between Managers and Entrepreneurs and between Low- and High-growth Entrepreneurs: A Reply in a More Conservative Vein. *Journal of Applied Psychology, 89,* 3–13.

Miner, John B., Smith, Norman R., and Bracker, Jeffrey S. (1989). Role of Entrepreneurial Task Motivation in the Growth of Technologically Innovative Firms. *Journal of Applied Psychology, 74,* 554–60.

Nathan, Barry R., and Alexander, Ralph A. (1985). An Application of Meta-Analysis to Theory Building and Construct Validation. *Academy of Management Proceedings, 45,* 224–28.

Oliver, John E. (1982). An Instrument for Classifying Organizations. *Academy of Management Journal, 25,* 855–66.

Rauch, Andreas, and Frese, Michael (2000). Psychological Approaches to Entrepreneurial Success: A General Model and an Overview of Findings. *International Review of Industrial and Organizational Psychology, 15,* 101–41.

Russell, Craig J. (2001). A Longitudinal Study of Top-level Executive Performance. *Journal of Applied Psychology, 86,* 560–73.

Sathe, Vijay (2003). *Corporate Entrepreneurship: Top Managers and New Business Creation.* Cambridge, UK: Cambridge University Press.

Schneider, Benjamin, Ehrhart, Karen H., and Ehrhart, Mark G. (2002). Understanding High School Student Leaders II. Peer Nominations of Leaders and Their Correlates. *Leadership Quarterly, 13,* 275–99.

Schoonhoven, Claudia B., and Romanelli, Elaine (2001). *The Entrepreneurship Dynamic: Origins of Entrepreneurship and the Evolution of Industries.* Stanford, CA: Stanford University Press.

Schriesheim, Chester A., Castro, Stephanie L., Zhou, Xiaohua, and Yammarino, Francis J. (2001). The Folly of Theorizing "A" But Testing "B"—A Selective Level-of-Analysis Review of the Field and a Detailed Leader–Member Exchange Illustration. *Leadership Quarterly, 12,* 515–51.

Scott, W. Richard. (2001). *Institutions and Organizations.* Thousand Oaks, CA: Sage.

Shane, Scott, Locke, Edwin A., and Collins, Christopher J. (2003). Entrepreneurial Motivation. *Human Resource Management Review, 13,* 257–79.

Shaw, Jason D., Duffy, Michelle K., and Stark, Eric M. (2000). Interdependence and Preference for Group Work: Main and Congruence Effects on the Satisfaction and Performance of Group Members. *Journal of Management, 26,* 259–79.

Smith, Norman R., and Miner, John B. (1983). Type of Entrepreneur, Type of Firm, and Managerial Motivation: Implications for Organizational Life Cycle Theory. *Strategic Management Journal, 4,* 325–40.

Stewart, Wayne H., and Roth, Philip L. (2001). Risk Propensity Differences between Entrepreneurs and Managers: A Meta-Analytic Review. *Journal of Applied Psychology, 86,* 145–53.

——. (2004). Data Quality Affects Meta-Analytic Conclusions: A Response to Miner and Raju (2004) Concerning Entrepreneurial Risk Propensity. *Journal of Applied Psychology, 89,* 14–21.

Streiner, David L. (2003). Starting at the Beginning: An Introduction to Coefficient Alpha and Internal Consistency. *Journal of Personality Assessment, 80,* 99–103.

Taggar, Simon, Hackett, Rick, and Saha, Sudhir (1999). Leadership Emergence in Autonomous Work Teams: Antecedents and Outcomes. *Personnel Psychology, 52,* 899–926.

Tinsley, Howard E.A. (2000). The Congruence Myth: An Analysis of the Efficacy of the Person–Environment Fit Model. *Journal of Vocational Behavior, 56,* 147–79.

Vecchio, Robert P. (2003). Entrepreneurship and Leadership: Common Trends and Common Threads. *Human Resource Management Review*, 13, 303–27.

Wiklund, Johan, and Shepherd, Dean (2003). Aspiring for, and Achieving Growth: The Moderating Role of Resources and Opportunities. *Journal of Management Studies*, 40, 1919–41.

Wilderom, Celeste P.M., and Miner, John B. (1991). Defining Voluntary Groups and Agencies within Organization Science. *Organization Science,* 2, 366–78.

Winter, David G. (2002). The Motivational Dimensions of Leadership: Power, Achievement, and Affiliation. In Ronald E. Riggio, Susan E. Murphy, and Francis J. Pirozzolo (Eds.), *Multiple Intelligences and Leadership*. Mahwah, NJ: Lawrence Erlbaum, 119–38.

Yukl, Gary (2002). *Leadership in Organizations*. Upper Saddle River, NJ: Prentice-Hall.

Zenger, Todd, R., Lazzarini, Sergio G., and Poppo, Laura (2002). Informal and Formal Organization in New Institutional Economics. *Advances in Strategic Management,* 19, 277–305.

CHAPTER 18

CHARISMATIC LEADERSHIP THEORY

ROBERT HOUSE

Background
The Diverse Array of Propositions
    The Initial 1976 Theory
    Personality and Charisma
    Motivational Effects of Charismatic Leadership
    Integrating Charismatic Theory
    The Rhetoric of Charisma
    Homogeneity of Charisma Among Followers
    Reformulations for the Future
    Phases of Charismatic Change
Evaluation and Impact
    The Presidents Research Program
    The Authors' Compendium of Support
    Research Evidence—Personality
    Research Evidence—Crises
    Research Evidence—Behavior
    Role of Close and Distant Leaders
    Applications
    Research in Review
    Back to Weber
Conclusions

Importance rating	★ ★ ★ ★
Estimated validity	★ ★ ★ ★
Estimated usefulness	★ ★
Decade of origin	1970s

There are a number of leadership theories that emphasize such matters as the emotional attachment followers feel for the leader, the arousal of followers by the leader, enhancement of follower commitment to the mission set forth by the leader, follower trust and confidence in the leader, follower value orientations, and follower intrinsic motives. Leadership of this kind gives meaningfulness to follower activities by providing a sense of moral purpose and commitment. Leader behavior remains of concern, but it deals with symbolic acts, visionary messages, intellectual stimulation, displays of confidence in self and followers as well, expectations of personal sacrifice, and exhortations to performance beyond normal requirements (Shamir, House, and Arthur 1993). Theories of this nature have their origins in the concept of charisma as articulated by Weber (see Miner 2002a). They attempt to build on that construct, to fill in the blanks and iron out the inconsistencies, as well as to formulate propositions and hypotheses that are readily testable.

    Two theories of this kind are detailed and evaluated in this and the following chapter—Robert

House's charismatic leadership theory and Bernard Bass's theory of transformational, as opposed to transactional, leadership. These formulations are the best known and most widely researched of the genre. They are not identical, nor are they the same as other theories on the same topic, but all of these theories have much in common, presumably because all are rooted in Weber's writings. I consider House's charismatic leadership theory first, simply because it came into being first.

In 1996 House formulated an updated version of his path–goal theory concerned with work unit leadership (see Miner 2002a), which lists twenty-six propositions. One of the categories of propositions used is labeled value-based behavior (articulate a vision, display passion for the vision, demonstrate confidence in vision attainment, arouse nonconscious relevant follower motives, take risks to attain the vision, communicate high expectations, use symbolic behaviors to emphasize vision values, exhibit positive evaluations of followers frequently). Three propositions dealing with value-based leadership are specified.

All this sounds very much like charismatic leadership, and in fact it is. The charismatic theory had existed for almost twenty years at this point, and the three propositions of path–goal theory represent an attempt to bridge the two approaches. Yet in many respects path–goal theory is an effort to deal with the task of supervising work units within hierarchic organizations, while charismatic theory more often deals with leading organizations as a whole. In spite of the three propositions, the two theories tend to function in separate domains.

BACKGROUND

Robert House was born in 1932 in Toledo, Ohio. He has had a varied career. After graduating from the University of Detroit he worked for Chrysler and started on an MBA at his alma mater. Later he moved to the Ph.D. program in business at Ohio State, where he obtained the degree in 1960, and continued as a faculty member. During this period his basic education was in classical management with practically no organizational behavior included (House 1993). In the latter respect he has been self-taught. House left Ohio State in 1963 for McKinsey and Company and later moved to the City University of New York. In 1972, he went to the University of Toronto, and more recently he has joined the faculty at the University of Pennsylvania's Wharton School, where he remains.

The background of his charismatic theory is of interest. The debt to Weber has already been noted. In addition, a major influence stemmed from the political science and sociological literature that built upon Weber. Into this background, House integrated certain of the relevant research from psychology. He was particularly influenced by the thinking of David McClelland (see Chapter 4), which was interpreted for him by David Berlew, a former student of McClelland's. He says, "I learned a great deal from my conversations with Dave. He was a major influence on my thinking and the stimulus for the development of the 1976 theory" (House 1993, 63).

To avoid confusion, I should note that McClelland's theory also spawned a theoretical thrust of House's (1988), which focused specifically on power in organizations and the role of power motivation. This thrust ultimately was extended to the nature of power relationships in organic and mechanistic organizations (House 1991). This work by House on power is closely related to the charismatic leadership theory, but it is an independent theory and is not treated directly here.

THE DIVERSE ARRAY OF PROPOSITIONS

House's charismatic theory is stated in terms of various sets of propositions that extend from 1977 onward, and which may in fact not yet be ended. However, the key propositions of the theory appear, at least at this point, to have already been set in print. The theory was first presented at a professional meeting in 1976, but was not published until the following year.

The Initial 1976 Theory

House (1977) defines charismatic leadership as referring to a leader who has charismatic effects on followers to an unusually high degree. These effects include devotion, trust, unquestioned obedience, loyalty, commitment, identification, confidence in the ability to achieve goals, and radical changes in beliefs and values. This definition is said to be free of tautology because the effects are operationally determined by independent observers. The propositions follow:

1. Characteristics that differentiate leaders who have charismatic effects on subordinates from leaders who do not have such charismatic effects are dominance and self-confidence, need for influence, and a strong conviction in the moral righteousness of their beliefs. (In a footnote House indicates he would accept intellectual fortitude and integrity of character, as well as speech fluency or capacity for ready communication as additional characteristics.)

2. The more favorable the perceptions of the potential follower toward a leader, the more the follower will model: (a) the valences of the leader; (b) the expectations of the leader that effective performance will result in desired or undesired outcomes for the follower; (c) the emotional responses of the leader to work-related stimuli; (d) the attitudes of the leader toward work and toward the organization. Here "favorable perceptions" is defined as the perceptions of the leader as attractive, nurturant, successful, or competent.

3. Leaders who have charismatic effects are more likely to engage in behaviors designed to create the impression of competence and success than leaders who do not have such effects.

4. Leaders who have charismatic effects are more likely to articulate ideological goals than leaders who do not have such effects.

5. Leaders who simultaneously communicate high expectations of, and confidence in followers are more likely to have followers who accept the goals of the leader and believe that they can contribute to goal accomplishment, and are more likely to have followers who strive to meet specific and challenging performance standards.

6. Leaders who have charismatic effects are more likely to engage in behaviors that arouse motives relevant to the accomplishment of the mission than are leaders who do not have charismatic effects. (In a footnote, House indicates that the leader's ability to arouse subordinate motives is hypothesized to be a function of the extent to which subordinates hold favorable leader perceptions as specified in number 2 above).

[7.] Leaders are more likely to have charismatic effects in situations stressful for followers than in nonstressful situations. Further, it can be hypothesized that persons with the characteristics of dominance, self-confidence, need for influence, and strong convictions will be more likely to emerge as leaders under stressful conditions. Whether or not follower distress is a necessary condition for leaders to have charismatic effects or for persons with such characteristics to emerge as leaders is an empirical question that remains to be tested. (This is not stated as a numbered proposition, although it would appear to be number 7.)

8. A necessary condition for a leader to have charismatic effects is that the role of followers be definable in ideological terms that appeal to the follower. (House 1977, 194, 196–198, 201, 203–5)

Figure 18.1   **The Initial Model of Charismatic Leadership**

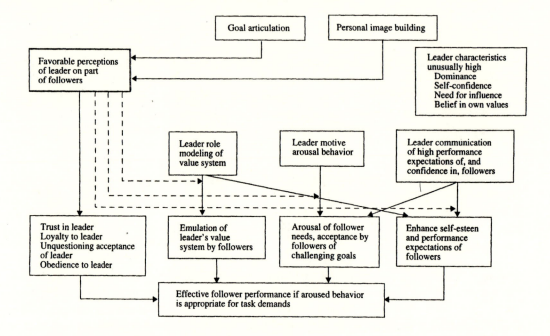

Source: House (1977, 206). Copyright © 1977 Southern Illinois University Press. Reprinted with permission.
Note: --- indicates a moderated relationship between leader and follower responses; leader characteristics are combined in a "possibly additive and possibly interactive" manner.

Figure 18.1 is presented as a summary statement of the theory. Note that what would have been proposition #7, regarding situations stressful for followers, is not depicted in the figure. Also, a subsequent restatement of the theory (House and Baetz 1979) fails to include the enigmatic proposition #7.

Personality and Charisma

There is roughly a ten-year gap in the published work on charisma theory at this point, although efforts in this area appear to have continued (House 1993). What finally did emerge, however, on the theoretical front is a set of finely tuned hypotheses suitable (and indeed used) for empirical testing purposes. These hypotheses were a component of a research program in which documents related to the behavior and personality characteristics of U.S. presidents were analyzed. The research itself will be considered later, but what is important at this point is how these hypotheses tie into the theoretical perspective.

In the first instances the hypotheses are as follows:

1. The biographies of cabinet members reporting to charismatic U.S. presidents (will) include more incidents of positive affective relations with the presidents and more positive affective reactions to their positions than (will) noncharismatic U.S. presidents.

2. The biographies of cabinet members reporting to charismatic U.S. presidents (will) include more incidents of charismatic behaviors on the part of the presidents than (will) biographies of noncharismatic presidents (House, Woycke, and Fodor 1988).

In the second instance, hypotheses dealing with charisma are specified as follows:

1. Presidential behavioral charisma will be positively related to presidential need for power and presidential activity inhibition and negatively related to presidential needs for achievement and affiliation.
2. Presidential behavioral charisma will be positively related to presidential performance. This relationship will remain after controlling for the effects of presidential motives on overall performance and on presidential behavioral charisma.
3. There will be positive relationships between presidential performance and need for power and activity inhibition, and there will be negative relationships between presidential performance and needs for achievement and affiliation, independent of any effects of motives on performance via behavioral charisma.
4. Crises are positively related to presidential behavioral charisma and presidential performance.
5. The institutional age of the presidency is positively related to presidential motives, level of crises within administrations, presidential behavioral charisma, and presidential performance (House, Spangler, and Woycke 1991, 368–71).

These hypotheses derive from what is referred to as the integrated House-McClelland model. This model is developed further elsewhere (House and Howell 1992) with the specification of the characteristics of what are termed socialized and personalized charismatic leaders. The model does indeed draw upon ideas advanced by McClelland regarding managers in hierarchic organizations, and it does appear to be aligned with House's (1977) earlier propositions regarding charismatic leaders. Yet it is well to recognize that McClelland (see Chapter 4) in his research was not dealing with charismatic leaders, only effective line managers.

Socialized charismatic leadership is defined to include (1) a basis for egalitarian behavior, (2) the services of collective interests rather than the leader's self-interest, and (3) the development and empowerment of others. Hypothesized characteristics of the socialized type are a high need for power combined with high activity inhibition, a low level of Machiavellian behavior, nonauthoritarianism, internal beliefs, and high self-esteem.

Personalized charismatic leadership on the other hand is defined as (1) being based on personal dominance and authoritarian behavior, (2) serving the self-interest of the leader and consequently self-aggrandizing, and (3) being exploitive of others. Such people are hypothesized to possess a high need for power in conjunction with low activity inhibition, high levels of Machiavellian behavior, high narcissism, high authoritarianism, external beliefs, and low self-esteem.

Motivational Effects of Charismatic Leadership

The next major extension of the theory involved an attempt to explain more fully the relationships between leader behaviors and their effects on followers (Shamir, House, and Arthur 1993). These formulations begin with a set of assumptions about human motivation and the self-concept:

1. People are not only pragmatic and goal-oriented but also self-expressive.
2. People are motivated to maintain and enhance their self-esteem and self-worth.
3. People are motivated to retain and increase their sense of self-consistency.
4. Self-concepts are composed at least partially of identities that include values and links to society.
5. People may be motivated by faith, which is not the same as expectancies (580).

Charismatic leaders achieve their effects by implicating followers' self-concepts. This in turn is accomplished by:

1. Increasing the intrinsic valence of effort
2. Increasing effort–accomplishment expectancies
3. Increasing the intrinsic valence of goal accomplishment
4. Instilling faith in a better future
5. Creating personal commitment

These motivational processes are activated by *role modeling,* whereby the leader assumes the role of a representative character, and by *frame alignment,* in accordance with which a set of follower values and beliefs become congruent and complementary with the leader's activities, goals, and ideology.

The theoretical propositions are then stated as follows:

1. In order to implicate the followers' self-concepts, compared to noncharismatic leaders, the deliberate and nondeliberate messages of charismatic leaders will contain:
   a) more references to values and moral justifications,
   b) more references to the collective and to collective identity,
   c) more references to history,
   d) more positive references to followers' worth and efficacy as individuals and as a collective,
   e) more expressions of high expectations from followers, and
   f) more references to distal goals and less reference to proximal goals.
2. The more leaders exhibit the behavior specified above, the more their followers will have:
   a) a high salience of the collective identity in their self-concept,
   b) a sense of consistency between their self-concept and their actions on behalf of the leader and the collective,
   c) a high level of self-esteem and self-worth,
   d) a similarity between their self-concept and their perception of the leader, and
   e) a high sense of collective efficacy.
3. The more leaders exhibit the behaviors specified in the theory, the more followers will demonstrate:
   a) personal commitment to the leader and the mission,
   b) a willingness to make sacrifices for the collective mission,
   c) organizational citizenship behavior, and
   d) meaningfulness in their work and lives.
4. A necessary condition for a leader's messages to have charismatic effects is that the message is congruent with the existing values and identities held by potential followers.

5. The more the potential followers have an expressive orientation toward work and life, the more susceptible they will be to the influence of charismatic leaders.
6. The more the potential followers have a principled orientation to social relations, the more susceptible they will be to the influence of charismatic leaders.
7. The emergence and effectiveness of charismatic leaders will be facilitated to the extent to which:
    a) there is an opportunity for substantial moral involvement on the part of the leader and the followers,
    b) performance goals cannot be easily specified and measured,
    c) extrinsic rewards cannot be made clearly contingent on individual performance,
    d) there are few situational cues, constraints, and reinforcers to guide behavior and provide incentives for specific performance, and
    e) exceptional effort, behavior, and sacrifices are required of both the leaders and followers (Shamir, House, and Arthur 1993, 586–90).

In this context the authors indicate that exceptional circumstances are not necessary for charismatic leadership to emerge; that exceptional conditions do not necessarily carry the implication of crisis, since opportunities may be involved as well; and that when crisis-handling and charisma occur together the effects tend to be short-term. Here charismatic leadership and crises are clearly unbundled in seeming contradiction to the House (1977) position.

Integrating Charismatic Theory

In a 1993 book chapter, House and Shamir attempt an integration of the various theories with roots in Weber's charisma, focusing on the treatment of charismatic behaviors. They do this by again specifying a set of propositions that collectively are said to accomplish this integrative purpose. The *first* such proposition is in reality a version of proposition #2 given in the previous section. However, a sixth consequence is now added, apparently taken from proposition #3 of the same set—a higher sense of meaningfulness in their work and lives.

The following three propositions are closely aligned with those stated previously as well:

2. Leaders who have charismatic effects are more likely to engage in behaviors that arouse motives relevant to the accomplishment of the mission than are those who do not have charismatic effects.
3. Leaders who have charismatic effects are more likely to arouse motives in the context of references to the mission and the collective than are those who do not have charismatic effects.
4. Leaders who have charismatic effects are more likely to behave in a manner that provides a personal and vivid example of the values of the mission than are leaders who do not.

Yet the last two propositions reflect an acceptance of ideas previously embodied in theories other than House's:

5. Leaders who have charismatic effects are more likely to challenge the assumptions, stereotypes, generalizations, and worldviews (weltanschauung) of followers than are leaders who do not have such effects.

Figure 18.2 **Model of the Charismatic Leadership Process**

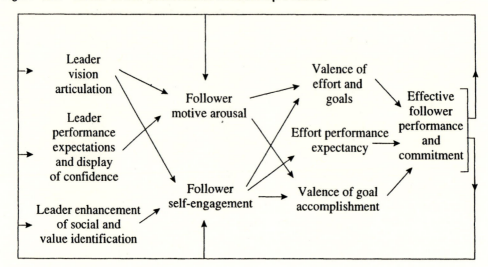

Source: House and Shamir (1993, 88). Copyright © 1998 Academic Press. Reprinted with permission.

6. Followers who are in a charismatic relationship with their leader are more likely to be intellectually stimulated by their leader's challenges to their assumptions, stereotypes, generalizations, and worldviews than are followers who are not in such a relationship. (House and Shamir 1993, 90–91, 95, 100)

In spite of these latter formulations and the goal of producing an integrated theory, as well as the use of terminology from expectancy and path–goal approaches to theorizing as reflected in Figure 18.2, there remain a number of differences among theories. Certain of these indeed are noted by House and Shamir (1993).

In another book chapter published at roughly the same time, House and Podsakoff (1994) also argue for integration, and apply the term *outstanding* (and outstanding leadership theory) to the various ideas dealing with charismatic, transformational, and visionary leadership phenomena; in this view charismatic leadership is one form of the outstanding type, but all three constructs are closely related. In this same publication the authors note certain behaviors "not associated with outstanding leadership," but advocated by other theorists. Among these are individualized consideration, environmental monitoring, leader adaptability, and intellectual stimulation. Yet in proposition #6 of House and Shamir (1993) intellectually stimulating behavior is accepted into charismatic leadership theory.

The Rhetoric of Charisma

Based on prior theorizing, especially that dealing with motivational effects (Shamir, House, and Arthur 1993), Shamir, Arthur, and House (1994, 29) set forth a set of propositions regarding the content of charismatic leaders' speeches (as opposed to the content of speeches by noncharismatic leaders) as follows:

1. more references to collective history and to the continuity between the past and the present;
2. more references to the collective and to collective identity, and fewer references to individual self-interest;
3. more positive references to followers' worth and efficacy as individuals and as a collective;
4. more references to the leader's similarity to followers and identification with followers;
5. more references to values and moral justifications, and fewer references to tangible outcomes and instrumental justifications;
6. more references to distal goals and the distant future, and fewer references to proximal goals and the near future; and
7. more references to hope and faith.

Homogeneity of Charisma Among Followers

A set of propositions dealing with the homogeneity of charismatic reactions among followers is proposed by Klein and House (1995). The idea is that charisma may flow from the leader fairly evenly to the various group members, or it may settle in pockets within the group. These propositions regarding the diffusion of charismatic effects are as follows:

1. A leader may share charismatic relationships with: a) all of his or her followers (high group-level charisma); b) some of his or her followers (variable, dyad-level charisma); or c) none of his or her followers (low group-level charisma).
2. The more a leader treats all of his or her followers in a consistent fashion, the more homogeneous the level of charisma characterizing each of the follower's relationship with the leader.
3. The greater the homogeneity in the nature of subordinates' values and orientations to work and to social relations, the greater the homogeneity of the charisma shared by each subordinate and the leader.
4. Charisma among the followers of a leader with charismatic qualities is likely to be homogeneous when: a) followers have sought membership in the leader's following; b) followers were selected by the leader; and c) both the leader and the followers have opted to keep the followers within the group.
5. The greater the follower's task interdependence and interaction, the more homogeneous the charisma that characterizes each follower's relationship with their common leader.
6. The higher the average level of charisma *and* the greater the homogencity of charismatic relations between a leader and his or her follower, the higher the morale and performance of the group.
7. The higher the average level of charisma *and* the greater the homogeneity of charismatic relations between a leader and his or her followers, the higher the risk of groupthink among the group.
8. Task interdependence and social interaction moderate the consequences of low homogeneity of charisma among the followers of a leader. When task interdependence and interaction are low, low homogeneity of charisma yields independent, dyadic relations with the leader. When task interdependence and interaction are high, high homogeneity of charisma yields intergroup conflict (Klein and House 1995, 187, 189–90, 192–93).

In addition to the ideas regarding homogeneity inherent in these propositions, this article contains certain other significant statements. Not only crises, but a variety of environmental conditions that merely arouse uncertainty, may give rise to charismatic leadership. The confluence of events that produce true, group-level charisma occurs only rarely; in this respect charisma seems like Maslow's view of self-actualization (see Miner 2002a). Thus, charismatic leadership training may well produce better subordinate relations, but it is unlikely to yield group-level charisma. The building of a group of subordinates who are open to charisma is a gradual process.

Reformulations for the Future

A chapter written by House (1995) covers much of the ground included in previous sets of propositions. However, there are some new ideas and some different ways of looking at old ones as well. The generic behaviors of outstanding leaders are described in a manner that appears to invoke "outstanding" as used in House and Podsakoff (1994). The behaviors are vision; passion and self-sacrifice; confidence, determination, and persistence; selective motive arousal; risk taking; expectations of and confidence in followers; developmental orientation; role modeling; demonstration of integrity; frame alignment; and symbolic behavior. Some of these are more closely aligned with House's earlier positions than others, although he now appears to accept all.

Propositions dealing with charisma are sprinkled throughout the chapter:

- The aforementioned leader behaviors will differentiate outstanding leaders from others in the twenty-first century.
- When followers experience a high degree of stress or stressful uncertainty, the emergence and perceived effectiveness of leaders who engage in the aforementioned leadership behaviors will be enhanced.
- Whenever the roles of followers can be authentically described or defined as providing an opportunity for moral involvement, the potential leader can articulate ideological goals and values and have a strong influence on the motivational states of followers.
- The emergence of outstanding leadership will be enhanced to the extent that

    1. performance goals cannot be easily specified and measured,
    2. extrinsic rewards cannot be made clearly contingent on individual performance,
    3. few situational cues, constraints, and reinforcers exist to guide behavior and provide incentives for specific performance,
    4. exceptional effort, behavior, and sacrifices are required of both leaders and followers, and
    5. potential followers experience feelings of unfair treatment, persecution, and oppression from sources other than the leader.

- Neocharismatic leadership . . . causes followers to recognize values that are shared with the leader and among the members of the collective; arouses in followers powerful nonconscious motives; engages followers' strongly held self-concepts such as self-efficacy and self-worth; and brings about strong follower identification with the vision and the collective. (House 1995, 421–22, 424, 438)

Phases of Charismatic Change

A recent set of propositions utilizes the unfreezing-moving-refreezing model proposed by Lewin (see Chapter 3) to specify what happens at each phase of a charismatic transformation (Fiol, Harris, and House 1999). These ideas are predicated on the finding from Spangler and House (1991) that the use of the word "not" in presidential writings and speeches may reflect a leader's motivation to break current frames through negation. This interpretation differs from McClelland's position that the use of "not" provides a measure of activity inhibition. The propositions advanced are:

1. Charismatic leaders will use the word "not" more often than noncharismatic leaders.
2. a) During a transformation, charismatic leaders will use the word "not" frequently during the initial phase, more frequently during the middle phase, and infrequently during later phases.
   b) The use of "nots" by noncharismatic leaders will not follow the curvilinear pattern of charismatic leaders.
3. Charismatic leaders will use more inclusive language than noncharismatic leaders.
4. Charismatic leaders will communicate at higher levels of abstraction than noncharismatic leaders.
5. All effective leaders will use more inclusive language with higher levels of abstraction.
6. a) During a transformation, charismatic leaders will use higher levels of inclusion and abstraction during the middle phase than in earlier or later phases.
   b) The use of inclusion and abstraction by noncharismatic leaders will not follow the curvilinear pattern of charismatic leaders (Fiol, Harris, and House 1999, 462–63).

Although this is the end of formal theorizing for present purposes, House (1999) does take the occasion of a response to criticism to clarify certain theoretical points. One such clarification is to emphasize that charisma in any form is in his view a rare phenomenon. Another relates to the relation of crisis and follower stress to charismatic leadership. The position stated is that some form of severe threat or stress experienced by followers operates to facilitate charismatic leadership, both as to its emergence and as to its effectiveness.

Later, a more comprehensive statement of charismatic leadership dynamics was proposed as follows:

> First is the encounter of the leader with a constituency that results in follower's *identification* with the leader's personality. After that the articulated vision arouses followers to *activity.* The leader's personal sacrifices and role modeling then inspire an elite of the followers to emulate the leader by *committing* themselves to the mission. But the improved performance of dedicated followers also brings routinization, which leads to their *disenchantment* and to bureaucratization and to *depersonalization* of other followers. From these it is only a small step to the final phase of follower's *alienation* from the leader, the mission, and the organization. (Jacobsen and House, 2001, 78)

The six italicized stages may eventuate in the routinization of charisma into a bureaucracy, but that depends on many factors; the outcomes of charisma are unpredictable.

At the moment this represents the sum total of House's theorizing on charismatic leadership. A theoretical contribution is contained in Antonakis and House (2002), but this is primarily in the form of an addendum to the theory proposed by Bass. Thus I consider it in the next chapter.

EVALUATION AND IMPACT

There is a chicken and egg problem in relating research to theory in the charismatic leadership domain. Undoubtedly the 1976 theory did precede the research to be considered, and thus that research, to the extent it is relevant, can be treated as theory testing. But as the theoretical propositions have evolved since, from 1988 to 1999, it becomes very difficult to disentangle research that prompted theory from research that evaluates it. This problem of theoretical source is compounded as House and his colleagues have moved from the basic charismatic theory to more integrated positions dealing with outstanding or neocharismatic leadership, which attempt, not always successfully, to bring together the theories of House and Bass, and other related formulations.

The Presidents Research Program

This program involves a series of studies undertaken by House and others working with him to look into the charismatic leadership process using U.S. presidents and documents relating to them. This research program appears to provide some direct tests of stated theory.

The initial study tested the hypotheses stated by House, Woycke, and Fodor (1988), which in turn relate closely to the 1976 theory. The biographies of cabinet members of presidents determined by historians to be charismatic leaders were content analyzed and compared with similar data on noncharismatic leaders. Although sample sizes are small, significance was obtained. There was evidence that charismatic presidents had more charismatic effects on their cabinet members in terms of the frequency of affective responses aroused. Also, these same presidents were found to exhibit more charismatic behaviors—display of self-confidence, high performance expectations, confidence in follower abilities, strong ideological goals, and individualized consideration for followers. The hypotheses were confirmed.

The next study utilized the cabinet member biographies plus a host of other sources to derive measures of presidential motivation (power, achievement, affiliation), activity inhibition (the use of "not"), crises faced, charisma, and performance (House, Spangler, and Woycke 1991). The results provide considerable support for the five hypotheses, particularly those involving power motivation. Personality factors in a president do appear to make a difference in both charisma and performance. The data are least strong for the hypothesized negative relationships involving affiliation motivation. Consistent with hypothesis 4, crises faced were positively related to both charisma and performance. Thus both leader personality and contextual variables appear to be operating when charisma is engaged.

A less compelling study utilized content analysis of a speech given by Jesse Jackson to the Democratic National Convention to exemplify the seven propositions advanced by Shamir, Arthur, and House (1994). The data are consistent with the propositions, but the findings are not presented in quantitative terms and involve one speech by one former presidential candidate widely considered to be a charismatic leader.

In Fiol, Harris, and House (1999), the authors return to the data on past presidents, and specifically to the use of negation in presidential speeches. The findings consistently support the propositions. Charismatic leaders do exhibit patterns of rhetoric involving not only the use of negation, but also inclusive language and high levels of abstraction. The phase variations anticipated based on Lewin's concept of change are clearly in evidence.

A test of the six-stage model of charismatic leadership dynamics was conducted using a computer simulation and matching historical time series information on six charismatic leaders, one of whom was a U.S. president, against this model (Jacobsen and House 2001). In all instances the simulation reproduced a sizable proportion of the variance (in the 62 to 90 range), thus confirming the adequacy of the theory—at least for charismatic leadership of the past.

Yet the outcomes from charisma remain something of an enigma, especially as they relate to the achievement of a vision. To investigate this issue Waldman, Ramírez, House, and Puranam (2001) conducted a study involving the CEOs of large corporations. They found a marginal relationship between CEO charisma and corporate profits, which became highly significant for those individuals whose companies were experiencing a high degree of perceived uncertainty in their environments. The evidence thus appears to support a view that charisma is particularly important under conditions of stress; it helps little or may even detract from performance otherwise.

Recently, House has taken the study of charisma global, working with a large number of colleagues in countries around the world. Only preliminary results on this program are available at this writing, but data from managers in over fifty countries indicate considerable agreement on the attributes and behaviors perceived to enhance charismatic leadership. The results indicate that charismatic leaders are universally seen as positive, encouraging, foresightful, planning ahead, motive arousers, confidence builders, dynamic, and motivational (DenHartog, House, Hanges, Ruiz-Quintanilla, and Dorfman 1999). Thus considerable cross-cultural consistency exists in the way charisma is defined. Furthermore, this consistency appears around factors that are often the same as those hypothesized by House earlier.

The Authors' Compendium of Support

In presenting many of their theoretical statements, the theory's authors open with a quick overview of existing studies said to support charismatic leadership theory in some form. These treatments refer to "at least twenty empirical investigations" (House, Spangler, and Woycke 1991), "at least 35 empirical investigations" (Shamir, House, and Arthur 1993), "numerous studies" (House and Shamir 1993), "over 30 studies" (House and Podsakoff 1994), and the like. In most instances there is little discussion of the content of these studies, only the statement that they contain supporting evidence. The uncritical reader might well jump to the conclusion that this is proven theory.

These are reports of research in some form, a number of them qualitative studies, which are dated as of sometime during the 1980s or early 1990s. A large number have not been formally published (dissertations, working papers, speeches, etc.) and thus are not readily available for review. Several relate primarily to Bass's transformational theory and will be considered in the next chapter. In other instances the studies appear to bear on charismatic leadership theory, but they were not undertaken specifically for the purpose of testing it. The authors cast a wide net and sometimes find research of a very tangential nature. There is nothing wrong with attempting to put a positive spin on one's theory, but the uncritical reader does need to be forewarned—things are not quite as positive as they are made out to be.

An example of a study cited to support charismatic theory, but clearly not conducted to test that theory, is Yukl and Van Fleet (1982). Yet there are tests in this period, and good ones. This point is best illustrated with reference to two laboratory studies, not exactly the kind of research one would anticipate in the charismatic leadership domain.

In the first of these studies, charismatic leadership as portrayed by professional actresses was compared with the more traditional initiating structure and consideration (Howell and Frost 1989). Individuals working under charismatic leaders had higher task performance on various indexes, higher satisfaction, and less role conflict than those working under consideration behavior. In comparison to initiating structure, charisma produced much the same effects as with consideration, but overall the differences were somewhat less pronounced. The findings are interpreted as consistent with House's 1976 theory.

The other study, also conducted with students, dealt with the effects of a crisis related to course grades. The reported results are that

> conditions of crisis facilitate the emergence of leaders who are perceived to be charismatic. Furthermore, such leaders are also perceived as more effective and more satisfying to followers than their less charismatic counterparts. . . . The increased charismatic appeal of leaders under conditions of crisis is particularly noteworthy in the absence of any evidence of the impact of crisis on ratings of transactional leadership. (Pillai and Meindl 1991, 238)

To the extent that charismatic theory anticipates such crisis effects, the theory is supported. But there has been some uncertainty in this regard.

Before turning to the more recent research, mention should be made of a study from the early period that has not been cited by House and his colleagues. This study involved the creation of an instrument directly from the charismatic effects specified in House (1977). An argument is then developed indicating that these effects may be reduced to the more mundane constructs of expert power, referent power, and job involvement (Halpert 1990). Correlational analyses were then carried out indicating that indeed the reduction appears justified. The equating of charisma with power is certainly consistent with theory, but the findings also seem to remove any heroic quality from charismatic leadership. This is a finding that clearly calls for further research.

Research Evidence—Personality

The second half of the 1990s saw a substantial number of research publications that advanced understanding of charismatic leadership considerably. Among these studies was one bearing on the Halpert (1990) assertions. Kudisch, Poteet, Dobbins, Rush, and Russell (1995) found that leader charisma added to the prediction of subordinate attitudes above and beyond the variance accounted for by expert and referent power; thus, charisma is distinguishable from these two types of power. However, the study did not consider job involvement and measured charisma quite broadly. Furthermore, the findings do replicate Halpert's (1990) results as to the important role played by expert and referent power in charismatic leadership.

Other studies add to the understanding of personality factors in charismatic leadership. In one such instance historical figures categorized as exhibiting socialized or personalized charismatic leadership from biographical documents were compared to establish the distinguishing characteristics of the latter. Personalized leaders were viewed as more harmful to others, more aggressive, less moral, and generated more negative comments from biographers. In terms of personality they exhibited an uninhibited need for power, a view of others as instruments to be used for one's own purposes, a destructive image of the world, a belief that personal goals would not be achieved because of prevailing uncertainties, narcissism (selfishness and a propensity to overvalue one's own achievements), and a fear that promoted strong self-protective tendencies. However, self-regulation and self-monitoring did not distinguish the two groups (O'Connor, Mumford, Clifton, Gessner, and Connelly 1995). The theoretical distinction between socialized and personalized charismatic leadership receives considerable support. Subsequent research (Strange and Mumford 2002) reinforces this latter conclusion, but it does not entertain the possibility that socialized and personalized charismatic leadership may not be mutually exclusive types.

Another biographical study focused on U.S. presidents and found that narcissism was not only associated with charisma, but also with a variety of indexes of performance effectiveness (Deluga 1997). Unfortunately, this research did not deal directly with the socialized versus personalized distinction. Yet a subsequent effort utilized the same data base to focus on the role of proactivity, defined as a disposition to influence the environment (Deluga 1998). This characteristic deals with such behaviors as influencing followers, seizing opportunities for change, demonstrating initiative, and persevering in actions. Again, the personality variable emerges as playing an important role in both charismatic leadership and presidential effectiveness. This role appears to extend beyond any such roles played by the needs for power, achievement, or affiliation.

Deluga (2001) returns to the American presidency, charisma, and rated performance, but this time to study the role of Machiavellianism, defined as "a social influence process embracing the use of politics, power, and expressive behaviors" (340). This can mean becoming actively involved in unsavory manipulation of others, and has been proposed as a predictor of exploitive, self-aggrandizing personalized charismatic leadership (House and Howell 1992). Machiavellianism emerges as related to both charismatic leadership and rated performance in the presidency. Also, personalized and socialized charismatic leadership were shown not to be mutually exclusive concepts; a person can be high on both. All in all the Deluga research raises considerable doubt concerning any exclusive tie between socialized charisma and leader effectiveness.

A topic that has received little research attention, though included in House's propositions, is the characteristics of followers who form charismatic relationships with their leaders. A study by Ehrhart and Klein (2001) takes up this follower side of the charismatic equation. Values held by followers proved to be especially important—in particular strong worker participation values and being low in security work values. Leaders displaying charismatic behaviors attracted followers with both sets of values. Personality factors did not exhibit a relationship, and there was nothing to indicate any sharing of similar characteristics between leader and follower, as hypothesized.

Research Evidence—Crises

The role of crises in promoting charismatic leadership has continued to be a topic of research interest. Pillai and Meindl (1998) found in a retrospective analysis that crises and stress were associated with *reduced* perceptions of leader charisma, apparently because after the crisis ends there is a fall-off in the attribution of charisma by followers. This, however, does not controvert the previous conclusion that crises facilitate the *emergence* of charismatic leadership. This study is also significant in indicating that other situational factors in addition to crises, namely organic structures and work group collective values, are related to charismatic leadership; both are important to the nurturance of charisma.

A longitudinal study by Hunt, Boal, and Dodge (1999) provides considerable support for the previous findings. These researchers identified two kinds of charismatic leadership—a visionary type and a crisis-responsive type. Over time the effects of crisis-responsive charismatic leadership tend to decay, while this decline does not appear with the visionary type. However, this study did not find the same consistent positive effects of charisma on performance that others have observed. Overall it appears that House's initial uncertainty regarding the effects of crises was justified. The relationships involved are complex, but crises are clearly more strongly related to charisma emergence and the early phases than to continued manifestation and termination.

I noted previously that Waldman, Ramírez, House, and Puranam (2001) found that perceived environmental uncertainty (and thus presumably a degree of crisis) moderated the charisma–performance relationship in large corporations. This would appear to be consistent with the focus on charisma emergence in other studies of similar phenomena. However, an attempt to replicate this finding (Waldman and Javidan 2002) produced discrepant results. The main effect from CEO charisma to profit was significant, but environmental uncertainty added nothing more. Given that the range on the uncertainty variable in this second study was severely restricted, obtaining results involving it may well have been out of the question. But we do not know.

Research Evidence—Behavior

An aspect of charismatic behavior that has received recent attention is some type of self-sacrificing activity where there is either abandonment or postponement of personal interests or welfare (Choi and Mai-Dalton 1999); this is part of the House theory. As hypothesized, self-sacrificing behavior is found to exhibit positive effects on charisma in both student and industrial samples. In a laboratory study Yorges, Weiss, and Strickland (1999) obtained much the same result. Sacrifice led to charismatic ascriptions and thus greater influence over followers. In contrast, apparent personal benefit tended to deprive a leader of charisma, and this effect was particularly striking. Perhaps this is why charisma is less common in the business context (with its widely publicized high levels of compensation, stock options, and perquisites) than in politics and religion.

Another laboratory study looked specifically into the effects of communicating a vision, implementing the vision through task cues, and demonstrating a charismatic communication style—all core components of charismatic leadership theory (Kirkpatrick and Locke, 1996). The results were mixed. Vision affected follower attitudes, but influenced performance primarily in an indirect manner. Task cues to implement the vision had the most pronounced direct impact on performance. Charismatic communication demonstrated few effects of any kind, suggesting that substance or content may be more important than style and rhetoric, at least for the influence of charismatic behavior on close, face-to-face followers.

Yet a study by Awamleh and Gardner (1999) that considered the effects of vision content, vision delivery (communication), and organizational-level performance on perceived leader charisma and effectiveness found all three independent variables played an important role. Charismatic communication clearly did have an impact here. Similarly, the image-based rhetoric of U.S. presidents was found to relate to both charisma and greatness (Emrich, Brower, Feldman, and Garland 2001). Yet the Kirkpatrick and Locke (1996) results suggest that this result cannot be assumed in all instances.

Further evidence in support of charismatic leadership theory comes from a study by Shea and Howell (1999), which found that charismatic behaviors produced high levels of task performance whether or not feedback on performance was provided. Yet research conducted within the Israeli armed forces to test certain aspects of the self-concept extensions to charismatic leadership theory (Shamir, House, and Arthur 1993) did not yield the expected results. Certain follower effects were found for leader behaviors that reflect an emphasis on the group's collective identity, but other leader behaviors did not operate in accordance with the theory at all. The authors say that "in general the self-concept-based theory did not receive much support in our study" (Shamir, Zakay, Breinin, and Popper 1998, 404). The particular military context may have been a factor, but still some correction to the prevailing optimism regarding charismatic theory seems warranted.

Role of Close and Distant Leaders

A theoretical distinction that might have been made, but has not, is between charismatic behaviors addressed to and assessed by close, face-to-face followers and such behaviors as they are experienced at a distance, often through the medium of intervening processes. An example would be the close charismatic leadership of a U.S. president experienced by cabinet members versus the distant leadership experienced by members of the voting public. Charismatic leadership theory does not make such a distinction, but in fact almost all of its tests have been close in nature. However, Shamir (1995) has raised the possibility that perceptions at a distance are more idealized, more susceptible to image building, more prototypical, depend less on observable behavior, are based more on leader visions, and are influenced greatly by rhetoric. In this view, close and distant charisma are far from being the same thing.

Shamir (1995) also presents data bearing on this matter. Students were asked to identify charismatic leaders with whom they had and had not had direct relationships, and they were interviewed for details on each. As it turned out, over 80 percent of the distant leaders were political, while the close leaders were much more varied. Leader traits, behaviors, and effects as perceived by the followers were identified and compared for close and distant relationships. In over 65 percent of these comparisons, differences of a significant nature were observed. In general these differences followed a pattern very similar to that hypothesized.

A second attempt to look into this issue, also conducted in Israel, is described by Yagil (1998). The followers were in the military and were asked to provide information regarding their attributions of charisma to their platoon leaders (close) and their battalion commanders (distant). The study was limited to a circumscribed set of characteristics, some of which proved to differentiate close and distant charisma and some of which did not. The data continue to suggest that the two types of charisma are not the same, but a clear picture of exactly what is involved in each instance requires further study. This is an issue that seems to be allied with the direct and indirect leadership distinction as developed by Lord (Chapter 15). Leadership theory has not given enough attention to such matters, and it should (see Waldman and Yammarino 1999).

Applications

In his writings about charisma, House has given little attention to matters of application, except perhaps to convey the very general impression that being a charismatic leader is a good idea. Recently, however, he has set forth certain "principles for leading through vision and values" (Hauser and House 2000, 260). These are inductive statements derived from the research of others and his own. Together they appear to represent an outline of a training program to teach charismatic leadership, although they are not stated as such. These principles follow:

1. The vision statement should meet the following criteria: brevity, clarity, abstractness, challenge, future orientation, stability, desirability or ability to inspire, identification of intended products, markets, and strategy.
2. The vision should deal with issues of change, an idealized future for the followers, ideal goals, and people working together.
3. The vision should be situation-specific, appropriate, and yet unique in the industry.
4. In articulating a challenging new vision, relate it to the past of the organization and align it with the values of the employees and the dominant society.
5. Build cohesive understanding of the vision among the top management team.
6. Encourage a high degree of participation in the implementation of the vision.
7. Articulate the vision in a dramatic way.
8. Communicate the vision first to highly influential and cooperative individuals in the organization in order to generate its rapid adoption.
9. Link the vision to task cues and goals.
10. Engage in behaviors that are consistent with the vision, highly visible, and involve personal sacrifice.

11. Use symbols, metaphors, and images that are consistent with the vision (Hauser and House 2000, 260–65).

These principles have not been tested as a unit in the way that they might be presented in a management development program, for instance; thus their usefulness in practice is unknown.

Although House has not developed any training program of this kind, others have created related courses and have tested their impacts. Thus, Towler (2003) studied the effects of an effort that taught articulating a vision; appealing to followers' values; use of autobiography; use of metaphors, analogies, and stories; and self-efficacy language. Role playing was a key element. In comparison with control groups, those who experienced training did change on some of the variables measured, and thus there was some support for the effectiveness of the program. However, it would be stretching the findings to say that charismatic leaders were created.

A second study on a course designed to improve skills in charismatically communicating a vision, with particular emphasis on being inspirational, appears to have covered much the same ground as the Towler (2003) program, and with similar methods (Frese, Beimel, and Schoenborn 2003). Again, only a portion of the agenda set forth by Hauser and House (2000) was covered. The results in comparison with control conditions were encouraging, but the study failed to measure "long-term objective effects of the training on the units' performance and organizational commitment by the subordinates."

These studies are a good beginning, but their results are a long way from validating the eleven principles set forth by Hauser and House (2000). Much more is needed.

Research in Review

In closing, in an extensive review of charisma and leadership theory and research, Bryman (1992) notes that he has been rather critical, but adds that developments in this area are at an early stage and that he does not wish to "nip in the bud" what the future may hold. Given the outburst of activity in the latter 1990s and since, it is no longer possible to consider this an undernourished field, and Bryman appears to have been right in anticipating this state of affairs. The research base is rapidly becoming the equal of that available for numerous other organizational behavior theories. Furthermore, this research is often of an experimental nature, where charisma and variables with a theoretical relation to it are manipulated in the laboratory. This is not exactly what would have been expected, but it has been a felicitous development and appears to have contributed both to an understanding of causality and to the generalizability of findings.

A comparison of House's many propositions against this research base clearly leaves many propositions unaccounted for insofar as available studies are concerned. This is particularly true of some of the more recent propositions, although since the recent theorizing has often incorporated ideas from other related theories, particularly Bass's, there are additional studies that need to be brought to bear; we will get to these in the next chapter. It can be said now, however, that these attempts at integration have both expanded the horizons of charismatic leadership theory and added a measure of ambiguity to it. There are some inconsistencies, on such matters as the role of crises and the scope of charisma, for instance.

Overall, the research appears to provide considerable support for the basic theory, if not for each specific formulation, at least for the major thrusts. Something like charisma does appear to be a meaningful and important leadership construct, and personality, as well as follower (or group), variables do seem to play an important role in that construct (van Knippenberg and Hogg 2003).

Charismatic leadership appears to work because it creates a match between followers and their values and the values and culture of the organization (Fry 2003).

As has been indicated, "the self-concept theory of charismatic leadership provides the most detailed explanation of leader influence on followers, but even this theory needs more clarification of how the various types of influence processes interact, their relative importance, and whether they are mutually compatible" (Yukl 2002, 262).

The theory as stated emphasizes a leader who empowers followers rather than placing them in a dependent role. Perhaps this is one reason the self-concept views have not found support in a military setting (Shamir, Zakay, Breinin, and Popper 1998). In any event, charismatic leadership theory in its self-concept version exhibits considerable convergence with Lord's views on the subject (see Chapter 15). The parallels and divergences between the two approaches need to be spelled out, but even more important is the need for research in this area. To date, the issue is clouded, at least within charismatic theory.

A problem that charismatic leadership theory faces is that charisma clearly can be a source of negative outcomes—people rise to the top who do not have the capability to produce positive outcomes once they get there (Hogan, Raskin, and Fazzini 1990). Yet charismatic leadership needs to exist in an environment of positive outcomes in order to thrive; that is what the research says. Under failure conditions followers will turn away. Theory has not really dealt effectively with this particular dark side of charisma. Three types of flawed charismatics have been described—the high-likeability floater, the resentful person, and the narcissist. The latter in particular represents a problem in that Deluga (1997) has found narcissism to represent a characteristic of charismatic leaders generally. Clearly, we need a theory that will handle the role of narcissism, and Machiavellianism too, in charismatic relationships. Are they tied in some way to self-efficacy?

One of the charismatic behaviors that House describes is personal image building, and on the evidence this is important. The implication is that charismatic leaders are exceptionally expressive people whose use of rhetoric and drama comes naturally; they are actors and actresses, always on stage and at the center of attention. Their personalities are those of dramaturgy. This type of formulation has indeed been made the centerpiece of a theory of the charismatic relationship (Gardner and Avolio 1998). It may be why professional actors and actresses appear to be so easily trained for performances in the laboratory experiments; indeed, there is some research support for these formulations (Sosik, Avolio, and Jung 2002).

The difficulty, however, is that this same desire to be at the center of attention, to stand out from the group and act out a role, often has been found to characterize successful managers in general (see the discussion of hierarchic role motivation theory in Chapter 17). In this regard, as in certain others, charismatic theory needs to make a clear distinction between characteristics and behaviors that typify charismatic managers and other kinds of effective managers. The research often raises questions in this area.

A review of the research literature on top-level executive leadership concludes that visionary and inspirational leadership are important for organizational effectiveness (Zaccaro 2001). Yet, in this and other discussions of this subject, it becomes apparent that this conclusion holds specifically for hierarchic, bureaucratic organizational forms (Zaccaro and Banks 2001). Research within organizations structured differently, using House's charismatic theory and focused on the personalities and behaviors that are involved there, is distinctly lacking (see Miner 2002b). In fact, as House himself notes, there are many aspects of charismatic theory that still need to be tested, both to validate some of the propositions and to demarcate the theory's domain more clearly (Aditya, House, and Kerr 2000).

Finally, I should mention a review of the charismatic leadership literature from the viewpoint of recognizing and appropriately applying levels-of-analysis considerations. This review ends by castigating both theorists and researchers for their failures in this regard (Yammarino, Dionne, and Chun 2002). The authors note that the entire field is built "upon empirical publications of which over 90% do not address, incorrectly address, ignore, misspecify, misuse, or abuse levels-of-analysis issues" (47).

Does this mean that we should throw out all that has been discussed here? I do not think so. We do not know how much error is actually introduced by these considerations, or how frequently conclusions are incorrectly specified. On the evidence it would appear that this can happen, but certainly not at the 90 percent level, and probably rather rarely.

Back to Weber

One of the major sources of criticism that charismatic leadership theory has faced comes from certain more sociologically oriented scholars who feel that House in his writings has not been true to the Weberian origins (Nur 1998). Is this type of criticism justified? For several reasons I do not believe it is, but that conclusion requires amplification.

The biggest difference is that Weber was concerned with a quality that had strong religious overtones. Charismatics were treated as endowed with supernatural, superhuman powers with divine origins. This belief was the source of their power over followers. Congruent with this power, charismatic leaders were sources of change who operated to mobilize efforts to subvert the status quo and existing routines within bureaucracy. They were rare because the attribution of divine powers is no everyday affair. They tended to thrive on crises.

House's propositions, on the other hand, do not deal with divine attributions, and thus they serve to tame charisma; they focus on different sources of power; they do not necessarily concern themselves with revolutionary change; they are inconsistent in their consideration of the role of crises; and they seem on occasion to imply a wide dispersion of charisma, even though House often says charisma is rare. Furthermore, his research utilizes measures that seem far removed from Weber's concept of charisma. The operationalizations developed by Conger and Kanungo (1998), for instance, came much closer to the constructs proposed by Weber.

Yet House, in spite of his debt to Weber, was proposing his own theory, one which he hoped would spark the leadership research that Weber had not. He has succeeded in that objective, and the research has given his ideas considerable, although not universal, support. He certainly has every right to propose any theory he wishes; that is how science advances. His formulations were not intended to be a mere reinterpretation of Weber, and they are not.

Furthermore, departures from Weber are to be found among those with a sociological approach to the field also. Etzioni placed charisma in many organizational contexts that Weber, with his emphasis on rarity, did not (see Miner 2002a). Bryman (1992) is critical of Etzioni's approach, indicating that "in redefining charisma so that it has a broad application across a wide span of organizations, the resulting definition is so inclusive that it lacks a specific referent" (92). Bryman feels that this is the reason that Etzioni's views on charisma in his opinion have lacked impact. However, an alternative view is that the lack of operationalization has undermined the conduct of research. House's approach, on the other hand, has been operationalized and its expanded scope has made for a much more potentially significant and useful theory insofar as dealing with the topic of leadership is concerned.

A final point on which Weber and House differ is the extent to which the routinization of charisma—the processes through which charismatically introduced changes are institutionalized and carried on into the future—is a major theoretical focus. This was a primary concern for Weber; it is given much less attention by House. Trice and Beyer (1986), among others, have argued that a complete theory of charismatic leadership must deal with the routinization issue. I am inclined to agree. Routinization requires that matters of succession be considered, and that positive outcomes be maintained long enough so that charisma can be retained to be institutionalized. These are important matters for charismatic leadership theory; they need to be addressed more fully.

CONCLUSIONS

With regard to the ratings, charismatic leadership theory does well, except with regard to practical applications. The importance rating of 4.76 is toward the top of the leadership theories, indicating that the field has a quite favorable perception. The estimated validity with 4 stars is very good, consistent with what reviewers have to say in assessing the charismatic theory. Yet there are gaps in the research coverage and in the logical consistency of the formulations. These do not appear to be excessive, or to threaten the overall validity of the theory, but they are sufficient to require both further research and some theoretical alterations. House, until recently, has not addressed the usefulness issue, probably because he tends to view charisma as a rare phenomenon. Given what has been happening on the training front, he probably should do something in this regard, if only to be sure that practice is correctly aligned with theory. His principles represent a beginning. However, the next step of undertaking a training evaluation study remains to be applied. Thus, the 2 star rating appears appropriate.

REFERENCES

Aditya, Ram N., House, Robert J., and Kerr, Steven (2000). Theory and Practice of Leadership: Into the New Millennium. In Cary L. Cooper and Edwin A. Locke (Eds.), *Industrial and Organizational Psychology: Linking Theory with Practice*. Oxford, UK: Blackwell, 130–65.

Antonakis, John, and House, Robert J. (2002). The Full-range Leadership Theory: The Way Forward. In Bruce J. Avolio and Francis J. Yammarino (Eds.), *Transformational and Charismatic Leadership: The Road Ahead*. Oxford, UK: Elsevier Science, 3–33.

Awamleh, Raed, and Gardner, William L. (1999). Perceptions of Leader Charisma and Effectiveness: The Effects of Vision Content, Delivery, and Organizational Performance. *Leadership Quarterly*, 10, 345–73.

Bryman, Alan (1992). *Charisma and Leadership in Organizations*. London: Sage.

Choi, Yeon, and Mai-Dalton, Renate R. (1999). The Model of Followers' Responses to Self-Sacrificial Leadership: An Empirical Test. *Leadership Quarterly*, 10, 397–421.

Conger, Jay A., and Kanungo, Rabindra N. (1998). *Charismatic Leadership in Organizations*. Thousand Oaks, CA: Sage.

Deluga, Ronald J. (1997). Relationship among American Presidential Charismatic Leadership, Narcissism, and Rated Performance. *Leadership Quarterly*, 8, 49–65.

——— (1998). American Presidential Proactivity, Charismatic Leadership, and Rated Performance. *Leadership Quarterly*, 9, 265–91.

——— (2001). American Presidential Machiavellianism: Implications for Charismatic Leadership and Rated Performance. *Leadership Quarterly*, 12, 339–63.

DenHartog, Deanne N., House, Robert J., Hanges, Paul J., Ruiz-Quintanilla, S. Antonio, and Dorfman, Peter W. (1999). Culture Specific and Cross Culturally Generalizable Implicit Leadership Theories: Are Attributes of Charismatic/Transformational Leadership Universally Endorsed? *Leadership Quarterly*, 10, 219–56.

Ehrhart, Mark G., and Klein, Katharine J. (2001). Predicting Followers' Preference for Charismatic Leadership: The Influence of Follower Values and Personality. *Leadership Quarterly*, 12, 133–79.

Emrich, Cynthia G., Brower, Holly H., Feldman, Jack M., and Garland, Howard (2001). Images in Words:

Presidential Rhetoric, Charisma, and Greatness. *Administrative Science Quarterly*, 46, 527–57.

Fiol, C. Marlene, Harris, Drew, and House, Robert J. (1999). Charismatic Leadership: Strategies for Effecting Social Change. *Leadership Quarterly*, 10, 449–82.

Frese, Michael, Beimel, Susanne, and Schoenborn, Sandra (2003). Action Training for Charismatic Leadership: Two Evaluations of Studies of a Commercial Training Module on Inspirational Communication of a Vision. *Personnel Psychology*, 56, 671–97.

Fry, Louis W. (2003). Toward a Theory of Spiritual Leadership. *Leadership Quarterly*, 14, 693–727.

Gardner, William L., and Avolio, Bruce J. (1998). The Charismatic Relationship: A Dramaturgical Perspective. *Academy of Management Review*, 23, 32–58.

Halpert, Jane A. (1990). The Dimensionality of Charisma. *Journal of Business and Psychology*, 4, 399–410.

Hauser, Markus, and House, Robert J. (2000). Lead through Vision and Values. In Edwin A. Locke (Ed.), *Handbook of Principles of Organizational Behavior.* Oxford, UK: Blackwell, 257–73.

Hogan, Robert, Raskin, Robert, and Fazzini, Don (1990). The Dark Side of Charisma. In Kenneth E. Clark and Miriam B. Clark (Eds.), *Measures of Leadership.* West Orange, NJ: Leadership Library of America, 343–54.

House, Robert J. (1977). A 1976 Theory of Charismatic Leadership. In James G. Hunt and Lars L. Larson (Eds.), *Leadership—The Cutting Edge.* Carbondale: Southern Illinois University Press, 189–207.

——— (1988). Power and Personality in Complex Organizations. *Research in Organizational Behavior*, 10, 305–57.

——— (1991). The Distribution and Exercise of Power in Complex Organizations: A Meso Theory. *Leadership Quarterly*, 2, 23–58.

——— (1993). Slow Learner and Late Bloomer. In Arthur G. Bedeian (Ed.), *Management Laureates: A Collection of Autobiographical Essays*, Vol. 2. Greenwich, CT: JAI Press, 39–78.

——— (1995). Leadership in the Twenty-First Century: A Speculative Inquiry. In Ann Howard (Ed.), *The Changing Nature of Work.* San Francisco, CA: Jossey-Bass, 411–50.

——— (1996). Path–Goal Theory of Leadership: Lessons, Legacy and a Reformulated Theory. *Leadership Quarterly* 7, 323–52.

——— (1999). Weber and the Neo-charismatic Leadership Paradigm: A Response to Beyer. *Leadership Quarterly*, 10, 563–74.

House, Robert J., and Baetz, Mary L. (1979). Leadership: Some Empirical Generalizations and New Research Directions. *Research in Organizational Behavior*, 1, 341–423.

House, Robert J., and Howell, Jane M. (1992). Personality and Charismatic Leadership. *Leadership Quarterly*, 3, 81–108.

House, Robert J., and Podsakoff, Philip M. (1994). Leadership Effectiveness: Past Perspectives and Future Directions for Research. In Jerald Greenberg (Ed.), *Organizational Behavior: The State of the Science.* Mahwah, NJ: Lawrence Erlbaum, 45–82.

House, Robert J., and Shamir, Boas (1993). Toward the Integration of Transformational, Charismatic, and Visionary Theories. In Martin M. Chemers and Roya Ayman (Eds.), *Leadership Theory and Research: Perspectives and Directions.* San Diego, CA: Academic Press, 81–107.

House, Robert J., Spangler, William D., and Woycke, James (1991). Personality and Charisma in the U.S. Presidency: A Psychological Theory of Leader Effectiveness. *Administrative Science Quarterly*, 36, 364–96.

House, Robert J., Woycke, James, and Fodor, Eugene M. (1988). Charismatic and Noncharismatic Leaders: Differences in Behavior and Effectiveness. In Jay A. Conger and Rabindra N. Kanungo (Eds.), *Charismatic Leadership: The Elusive Factor in Organizational Effectiveness.* San Francisco, CA: Jossey-Bass, 98–121.

Howell, Jane M., and Frost, Peter J. (1989). A Laboratory Study of Charismatic Leadership. *Organizational Behavior and Human Decision Processes*, 43, 243–69.

Hunt, James G., Boal, Kimberly, B., and Dodge, George E. (1999). The Effects of Visionary and Crisis-Responsive Charisma on Followers: An Experimental Examination of Two Kinds of Charismatic Leadership. *Leadership Quarterly*, 10, 423–48.

Jacobsen, Chanock, and House, Robert J. (2001). Dynamics of Charismatic Leadership: A Process Theory, Simulation Model, and Tests. *Leadership Quarterly*, 12, 75–112.

Kirkpatrick, Shelley A., and Locke, Edwin A. (1996). Direct and Indirect Effects of Three Charismatic Leadership Components on Performance and Attitudes. *Journal of Applied Psychology*, 81, 36–51.

Klein, Katherine J., and House, Robert J. (1995). On Fire: Charismatic Leadership and Levels of Analysis. *Leadership Quarterly*, 6, 183–98.

Kudisch, Jeffrey D., Poteet, Mark L., Dobbins, Gregory H., Rush, Michael C., and Russell, Joyce E.A. (1995). Expert Power, Referent Power, and Charisma: Toward the Resolution of a Theoretical Debate. *Journal of Business and Psychology*, 10, 177–95.

Miner, John B. (2002a). *Organizational Behavior: Foundations, Theories, and Analyses.* New York: Oxford University Press.

——— (2002b). The Role Motivation Theories of Organizational Leadership. In Bruce J. Avolio and Francis J. Yammarino (Eds.), *Transformational and Charismatic Leadership: The Road Ahead.* Oxford, UK: Elsevier Science, 309–38.

Nur, Yusuf A. (1998). Charisma and Managerial Leadership: The Gift that Never Was. *Business Horizons*, 41(4), 19–26.

O'Connor, Jennifer, Mumford, Michael D., Clifton, Timothy C., Gessner, Theodore L., and Connelly, Mary S. (1995). Charismatic Leaders and Destructiveness: An Historiometric Study. *Leadership Quarterly*, 6, 529–55.

Pillai, Rajnandini, and Meindl, James R. (1991). The Effect of a Crisis on the Emergence of Charismatic Leadership: A Laboratory Study. *Academy of Management Proceedings*, 51, 235–39.

——— (1998). Context and Charisma: A Meso Level Examination of the Relationship of Organic Structure, Collectivism, and Crisis to Charismatic Leadership. *Journal of Management*, 24, 643–71.

Shamir, Boas (1995). Social Distance and Charisma: Theoretical Notes and an Exploratory Study. *Leadership Quarterly*, 6, 19–47.

Shamir, Boas, Arthur, Michael B., and House, Robert J. (1994). The Rhetoric of Charismatic Leadership: A Theoretical Extension, a Case Study, and Implications for Research. *Leadership Quarterly*, 5, 25–42.

Shamir, Boas, House, Robert J., and Arthur, Michael B. (1993). The Motivational Effects of Charismatic Leadership: A Self-Concept Based Theory. *Organization Science*, 4, 577–94.

Shamir, Boas, Zakay, Eliav, Breinin, Esther, and Popper, Micha (1998). Correlates of Charismatic Leader Behavior in Military Units: Subordinates' Attitudes, Unit Characteristics, and Superiors' Appraisals of Leader Performance. *Academy of Management Journal*, 41, 387–409.

Shea, Christine M., and Howell, Jane M. (1999). Charismatic Leadership and Task Feedback: A Laboratory Study of Their Effects on Self-Efficacy and Task Performance. *Leadership Quarterly*, 10, 375–96.

Sosik, John J., Avolio, Bruce J., and Jung, Dong I. (2002). Beneath the Mask: Examining the Relationship of Self-Presentation Attributes and Impression Management to Charismatic Leadership. *Leadership Quarterly*, 13, 217–42.

Spangler, William D., and House, Robert J. (1991). Presidential Effectiveness and the Leadership Motive Profile. *Journal of Personality and Social Psychology*, 60, 439–55.

Strange, Jill M., and Mumford, Michael D. (2002). The Origins of Vision: Charismatic versus Ideological Leadership. *Leadership Quarterly*, 13, 343–77.

Towler, Annette J. (2003). Effects of Charismatic Influence Training on Attitudes, Behavior, and Performance. *Personnel Psychology*, 56, 363–81.

Trice, Harrison M., and Beyer, Janice M. (1986). Charisma and Its Routinization in Two Social Movement Organizations. *Research in Organizational Behavior*, 8, 113–64.

van Knippenberg, Daan, and Hogg, Michael A. (2003). A Social Identity Model of Leadership Effectiveness in Organizations. *Research in Organizational Behavior*, 25, 243–95.

Waldman, David A., and Javidan, Mansour (2002). Charismatic Leadership at the Strategic Level: Taking a New Look at Upper Echelons Theory. In Bruce J. Avolio and Francis J. Yammarino (Eds.), *Transformational and Charismatic Leadership: The Road Ahead.* Oxford, UK: Elsevier Science, 173–99.

Waldman, David A., Ramírez, Gabriel G., House, Robert J., and Puranam, Phanish (2001). Does Leadership Matter? CEO Leadership Attributes and Profitability under Conditions of Perceived Environmental Uncertainty. *Academy of Management Journal*, 44, 134–43.

Waldman, David A., and Yammarino, Francis J. (1999). CEO Charismatic Leadership: Levels-of-Management and Levels-of-Analysis Effects. *Academy of Management Review*, 24, 266–85.

Yagil, Dana (1998). Charismatic Leadership and Organizational Hierarchy: Attribution of Charisma to Close and Distant Leaders. *Leadership Quarterly*, 9, 161–76.

Yorges, Stefani L., Weiss, Howard M., and Strickland, Oriel J. (1999). The Effect of Leader Outcomes on Influence, Attributions, and Perceptions of Charisma. *Journal of Applied Psychology*, 84, 428–36.

Yukl, Gary (2002). *Leadership in Organizations*. Upper Saddle River, NJ: Prentice-Hall.

Yukl, Gary A., and Van Fleet, David D. (1982). Cross-Situational, Multimethod Research on Military Leader Effectiveness. *Organizational Behavior and Human Performance*, 30, 87–108.

Zaccaro, Stephen J. (2001). *The Nature of Executive Leadership: A Conceptual and Empirical Analysis of Success*. Washington, DC: American Psychological Association.

Zaccaro, Stephen J., and Banks, Deanna J. (2001). Leadership, Vision, and Organizational Effectiveness. In Stephen J. Zaccaro and Richard J. Klimoski (Eds.), *The Nature of Organizational Leadership*. San Francisco, CA: Jossey-Bass, 181–218.

CHAPTER 19

TRANSFORMATIONAL LEADERSHIP THEORY

BERNARD BASS

Background
Theoretical Statements
    Leadership and Performance Beyond
      Expectations
    The Transactional Leader
    Role of Personality
    Reemphases and Extrapolations
    Multiple Levels of Analysis and the
      Pseudotransformational
Evaluation and Impact
    Research in the 1980s
    Subsequent Research and Conclusions from
      Binghamton
    Outcome Relationships as Viewed from
      Binghamton
    Meta-Analyses
    Research from Beyond Binghamton
    Transformational Training
    Explaining How Transformational Leadership Works
    Strengths and Weaknesses
    Comparing the Theories
Conclusions

Importance rating	★ ★ ★ ★ ★
Estimated validity	★ ★ ★ ★
Estimated usefulness	★ ★ ★ ★
Decade of origin	1980s

Transformational theory was developed by Bass relatively late in his professional career. Unlike House, he was not primarily a theorist in his earlier years, having been much more concerned with research. Yet the two theorists do have in common that both came out of Ohio State during the period when the behavioral study of leadership was in its heyday there. That both should develop parallel theories, which at least in their Weberian origins go beyond the behavioral, seems a strange coincidence. Yet Ohio State had a very pervasive influence on leadership theorizing and research in that period.

BACKGROUND

Bernard Bass was born (in 1925) and grew up in New York City, attending the College of the City of New York for several years before a stint in the Air Force. Subsequently, he went to Ohio State where he received all his degrees in industrial psychology. He obtained the Ph.D.

Figure 19.1 Outline of the Work Pursued by Bernard Bass Until the Early 1980s

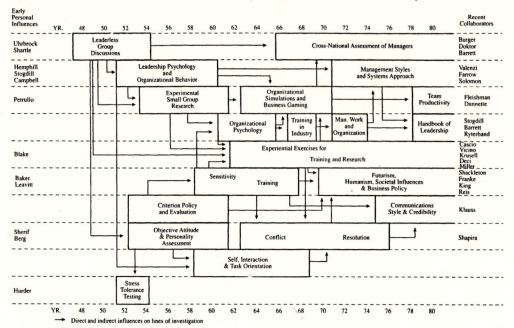

Source: Bass (1981a, 65). Copyright © 1981 *Journal of Management.* Reprinted with permission.

in 1949 at age twenty-four. He was educated in the context of the Ohio State leadership program and did his dissertation on leaderless group discussion, which was really concerned with emergent leadership.

After Ohio State he joined the faculty in psychology at Louisiana State University. Subsequent to a visiting year in the psychology department at Berkeley, in 1962, he moved to the business school at the University of Pittsburgh. He has continued his association with business schools throughout his career, although at different universities. The next of these was the University of Rochester, and later the State University of New York at Binghamton. He is now emeritus from the latter, although until very recently he continued to work and publish from there (Hooijberg and Choi 2000).

In moving from leaderless group discussions to transformational leadership, Bass followed a highly differentiated scholarly route, albeit a route filled with many significant contributions, not only to leadership study but to numerous other topic areas within organizational behavior. Figure 19.1 outlines the subjects of his endeavor over this period, up to the early 1980s, when he turned to the study of transformational leadership and developed his theory of the processes involved therein (Bass 1981a).

THEORETICAL STATEMENTS

Bass does not appear to have been influenced primarily by House's earlier formulations on charismatic leadership, at least initially. The main source for his early ideas, in addition to Weber, was James Burns and his book on political leadership entitled *Leadership* (1978).

This book stimulated Bass's work on transformational leadership; he saw this work as providing a way to bridge the gap between group dynamics and the leadership demonstrated by the world's movers and shakers (Bass 1992a). Not long after reading the Burns book, he began to develop what amounted to an agenda for studying the application of transformational leadership at the mass level to the small group situation (Bass 1981b). Before long he had characteristically initiated a pilot study on the subject, utilizing South African executives to describe transformational leaders they had known (Bass 1982). However, the first formal theoretical presentation was his book *Leadership and Performance Beyond Expectations* (1985b).

Leadership and Performance Beyond Expectations

This book was in fact preceded by a brief digest in article form (Bass 1985a). I will draw on both publications in what follows but primarily on the book. The baseline against which transformational leadership is compared is set by transactional leadership. A leader of this latter kind:

1. recognizes what it is we want to get from our work and tries to see that we get what we want if our performance warrants it,
2. exchanges rewards and promises of reward for our effort, and
3. is responsive to our immediate self-interests if they can be met by our getting the work done (Bass 1985b, 11).

A leader of the transformational kind, however, motivates people to do more than they had previously expected to do. This is accomplished

1. by raising our level of awareness, our level of consciousness about the importance and value of designated outcomes, and ways of reaching them,
2. by getting us to transcend our own self-interest for the sake of the team, organization, or larger polity, and
3. By altering our need level on Maslow's (or Alderfer's) hierarchy or expanding our portfolio of needs and wants (Bass 1985b, 20).

Thus, the theory accepts and incorporates Maslow's hierarchy of needs and the prepotency concept, as well as the idea of self-actualization (see Miner 2002a), although other processes may be engaged by transformational leaders. Most leaders behave in both transactional and transformational ways in different intensities and amounts; this is not an entirely either-or differentiation. Figure 19.2 outlines the processes involved in both types of leadership.

Charismatic and transformational processes are closely related, but a person can be charismatic without being transformational in the influence exerted, as is the case with many celebrities. Thus charisma is necessary for transformational leadership, although in and of itself it is not sufficient for the process to evolve. This suggests the operation of other factors within the context of transformational leadership. In addition to *charisma,* which includes inspirational leadership, these are *individualized consideration* and *intellectual stimulation*. There are two transactional factors—*contingent reward* and *management-by-exception*. These five factors were identified through and emerged from factor analytic studies. Yet it is important to remember that what comes out of factor analysis is a function of what goes in. Some theory, implicit or explicit, must have guided the writing and selection of potential items in the first place.

In discussing the charisma components of his theory, Bass (1985b) draws heavily on House

Figure 19.2 **Transactional and Transformational Leadership**

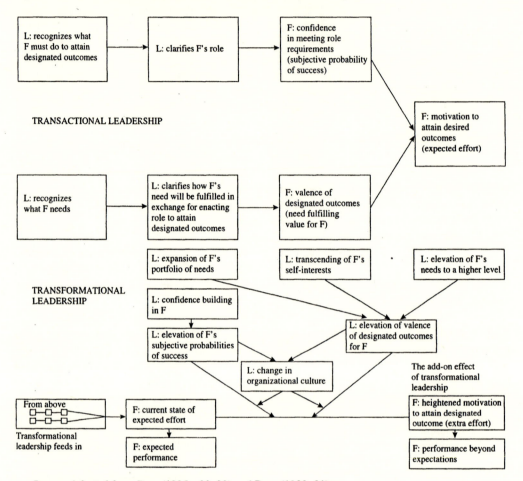

Source: Adapted from Bass (1985a, 30, 32) and Bass (1988, 31).
Note: L = Leader; F = Follower.

(1977). In fact he accepts the propositions and incorporates them in his own theory, describing them as "seven propositions about the more overt aspects of charismatic leadership in complex organizations that fit with social and organizational psychology" (Bass 1985b, 53). He does not incorporate the hypothesis with regard to stress at this point, but he does include the Initial Model of Charismatic Leadership (Figure 18.1 in this volume).

He then goes on to propose an additional set of propositions on the same subject, designed to capture the more emotional aspects of charisma (the luster, the excitement) that he believes House (1977), with his emphasis on the observable and rational, fails to incorporate in the first seven:

8.   The charismatic leader reduces resistance to attitude change in followers and disinhibitions of behavioral responses by arousing emotional responses toward the leader and a sense of excitement and adventure, which may produce restricted judgments and reduced inhibitions.

9. The larger-than-life status of charismatic leaders make[s] them useful targets of their followers' projections and catalysts for rationalization, repression, regression, and disassociation.

10. Shared norms and group fantasies among followers facilitate the emergence and success of the charismatic leader.

11. The charismatic leader may make extensive use of successful argumentation in influencing others and justifying his position. The charismatic leader may display superior debating skills, technical expertise, and ability to appropriately muster persuasive appeals.

12. Analogous to thesis and antithesis, the very behaviors and qualities that transport supporters into extremes of love, veneration, and admiration of the charismatic personality, send opponents into extremes of hatred, animosity, and detestation.

13. Charismatic leaders vary greatly in their pragmatism, flexibility, and opportunism.

14. Charismatic leadership is more likely to be seen when groups, organizations, cultures, and societies are in a state of stress and transition. (Bass 1985b, 56–59)

The last of these propositions appears designed to fill in the gap created by the failure to consider House's hypothesis dealing with stress effects.

Inspirational leadership is said to be a subfactor within charisma. As such, it can be self-generated and occur outside the charismatic context. Within charisma it involves providing models for followers; emotional appeals to competitiveness, power, affiliation, altruism, and the like; and the use of persuasive words, symbols, and images.

Individualized consideration is transformational but not charismatic. Its essence is a developmental orientation. One aspect is mentoring—which includes, on the one hand, an enhanced self-image, security, integration of needs, and visibility, and, on the other hand, fulfillment of follower desires for information and fate control. The second aspect is individualization, which means for the leader the fostering of one-on-one contact and two-way communications (a dyadic relationship), attention to individual differences in needs, and delegation of responsibilities. For the follower individuation involves the fulfillment of unique needs as well as a sense of ownership, personal responsibility, and fate control.

Intellectual stimulation can also serve to evoke heightened efforts on the part of followers. This means for the leader an orientation that is rational, empirical, existential, and idealistic; it also means competence in the form of intelligence, creativity, and experience. As a result, the leader is alert to threats, challenges, and opportunities; possesses diagnostic skills; and is capable of solution generation. In turn followers experience easier comprehension, enhanced role clarity, the capturing of their attention, and enhanced role acceptance.

Transformational leaders will display some combination of the three factors—charisma, individualized consideration, and intellectual stimulation. They are likely to be high on all three.

The Transactional Leader

The theory is equally specific regarding transactional leaders, who are most likely to be found at the lower levels of hierarchic organizations. The key factors involved here are contingent reward and management by exception (to include negative feedback and contingent aversive reinforcement).

Contingent reward is said to be supported by a goodly body of research of the kind discussed in Chapter 8. It may well incorporate the advantages of goal setting (see Chapter 10) as well. Pay for performance operates in this manner.

Management-by-exception is described as involving a situation where the leader intervenes only when something goes wrong. This is not the exception principle as described by Frederick Taylor (see Miner 2002a) since in that instance both negative deviations in the form of ineffective performance *and* positive deviations in the form of outstanding performance were to be given special attention.

Role of Personality

Bass (1985b) discusses the role of both the organizational environment and personality factors as antecedents of transformational leadership. In the former instance he deals with such considerations as the association between transformational leadership and organic systems, the role of stress and rapid change (proposition 14), and the tendency for transformational leadership to blossom at higher organizational levels. However, the treatment of personality is the more specific.

On the latter score he recognizes that personality factors play a role at both the follower and leader levels. Equalitarian, self-confident, highly educated, and high-status followers, among others, are likely to be resistant to charismatic leadership. Inflexible followers will not respond well to individualized consideration and intellectual stimulation. Those who are more predisposed to extrinsic motivation will be particularly receptive to transactional leadership. The point is that follower personality makes a difference; dependent people should be attracted to transformational leaders and should exhibit more compliance as a result.

Leader personality also is important. Social boldness, introspection, thoughtfulness, and activity level (but not sociability, cooperativeness, and friendliness) should be at a high level among the transformationals; probably authoritarianism, assertiveness, need for achievement, maturity, integrity, creativity, and originality as well. Transactionals should be high on conformity, sense of equity, and a preference for social as opposed to political approaches. Thus power needs should predominate in transformational leaders and affiliation needs in transactional ones. Overall, personality factors would be expected to play a more significant role in transformational leadership.

Reemphases and Extrapolations

The theory as a whole has remained remarkably stable over time. However, Bass has tended to place his emphases in different places and to extend the theory's coverage in various respects. In most cases these alterations reflect a response to new research data, but on occasion the changes represent an attempt to deal with input from other theoretical positions as well.

At an early point Bass took steps to emphasize that transformational leadership is a widespread phenomenon, in contrast to Weber's charisma. Consonant with this view, he also emphasized that such leadership can be learned, and that training to accomplish this should be instituted (Bass 1990).

Bass also has given increased theoretical attention to the matter of stress as it relates to transformational and transactional leadership (Bass 1992b). The position is that transformational leadership will act to reduce feelings of burnout and symptoms of stress. It does this by helping followers transcend their self-interest, increase their awareness, and shift their goals away from personal safety to achievement and self-actualization. Charisma acts to satisfy frustrated identity needs and any lack of social support. Individualized consideration helps convert crises to developmental challenges. Intellectual stimulation promotes thoughtful and creative solutions to stressful problems. Thus transformational leadership adds to what transactional leaders can accomplish in the face of crisis.

A particularly interesting essay deals with certain changes in the factors of leadership and with certain critiques that have been advanced against the theory—attempting to eliminate the "strawmen" thus created (Bass and Avolio 1993). The factors now specified and a typical item measuring each are:

A. Transformational leadership
1) Charisma (idealized influence)—has my trust in his or her ability to overcome any obstacle
2) Inspirational motivation—uses symbols and images to focus our efforts
3) Intellectual stimulation—enables me to think about old problems in new ways
4) Individualized consideration—coaches me if I need it
B. Transactional leadership
5) Contingent reward—makes sure that there is close agreement between what he or she expects me to do and what I can get from him or her for my effort
6) Management-by-exception—takes action only when a mistake has occurred
C. Nonleadership
7) Laissez-faire—doesn't tell me where he or she stands on issues (Bass and Avolio 1993, 51–53)

The last of these (#7) extends the variance in leader behaviors considered; it harks back to the days of Lewin (see Chapter 3) and thus is not original with this theory. There is also reference to two higher-order factors of an *active* and *passive* nature but without much by way of detail on these factors.

The critiques are dealt with through ten position statements, or arguments, as they are called. Some of these represent theoretical statements and some are empirical generalizations from research; in the interest of completeness of coverage all are noted below:

1. Questionnaires/surveys are being used appropriately.
2. Some attributions and effects on followers are being measured, but much is description of leadership behavior (the prototypical leader has many attributes and behaviors that have been linked to transformational leadership).
3. The factor structure underlying the MLQ is empirically supportable (MLQ = Bass's multifactor leadership questionnaire).
4. Charisma and transformational leadership are not synonymous (the three additional transformational factors . . . are conceptually distinct from charisma).
5. Individualized consideration is not a reincarnation of the consideration scale of the Leader Behavior Description Questionnaire (LBDQ) (although . . . there is overlap between the two).
6. Initiation of structure and consideration cannot conceptually and empirically account for transformational and transactional leadership.
7. Transformational leadership can be either directive or participative, as well as democratic or authoritarian, elitist or leveling.
8. Transformational leadership is not necessarily synonymous with effective leadership, nor is transactional leadership (especially MBE [management-by-exception]) synonymous with ineffective leadership.

9. The best of leaders are both transformational and transactional; the worst are neither; the worst avoid displaying leadership.
10. Leaders can be taught and motivated to be more transformational with consequential effects on the organization's programs and policies for improving itself (Bass and Avolio 1993, 55–73).

In a book published a year later (Bass and Avolio 1994), certain trends noted previously are solidified. Charisma is renamed "idealized influence"—thus creating the four I's of transformational leadership (idealized, inspirational, intellectual, individualized). Management-by-exception is divided into active (proactive monitoring) and passive (waiting for deviances) types. A factor hierarchy is established extending from laissez-faire to passive management-by-exception, to active management-by-exception, to contingent reinforcement, to the four I's. This hierarchy is expected to be positively related to both the ineffective-effective dimension and the passive-active (which are distinct from each other). This book is primarily concerned with various ways in which the full-range model may be applied to specific problem areas; it is not intended to be a source of new theory, and it is not.

Bass (1997) provides an overview of previous theory and research on it. This article also contains three corollaries for the theory, which although not new, do serve to emphasize important theoretical points:

1. There is a hierarchy of correlations among the various leadership styles and outcomes in effectiveness, effort, and satisfaction (this runs from laissez-faire to transformational).
2. There is a one-way augmentation effect (transformational leadership adds explained variances in outcomes to that explained by transactional leadership).
3. In whatever the country, when people think about leadership, their prototypes and ideas are transformational (Bass 1997, 134–35).

Multiple Levels of Analysis and the Pseudotransformational

Two theoretical extensions appeared in the latter 1990s that indeed do move onto new ground. Let us take up the multiple levels matter first. Individualized consideration is the focus of this treatment, and the contention is that this construct may be considered and operationalized at three levels—as a characteristic of the leader's behavior (individual), as representing a group's behavior toward individuals (group), and as a characteristic of the organization's culture (organizational) (Avolio and Bass 1995). The individualized consideration construct is the linchpin between transactional models of leadership and the transformational in that to a degree it has a foot in both camps. In some organizations at least, individualized consideration emerges initially at the organizational level in top management, then diffuses down through the hierarchy to group leadership, and finally characterizes the work group itself, and its members. In such cases the construct becomes part of the culture, but it needs to be measured in a different way at each level.

The theoretical proposition involved is:

1. Individualized consideration needs to be operationally defined, measured, and interpreted relative to the level and context in which it is embedded. The context, accrued over time, sets a threshold on how such behavior is interpreted.

Example items for measures of each level are:

- Organization—Individuals are considered an essential building block for organizational development.
- Group—Members provide useful advice for each other's development.
- Individual—The leader diagnoses each follower's needs.

Also:

2. A behavior exhibited by a leader that is reinforced by the leader over time and within the context (which includes the people) can emerge at subsequently higher levels of analysis representing a group norm or characteristic of the culture. This, in part, represents the core of what is transformed by a leader at multiple levels of analysis (Avolio and Bass 1995, 210–11, 214).

Measures of the type needed to study a construct at multiple levels as indicated by these propositions have in fact been created (Bass 1998). Previously the theory operated only at the individual leader level.

The second change in the theory introduces the concept of pseudotransformational leadership to deal with the personalized power factor (see Chapter 18). What happened in this instance is described as follows:

> Originally, the dynamics of transformational leadership were expected to be the same whether beneficial or harmful to followers (Bass 1985[b]), although Burns (1978) believed that to be transforming, leaders had to be morally uplifting. I have come to agree with Burns. Personalized transformational leaders are *pseudotransformational*. They may exhibit many transforming displays but cater, in the long run, to their own self-interests. Self-concerned, self-aggrandizing, exploitative, and power-oriented, pseudotransformational leaders believe in distorted utilitarian and warped moral principles. This is in contrast to the truly transformational leaders who transcend their own self-interests. (Bass 1998, 15)

Bass goes on to describe this type, which in fact had not truly been included previously within the theory, as narcissistic, impetuous, and impulsively aggressive. These people bring about compliance, but the commitment of followers is not internalized and is of a public nature only. They tend to manufacture crises. They can well be charismatic, inspirational, intellectually stimulating and individually considerate, but this is all in the service of their own self-interest.

In contrast to the immorality of the pseudotransformational, true, socialized transformationals have followers who identify with them and their aspirations, wishing to actually emulate their leaders. Here the discussion follows Shamir, House, and Arthur (1993) closely. Authentic transformational leaders expand the effective freedom available to their followers, as well as the scope for altruistic intention. Their actions are noble and moral; "they should be applauded, not chastised" (Bass and Steidlmeier 1999). In contrast Bass really does not like the pseudotransformationals, among whom Hitler appears to represent the essential prototype in his mind.

A comprehensive, up-to-date statement of the total theory is provided in the Introduction to Avolio and Bass (2002). To this should be added the prediction that in the future transformational leader behavior will be more prevalent, and transactional leader behavior less so (Bass 2002b).

EVALUATION AND IMPACT

The availability of an array of theory-related measuring instruments has served to foster a great deal of research bearing on transformational theory. Bass and his colleagues at SUNY–Binghamton have been at the forefront of this research, and in the early years they produced almost all of what was done. Interest has diffused, however, to the point where in recent years the research has been widely dispersed. Yet Bass and those working with him have continued to do significant work. This is an instance, like Fiedler's theories (see Chapter 13), where the interplay between theory and research has been continual.

Research in the 1980s

In the early pre-theory period, there were a number of hypotheses that did not fit the data and other blind alleys, often involving attempts to make factor analyses fit with constructs in ways that they stubbornly refused to accommodate (Bass 1995). Much of this research involved aspects of consideration and initiating structure.

Finally, with the construction of a completely new item pool, meaningful factors began to emerge. At first there were five of them—charismatic leadership, contingent reward, individualized consideration, management-by-exception, intellectual stimulation. The charisma factor accounted for 65 percent of the total variance of consequence; no other factor accounted for as much as 10 percent. There was also some evidence to support a scale for extra effort, a scale for inspirational leadership, an active-proactive factor, and a passive-reactive factor (Bass 1985b). Reliability of measurement was good. Preliminary support for validity against satisfaction and effectiveness, and an add-on effect from transformational leadership, was obtained, although problems with common method variance confounded these findings. This research produced the first version of the Multifactor Leadership Questionnaire (MLQ).

A study followed in which construct validity was investigated using ratings of world-class leaders based on biographical data (Bass, Avolio, and Goodheim 1987). Another study used the MLQ in a government agency in New Zealand and established that the degree of transformational leadership found at one managerial level tended to be evident at the next lower level as well (Bass, Waldman, Avolio, and Bebb 1987). Another study compared MLQ results with measures of satisfaction and rated performance from a management-by-objectives program in a manufacturing firm (Waldman, Bass, and Einstein 1987). The correlations were low for performance, although charisma and individualized consideration did achieve significance; add-on effects were mixed overall. Another study utilized the MLQ in the context of a management game where financial results were available, and it found significant relationships for all MLQ factors but management-by-exception (Avolio, Waldman, and Einstein 1988). However, only individualized consideration, and to a lesser degree charisma, contributed unique variance to the financial performance criterion.

In a study conducted at Federal Express (Hater and Bass 1988), top-performing managers, when rated by subordinates on the MLQ and on effectiveness, clearly produced superior results; the augmentation or add-on hypothesis was supported, they had higher transformational scores (except on intellectual stimulation), and even the transactional scores produced significant positive, though low, correlations (except for management-by-exception). Yet when performance ratings by the manager's superiors were used as criteria, only weak support for theory of any kind was obtained.

These studies, and certain others not mentioned, gave transformational theory a good start, especially the Hater and Bass (1988) research, which is widely cited. Certain problem areas remained, however.

Subsequent Research and Conclusions from Binghamton

The MLQ is almost invariably used in research on transformational theory. Yet as Bass (1998, 165) notes, there are problems here, in spite of the fact that numerous versions of this measure have been devised over the years in an attempt to provide an improved instrument. One such problem is multicollinearity between factors, specifically those of a transformational nature. The correlations are high and efforts to eliminate them have consistently failed. In particular, inspirational motivation is so highly correlated with charisma that the two are not statistically differentiable. The rationale for the inspirational factor lies not in factor analysis, but in the existence of a separate literature.

Although the internal consistency reliabilities of the scales have generally been good, that has not always been the case for active management-by-exception, when an active-passive distinction is made. It appears to be difficult to write items that clearly identify this factor, and as a result, ambiguity intrudes into the factor.

Finally, Bass notes problems with the universality of the factor structure. Different studies with different samples, measured at different times, with somewhat different instruments have not always produced the same results. This has been a continuing source of difficulty because the basic theory is predicated to a large extent on factor analytic findings. Avolio, Bass, and Jung (1999) have attempted to cope with this issue by extracting an optimal structure from fourteen samples where the same MLQ version was used in all instances. The best fit involved six primary factors—charisma, intellectual stimulation, individualized consideration, contingent reward, management-by-exception-active, and passive-avoidant. The first four of these are highly and positively intercorrelated. The last two are positively correlated with each other and negatively correlated with the first four. In addition, three higher-order factors emerge—transformational, developmental exchange, and corrective avoidant. The former loads highest on charisma and the second on contingent reward, but both are correlated with each other; corrective avoidant loads highest on passive-avoidant and is negatively correlated with transformational.

This pattern is not entirely consistent with earlier theory, and to the extent it bundles the transformational factors with contingent reward, it appears to depart from theoretical expectations. Either the theory needs to be changed, or the measure, or the theory needs to explicitly divorce itself from the results of factor analysis. The authors do none of these; they simply call for further study. The three problems that Bass (1998) noted clearly remain.

Bass (2002a) has recently reported as well on the research dealing with different aspects of intelligence. He concludes that "the most extensive empirical evidence of correlations with transformational leadership rests with the traits of emotional intelligence, less so for social intelligence, and least with cognitive intelligence" (113). Yet qualifications should be entered. When cognitive intelligence is considered, measures of this kind do not distinguish at all between transformational leaders and leaders who do not match this criterion when both are working at the same level in hierarchic organizations; thus general intelligence does not really appear to be distinctive. Consistent with the social intelligence conclusions (Bass 2002a), a comprehensive analysis supports both agreeableness and extroversion (Judge and Bono 2000). Yet this same study did not conclude in favor of conscientiousness, self-esteem, or locus of control, all of which are said to be defined as within emotional intelligence (Bass 2002a). The problem in the latter instance may well be a function of the ambiguity that has often characterized the emotional intelligence construct. I should add that this comprehensive study did not yield very strong correlations with transformational leadership using any of its personality variables.

Finally, a study emanating from Binghamton concludes that, as hypothesized, "Leaders perceived by followers and/or peers as more transformational, produced vision statements that were rated as stronger in terms of optimism and confidence content" (Berson, Shamir, Avolio, and Popper 2001, 67).

Outcome Relationships as Viewed from Binghamton

Next we need to consider the data presented by Bass and his colleagues as they relate to the three corollaries (Bass 1997), and to the matter of outcome relationships generally. With regard to the hierarchy of relationships between MLQ variables and effectiveness, effort, and/or satisfaction (also measured in the MLQ), Bass and Avolio (1993) present evidence that strongly supports the theory. Correlations in the 0.60 to 0.80 range are reported for the transformational factors, with charisma producing the highest; in the 0.40 to 0.60 range for contingent reward; in the –0.30 to 0.30 range for management-by-exception; and in the –0.30 to –0.60 range for laissez-faire leadership. Actual median correlations from seventeen studies are 0.71 for charisma, 0.65 for inspirational motivation, 0.54 for intellectual stimulation, 0.55 for individualized consideration; then moving to transactional factors, 0.35 for contingent reward, 0.07 for management-by-exception, and –0.41 for laissez-faire.

These results appear striking, but they are confounded to an uncertain degree by common method variance. Bass (1997) says the results are similar when independent outcome criteria are used, although the differentiation is less. Yet the early studies produced mixed results in this regard. A study in which criterion data were separated from MLQ scores by having different subordinates provide each, produced validities in the 0.22 to 0.34 range for charisma and from 0.18 to 0.35 for individualized consideration. Intellectual stimulation did not yield significant correlations (Seltzer and Bass 1990). In another instance (Howell and Avolio 1993), management-by-objectives performance was used as a criterion with the result that common method bias was minimized, and the transformational factors produced validities in the 0.26 to 0.36 range. This study is unusual in that predictive validity (over a one-year period) was involved.

These studies in the 1990s provide evidence for the add-on or augmentation effect, thus supporting corollary two, but not with all criteria. A problem here is that when independent criteria are used, the transactional correlations with criteria may decrease, so that they are not significantly different from zero, or may even be negative. As a result, the "augmentation" is at best merely a consequence of the significant transformational findings; there is no positive transactional result to add on to.

Corollary three says that the positive results indicated for corollary one and two may be generalized internationally. Considerable data to support this conclusion are provided (Bass 1997), but they are based primarily on studies that do not use a separate outcome measure. Some differences between cultures on MLQ factors are noted as well. However, a recent study in which U.S. and Asian university students were compared suggests caution; the authors conclude "the effects of transformational and transactional leadership may not always generalize across Caucasian and Asian followers" (Jung and Avolio 1999, 217).

Bass (1997) notes certain other findings that depart from theoretical expectations. Organic and mechanistic organizations have not always been found to differ in the proportion of leaders of different types found within them. Inspirational motivation and satisfaction are usually highly correlated, but in one professional organization this figure was actually *negative* in direction. The tendency for intellectual stimulation to operate in unexpected ways, which has been noted previously, was compounded in a study of stress relationships that indicated that when other factors were held constant, stress and burnout *increased* under this type of leadership; charisma and individualistic consideration yielded the expected decrease in stress (Bass 1998). There is some suggestion in these findings that professional and intellectual leadership may not operate in a manner entirely consistent with transformational theory.

An additional study from Binghamton that bears mentioning dealt with the theory as it relates to multiple levels of analysis (Yammarino, Spangler, and Dubinsky 1998). The data for the sales personnel studied did not support theoretical expectations well. Transformational leadership was unrelated to actual sales figures, although it did relate to affective outcome and rated performance variables. Analyses, which considered data for the group level and below but not for the organizational level, indicated that the relationships held only at the individual level and were unaffected by dyad and group membership. Furthermore, transformational and contingent reward leadership operated similarly, suggesting that the two may not be as different as the theory presupposes. These data appear to be free of same-source biases.

A recent study of U.S. Army platoons under simulated combat conditions serves to confirm the relation of both transformational and transactional leadership to independently established performance levels (Bass, Avolio, Jung, and Berson 2003). Thus same source bias was not an issue, but at the same time correlations tended to be low, though consistently significant. The augmentation effect was not in evidence initially, but it did appear under specific circumstances. Overall, this research adds evidence of the theory's validity, while providing reason to believe that its effects are modest when common source bias is removed.

The Meta-Analyses

The major meta-analytic study evaluating transformational theory utilized a large number of unpublished sources as well as those we have been considering (Lowe, Kroeck, and Sivasubramaniam 1996). Intercorrelations among the three transformational measures ranged from 0.68 to 0.85 and the management-by-exception measure correlated from 0.05 to 0.10 with these three, but contingent reward was much more highly correlated with the transformational measures (0.63 to 0.70) than with management-by-exception (0.21). Internal consistency reliability was entirely adequate for all measures except management-by-exception (0.65).

The major findings are given in Table 19.1. These involve effectiveness outcomes only, but note the huge differences in validity coefficients when common method variance is removed. Yet charisma and individualized consideration remain significant even so; the other scales are not, including intellectual stimulation. The organizational measure values for transformational leadership are generally in line with the validities typically obtained in studies of predictors of managerial performance. There is no evidence of an extraordinary effect here. Also, contrary to the original hypothesis, transformational leadership is neither more prevalent nor more effective in higher management.

This meta-analysis has been replicated bringing the data up to 2002 and adding in some forty-nine studies (Dumdum, Lowe, and Avolio 2002). The results for the dimensions of transformational leadership are essentially the same. Management-by-exception tends to yield more negative correlations, and laissez-faire leadership produces distinctly negative values. Satisfaction as a criterion behaves much like effectiveness. Although there are other similar meta-analyses, all are of an earlier vintage and/or are less comprehensive in coverage.

A meta-analysis comparing male and female managers, however, does yield some interesting results (Eagly, Johannesen-Schmidt, and van Engen 2003). The findings indicate that women

Table 19.1

Mean Corrected Correlations Between MLQ Scales and Effectiveness Criteria With (Subordinate Ratings) and Without (Organizational Measures) Common Method Bias

Scale	Subordinate ratings	Organizational measures	Correlations differ
Charisma	0.81[a]	0.35[a]	Yes
Individualized consideration	0.69[a]	0.28[a]	Yes
Intellectual stimulation	0.68[a]	0.26	Yes
Contingent reward	0.56[a]	0.08	Yes
Management-by-exception	0.10	-0.04	Yes

Source: Adapted from Lowe, Kroeck, and Sivasubramaniam (1996, 410).
[a]Correlation is significantly different from 0.

consistently score higher than men on transformational leadership measures. On transactional measures the results are split, but men score higher than women on laissez-faire leadership, indicating a tendency toward less effective performance. With few exceptions, these results are significant, yet they are small, running at roughly 5 percent. Given that transformational managers tend toward participative leadership, and given the finding by Jago and Vroom (see Chapter 12) that women are more participative than men, this result might have been anticipated. Nevertheless, it may come as a shock to many.

Research from Beyond Binghamton

Although the great majority of the research on transformational theory has been conducted by Bass and his colleagues at SUNY–Binghamton, significant research has been conducted elsewhere as well; on occasion, however, these more distant studies do exhibit certain ties to the Binghamton group.

A particularly important finding derives from the Podsakoff, MacKenzie, and Bommer (1996) study of transformational leadership and substitutes for leadership discussed in Chapter 16. In this regard the authors say:

> [T]he results of the aggregate analysis indicate that because of the large proportion of the shared variance between the transformational leader behaviors and substitutes for leadership, it is essential to include the substitutes variables in any test of the effects of transformational leadership. (289–90)
>
> [T]hree reasons why the substitutes variables might be correlated with leader behaviors. First, . . . the relationships between the substitutes and leader behaviors might . . . be caused by other unrecognized factors. Second, . . . the substitutes may influence or constrain a leader's behavior in some way. A final possibility . . . is that leaders can influence the substitutes variables. (295)

Thus it seems entirely possible that the failure to find a greater impact of transformational behaviors at higher levels is a consequence of the failure to incorporate substitutes for leadership in the research. Certainly top management has the greater influence over these variables. In any event, the presence of contextual factors including substitutes in transformational leadership research has been a rather rare phenomenon.

The uncertainty over the factor structure of the MLQ has not been limited to the Binghamton group. Other studies have found various departures from theoretical expectations including a failure to differentiate within the transformational domain and the fact that the transactional contingent reward component emerges as closely aligned with the transformational components (see DenHartog, Van Muijen, and Koopman 1997; also Tejeda, Scandura, and Pillai 2001). These problems with the factor structure of the MLQ, the dominant instrument used to test transformational theory, have begun to produce a number of competing measures and some disparate results as well (e.g., see Alimo-Metcalfe and Alban-Metcalfe 2001; Parry 2002).

The question of the role of follower trust in transformational leadership has been a concern for some time, but it now is apparent that trust plays a positive mediating role between transformational leadership and organizational citizenship behaviors, which involve performances that go beyond expectations and role requirements (Podsakoff, MacKenzie, Moorman, and Fetter 1990; Pillai, Schriesheim, and Williams 1999). Transactional leadership does not relate to trust in this same way. Interestingly, however, in a predominantly professional context, intellectual stimulation related negatively to trust, but this effect was overridden by the positive impact of charisma and individualized consideration. These findings regarding trust offer the possibility of bridging the void between personalized and socialized charismatics. Quite possibly, in spite of the wide differences between the two types, the capacity to inspire trust in followers characterizes both and provides them with common ground.

The uncertainties that often seem to arise when transformational leadership is studied in a professional context are at least partially illuminated by a number of studies undertaken in the R&D environment (see Elkins and Keller 2003). Transformational leadership, including intellectual stimulation, is a good predictor of outcomes from research projects. These results appear to be independent of any same-source bias. Another similar finding is that charisma, inspirational motivation, and intellectual stimulation, but not individualized consideration, serve to differentiate emergent, informal leaders who take the role of product champions involving technological innovations from those who do not take this role (Howell and Higgins 1990). This tie between transformational leadership and innovative endeavor (Jung, Chow, and Wu 2003), as well as creativity (Shin and Zhou 2003) seems now to be well established.

Transformational Training

The most significant application of transformational theory that has appeared to date involves the training of leaders to become more transformational. Bass (1998) describes certain efforts along these lines.

One such approach involves individual counseling by organizational development practitioners or others, who feed back MLQ profile results, interpret them, and aid the target person in developing a set of priorities, plans, and goals. The counselor is consistently supportive in encouraging movement to a more active, transformational style. Limited evaluation data are reported, but the available evidence indicates that such a program can improve MLQ scores beyond any changes occurring in a control group. A book containing multiple cases has been published recently to aid in this type of development or in self-development (Avolio and Bass 2002).

Planning and goal setting of this kind may also be embedded in a formal training program. Such a program involves some simulations and exercises but focuses mostly on action learning to deal with on-the-job issues. The training emphasizes, in order of coverage:

1. increasing awareness of the leadership paradigm;
2. learning about alternatives that are conducive to improving oneself as well as one's followers; and
3. adapting, adopting, and internalizing the new ways of thinking and acting (Bass 1998, 103).

The fourteen modules are spread over several days of both basic and advanced training with an interval of three months between to practice key skills.

Significant training effects on MLQ and outcome variables are reported from studies conducted to evaluate this type of training. The most striking change was a substantial reduction in management-by-exception behavior. Increases in inspirational motivation and intellectual stimulation were also evident, thus supporting the transformational objective. In general, those transformational variables that were the specific focus of a participant's leadership development plan were the ones most likely to rise from pretest to posttest.

In addition to the evaluation research reported in Bass (1998), several other studies bear mention. These utilized variants of the standard training, but they appear to be sufficiently similar to justify attention here. Spreitzer and Quinn (1996) report an extensive application within the Ford Motor Company that was successful in stimulating meaningful transformational change efforts on the part of slightly less than half of the participants. These change behaviors, though self-reported, do not appear to have been a function of social desirability factors and are described as being dramatic. Yet no ties between training effects and promotion rates subsequently could be established.

A second study involved a more abbreviated training effort, but it did utilize a control group (Barling, Weber, and Kelloway 1996). The results indicated substantial improvements in transformational leadership, especially in intellectual stimulation, which was the major focus of the training. There was also evidence of an impact on financial outcomes. Common source bias does not appear to have operated anywhere within this study.

A major research effort in Israel contrasted effects of transformational leadership training with "eclectic" training by comparing follower reactions down through a military hierarchy (Dvir, Eden, Avolio, and Shamir 2002). The training produced changes in the direct followers (noncommissioned officers) of the focal transformationally trained leaders (officers) with the result that the performance of their followers (recruits) improved significantly over the controls. This was a highly stressful context, and one of the primary effects of training in transformational behaviors was to ameliorate the impact of this stress.

Overall, the research appears to have been sufficient in quantity and scientific controls to justify a conclusion that transformational leadership training can achieve the intended results; the changes appear to be based on actual increases in leader uses of transformational behaviors. Furthermore, the number of such training efforts noted in the literature appears to be on the increase (e.g., see Ayman, Adams, Fisher, and Hartman 2003).

Explaining How Transformational Leadership Works

Bass (1998) indicates that little research has been done to explicate exactly how transformational leadership works. He does note, however, the research on trust by Podsakoff, MacKenzie, Moorman, and Fetter (1990) and the theoretical contributions of Shamir, House, and Arthur (1993) dealing with follower self-concepts, as well as Howell and Frost's (1989) finding that charismatic leaders are able to maintain productivity in the face of sizable obstacles. In a prior article, Bass (1995) lists these same publications as offering promising insights, but in that instance he does make some reference to the Maslow hierarchy that he initially (Bass 1985) invoked to explain how transformational leadership works.

These indications by the theory's author that a need exists for more research on the processes of transformational leadership have elicited considerable subsequent response. A number of different motivational processes have been proposed as acting to propel transformational behavior, and several have been shown to actually operate. Thus a study of high school students found that those students who behaved as transformational leaders perceived their fathers as acting in the same manner toward them (Zacharatos, Barling, and Kelloway 2000); a desire to emulate the father seemed to be characteristic. In another instance, an association was found between transformational leadership and moral reasoning, suggesting that the leadership behavior may be motivated by a desire for morality (Turner, Barling, Epitropaki, Butcher, and Milner 2002).

Also operative may be an enhanced level of intrinsic work motivation in followers. Research indicates that those who are followers of transformational leaders experience a greater sense of meaningfulness and personal engagement in their work; they see it as more fulfilling, enjoyable, and important (Bono and Judge 2003). Followers may experience both dependence and empowerment as a consequence of exposure to transformational leadership (Kark, Shamir, and Chen 2003). Dependence seems to result from a personal identification with the leader, and empowerment is associated with a social identification with a work group composed of followers subject to transformational leadership. In both instances the particular kind of leadership style involved appears to prime aspects of the self (relational and collective, respectively). Thus, followers who seek dependence and/or empowerment may be drawn to transformational leaders.

These findings would seem to provide much by way of building blocks to explain why and how transformational leadership works. Yet alternative positions need to be considered. One such departure from current thinking is this:

> Transformational leadership clearly represents a combination of the recognition-based and inferential modes of leadership perception. . . . Many researchers describe transformational leaders as conforming to the notions of followers—recognition-based processes. It is also clear that transformational leadership involves the perception by followers that leaders have an agenda for producing favorable performance outcomes—inferential processes. Critical evaluation of the construct should ask whether transformational leadership is anything more than categorizing someone as an effective leader. . . . We would caution researchers interested in the topic to keep in mind the lessons learned from prior research on questionnaires and leadership perception. Like other "behavioral" measures, transformational leadership scales may tell us as much about how leaders are integrated with subordinates' implicit theories as they do about the actual behaviors of transformational leaders. (Lord and Maher 1991, 290)

A position of a similar nature is advocated by Meindl (1990, 1995) under the romance of leadership label. This view holds that people, including followers, often attribute more to leadership-as-cause than is warranted. When organizations are transformed, people tend to search for and to find a great leader to explain what has happened. Leadership is emphasized more when productivity changes occur, and there is a disproportionate tendency to explain extreme and unexpected changes as leadership effects. Biases of this kind are most likely in the emotion-laden situations that appear to provoke charismatic or transformational leadership. Romanticizing the leader in this way can be so extreme that charismatic leadership becomes nothing more than a set of follower attributions; it is highly contagious and is transmitted among followers through their networks of interpersonal relationships (friendships) as indicated by Pastor, Meindl, and Mayo (2002).

These views have received support from research (e.g., see Chen and Meindl 1991). Furthermore, these findings are clearly antithetical to Bass's theory and House's too. If charismatic leadership is a mirage, it needs to be studied at the level of follower perceptions; much of current theory and research thus would seem to miss the point. From the evidence the romance of leadership is a real enough phenomenon on occasion. However, we do not know how often it occurs, and when it does, how much variance it accounts for. There is good evidence that leadership effects do occur (see Chapter 15) and that the romance of leadership may not always operate (Awamleh and Gardner 1999). Probably certain followers in certain states are more susceptible to romance of leadership effects. Meindl, and Lord also, have indeed unearthed important factors for the study of leadership, but not, on the current evidence, one that totally explains away the charismatic phenomenon; quite the contrary.

Strengths and Weaknesses

Antonakis and House (2002) endorse Bass's transformational theory in its extended form and congratulate him on producing a major theoretical breakthrough. They feel, however, that research on the theory is weighted too heavily on the behavioral side and does not give enough attention to personality considerations in the leader; they call for research and theory along the lines of McClelland (see Chapter 4). This would allow transformational theory to be applied to selection decisions in a way that it currently is not, since followers are needed to define a leader as transformational. Judge and Bono (2000) in fact have suggested that three of the "big five" dimensions of personality might be applied to assist organizations in choosing transformational leaders, but I am not aware of any follow-up on this proposal.

Another of Antonakis and House's (2002) suggestions is that more research be devoted to establishing that transformational leaders actually have the ability to transform organizations and followers. This is implicit in both the House and Bass theories and is relevant to the routinization of charisma issue, which has rarely been addressed in research to date. A study that does touch upon the matter of organizational transformation, however, serves to test the hypothesis that charismatic leadership can influence investors to buy stock in a company, and thus drive its stock value up (Flynn and Staw 2004). This was found to be true, the implication being that transformational leaders actually can bring about changes in a firm's economic and social environment.

Bryman (1996), in discussing transformational theory, notes the impressive set of research findings and the very substantial impact on the study of leadership. Undoubtedly, the theory has done a great deal to revive the leadership area. Yet Bryman and others have bemoaned the limited attention to situational or contextual factors within the theory. There is some concern with the effects of crises, uncertainty, follower stress and the like, largely because Weber indicated similar concerns, but beyond that there is much more in the research findings than in the theoretical formulations.

The issue can be epitomized by considering the finding noted previously that female managers are more transformational than men. Yet studies of world leaders consistently identify more males, and more male charismatics. For instance, in the Bass, Avolio, and Goodheim (1987) study of "movers and shakers," 87 percent of the nominees were men. When one narrows the data down to focus on those who score high (3.0 or more) on charisma, individualized consideration, and intellectual stimulation, the percentage of males is 82, 79, and 86, respectively. Most people would attribute this differential to opportunity differences, or put differently, to lack of opportunity for females. But that is exactly the point—theory, and research, dealing with opportunity and its effects are totally lacking. What type of context nurtures transformational and charismatic leadership, and how does one get into that context?

The need to theorize about context has in fact been recognized, and indeed propositions regarding transformational leadership-maximizing conditions have been advanced. The following provide examples for consideration:

1. Organizations will be more receptive to transformational leadership during adaptation orientation than during efficiency orientation.
2. Organizations with dominant boundary-spanning units will be more receptive to transformational leadership than will organizations with dominant technical cores.
3. Both simple structure and adhocracy forms will be more receptive to transformational leadership than will the machine bureaucracy, professional bureaucracy, or divisional structure forms.
4. Organizations with a clan mode of governance will be more receptive to transformational leadership than will organizations with either market or bureaucratic modes of governance (Pawar and Eastman 1997, 92, 94–95, 97).

I am not advocating these particular propositions, only the need for some such formulations. Indeed, elsewhere I have advocated that transformational leadership may take entirely different forms in different organizational contexts (Miner 2002b). The behaviors exhibited may be very similar, but the motivational base may differ substantially. Most of the research has been conducted in hierarchic, bureaucratic organizations, consistent with the origins of the charisma concept in Weber's theory of bureaucracy. As noted, transformational leadership in professional contexts does not always operate in quite the same manner, and it may differ as well in entrepreneurial (task) and group contexts (in the latter respect, see Peters and Williams 2002). The research to establish what type of personality is behind transformational behavior outside of bureaucracies simply does not exist, nor does the theory advance propositions in this regard.

The context issue is raised in a somewhat different manner by Porter and Bigley (2003). They note that if a firm encourages transformational leadership throughout the managerial ranks of the company, the change agenda of one such leader can well conflict with that of another, placing many followers in positions of role conflict and consequently demotivating them, rather than achieving the desired peak motivational levels. The person simply does not know whose agenda to follow. This becomes a major problem when transformational training is used widely within an organization.

The problem in this situation is that a construct originally proposed by Weber for application at the top levels of bureaucracies (where there is no room for alternative agendas) is now applied throughout the organization (where conflicting agendas are inevitable). This is the levels-of-analysis issue considered in the last chapter, and it represents an instance in that regard where organizational performance can in fact be damaged. A number of critics have noted the vulnerability of transformational leadership theory on this score (see Schriesheim 2003; Schriesheim, Castro, Zhou, and Yammarino 2001). The theory needs to be more specific as to its contextual domain and its reason for making choices in this regard.

On a different topic, Yukl (1999) presents an excellent critique of transformational theory, and in doing so emphasizes his concern about basing the theory on a factor analytically derived structure, which can change as a function of many considerations including the particular item input to a given factor analysis. This situation means that the constructs and the relations among them can change also, and theoretical constructs are not supposed to change except in some predetermined manner specified by a theory. Thus there are definite construct validity problems. This is particularly true of the transactional factors that do not appear to possess a common rationale. As a result, under certain research conditions, contingent reward tends to drift into the domain of transformational leadership, and the relationship indicated by the key augmentation hypothesis loses any clear meaning.

There are numerous aspects of the theory that simply have not been tested, including the propositions Bass added to House's initial theory of charisma. Also, although the theory is strong on the positive aspects of transformational leadership, it is weak on the detrimental or negative aspects. Socially acceptable behaviors are emphasized, and manipulative behaviors such as intimidation are ignored. Bass has recognized this problem recently and has introduced the concept of pseudotransformational leadership.

This shift, however, carries with it its own set of problems. Chief among these is the fact that existing measures do not deal with pseudotransformational behaviors, and operationalizations of the construct do not exist. Thus, what has been one of the major strengths of transformational theory is lost in this particular instance. The kinds of behaviors that would appear to need measuring are:

> manipulative behaviors that increase follower perceptions of leader expertise and dependence on the leader . . . misinterpreting events or inciting incidents to create the appearance of a crisis; exaggerating the leader's positive achievements and taking unwarranted credit for achievements . . . covering up mistakes and failures . . . limiting member access to information about operations and performance . . . limiting communication of criticism or dissent; [and] indoctrinating new members. (Yukl 1999, 296)

Bass (1998) says that pseudotransformationals can be charismatic, inspirational, intellectually stimulating, and individually considerate much like authentic transformationals, but that they use these behaviors in their own self-interest, not for the benefit of others. That seems to compound the measurement problem. Yet measures of personalized and socialized power do exist, and these may provide entrée to the problem.

Conceptually, however, there is the issue of whether self-interest is sufficient to differentiate the two types. Overdetermination may well operate so that a transformational leader acts out of multiple motives, some of which are self-oriented and some of which are not. People can serve their own interests and still produce products that benefit the common good (as in the case of capitalism). My point is that hinging the pseudo-authentic differentiation on self-interest alone seems unlikely to work. Yet understanding the dark side of transformational leadership is important, and that Bass has raised this issue, even if he has not solved it, is a significant contribution.

In spite of his numerous criticisms and his belief that further refinement of transformational theory is needed, Yukl (2002) concludes that overall the empirical research on the theory is supportive. In the application area, Gist and McDonald-Mann (2000) indicate that transformational training has been found to yield promising results, and they encourage the use of the approach in management development programs while at the same time indicating the need for further research on the subject.

Comparing the Theories

Both charismatic (Chapter 18) and transformational (this chapter) theory have considerable research support, even though both have sizable untested gaps and some instances where aspects of the theories have not been confirmed by the research. To some degree the confirmatory studies apply to both theories, although investigations are typically initiated to focus on one theory or the other. This implies overlap between the theories. Such overlap has clearly existed from the beginning, and both House and Bass have made efforts to integrate the theories further.

Such attempts to achieve integration have not been successful; nor do either charismatic theory or transformational theory match up very well with Weber—both lack the emphasis on divine attributions and the definition of charisma as rare in scope, for instance, although House appears closer to Weber as regards the latter than Bass. As currently specified, the theories are obviously different, even though each has responded to the research evidence by moving closer to the other.

The question that remains is if these two somewhat different theories are nevertheless wrestling with the same constructs. Yukl (1999) believes they are not. He raises a question as to whether or not charismatic and transformational leadership can occur at the same time in the same person and whether or not this is common or uncommon, stable or unstable. He believes that any such simultaneous occurrence will inevitably be uncommon and unstable.

Unfortunately, the data to answer Yukl's questions are not presently available. It seems unlikely that research of this kind can be conducted effectively until the theories deal more completely with the various aspects of the dark side of charisma, and measure them too, and until the routinization phenomenon is mapped into the theories. In any event, whether the constructs involved are the same, or partially overlapping, or completely separate is not answerable on either theoretical or data-based grounds right now. This is part of an agenda for the future.

Finally, there is a need to scale down the rhetoric regarding these theories. They are not supertheories, with superexplanatory powers, modeled after their charismatic subject matter. The correlations and dependent variable relationships are commendable, but after biases are removed, much the same as those reported for other good theories in this volume. There is no evidence so far that would warrant a claim for extraordinary accomplishments for either theory.

CONCLUSIONS

Going back to the ratings, transformational leadership theory is evaluated as the most important of the theories considered in Part III with a value of 5.06, the only leadership theory to attain 5 stars. The theory is also one of the most widely researched and discussed. As to estimated validity, the theory's 4 star status reflects the fact that a large proportion of this research is supportive. But, as noted, gaps exist in both the research and the theorizing. In particular, many context issues remain to be considered, and although Bass has succeeded in sparking research to explain how transformational leadership works, we still do not have a full answer, and the theory itself has been mute on the issue since the ill-fated effort to mobilize Maslow's need hierarchy theory in this regard (see Miner 2002a).

Transformational training has proven a valuable asset in management development, and it serves to justify the 4 star rating on estimated usefulness. However, longitudinal research over a considerable period of time is still needed to determine exactly what happens when a large number of transformationals are set loose in an organization at the same time. Also, it would be very helpful to be able to identify in advance individuals who are particularly likely to mobilize transformational behaviors. The lack of applications to bring to bear on selection decisions represents a real limitation.

REFERENCES

Alimo-Metcalfe, Beverly, and Alban-Metcalfe, Robert J. (2001). The Development of a New Transformational Leadership Questionnaire. *Journal of Occupational and Organizational Psychology*, 74, 1–27.

Antonakis, John, and House, Robert J. (2002). The Full-range Leadership Theory: The Way Forward. In Bruce J. Avolio and Francis J. Yammarino (Eds.), *Transformational and Charismatic Leadership: The Road Ahead.* Oxford, UK: Elsevier Science, 3–33.

Avolio, Bruce J., and Bass, Bernard M. (1988). Transformational Leadership, Charisma, and Beyond. In James G. Hunt, R. Rajaram Baliga, H. Peter Dachler, and Chester A. Schriesheim (Eds.), *Emerging Leadership Vistas.* Lexington, MA: D.C. Heath, 29–49.

——— (1995). Individual Consideration Viewed as Multiple Levels of Analysis: A Multi-Level Framework for Examining the Diffusion of Transformational Leadership. *Leadership Quarterly*, 6, 199–218.

——— (2002). *Developing Potential Across a Full Range of Leadership: Cases on Transactional and Transformational Leadership.* Mahwah, NJ: Lawrence Erlbaum.

Avolio, Bruce J., Bass, Bernard M., and Jung, Dong I. (1999). Re-examining the Components of Transformational and Transactional Leadership Using the Multifactor Leadership Questionnaire. *Journal of Occupational and Organizational Psychology*, 72, 441–62.

Avolio, Bruce J., Waldman, David A., and Einstein, Walter O. (1988). Transformational Leadership in a Management Game Simulation: Impacting the Bottom Line. *Group and Organization Studies*, 13, 59–80.

Awamleh, Raed, and Gardner, William L. (1999). Perceptions of Leader Charisma and Effectiveness: The Effects of Vision Content, Delivery, and Organizational Performance. *Leadership Quarterly*, 10, 345–73.

Ayman, Roya, Adams, Susan, Fisher, Bruce, and Hartman, Erica (2003). Leadership Development in Higher Education Institutions: A Present and Future Perspective. In Susan E. Murphy and Ronald E. Riggio (Eds.), *The Future of Leadership Development.* Mahwah, NJ: Lawrence Erlbaum, 201–22.

Barling, Julian, Weber, Tom, and Kelloway, E. Kevin (1996). Effects of Transformational Leadership Training on Attitudinal and Financial Outcomes: A Field Experiment. *Journal of Applied Psychology*, 81, 827–32.

Bass, Bernard M. (1981a). From Leaderless Group Discussions to the Cross-National Assessment of Managers. *Journal of Management*, 7(2), 63–76.

——— (1981b). *Stogdill's Handbook of Leadership: A Survey of Theory and Research.* New York: Free Press.

——— (1982). Intensity of Relation, Dyadic–Group Considerations, Cognitive Categorization, and Transformational Leadership. In James G. Hunt, Uma Sekaran, and Chester A. Schriesheim (Eds.), *Leadership—Beyond Establishment Views.* Carbondale, IL: Southern Illinois University Press, 142–50.

——— (1985a). Leadership: Good, Better, Best. *Organizational Dynamics*, 13(3), 26–40.

——— (1985b). *Leadership and Performance Beyond Expectations.* New York: Free Press.

——— (1990). From Transactional to Transformational Leadership: Learning to Share the Vision. *Organizational Dynamics*, 18(3), 19–31.

——— (1992a). A Transformational Journey. In Arthur G. Bedeian (Ed.), *Management Laureates: A Collection of Autobiographical Essays,* Vol. 1. Greenwich, CT: JAI Press, 65–105.

——— (1992b). Stress and Leadership. In Frank Heller (Ed.), *Decision Making and Leadership.* Cambridge, UK: Cambridge University Press, 133–55.

——— (1995). Theory of Transformational Leadership Redux. *Leadership Quarterly*, 6, 463–78.

——— (1997). Does the Transactional–Transformational Leadership Paradigm Transcend Organizational and National Boundaries? *American Psychologist*, 52, 130–39.

——— (1998). *Transformational Leadership: Industrial, Military, and Educational Impact.* Mahwah, NJ: Lawrence Erlbaum.

——— (2002a). Cognitive, Social, and Emotional Intelligence of Transformational Leaders. In Ronald E. Riggio, Susan E. Murphy, and Francis J. Pirozzolo (Eds.), *Multiple Intelligences and Leadership.* Mahwah, NJ: Lawrence Erlbaum, 105–17.

——— (2002b). Forecasting Organizational Leadership: From Back (1967) to the Future (2034). In Bruce J. Avolio and Francis J. Yammarino (Eds.), *Transformational and Charismatic Leadership: The Road Ahead.* Oxford, UK: Elsevier Science, 375–84.

Bass, Bernard M., and Avolio, Bruce J. (1993). Transformational Leadership: A Response to Critiques. In Martin M. Chemers and Roya Ayman (Eds.), *Leadership Theory and Research: Perspectives and Directions.* San Diego, CA: Academic Press, 49–79.

————— (1994). *Improving Organizational Effectiveness Through Transformational Leadership*. Thousand Oaks, CA: Sage.

Bass, Bernard M., Avolio, Bruce J., and Goodheim, Laurie (1987). Biography and the Assessment of Transformational Leadership at the World-Class Level. *Journal of Management*, 13, 7–19.

Bass, Bernard M., Avolio, Bruce J., Jung, Dong I., and Berson, Yair (2003). Predicting Unit Performance by Assessing Transformational and Transactional Leadership. *Journal of Applied Psychology*, 88, 207–18.

Bass, Bernard M., and Steidlmeier, Paul (1999). Ethics, Character, and Authentic Transformational Leadership Behavior. *Leadership Quarterly*, 10, 181–217.

Bass, Bernard M., Waldman, David A., Avolio, Bruce J., and Bebb, Michael (1987). Transformational Leadership and the Falling Dominoes Effect. *Group and Organization Studies*, 12, 73–87.

Berson, Yair, Shamir, Boas, Avolio, Bruce J., and Popper, Micha (2001). The Relationship Between Vision Strength, Leadership Style, and Context. *Leadership Quarterly*, 12, 53–73.

Bono, Joyce E., and Judge, Timothy A. (2003). Self-Concordance at Work: Toward Understanding the Motivational Effects of Transformational Leaders. *Academy of Management Journal*, 46, 554–71.

Bryman, Alan (1996). Leadership in Organizations. In Stewart R. Clegg, Cynthia Hardy, and Walter R. Nord (Eds.), *Handbook of Organization Studies*. London: Sage, 276–92.

Burns, James M. (1978). *Leadership*. New York: Harper and Row.

Chen, Chao C., and Meindl, James R. (1991). The Construction of Leadership Images in the Popular Press: The Case of Donald Burr and People Express. *Administrative Science Quarterly*, 36, 521–51.

DenHartog, Deanne N., Van Muijen, Jaap J., and Koopman, Paul L. (1997). Transactional Versus Transformational Leadership: An Analysis of the MLQ. *Journal of Occupational and Organizational Psychology*, 70, 19–34.

Dumdum, Uldarico R., Lowe, Kevin B., and Avolio, Bruce J. (2002). A Meta-Analysis of Transformational and Transactional Leadership Correlates of Effectiveness and Satisfaction: An Update and Extension. In Bruce J. Avolio and Francis J. Yammarino (Eds.), *Transformational and Charismatic Leadership: The Road Ahead*. Oxford, UK: Elsevier Science, 35–66.

Dvir, Taly, Eden, Dov, Avolio, Bruce J., and Shamir, Boas (2002). Impact of Transformational Leadership on Follower Development and Performance: A Field Experiment. *Academy of Management Journal*, 45, 735–44.

Eagly, Alice H., Johannesen-Schmidt, Mary C., and van Engen, Marloes L. (2003). Transformational, Transactional, and Laissez-Faire Leadership Styles: A Meta-Analysis Comparing Women and Men. *Psychological Bulletin*, 129, 569–91.

Elkins, Teri, and Keller, Robert T. (2003). Leadership in Research and Development Organizations: A Literature Review and Conceptual Framework. *Leadership Quarterly*, 14, 587–606.

Flynn, Francis J., and Staw, Barry M. (2004). Lend Me Your Wallets: The Effect of Charismatic Leadership on External Support for an Organization. *Strategic Management Journal*, 25, 309–30.

Gist, Marilyn E., and McDonald-Mann, Dana (2000). Advances in Leadership Training and Development. In Cary L. Cooper and Edwin A. Locke (Eds.), *Industrial and Organizational Psychology: Linking Theory with Practice*. Oxford, UK: Blackwell, 52–71.

Hater, John J., and Bass, Bernard M. (1988). Superiors' Evaluations and Subordinates' Perceptions of Transformational and Transactional Leadership. *Journal of Applied Psychology*, 73, 695–702.

Hooijberg, Robert, and Choi, Jaepil (2000). From Selling Peanuts and Beer in Yankee Stadium to Creating a Theory of Transformational Leadership: An Interview with Bernie Bass. *Leadership Quarterly*, 11, 291–306.

House, Robert J. (1977). A 1976 Theory of Charismatic Leadership. In James G. Hunt and Lars L. Larson (Eds.), *Leadership—The Cutting Edge*. Carbondale: Southern Illinois University Press, 189–207.

Howell, Jane M., and Avolio, Bruce J. (1993). Transformational Leadership, Transactional Leadership, Locus of Control, and Support for Innovation: Key Predictors of Consolidated-Business-Unit Performance. *Journal of Applied Psychology*, 78, 891–902.

Howell, Jane M., and Frost, Peter J. (1989). A Laboratory Study of Charismatic Leadership. *Organizational Behavior and Human Decision Processes*, 43, 243–69.

Howell, Jane M., and Higgins, Christopher A. (1990). Champions of Technological Innovations. *Administrative Science Quarterly*, 35, 317–41.

Judge, Timothy A., and Bono, Joyce E. (2000). Five-factor Model of Personality and Transformational Leadership. *Journal of Applied Psychology*, 85, 751–65.

Jung, Dong I., and Avolio, Bruce J. (1999). Effects of Leadership Style and Followers' Cultural Orientation on Performance in Group and Individual Task Conditions. *Academy of Management Journal*, 42, 208–18.

Jung, Dong I., Chow, Chee, and Wu, Anne (2003). The Role of Transformational Leadership in Enhancing Organizational Innovation: Hypotheses and Some Preliminary Findings. *Leadership Quarterly*, 14, 525–44.

Kark, Ronit, Shamir, Boas, and Chen, Gilad (2003). The Two Faces of Transformational Leadership: Empowerment and Dependency. *Journal of Applied Psychology*, 88, 246–55.

Lord, Robert G., and Maher, Karen J. (1991). *Leadership and Information Processing: Linking Perceptions and Performance*. Boston, MA: Unwin Hyman.

Lowe, Kevin B., Kroeck, K. Galen, and Sivasubramaniam, Nagaraj (1996). Effective Correlates of Transformational and Transactional Leadership: A Meta-Analytic Review of the MLQ Literature. *Leadership Quarterly*, 7, 385–425.

Meindl, James R. (1990). On Leadership: An Alternative to the Conventional Wisdom. *Research in Organizational Behavior*, 12, 159–203.

——— (1995). The Romance of Leadership as a Follower-Centric Theory: A Social Constructionist Approach. *Leadership Quarterly*, 6, 329–41.

Miner, John B. (2002a). *Organizational Behavior: Foundations, Theories, and Analyses*. New York: Oxford University Press.

——— (2002b). The Role Motivation Theories of Organizational Leadership. In Bruce J. Avolio and Francis J. Yammarino (Eds.), *Transformational and Charismatic Leadership: The Road Ahead*. Oxford, UK: Elsevier Science, 309–38.

Parry, Ken W. (2002). Four Phenomenologically Determined Social Processes of Organizational Leadership: Further Support for the Construct of Transformational Leadership. In Bruce J. Avolio and Francis J. Yammarino (Eds.), *Transformational and Charismatic Leadership: The Road Ahead*. Oxford, UK: Elsevier Science, 339–72.

Pastor, Juan-Carlos, Meindl, James R., and Mayo, Margarita (2002). A Network Effects Model of Charisma Attributions. *Academy of Management Journal*, 45, 410–20.

Pawar, Badrinarayan S., and Eastman, Kenneth K. (1997). The Nature and Implications of Contextual Influences on Transformational Leadership: A Conceptual Examination. *Academy of Management Review*, 22, 80–109.

Peters, Ronald M., and Williams, Craig A. (2002). The Demise of Newt Gingrich as a Transformational Leader: Does Organizational Leadership Theory Apply to Legislative Leaders? *Organizational Dynamics*, 30, 257–68.

Pillai, Rajnandini, Schriesheim, Chester A., and Williams, Eric S. (1999). Fairness Perceptions and Trust as Mediators for Transformational and Transactional Leadership: A Two-Sample Study. *Journal of Management*, 25, 897–933.

Podsakoff, Philip M., MacKenzie, Scott B., and Bommer, William H. (1996). Transformational Leader Behaviors and Substitutes for Leadership as Determinants of Employee Satisfaction, Commitment, Trust, and Organizational Citizenship Behaviors. *Journal of Management*, 22, 259–98.

Podsakoff, Philip M., MacKenzie, Scott B., Moorman, Robert H., and Fetter, Richard (1990). Transformational Leader Behaviors and Their Effects on Followers' Trust in Leader, Satisfaction, and Organizational Citizenship Behaviors. *Leadership Quarterly*, 1, 107–42.

Porter, Lyman W., and Bigley, Gregory A. (2003). Motivation and Transformational Leadership: Some Organizational Context Issues. In Lyman W. Porter, Harold L. Angle, and Robert W. Allen (Eds.), *Organizational Influences Processes*. Armonk, NY: M.E. Sharpe, 263–74.

Schriesheim, Chester A. (2003). Why Leadership Research Is Generally Irrelevant for Leadership Development. In Susan E. Murphy and Ronald E. Riggio (Eds.), *The Future of Leadership Development*. Mahwah, NJ: Lawrence Erlbaum, 181–97.

Schriesheim, Chester A., Castro, Stephanie L., Zhou, Xiaohua, and Yammarino, Francis J. (2001). The Folly of Theorizing "A" But Testing "B"—A Selective Level-of-Analysis Review of the Field and a Detailed Leader–Member Exchange Illustration. *Leadership Quarterly*, 12, 515–51.

Seltzer, Joseph, and Bass, Bernard M. (1990). Transformational Leadership: Beyond Initiation and Consideration. *Journal of Management*, 16, 693–703.

Shamir, Boas, House, Robert J., and Arthur, Michael B. (1993). The Motivational Effects of Charismatic Leadership: A Self-Concept Based Theory. *Organization Science*, 4, 577–94.

Shin, Shung Jae, and Zhou, Jing (2003). Transformational Leadership, Conservation, and Creativity: Evidence from Korea. *Academy of Management Journal*, 46, 703–14.

Spreitzer, Gretchen M., and Quinn, Robert E. (1996). Empowering Middle Managers to Be Transformational Leaders. *Journal of Applied Behavioral Science*, 32, 237–61.

Tejeda, Manuel J., Scandura, Terri A., and Pillai, Rajnandini (2001). The MLQ Revisited: Psychometric Properties and Recommendations. *Leadership Quarterly*, 12, 31–52.

Turner, Nick, Barling, Julian, Epitropaki, Olga, Butcher, Vicki, and Milner, Caroline (2002). Transformational Leadership and Moral Reasoning. *Journal of Applied Psychology*, 87, 304–11.

Waldman, David A., Bass, Bernard M., and Einstein, Walter O. (1987). Leadership and Outcomes of Performance Appraisal Processes. *Journal of Occupational Psychology*, 60, 177–86.

Yammarino, Francis J., Spangler, William D., and Dubinsky, Alan J. (1998). Transformational and Contingent Reward Leadership: Individual, Dyad, and Group Levels of Analysis. *Leadership Quarterly*, 9, 27–54.

Yukl, Gary (1999). An Evaluation of Conceptual Weaknesses in Transformational and Charismatic Leadership Theories. *Leadership Quarterly*, 10, 285–305.

Yukl, Gary (2002). *Leadership in Organizations*. Upper Saddle River, NJ: Prentice-Hall.

Zacharatos, Anthea, Barling, Julian, and Kelloway, E. Kevin (2000). Development and Effects of Transformational Leadership in Adolescents. *Leadership Quarterly*, 11, 211–26.

NAME INDEX

A

Abelson, Michael A., 311, 318
Abelson, Robert P., 156
Adam, Everett E., 115, 131
Adams, Alice M., 5, 16
Adams, J. Stacy, 134–145, 148, 150, 155–156, 170
Adams, Susan, 246, 253, 376, 382
Aditya, Ram N., 56, 58–59, 225, 227–229, 244, 247, 251–253, 267, 270, 273, 276, 278, 294–298, 355, 357
Adler, Seymour, 197, 203, 330, 334
Agger, Ben, 25, 32
Ahearne, Mike, 313, 383
Ajzen, I., 170
Alavi, Maryam, 223–224, 230
Alban-Metcalfe, Robert J., 375, 382
Alderfer, Clayton P., 89–91, 363
Aldis, Owen, 115, 131
Alexander, Ralph A., 330, 335
Alge, Bradley J., 176, 186
Alimo-Metcalfe, Beverley, 375, 382
Allen, Robert W., 133, 317, 384
Alvarez, José L., 5, 16
Alvesson, Mats, 24–25, 32
Ambrose, Maureen L., 111–112, 145–146, 154, 156–157
Anderson, James K., 320, 334
Angle, Harold L., 317, 384
Anonyuo, Chigozie, 198, 202
Antonakis, John, 200–201, 347, 357, 378, 382
Arad, Sharon, 223, 230
Argyris, Chris, 25, 32
Arrowood, A. J., 140
Arthur, Michael B., 334, 337, 341, 343–344, 348–349, 352, 359, 369, 384
Ash, Mitchell G., 38, 44
Ash, Ronald A., 53, 58, 60
Ashforth, Blake E., 321, 334
Ashkanasy, Neal M., 196, 201
Astley, W. Graham, 8, 15, 26, 32
Atkinson, John W., 47–48, 59
Atwater, Leanne E., 313, 317
Audia, Pino G., 169, 180

B

Avolio, Bruce J., 124, 132, 224, 230, 335, 355, 357–359, 367–373, 375–376, 378, 382–384
Awamleh, Raed, 352, 357, 378, 382
Ayman, Roya, 241–242, 244–246, 253–254, 358, 376, 382

Bacharach, Samuel B., 7, 10, 15
Bachrach, Daniel G., 268, 279
Badin, Irwin J., 128, 132
Baetz, Mary L., 340, 358
Bagozzi, Richard P., 20, 32, 178, 181
Baillie, James, 13, 16
Baker, Douglas D., 125, 132
Baker, Paul, 362
Baldes, J. James, 175, 181
Baliga, B. Rajaram, 382
Balkin, David B., 154, 158
Bandura, Albert, 120, 122, 124, 131, 163, 170, 179, 181
Banks, Deanna J., 355, 360
Barling, Julian, 376–377, 382, 385
Barnard, Chester I., 259, 276
Barnes, Valerie, 248, 253
Barnes-Farrell, Janet L., 200–201
Barrett, Edward, 25, 32
Barrett, Gerald V., 58–59, 362
Barrett, Kelley M., 251, 254
Bartol, Kathryn M., 106–107, 109, 111–112, 144, 148, 156, 164, 181
Bartunek, Jean M., 5, 17
Bass, Bernard M., 182, 243, 247, 253, 338, 347–349, 354, 361–373, 375–378, 380–385
Bateson, Allan G., 294–295, 297
Battista, Mariangela, 53, 58, 60
Bauer, Tayla N., 111, 113, 269, 276
Baum, J. Robert, 54, 59, 169, 178, 181
Baum, Joel A. C., 33
Baumgardner, Terri L., 285, 297
Beach, Lee Roy, 196, 202
Bebb, Michael, 370, 383
Bedeian, Arthur G., 5, 16, 74, 92, 112–113, 132, 149, 158, 182, 230, 254, 277, 335, 358, 382

Beimel, Susanne, 354, 358
Belasco, James A., 21, 32
Benne, Kenneth D., 42, 44
Berelson, Bernard, 6, 15
Berg, Irwin A., 362
Bergami, Massimo, 178, 181
Berkes, Leslie J., 311, 317
Berkowitz, Leonard, 92, 156, 254
Berlew, David, 338
Bernstein, Susan D., 28, 32
Berscheid, Ellen, 135, 139, 158
Berson, Yair, 372–373, 383
Beyer, Janice M., 8, 15, 357–359
Biderman, Michael, 87, 92
Bies, Robert J., 152, 156
Biglan, Anthony, 238, 255
Bigley, Gregory A., 131, 157, 379, 384
Binning, John F., 281, 297–298
Blackburn, Richard S., 23, 31–32
Blake, Robert R., 362
Blakely, Gerald, 88, 92
Blood, Milton R., 316
Blyth, Dewey, 251, 255
Boal, Kimberly B., 351, 358
Bobocel, D. Ramona, 151, 156
Böhnisch, W., 220, 229
Bommer, William H., 270, 279, 313–314, 318,
      374, 384
Bono, Joyce E., 72, 74, 87, 92, 371,, 377–378,
      383
Bons, P. M., 240, 254
Boswell, Wendy R., 5, 13, 17, 106, 112
Bowen, David E., 308–309, 317
Boyatzis, Richard E., 56, 59
Boyd, Nancy G., 271, 277
Bracker, Jeffrey S., 327, 335
Bradford, Leland P., 42, 44
Breinin, Esther, 352, 355, 359
Bretz, Robert D., 150, 156
Brewer, J. Frank, 187, 202
Bright, Andrea, 52, 60
Briner, Rob B., 173, 183
Broedling, Laurie, 316–317
Brooks, Margaret E., 5, 16
Brower, Holly H., 352, 357
Brown, Clarence W., 6, 16
Brown, Douglas J., 289–291, 296–298
Brown, Karen A., 192–193, 195, 199, 201
Brown, Kenneth G., 5, 17
Brown, Michelle, 146, 156
Bryan, Judith F., 161, 174, 181–182
Bryman, Alan, 354, 356–357, 378, 383

Bunker, Archie, 310
Burger, Philip C., 362
Burke, Lisa A., 88, 91
Burke, Michael J., 246, 253
Burke, W. Warner, 40, 45
Burnham, David H., 47, 50, 59
Burns, James M., 362–363, 369, 383
Burns, Tom, 79, 91, 304
Burr, Donald, 383
Burrell, Gibson, 24, 32
Butcher, Vicki, 377, 385
Byrne, Zinta S., 151, 156

C

Calder, Bobby J., 186, 201
Camerer, Colin, 292, 299
Cameron, Kim S., 28, 32, 132
Campbell, Donald T., 22, 33, 262
Campbell, John P., 7, 16
Campion, Michael A., 22, 34
Cannell, Charles F., 38, 45
Capps, Michael H., 145, 157
Capwell, Dora F., 61, 74
Carland, James D., 329, 334
Carland, Jo Ann C., 329, 334
Carr, Linda, 53, 59, 60
Carson, Kenneth P., 72, 74, 330, 334
Cartledge, Norman, 162–163, 174, 182
Cascio, Wayne F., 362
Cashman, James F., 257–258, 262–264, 277
Cason, Kathryn, 151, 157
Cass, Eugene L., 230
Castro, Stephanie L., 267, 276, 279, 315, 318,
      329, 335, 379, 384
Cavanaugh, Marcie A., 5, 17
Chan, Fiona S., 8, 16
Chan, Kim-Yin, 333–334
Chemers, Martin M., 225, 229, 238–239, 241–246,
      253–254, 269, 277, 293–295, 297, 316–317,
      358, 382
Chen, Chao C., 147, 156, 330, 334, 378, 383
Chen, Gilad, 377, 384
Chen, Xiao-ping, 224, 230
Cheng, Tsz-kit, 8, 16
Chesney, Amelia A., 169, 177, 181
Choi, Jaepil, 233, 255, 383
Choi, Yeon, 352, 357, 362
Chow, Chee, 375, 384
Chreim, Samia, 294, 299
Christensen, Clayton M., 12, 16
Chun, Jae Uk, 356, 359

Church, Allan H., 72–74, 90, 92
Clark, Kenneth E., 358
Clark, Miriam B., 358
Clark, Russell A., 48, 59
Clarke, Linda D., 149, 157
Clegg, Stewart R., 4, 16, 25, 28–29, 32–34, 93, 383
Cleveland, Jeannette, 203
Cleven, Walter A., 235, 253
Clifton, Timothy C., 350, 359
Cogliser, Claudia C., 267, 279
Cohen-Charnash, Yochi, 153, 156
Colbert, Amy L., 5, 17
Coleman, Peter T., 25, 34
Collins, Christopher J., 58, 60, 331, 335
Colquitt, Jason A., 151–153, 156
Conger, Jay A., 356–358
Conlon, Donald E., 153, 156
Connelly, Mary S., 350, 359
Connolly, Terry, 179, 181
Conrad, Kelley A., 202
Cook, Thomas D., 22, 33
Coombs, Timothy, 127–128, 131
Cooper Cary L., 5, 16, 59, 74, 92, 112, 156–157, 183, 229, 253, 255, 276, 297, 357, 383
Cooper, Elizabeth A., 145, 158
Cooper, R., 182
Cordery, John L., 83, 93
Cornelius, Edwin T., 330, 334
Cortina, José M., 20, 33
Cronshaw, Steven F., 200–201
Cropanzano, Russell, 151–152, 156–157
Crouch, Andrew, 221, 229
Culbert, Samuel A., 208, 229
Cummings, Larry L., 70, 74, 96, 100, 112
Cummings, Thomas G.., 25, 33

D

Dachler, H. Peter, 88, 92, 382
Daft, Richard L., 5, 17
Danehower, Carol, 177, 183
Daniel, David L., 315, 318
Dansereau, Fred, 257–258, 262–264, 271–272, 277–279, 291, 297
Das, T. K., 5, 16
Davenport, Thomas H., 15, 17
Davis, Tim R. V., 122, 127, 131–132
Davis, William N., 50, 60
Davis-Blake, Alison, 27, 33, 89–91
Day, David V., 267–269, 276–277, 281, 288, 297
Day, Russell R., 246, 253

deCharms, Richard, 55, 59
Deci, Edward L., 103, 109–110, 112–113, 170, 179, 181, 362
deJonge, Jan, 87, 91
Deluga, Ronald J., 350–351, 55, 357
Dembo, Tamara, 43, 45, 160, 164, 182
DenHartog, Deanne N., 349, 357, 375, 383
DeNisi, Angelo S., 93
Depinet, Robert L., 58–59
DeShon, Richard P., 176, 181
DeVader, Christy L., 281, 294–295, 297–298
DeVitt, H. William, 70, 74
Dickinson, Alyce M., 128, 132
Dies, Robert R., 58, 60
Dionne, Shelley D., 313, 317, 356, 359
Dirks, Kurt T., 268, 277
Dobbins, Gregory H., 197–198, 201, 203, 350, 359
Dodge, George E., 351, 358
Doh, Jonathan P., 227, 229
Doktor, Robert, 362
Dollard, Maureen F., 87, 91
Donahue, Lisa M., 185, 202
Donaldson, Lex, 5, 14, 16, 25–26, 30, 33
Donovan, John J., 176–177, 181
Dorfman, Peter W., 304, 307–309, 311–315, 317–318, 349, 357
Dormann, Christian, 87, 91
Dornstein, Miriam, 147, 156
Doty, D. Harold, 14, 16
Dowling, Michael J., 29, 34
Dowling, William F., 115, 132
Drake, Bruce H., 46, 60
Drasgow, Fritz, 333–334
Drazin, Robert, 8, 17
Drucker, Peter F., 170, 181
Dubin, Robert, 6–7, 11, 16
Dubinsky, Alan J., 373, 385
Duchon, Dennis, 268, 277
Duffy, Michelle K., 330, 335
Dugan, Kathleen W., 198, 201
Dukerich, Janet M., 329, 334
Dulebohn, James, 148, 156
Dumdum, Uldarico R., 373, 383
Duncan, W. Jack, 5, 16
Dunegan, Kennth J., 268, 277
Dunham, Randall B., 83, 93
Dunnete, Marvin D., 16, 33, 59, 156, 202, 230, 277–278, 298, 362
Durham, Cathy C., 107, 112, 144, 156, 176, 181
Dutton, Jane E., 28, 32, 132
Dvir, Taly, 376, 383
Dwyer, Deborah J., 91

E

Eagly, Alice H., 40, 45, 330, 334, 373, 383
Earley, P. Christopher, 179, 181
Eastman, Kenneth K., 379, 384
Ebadi, Yar M., 220, 230
Ebrahimi, Bahman, 330, 333–335
Eden, Dov, 376, 383
Edwards, Jeffrey R., 19–20, 33–34
Ehrhart, Karen H., 332, 335
Ehrhart, Mark G., 332, 335, 351, 357
Einstein, Walter O., 370, 382, 385
Eisenbach, Regina J., 95, 113
Eisman, Elena J., 58, 60
Elkins, Teri, 276–277, 375, 383
Emrich, Cynthia G., 291, 298, 352, 357
Emsley, David, 178, 181
Engle, Elaine M., 269, 277, 289, 297
Ensley, Michael D., 329, 334
Epitropaki, Olga, 377, 385
Erdogan, Berrin, 271–273, 276–277
Erez, Amir, 111–112, 179, 181
Erez, Miriam, 30, 33, 113, 132, 177, 181–182, 278
Ettling, Jennifer T., 221–222, 229
Etzioni, Amitai, 356
Evangelista, A. S., 88, 91
Evans, Martin G., 22, 33, 108, 112
Eyde, Lorraine D., 53, 58, 60

F

Fabian, Frances H., 29, 33, 329, 334
Fairhurst, Gail T., 196, 201
Fang, Yongqing, 87, 92
Farh, Jiing-Lih, 268, 278
Farrow, Dana L., 362
Fazzini, Don, 355, 358
Fedor, Donald, 85, 93
Feldman, Jack M., 352, 357
Fernandez, Carmen F., 267, 277
Ferrier, Walter J., 193, 195, 201
Ferrin, Donald L., 268, 277
Ferris, Gerald R., 85–86, 91, 93
Festinger, Leon, 43, 45, 134, 157, 160, 164, 182
Fetter, Richard, 313–314, 318, 375–376, 384
Fiedler, Fred E., 92, 185, 232–255, 331, 370
Field, Richard H. G., 219–220, 222, 229–230
Filley, Alan C., 301, 317
Finegold, David, 106, 112
Finn, Stephen E., 58, 60
Fiol, C. Marlene, 346–348, 358
Fisher, Bruce M., 246, 253, 276, 382

Fitzgerald, Michael P., 86, 92
Flanagan, John, 62, 68, 74
Fleishman, Edwin A., 253, 296, 299, 362
Flynn, Francis J., 378, 383
Foa, Uriel G., 239, 254
Fodor, Eugene M., 341, 348, 358
Folger, Robert, 151, 157
Ford, Eric W., 5, 16
Ford, Robert N., 67, 74
Foti, Roseanne J., 281, 283, 292, 296–298, 329–330, 334
Foucault, M., 32
Fox, Marilyn L., 91
Fox, Suzy, 27, 34, 90, 93
Frank, Linda L., 85, 91
Franke, Richard H., 362
Franz, Timothy M., 196, 202
Fraser, Scott L., 281, 297
Frayne, Colette A., 130–131
Fredrickson, James W., 194, 202
Freedman, Sara, 139, 145, 156
Freiberg, Steven J., 289–290, 298
Frese, Michael, 57, 60, 331, 335, 354, 358
Fried, Yizhak, 86–87, 91, 93
Frink, Dwight D., 176, 183
Frost, Peter J., 23–24, 30, 33–34, 316–317, 349, 358, 376, 383
Fry, Louis W., 355, 358
Fuller, Jack, 88, 92

G

Gaertner, Stefan, 267, 278
Galbraith, Jay, 96, 100, 112
Gallois, Cynthia, 196, 201
Garb, Howard N., 331, 334
Garcia, Joseph E., 242, 246, 248–251, 254–255
Gardner, William L., 296, 299, 352, 355, 357–258, 378, 382
Garland, Howard, 352, 357
Gavin, Mark B., 196, 201
George, Jennifer M., 8, 16, 27–28, 33, 90–91
George-Falvy, Jane, 178, 182
Georgopoulos, Basil S., 94–97, 101–102, 112
Gerhart, Barry, 74, 112, 156, 181
Geringer, J. Michael, 130–131
Gerstner, Charlotte R., 267–269, 276–277
Gessner, Theodore L., 350, 359
Ghate, Onkar, 24, 33, 159, 181
Ghiselli, Edwin E., 6, 16, 251, 254
Gholson, Barry, 34
Giacalone, Robert A., 145, 157

Gibb, Jack R., 42, 44
Gibson, Frederick W., 251–252, 254
Gilliard, Debora J., 330, 334
Gingrich, Newt, 384
Ginsburg, Sol W., 320, 334
Ginsburgh, Steven, 264, 277–278
Ginter, Peter M., 5, 16
Ginzberg, Eli, 320, 334
Gioia, Dennis A., 198, 201, 294, 297
Gist, Marilyn E., 196, 203, 252, 254, 380, 383
Glaser, Barney G., 15–16
Glick, William H., 14, 16, 89, 91
Glube, R., 220, 230
Godfrey, Eleanor P., 234–235, 255
Goffee, Rob, 334
Golden, Brian R., 329, 334
Goldstein, Arnold P., 129, 131
Goldstein, Jeffrey, 40, 45
Gómez, Carolina, 269, 277
Goodheim, Laurie, 370, 378, 383
Gooding, Richard Z., 200–201
Goodwin, Vicki L., 176, 183
Gottfredson, Linda S., 10, 16
Gowing, Marilyn K., 52, 60
Grabbe, Paul, 42, 45
Graen, George B., 96, 107, 112, 256–266, 269–273, 275, 277–279
Graen, Martin G., 266, 278
Graen, Michael R., 266, 273, 278
Grauer, Eyal, 5, 16
Green, Stephen G., 184–185, 187–191, 194–196,, 200–203, 269, 276, 292, 297
Greenberg, Jerald, 16, 33, 91, 142–143, 145, 151, 153–157, 198, 202, 358
Greenberger, David B., 198, 202
Greenhaus, Jeffrey H., 128, 132, 198, 202
Greenwood, Royston, 42, 45
Gregory, Donna, 52, 60
Greiner, Larry E., 301, 317
Griffeth, Roger W., 267, 278
Griffin, Mark A., 26, 34, 83, 93
Griffin, Ricky W., 87–88, 91
Grover, Richard A., 312, 318
Grush, Joseph E., 107, 113
Gueutal, Hal G., 89, 93
Gully, Stanley M., 270, 278
Gupta, Nina, 88, 91, 223, 230

H

Haas, J. A., 182
Häcker, Hartmut, 182, 277

Hackett, Rick D., 268, 278, 330, 335
Hackman, J. Richard, 75–86, 91–93, 104, 112, 170
Hackman, Ray C., 71, 74
Haga, William J., 257–258, 263–264, 277–278
Hall, D. M., 234–235, 255
Hall, Rosalie J., 289, 291, 297–298
Halpert, Jane A., 350, 358
Hamner, Ellen P., 117–118, 131
Hamner, W. Clay, 114, 116–120, 128, 131
Hanges, Paul J., 349, 357
Hansemark, Ove C., 58–59
Hansen, Curtiss P., 202
Harder, Joseph W., 150, 157
Harding, Francis D., 296, 299
Hardy, Cynthia, 4, 16, 28, 32–34, 93, 383
Harris, Drew, 346–348, 358
Harris, Karen L., 89, 92, 269, 279
Hartke, Darrell D., 243, 255
Hartley, Eugene L., 45
Hartman, Edwin, 12, 16, 28, 33
Hartman, Erica, 246, 253, 376, 382
Harvey, Jennifer L., 291, 298
Hastings, Limda L., 240, 254
Hater, John J., 370, 383
Hatfield, John D., 148, 157
Hauenstein, Neil M. A., 292, 297
Hauser, Markus, 353–354, 358
Hayton, James C., 72, 74
Heerwagen, Judith H., 196, 202
Heggestad, Eric D., 54, 59
Heider, Fritz, 185, 202
Heller, Frank A., 208, 223, 228–229, 254, 382
Hemphill, John, 362
Hendrix, William H., 144, 158
Heneman, Robert L., 198, 202
Herma, John L., 320, 334
Herald, David M., 27, 33, 90, 92
Herzberg, Frederick, 30, 58, 61–74, 76, 80, 85, 88, 135, 170
Hesketh, Beryl, 53, 58, 60
Hibbard, Stephen, 331, 334
Higgins, Christopher A., 375, 383
Highhouse, Scott, 5, 16
Hill, Kenneth D., 316–317
Hinings, C. Robert, 42, 45
Hinson, Thomas D., 149, 157
Hinton, Michelle, 87, 92
Hitler, Adolf, 37, 233, 369
Hitt, Michael A., 93
Ho, Violet T., 72, 74
Hodgetts, Richard M., 125, 132

Hoel, William, 265, 278
Hofer, Charles W., 4, 17
Hofmann, David A., 93
Hogan, Robert T., 54, 59, 355, 358
Hogg, Michael A., 273, 279, 298, 354, 359
Hollenbeck, John R., 176, 181
Hom, Peter W., 267, 278, 292, 299
Homans, George C., 134, 157
Hooijberg, Robert, 233, 255, 362, 383
Horgan, Dianne D., 221, 229
Hough, Leaɔtta M., 16, 33, 59, 278, 298
House, Robert J., 13, 16, 27, 33, 56, 58–59, 90,
    92, 219, 225, 227–229, 244, 247, 250–254,
    267, 270, 273, 276, 278, 294–298, 300–301,
    317, 337–341, 343–359, 362–365, 369, 378,
    380–384
Houts, Arthur C., 34
Howard, Ann, 358
Howell, Jane M., 341, 349, 351–352, 358–359,
    372, 375–376, 383
Howell, Jon P., 304, 307–309, 311–315,
    317–318
Huber, Vandra L., 311–312, 318
Hui, Chun, 262, 278
Hulin, Charles L., 84, 92
Humphreys, John, 171, 181
Hunt, J. McVicker, 45, 182
Hunt, James G., 229–230, 253–254, 277, 298,
    351, 358, 382–383
Hunter, John E., 171, 176, 183
Hurder, W. P., 362
Huseman, Richard C., 148, 157

I

Icenogle, Marjorie L., 177, 183
Ilgen, Daniel R., 108, 112, 194, 202, 238, 247,
    254, 299, 317
Ilies, Remus, 111–112, 176, 181, 257, 278
Isen, Alice M., 111–112, 179, 181

J

Jackson, Jesse, 348
Jackson, Susan E., 93
Jacobs, Ruth L., 57, 59
Jacobs, T. Owen, 257, 278, 296, 299
Jacobsen, Chanock, 347–348, 358
Jacobsen, Patricia R., 141–142, 156
Jago, Arthur G., 207–208, 213–214, 216, 218–222,
    225–227, 229–231, 246, 255, 374
Jaɔnes, Lawrence R., 8, 7, 313, 317

Janssen, Peter P. M., 87, 91
Jaques, Elliott, 151, 157
Javidan, Mansour, 351, 359
Jenkins, G. Douglas, 88, 91, 223, 230
Jermier, John M., 25, 33, 302–303, 308, 310–312,
    314, 317–318
Jerome, William T., 321, 334
Johannesen-Schmidt, Mary C., 40, 45, 373, 383
Johns, Gary, 87, 92
Johnson, Blair T., 330, 334
Johnson, Thomas W., 263–264, 278
Jones, Candace, 329, 334
Jones, Edward E., 186, 192, 202
Jones, Gareth R., 8, 16
Jones, Nyle W., 94–97, 101–102, 112
Judge, Timothy A., 72–74, 87, 90, 92, 111–112,
    176, 181, 196, 202, 257, 278, 371, 377–378,
    383
Jung, Dong I., 355, 359, 371–373, 375,
    382–384

K

Kabanoff, Boris, 26, 34, 247, 255
Kacmar, K. Michele, 270, 278
Kahai, Surinder S., 224, 230
Kahn, Robert L., 38, 45, 71–72, 74, 257, 278
Kahnweiler, William M., 221, 230
Kalb, Laura S., 195, 203
Kalin, Rudolph, 50, 60
Kanfer, Ruth, 54, 59
Kanungo, Rabindra N., 356–358
Kaplan, Abraham, 7, 16
Karau, Steven J., 330, 334
Kark, Ronit, 377, 384
Kärreman, Dan, 25, 32
Kassner, Marcia W., 85, 93
Katz, Daniel, 257, 278
Kaufman, Stanley, 85, 92
Kavanagh, Michael, 147, 157
Kay, Gary G., 58, 60
Kehoe, Jerry, 53, 58, 60
Kelemen, Michaela, 24, 33
Keller, Robert T., 276–277, 375, 383
Keller, Tiffany, 293, 298
Kelley, Harold H., 186–187, 190
Kelloway, E. Kevin, 376–377, 382, 385
Kemmerer, Barbara, 87, 92
Kendall, Lorne M., 161, 182
Kennedy, John K., 244, 255
Keon, Thomas L., 109, 113
Kernan, Mary C., 281, 298

Kerr, Steven, 58–59, 225, 227–229, 244, 247, 251, 253, 267, 273, 276, 296–297, 300–304, 306–314, 316–318, 355, 357
Ketchen, David J., 14, 16
Kickul, Jill, 149, 157
Kiker, Scott, 315, 318
Kilduff, Martin, 24, 33
Kim, Jay S., 267, 270, 278
King, Bert T., 92, 253, 362
King, Wesley C., 149, 157
Kinicki, Angelo J., 72, 74, 200–201
Kinne, Sydney B., 174, 182–183
Kipnis, David, 193, 202
Kirkpatrick, Shelley A., 54, 59, 169, 178, 181, 352, 358
Kisfalvi, Veronika, 294, 299
Klaas, Brian S., 199, 202
Klauss, Rudi, 362
Klein, Howard J., 175–176, 181, 267, 270, 278
Klein, Katherine J., 345, 351, 357, 359
Kleinbeck, Uwe, 113, 132, 182, 277–278
Klieman, Rhonda S., 89, 92, 269, 279
Klimoski, Richard J., 185, 202, 360
Knerr, Claramae S., 162–163, 182
Knez, Marc, 292, 299
Knight, Don, 176, 181
Knowlton, William A., 194, 202, 248, 254
Koch, Sigmund, 113
Koeppel, Jeffrey, 174, 182
Koestner, Richard, 54, 60, 110, 112
Köhler, Wolfgang, 38
Komaki, Judith L., 116, 127–128, 131–132
Konovsky, Mary A., 143, 152, 157
Koopman, Paul L., 375, 383
Korman, Abraham K., 128, 132
Kornberger, Martin, 25, 33
Kraimer, Maria L., 196, 202
Kray, Laura, 145, 157
Kreitner, Robert, 114, 119–123, 130, 132
Kroeck, K. Galen, 373–374, 384
Krusell, J., 362
Kubiszyn, Tom W., 58, 60
Kudisch, Jeffrey D., 350, 359
Kuhn, Thomas, 32–33
Kulik, Carol T., 79, 84, 92, 111–112, 145–146, 157

L

Lam Simon S. K., 22, 33, 224, 230
Lammers, Cornelis, 14, 16
Landeweerd, Jan A., 87, 91
Landy, Frank J., 203

Langan-Fox, Janice, 57, 59
Langner, Paul H., 84, 92
Lankau, Melenie J., 271, 279
Lapierre, Laurent M., 268, 278
Larson, J., 187, 203
Larson, James R., 292, 298
Larson, Lars L., 229–230, 254, 277, 358, 383
Larwood, Laurie, 147, 157
Latack, Janina C., 109, 113
Latham, Gary P., 30, 33, 130, 132, 160, 163–164, 166–175, 177, 180–183, 330, 334
Lattal, Kennon A., 115, 132
Lawler, Edward E., 25, 33, 75–79, 83–85, 92, 94–96, 98–101, 103–104, 106, 108, 111–113, 143, 149, 156–157, 257
Lawrence, Paul R., 77, 82–84, 93
Lazzarini, Sergio G., 329, 336
Leana, Carrie R., 270, 279
Leavitt, Harold J., 329, 334, 362
Ledford, Gerald E., 25, 33
Lee, Cynthia, 179, 181
Lee, Felissa K., 177, 182
Lee, Jeong-Yeon, 23, 34, 315, 318
Lee, Thomas W., 200, 202–203
Leone, Luigi, 178, 181
LePine, Jeffrey A., 199, 202
Lester, Scott W., 149, 157
Leventhal, Gerald S., 145, 157
Levine, Richard, 147, 157
Levinson, Harry, 46, 59–60
Lewin, Kurt, 5, 15–16, 37–45, 47, 58, 94–95, 112–113, 159–160, 164, 182, 223, 328, 367
Lichtenstein, Benyamin M. B., 329, 334
Liddell, W. W., 220
Liden, Robert C., 192–193, 195–196, 202, 223, 230, 264–265, 267, 269, 271–273, 276–279
Lilienfeld, Scott O., 331, 334
Lind, E. Allan, 145, 154–155, 157
Lindell, Michael K., 23, 33
Lippitt, Ronald, 39, 45
Litwin, George H., 51, 59
Locke, Edwin A., 5, 8, 16, 20–21, 24–25, 30, 32–33, 54, 58–60, 74, 87, 92–93, 104, 106, 109, 111–113, 127, 132, 148, 156–157, 159–183, 202, 223–224, 229–230, 253, 255, 276, 297, 331, 335, 352, 357–358, 383
Loher, Brian T., 86, 92
London, Manuel, 185, 201–203, 297
Long, Gary, 145, 157
Loo, Robert, 19, 33
Lord, Robert G., 199–202, 269, 277, 280–299, 303, 315, 317, 355, 377–378, 384

Lorsch, Jay W., 32, 92
Louviere, Jordan J., 222, 229
Lowe, Kevin B., 296, 299, 373–374, 383–384
Lowell, Edgar L., 48, 59
Luthans, Brett C., 125, 132
Luthans, Fred, 87, 92, 99, 113–116, 119–128, 130–133, 176, 183
Luthans, Kyle W., 125, 132

M

Macaulay, Jennifer L., 252, 254
Maccoby, Eleanor E., 45
Maciag, Walter S., 125–126, 132
MacKenzie, Scott B., 23, 34, 268, 279, 310, 312–315, 318, 374–376, 384
Mahar, Linda, 246, 254
Maher, John R., 92
Maher, Karen J., 280–281, 283–287, 289, 292–295, 297–298, 303, 377, 384
Mahoney, Gerald M., 94–97, 101–102, 112
Mai-Dalton, Renate R., 352, 357
Maier, Norman R. F., 208, 227, 230
Maierhofer, Noami I., 26, 34
Maitlis, Sally, 173, 183
Mannix, Elizabeth A., 147, 157
Manz, Charles C., 315, 318
Margerison, Charles, 220, 230
Margulies, Newton, 25, 34
Markham, Steven E., 22, 34
Marrow, Alfred J., 42–43, 45
Marshak, Robert J., 40, 45
Martin, Joanne, 24, 34
Martinko, Mark J., 124, 132, 184, 186, 201–202
Martocchio, Joseph J., 148, 156, 176, 183, 196, 202
Maslow, Abraham H., 46, 76, 114, 170, 346, 363, 377, 381
Maslyn, John M., 195, 202, 270, 275, 279
Massarik, Frederick, 25, 34
Masters, Marick, 85, 93
Mathapo, J., 70, 74
Mausner, Bernard, 61–63, 68–69, 71, 74
Mayo, Margarita, 378, 384
Mazza, Carmelo, 5, 16
McAdams, Dan P., 54, 60
McClelland, David C., 44, 46–52, 54–60, 170, 186, 327, 338, 341, 347, 378
McDonald-Mann, Dana, 252, 254, 380, 383
McFarlin, Dean B., 177, 182
McGregor, Douglas, 114
McGuire, Mark A., 251, 254

McKee, Gail H., 22, 34
McKee-Ryan, Frances M., 72, 74
McKelvey, Bill, 9, 12, 16, 26, 33
McKenna, Jack F., 229, 258
McKinley, William, 13, 17, 29–30, 34
McMahan, Gary C., 88, 91
McNatt, D. Bryan, 5, 17
Meckler, Mark, 13, 16, 46, 60
Mehra, Ajay, 24, 33
Meindl, James R., 350–351, 359, 377–378, 383–384
Mento, Anthony J., 175, 183
Meyer, Gregory, 58, 60
Miles, Edward W., 148, 157
Miles, Raymond E., 289, 299
Miller, Danny, 14, 16
Miller, John A., 362
Miller, Lynn E., 107, 113
Millman, Zeeva, 130, 132
Milner, Caroline, 377, 385
Minami, Takao, 262, 277
Miner, John B., 4–5, 9, 14, 17, 20, 26–27, 31, 34, 37, 39, 44–45, 54, 56–57, 60, 88, 92, 145, 157, 167, 170, 182, 187, 195, 200, 202, 257, 279, 285, 293, 296–297, 299, 301, 304, 318–322, 324, 326–338, 346, 355–356, 359, 363, 366, 379, 381, 384
Minnich, Michelle R., 128, 131
Miron, David, 47, 57, 60
Mitchell, Terence R., 8, 17, 128, 132, 145, 157, 178, 182, 184–196, 199–203, 238–239, 254–255, 292, 297
Mitra, Atul, 223, 230
Moeller, Gerald H., 55, 59
Moeller, Nancy L., 86, 92
Mohler, Carolyn J., 151–152, 156
Mohrman, Alan M., 25, 33
Mohrman, Susan A., 25, 33
Mone, Mark A., 13, 17
Moore, Larry F., 334
Moorman, Robert H., 88, 92, 375–376, 384
Moreland, Kevin L., 58, 60
Morgan, Wesley G., 53, 60
Morgeson, Frederick P., 22, 34
Morris, Charles G., 81, 92
Morris, Timothy, 334
Mowday, Richard T., 143, 147, 157
Moynihan, Lisa M., 5, 17
Mueller, Charles W., 18, 34
Mueller, Stephen L., 149, 157
Mumford, Michael D., 271, 279, 296, 299, 350, 359

Murphy, Susan E., 230, 251–255, 279, 336, 382, 384
Murray, Henry A., 46–47, 53, 60

N

Nathan, Barry R., 330, 335
Neale, Margaret A., 147, 157
Nebeker, Delbert M., 108, 112
Neider Linda L., 74, 269–270, 277, 279, 359
Neimeyer, Robert A., 34
Newcomb, Theodore M., 45
Newell, Allen, 281, 299
Ng, K. Yee, 153, 156
Niehoff, Brian P., 88, 92, 312, 318
Nielson, Troy R., 95, 113
Nijhuis, Frans J. N., 87, 91
Noe, Raymond A., 86, 92
Nord, Walter R., 4, 16, 27–28, 32–34, 90, 93, 115, 122, 132, 383
Northcraft, Gregory B., 147, 157
Nottenburg, Gail, 85, 93
Novak, Michael A., 265, 273, 278
Nur, Yusuf A., 356, 359
Nuttin, J. R., 166, 183
Nystrom, Paul C., 317

O

O'Brien, Gordon E., 238, 247, 254
O'Brien, Richard M., 128, 132
O'Connor, Jennifer, 350, 359
O'Leary-Kelly, Anne M., 176, 183
O'Reilly, Charles A., 191, 195, 203
Oldham, Greg R., 75–86, 92–93, 170
Oliver, John E., 328, 335
Oncken, Gerald R., 238, 255
Ones, Deniz S., 20, 34
Ong, Mark, 177, 183, 224, 230
Orris, James B., 263–264, 278
Otteman, Robert, 119, 132

P

Paine, Julie Beth, 268, 279
Palich, Leslie E., 292, 299
Papanek, Miriam Lewin, 38, 42, 45
Parasuraman, Saroj, 198, 202
Parker, Sharon K., 83, 93
Parry, Ken W., 15, 17, 375, 384
Pastor, Jaun-Carlos, 378, 384
Patel, Rita, 52, 60

Patton, Gregory K., 72, 74
Paul, Robert J., 87, 92, 125, 132, 220, 230
Pawar, Badrinarayan S., 379, 384
Payne, Roy L., 46, 60
Pearce, Jone L., 85–86, 93
Pearlman, Kenneth, 53, 58, 60
Peiperl, Maury A., 334
Pence, Earl C., 197, 203
Pendleton, William C., 197, 203
Peracchio, Laura, 22, 33
Pescosolido, Bernice A., 26, 34
Peters, Lawrence H., 243, 255
Peters, Thomas J., 168, 183
Peters, Ronald M., 379, 384
Peterson, R. O., 61, 74
Petrullo, Luigi, 362
Pfeffer, Jeffrey, 4, 13, 17, 27–29, 33–34, 87–91, 93
Phillips, James S., 281, 298–299
Phillips, Lynn W., 20, 32
Piccolo, Ronald F., 257, 278
Pierce, Hawkeye, 310
Pierce, Jon L., 83, 93
Pillai, Rajnandini, 350–351, 359, 375, 384–385
Pinder, Craig C., 111, 113, 178, 183, 334
Pirozzolo, Francis J., 253–255, 336, 382
Pitcher, Patricia, 294, 299
Podsakoff, Nathan P., 23, 34, 315, 318
Podsakoff, Philip M., 23–24, 268, 279, 308–315, 317–318, 344, 346, 349, 358, 374–376, 384
Pohlman, John T., 243, 255
Popper, Micha, 352, 355, 359, 372, 383
Poppo, Laura, 329, 336
Porter, Christopher O. L. H., 153, 156
Porter, Lyman W., 94–96, 98–99, 103–104, 106, 108, 111–113, 131, 133, 157, 257, 317, 379, 384
Posthuma, Richard A., 152, 158
Poteet, Mark L., 350, 359
Potter, Earl H., 248, 251, 253–255
Premack, Steven, 176, 183
Price, James L., 18, 34
Priem, Richard L., 5, 17
Prien, Erich P., 53, 58, 60
Pritchard, Robert D., 108, 112
Prusack, Laurence, 15, 17
Pulakos, Elaine E., 299, 317
Puranam, Phanish, 349, 351, 359
Pusic, Eugen, 223, 229
Putka, Dan J., 178–179, 183

Q

Quast, Hans-Henning, 182, 277
Quinn, Julie A., 89, 92, 269, 279
Quinn, Robert E., 132, 376, 385
Quinn, Robert F., 28, 32
Quiñones, Miguel A., 251, 255

R

Radosevich, David J., 176–177, 181
Ragan, James W., 246, 255
Raju, Nambury S., 54, 60, 329, 332, 335
Ramirez, Gabriel G., 349, 351, 359
Rand, Ayn, 159
Raskin, Robert, 355, 358
Rauch, Andreas, 57, 60, 331, 335
Raynor, Michael E., 12, 16
Read, Peter C., 222, 229
Reber, G., 220, 229
Redding, Thomas P., 128, 131
Rediker, Kenneth J., 193, 195, 201
Reed, Geoffrey M., 58, 60
Reis, H. T., 362
Renn, Robert W., 87, 93, 177, 183
Rentsch, Joan R., 87, 93
Rice, Robert W., 177, 182, 247, 255
Rich, Philip, 14, 17
Richards, Mary, 310
Riggio, Ronald E., 230, 253–255, 279, 336, 382, 384
Roberts, Sharon, 111, 113
Rodgers, Robert, 171, 176, 183
Rodriguez, Donna, 52, 60
Roehling, Mark V., 5, 17
Romanelli, Elaine, 329, 335
Ronan, W. W., 174, 183
Rosen, Benson, 269, 277
Rosenbaum, William B., 140, 156
Rosenkrantz, Stuart A., 125–126, 132
Rosenstein, Joseph, 5, 17
Rosow, Michael P., 128, 132
Ross-Smith, Anne, 29, 33
Roth, Philip L., 54, 60, 332, 335
Roth, Susanna, 57, 59
Rottenstreich, Yuval, 292, 299
Rotter, Julian B., 186–187
Rousculp, Mathew D., 5, 16
Rousseau, Denise M., 13, 16, 72, 74, 178, 183, 270, 279
Rozell, Elizabeth J., 173, 183
Rubin, Beth A., 26, 34

Ruiz-Quintanilla, S. Antonio, 349, 357
Rupp, Deborah E., 151–152, 156
Rush, Michael C., 281, 298–299, 350, 359
Russell, Craig J., 329, 335
Russell, Jeanne M., 198, 201
Russell, Joyce E. A., 350, 359
Ryan, Richard M., 109–110, 112
Ryan, Thomas A., 159–160, 173, 183
Rynes, Sara L., 5, 17, 74, 112, 156, 181
Ryterband, E. C., 362

S

Sagie, Abraham, 223–224, 230
Saha, Sudhir, 330, 335
Salancik, Gerald R., 87–91, 93, 201
Sanchez, Juan I., 53, 58, 60
Sanchez, Julio C., 14, 17
Sanchez, Rudolph J., 111, 113
Sandberg, Jörgen, 53, 60
Sandelands, Lloyd E., 8, 17
Sathe, Vijay, 329, 335
Sauley, Kerry S., 149, 158
Scandura, Terri A., 20, 34, 259–262, 266, 269–271, 273, 278–279, 375, 385
Scarpello, Vida, 72, 74
Schaubroeck, John, 22, 33, 224, 230
Schein, Edgar H., 285–286
Schendel, Dan E., 4, 17
Schepman, Stephen, 127–128, 131
Scherer, Andreas G., 29, 34
Schiemann, William, 257, 259, 264, 277–278
Schmidt, Frank L., 20, 34, 131
Schmidt, Warren H., 207–211, 230
Schminke, Marshall, 151–152, 154, 156
Schneider, Benjamin, 332, 335
Schoenborn, Sandra, 354, 358
Scholl, Richard W., 145, 158
Schoonhoven, Claudia B., 329, 335
Schriesheim, Chester A., 72, 74, 227, 230, 243–244, 246–247, 253, 255, 267, 269–270, 276–277, 279, 298, 301, 315, 318, 329, 335, 359, 375, 379, 382, 384
Schriesheim, Janet F., 302, 317
Schwab, Donald P., 70, 74
Scott, K. Dow, 22, 34
Scott, Kimberly S., 154, 157
Scott, W. Richard, 329, 335
Scott, William E., 115, 131
Sculli, Domenic, 8, 16
Seabright, Mark A., 154, 156
Sears, Pauline S., 43, 45, 160, 164, 182

Segall, Marshall H., 55, 60
Sekaran, Uma, 298, 382
Seltzer, Joseph, 372, 384
Sgro, Joseph A., 197, 203
Shackleton, V. J., 362
Shadish, William R., 31, 34
Shalley, Christina E., 179, 183
Shamir, Boas, 337, 341, 343–344, 348–349, 352–353, 355, 358–359, 369, 372, 376–377, 383–384
Shane, Scott A., 27, 33, 58, 60, 90, 92, 331, 335
Shapira, Zur, 362
Shartle, Carroll L., 362
Shaw, Jason D., 223, 230, 330, 335
Shea, Christine M., 352, 359
Sheldon, Kennon M., 177, 182
Shepherd, Dean, 330, 336
Sheridan, John E., 311, 318
Sherif, Muzafer, 362
Shiflett, Samuel C., 247, 255
Shin, Shung Jae, 375, 384
Shippmann, Jeffrey S., 53, 58, 60
Shook, Christopher L., 14, 16
Shore, Lynn M., 270, 279
Siebrecht, Adrienne, 51, 59
Sierad, Jack, 186, 203
Silver, William S., 196, 203
Silverman, David, 25, 34
Simeon, Rebecca J., 221, 229
Simon, Herbert A., 281, 299
Sims, Henry P., 198, 201, 315, 318
Singer, Marc G., 111, 113
Singleton, W. T., 254
Sire, Bruno, 154, 158
Sivasubramaniam, Nagaraj, 373–374, 384
Skinner, B. F., 114–117, 119, 127, 130–132
Skov, Richard B., 197, 203
Slocum, John W., 304, 306, 312, 316–317
Smiddy, Harold, 170
Smith, Blanchard B., 226, 230
Smith, Ken G., 169, 180–181, 193, 195, 201
Smith, Norman R., 327, 335
Smith, Patricia C., 160
Smith, Wendy G., 289, 298, 315, 317
Smither, James W., 197, 203
Smyser, Charles M., 187, 203
Snavely, B. Kay, 196, 201
Snow, Charles C., 289, 299
Snyderman, Barbara S., 61–63, 68–69, 71, 74
Solomon, R. J., 362
Sommer, Steven M., 95, 113, 125, 133
Sommerkamp, Patricia, 265, 273, 278

Song, Lynda J., 268, 278
Sorcher, Melvin, 115, 129, 131–132
Sosik, John J., 224, 230, 355, 359
Spangler, William D., 54, 56, 59–60, 341, 346, 348–349, 358–359, 373, 385
Sparrowe, Raymond T., 196, 202, 267, 269, 272, 279
Spector, Paul E., 86, 93, 153, 156
Spencer, Lyle M., 52, 54, 57–58, 60
Spencer, Signe M., 52, 54, 57–58, 60
Spreitzer, Gretchen M., 376, 385
Spurgeon, P., 254
Stablein, Ralph E., 23, 30, 33
Stajkovic, Alexander D., 124, 126–127, 132–133, 176, 183
Stalker, G. M., 79, 91, 304
Starbuck, William H., 12, 17, 317
Stark, Eric M., 330, 335
Staw, Barry M., 7, 13, 17, 201, 378, 383
Steel, Robert P., 87, 93
Steers, Richard M., 131, 157
Steidlmeier, Paul, 369, 383
Steiner, Gary A., 6, 15
Steiner, George A., 9, 17
Steinmetz, Lawrence L., 187, 195, 203
Stephens, Gregory K., 95, 113
Stewart, Wayne H., 54, 60, 332, 335
Stilwell, Dean, 269, 279
Stogdill, Ralph M., 253, 362, 382
Stone, Eugene F., 86, 89–90, 93
Strange, Jill M., 350, 359
Strassberg, Zvi, 201, 203
Strauss, Anselm L., 15–16
Strauss, George, 223, 229
Streiner, David L., 312, 318, 331, 335
Streufert, Siegfried S., 92, 253
Strickland, Oriel J., 352, 360
Stroh, Linda K., 271, 279
Strube, Michael J., 242, 255
Suddaby, Roy, 42, 45
Sue-Chan, Christina, 177, 183, 224, 230
Summers, Timothy P., 144, 158
Suttle, J. Lloyd, 92
Sutton, Robert I., 7, 17
Swiercz, Paul M., 177, 183

T

Taber, Tom D., 84, 93
Taggar, Simon, 330, 335
Tang, Thomas L., 111, 113
Tannenbaum, Robert, 25, 34, 207–211, 229–230

Taylor, Elisabeth, 84, 93
Taylor, Frederick W., 38, 366
Taylor, Lew, 87, 92
Taylor, Robert R., 271, 277
Tejeda, Manuel J., 375, 385
Tepper, Bennett J., 243–244, 247, 255
Terman, Lewis, 38
Terpstra, David E., 173, 183
Tetrault, Linda A., 243–244, 247, 255
Tetrick, Lois E., 87, 93, 270, 279
Thierry, Henk, 108, 111, 113, 132, 182, 277–278
Thomas, Jay C., 281, 298–299
Thomas, Steven L., 150, 156
Thomas-Hunt, Melissa, 13, 16
Thompson, Charles M., 178–179, 183
Thompson, Kenneth R., 122, 133, 178, 182
Thompson, Leigh, 145, 157
Thompson, Margaret A., 221, 230
Thoreson, Carl J., 72, 74
Thornbury, Erin E., 5, 16
Thorndike, Edward, 301
Tiegs, Robert B., 87, 93
Tindale, R. Scott, 298
Tinsley, Howard E. A., 328, 335
Tischner, E. Casey, 179, 183
Tjosvold, Dean, 196, 203, 220, 230
Todor, William D., 311–312, 318
Tolman, Edward C., 94–95, 113
Tomkins, Silvan S., 320
Tosi, Henry L., 13, 17, 131, 315, 318
Towler, Annette J., 354, 359
Trumblay, Michel, 154, 158
Trice, Harrison M., 21, 32, 357, 359
Truxillo, Donald M., 111, 113
Turban, Daniel B., 177, 182
Turner, Arthur N., 77, 82–84, 93
Turner, Barry A., 15, 17
Turner, Nick, 83, 93, 377, 385

U

Uhl-Bien, Mary, 259, 262, 265, 268, 270, 275, 277–279
Uhrbrock, R. S., 362

V

Valenzi, Enzo R., 362
Vancouver, Jeffrey B., 178–179, 183
Vandenberg, Robert J., 20, 34, 87, 93
Van de Ven, Andrew H., 5–6, 17
Van Dyne, Linn, 199, 202

Van Eerde, Wenderlein, 108, 111, 113
Van Engen, Marloes L., 40, 45, 373, 383
Van Fleet, David D., 349, 360
Van Knippenberg, Daan, 273, 279, 354, 359
Van Maanen, John, 29, 34
Van Muijen, Jaap J., 375, 383
Vardi, Yoav, 155, 158
Varma, Arup, 271, 279
Vecchio, Robert P., 58, 60, 144, 147, 149, 158, 252, 255, 267, 277, 279, 331, 336
Veroff, Joanne B., 51, 60
Veroff, Joseph, 51, 60
Vicino, F. L., 362
Villa, Jennifer R., 315, 328
Viswesvaran, Chockalingam, 20, 34
Von Glinow, Mary Ann , 302, 317
Voronov, Maxim, 25, 34
Vredenburgh, Donald J., 311, 318
Vroom, Victor H., 94–100, 102–103, 105, 108, 111, 113, 170, 207–214, 216–231, 251, 257, 374

W

Wachtel, Jeffrey M., 333, 335
Wagner, John A., 223–224, 230–231
Wakabayashi, Mitsuru, 261, 266, 278–279
Waldman, David A., 349, 351, 353, 359, 370, 382–383, 385
Walker, Charles R., 62, 74
Wall, Toby D., 83, 93
Walster, Elaine, 135, 139, 156, 158
Walster, G. William, 135, 139, 158
Wanner, Eric, 50, 60
Wanous, John P., 109, 113
Waterman, Robert H., 168, 183
Wayne, Sandy J., 196, 202, 267, 269–270, 272, 279
Weber, Max, 49, 324, 337–338, 356, 358, 361–362, 366, 378–379, 381
Weber, Roberto, 292, 299
Weber, Tom, 376, 382
Webster, Jane, 12, 17
Wedley, W. C., 220, 230
Weed, Stan E., 187, 203
Weick, Karl E., 33, 294, 299
Weinberger, Joel, 54, 60
Weiner, Bernard, 170, 186, 190, 203
Weingart, Laurie R., 179, 183
Weiss, Howard M., 330, 334, 352, 360
Weiss, Richard M., 13, 17, 26, 34
Weiss, Thomas, 145, 157
Weitz, Ely, 155, 158

Welch, Jack, 317
Welchans, Thomas D., 154, 157
Welsh, Dianne H. B., 125, 133
Wertheimer, Max, 38
Wesson, Michael J., 153, 156, 176, 181
Wheeler, Hoyt N., 199, 202
Wheeler, Kenneth G., 149, 158
White, Donald D., 115, 132
White, Ralph K., 39, 45
Whitney, David J., 23, 33
Wiener, Yoash, 70, 74
Wiersma, Uco J., 110, 113
Wiesen, L., 70, 74
Wiklund, Johan, 330, 336
Wilderom, Celeste P. M., 328, 336
Williams, Amy A., 178, 183
Williams, Craig A., 379, 384
Williams, Eric S., 375, 384
Williams, Ethlyn A., 20, 34
Williams, Larry J., 20, 34
Williams, Margaret L., 311–312, 318
Williams, Scott, 129, 133
Wilpert, Bernhard, 223, 229
Winter, David G., 51–52, 56–57, 60, 330, 336
Witt, L. A., 270, 278
Wofford, J. C., 176, 183
Wofford, Jerry C., 46, 59
Woike, Barbara A., 54, 60
Wolf, William B., 44–45
Wood, James M., 331, 334
Wood, Robert E., 168–169, 175, 183, 187,
    189–191, 194–195, 203
Wortman, Camille B., 192, 202
Woycke, James, 56, 59, 341, 348–349, 358
Wright, Patrick M., 13, 17, 175–176, 181, 183
Wu, Anne, 375, 384

X

Xie, Jia Lin, 87, 92

Y

Yagil, Dana, 353, 359
Yamaguchi, Ikushi, 149, 158
Yammarino, Francis J., 271, 276, 279, 313, 315,
    317–318, 329, 335, 353, 356–357, 359, 373,
    379, 382–385
Yearta, Shawn K., 173, 183
Yetton, Philip, 207–214, 217–219, 221, 226, 229–231
Yi, Youjae, 20, 32
Yorges, Stefani L., 352, 360
Yu, K. C., 330, 334
Yukl, Gary, 224, 231, 251, 255, 275, 279, 315,
    318, 330, 336, 349, 355, 360, 379–381, 385

Z

Zaccaro, Stephen J., 293, 296, 299, 316, 318, 355,
    360
Zacharatos, Anthea, 377, 385
Zais, Mitchell M., 248, 254
Zakay, Eliav, 352, 356, 359
Zammuto, Raymond F., 8, 15, 26, 32
Zautra, Alex, 67–68, 74
Zedeck, Sheldon, 203
Zenger, Todd R., 329, 336
Zhou, Jing, 375, 384
Zhou, Xiaohua, 276, 279, 315, 318, 329, 335,
    379, 384
Zimmer, Frederick G., 230
Zimmer, R. J., 220
Zivnuska, Suzanne, 270, 278

SUBJECT INDEX

A

ABAB research design, 125
Ability, 58, 77, 96, 98–99, 103, 167, 172, 176–177, 198, 200, 260, 310
Absenteeism, 82, 87, 124, 130, 144, 151
Academic settings, 221. *See also* University, settings
Academy of Management, 301, 327, 330
Accountants, 68
Accounts, 198–199
Achievement, 39, 65, 71, 73, 82, 160, 366
    motivation, 54–55, 167, 186, 244, 324, 327, 348
        theory, 46–58, 319, 330
    need for, 48–49, 52, 167, 186, 341, 351, 366
    situations, 48
    training, 129, 333
The Achieving Society, 55
Action(s),
    alternatives, 87
    corrective, 197*t*
    goal, 43
    principles, 79–80
    research, 37–38, 42
Activity inhibition, 341, 347–348
Actors, professional, 355
Actresses, professional, 349, 355
Adaptive organisms, 87
Affect, 167
Affective
    outcome, 373
    reactions, 269
Affiliation
    motivation, 47, 50–51, 82, 244, 348
    need for, 56, 341, 351, 366
Age, 137, 146, 271, 341
Aircraft maintenance units, 67
Ambiguity, 8, 150, 237–238
    role, 263, 268, 310
America, *See* United States
American
    goods, 125
    leadership, 39. *See also* Leadership

American *(continued)*
    presidency, 351. See also United States, presidents.
American Institutes for Research (AIR), 62, 160
American Jewish Committee, 42
American Psychological Association (APA), 42
American Pulpwood Association, 160
American Telephone and Telegraph Company (AT&T), 56–57, 67
Anger, 137, 139, 144, 150
Anomie, 82
Anthropology, 26
Anxiety, 167, 250–251, 321, 324
Apologies, 191, 195
Apprentices, 43
Aptitudes, 58
Aspiration, level of, 43, 159–160
Assertiveness, 366
Assessment, 333
    centers, 266
Assumed Similarity between Opposites score (ASo), 234–235
Atlantic Refining Company, 320–321, 330, 332
Attitude(s), 208, 234, 239, 364
    subordinates, 350
    to superiors, 324
Attribute(s), 106, 215, 217, 222, 284, 295
Attribution(al)
    model, 188*f*, 189–191, 192*t*
        of leader response, 190*f*
    process, 185, 187–190
    theory, 124, 180, 184–201, 281, 283, 292, 294–295
Attributions, 197*t*
    managerial, 142*t*
Augmentation (add-on) effect, 368, 370, 372, 380
Australia, 146, 196
Austria, 83, 208, 221, 233
Authoritarian leadership, 39–40, 367. *See also* Leadership
Authoritarianism, 341, 366
Authority, 199, 223
    figures, 152–153, 169
    formal, 258

Authority *(continued)*
    legitimate, 172, 236, 258
Autocratic behavior, 217, 219, 227
Automatic processes, of leadership perceptions,
    285–286
Autonomous work groups, 328–329
Autonomy, 77–78, 80, 83, 85

B

Baseball players, 150
Basketball
    players, 150
    teams, 234
Battalion commanders, 353
Behavior(s), 116, 119, 121–122, 124–125, 128,
    207, 212–213, 218, 225, 283, 343, 346
    considerate, 250
    directive, 250–252
    employee, 115
    modeling, 129
    modification, 165. *See also* Organizational,
        behavior modification (O.B. Mod.)
    role, 328
    shaping, 117
    subordinate, 187
    symbolic, 346
    value-based, 338
    work, 105
Behavioral
    contingency management model, 119–120
    observation scale, 172
    science, 26
Behaviorism, 115, 127, 129–131, 165
Behaviorist(s), 120, 127, 129, 165–166
Belief(s), 341
Bell Labs, 135
Benevolents, 148
Berlin, Germany, 38
Beyond Freedom and Dignity, 130
Bias, 187, 194, 199–200, 219, 375, 377
"Big five" personality measure, 111, 176, 378
Biographical studies, 340–341, 348, 350
"Black box," 245, 252
Blacks, 57, 197–198
Blue-collar workers, 67, 82
Board of directors, 235
Bomber crews, 234
Boredom, 161
Boston University, 47
Boundary,
    conditions, 56, 107, 162, 191

Boundary *(continued)*
    definitions, 8, 177
    organizational, 270
    spanning, 135
Boundaries, 3, 8, 147, 167
Brainstorming tasks, 173
Brooklyn College, 320
Brown University, 95
Bureaucracies, 379
Bureaucracy, 107, 329, 347, 356
    theory applied to, 324
    theory of, 379
Bureaucratic
    organizations, 223, 324, 331, 379
    theory, 56
Burnout, 366, 373
Business
    development, 49
    failure, 145
    organizations, 49
    policy, 9
Business schools, 47

C

Cabinet members, 340–341, 348, 352
"Cafeteria" compensation systems, 106
California, 95
Cambridge, MA, 38
Canada, 154, 160
Careers, 264, 328–329
Carnegie Mellon University, 103, 207–208, 280–281
    Graduate School of Industrial
        Administration, 95
Case
    method, 9
    studies, 155
Case Western Reserve University, 62
Catastrophe
    model, 286*f*
    theory, 285, 287, 294
Categorization, 283, 285, 292–293
Catholic religion, 49, 82
Causal
    model, 307*f*
    modeling, 20
    relationships, 7, 21
    research, 21
Causality, 173, 354
Causation, 9, 20
Change(s), 42
    automatic processes, 285, 292–293, 295

Change(s) *(continued)*
    controlled processing, 285, 292–293, 295
    discontinuous, 285, 287, 293
    motivational, 52, 57
    perceptual, 293
    process(es), 40–43, 41*f*, 287
Charisma, 337, 340–341, 343–346, 349–352, 354–356, 363–364, 366–368, 370–373, 375, 378–381. *See also* Leadership, charismatic theory
Charismatic
    behaviors, 343, 352
    initial model of, 340*f*
    leadership theory, 337–357, 381
    process, model of, 344*f*
Chief executive officers (CEO), 349, 351
Child development, 38
Children, 57, 110, 115, 128
China, 147, 269, 273, 330
Chinese studies, 268–269
Choice
    free, 109
    occupational, 98
Chrysler Corporation, 338
City University of New York (CUNY), 62, 116, 338
    Baruch College, 300–301
Clark University, 319
Classical
    management, 170
    theory, 26, 301
Clerical employees, 67, 263
Cleveland, OH, 62
Coercion, 263
Cognitive
    abilities, 250
    complexity, 239
    dissonance theory, 134
    evaluation theory, 109–110
    processes, 105
    resource theory, 247–252
        decision tree for, 249*f*
    schema, 282*f*, 283, 287
    skills training, 251–252
    tests, 58
    theory, 289
    variables, 127
Collectivism, 224
College of the City of New York, 361
Colleges. *See* University.
Columbia University, 141, 321
    Conservation of Human Resources project, 320
    Graduate School of Business, 320

Commitment, organizational, 266, 310–311, 354
Common method
    bias, 22–23, 153, 266–267, 313, 372–373, 374*t*, 376
    variance, 22–23, 84, 88, 223, 313–314, 370, 372
Compensation. 106, 139–140, 150–151, 164, 223. *See also* Monetary incentives; Pay; Salary
Competency, 54
    modeling, 52–53, 58
    testing, 58
Competition, 162
Competitiveness, 324
Computer
    feedback, 226
    personnel, 265
    simulations, 21, 348
Concurrent validity, 245
Conflict, 14, 81, 147, 149, 194, 199
    role, 83
    subordinate, 211–213, 215, 217–219, 221, 228
Conformity, 20, 366
Conscientiousness, 371
Consensus
    and competing theories, 29–30
    information, 187–189, 196
    obtaining, 31
    problems in, 28–29
    role of, 28–31
Consideration, 237, 256–257, 262, 295, 302–303, 310, 312, 314, 333, 349, 367, 370
    individualized, 363, 365–373, 375, 378, 380
Consistency, of information, 187–189, 196
Construct validity, 20, 110, 149, 221–222, 244–245, 312, 331–332, 370, 380
Constructs, 7, 19–20, 27, 54, 108, 120, 146, 177, 194, 234, 271, 354, 369, 380–381
Content analysis, 348
Contextual factors, 378
Contingencies, types of, 116–117
Contingency variables, 109, 228, 236, 242*t*
Contingency theory, 310
    of leadership, 232–253, 331
    octants, 240*f*, 241, 243*f*, 243–244
"Contra" position, to scientific dictates, 24–25
Control, 128, 324
    groups, 67, 125, 321, 376
    leader, 304
    organizational, 304, 316
    performance, 304

Control *(continued)*
    process, 323*f*
    in scientific inquiry, 9–10
    variables, 21
Cooptation, 88, 178
Coping strategies, 309*t*
Cornell University, 159
    School of Home Economics, 38
Corrective avoidant factor, 371
Correlation coefficient, 19, 311
Correlational analyses, 22, 221, 350
Correlations, 108, 223, 310, 312
Cost, 150–151
    as an outcome, 139
    rule, 215
Covariation, principle of, 187
Coworkers, 128
Creativity, 83, 179, 250, 276, 365–366
Crises, 341, 343, 345, 348, 350–352, 354, 356,
    366–367, 369
Criterion variance, 314
Critical
    incident technique, 62, 68, 71–72
    psychological states, 84, 86–87
    theory, 25
Cross-cultural studies, 238, 349
Crotonville, NY, 135, 301
Cultural
    differences, 147, 295
    values, 149
    variations, 154, 221
Culture(s), 285–286, 293
    change, 332
    organizational, 227–228, 293
Customer service representatives, 155
Cybernetics, 175, 286. *See also* Information
    processing, cybernetic model of
Czech Republic, 149
Czechoslovakia, 221

D

Dalhousie University, 160
Decision(s), 287
    acceptance, 208, 210–211, 219, 222, 225
    autocratic, 211, 221
    group, 196. *See also* Group(s), decision
        making; decision sharing
    mathematical functions, 216
    quality, 208, 210–211, 219, 225, 228
    sharing theory, individual, 212–213, 216–217
    theory, 105

Decision making, 152, 200
    managerial, 226
Decision rules, 210–213, 216, 218–219,
    226–227
    acceptance priority, 218–219
    commitment, 215–216, 222
    conflict, 211–213, 218, 220–222
    cost, 215
    development, 215–216
    equations, 216, 222
    fairness of, 211, 218
    goal congruence, 210, 213, 218
    group, 215–216
    individual, 215–216
    information, 210, 213, 219
    quality, 215–216, 218, 222
    subordinate information, 213
    time penalty, 215, 226
    unstructured problem, 210, 213
Decision-tree, 207, 211*f*, 211–214, 214*f*, 216–217,
    226, 248, 249*f*, 308
Deductive theory, 10–11, 245
Delegation, 223, 269, 365
Democracy, 39, 65
Democratic leadership, 39–40, 42, 227–228, 367
Democratic National Convention, 348
Department stores, 124–125
Dependence, 377
Description, in scientific method, 7
Descriptive theory, 225, 228, 265, 267
Disability, 271
Discipline, 196
Discretion, 151, 286, 293
Dispositions, 27–28, 89–90, 221, 311, 351
    defined, 27
Distinctiveness of information, 187–189, 196
Distortion, 138–139
Distributive justice, 143, 152–155
Domain(s), 8, 224–225, 235
    limited, 10, 14, 40, 49
    of a theory, 7–8, 11, 168, 238, 270
Duke University, 116, 185
Dust-bowl empiricism, 11
Dyad(s), 259, 262, 270, 373. *See also* Vertical
    dyad linkage theory (VDL)
    leader-member, 199
Dyadic
    approach to leadership, 272*t*
    career reality (DCR), 257, 259–260, 260*t*
    exchanges, 287
    loyalty, 261, 263
    model, 100

Dyadic *(continued)*
    partnership building, 261–262, 265–266
    relationships, 257–260, 263, 267, 269–270,
        273, 276, 365
Dynamic theory, 178

E

Economic
    development, 49, 55, 58
    motivation, 142
Economics, 4, 26
Ecuador, 54
Effort, 98–99, 103–104, 106–107, 146, 162, 186,
    197–198, 200, 343, 346, 370, 372
Effort-reward probability, 98–99, 103–104, 104*t*
Ego, 252, 321
Electronics firm, 224
Emotional distance, 234
Empathic supersalespeople, 327
Employee(s), 67, 106, 111, 119, 148, 154, 167, 262
    health, 91
    loyalty, 88
    motivation, 134
Empowerment, 223, 228, 269, 341, 377
Engineers, 68
England, 38, 185, 208, 328
Enhancers, 304, 308, 309*t*, 316. *See also*
    Leadership, substitutes for
Entitleds, 148
Entrepreneurial
    firms, 331
    job, 109
    success, 51
Entrepreneurs, 48–49, 54, 100, 167, 178, 324,
    327, 329
    female, 57
    high-tech, 327, 330
Entrepreneurship, 49, 54–55, 169, 327
    development program, 327
Environment(s), 116, 351
    organizational, 287, 366
    person, 79
    social, 281, 283
Environmental
    fit, 287
    stress, 238
    turbulence, 241
    uncertainty, 349, 351–352
Equity, 142*t*, 149–150, 366
    sensitivity, 148–149
    theory, 131, 134–155, 180, 262

Esteem needs. *See* Self-esteem
Europe, 62, 151, 221
Event-based processing, 285
Exchange relationships. *See* Equity, theory.
Expectancy, 163–165, 167, 176
    effort-to-performance, 100
    motivation, 111
    performance-to-outcome, 100
    theory, 19, 23, 76, 94–112, 127, 130,
        149, 163, 177, 208, 229, 257, 262,
        344
    model, 101*f*
Expectations, 122, 263
Experience, 247, 250–251, 284, 310, 365
    managerial, 240–241
Experimental
    designs, 101, 127
    groups, 67, 125
    quasi-designs, 22
    research, 23, 354. *See also* Laboratory,
        experiments; Field, experiments
Expert idea generators, 327
Explanation, in scientific method, 7
Explicit theory, 173, 363
Externals, 107
Extinction, 116–117
Extrinsic
    motivation, 109–110, 366
    outcomes, 100
    rewards, 100, 106, 125, 343, 346

F

Factor
    analysis, 84, 312, 363, 370–371, 379–380
    hierarchy, 368
Factory workers, 38
Failure, 48, 167, 186, 193, 195–196, 198, 219,
    292, 320–321
    administrative, 64
    conditions, 355
    fear of, 43, 47
Fairness, 195. *See also* Organizational, justice.
Farm
    supply cooperative, 234–235
    workers, 38
Fast track status, 273–276
Federal Express, 370
Feedback, 78, 84, 109, 165–166, 166*f*, 177, 195
    computer, 308
    job, 77, 80
    loop, 99–100, 122, 178

Feedback *(continued)*
    performance, 126, 161, 172, 262, 302
    task, 283, 314
Females, 56–58, 197, 285, 293, 373, 378–379.
    See also Women
Field
    experiments, 21–22
    research, 163, 172, 195
    studies, 86, 196–198, 243, 294, 312
Follower(s), 337, 339, 341–348, 351–353, 355–356,
    365–366, 369, 376, 378
    attitude change, 364
    face-to-face, 352
    homogeneity of charisma, 345–347
    self-concepts, 289–291, 342, 376
    stress, 339–340
    trust, 337, 339, 375
    values, 354–355
    work motivation, 377
Force, of an action, 98, 108
Force-field analysis, 39–40, 41*f*, 44
Ford Foundation Doctoral Dissertation Series,
    95
Ford Motor Company, 376
Formalization, 311, 314, 316
Frame alignment, 342, 346
France, 221
Free time study, 110
Freezing, 346. *See also* Unfreezing
Friendships, 271, 278

G

Gender, 271, 285, 331–333
    differences, 197–198, 221
General Electric Corporation, 135, 150, 170, 301,
    317
    Corporate Leadership Development, 301
Generalization, 25, 127
Georgia Institute of Technology, 160, 320
Georgia State University, 320
German
    army, 48
    leadership, 39
Germany, 37–38, 221
Gestalt psychology, 38
Goal(s), 96, 102, 161, 163–164, 169*f*, 236
    achievement, 162, 172, 176
    assigned, 163, 172–173, 177
    attainment, 43, 97, 129, 167, 176
    choice, 164–165
    commitment, 165, 176–178, 270–271

Goal(s) *(continued)*
    content, 162
    difficulty, 169, 176–178, 180
    distal, 342, 345
    intensity, 162
    mechanisms, 164
    participative, 173, 177, 180
    performance, 192, 343, 346
    personal, 176
    proximal, 342
    self-set, 169, 173, 178
    specificity, 180
Goal-setting, 43–44, 129, 223, 365, 375
    participative, 169, 172–173
    theory, 124, 127, 130–131, 155, 159–180,
        229, 270
Goldman Sachs, 301, 317
Government, 221
    agencies, 370
    employees, 265
Great Britain, 208
Grounded
    research, 294, 333
    theory, 14–15, 25, 264, 321
Group(s), 38, 134, 139, 148, 214, 273, 288
    cohesiveness, 311, 313–314, 316
    decision
    making, 41–42, 159, 196
      -sharing, 210–212, 216
    dynamics, 21, 37, 44, 310
    effectiveness, 236–237
    goal-setting, 176
    in, 258–259, 263–264, 267
    interpersonal processes, 81
    leadership, 236–237
    members, 81, 147, 270, 369, 373
    norms, 329
    out, 258–259, 263–264, 267, 269
    performance, 193, 195, 250–252, 301
      poor, 192*t*. *See also* Performance, poor;
        Performance, ineffective
    processes, 81
    role motivation theory, 326*f*, 328, 330
    support, 250
    system, 324, 326*f*, 329
    task, 81–82, 235–236, 236*t*, 238, 248
    theory, 328, 333
    types, 236–237, 304
      problem, 211*f*, 212*t*
Growth
    need strength, 78, 86*t*, 90, 266, 273
    orientation, 330

Growth *(continued)*
    personal, 81
Guilt, 137, 139, 144, 147, 150, 324

H

Halifax, Nova Scotia, 160
Harvard Business Review, 12, 15, 62
Harvard Psychological Clinic, 47
Harvard University, 47, 94, 115, 134, 160
Harwood Manufacturing Company, 42–43
Hawthorne effect, 22
Hay Associates, 58
Hedonism, 104–105
Heuristics, 185, 282–283
Hierarchic
    organizations, 129, 223, 304, 316, 329,
        338, 365, 379
    role motivation theory, 325*f*, 330, 355
    systems, 300, 316, 324, 325*f*
    theory, 330, 333
Hierarchy
    motivational, 239, 244
    of needs, 363
    need theory, 46, 76, 82, 381
    substitutes for, 304
High-performance cycle, 167–168, 168*f*, 177
High school students, 377
Hill Air Force Base, 67
Hong Kong, 22
Household appliance company, 101–102
Housewives, 40–41
Human Relations, 38
Human resource(s),
    management, 116, 172
    managers, 221
Humanism, 28
Humanist, 62
Hygienes, 61, 63–67, 70–73
Hypotheses, 10, 31

I

Idealized influence, 368. *See also* Charisma
Identity
    collective, 290, 342, 352
    personal, 290, 377
    self, 290–292
    social, 290, 377
    task, 77, 80, 84
Image building, 353, 355
Imitation, 127

Implicit theories, 173, 199–200, 283, 292–294,
    314, 321, 363, 377
Impression management, 191, 195, 198
Incentive system, 100, 102
Incentives, 161–162, 343
Incommensurability, 32
India, 54, 273
Indiana University, 310
    studies at, 312–314
Individual(s), 38, 78, 81, 87–88, 90, 96, 105, 107,
    135, 138–139, 146–147, 164–165, 180,
    192*t*, 193, 245, 308
    differences, 27, 43, 88–89, 105, 108, 111,
        127, 130–131, 147–150, 167, 186,
        196, 217, 221, 223–224, 293, 295,
        321, 365, 369
    motivation, 328
    problem types, 214*f*
Individualism, 224
Individualization, 365
Inducement systems, 324
Inducements-contributions theory, 259
Inductive theory, 10–11, 24, 232, 238, 245, 252,
    321
Industrial
    psychology, 38
    relation departments, 64, 73
    samples, 352
Inequity. *See* Equity, theory
Inferential processes, 283–285
Influence, 261, 264, 339
    idealized, 368
Influence-power continuum theory, 208, 229
Information, task-relevant, 305*t*
Information processing, 185
    and change, 285
    cybernetic model of, 283, 285–286, 292–293
    expert, 283, 285–286, 292–293, 295
    human, 283
    limited capacity, 283, 285–286, 292
    multiplicative, 108
    rational model of, 282*f*, 283, 284*t*, 286, 292
    social, 87–88
    theory of leadership, 280–297
Information processors, collective, 288
Informational justice, 152–154
Ingratiation, 192–193, 195
Inhibition, 56
Initial Model of Charismatic Leadership, 340*f*,
    364
Initiating structure, 237, 250, 256–257, 262, 295,
    302–303, 310, 312, 314, 333, 349, 367, 370

Innovation, 276
Inputs, 136*t*, 136–141, 137*t*, 148, 150
Inspirational leadership. *See* Leadership, inspirational
Institutionalization, xii, 74, 111, 329, 356
Instrumentality, 96–98, 100, 102–103, 105
Integrated House-McClelland model, 341
Integration, 344, 354, 381
Integrity, 346, 366
Intellectual stimulation, 363, 365–373, 375–376, 378, 380
Intelligence, 20, 58, 241, 246, 250–252, 365, 371
Interaction,
    effects, 303
    process of, 84
Interactional justice, 152–154
Internal states, 119, 122, 131
Internals, 107
International Business Machines (IBM), 62, 78
Interpersonal justice, 152–154
Intimidation, 380
Intrinsic
    motivation, 109–110, 172–173
    outcomes, 100
    satisfaction, 268, 308
    work motivation, 377
Investors, 378
Israel, 147, 353
Israeli armed forces, 352

J

Japan, 257, 267, 269, 273, 293, 295
Japanese Americans, 295
Japanese corporations, 266
Jews, 37
Job
    analysis, 172
    attitudes, 61, 68
    characteristics
        core, 80*f*
        model, 78*f*
        theory, 75–91, 100, 108, 266
    choice, 109
    design, 38
    effort, 104, 104*t*
    enlargement, 62, 64, 88
    enrichment, 38, 58, 61–62, 65–68, 72–74, 88, 125, 258, 266
        pre- and post-measures of, 68*t*
    goals, 103
    insecurity, 140, 142
    involvement, 350
    performance, 68, 87, 98, 103, 104*t*, 107, 257–258
    problems, 257–259, 263–264
    redesign, 65
    rotation, 240
    satisfaction, 63, 67–68, 70, 79, 82, 85, 90, 98, 103, 106, 148, 162–163, 167, 177, 223, 257–259, 263–264, 311, 349
        pre- and post-measures of, 68*t*
    scope, 88–89
    study, 62
    tenure, 263
Job Diagnostic Survey, 83–84

K

Keio University, 257
Knowledge, 26–28, 58, 78, 81, 84, 96, 164, 172, 250, 308, 310
    development of, 18–32
    of results, 161–162, 176
    structure, 283

L

Laboratory
    experiments, 21, 38, 196, 281, 355
    research, 144, 163, 170, 172, 176–177, 195, 224, 289, 293, 354
    studies, 25, 86, 111, 153, 194, 197–198, 220, 222, 243, 294–295, 349, 352
    testing, 160
    training. *See* Sensitivity training; T-groups
Laissez-faire leadership, 39–40, 367–368, 372, 374
Latitude, 260, 263, 267, 269
Law of effect, 301
Leader Behavior Description Questionnaires (LBDQ), 262, 367
Leader-member exchange theory (LMX), 198, 256–276, 268*t*
Leader(s), 187–191, 197, 199, 236, 244, 248, 259, 301, 328–329, 333, 339, 343
    authentic transformational, 369
    behavior, 187–188, 209, 211*f*, 212*t*, 214*f*, 217, 218*t*, 220, 226, 293, 303*t*, 304, 307, 307*f*, 310, 312–315, 319, 337–338, 341, 352
    behavior ratings, 295
    close, 352–353
    control, 239–241, 304

Leader(s) *(continued)*
      distant, 352–353
      influence, 239–241
      match, 245–247, 252
      -member relations, 236–238, 240–241, 246,
          250
      power, 193
      prototypical, 367
      romanticizing, 377
      socialized transformational, 369
      succession, 293, 357
Leadership, 362
Leadership, 13, 262, 265, 267, 294, 296,
      332–333
      autocratic, 228. *See also* Autocratic,
          behavior
      automatic processes, 283
      as careers, 328–330
      categorization theory, 283
      charismatic, 337–357, 362, 365, 369, 376,
          378, 380–381
      climates, 39–40, 40*f*, 43
      contingency theory, 232–253, 331
      direct, 287–288, 293, 302–303, 316, 353
      directive, 367
      dyadic approach to, 272*f*
      dynamics, 240–241
      effectiveness, 308, 367, 370, 372–373, 377
      elitist, 369
      indirect, 287–288, 293, 302–303, 353
      inferential, 283–285, 292, 377
      inspirational, 355, 363, 365, 369, 380
      intellectual, 373
      leveling, 367
      neocharismatic, 346
      outstanding, 344, 346
      personalized charismatic, 341, 350–351,
          375, 380
      problems, 309*t*
      professional, 373, 379
      pseudotransformational, 368–369, 380
      recognition-based, 283–285, 292, 377
      socialized charismatic, 341, 350–351, 375,
          380
      substitutes for, 300–317, 374
          neutralization effects on, 303*t*
      training. *See* Training
      transactional, 338, 350, 363, 364*f*,
          365–366, 368–370, 372–374, 380
      transformational, 313, 338, 344, 349,
          361–381, 364*f*
      visionary, 344, 351, 355

Leadership and Information Processing:
      Linking Perceptions and Performance,
      280, 294
Leadership and Performance Beyond
      Expectations, 363–365
Learning, 117, 119–120
      A-B-C model, 122, 124
      avoidance, 116–117, 130
      defined, 116
      process, social, 123*f*
      sign-gestalt theory, 95
      S-O-B-C model, 122, 124
      theory, 94, 111
Least preferred coworkers (LPC), 234–241, 244,
      247, 249–250, 252
Legitimacy, 263
Leniency, 198
Levels-of-analysis, 356, 379
Limited domain, 40, 49
      theories, 10, 14
Linear relationship models, 285
Line-of-sight, 106
Locus of control, 167, 187–188, 371
Longitudinal
      analysis, 87, 266
      measures, 21, 23
      research, 381
      studies, 269, 333, 351
Louisiana State University, 362
Loyalty, 260–261, 272

M

Machiavellian behavior, 341
Machiavellianism, 351, 355
Macro
      analysis, 26
      organizational behavior, 124, 155
      research, 180
      studies, 308
      theory, 13–14, 169, 270, 294, 310
      variables, 99
Main effects, 314
Malawi, 54
Male children, 49
Males, 56–57, 197, 373, 378
Management, 61, 159
      classical, 26, 170, 301
      development, 21, 214, 217, 235, 246, 354,
          380–381
      game, 370
      strategic, 4, 9, 62, 289

Management-by-exception, 363, 365–368, 370–373, 376
Management-by-objectives (MBO), 159, 170–172, 176, 370, 372
Managerial
    jobs, 87, 109
    motivation, 247, 323–324, 327, 332. *See also* Role motivation theory
    performance, 51, 51*t*, 247, 251
    role motivation
        theory, 320–324, 325*f. See also* Role motivation theory
        training, 57, 200
    success, 50, 219, 324. *See also* Success
    talent, 251
    work, 128
Managerial Choice, 64–65
Managers, 21, 30, 51, 56, 56*t*, 87, 103–104, 128–129, 155, 178, 180, 186–187, 195, 198–200, 207–213, 216–221, 224–227, 237, 240, 246, 256–260, 262, 265, 315, 319–321, 329, 332, 355, 370
    female, 285, 293, 373, 378
    human resource, 5
    line, 341
    male, 373
    scientist, 320
Manchester Business School, 208
"Managing Involvement," 226
Manufacturing
    employees, 153
    firms, 370
    organizations, 127
    study, 125
Marxism, 25
Masculinity, 324
Massachusetts Institute of Technology (MIT), 38, 42, 328
Masters of Business Administration (MBA), 320, 327
Maturity, 366
Mayview State Hospital, 62
McBer & Company, 47
McGill University, 95
McKinsey and Company, 320, 338
Measurement, 83–85, 101, 235, 302–303
    procedures, 53–54
    process, 233
    reliability of, 19, 370
    semantic differential approach, 235
Mechanistic
    climate, 79

Mechanistic *(continued)*
    organizations, 304, 305–306*t*, 338, 372
Mediators, 165, 187, 307*f*, 313
Medical tests, 58
Men, 374, 378. *See also* Males
Mental
    health, 116
    patients, 70, 128
    states, 89
Mentally ill, 70
Mentoring, 221, 269, 365
Meso theory, 13–14, 328
Meta-analysis, 86, 109–111, 127, 153–154, 171, 176–177, 179, 223, 242–243, 246, 267, 269, 276, 294–295, 314, 330, 332, 373–374
Michigan State University, 116
Micro
    analysis, 26
    research, 180
    theory, 13–14, 169
Military, the, 221, 252, 352–353, 355, 376
Miner Sentence Completion Scales, 327–328, 331, 333
    Form P, 327
    Form T, 327
Minneapolis, MN, 140
Modeling, 120–121, 121*t*, 127
Moderator(s), 78–79, 84, 86–87, 122, 165, 167, 177, 190, 221, 224, 235–236, 266, 273, 307*f*, 308, 313
    analyses, 312–313
    effects, 312–313, 315
    process, 82–83
    variables, 302, 304
Monetary incentives, 161, 164, 177. *See also* Pay; Salary
Money, 48, 65, 102, 126 *See also* Compensation; Monetary incentives; Pay; Salary
Montreal, Canada, 95
Moral(s), 149, 337, 339, 342, 350, 377
    involvement, 343, 346
    justification, 345
Motivation, 5, 13, 97, 100, 108, 111, 119, 148, 176, 179, 257, 294, 305*t*
    decline in, 331, 333
    group, 324
    human, 63–64, 108, 124, 341
    hygiene theory, 30, 61–74, 135
    inspirational, 367, 371–372, 375–376
    job, 61
    presidential, 348–349

Motivation *(continued)*
    professional, 324, 327. *See also*
        Professional, role motivation
    sequence, 170*f*, 179–180
    task, 249, 324
    test-taking, 111
    theory, 208
    work, 84
Motivating potential score (MPS), 78–79, 84, 86*t*,
    87
Motivation to manage, 321, 333. *See also* Role
    motivation theory, managerial
Motivation to Work, 63
Motivational
    constructs, 319
    development, 57
    process, 105
Motivator(s), 64, 66–67, 69, 71–72, 106
Motives, 58
    unconscious, 53
Moving, 42, 346. *See also* Unfreezing; Freezing
Multifactor Leadership Questionnaire (MLQ),
    367, 370–372, 375–376
Multiple
    correlation analyses, 104
    regression analysis, 216. 314

N

Narcissism, 341, 350, 355, 369
National Training Laboratories (NTL), 38
Nazis, 37
Nebraska State Mental Health System, 116
Need(s)
    achievement, 48–49, 52, 167, 186, 341,
        351, 366
    affiliation, 47, 50–51
    autonomy, 47
    harmavoidance, 47
    hierarchy theory, 46, 76, 82, 381
    human, 63
    hunger, 47–48
    of individuals, 76–77, 365
    social, 81
    strength,
        growth, 84–85, 86*t*
        higher-order, 78, 84
    understanding, 47
Negation, 347–348
Neutralization effects, 303*t*
Neuroticism, 176
Neutralizers, 302–304, 307*f*, 308, 316

New Britain, CT, 42
New England, 43
New York City, NY, 62, 140, 300–301, 320, 361
New York University, 140
New Zealand, 370
Normative
    decision theory, 207–229, 256
    model, for dyadic career realities (DCR), 260*t*
    tests, 219–220, 220*t*
    theory, 205, 267, 273
Norms, 147, 149
    middle class, 82
    need-based, 273
Northwestern University, 94–95, 116

O

Objectivism, 159
Occupational choice, 103, 106
Octants, in contingency theory, 240*f*, 241, 243–244,
    243*f*
Ohio State Leadership Studies, 281
Ohio State University, 250, 256, 276, 300–301,
    303, 308, 333, 338, 361–362
Oliver Organization Description Questionnaire, 328
Open hearth steel shops, 234
Operant
    behavior, 114–131
    conditioning techniques, 117, 130
    defined, 116
Organic
    climate, 79
    organizations, 14, 304, 305*t*-306*t*, 316,
        338, 372
    systems, 366
Organism, 122, 130
Organization(s), 167, 288
    design, 301–302
    development, 65, 301, 304, 328, 369
        theory, 75
Organizational
    choice, 102–103, 109
    citizenship, 268–269, 342, 375
    effectiveness, 293, 355
    expectations, 375
    forms, 328–329, 355
    inflexibility, 314
    justice, 151–155, 152*f*, 268
    measures, 374*t*
    norms, 20
    performance. *See* Performance,
        organizational

Organizational *(continued)*
    process, 75
    science, 4
    structure, 175
    studies, 4
    tenure, 251
    theory, 107
    types, 328
Organizational behavior
    defined, 3
    modification (O.B.Mod), 114–131, 123*f*, 126*f*, 155, 169
    theoretical knowledge of, 24–26
    values in, 26–27
Organizational Behavior: Foundations, Theories, and Analyses, xi
Organizational Behavior Modification, 119
Organizational Behavior Modification and Beyond, 119
Orthodox job enrichment, 65–67, 80
Outcome(s), 79, 83, 98–99, 103, 104*t*, 108, 111, 136*t*, 137*t*, 136–139, 141, 144–156, 147–148, 150, 153–154, 224, 310–311, 329
    relationships, 267–268
    variables, 86*t*, 267, 268*t*, 314
Output, 161
Outstanding leadership theory, 344, 346
Overreward, 136–137, 147–150, 154–155
    research on, 143–144

P

Paradigm, 32
Parsimony, 124, 127, 178, 194, 224–225
Participation, 217, 222, 226, 228, 232
Participative
    decision making, 44, 125, 208, 221, 258
    leadership, 216, 251, 374
    management, 44, 65, 107, 162, 223–224, 241
Passive-avoidant factor, 371
Path perceptions, 97
Path-goal theory, 301, 311, 313, 315, 338, 344
Pay, 66, 72, 100, 103, 106–109, 125–126, 137–138, 144–145, 150–152, 154. *See also* Compensation; Monetary incentives; Money; Salary
    for performance, 107, 147, 365
    research on, 139–142
Perceived
    environmental uncertainty, 349, 351
    equitable rewards, 103–104
    reality, 233

Perception(s), 185, 269, 283–289
    instrumental, 102*t*
    of raters, 292
    role, 99, 103–104
    social, 286*f*
Perceptual
    bias, 292–293
    control theory, 178–179
    theory, 292–293
Performance, 70, 72, 97–100, 103–104, 106, 109, 111, 126–127, 129, 144, 147, 160–161, 167–178, 169*f*, 173–180, 196, 197*f*, 198, 223, 240*f*, 241, 245–246, 250, 268–269, 273, 283–289
    appraisal, 62, 172, 201, 266, 294
    effectiveness, 350
    ineffective, 185–187, 200, 320, 322*t*, 323*f*, 366. *See also* Performance, poor
    leadership effects on, 286–289
    maximization, 118
    objective, 267
    organizational, 250, 287, 288*t*
    people, 304
    poor, 64, 184–201, 190*f*, 192*t*, 293, 295. *See also* Performance, ineffective
    presidential, 348–349. *See also* United States presidents
    rated, 351, 370, 373
    ratings, 270, 370
    reward, 107
    subjective, 267
    task, 81, 349, 352
Performance-to-outcome expectancy, 106
Person
    -based processing, 285
    -organization fit, 328
Personal
    achievers, 167
    identity, 270, 377
Personality, 167, 177, 180, 244, 247, 294, 340–341, 348, 350–351, 354, 378
    characteristics, 149, 155, 176, 179, 224
    research on, 89–90
    role of, 366
    theory of, 27, 37–44, 46, 58, 89–90
    variables, 76
Philadelphia, PA 320
Philosophy, 4, 10
Piece-rate pay, 43, 140–141, 144, 149
Planning, 179, 375
Plans, 168, 169*f*, 283
Platoon leaders, 353

Poland, 221
Police departments, 310–311
Policy, 195, 266, 287
Political
    leaders, 281
    science, 26, 338
Positivist theory, 32
Postmodernism, 25–26, 28
Poststructuralism, 25
Power, 47, 51–52, 195–196, 201, 208, 224, 228,
    313, 338, 356
    concepts of, 51–52
    expert, 222, 350
    motivation, 49–50, 55–57, 324, 330, 348
    motive, development of, 51*t*
    need for, 341, 351, 366
    personalized, 50, 369
    position, 236, 238, 241, 246
    referent, 350
    shared, 232
    socialized, 50, 52, 56, 56*t*
Practitioners, 30. *See also* Managers
Prepotency, concept of, 363
Presidential charisma, 340–341
Pressure, feelings of, 167
Pretest sensitization, 88
Princeton University, 319
Prisoners, 128
Proactivity, 351
Procedural justice, 143, 152–154
Production workers, 101
Productivity, 96, 101, 109, 140, 179, 266
Professional
    education, 308
    jobs, 87, 109
    organizations, 329
    orientation, 304
    role motivation theory, 325*f*, 327, 330, 333
    systems, 304, 316, 324, 325*f*
    work, 128
Professionals, 147, 302
Projective
    measurement, 53–54
    measures, 57, 331, 333
    technique, 23, 329, 331, 333
Promotion, 22, 56*t*, 88, 103, 240, 266, 333, 376
Proofreading tasks, 141, 142*t*
Propositions, 7, 110
Protestant ethic, 49, 55, 82
Protestant Reformation, 49
Prototypes, 283–284, 287, 329
Prussia, 38

Psychoanalysis, 46, 321
Psychological
    distance, 197–198, 234, 239
    processes, 146*f*
    tests, 58
    variables, 31
Psychological Service of Pittsburgh, 61–62
Psychologists, social, 124
Psychology, 13, 26, 37, 44, 55, 95, 115, 159,
    184–186, 201, 338
    clinical, 129, 201, 331
Psychometric research, 311–312, 332
Public utility company, 265
Punishment(s), 116–118, 129–130, 196, 312,
    314
    status of, 121–122
Purdue University, 185

Q

Q-technique methodology, 233–234
Qualitative studies, 349
Quantitative analysis, 49
Questionnaire(s)
    measures, 100, 102–103
    ratings, 103

R

Race, 271
Rate busters, 138
Ratings, of theories
    importance, xii, 37, 44, 61, 73, 75, 91, 94,
        110–111, 114, 131, 134, 159, 180,
        184, 201, 207, 210, 229, 232, 252,
        256, 276, 280, 296, 300, 317, 319,
        333, 337, 357, 361, 381
    institutionalized, xii, 37, 44, 58, 61, 73–74,
        91, 94, 111, 114, 131, 134, 155, 159,
        180, 184, 207
    usefulness (estimated), xii, 37, 58, 61, 74–75,
        91, 94, 110, 114, 131, 134, 155, 159,
        180, 184, 201, 207, 210, 229, 232,
        252, 256, 276, 280, 297, 300, 317,
        319, 337, 357, 361, 381
    validity (estimated), xii, 37, 58, 61, 73, 75,
        91, 94, 110–111, 114, 131, 134, 155,
        159, 180, 184, 201, 207, 210, 229,
        232, 252, 256, 276, 280, 297, 300,
        317, 319, 333, 337, 361, 381
Rationality, 105
Reciprocity, 272

Recognition, 65, 67, 73, 283–285
    social, 124–126
    Referent selection, 145–147, 146f, 155
Reinforcement, 116–120, 127
    contingent, 112, 128
    continuous, 117–118, 128
    partial, 118, 128
    schedules of, 117–118, 128, 131
Reinforcers, 116, 121, 343, 346
Reliabilities
    internal consistency, 310–312, 331–332,
        371, 373
Reliability, 84, 164, 332
    coefficient, 19
    of measurement, 19, 370
    scorer, 53–54, 331
    test, 54, 149
      -retest, 331–332
Religion, 356
Requisite Task Attribute Index, 83
    Research
    conduct of, 18–32
    design of, 20–23
    qualitative, 23–24
Research Center for Group Dynamics, 38
Research and development (R&D) companies,
    276, 320–321, 375
Responsibility, social, 147
Rewards, 106–107, 116–117, 129–130, 139, 144,
    149, 303, 312, 314
    contingent, 363, 365, 367, 371–373, 375, 380
    distribution of, 147
    extrinsic, 100, 106, 125, 343, 346
    intrinsic, 100, 106
    social, 125
    system, 106, 268
    value of, 98–99, 103, 104t, 106
Risk(s)
    avoidance, 57, 332
    taking propensity, 54, 346
Rockefeller Foundation, 38
Role(s), 257
    acceptance, 365
    clarity, 167, 365
    conflict, 83, 167, 263, 268, 349
    making, 261, 263, 269
      description of, 261f
    modeling, 265, 320, 342, 346
    motivation training, 320–321, 331, 333
    playing, 155, 354
    prescriptions, 106, 236, 321, 324, 327, 329
    routinization, 259–260, 261f, 269

Role(s) (continued)
    taking, 257, 261f
Role motivation theory, 316, 319–333
    four forms of, 325f-326f
    group, 326f, 328, 333, 379
    hierarchic, 56, 324, 325f
    managerial, 320–324, 325f
    professional, 325f, 327
    task, 54, 326f, 327, 379
Routinization, 314, 356–357, 378, 381
Rural
    -urban moderator, 82
    workers, 82
Russia, 125
Russian factory study, 125

S

Sabotage, 154
Sacrifices, 343, 346, 352
Safety, 83, 366
Salary, 65, 70–71, 73, 198. See also Compensation;
    Monetary incentives; Money; Pay
Salespeople, 50, 66, 124, 220, 373
Satisfaction, 69, 71, 84, 86t, 99, 103–104, 149,
    370, 372–373
Satisficing, 283
Schemas, 285–286, 320, 322t. See also Cognitive,
    schemas
Science, 25, 28–30, 44
    assumptions of, 9
    defined, 6
    normal, 32
    role of theory in, 7–8, 15
Scientific
    concepts, objections to, 24–25
    dictates, objections to, 24–26
    inquiry, rules of, 9–10
    management, 38, 62, 87, 170
    method, 3, 7
    research, 28
    theory, 4, 7, 31
Scientists, 283, 320
Scripts, 283, 285
Selection, 5, 251, 333
Self-
    actualization, 71, 246, 363, 366
    concepts, 233–234, 272, 290, 341–343,
      346, 355
    concepts, follower, 289–291, 342, 376
    control, 120–122, 127, 129–130, 315
    efficacy, 111, 163–164, 167, 176–179, 196,
      199, 224, 247, 252, 271, 346, 354

Self- *(continued)*
    efficiency construct, 124
    esteem, 167, 341, 371. *See also* Esteem
        needs
    evaluation, 145–146
    identities, 290–292, 295–297
    management, 122, 124, 129, 169, 172, 178,
        315
    ratings, 104
    -report, 102, 109, 329, 376
        data, 72, 217
        measures, 53–54, 57
    views, 290
    worth, 290–291, 346
Sensitivity, 264
Sensitivity training, 38, 42, 328. *See also* T-groups
Sentence-completion
    format, 327
    instrument, 321, 331
    method, 54, 329
Service organizations, 127
Sewing-machine operators, 41, 43
Shaping, 120–121, 121*t*
Situation(al)
    constraints, 167, 177, 343, 346
    control, 238, 249–250. *See also*
        Situation(al), favorableness
    differences, 147–149
    engineering, 245–247
    favorableness, 236–241, 240*f*, 245–246
    influences, 89–90, 238, 249
    interview, 172
    management, 251
    problem, 218*t*
    stress, 238
Situation(s), 27, 122
Skill(s), 77–78, 81, 83–84, 103, 164, 308
    variety, 80, 83
Social
    cognitive theory, 124, 131
    desirability, 376
    exchange theories, 134
    identity, 290, 377
    learning
        process model, 123*f*
        theory, 122, 124, 129, 131
    network analysis, 272
    perception, 281, 286*f*
    psychology, 37–44, 169, 180, 184, 192
    sciences, 3–4, 11, 25
    sensitivity, 145
Socialization, 293

Society for the Psychological Study of Social
    Issues, 42
Sociologists, 134
Sociology, 13
Sociophilia, 244
Sociophobia, 244
Sociotechnical
    systems, 65
    theory, 75
Soldiers, 320
Spatial distance, 310–311
Special education teachers, 333
Stanford-Binet tests, 38
Stanford University, 38, 134–135
State Teachers College, 42
State University of New York, Binghamton, 362,
    369, 371–375
State University of New York, Buffalo, 320
Strategic management, 4, 9, 62, 289
Stress, 238, 240, 246–251, 262, 339–340, 346–347,
    349, 351, 364–367, 372–373. 376
Student(s), 153, 194, 352–353
    Asian university, 372
    business, 103, 149, 221
    college, 21, 140–141, 173–174, 310–311
    European, 149
    high school, 332, 377
    Master of Business Administration (MBA), 5
    United States university, 372
Subordinate(s), 170–171, 187, 194, 196, 198–199,
    207–213, 217–219, 250, 256–257, 264, 269,
    287, 296, 301, 339, 346, 354, 370, 372,
    374*t*, 377
Substitutes, 302, 307–308, 309*t*, 310–313, 315–317.
    See also Leadership, substitutes for
Success, 43, 47–48, 57, 167, 186, 193, 196, 198,
    219, 266, 292
    fear of, 57
Superiors, 170–171, 219, 256–259, 264, 269
Supervisors, 103, 125, 197, 266, 300
Supplements, 307, 316. *See also* Leadership,
    substitutes for
Survey parties, 234
Switzerland, 221
Syracuse University, 38

T

Tank crews, 234
Task(s), 259, 304
    attributes, 77
    complexity, 167–168, 177, 179

Task(s) *(continued)*
  design, 301
  difficulty, 176, 197–198, 200
  identity, 77, 80, 84
  role motivation theory, 54, 326*f*, 327, 379
  significance, 77, 80
  strategies, 164, 168, 169*f*
  structure, 236, 238, 246
  systems, 324, 326*f*, 329–330
  theory, 327, 331
  variety, 77
Tautology, 339
Tavistock Institute of Human Relations, 38, 328
Taxonomy
  decisions, 222. *See also* Decision rules
  defined, 14
  task groups, 236
Team(s), closely knit, 307, 311
Technological obsolescence, 64
Telephone company service representatives, 104
TELOS, 226
Tension, 137, 139, 141, 145, 148
Test-retest reliability, 331
Textile workers, 38
T-groups, 38, 42. *See also* Sensitivity training
Theft, 145, 151, 155
Thematic Apperception Test (TAT), 47, 53–55, 57–58, 68
Theories of Organizational Behavior, xi
Theory
  building, 10–11
components of a, 7–8, 8*f*
  decade of origin, xii, 37, 61, 75, 94, 114, 134, 159, 184, 207, 232, 256, 280, 300, 319, 337, 361
  defined, 5, 7
  field, 43
  good, 5–6, 11–13, 30, 40, 224, 281
  grand, 11, 44
  and practice, 5–6
  testing, 32, 251
A Theory of Goal Setting and Task Performance, 163
Threshold, 137, 143–144, 148, 150, 303, 368
Time
  penalty, 215, 226
pressures, 228
Toledo, OH, 338
Training, 43, 55, 129–130, 155, 169, 172, 200, 221, 225–228, 237–238, 240–241, 265–266, 273, 296, 301, 304, 308, 310, 332–333, 353, 357, 366. *See also* Sensitivity, training; T-groups

Training *(continued)*
  achievement motivation, 57, 129, 333
  cognitive skills, 251–252
  human relations, 241, 301
  leader match, 245–246
  leadership, 240*f*
  power motivation, 57
  stress-reduction, 251
  transformational, 375–376, 380–381
Traits, 58, 98–99
Transactional leadership, 363, 364*f. See also*
  Leadership, transactional
Transformational leadership theory, 361–381
Transitivity, 105
Trust, 260–261, 269, 375
Turnover, 43, 67, 87, 109, 144–145, 151, 200, 257–258, 263–265, 267
Type A behavior, 167
Typology
  defined, 14
  of workers, 64

U

Uncertainty, 150
  environmental, 349, 351–352
  perceived, 349
Underreward, 137, 144–145, 149, 151
Unfreezing, 42, 346.
United Kingdom, 83, 273
United States (U.S.) 25, 37–39, 55, 57, 95, 147, 149, 151, 208, 221, 233, 267, 273, 293, 295
  Air Force, 361
  Army platoons, 373
  corporations, 88
  Department of Health, Education and Welfare, 62
  military, 250. *See also* Military, the
  Office of Naval Research, 160
  presidents, 56, 340–341, 350, 352
  presidents research program, 348–349
University
  campuses, 331
  clerical employees, 364
  housing and food managers, 263–264
  settings, 263–264, 266
University of Akron, 160, 281
University of Berlin, 38
  Psychological Institute, 38
University of California, Berkeley, 76, 94–95, 320, 362
  Department of Psychology, 95
  Tolman Hall, 95

University of California, Irvine, Graduate School of Administration, 96
University of California, Los Angeles (UCLA), 208
University of Chicago, 233
University of Cincinnati, 185, 257
University of Detroit, 338
University of Exeter, 185
University of Freiberg, 38
University of Houston, 208
University of Illinois, 76, 82, 185, 233, 241, 257
University of Indiana, 115
University of Iowa, 39, 42, 115
    Child Welfare Research Station, 38
University of Maryland, 160, 320
University of Michigan, 76, 97, 208, 280, 301, 328
    Institute for Social Research, 38, 96
    School of Business, 28
    Survey Research Center, 95–96
University of Minnesota, 115, 257
University of Mississippi, 135
University of Missouri/St. Louis, 281
University of Munich, 38
University of Nebraska, 115, 127
University of New South Wales, Graduate School of Management, 208
University of North Carolina, Chapel Hill, 135
University of Oregon, 320
University of Pennsylvania, 95
    Wharton School, 320, 338
University of Pittsburgh, 62, 362
University of Rochester, 362
University of Southern California, 300–301
University of Southwestern Louisiana, 257
University of Toronto, 160, 338
University of Washington, 160, 185, 192, 194, 196, 233, 241
Urban workers, 82
Utah, 67

V

Valence(s), 43, 98, 100, 103, 104*t*, 106, 137, 148–149, 165, 339
    of outcomes, 97–98
    variable, 43
Validity, 19–20, 101, 107, 112, 217, 219–221, 225, 332–333, 370, 372–373
    coefficients, 222
    face, 20
    predictive, 372
    studies, 333

Values, 49, 82, 162, 167, 224, 351, 353
    democratic, 44
    humanistic, 44
Variable(s), 7, 19, 84, 103
    criterion, 302
    expectancy, 98
    measuring, 18–20, 108
    predictor, 302
    ratio schedule, 128
    sociological, 31
    suppressor, 302, 307
Venture growth, 169
Vertical dyad linkage theory (VDL), 96, 256–276.
Veterans Administration, 320
Vienna, Austria, 233
Virginia, 43
Vision(s), 169, 338, 346, 349, 352–354
    statements, 178

W

Wage and salary administrators, 135
Washington, D.C., 160, 164
Wealth
    creators, 58
    relational, 270
Wesleyan University, 47
West Point Academy, 115
Weyerhaeuser Company, 160
Women, 198, 221, 285, 324, 373–374. *See also* Females
Work
    groups, 81, 301–302, 304, 314
        autonomous, 328–329
    manual, 128
    structure, 241
    values, 82
Work and Motivation, 95
Work and the Nature of Man, 63–64
Workers, 128. *See also* Employees
    city, 82
    town, 82.
World War II, 40, 42, 62, 320

Y

Yale University, 47, 207–208, 222
    School of Industrial Administration, 76, 95–96

Z

Zeitgeist, 115